THE EGYPTIAN WORLD

——— .•. ———

The Nile valley produced one of the most sophisticated, and certainly the longest-lived, civilizations of the ancient world. Yet remarkably few books have looked at the broad topics of ancient Egyptian culture as expressed down the centuries. *The Egyptian World* presents an authoritative, up-to-date, single-volume work on Egyptian civilization, organized along thematic lines. Readers will gain a broader understanding of ancient Egyptian society in all its complexity without having to contest with the rigid chronological divisions often imposed on pharaonic history.

The volume comprises 32 original contributions written by leading specialists from the UK, USA, Canada, Australia, New Zealand, Austria, Germany and Egypt. Each chapter aims to give a broad overview of its particular topic, while also reflecting its author's specialist research interests. With previously unpublished drawings and photographs, the volume as a whole presents a digest of current research trends in Egyptology as well as a unique examination of the Egyptian world. Throughout, the contributors have drawn on the latest fieldwork and analysis to provide a fresh perspective on an ancient culture.

Toby Wilkinson is a Fellow of Clare College, Cambridge, and an Honorary Research Fellow in the Department of Archaeology, University of Durham. His publications include *Early Dynastic Egypt*, *The Thames and Hudson Dictionary of Ancient Egypt*, and *Lives of the Ancient Egyptians*.

THE ROUTLEDGE WORLDS

THE VIKING WORLD
Edited by Stefan Brink in collaboration with Neil Price

THE BABYLONIAN WORLD
Edited by Gwendolyn Leick

THE EGYPTIAN WORLD
Edited by Toby Wilkinson

THE ISLAMIC WORLD
Edited by Andrew Rippin

THE WORLD OF POMPEII
Edited by Pedar W. Foss and John J. Dobbins

THE RENAISSANCE WORLD
Edited by John Jeffries Martin

THE EARLY CHRISTIAN WORLD
Edited by Philip F. Esler

THE GREEK WORLD
Edited by Anton Powell

THE ROMAN WORLD
Edited by John Wacher

THE HINDU WORLD
Edited by Sushil Mittal and Gene Thursby

Forthcoming:
THE OTTOMAN WORLD
Edited by Christine Woodhead

THE ELIZABETHAN WORLD
Edited by Susan Doran and Norman Jones

THE BYZANTINE WORLD
Edited by Paul Stephenson

THE EGYPTIAN WORLD

Edited by

Toby Wilkinson

LONDON AND NEW YORK

First published 2007
First published in paperback 2010
by Routledge
2 Park Square, Milton Park, Abingdon, Oxon OX14 4RN

Simultaneously published in the USA and Canada
by Routledge
270 Madison Ave, New York, NY 10016

Routledge is an imprint of the Taylor & Francis Group, an informa business

© 2007, 2010 Edited by Toby Wilkinson

Typeset in Garamond by
Florence Production Ltd, Stoodleigh, Devon
Printed and bound in Great Britain by
The Cromwell Press Group, Trowbridge, Wiltshire

British Library Cataloguing in Publication Data
A catalogue record for this book is available from the British Library

Library of Congress Cataloging in Publication Data
A catalog record for this book has been requested

ISBN 13: 978–0–415–42726–5 (hbk)
ISBN 13: 978–0–415–56295–9 (pbk)

CONTENTS

————•◆•————

— Contents —

PART VI: AESTHETICS

PART VII: INTERACTIONS

ILLUSTRATIONS

——— ·◆· ———

FIGURES

Psusennes I *c.*1040–*c.*985
Amenemope *c.*985–*c.*975
Osochor (Osorkon 'the elder') *c.*975–*c.*970
Siamun *c.*970–*c.*950
Psusennes II *c.*950–*c.*945

22nd Dynasty *c.*945–*c.*715

Shoshenq I *c.*945–*c.*925
Osorkon I *c.*925–*c.*890 and Shoshenq II *c.*890
Takelot I *c.*890–*c.*875
Osorkon II *c.*875–*c.*835
Shoshenq III *c.*835–*c.*795
Shoshenq IV *c.*795–*c.*785
Pimay *c.*785–*c.*775
Shoshenq V *c.*775–*c.*735
Osorkon IV *c.*735–*c.*715

23rd Dynasty *c.*830–*c.*715

Takelot II *c.*840–*c.*815
Pedubast I *c.*825–*c.*800 and Iuput I *c.*800
Shoshenq VI *c.*800–*c.*780
Osorkon III *c.*780–*c.*750
Takelot III *c.*750–*c.*735
Rudamun *c.*755–*c.*735
Peftjauawybast *c.*735–*c.*725
Shoshenq VII *c.*725–*c.*715

24th Dynasty *c.*730–*c.*715

Tefnakht *c.*730–*c.*720
Bakenrenef *c.*720–*c.*715

25th (Kushite) Dynasty *c.*800–657

(Some scholars place the 25th Dynasty in the Late Period)

Alara *c.*800–*c.*770
Kashta *c.*770–*c.*747
Piye *c.*747–*c.*715
Shabaqo *c.*715–*c.*702
Shabitqo *c.*702–*c.*690
Taharqo 690–664
Tanutamani 664–657

LATE PERIOD 664–332 BC

26th Dynasty/Saite Period 664–525

Nekau I 672–664
Psamtik I 664–610
Nekau II 610–595
Psamtik II 595–589
Apries 589–570
Amasis 570–526
Psamtik III 526–525

27th Dynasty (First Persian Period) 525–404

Cambyses 525–522
Darius I 521–486
Xerxes 486–466
Artaxerxes I 465–424
Darius II 424–404

28th Dynasty 404–399

Amyrtaeos 404–399

29th Dynasty 399–380

Nepherites I 399–393
Psammuthis 393
Hakor 393–380
Nepherites II 380

30th Dynasty 380–343

Nectanebo I 380–362
Teos 365–360
Nectanebo II 360–343

31st Dynasty (Second Persian Period) 343–332

Artaxerxes III 343–338
Arses 338–336
Darius III 335–332

MACEDONIAN PERIOD 332–309 BC

Alexander III (the Great) 332–323
Philip Arrhidaeus 323–317
Alexander IV 317–309

PTOLEMAIC PERIOD 305–30

Ptolemy I 305–282
Ptolemy II 285–246
Ptolemy III 246–221
Ptolemy IV 221–205
Ptolemy V 205–180
Ptolemy VI 180–145
Ptolemy VIII and Cleopatra II 170–116
Ptolemy IX 116–107 and Cleopatra III 116–101
Ptolemy X 107–88
Ptolemy IX (restored) 88–80
Ptolemy XI and Berenice III 80
Ptolemy XII 80–58
Cleopatra VI 58–57 and Berenice IV 58–55
Ptolemy XII (restored) 55–51
Cleopatra VII and Ptolemy XIII 51–47
Cleopatra VII and Ptolemy XIV 47–44
Cleopatra VII and Ptolemy XV 44–30

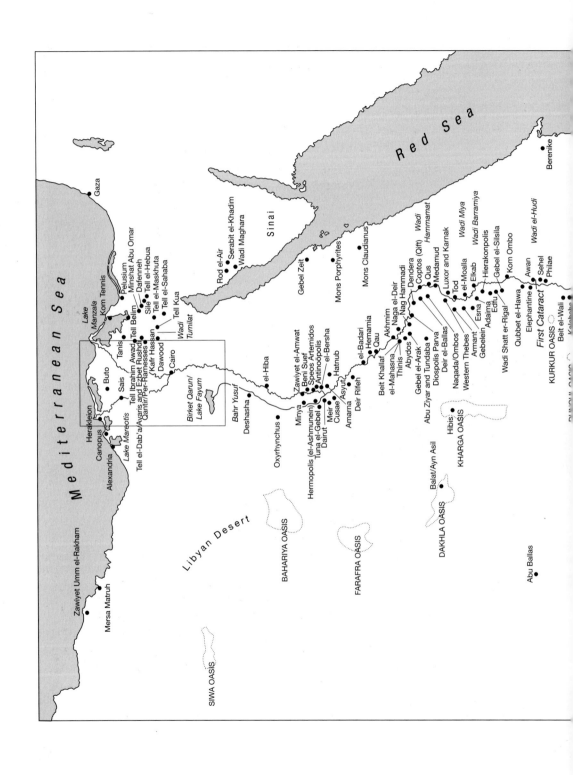

Mediterranean Sea

Zawiyet Umm el-Rakham

Mersa Matruh

Herakleion
Canopus
Alexandria
Lake Mareotis

Buto
Sais

Gaza

Pelusium
Minshat Abu Omar
Dafenneh
Sile
Tell el-Hebua
Tell el-Maskhuta
Tell el-Sahaba
Tell Kua

Kom Tennis
Lake Manzala

Tanis
Tell Belim
Tell el-Dab'a/Avaris and Ezbet Rushdi
Tell Ibrahim Awad
Qantir/Per-Ramesses
Kafr Hassan
Dawood

Wadi Tumilat

Cairo

Birket Qarun/ Lake Fayum

Bahr Yusuf

Deshasha

Oxyrhynchus

el-Hiba

Minya
Hermopolis (el-Ashmunein)
Tuna el-Gebel
Dairut
Meir
Cusae
Amarna

Zawiyet el-Amwat
Beni Suef
Speos Artemidos
Antinoöpolis
Hatnub
el-Bersha

Asyut
Deir Rifeh

el-Badari
Qau
Hemamia

Akhmim
Thinis
Abydos

el-Mahasna
Naga el-Deir
Nag Hammadi

Beit Khallaf

Gebel el-Arak
Abu Ziyar and Tundaba
Diospolis Parva
Deir el-Ballas
Naqada/Ombos
Western Thebes
Armant
Gebelein

Dendera
Coptos (Qift)
Qus
Medamud
Luxor and Karnak
Tod
el-Moalla
Elkab
Esna
Hierakonpolis
Adaima
Edfu
Gebel el-Silsila

Kom Ombo

Wadi Shatt er-Rigal

Qubbet el-Hawa
Elephantine
Awan
Sehel
Philae

First Cataract

Beit el-Wali

Red Sea

Berenike

Rod el-Air
Serabit el-Khadim
Wadi Maghara

Sinai

Gebel Zeit

Mons Porphyrites

Mons Claudianus

Wadi Hammamat

Wadi Miya

Wadi Barramiya

Wadi el-Hudi

KURKUR OASIS

Hibis
KHARGA OASIS

Balat/Ayn Asil

DAKHLA OASIS

FARAFRA OASIS

BAHARIYA OASIS

Abu Ballas

Libyan Desert

SIWA OASIS

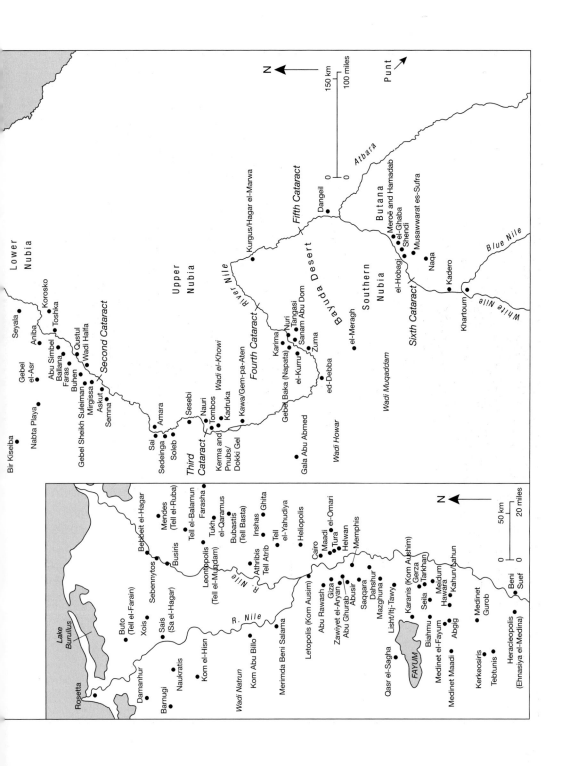

INTRODUCTION

———————

Toby Wilkinson

This volume is intended to fill a gap in the extensive literature on ancient Egypt, by presenting an authoritative, up-to-date, single-volume work on pharaonic civilization, organized along thematic lines. By eschewing the usual chronological approach, the book has been able to concentrate instead on exploring each individual topic from a variety of angles. In this way, it is hoped that readers will gain a broader understanding of ancient Egyptian society in all its complexity, liberated from the rather artificial chronological divisions that we impose on pharaonic history.

The book comprises 32 original contributions written by leading specialists from the UK, USA, Canada, Australia, New Zealand, Austria, Germany and Egypt. Each chapter aims to give a broad overview of the subject under discussion, while also reflecting its author's particular research interests. The volume as a whole, therefore, presents a digest of current research trends in Egyptology as well as a unique examination of the Egyptian world. Throughout, the contributors have drawn on the latest fieldwork and analysis to provide fresh perspectives on an ancient culture. The chapters are arranged in seven thematic sections.

Part I, Environments, looks at the physical parameters within which ancient Egyptian civilization developed and operated. Egypt is often taken to be synonymous with the Nile Valley, and this most important geographical feature is, indeed, the subject of the opening chapter. However, the ancient Egyptians had to come to terms with, and learn to exploit, a range of distinctive environments. Each of these is examined in turn, from the broad, green expanses of the delta – with all the constraints its environment imposed on settlement and communication – to the harsher, arid conditions of the eastern and western deserts. New archaeological work is transforming our understanding of both regions, and the chapters take full account of recent discoveries. The oases of the Western Desert have, likewise, emerged from relative obscurity to a much more central place in our picture of the ancient Egyptian world. Finally, in this part, a chapter explores the urban environment; towns and cities formed the backdrop for the lives of large numbers of Egyptians, but this facet of their experience is often neglected because of its relative invisibility in the artistic record of temples and tombs.

Part II, Institutions, concentrates on the human groupings that characterized the structure of ancient Egyptian society. At the very apex was the king, supported by his close relatives. The monarchy exercised a tremendous influence on all areas of Egyptian culture, dictating the styles of art, architecture and literature that dominate in the surviving record. The nature of royal power and the true extent of its political influence are important questions that go to the heart of Egyptian civilization. Besides the king and the royal family, other self-interest groups emerge as key players in internal politics. The literate bureaucracy of central and regional government, the powerful priesthoods attached to the major state temples, and the military hierarchy: all were at some times supporters, at other times rivals, of royal power. By exploring the ambitions and internal strains of these institutions, the fabric of authority in ancient Egypt can be laid bare.

Part III, Economies, examines the patterns of economic activity in ancient Egypt. The productive sector was dominated by farming, and by the complex system of land tenure, taxation and redistribution that maintained the royal court and financed its lavish building projects. The organization of labour required for pyramid-building ranks as one of the ancient Egyptians' greatest achievements, yet the composition and control of the workforce is rarely studied. Other chapters focus on the technologies employed in craft production, and on the balance between state and private enterprise, an evolving debate within Egyptology.

Part IV, Societies, forms the core of the book, both spatially and conceptually, and represents one of its most distinctive aspects. There have been very few detailed discussions of ancient Egyptian social factors, even though topics such as gender, sexuality, ethnicity, morality and law lie at the heart of any society, ancient or modern. They circumscribed the lives of the ancient Egyptians as much as any geographical, political or economic factors, yet social influences are rarely given due consideration in studies of pharaonic civilization. Moreover, there is a tendency to regard ancient Egyptian culture as monolithic, rarely departing from the dictates of the royal court except during periods of political turmoil. Yet, throughout pharaonic history, local identities existed, even if they left weak traces in the official record. The chapters of Part IV comprise an original and ground-breaking series of insights into the fundamental nature of ancient Egyptian culture.

Part V, Ideologies, looks at ancient Egyptian beliefs in their many forms. The ideology of kingship permeated, indeed defined, state religion. Inextricably bound up with the myths about Egypt's creation and the daily rites of the major cults, it was one of the most important determinants of ancient Egyptian court culture. While the great temples are enduring symbols of pharaonic civilization, they have little to say about the spiritual beliefs and practices of ordinary people. Our knowledge of private religion is, instead, based upon the study of smaller artefacts and is constantly evolving. The belief in an afterlife, reflected in the elaborate preparations made for burial, was a universal concern for all levels of society, and – from pyramids to mummies – has provided many of the quintessential symbols of ancient Egypt.

Part VI, Aesthetics, focuses on the cultural expressions that have survived from ancient Egypt, and which continue to entrance the modern mind. The Egyptians' highly distinctive artistic and architectural legacies are, perhaps, more familiar than their literary output; yet all three areas provide important insights into ancient

Egyptian sensibilities and modes of self-expression. All three represent means by which the ancient Egyptians projected their consciousness onto the world around them.

Part VII, Interactions, which forms the final section of the book, examines the contacts between ancient Egypt and its neighbours, and the influence that pharaonic civilization had on the development of other cultures. Egypt stands at the meeting-point of Africa, Asia and Europe, and has always been a melting-pot of peoples, beliefs and cultural influences. Egypt's significance in the ancient world extended far beyond its own borders. Only by looking at ancient Egypt from without, as well as from within, can its distinctive achievements be placed in proper context. Of course, ancient Egypt continues to have an impact on today's world, and the final chapter will look at our enduring fascination for 'The Egyptian World'.

PART I

ENVIRONMENTS

CHAPTER ONE

THE NILE VALLEY

—·◆·—

David Jeffreys

The geography of the Nile Valley is, of course, familiar to anyone with an interest in pharaonic civilization, but that familiarity tends perhaps to cloud our appreciation of its unusual and even unique qualities. Essentially a major river system passing through a hyper-arid desert (it has sometimes been described as a 'linear oasis'), the valley consists of the river itself, with an average width of about 500 metres, and a strip of arable alluvial soil either side, giving a flood plain width varying from three to 12 kilometres. The edges of the valley are of only seasonal potential use, and in times of low floods and during the dry season were used for occasional grazing or abandoned altogether.

The northern Nile Valley (from Khartoum to Cairo) is fed by three main tributary sources (the White Nile rising in Uganda, the Blue Nile flowing from Ethiopia, and the Atbara which joins the main course in Sudan, north of the confluence of the other two at Khartoum); its regime within Egypt is not conditioned by local precipitation (except for the Mediterranean coastal region) but by weather events thousands of kilometres to the south, where the monsoon rains fall over the Ethiopian highlands, swelling the Blue Nile during the summer months. The White Nile, by contrast, provides a smaller and relatively even supply throughout the year, while the Atbara is largely seasonal and supplies comparatively little.

The history of formation of the northern Nile Valley is complex, and involves several geological stages (Eonile, palaeonile, prenile, proto-Nile, Neonile) whose formation is explained by responses to tectonic movement, climate change and sea levels (Said 1975, 1990). Only the last two of these phases coincide with human occupation: river terraces of Palaeolithic times can be traced at some points in the sides of the escarpment, and for the whole of the Neolithic, from about 12,000 BP, the valley has been gradually building. To a large extent this explains why very few Palaeolithic sites are located in or near the present flood plain, especially in the north: they are found either in the high desert and correspond to moister, savannah conditions in the eastern Sahara (McHugh *et al.* 1988; Wendorf *et al.* 1992/3), or occur in older riverbank deposits which have been cut by later channels and are now well above the valley floor (Sandford and Arkell 1929; Sandford 1934: 61; Vermeersch 2000). The desert limestones and sandstones underlying the earliest recent riverine deposits have been found (near Cairo) sometimes at depths of over half a kilometre (Said and Yousri 1968).

The Nile Valley today presents as a long thin ribbon of alluvial silts and clays along the river sides, with the highest ground usually lying along the riverbanks where the heaviest suspended material in the floodwaters has been deposited. These banks or levees most often show an eastward progression across the valley floor (Butzer 1976), although trends in the opposite direction are also evident (Kubiak 1998; Graham and Bunbury 2005). This movement is important for the study of settlement patterns: some east-bank sites may have been wholly or partially removed by the changing course of the river, while those on the other side will either have followed the river or been left lying inland.

The Egyptian Valley north of the First Cataract ('Upper Egypt') is often conventionally divided into three sections (e.g. Baines and Malek 1980): southern and northern upper (Aswan to Abydos or Asyut); middle (Abydos or Asyut to Fayum) and lower (Fayum to Cairo). This schema corresponds to the general width of the flood plain at various points: it is conspicuously narrow between Aswan and Kom Ombo, relatively broad throughout the region between Luxor and the Fayum, especially north of Asyut, and narrow again between the Fayum and Cairo. Upstream of the First Cataract at Aswan (usually taken as the southern frontier of pharaonic Egypt), the valley was exceptionally narrow before the construction of the Aswan Dam, and was interrupted by a series of other cataracts that result from bands of harder rocks such as granite crossing the course of the river. These, and one ex-cataract within Egyptian territory at Gebel el-Sisila, were traditionally exploited by the Egyptian state as useful sources of specialist building or sculptural stone.

Following the most recent drying phase of the Sahara from the fourteenth to the twelfth millennia BC onwards, and especially from the fourth to the third millennia BC, the Nile Valley and delta became a magnet for population movement and settlement from the former savannah areas to the west (Hassan 1988), and from the Levant and the south. Human exploitation of the Nile's resources almost certainly began in prehistoric times: designs on painted pottery of the Naqada II Period have, for example, been interpreted as proto-images of an irrigated landscape, although there is debate on the question of how early a full, man-managed pattern of flood-recession agriculture was established. The assumption is that, by the time a fully functioning state apparatus for the Nile Valley evolved (probably by the 3rd Dynasty), the agricultural infrastructure was, if not centrally controlled, then at least organized as a series of networks at a regional level for maximum yield and storage capability. Throughout pharaonic history and, indeed, into modern times, agriculture was dependent on basin irrigation, which used the annual floodwaters to be stored in basins (Arabic *ahwad*, singular *hod*), bounded by earthwork dykes, until the suspended silts were deposited; the water was then drained off in a controlled sequence by breaching the boundaries between the basins. Only with the construction of the Aswan Dam at the end of the nineteenth century, and more crucially with the High Dam in the 1960s, did this system end and perennial irrigation become possible. With these modern constructions the traditional Nile regime and much of the Nilotic landscape has changed out of all recognition, as has the habitation pattern. The High Dam no longer allows the natural suspended silts to be carried over the flood plain; instead, these are mostly blocked and collect within the reservoir (Lake

Nasser). Construction within Egypt, especially in high-value urban and suburban environments (most notably around Cairo), has been allowed to continue almost unchecked and is now at a critical stage (see below). The long-term rise in the flood-plain due to natural sedimentation has also been arrested, and there are other ecological consequences (salination, local changes in weather, a rising groundwater table) that affect the economic sustainability of the country, and, by extension, its cultural heritage.

The periodicity of the flood recession cycle is, in some ways, crucial to an understanding of other features of the Egyptian social and economic calendar. The Nile in Egypt began to rise in late summer, reached its maximum in September, and subsided in late autumn. This reversal of the normal timing, with planting and cropping taking place in the winter months, was commented on by early visitors to Egypt, as was the observation that the Nile flowed in the 'wrong' direction (i.e. from south to north). Since a close record was kept of the dates and levels of inundations, it became apparent that celestial calendars (especially lunar) required compensation for annual environmental events.

Both the ancient Egyptian and the Arabic terminology for different parts of the flood plain suggest that there was a sophisticated understanding not only of the timing but also of the processes at work, or at least of the effects that these processes would have on a successful harvest. There were, for example, different terms for land regularly inundated, land only occasionally inundated, and land newly created or reclaimed from the river, as well as specific terms for different soil types. There must have been some awareness of the long-term properties of the river regime, such as the gradual rise in level of the plain, as well as the lateral movement of the river across it; although to what extent any action could be taken to counter or accommodate this behaviour is less clear. There are certainly instances of very old standing structures, found at levels that were once dry throughout the year, becoming gradually waterlogged or seasonally flooded; there is also some evidence in recent times of competition between municipalities over islands and other new productive or potentially productive land, and it is reasonable to suppose that this existed at earlier periods too. Individual towns and villages certainly had their own river defences, which might also act as military features in time of need, and the maintenance of municipal dykes was a carefully managed business.

The length and narrowness of the valley are among its most conspicuous features and these almost certainly contributed to the emergence of Egypt as one of the earliest, if not the earliest, of the world's territorial states. Although stretches of alluvial deposition are found throughout the Nile Valley north of the First Cataract, the width of the valley floor varies from four to 12 kilometres across. Areas of particular constriction occur north of Aswan, prompting the suggestion at one time that this might account for competition and the early rise of state society in this area (Bard and Carneiro 1989); and just south (upriver) of the head of the delta branches, which is again very probably the reason for the location of the first capital of the unified state (White Walls, later Memphis; modern Mit Rahina) at this point (Jeffreys and Tavares 1994). It is not altogether clear how the hydropolitics of the valley operated in pharaonic times: there was almost certainly no real competition for water resources, since the technology needed for damming or for massive water storage did not exist, although some temporary arrangements for diverting river channels may have been introduced in the cataract regions (Vercoutter 1994; but see de Putter 1992, 1993). However, the need to cooperate in the maintenance of river defences and containing earthworks must have involved organization at the local, if not the national level. The interrelationships between the different nomes is of considerable interest, since the formal, normative documents from periods of settled rule rarely shed light on them. There are occasional eulogies of individual cities, and some administrative texts that record travel up and down the river, and temple landholdings; but only recently has evidence been produced for tension and even hostility between neighbouring nomes, significantly during the intermediate periods (Darnell and Darnell 1997a). In some cases new political foundations seem to be deliberately sited between existing power centres (e.g. Itj-tawy and Amarna; and possibly Thebes in the 12th Dynasty).

Similarly, interpretations of the relations between Egypt and Nubia have, until recently, rested on a fairly small corpus of official/ceremonial pharaonic texts. There is no very good reason for treating Egypt as a separate entity, isolated from societies further south: recent work has tended to reflect an awareness that Nilotic cultures in both Egypt and Sudan are, perhaps, more helpfully considered together (Welsby 1996), even to the extent of tracing the roots of pharaonic civilization to south of the First Cataract (Williams 1980, 1987; but see Adams 1985). Certainly the traditional view of Nubia as a culture or culture group under the shadow of a politically dominant Egyptian state has come to be questioned if not deconstructed in recent years.

In section, the Nile Valley appears as a slightly inverted saucer (Butzer 1976), with low-lying areas, often marsh and backswamp environments, near the desert margin and the highest ground near the river where the heavier soil particles were precipitated soonest after the arrival of the flood. Habitation sites in the valley typically cluster at its edges or along these levees and riverbanks, where the highest alluvial ground is found, above the floodwaters all year round. Northwards from Dairut in Middle Egypt, where the valley is at its widest, a subsidiary stream, the Bahr Yusuf (probably a relic of an older course of the main river, maintained and periodically cleared by successive governments) runs parallel to the Nile, with its own flood plain and associated settlement sites. Just north of Beni Suef, a branch of the Bahr Yusuf flows into the large wind-scoured depression of the Fayum with its (much reduced) lake, the Birket Qarun. The Fayum is a curious and interesting geographical feature and seems at times to have acted almost as an overflow facility to the Nile Valley: recent geoarchaeological work there is beginning to suggest that Egyptian water management might have been more ambitious than has been supposed (Hassan 2005).

Typically, settlements were located closest to the water resources, along riverbanks and the sides of subsidiary channels, where these allowed advantageous conditions. The question of transient populations, moving between towns and villages and the surrounding countryside, and even at times out into the desert regions, is not much discussed but they must have been a constant feature, though they appear only occasionally in the pictorial record.

Cemeteries were normally sited close to the settlements, or in the nearest available part of the desert margins. Only rarely, and for specific cult requirements, were burials made within settlements, and of necessity these were shallow enough to remain above the contemporary groundwater table during the inundation. The occasional reference to burials (and temples) being flooded makes it clear that these events were rare and were considered disastrous.

This historical settlement pattern has changed beyond all recognition during the twentieth century, once the successive Aswan dams had essentially created dry conditions throughout the year, allowing building to spread far beyond the original practical limits. The ecology of the Nile Valley is now, in fact, at a critical stage – one of the most acute in the world – in which the finite agricultural resources of the flood plain are in danger of being seriously depleted and eventually overrun by accelerating building programmes (Nasa Earth Observatory website). Overflow housing and irrigation schemes in the desert regions adjacent to the valley are only a partial solution to the problem, and create and perpetuate their own problems.

The river was vitally important to both practical agrarian behaviour and cognitive patterns, although it is perhaps curious that textual references are not more common. There was a distinct terminology for the 'ordinary' Nile (*iteru*), as opposed to the flood (*hapi*) which was deified and had an important shrine just south of Cairo (Zivie 1980), at the traditional meeting place of the valley and delta, the 'Two Lands'. In Roman times the river in flood was personified in sculpture as a bearded male deity, similar to the Tiber figures, attended by 16 cherub-like beings representing the cubits of an 'ideal' flood. Monitoring of the Nile flood was carefully, indeed almost obsessively, maintained, and we have a near-continuous sequence of flood records from the Roman Period onwards (Popper 1951; Hassan 1981), although the records from pharaonic times are, perhaps surprisingly, much less abundant. Observations were made at a number of sites – usually at a kind of building, often attached to a temple, known in Roman times as Nilometer or Niloscope (later *miqyas* or *manyal* in Arabic), of which the best known are at Aswan (Elephantine Island) and Cairo (Roda Island). Curiously, we know little about this practice before the Late and Ptolemaic Periods: although a few flood marks do occur, also notably recorded on outlying parts of temple complexes, it cannot be assumed that they were part of a system organized on a national or even a regional scale (Borchardt 1906; Bonneau 1971). The late antique tradition of a Nilometer at Alexandria (or Memphis?) shows how closely the responsibility for recording the flood was in the hands of the priesthood or clergy (Engreen 1943).

It is assumed that there must also have been an equally rigorous method of recording property boundaries in between floods: considering the extremely precise cadastral records for individual properties it would be surprising if the same detail were not kept for agricultural holdings. How this was managed on the ground is, however, again uncertain: a series of cult objects known as *cippi* (an Italian term meaning 'boundary stone') is certainly known from Egypt, almost always associated with the image of Horus as a child, but this is entirely a contrived modern Egyptological term and it is far from certain that this was the original purpose.

As far as we can tell, the remote sources of the Nile and the cause of the flood were unknown in ancient times, although there was a pious fiction of a source both at Thebes (Gabolde 1995) and Aswan, and a separate, notional 'source' of the delta branches was located in the Memphis region. Herodotus in the fifth century BC was only able to surmise (although quite accurately) on the reasons for the inundation.

The extraordinary, linear geography of the valley must have exercised a huge influence on the settlement and demography of different regions. The desert margins were policed at certain times, perhaps by local tribal groups, though it is uncertain how effective this form of control can have been – immigration, or at least ingress, at all points along the valley must have been regular, although perhaps less marked than in the delta with its hazier boundaries and more heavily used access routes. One record from Middle Egypt, apparently showing an incoming social group approaching and dealing with the regular inhabitants of the valley, places that group in a kind of limbo between open desert with its own fauna, and the conventional imagery of a settled agrarian population. Depending on season, the desert margins will have provided free passage and adequate grazing and life support, though there may have been competition for them.

The Nile's geography also dictated the administrative divisions of the country, known in later times as nomes, which in the valley (unlike the delta) are able to straddle the main course of the river (Helck 1974). The numbering of the 22 Upper Egyptian units begins with Aswan at the First Cataract, while the 'northern' capital, Memphis, occupying a position at the transition from valley to delta, was considered the first nome of Lower Egypt.

At the local and regional levels, settlement will have been dictated by the habitability of different zones throughout the flood cycle: the popular view of the Nile flood as a stable, regular event, providing guaranteed subsistence benefits at relatively little cost in effort and technology, certainly needs some revision. There was, for example, no certainty year on year of the flood reaching its optimum level (called euthemia or plenitude), irrigating the maximum area of the flood plain without causing structural damage, and the complete reliance on the flood as a means of livelihood (wells and cisterns seem to be almost unknown except in marginal low-desert environments) made Egypt extraordinarily vulnerable to variations in the flood level reached. Some, indeed, have seen the failure of the flood over periods of time as being instrumental in the weakening or loss of centralized control at certain points – Egypt's 'intermediate periods' (Bell 1971, 1975; Hassan 1981). Progressive cultivation of the flood plain may also sometimes have gone into reverse or been reduced in the short term: recent work on later (Mamluk) flood levels (Borsch 2000) has suggested that high levels early on in the season are not necessarily a sign of adequate floodwater cover, but might have resulted from inefficient or non-existent storage of floodwater in Upper Egypt.

Other accepted views of the Nile Valley also need to be questioned. The landscape is often assumed to be similarly constant and unchanging over time, but it is clear that at least from Early Dynastic times the valley floor, as well as the river bed and flood level, have been inexorably rising – an average of one centimetre per century has been estimated (Butzer 1976) – which means inevitably that the valley in antiquity must have been not only lower but also considerably narrower than at present. Palaeofan drainages such as those of the Wadi Hof and the Wadi Digla in the Memphis area will have intruded much more obviously into the flood plain and may even have affected the course of the river. Because of the constant remixing of newly laid sediments due to intensive arable farming, the buried stratigraphy of the valley floor is extremely amorphous and laminated layers are usually only found on undisturbed island shores. This helps to explain why we know surprisingly little about ground levels in the valley during dynastic times or, for that matter, any other period – pavement levels of temples and other structures at major sites will almost certainly have been higher than the general level of the valley floor. An interesting case is that of the 'valley temples', found with most, if not all, Old Kingdom pyramids and solar temples, which were once thought to provide functioning harbours for ceremonial and supply vessels reaching them across the inundation waters or by canals: it now seems unlikely that even abnormally high inundations would have come anywhere near these structures (Jeffreys 2001).

Archaeological exploration of the Egyptian Nile Valley in the last 200 years has, in general, been a remarkably uneven affair: the overwhelming concentration of excavation and survey has always been on the obvious, easily accessible temple and funerary sites on the low and high desert margins, with little work done on settlement sites in the flood plain. This is gradually changing, but the priority of many fieldworkers is still undoubtedly the monumental structures in the dry desert zone.

Much has been made of the urgent need for archaeological recording in the Nile delta, to the extent of the Supreme Council for Antiquities declaring a virtual moratorium on further fieldwork unless undertaken in the delta. It is, however, often overlooked that the problem, as it concerns settlements, is equally acute in the valley, and indeed in the extended valley created by ambitious irrigation projects such as Toshka: sites such as Amarna and the Khafra diorite quarries, once thought safe from modern development, are now directly threatened and there seems to be little sense of urgency about their protection on the part of the authorities.

The net result is that the archaeological picture from Egypt is hopelessly one-sided: in many cases we simply do not know where the settlement sites are, and are forced to infer them from an assumed proximity to concentrations of tombs and mortuary temples. A good example of this disparity is the Old Kingdom capital of Memphis, whose cemeteries and pyramid fields, stretching 36 kilometres from Giza and Abu Rawash in the north to Dahshur and Mazghuna in the south, are deservedly world-famous, while the location of the city itself remains almost entirely a matter of conjecture. The supposedly 'typical' town sites, of which only a handful are recorded (Amarna, Deir el-Medina, Kahun) are, in fact, anything but typical: Amarna is a new foundation town built to serve a highly individualized royal cult; Deir el-Medina is a purpose-built craft village; and Kahun is essentially a pyramid town which survived as a local administrative hub. Significantly, none of them was built in the flood plain, although there may have been some kind of a mental map of settlement patterning in operation: the famous case of the royal capital, Amarna, exhibits several nodes of settlement activity, clustering in the north, centre and south of the large desert embayment containing the total conurbation, rather than a highly centralized, nucleated organization. Could this be a reflection of the way that a true valley settlement would have been laid out, i.e. discontinuously, with palace and other specialist areas located, perhaps on islands, away from the 'core' site?

Because of its shape, settlement patterning within the flood plain tends to defy the usual attempts to formulate for spatial analysis (e.g. central place theory); instead, the series of provinces (nomes) has at the core of each a nome capital, which persists over long time periods (although some are still unlocated or conjectural). Some of the best-known urban sites (Thebes, Amarna), being new royal locations, never emerged, or were slow to become established, as regional centres. Satellite sites are, of course, known, although it is important to recognize that many of these may be only ephemeral, or only seasonally occupied. Some towns (e.g. el-Hiba) seem to be deliberately sited on the traditional boundaries between nomes, although these boundaries might shift over time and were probably never formally marked.

The naming of Egyptian sites can be initially confusing: it has become the practice in Egyptology to use pharaonic Egyptian, Greek or Roman, Coptic or Arabic versions, or any combination of these. Some modern placenames (e.g. el-Ashmunein) derive from the ancient Egyptian, some (e.g. Burumbul) from Greek; often toponyms are given in binary form (Avaris/Tell el-Dabʿa, Memphis/Mit Rahina) in the literature. It may be noted that modern toponyms can be quite inappropriate for referring to ancient sites: when these were large conurbations with extensive cemeteries (Memphis, Thebes, Per-Ramesses) they often lie beneath and beyond several modern towns or villages.

The Nile Valley naturally provides some unique landscapes: one of its characteristics is that the desert is ever-present on both the eastern and western horizons and in some places is extremely conspicuous; in such locations the landscape was clearly important to local cult activity (Amarna, Gebel Barkal) and itself became associated or identified with specific deities (the 'mistress of the mountain' at Thebes and Memphis). Elsewhere, as at Amarna/Akhetaten ('Horizon of the Aten'), whole towns are laid out with respect to features on the horizon: in the case of Amarna, the 'royal valley' housing the tombs of the royal family. Another interesting case study is the Memphis pyramid field, where the pyramids, as man-made simulacra of mountains, are specifically located in the landscape as a kind of visual relay between different parts of the capital, and even between Memphis and other towns (especially Heliopolis, centre of the sun cult). The pyramids, indeed, are located in an iconic stretch of land along the Nile, embracing as they do the abrupt transition from valley to delta, with its very different geography, landscape and culture.

CHAPTER TWO

THE NILE DELTA

Penelope Wilson

The triangular fan of the Nile delta has provided a rich natural environment with abundant resources for human habitation over the past six thousand years. The historical and archaeological details of some settlements in specific delta locations are better known for some periods than for others. It is likely that the contribution of the delta to Egyptian culture and civilization in antiquity varied and is only preserved in discrete parts. Calls for more work to be carried out on the archaeology of the northern part of Egypt in the last 40 years have begun to yield interesting results, not only for establishing a northern identity and dynamic, but also inviting comparison with the alluvial areas of the Nile Valley. By addressing the expectations of what can be extracted from the archaeological material of the north, a meaningful comparison of Egyptian culture in the north and south could be eventually attempted and, perhaps, the reality behind the Egyptian ideology of the 'Two Lands' explored more fully. In the delta, there are not the standing, inscribed temples and tombs or well-preserved cemeteries that have provided so much information about Upper Egypt. There are, however, significant *tell*-sites and the remains of large urban centres, as well as groups of cemeteries upon sand hills which have led to the development of a distinctive form of settlement archaeology. Investigative techniques, such as the study of the geological and riverine impacts on human life, the archaeological investigation of urban sites with complex and difficult stratigraphy, and combined ground and satellite regional surveys are contributing to a larger picture of human life dynamics throughout the delta and valley. The complexity and multidisciplinary nature of some of the work and the lack of emphasis on sensational burial finds has, however, limited the public perception of the progress made in delta archaeology. The threats of agricultural and modern urban pressures and the efforts of the Egyptian authorities to encourage coordinated work in Egypt are moving forward delta studies towards the complex synthesis of excavated material of all kinds. The results could lead towards the definition of a significant Lower Egyptian culture, an exploration of the political tensions within the unified complex state, and an understanding of the reasons why the controlling administrative centre of a united Egypt could only ever have been in the north, even if based in different locations.

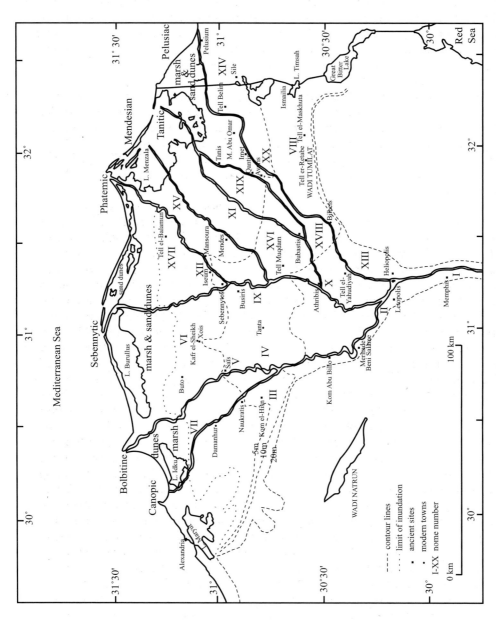

Figure 2.1 Map of the Nile Delta showing a reconstruction of river branches in ancient times, ancient sites, modern towns and contour lines. It is based on a compilation of data by Said (1993: 71).

GEOLOGY

The delta is a fan of mid-Pleistocene sands and gravels, covered in a layer of alluvial sediments and cut by a network of river channels and distributaries (Butzer 1975). The best alluvial land was situated in the upper delta plain, with a broad fan-like shape delineated at the side by 20-metre-high scarps of Late Pleistocene sediments. There is little topography, with the height of the land mass above sea level rising from zero metres at the coastline southward towards Cairo which lies around 18 metres above sea level. The modern total land area of the delta is estimated at 12,500 square kilometres (Sestini 1989).

The formation of the delta has been affected by various processes, including changes in sea level, subsidence of the delta fringe and plain, off-shore sedimentation patterns and the variable volume of the Nile flood. In some places, the underlying, undulating sand was higher than the alluvial mud of the flood plain. Such sand hills or *geziras* were exposed and weathered, cut and reworked by river channels and formed higher ground, until they were partially or completely subsumed beneath the accumulated sediments.

There were two main and significant river branches from around 8000 BC: one through the central delta plain, later the Sebennytic Branch, and the other to the west along the desert fringe, later the Canopic Branch (Butzer 2002: 89). There were a number of other minor distributaries, particularly on the east, reaching the Mediterranean Sea through a system of freshwater lakes, brackish lagoons, sand ridges and marshland. Until 2000 BC there was deep entrenchment of the distributary channels, creating five major branches known in the Ramesside Period, if not before, as the 'River of the West' (Canopic), the 'Water of Ptah' (Bolbinitic), the 'Great River' (Sebennytic), the 'Water of Amun' (Phatemic), and the 'Water of Pre' (Pelusiac) (Bietak 1975). The river branches ran in incised channels with banks or levees beside them, formed by the deposition of sediments at the point nearest to the channel during major floods. The levees, especially on the outer edges of river bends, formed high ground, which would have stood above the flood plain and above lesser floodwaters. The variability of the floods, in terms of energy of the flood, the volumes of water and the amounts of sediment, meant that distributaries incised new courses and old channels could be abandoned, filled with sediment and subsequently recut.

There were recurrent flood perturbations, however, with high floods for a century during the period 4250–4000 BC, in general between 4100 and 2400 BC and during the Middle Kingdom (Butzer 2002: 90). Low floods are measured and recorded on the Palermo Stone during the 2nd Dynasty (Bell 1970). After 1400 BC there was greater channel stability leading to the more 'modern' fluvial regime and continued accretion of overbank silts. The lower flood energy of the river led to the progressive atrophy of five Nile branches, with water being diverted to the modern Damietta (Phatemic) and Rosetta (Bolbitine) channels by the seventeenth century AD (Embabi 2004: 73) (Figure 2.2). The flood plain was watered and covered by alluvial sediments during the inundation, with the water courses dividing it and creating natural basins. The management of the basins meant that water was provided for the duration of a crop or crops and the land under cultivation could be increased by effective control of the irrigation systems. Changes in the pattern of flooding and of the river branches affected human settlement very greatly and, in consequence, are a significant factor in the economic and political development of the delta (Hassan 1997).

Figure 2.2   The Rosetta mouth of the Nile.

The area to the north of the 1 m above sea level contour line was dependent on low sea levels for human settlement, particularly in the Ptolemaic–Roman and Late Antique Periods. Parts of the city of Alexandria, all of Canopus and Herakleion in the north-west, small *koms* in and around Lake Burullus, as well as the formerly large settlement at Kom Tennis in Lake Menzala and the great city of Pelusium in the north-east have suffered due to sea level rise for one reason or another (Stanley 2005). The lagoonal and marsh fringe of the lower delta plain now comprises the reclaimed areas of lakes Mareotis, Burullus and Menzala. The steady reclamation of the marshes in the north-east may be one of the factors in the economic prosperity of this area, particularly from the New Kingdom onward.

South of the 1 m hinge, the delta can be divided geographically into three main portions, each with distinct geological and, perhaps, ethnic profiles, yet each a part of the same flood plain environment. The central delta is a thick mass of flood plain silt, intercalated with peat marshes and lying on sand with some sand hills and ridges running in a north–south line alongside sediment levees created by deep river channels. The north-western delta consists of beach sands overlying lagoon mud, peat marsh and marine sand, brought inland over the flood plain silt and the original sands. This area abuts the desert sands of the Western Desert along with its oasis areas. The north-eastern delta is a similar stratum of beach sands overlying peat and lagoon deposits, but with thicker layers of marine sand intercalated with silt and mud, overlying deepwater marine mud upon sand, flood plain mud and, finally, the original sand base (Stanley 2005). The hinge line provides some geological understanding for the environment and also allows a basis for a reconstruction of the human responses to the exploitation of the delta.

GEOGRAPHY AND CULTURE

The development of the delta as a contributory factor in the maintenance of the Egyptian state depended upon the availability of agricultural and pasture land and its management by the settling of people and animals there. The river routes to the west and east gave access to important resource areas and created flexible Egyptian 'frontiers' allowing people to pass in and out of Egypt, as well as being fixed and guarded so that transient peoples could be stopped and monitored (Quirke 1989).

The literary text, *The Teaching for King Merikara*, dating to the Middle Kingdom, acknowledges that in ancient times the divisions of the delta were recognized and had a specific character. Merikara ruled the north from his capital city at Heracleopolis, east of the Fayum, in opposition to the Theban rule of the south. His father, King Khety, counselled him to depend upon the delta, both for its revenues and as a buffer against incursions, particularly on the eastern side: 'It happened that I became lord of (my) city, one whose heart was heavy because of the delta (from) Hutshenu to Sembaq, whose southern boundary was at Two Fishes Canal' (lines 81–2). Though the exact location of these places is unknown, the subtext is that they are a domain, that is, a royal or temple estate, a town acting as a regional administrative and surplus storage centre, and a major canal system, perhaps artificially enhanced, in the delta. The western side provided Merikara with *meru*-wood and juniper wood, implying perhaps limited forestation, possibly in scrubland in the sandy areas of the western margins. It is likely that not only were the desert fringes an abundant resource for plants, bushes and wild animals, such as hares, gazelles, wild boar and wild cattle, but that the cultivated areas around Imau (Kom el-Hisn) were notable for their vineyards. The sandy soil would have created a reasonable growing environment for vines and they could have remained in place all year on the desert terraces above the flood level. Wine for the jubilee festivals of Amenhotep III came from the vintners of the 'Western River' (Leahy 1978: 31 no. XVII).

From the edge of the desert, near Kom Abu Billo, there was access to the south towards the Fayum and north-west towards the area of Wadi Natrun, a depression 25 metres below sea level at the northern end, 35 kilometres long and a maximum of 8 kilometres wide (Figure 2.3). There are now eight lakes lying in a line along the *wadi* and some of them dry up in the summer leaving a white salt crust residue, while others remain as marshes (Meinardus 1989: 48–51). The 'Hill of Nitria', located south-west of modern Damanhur and close to Barnugi, supplied natron (Evelyn White 1932: 19–20), a mixture of sodium bicarbonate and sodium carbonate, with some sodium sulphate and sodium chloride impurities. It was used in mummification, for the artificial drying and preservation of soft tissues, and in faience and glass manufacture. The most famous inhabitant of this area was the 'Eloquent Peasant', who brought from here to Egypt the herbs and plants of the area, the stones of the desert, natron and salt, and perhaps traded with the Farafra cattle herders for 'sticks' and with the local Tjemhu or Tjehenu inhabitants for jackal and leopard skins (Parkinson 1997: 58). These latter peoples seem to have ranged across the western

Figure 2.3   The Wadi Natrun looking towards the delta, with modern reclaimed land in the foreground.

desert and coastal margins from Early Dynastic times, with the Libu and Meshwesh attested further to the west by the New Kingdom (O'Connor 1990).

The 'Middle Islands' of the delta in Merikara's 'Teaching' were the patches of flood plain, *geziras* and levees between the river channels, which constituted the central settled areas with state temples and agricultural lands. The cultivated land was the rich agricultural zone subject to increased exploitation from the beginning of the Egyptian state. The ten oldest of the 20 Lower Egyptian nomes (districts) are situated in the area between the two main distributaries and date to before the 3rd Dynasty (Butzer 1976: 93–4), with recent work showing that Mendes and Buto have clear Predynastic settlement layers and Saïs has Neolithic material (Wilson and Gilbert 2003). The story of the delta is inextricably linked with the gathering pace of agricultural development and the extension of this central area, bringing large areas of fields under cultivation by improved drainage and irrigation. More importantly, manpower was provided through military campaigns to operate and develop the field systems (Redford 1993). The modern patchwork of small strip-like fields can be clearly seen on maps and from aerial and satellite images, but ancient field and domain patterns are well hidden beneath the mud. The flat landscape gives the impression that it can be traversed easily, but it is deceptive. Due to the nature of the cultivation, the land is also criss-crossed by irrigation ditches and the larger canals. They can be an impediment to direct movement from east to west, although local ferries would have made crossing larger waterways possible. The sand *geziras* stood up out of the mud and the early river distributaries wove around them in a sinuous pattern. Every thousand years, an average of 1.5 metres of sediment would have been added to the land surface.[1] Over time, many of the smaller *geziras* were buried by the accumulations of sediment or eroded and washed away by the undercutting of the water channels. The great cities of Saïs, Xois and Imet (Buto) took advantage of the agricultural hinterland and managed it for their temple towns situated on dispersed *geziras*. They were far enough away from one another that they did not encroach on each other's territory, but close enough to trade, participate in festivals and coordinate the management of the river channels and dykes. The flood plains supported a subsistence and surplus crop of grain, vegetable and fruit crops, along with flax and vines. Towns, villages and hamlets may have completed the dispersed settlement patterns spreading out from the main storage and cult centres.[2]

Merikara was finally warned that, although the eastern zone of the delta was full of foreigners, the area from Hebenu in the south to the 'Way of Horus' in the northeast was a buffer zone, settled with towns and people. Danger came from the nomadic Asiatic peoples, who were a constant source of unease and disorder. While the 'foreigners' of the east were tolerated because they paid taxes to the Egyptian king, the Asiatics were regarded as a source of chaos and incursions. In the eastern delta, there were a series of low depressions which formed a chain of marshy and lake areas between the Mediterranean Sea and Red Sea coast. The area was characterized by salt flats and impassable marshes, though pathways on higher and more compact ancient levees created state highways which were guarded by fortifications and garrisons of soldiers, at least from the Middle Kingdom, if not before. The fortress of Tell el-Hebua, just beyond Qantara in the middle of a now very desolate area, protected and monitored the 'Ways of Horus' into Sinai and beyond (Maksoud 1998). In the Early Dynastic Period, there were already a number of Egyptian settlements on the eastern side of the delta,[3] which demonstrate the presence of an elite, perhaps controlling early, overland trade routes to the east (Tassie and van Wetering 2003). They may either be seen as 'colonies' established by the newly founded state and populated from the great urban centres at Memphis, or pre-existing local elites who demonstrated their 'new' status by adopting the elite Memphite culture in their graves and by being buried in a manner similar to their contemporaries. They seem to have created a managerial network exploiting the agricultural hinterland of the area, supervising the Pelusiac Branch of the river and its distributaries and the land routes eastward through the Wadi Tumilat. They adopted or brought in the customs of the Memphite elite and their burial practices too, so that the cultures they represent are relatively homogeneous. A local east delta culture is more difficult to trace because it is not represented within this system.

The status of people indigenous to the Eastern Desert and salt-marsh areas is of some importance in understanding the tensions of control and culture in the eastern delta in particular, and the ramifications of the 'Hyksos' rule of 1700–1400 BC. The Egyptians characterized such people in the state ideology as *shatyu* and/or *pedjetyu-shu*, but archaeological evidence for them is, not surprisingly, meagre. Some of the nomadic tribes of the area may have acted as caravan leaders and ultimately as middlemen in the trade routes. Middle Kingdom settlements or foundations at Tell Ibrahim Awad and Ezbet Rushdi were established by the kings who brought the

Figure 2.4 Delta fields and tree-lined canal. The modern landscape, here at Sa el-Hagar, is deceptive. The tall Eucalyptus trees on the right and bamboo in the centre are modern imports.

middlemen into the eastern delta. The subsequent weakening of central rule allowed people with an Early Bronze Age II Palestinian cultural background to take over the strategically important nexus at Tell el-Dab'a (Avaris) and to create a centre of northern rule from here (Bietak 1997a). Their influence can be seen in the burials at Tell el-Maskhuta, and in the Tell el-Yahudiya juglets which are found from Middle Egypt to Palestine. The later positioning of Per-Ramesses (Qantir), the capital of the Ramesside kingdom, nearby to the north-east, emphasized that, in an eastward looking world order, the eastern delta provided an environment for coordination and contact between the Aegean and Mycenaean world, Anatolian and Eastern Mediterranean cultures, and the southern lands of Upper Egypt and Nubia. The eastern frontier continued to be a focus of strategic development into the 26th Dynasty and the Late Period, with royal refoundations at Mendes (Redford 2004a), Tell Belim and Dafenneh, while, under Nekau II, the first attempts were made to link the Red Sea to the Mediterranean by means of a canal.

RESOURCES

The whole of the delta was full of natural resources, from the migratory birds of the marshes to the tamarisk bushes full of bees and the fish of the waterways and ponds. The marsh areas would have seemed to be an impenetrable mass of reeds, but they contained channels, fishermen's huts, nets and baskets for catching fish. They also provided sport for fishers and fowlers (Caminos 1956). The careful husbandry of the swamps meant that the channels through the thick reed thickets would have been kept open, known to people in strategic 'ports' such as Buto, but possibly inaccessible to those from outside. By controlling these access points the Butoites would have been able to allow traders in or set sail themselves in order to connect with people in other areas such as the region of Canaan (Faltings 2002).

Both pasture lands in the alluvial plain and the islands in the marshes also provided for the pasturing of cattle, sheep, goats, pigs, donkeys and mules. Many of the ancient nome names of the delta are associated with cattle; for example, the name of the 2nd Lower Egyptian nome of Letopolis on the south-west fringe is written with the foreleg of a bull, while the 6th nome of Xois, extending from the mid-delta to the coast, is written 'Mountain Bull' and the 10th nome of Athribis in the south-east delta is 'Black Bull'.[4] It is likely that cattle were brought up from the Nile Valley, possibly from even further south along the great cattle routes from Nubia. They could have been fattened on the delta pastures, scrubland and marshes, before being brought to the central administrative zone near Memphis for slaughter. It made economic sense for them not to be too far from where they were needed, that is, at the urban centre of Memphis and also the concentration of specialist craftsmen working on the royal mortuary complexes at Giza and Saqqara. The islands in the marshes and the non-agricultural pastures of the north provided secure places in which to herd cattle; the unauthorized removal of cattle from these areas would have been difficult. The preponderance of cattle suggests that they became the status meat of choice sometime during the late Predynastic Period, but finds from Predynastic Saïs (Wilson and Gilbert 2003), Old Kingdom Kom el-Hisn (Wenke *et al.* 1988) and Middle Kingdom Tell Ibrahim Awad (Boessneck and von den Driesch 1992a) suggest that pigs were reared over and above cattle and caprids, since pig bones are more prominent in the faunal record. An ostracon from the reign of Ramesses II details the holdings of the estates of the Temple of Amun in the delta, and although it mentions swineherds, does not refer to pigs (Wente 1990: 118–19, No. 141). Although this could be an oversight, it may also imply that pigs were the staple meat and produced fat for the non-elite inhabitants of the north. There are also documentary references to wool being transported downriver, perhaps from the delta pastures, and it was presumably an important commodity of the north (Wente 1990: 120–2).

Fish were an important staple food, being caught either in nets in shallow pools after the flood or in deeper water from boats by harpoon. Fish provided a rich harvest that could be dried, salted or processed to make pastes, and therefore kept for some time. The marshes themselves provided reeds which were harvested for use in making basketry, matting and papyrus. In addition, flax-growing areas and linen workshops must have been a major part of northern life, although the technologies of these fragile organic materials are difficult to study because they do not survive in the wet delta conditions. While all of the above resources were available in the south and in the Fayum, the delta provided an abundance.

There were also disadvantages to the north. 'The arrowmaker goes north to the Delta to fetch himself arrows. He must work excessively in his activity. When the gnats sting him and the fleas bite him as well, then he is judged' (*Satire of the Trades*: 8; Simpson 2003: 433). The extra humidity under the hot Egyptian summer sun made conditions difficult, while the cold winter winds and rainfall were unpleasant. It is not known if malaria was endemic to the delta area in ancient times, but bilharzia and associated diseases could have been a damaging part of delta life (cf. Ayrout 2005: 72–4). The inundation was probably the most significant danger in the north. Aside from potential famine caused by lesser floods and destruction caused by high floods, the floodwaters themselves may not always have been potable as they were full of fine sediment. For a short time during the year effective sieving of water must have taken place, perhaps using linen gauzes; or wells were sunk in towns in order to provide clean, fresh water without having to rely on the river channels. Limestone-lined wells at Tell Abqa'in (Thomas 2002) and Qantir, as well as pottery-ring-lined wells at Saïs (Wilson 2005), reflect the fact that the groundwater and, perhaps, springs in the delta played an important part in everyday life (Vernus 1989b).

HISTORY AND ARCHAEOLOGY

Earlier historical surveys of the delta have focused on evidence from written sources. The organization of the united Egyptian state by the 3rd Dynasty led to the development of the massive resource potential of the delta in order to supply the building projects of the Egyptian kings. The Memphite area was the perfect administrative centre for the ideological 'Two Lands' as well as being in a position to exploit the combined economic resource base of north and south. The domains of the 4th Dynasty and later attest to the internal colonization of the delta (Kemp 1983: 89–92); the foreign expeditions of kings helped in the acquisition of people and animals for the lands and work centres. There may have been local northern rulers in the First Intermediate Period as well as attendant economic and social problems; these would have been caused by factors connected with the inundation and changes in river channels, and would have been devastating for the rural foundations of the north. In the Middle Kingdom, kings tried to reassert control of trade routes by building fortresses and reorganizing the agricultural land boundaries (according to the Chapel of Senusret I at Karnak). By the late Middle Kingdom, however, the large Asiatic presence in the eastern delta and an influx of western Semitic speakers combined with the wane of Memphite control, leading to the establishment of a Late Bronze Age II Canaanite/Palestinian culture in the eastern delta whose rulers claimed authority over a substantial part of northern and central Egypt. The Theban kings of the New Kingdom removed this intrusive political element, but some of the cultural traces remained and the pattern of development of the delta continued as before, except that many delta estates were under the direct control of the Temple of Amun at Karnak and the Theban court. New areas were reclaimed and brought into the economic holdings, for example, around Tell el-Balamun. The political focus shifted back to the eastern delta in the face of Egyptian interaction with the power centres of the Late Bronze Age. Per-Ramesses formed a highly suitable court centre, and the lands around it supplied workforces as well as the army, with military men acting as landlords. Increased pressure on land came from the west with the immigration of 'Libyan' groups who eventually offered their services as mercenaries in the army and operated fiefdoms, exchanging military service for land. The dissipation of delta lands to groups of immigrants and the fracturing of political power led to chiefdoms of the Ma, Meshwesh and Libu who were not inclined to unite with one another (Redford 1993: 315–17).

The extension of the agricultural land available in the delta since the Old Kingdom meant that certain cities were no longer 'marsh' towns, but had a rich agricultural hinterland and formed city-states in their own right. In the 26th Dynasty, Saïs developed a new strategic outlook with a port and warehousing centre at Naukratis in the west of the delta. Military control of the east was backed by the use of Aegean military units, while the northern control of Theban property was achieved by sending the daughter or sister of the Saïte king south as the God's Wife of Amun. The establishment of the united Egyptian state with a power base in the western delta acted as a precursor to the foundation of Alexandria, again combining port, strategic location and administrative centre of control for the agricultural lands.

The nature of archaeology in the delta gives a different emphasis to economic, political and religious information compared to archaeology in the south. Epigraphy and the recording of standing monuments are less important in the north, where such monuments have not survived to the same extent as in the south. On the other hand, settlements and towns are rather better preserved in the northern environment at several different levels. The geophysical mapping of Qantir has led to more targeted excavations (Pusch 1999b) and the phases of the town of Avaris can be followed from the Middle Kingdom through to the early New Kingdom (Bietak 1997a). The systematic excavation of clear *tell* areas is uncovering the history of Tanis from the 21st Dynasty to the Ptolemaic Period (Brissaud and Zivie-Coche 1998) and Mendes from the Early Dynastic to the Roman Period (Friedman 1992; Redford 2004a). Fieldwalking and survey have produced interesting results about the Saïte Greek foundation and subsequent development of the town at Naukratis (Coulson 1996). Consequently, the questions raised by the excavated remains pertain to the development of the infrastructure of cities and their individual houses, to the relationship between living areas, cemeteries and temple complexes, and to the pottery traditions of different regions. Whereas the valley evidence emphasizes elite culture, with a written background, the delta may furnish more information about lower levels of society in both rural and cosmopolitan milieux.

In some ways, it is the difficulty of dealing with the archaeological material from the northern environment that has caused the perceived lack of knowledge about the delta, rather than a lack of actual material. Furthermore, the challenge lies in unravelling the evidence for 'low' urban and rural culture, and in defining a method for exploring its interaction with elite culture and the political dimension. Careful exploration of the existing nome capitals of the delta, especially in the last 50 years, is slowly building up a picture of cities as bustling as those of medieval Europe, as polyglot and cosmopolitan as any of the Eastern ports, and as full of religious ritual and festivals. The extension of this work to outlying towns, hamlets and settlement work may lead to understanding the dynamics behind political and religious life.

THE DELTA DIFFERENCE

The possible contrast between the local 'Egyptian-state' and 'fringe-state' lifestyles is hardly addressed by the elite archaeological evidence. The delta, however, contains large town *tell* sites and offers the prospect of stratified cultural information mixed with regional cultural differentiation in pottery and other objects, building practices and burial customs. It would be at the lower end of society that a regional delta culture may emerge. An obvious area of immediate difference may have existed in the dialect of Egyptian spoken in the north. The only hints of this come, perhaps, from the names of the Late Period kings, such as Shoshenq and Psamtek, and in the variety of Coptic dialects, of which Bohairic is the northern version.

Other tantalizing hints of significant cultural and technical differences between Lower and Upper Egypt come from the study of pottery types and assemblages from the delta. An indigenous Lower Egyptian tradition has been suggested from the pottery of the Late Predynastic Period at Buto and at Mendes, which was subsumed by the incoming Upper Egyptian Naqada II material, providing the evidence for the cultural unification of Egypt. A particular type of 'fibrous-ware' has been identified at Buto, Maadi and Mendes (Köhler 1992: 16–17; Friedman 1992: 200), as well as small globular pots with pre-fired holes perhaps peculiar to Buto which seem to be distinctively Lower Egyptian and correspond to the Naqada IId2–III phase (Köhler 1992; Friedman 1992: 204). Seidlmayer has identified a pottery sequence by comparing Late Old Kingdom and First Intermediate Period pottery from the north and south and detected that northern vessels remained more slender, with a high shoulder than the scraped and wheel-made, bag-shaped vessels of the valley. Perhaps this was the result of a delay in the use of new wheel technology in the north (Seidlmayer 2000: 122–4). French has cautiously suggested that a Late Dynastic marl pottery production centre existed in the north, perhaps using white desert clays from the west, and that there was a black-silt ware production centre in the north in the Ptolemaic Period (French 1992) for which a kiln has been found at Buto (Ballet in Hartung *et al.* 2003). Some of the differences noted may be due to the use of northern marl-clay resources, and some to different pottery functions, for example, in fish-product processing or pig and beef fat rendering, or perfume and wine manufacture.

Burial in the delta was a problem (Figure 2.5). The nearest high desert ground was to the east or west, but for most settlements it was impractical to use such locations. The *geziras* and levees provided some high ground, and the tops of the high sand hills seem to have been preferred places for burials, while the settlements were placed on the hillside, remaining above the flood plain. The proximity of settlements and cemeteries was close, and they could expand into each other. Solid mud-brick walls formed a good basis for ready-built tombs, perhaps with vaulted ceilings, and so abandoned town-areas could be reused in this way. Pottery-coffin burials in separate areas of sites, and poorer burials without obvious surviving funerary goods, could eventually become part of a new settlement at a later time, as the settlement was refounded. Such arrangements mean that, archaeologically, multi-strata sites tend to be both cemeteries and settlements. The survival of separate burial mausolea in the delta made from mud-brick suggests an elite burial practice which allowed mass burial, perhaps around important or influential individuals, for example, the Middle Kingdom vault at Bubastis (Grajetzki 2003: 46). There were also separate necropolis areas on sandy *geziras* as at Quesna (el-Hegazy 2002) where a 26th–30th Dynasty mausoleum evidently served the elite of Athribis, or the Wahibra elite-cemetery at Saïs (Bakry 1968). Other burial sites were within town areas in carefully defined zones; these may have been built over later, giving the impression of burials under houses. There is no doubt that the pottery-encased burials at Tanis and Tell Belim (Spencer 2002) belonged to individual cemetery zones separated from, but within visible contact of, the temples of both sites. Pottery slipper coffins provided

Figure 2.5 Kom el-Ahmar on a levee in Beheira Province has been affected by *sebakh* digging, but the local cemetery is still built on top of one of the ancient mounds.

some protection for the body and seem to have been the basic type of funerary equipment available for the middle-ranking elite in the north. In addition, the hawk-faced burials of the Third Intermediate Period may have originated in the north; they range from bronze beak and eye fittings from Tell el-Balamun (Spencer 2001) to the splendid silver sarcophagus of Shoshenq II from Tanis.

Hard stone sources were absent from the delta proper, with the nearest being at the delta apex at Gebel el-Ahmar and the Memphite desert. There was thus no need for the kind of economic management of the desert quarries as occurred in the valley, negating the importance of local rulers in the supply of these commodities. The lack of building stone seems to have led to the specific practice of recycling stone as a building material. For example, Middle Kingdom installations at Tell el-Dabʿa were reused throughout the eastern delta; Per-Ramesses was dismantled to be reused at Tanis (Habachi 1972b); buildings from Saïs were reused in villages along the Rosetta branch of the Nile (Habachi 1943) and, along with blocks from Heliopolis, contributed to the Ptolemaic cities at Alexandria, Canopus and Herakleion.

The mud-brick enclosures of the temples may have served as much as flood defences in the north as markers of divine space. The continual renewal of enclosures suggests that their low, brooding presence on the horizon would have become truly impressive during the flood. Although the delta landscape is flat, the tree-lined canals make long-distance views across the landscape difficult. This may have been the reason behind a type of construction attested from the 26th Dynasty. There are a number of examples of casemate foundations which seem to have belonged to ramped, high platform structures. They may have been fortress-garrisons positioned in strategic places such as Tell Defenneh, Tell el-Balamun and Naukratis (Spencer 1999); but, they may also have served as watch towers, beacons and signal posts which could be used to send communications by light or fire more quickly than it would have been possible to traverse the land.

The plethora of ichneumon cults of Atum, the myths of the creatrix goddess Neith at Saïs, and the two aspects of Horus – as the hippopotamus harpooner at Mesen and as the child, protected in the delta marshes – all suggest that there were strong regional cult mythologies in the north, allusions to which were collected together in the 'The Delta Papyrus', P. Brooklyn 47.218.84 (Meeks 2006).

The north seems to have been a multi-ethnic environment, perhaps from the time of the first 'Egyptian' or 'Memphite' settlers who came to the delta, and it continuously adapted and changed, amalgamating 'Asiatics', 'Libyans' and 'Greeks'. All of these terms may mask a flexible, developing region whose people had a subtle, but profound, impact on Egypt. The economic strength of the north, based on its rivers, distributaries and flood plain, ensured the political power of the northern centres from Memphis to Alexandria, and subtly affected the direction of, and changes in, Egyptian culture as a whole.

NOTES

1 The figure given here is an average, as rates of sedimentation varied at different chronological periods according to the intensity of the inundation and depending upon where they were measured. Stanley estimates that an average of 1.4 mm of sediment was deposited each year in ancient times, based on the Smithsonian drill augers on the northern delta edge (Stanley *et al.* 1996). Butzer notes that there are too many local variables to make a general figure viable.

2 The modern Egyptian constitution describes the basic units of local administration as governorates (26), districts (163), major urban centres (4), provincial cities (8), towns (199) and village units (928). The latter consist of a mother village with the local people's council and executive council, then satellite villages (3,568) and hamlets (*ezbet*) (25,000) (Mayfield 1996: 74–7). The gradual increase in numbers reflects the outward spread of the population and, in effect, a dispersed settlement/population pattern, perhaps similar to that in antiquity.

3 The data should be seen in the light of excellent surveys of the east (Bietak 1975; van den Brink 1987) which have located 'settlement sites' and of the work done in cemetery sites, such as those at Kafr Hassan Dawood and Minshat Abu Omar. Some caution is expressed by van den Brink in the identification of sites from the mere presence of pottery sherds, as much soil material has been moved from place to place in the delta as *sebakh* for fertiliser (van den Brink 1987). In addition, monumental remains made from stone have had equally wandering lives. The actual definition of what constitutes a 'site' is yet to be achieved. There are undoubted *tells* and ancient sites, many of which have been levelled, but some have survived especially in Kafr el-Sheikh, Sharqiyah and Beheira provinces (Spencer 2006).

4 Others include the 11th nome of Pharbaethis in the central-eastern delta, which is 'Cattle Count', and the 12th nome stretching from Sebennytos to the coast in the north-eastern delta which is 'Calf and Cow'. In addition, the cow goddess Hathor was worshipped at Kom el-Hisn in the western delta, among other places.

CHAPTER THREE

THE DESERTS

——— ·◆· ———

John C. Darnell

The Nile Valley is a narrow ribbon of agricultural land cutting through the North African desert, and the oases of the Western Desert are but small islands of water and cultivable land afloat in a sea of rock and sand.[1] The majority of the territory that fell easily within the control of the pharaonic state was desert. This Red Land greatly exceeded the small areas of Black Land, as the Egyptians well understood, and they neither ignored nor feared either the rocky and mountainous wilderness to their east, or the even more awesome wastes to their west. The deserts contained many major routes, linking the Nile Valley with the oases and even more remote areas; they were the repository for most of the mineral wealth of Egypt and Nubia;[2] and the stones and minerals from these desert areas were the physical foundations for the architecture and economy of the pharaonic state.

The quarries and mining regions in the Eastern and Western Deserts were connected to the Nile Valley by often well-constructed roads (Murray 1939; Harrell and Brown 1995; Bloxam 2002; Shaw 2006), while additional road networks linked the Nile Valley with the Red Sea to the east and the oases and more distant points to the west (Figure 3.1). Pharaonic desert roads range from raised causeways to swept tracks to caravan routes formed by the tracks of numerous animals, and literally paved with sherds (D. Darnell 2002); the tracks often follow a relatively straight course, and are not averse to steep ascents, which people and donkeys negotiated with relative ease. Far from being limited to thoroughfares for stone and minerals, ancient Egyptian desert roads, particularly routes through the Western Desert, were important conduits for trade and travel. Tracks frequently ran parallel to the course of the Nile and cut off great bends of the river to bypass the cataracts and other areas of difficult navigation (Degas 1994; Darnell *et al.* 2002: 1–3; *contra* Graham 2005: 44), and would have continued to function when the Nile itself was low and closed to all but the smallest vessels. Even the gods themselves had to find their ways between the Nile Valley and the oases, and the roads might carry their divinity as well (cf. Kaper 1987; Klotz 2006: 9–10).

The deserts were important areas of cultural development before the rise of the Early Dynastic Egyptian state, and were fully integrated into the cultural topography of the pharaonic mind. The earliest pre-pharaonic cultures of north-east Africa emerged

Figure 3.1　Ancient caravan tracks along a major route between the Nile Valley (southern Thebaid) and Kharga Oasis.

from those deserts, and throughout pharaonic history the desert regions surrounding Egypt and Nubia formed part of the inscribed landscape of Nilotic civilization. While rock inscriptions could serve such mundane functions as sign posts and meeting places (for a rock inscription as a landmark for a desert patrol, see Smither 1945: pl. 3a, line 12), many reveal religious motives, and relate to a peculiarly Egyptian approach to annexing and 'Niloticizing' the desert. A number of desert sites are second only to larger temple complexes in terms of the importance and complexity of the inscribed material they preserve, and the information they provide regarding otherwise little known and poorly attested aspects of ancient Egyptian religion.

PREDYNASTIC AND PROTODYNASTIC EGYPT

The deserts that surround the Nile Valley and the western oases were once major centres of cultural change and interacton in north-east Africa. The desert hinterlands of Egypt – especially the vast expanses of the Western Desert – were the areas in which Neolithic traditions from the Sahara, the Sudan and south-western Asia met and combined to create the nascent pharaonic civilization.

During the last Ice Age the Sahara was much drier and larger than it is today. In one of many climatic fluctuations (Hassan 2002; Hoelzmann 2002), this period of hyper-aridity drew to a close around 12000 BC, when the southern monsoonal rains

– determined by the northern extent of the Intertropical Convergence Zone (Smithson in Barker *et al.* 1996: 52–9) – spread to the north, bringing with them an expansion of the Sahelian grasslands and acacia scrublands over 800 kilometres further north than their present extent. During this period of time, different versions of an essentially Neolithic lifestyle began to develop in north-eastern Africa and Western Asia.

Ceramic technology and cattle domestication are two important early developments in the Western Desert, the foundations of an otherwise Neolithic lifestyle, often centred around temporary occupation of wells and seasonal lakes (*playa* basins), in which agriculture and permanent settlements were not of primary importance. Pottery appears in the Sudan and in the Western Desert/Eastern Sahara during the ninth millennium BC, independent of the almost simultaneous development of a ceramic tradition in Western Asia. Two basic ceramic traditions appear in north-east Africa: an undecorated, northern (earlier Capsian and later Nilo-Nubian) style, the vessel shapes often pointed, present by 9000 BC at Regenfeld in the Great Sand Sea, by 7600 BC at Dakhla Oasis and elsewhere in the Western Desert, and by *c.*5500 BC at Nabta Playa in the south-east; and an overall decorated, southern (Saharo-Sudanese) style, most often on essentially globular vessels, established at Khartoum by 7000 BC (Nelson *et al.* 2002; Kuper 2002).

The deserts were also the centres of African cattle domestication and the adoption of Near Eastern caprid herding (Hassan 2002). Roughly coeval with the development of pottery, by societies that appear originally to have relied on hunting and fishing around seasonal lakes and streams, is the domestication of cattle, attested by 8500 BC at Bir Kiseiba and Nabta Playa, approximately 1,000 years earlier than in Western Asia (Kuper 2002; Wendorf and Schild 2002a, 2002b; Schild and Wendorf 2002). With the advent of a dry period *c.*7600 BC, cattle pastoralism appears to have spread out from its probable origin in areas nearer the Nubian Nile, and by 7000 BC had reached the Niger (Wendorf *et al.* 2001: 625–9, 631–2, 655–8, 671; Hassan 2002: 11–26, 198–201, 209–23; for linguistic evidence, see Ehret 1993). Sheep and goats, apparently introduced from south-western Asia, are in evidence in the area of Nabta Playa, the oases of Dakhla and Farafra, and the Eastern Desert during the fifth millennium BC, apparently earlier than in the Nile Valley (Wendorf *et al.* 2001: 623–5, 634–5, 663; Hassan 2002: 201–3). Plant domestication probably never occurred in the Western Desert, and the sewing of wild sorghum at seasonal sites seems, for a variety of reasons, not to have led to early domestication (Wendorf *et al.* 2001: 590–1; Hassan 2002: 111–22, 157–69). Nevertheless, later desert patrolmen (Clère and Vandier 1948: 19, §23, line 17) and nomads (cf. Murray 1939: 100–1) continued to engage in modest seasonal cultivation, probably in the old playa areas.

By the early sixth millennium BC, the centre for major cultural development was shifting from the desert to the Nile Valley, with the Badarians, present at Hemamia by about 6100 BC, leading in a direct line of development ultimately to pharaonic civilization. This new Nilotic culture may owe something to the Tasians, perhaps a desert component of Badarian culture, showing strong Libo-Nubian traits in their ceramic tradition. Evidence of Tasian activity – including pottery, rock art and burials – along routes through the Western and Eastern Deserts suggests that the Tasians were a conduit by which the incipient Nilotic cultures interacted with desert-dwelling and Nubian groups (D. Darnell 2002: 156–69; for more Western Desert Tasian material see Hope 1998, 2002a: 48; for Eastern Desert evidence, see Friedman and Hobbs 2002). Epigraphic and archaeological evidence in the Rayayna Desert south of Thebes further reveals the interaction of several Nilotic and desert cultures, including Tasian, Badarian and Abkan (D. Darnell 2002; Darnell and Darnell, forthcoming). The Cave of the Hands there, with red outlines of human hands covering the ceiling, finds parallels in Farafra Oasis and in the central Sahara (D. Darnell 2002: 161 and 175 n. 5). Certain Saharan cultural objects, tethering stones (Pachur 1991) and the so-called 'Clayton Rings' (Figure 3.2; D. Darnell 2002; Riemer 2004) persist well into the pharaonic era, and reveal the longevity of desert cultures, even as the desert ceased to support any sizable populations outside the oases.

Already during the earliest Predynastic, the Egyptians began to carve images, and later inscriptions as well, on the rocks of their surrounding deserts (Winkler 1938–9; Mark 1998: 81–7; Morrow and Morrow 2002; Darnell *et al.* 2002; Darnell 2002a, 2002b; Wilkinson 2003b). These rock inscriptions appear at an early stage to have provided the Egyptians with a means of labelling and even creating space in the deserts through which many of them moved, transforming what might be an otherwise monotonous desert landscape into an interactive component of human society (David and Wilson 2002; Chippindale and Taçon 2000; Bender 1999). During the early Predynastic Period, Upper Egyptian cultures developed a group of images to represent aspects of the solar cycle. By the late Predynastic, they were grouping these images into large tableaux (Figure 3.3), thereby transforming desert sites into cosmological

Figure 3.2 A cache of so-called Clayton Rings and perforated disks from the Rayayna Desert.

treatises within the landscape. At Vulture Rock in the Wadi Hilal east of Elkab, animals and boats – animate and inanimate carriers of the sun – revolve around the rocky outcrop (Huyge 2002); donkeys, chthonic images inimical to the sun, oppose in their orientation the solar rotation of the giraffes and boats (for giraffes as solar carriers, see Westendorf 1966a: 37 and 84–5; 1966b: 207–8). Generations of Elkab desert visitors created and updated a marriage of geology and art to create a model of the cosmos, around which human visitors could walk, thereby partaking in the solar cycle. Combined images of the old animal carrier and the solar barque also appear in Upper Egyptian rock art (Westendorf 1979; Váhala and Červiček 1999: No. 334; Darnell 2003b: 112), revealing inter-generational interactions at the rock art sites.

As human society became more complex, the solar animals required handlers, and just as the twin serpopards on the Narmer Palette must be held and intertwined by human minders, so in rock art human figures may hold giraffes by ropes (compare Váhala and Červiček 1999: nos. 24 and 25/A; Scharff 1929: 150–1 and pl. 14; Darnell, forthcoming a). Likewise, boats that may originally have depicted the solar vessel itself came to be towed by human helpers (Basch and Gorbea 1968: 179 and 191; Váhala and Červiček 1999: no. 307/B; Darnell 2003b: 113; forthcoming, b), echoing actual riverine processions. Did the evocation and reproduction of the cosmic order in the desert landscape somehow influence the organization of the increasingly complex human society? By the Naqada II Period a political association of cosmic and human order appears with the advent of a cycle of scenes that together presage the Jubilee Cycle of pharaonic kingship. Such tableaux appear on the Gebelein Shroud, in the Painted Tomb (Tomb 100) at Hierakonpolis and in rock art (compare Basch and Gorbea 1968: 35–6; Váhala and Červiček 1999: nos. 221 and 287).

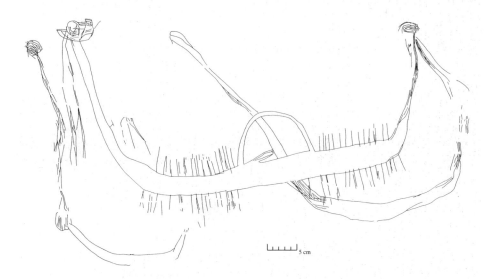

Figure 3.3 A large nautical tableau from the site called 'Dominion Behind Thebes' in the Western Desert, showing late Predynastic vessels. The largest boat is a close parallel in shape and adornment to a number of vessels on the famous Gebel el-Arak knife handle.

With the dawn of the Protodynastic Period, except for periodic invasions, especially by Libyan groups, the history of Egypt's deserts is predominantly a story of pharaonic Egyptian travel and intervention in those deserts by members of the Nilotic society. At least one late Predynastic ruler mounted a raid against the inhabitants of the Western Desert region of Tjehenu-Libya (Wilkinson 1999: 162). Protodynastic armies travelled along desert routes at the time of Upper Egyptian unification, and a ruler Horus Scorpion left an important tableau at Gebel Tjauti, apparently recording his use of a route crossing the desert filling the Qena Bend in order to outflank and subdue the region of Naqada (Darnell *et al.* 2002: 10–19; Hendrickx and Friedman 2003; Campagno 2004). By the beginning of the Naqada III Period, desert inscriptions combine the earlier symbolic imagery and the new hieroglyphic writing system both to record historical events (Williams and Logan 1987: 282–5; Ciałowicz 2001: 62–3) and to reveal the spread of royal hegemony – the image of the *serekh* annexes the cliff on which it is inscribed, just as a seal impressed in clay may establish ownership over objects and buildings (Winkler 1938–9: vol. 2, pl. 11; Žába 1974: 30–1, 239–41; Huyge 1984; Wilkinson 1995, 1999: 80–1; Váhala and Červiček 1999: no. 149; Darnell *et al.* 2002: 19–22; 2003b: 112; Darnell, forthcoming b). Through use of the imagery of the Jubilee Cycle these early historical tableaux celebrate terrestrial events in the terms of their cosmic significance (Hornung 1966; Serrano 2002).

THE OLD KINGDOM

The pharaohs of the Old Kingdom continued the precedent set by their Early Dynastic predecessors (Wilkinson 1999: 165–75) and maintained hegemony over the desert regions, while instituting new and ambitious programmes of building and expeditionary activity. An Old Kingdom ruler constructed a large dam in a desert wadi east of Helwan, in an attempt to create a water reservoir, perhaps a conscious attempt to reverse the final desiccation of the desert, but a flash flood destroyed the project before completion (Garbrecht 1983). The quarrying activities of Old Kingdom rulers are extensive, ranging well into the Sinai Peninsula to the north-east, to the Gebel el-Asr quarries in the far south-west, including Hatnub, Wadi Hammamat, and the routes to the Wadi Barramiya east of Edfu (Engelbach 1933; Rowe 1938; Peden 2001: 6–10, 12–13; Darnell and Manassa, forthcoming). During the Old Kingdom, private inscriptions appear to increase at desert sites, many of these the memorials of expedition members (Eichler 1993; Bell *et al.* 1984; Peden 2001: 4–13; Darnell, forthcoming b). Travel-related inscriptions appear at several Western Desert sites (Darnell *et al.* 2002: 26–9, 119; Kuhlmann 2002: 132–9) and in the Wadi Sheikh Ali (Meyer 1983), providing details of composition, equipment and route of travel (Schenkel 1965: 25–8, 222–5, 260–70; Eichler 1993).

Maintenance of desert routes was essential to exploiting the mineral wealth of the Eastern Desert; similarly, exploration of Western Desert routes granted access to mineral resources and, perhaps even more significantly, trade goods from Libya and Nubia (for Old Kingdom titles related to roads, see Fischer 1991). At an early period the region of Coptos became the starting point for the important Wadi Hammamat route and other Eastern Desert tracks, and Coptos controlled these routes to some extent continuously until late antiquity (Gabolde and Galliano 2000: 144–87). The Theban Desert Road Survey has recorded numerous Old Kingdom campsites between the Nile and Kharga Oasis (particularly west of the Tundaba site, see below); physical remains include Meidum bowl sherds of both Nilotic and oasis fabrics and fragmentary mud-seals. Such stopping points might have been used by the Old Kingdom expedition leader Harkhuf, whose autobiography attests to the use of desert routes – including the 'Oasis Road' – to track the movements of more distant groups, such as the ruler of Yam, who went to the 'western corner of heaven' in his military pursuit of the Tjemehu-Libyans (O'Connor 1986; for the identification of the Tjemehu with Berber speakers and the C-Group culture, see Behrens 1984/5, 1986).

The site of Balat in Dakhla Oasis became a centre of Old Kingdom activity in the south-western desert, and probably maintained connections with the Nile via the Darb Tawil (Minault-Gout 1985) and the main Girga Road. Desert scouts, often stationed on hilltops, guarded the oasis' periphery (Kaper and Willems 2002), and may have interacted with groups living beyond the oasis proper. Documents from Balat record what appear to be otherwise unknown desert toponyms (Pantalacci 1998), and use of a track leading out of Dakhla toward the south-west (Kuhlmann 2002: 149–58) may relate to the interactions of the oasis inhabitants with more distant groups. The fact that potters appear in the clay tablets from Balat, in conjunction with the impending arrival of officials from unknown places (Pantalacci 1998: 306–9), suggests that those potters may be involved in the establishment and maintenance of water depots, such as that at Abu Ballas. A series of sites along the Abu Ballas Trail preserves both epigraphic and archaeological evidence of official Old Kingdom presence (Kuhlmann 2002; Riemer *et al.* 2005), including stylized depictions of leather water sacks.[3] The ultimate goal of the Abu Ballas Trail may have been the region of Uweinat, itself perhaps a way station en route to a more distant area. On this track, as on all of the pharaonic desert roads, the chief pack animals were donkeys, the camel being of no consequence prior to the Persian Period (references in Darnell *et al.* 2002: 2, nn. 21–2).

THE FIRST INTERMEDIATE PERIOD

With the demise of the Old Kingdom and the outbreak of internecine strife in the south, warfare returned to the deserts. One of the first of the southern administrators to assert rule beyond his own domain was the governor of the Third Upper Egyptian nome, Ankhtifi, who employed both naval and land forces, and apparently some desert manoeuvring as well, against his neighbours (Vandier 1950; Seidlmayer 2000: 128–33), at one point attacking the hill fortress (*sega*) *Semekhsen*, west of the southern border of Thebes (for the term *sega* see Gasse 1988: 30; Hannig 2003: 1252).

The shortest route between the Upper Egyptian Nile and the Red Sea leaves the Nile at the Qena Bend; from the same area begins the shortest route to the great southern oases Kharga and Dakhla (Darnell 2002a; Darnell *et al.* 2002: 35–6). This concentration of routes led to the rise of Thebes, which alone could directly control tracks through the Eastern and Western Deserts. An inscription of the Coptite nomarch Tjauti – at the Gebel Tjauti site, a few metres to the right of the Scorpion tableau – states that an enemy nomarch, apparently the governor of Thebes, had 'annexed the escarpment'; Tjauti also records that he opened a new route across the bend, apparently an ultimately unsuccessful Heracleopolitan countermeasure (Darnell *et al.* 2002: 30–7). Just as Horus Scorpion appears to have employed the same route to outflank Naqada, so Thebes made use of the road in the reverse, and outflanked the important Coptite nome, probably descending on the northern forces in the region of Abydos. Indeed, the Stela of Hetepi from Elkab refers to an expedition travelling 'in the dust' (Gabra 1976); the Cairo stela of Djari, from the reign of Intef II, refers to fighting between Thebes and the Heracleopolitans 'west of Thinis' (Darnell 1997); and the 'shock troops of the Son of Ra Intef' – apparently the elite troops of Tjauti's Theban nemesis – left a memorial of their own passage near Tjauti's inscription, perhaps on their way north to the combat west of Thinis (Darnell *et al.* 2002: 38–46). Exploiting both her location and her desert-savvy Nubian allies (Fischer 1961), Thebes waged a war of manoeuvre by specialized forces in a marginal area, allowing for an economy of force and a classic indirectness of approach (for these concepts see Liddel Hart 1991).

Although the main northern routes of the Theban Western Desert preserve ample evidence of early contacts between the Nile and Kharga Oasis (Darnell *et al.* 2002: 28–9, 43–6; Darnell 2002a: 147–9; D. Darnell 2002: 165–73), an officially sponsored push to develop the route and the southern oases first occurred during the early Middle Kingdom. After Mentuhotep II asserted Theban domination over all of Egypt, he turned his attention to securing routes into the Eastern and Western Deserts, the latter being important in providing access to both the oases and routes south into Nubia. During the Middle Kingdom, the Girga Road appears to have become the major artery between the southern oases and the Nile.

THE MIDDLE KINGDOM

Even before the final subjugation of criminals who had fled to the oases during the First Intermediate Period, Mentuhotep II altered the economic status of the oases and desert regions, an action that would have considerable implications for the use of desert routes. The Ballas Inscription of an early Middle Kingdom ruler – probably Mentuhotep II – refers to the annexation of Lower Nubia and an oasis area to the burgeoning Theban realm (Fischer 1964: 112–13; Darnell, forthcoming d):

> x + 5:   . . . [. . .] . . . Wawat and the o[asis . . .]
> x + 6:   . . . [. . .] [the trouble-makers] there [in].
>   To Upper Egypt did (I) attach it.
>   There is no king for whom they worked [during the former reigns]
>   [of the ancestors/forefathers(?)] . . . [. . .]
>   in as much as he loves [me] . . .
> x + 12: [. . .] Wawat and the oasis –
>   That (I) attached them to Upper Egypt
>   was after (I) drove out the [reb][ellious ones(?). . .]

Although desert regions had delivered income/tribute to his predecessors (Blackman 1931: pl. 8, line 6; Clère and Vandier 1948: 15), Mentuhotep II appears to indicate that Lower Nubia and *Wehat* ('oasis') first made obligatory (tax) payments into the Egyptian economy during his own reign (Bleiberg 1988; Moreno Garcia 2000: 129–30 n. 41; Smith 2003: 182–3). In expanding into Wawat, the Thebans appear to have employed the Darb Gallaba and Darb Bitan routes of the Western Desert, leading through the oases of Kurkur and Dunqul on the Sinn el-Kaddab. A chief reason for interest in those routes would have been to secure access to the military recruiting grounds of Lower Nubia (Darnell 2004a). The Nubian desert dwellers also still herded their 'Saharan' cattle, as a number of Middle Kingdom texts and scenes reveal (Blackman 1914: pls 9 and 10; 1915: pls 3, 6 and 11; Vernus 1986: 141–4), and continued to drive them along desert roads in the post-New Kingdom Period (compare the text of Taharqa referring to the 'cattle road' – Hintze 1959/60). A link between Thebes, Nubia and the Western Desert is clear in the title in a rock inscription at Kumma: *iry-pat haty-a ra-aa Shemau Waset Ta-Sety*, 'prince and count of the (narrow) door (of the desert) of Upper Egypt, of Thebes and Nubia' (Reisner *et al.* 1960: 156 and pl. 100G; Ward 1982: 101, no. 844a).

In spite of Mentuhotep's exertions, troublemakers lingered in the Kharga and Dakhla region. The early Middle Kingdom policeman Kay travelled to the oasis region to bring back a fugitive (rebel leader?) (Anthes 1930: pl. 7, lines 4–6; Freed 1996: 304), and 12th Dynasty policeman Beb 'policed for the king in all the deserts' (Boeser 1909: 5 and pl. 10, lines 7–8; Andreu 1987: 19–20). They appear to have used Theban routes to the west, and the Steward Dediku states on his stela that he set out from Thebes to secure the land of the oasis dwellers (Schäfer 1905). In keeping with the economic and administrative changes in Egyptian activity in the deserts, the early Middle Kingdom also sees the end of the use of naval officers in command of desert expeditions (Abd el-Raziq *et al.* 2002: 43).

Under Amenemhat I a civil war appears to have erupted, perhaps exacerbated by the mercenaries who flooded the ranks of the local armies during the First Intermediate Period (Darnell 2003a, 2004a). Mentuhotep II's Nubian recruits, who travelled the roads of the Theban-controlled Western Desert, may have been among the bands of Egyptians and Nubians who terrorized Middle Egypt. The fact that much of the warfare of the First Intermediate Period took place in marginal areas, and the use of desert sites already during the Old Kingdom for atypical and more 'self-centred' private inscriptions, may explain the presence of important inscriptions describing the social and political turmoil of the early Middle Kingdom in the Hatnub quarries (Anthes 1928; Willems 1983–4).

The re-establishment of centralized control over the Nile Valley fuelled the construction of a physical basis for pharaonic hegemony in the Egyptian and Nubian deserts. Together with the great fortress complex along the Second Cataract in Nubia, the Middle Kingdom appears to have maintained a string of fortresses in the eastern delta (Quirke 1989), and at least one desert temple outpost overlooked the Wadi Natrun (Fakhry 1940) and its desert routes (Kuhlmann 1992; Kurth 2003: 14–17). The temple may in fact be located within a fortified enclosure, although it may also be a temple within an enclosure wall, as is the case with other, fortified structures (cf. Schmitt 2005). Concentrations of hut emplacements and shelter areas along desert roads probably served as outposts for perambulating desert patrols; the consistent kits of pottery – ovoid jars of silt, small globular vessels of Marl A3 fabric, and hemispherical cups – associated with these huts suggest the presence of state-supplied policemen and soldiers (D. Darnell, forthcoming; 2002: 172; Darnell and Darnell 1997b: 72–3; cf. Dunham 1967: 141–2; Chartier-Raymond *et al.* 1994:

61–4). The policemen and soldiers are in evidence from their inscriptions in the Theban Western Desert (Darnell *et al.* 2002: 56–65, 70, 73–4, 123–4, 137–8, 141, 143; Darnell 2002a: 145), and concentrations of Middle Kingdom name inscriptions at elevated positions in Nubia may be the signatures of desert patrolmen (Smith 1966: 330–4; 1972: 55–8; Obsomer 1995: 284–6).

Whereas Old Kingdom Dakhla was apparently an outpost of the central government in an economically foreign territory, an economic lifeline tied Middle Kingdom Kharga to the Nilotic administration. Middle Kingdom governors of Dakhla continued to maintain desert routes (Baud *et al.* 1999; for Middle Kingdom use of the Darb el-Ghubari between Dakhla and Kharga, see Winkler 1938: 12, pl. 8.1; Osing 1986: 81–2), and Dakhla continued to serve as a base for expeditions toward the far south-west (Burkard 1997, with corrections in Darnell *et al.* 2002: 73). Middle Kingdom inscriptions near Bahariya (Castel and Tallet 2001) also suggest a use of the entire oasis ring route.

A Middle Kingdom pot depot of considerable size, approximately one third of the distance from the Nile Valley on the northern Girga Road, reveals a new level of official sponsorship on routes between the Nile and the oases. The site of Abu Ziyar (Figure 3.4) appears originally to have comprised several hundred large Marl C vessels of early Middle Kingdom type (Figure 3.5; compare Bader 2001: 155–60), centred to the east of a rectangular, dry stone structure. The jars appear to have been produced in the area of Lisht (Arnold 1988: 112–16), dispatched from the Nile Valley as part of an official opening of Kharga. Most of the other ceramic remains at the site are of Nilotic manufacture, with a few of oasis fabrics. Remains of mud seals and document sealings support the 12th Dynasty date of the Abu Ziyar outpost, and are evidence for careful administrative control of the activities at the site (J.C. Darnell and D. Darnell, forthcoming; cf. Gratien 2001; von Pilgrim 2001). Although the main Girga to Kharga route was travelled and patrolled prior to the establishment of Abu Ziyar, the closest parallels to the site, expedition bases such as the Gebel el-Asr quarry site (Shaw 1999; Shaw and Bloxam 1999; Darnell, forthcoming e), reveal an application of official expedition patronage and outfitting to the control and provisioning of a route connecting the Nile Valley to the southern oases.

An ostracon from Abu Ziyar (Abu Ziyar 2), in a Middle Kingdom bureaucratic hieratic hand, refers to a work foreman (Quirke 2004b: 83, 102) and his crew of apparently 300 men, revealing the use of tax labourers, and of government overseers (cf. Simpson 1963a), at Abu Ziyar. Perhaps involved in setting up the outpost, they may also have been en route to an outpost in one of the oases, perhaps Gebel Ghueita in Kharga Oasis, where archaeological remains indicate a Middle Kingdom settlement of no mean size (D. Darnell 2002: 172–3).

Large and carefully organized (cf. Farout 1994) Middle Kingdom expeditions frequented the Wadi Hammamat, and several other routes through the Eastern Desert (Couyat and Montet 1912–13; Goyon 1957; Seyfried 1981: 241–83; Peden 2001: 35–7; Abd el-Raziq *et al.* 2002; Morrow and Morrow 2002). The Ballas Inscription (line x + 9) already suggests interest in the Red Sea, and the Wadi Hammamat inscription of Henenou (Lichtheim 1988: 52–4) refers to an expedition to the Red Sea, via the Wadi Hammamat, bound ultimately for the land of Punt (Bradbury 1988; Kitchen 1993a, 2004).

Figure 3.4 The early Middle Kingdom outpost at Abu Ziyar (photograph by kite). The plume of red sherds, of greatest density to the east (top) of the dry stone rectangular structure, is almost exclusively made up of Marl C storage jar sherds. The area depicted measures approximately 30.5m by 21.25m, and north is to the upper left (the building is oriented to just west of north).

In the Sinai, at sites such as Rod el-Air and Serabit el-Khadim, Middle Kingdom inscriptions attest to considerable activity, and provide interesting mineralogical and climatological descriptions of the desert (Gardiner *et al.* 1952, 1955; Seyfried 1981: 153–237; Iversen 1984; Aufrère 1991; Kurth 1996; Peden 2001: 32–4). Middle

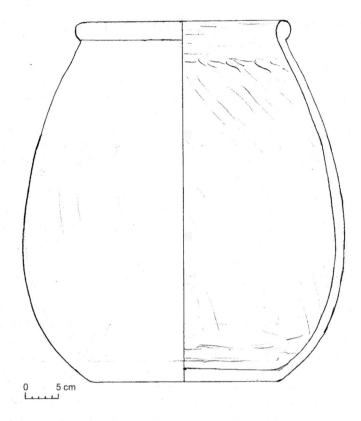

0   5 cm

Figure 3.5   A drawing of one of the early 12th Dynasty Marl C storage jars
from the early Middle Kingdom outpost at Abu Ziyar.

Kingdom expeditions into the desert margins reproduced to some extent the desert
melting pot of the Predynastic Period, and Egyptian officers and officials interacted
with foreign mercenaries and conscripts to provide a unique mechanism of acculturation
similar to that of the later Roman legions. Beginning already in the late Old Kingdom
and First Intermediate Period, large numbers of Nubian recruits and prisoners
contributed to the creation of an acculturated Nubian population in Upper Egypt
and Lower Nubia; specialized and state-supplied Nubian patrolmen within the Thebaid
and along Western Desert routes are well attested (Scharff 1922: 60–1; Spalinger
1986: 222; Quirke 1990a: 19–22; Darnell 2002a: 145).

Middle Kingdom inscriptions from Sinai record Asiatics (*aamu*) as integral, even
armed, elements of Egyptian expeditions (Gardiner *et al.* 1952; 1955: 19 and 206;
Valbelle and Bonnet 1996: 34–5 and 147). Taking part in Egyptian desert expeditions,
these speakers of Asiatic languages interacted with Egyptian military scribes and
produced an alphabetic script for writing non-Egyptian languages (Sass 1988; Darnell,
Dobbs-Allsopp *et al.* 2005; Hamilton 2006). Early examples appear in both the
Western Desert and Sinai, suggesting either several independent developments, or
the rapid spread of the practice due to the reassignment of various desert platoons
from one region to another.

40

THE SECOND INTERMEDIATE PERIOD AND THE EARLY NEW KINGDOM

The routes of the Western Desert appear to have achieved a self-sufficient status by the time of the 13th Dynasty, by which time the great depot at Abu Ziyar was no longer maintained. An often-assumed Hyksos control of the deserts (Bourriau 1999) finds little support from epigraphic or archaeological remains (Darnell 1990: 72; Ryholt 1997: 140–2 and 327; Baud 1997: 27–8). Likewise, the southern kingdom of Kerma does not appear to have been in firm control of the desert roads to its north, although a Nubian raid reached at least as far north as Elkab (Davies 2003a, 2003b). Thebes appears as well not to have maintained any major presence on the routes of the Western Desert during the early Second Intermediate Period. In Kharga, occupation continued at Gebel Ghueita, with local Middle Kingdom styles persisting, and little evidence of any contact with the outside world, except for the appearance of Theban styles, these becoming more prevalent as the 17th Dynasty progressed (D. Darnell 2002: 173). Within the Qena Bend, however, Theban activity never ceased throughout the 17th Dynasty, and grew exponentially during the latter part of the dynasty. The Wadi el-Hôl was the midpoint between Thebes and her garrison at Abydos (Franke 1985; Snape 1994: 311–13), and with Gebel Qarn el-Gir was one of the stops between Thebes and Abydos; Thebes appears to have occupied these sites without break throughout the 17th Dynasty. By the late 17th Dynasty Thebes exerted considerable effort to travel and probably control most of the major desert routes of the Thebaid (Darnell 2002a: 132, 139–41; D. Darnell 2002: 169–74), and the Hyksos appear to have maintained some presence in Bahariya (Colin 2005), perhaps a belated response to Theban control of the major desert roads. By the late 17th Dynasty, Thebes also controlled the northern Girga route, ultimately allowing Kamose to capture a Hyksos messenger (Habachi 1972a).

Economically, Mentuhotep II's integration of the oases into the Nilotic economy, and his successors' efforts and expenditures in opening the Girga Road and developing Kharga Oasis, bore fruit by the end of the Second Intermediate Period. The success of the Theban military and economic control of the Western Desert is particularly in evidence at a desert outpost, Tundaba, at the midpoint of the main northern route between the Nile and the north-eastern wells of Kharga Oasis (D. Darnell 2002: 169–72; Darnell *et al.* 2002: 45; Darnell 2002a: 147–9). Structures at the site, and a small cooking area to the south (at which ostrich eggs were cooked in large quantities), appear to have housed a small garrison to guard the strategic desert road. The central feature of the site was a cistern (Figure 3.6), just over 28 metres in depth, designed to augment the earlier water depots on the route.

The outpost at Tundaba seems to have begun to pay for itself at an early stage, delivering income into Egypt's administrative coffers. An ostracon from Tundaba of early 18th Dynasty date records the calculation of an obligatory payment to the administration (Warburton 1997: 281), probably duty paid as well-tax. A well-tax is known from the time of the Old Kingdom (Weill 1912: pl. 3; Goedicke 1967: 72 n. 30, fig. 5), and for the New Kingdom is mentioned in the Turin Taxation Papyrus (Warburton 1997: 159–64). According to the Turin document, each controller of a well in the 'southern and northern oases' oversaw the collection and delivery of some payment that formed part of the tax of the wells.

41

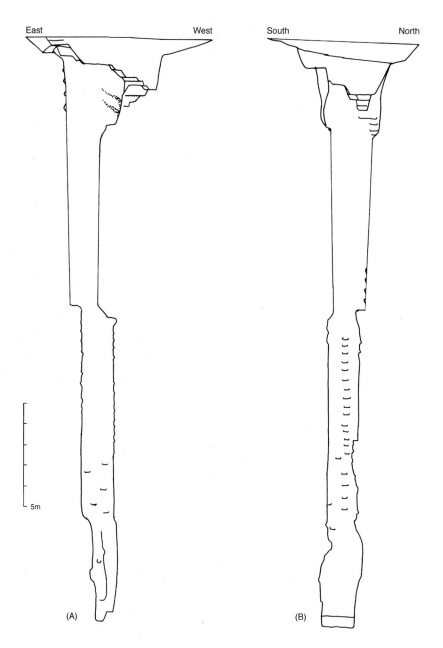

Figure 3.6 East to west (A) and north to south (B) sections of the cistern at Tundaba, probably a late 17th/early 18th Dynasty enlargement of an earlier excavation.

THE NEW KINGDOM

At the beginning of the New Kingdom, many of the outposts for militarized desert patrols were abandoned or converted into forward economic bases and administrative centres, and concentrations of remains are larger and more widely spaced than in the Middle Kingdom. Along the Girga Road, sherds from imported and oasis-fabric amphorae are prominent, including a Canaanite amphora stamped with the cartouche of Thutmose I (the political implications of the manufacture of vessels in Palestine for the Egyptian court at this early date in the New Kingdom will be discussed in J.C. Darnell and D. Darnell, forthcoming); wine amphorae from the oases – including the vineyards of *Perwesekh* at Gebel Ghueita – appear at a number of sites in the Nile Valley and represented an important commodity travelling the Western Desert routes (Marchand and Tallet 1999; Hope 2002b; D. Darnell 2002: 172–3), augmenting the more traditional oasis exports (Giddy 1980, 1987: 64; Zauzich 1987).

Activity in the mines of Sinai may have surpassed that of the Middle Kingdom (Peden 2001: 76–81; Hikade 2001; Tallet 2003: 470–3) and New Kingdom mining interests spread as far as the desert of the Arabeh (Rothenberg 1988). New Kingdom expeditions into the Sinai and the deserts of southern Syria-Palestine, under the command of a bipartite civil (royal) and military (local) command, departed from a staging area near the mouth of the Wadi Tumilat, a region known as the 'Frontier of Ra' (Tallet 2003).

In order to control the Upper Nilotic termini of routes to the far south-east, and to control access to the roads crossing the Bayuda Desert, Thutmose I – confirmed by Thutmose III – established the farthest Egyptian outpost at Kurgus (Davies 1998, 2001b, 2003c, 2004). Egyptian hegemony over Nubia was further supported by the creation of the 'Western Wall of Pharaoh', apparently a string of outposts and patrol routes (Darnell 2004c). The defensive ensemble appears to have been governed out of the fortress of Faras, and extended at least as far north as the oasis of Kurkur. Elsewhere in the Upper Egyptian and Nubian deserts, pharaohs of the 19th Dynasty set about improving conditions along the roads. Seti I dug a well in the Wadi Mia to provide a watering point for travellers east of Edfu, particularly miners working in the Wadi Barramiya (Schott 1958). Seti also attempted to provide such a resource for miners in the Wadi Allaqi, but failed; his son Ramesses II succeeded (Kitchen 1975–89: vol. 2, 353–60; 1999a: 214; Gabolde and Galliano 2000: 153). Merenptah also claims to have been energetic in reopening neglected wells, making them 'function again for messengers' (Kitchen 1975–89: vol. 4, 18, lines 5–8).

The New Kingdom also witnessed the growth of enormous caravanserais within the Thebaid that attest to a steady flow of traffic (Darnell *et al.* 2002: 91; Darnell 2002a: 138–9). The caravanserai deposit above the Wadi el-Hôl, atop Gebel Roma (Figure 3.7), represents a stratified accumulation of debris, consisting primarily of animal dung, pottery and botanical remains; the deposit began to develop during the Middle Kingdom, and grew rapidly beginning with the 17th Dynasty, with major accumulation across the entire site ending with the late Ramesside Period. The majority of the botanical remains are barley and wheat, although other plants are in evidence (Sikking and Cappers 2002). Most of the grain shows no sign of digestion by animals, and was probably intended for human consumption. The temple of Karnak appears to have possessed fields at Hu (Caminos 1958: 126–7, 132–3; Vleeming 1991: 8, 21, 37), and the route may have seen the transportation of considerable grain

Figure 3.7 An early New Kingdom level at the Gebel Roma caravanserai.

shipments for offerings to the god Amun; just as duty was calculated at Tundaba, so was grain weighed at Gebel Roma (Figure 3.8; Darnell *et al.* 2002: 154–5).

In the Wadi el-Hôl a number of Middle Kingdom inscriptions refer to runners and royal messengers using the Farshût Road (Darnell and Dobbs-Allsopp *et al.* 2005: 87–90, 102–5), and by the time of the New Kingdom these included mounted patrols and letter-carriers (Darnell *et al.* 2002: 139; Darnell 2002a: 135–8, 143–4). At least some of these patrols were Nubians, mounted Medjay (Zivie 1985; Darnell

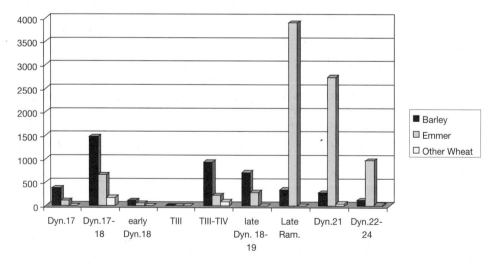

Figure 3.8 Grain distribution at Gebel Roma: amounts of wheat and barley in 1-litre samples of the caravanserai deposit (level numbers converted to dates based on the ceramic analysis of the deposit by Deborah Darnell).

2002a: 143–4, 152 n. 8). Two stelae of the 21st Dynasty high priest and king Menkheperra, set up at either end of the high plateau on the Farshût Road, refer to that route as the 'Road of Horses' (Darnell 2002a: 132–5). The inscription of a chief of the stable at the Wadi el-Hôl (Darnell *et al.* 2002: 139) and a depiction of a mounted rider there (Darnell 2002a: 137) support the use of horses on the route. The stratified deposit atop Gebel Roma further suggests the maintenance of horse relays on the high plateau, and the increase in amounts of animal droppings led to particular sanitation measures. During the early 18th Dynasty a series of gypsum floors sealed off the debris and, beginning with the early Ramesside Period, many layers reveal sherds that were apparently purposely pulverized for animal bedding. Together this information supports the conclusion that the main Farshût Road was, in antiquity, a major postal 'pony express' route.

POST-NEW KINGDOM

Libyan troops appear in the royal bodyguard of the Amarna kings (Davies 1903: pls 10, 15, 20, 26; 1905: pls 10, 13, 17; 1906: pls 10, 13, 22, 40; 1908: pls 20, 29) and some conflict involving Egyptians, Libyans and probable Mycenaeans appears on a papyrus from Amarna (Schofield and Parkinson 1993). By the reign of Ramesses II the Libyans were restive and required the construction of a string of fortresses in the north-western desert (Habachi 1980; Thomas 2000; Snape 2003: 98–105), perhaps an elaboration of an earlier Middle Kingdom system. During the reign of Merenptah, Libyans, apparently armed and assisted by Mediterranean allies – the 'Sea Peoples' – began to mount a series of invasions of Egypt using the road networks connecting the Western Desert oases and the Nile Valley (D. Darnell 2002: 171–2; Manassa 2003). At the same time, certain Libyan groups appear to have functioned as desert scouts for the Egyptians (Caminos 1954: 176–81), not unlike the earlier Nubian Medjay. Late Ramesside Egypt appears to have been hard-pressed to defend itself against the less-organized, smaller bands of Libyans who continued to prey on the Nile Valley (Haring 1993), even after the defeat of their last major invasion during the reign of Ramesses III. The Libyan raids may have had a deleterious effect on desert trade and use of desert roads.

These effects may even have contributed to the major economic crisis that helped usher in the fall of the Ramesside state, apparent in the archaeological record in the caravanserais of Gebel Roma and Gebel Qarn el-Gir. Earlier layers at the site reveal constant traffic with a variety of ceramic fabrics and forms, and plant remains dominated by – but not limited to – barley and emmer. During the late Ramesside Period, the caravanserais reveal periods of infrequent use, with sand accumulation, and the remains of what appear to be less frequent visits by large caravans, equipped with a limited corpus of ceramic shapes and fabrics, suggesting official sponsorship (as earlier at Abu Ziyar). The shipments were predominately grains, probably travelling from the fields of Amun in the region of Hu, filling the treasuries of the domain of Amun at the time when much of Egypt groaned under famine and impending civil war (Janssen-Winkeln 1992, 1995) – the desert routes became the avenues along which a dying state transported its remaining agricultural wealth in a terminal hoarding economy. Whereas barley is more prevalent than wheat in the earlier caravanserai levels, an abrupt inversion of the relative ratios of wheat and barley occurs in late Ramesside levels, corresponding to a period of sharp increases in grain prices (Janssen 1975b).

With the end of the Ramesside Period, the oases appear once again to have become areas controlled by brigands and rebels beyond the reach of the pharaonic state. With the pontificate of Menkheperra during the 21st Dynasty, the Theban government began once again to assert control over the oases and the routes connecting them with the Nile Valley. In addition to promulgating a general amnesty for exiles in the oases (von Beckerath 1968), Menkheperra also constructed fortresses at the Nile Valley termini of Western Desert routes (Kitchen 1986: 249, 269–70); on at least one of these tracks he erected a series of stelae (Darnell 2002a: 132–6).

The desert roads evince considerable traffic again by the Saite Period, and this traffic increases exponentially with the continual rise in importance of the oases, particularly during the Persian and Greco-Roman Periods. Although during the height of pharaonic control over the desert hinterlands during the Middle Kingdom and New Kingdom most desert traffic followed a limited number of major desert arteries, Late Period and especially Roman travel through Egypt's deserts became, as it was during the Predynastic Period and to some extent still during the Old Kingdom, a vast network of larger and smaller routes, with little evidence for any major governmental control of the traffic within the desert regions proper.

CULTIC ACTIVITY AND RELIGIOUS ARCHITECTURE IN THE DESERT

Although certain deities were linked to the desert, because of associations both geographical – Sopdu as lord of the east (Giveon 1984; Valbelle and Bonnet 1996: 38–9), Ha as personification of the Western Desert (Leitz 2002: 10–11), Ash as a Libyan deity (Willeitner 2003: 146 n. 51), and Igay as a lord of the oases (Fischer 1957: 230–5; Kuhlmann 2002: 138) – and theological – Seth as god of the Red Land (Te Velde 1967; Kaper 1997) – the deities most prominent at pharaonic desert sites are Hathor and Horus, the latter often in the guise of the deified ruler (Darnell *et al.* 2002: 29; Darnell, forthcoming e). Quarries possessed their own divinities (Meeks 1991), to whom a number of graffiti – especially later demotic and Greek inscriptions – address themselves (cf. de Morgan *et al.* 1894: 366 [b and c] and 369; Preisigke and Spiegelberg 1915: pl. 22 [no. 306]).

Just as some rock inscriptions at desert sites near the Nile Valley refer to Nilotic festivals (Winlock 1947: 77–90; Peden 2001: 29–32), so a number of desert inscriptions attest to religious practices and celebrations peculiar to the desert environment (Darnell 2002b: 112–14). Because some of the desert routes could represent the actual tracks on which the goddess of the Eye of the Sun might return to Egypt with her entourage (Darnell 1995), and because some of those routes were the avenues by which the mineral wealth of the deserts – the raw materials of the Eye of the Sun (Aufrère 1991) – would actually reach Egypt, much of the religious activity in Egypt's deserts during the pharaonic period appears to have related to the worship of the solar eye. Apart from temples within the oases, the ancient Egyptians maintained some permanent religious structures in the desert proper, and appear not infrequently to have celebrated religious ceremonies within the deserts themselves.

Several Middle Kingdom visitors to the Wadi el-Hôl vividly describe their visit as 'spending the day beneath this mountain on holiday' (Darnell *et al.* 2002: 129–38) – evidence, along with depictions of singers and the goddess in her bovine form

(Darnell *et al.* 2002: 93–4, 126–7), of the worship of Hathor in the remote desert. A deposit of ostrich feathers with inscribed sandstone flakes at the site of Hk64, at the north-west desert edge of Hierakonpolis, also suggests the veneration of the goddess Hathor, and provides tangible evidence for desert travellers bringing objects of cultic significance to trade or offer in Egypt (Friedman *et al.* 1999; Friedman 1999). Figures in festal garb and poses (holding flowers, etc.) (cf. Váhala and Červiček 1999: no. 292; Darnell *et al.* 2002: 65–7) also appear to relate to festival activities at desert inscription sites.

Textual and archaeological evidence for royal statues in the desert reveals a further facet of priestly presence at rock inscription sites (Darnell *et al.* 2002: 103–4). The liminal nature of the desert regions might have been considered particularly appropriate to the worship of the deified king as early as the Middle Kingdom; manifestations of this phenomenon include a probable depiction of Mentuhotep II as divine ruler in the Shatt er-Rigal on a track linking the Thebaid with Lower Nubia (Berlev 1981; Darnell 2004a), and votive hawks inscribed with the Horus names of Senusret II and Amenemhat III in the 'cairn shrines' at the Gebel el-Asr quarries (Engelbach 1933; Darnell and Manassa, forthcoming). A New Kingdom reflection of these monuments includes a healing statue of Ramesses III to the east of Gebel Ahmar, once located on a desert road, where the Nile was just visible to a traveller (Drioton 1939).

Religious structures in the desert could be formal temples near the Nile Valley, and small atypical structures at deep desert sites; the landscape itself could even provide natural grottos as foci for worship. Rock inscriptions of cultic significance may cluster at areas providing shade and something of a natural 'shrine', as at Gebel Agg near Toshka East in Nubia (Simpson 1963b: 36–44), the Gebel Tjauti shelf (Darnell *et al.* 2002: pls 2, 3 and 8), and the *Paneia* of the Coptos to Berenike route (Colin 1998). At times, rough stone walls could augment these natural shrines, as at Timna in the Arabeh (Ventura 1974), and less substantial materials, such as tent elements, may have augmented that and other desert shrines. Most of these natural centres were located along desert roads, and indications of the worship that occurred at such places reveal a direct association with the use of the roads themselves. Members of the priesthood left inscriptions at several desert sites, some as members of expeditionary forces (Seyfried 1981), and others travelling as part of their religious duties between temples at the termini of desert routes (Darnell *et al.* 2002: 95, 102, 120). A number of New Kingdom rock inscriptions record hymns and prayers, most addressed to Amun (e.g. Spiegelberg 1921: nos 904 and 914; Černý 1956: nos 1345 and 1394; Klemm and Klemm 1993: 204; Darnell, forthcoming d). Some rock inscriptions served apotropaic functions, even recording spells for magical protection, and the simple viewing or reading of texts might receive a promise of health and safety (cf. Darnell *et al.* 2002: 103–4).

An interplay of 'formal' and 'informal' architecture appears in the earliest surviving temples of Egypt (Friedman 1996), and appears throughout the pharaonic era at desert sites. By the late New Kingdom an ensemble of temples in the Wadi Hilal, east of Elkab, was a site for the worship of the Eye of the Sun in her local guise of Shemytat (Derchain 1971). Inscriptions of Old Kingdom priests at the Wadi Hilal refer to an earlier temple in the area (Vandekerckhove and Müller-Wollermann 2001: 341–2; Darnell 2004b: 154–5), and indeed a Predynastic image at Vulture Rock may depict an even earlier desert temple at the site. The embattled late 17th Dynasty managed to construct a small chapel at the Theban terminus of the Farshût Road (Darnell *et al.* 2002), echoing the temple of Sankhkara Mentuhotep III at the terminus of a less frequented branch of the same route. Both temples were located at the western Theban termini of a road with a branch leading to Abydos, where the cult of Osiris enjoyed immense popularity during the 13th Dynasty (Leahy 1989: 59–60). The religious significance of the routes from Thebes to Abydos, and Mentuhotep III's activities at Abydos (Leahy 1989: 56), may explain the presence of the temples. At least one priest from Abydos travelled the road from Abydos on his way to perform ritual duties at Thebes, and left an elaborate inscription at the Wadi el-Hôl (Darnell *et al.* 2002: 97–101).

The temple of Serabit el-Khadim in Sinai reveals a mingling of styles (Valbelle and Bonnet 1996). Even less formal are the shrines of Gebel Zeit, overlooking the Red Sea (Merz *et al.* 1980; Castel and Soukiassian 1985; Castel 1988). Least formal of all, but imminently suited to the desert landscape, were small cairn shrines, of the sort known from the Gebel el-Asr quarries, essentially stone cairns with arms creating courtyards enclosing votive objects and stelae (Engelbach 1933). Perhaps the poor and more rapidly made descendants of such structures are the small votive cairns, present at the termini of numerous desert routes, a small forest of which was erected at Gebel Tingar west of Aswan (Jaritz 1981: 246, pls 39–40).

The deserts of Egypt were the places in which the various Neolithic traditions of northern Africa and south-western Asia met and combined to create the formative cultures of the Egyptian Predynastic. The deserts never frightened the Egyptians, as some have assumed, but rather remained the treasuries of the pharaonic state, the sites of the quarry roads, and the homes of great networks of trade and travel routes, linking the various portions of Egypt with each other, and with the outside world. During times of turmoil in the Nile Valley, they were the cockpits of desert warfare.

NOTES

1 Much of the material on which major sections of this chapter are based is only partially published, being the results of the work of the Theban Desert Road Survey and Yale Toshka Desert Survey, and studies prompted by this fieldwork; provisionally, readers are referred to www.yale.edu/egyptology, where they will find routinely updated summaries and images of work at all the major sites. Certain elements of the text discussing the archaeological material derive from season reports of the Theban Desert Road Survey, by J.C. Darnell and D. Darnell. The author would like to thank Deborah Darnell and Colleen Manassa for assistance in the preparation of this chapter.

2 For an overview of Egyptian mines and quarries, see G. Goyon 1974; Castel and Soukiassian 1989; Klemm and Klemm 1993; Shaw 1998, 2002; Harrell 2002; Klemm *et al.* 2002; economic and social implications of quarry activity are addressed in Shaw 1994 and 1998. Since many quarries are located close to the Nile Valley and the overall significance of stone extraction remains fairly constant throughout the pharaonic period, discussion of mining activity will be placed within the context of exploitation of the desert realms in general, particularly the network of desert routes.

3 Kuhlmann 2002: 132–8; Kuper and Förster 2003; Kuhlmann 2005. The image interpreted as a 'water mountain' is probably not a deformed mountain sign, however, but a representation of a leather canteen, or pot-holder. The shape and etchings on the upper corners is identical to an 18th Dynasty clay vessel made to look like a ceramic canteen within its leather container (Roehrig 2005: 230–1).

CHAPTER FOUR

THE OASES

—— .◆. ——

A.J. Mills

The Western Desert of Egypt is the area between the Nile and the frontier of Libya, and from the Mediterranean littoral southwards to the Sudan border. It is a vast area, some two-thirds of the land mass of modern Egypt. However, it should be realized that the real Egypt of ancient times was only the Nile Valley and the delta, and the remainder of the area now known as Egypt was 'foreign' to the Egyptians. This means that the oases of the Western Desert were not an official part of the Egypt of the Pharaohs, but were somehow apart, a foreign region, although under the control of the central government. Nonetheless, there was a long association between pharaonic Egypt and the western oases, and it is not inappropriate to see the oases as an integral part of Egyptian history.

There are five major oases in the Egyptian Western Desert (Giddy 1987): (from north to south) Siwa (Fakhry 1973), Bahariya, Farafra (Fakhry 2003), Dakhla (cf. Winlock 1936) and Kharga. Throughout historical times they have all supported permanent settlement. There is also a depression close to the Nile, the Fayum, which, although technically an oasis, is generally considered to be, culturally, an integral part of 'Nile Valley' Egypt. In addition, there are many smaller places – such as Bir Terfawi, el-Areg and Bir Murr – which are too small to support any permanent habitation, but which have served the people of the desert as occasional water sources, some flowing, others that needed digging out. These smaller water holes played a less significant role in Egyptian history, although they are of interest to those who explore the prehistory of the region. The author of this chapter has spent over 25 years investigating the Dakhla Oasis and perforce many of the facts and ideas written here are the product of that study.[1] Other oases are rather less well known, although work is currently under way by an increasing number of teams.

THE OASES TODAY

Hollywood has typified the Saharan oasis as having a spring-fed quiet pool of water, a cluster of date palm trees, at most a few houses or perhaps just tents, occasional grazing camels and some goats as the major livestock. Humans are few and have a hard, but tranquil time eking a living out of the harsh environment. The reality is

49

quite different. The oases are each rather large – the largest is Dakhla Oasis with an area of over 2,000 square kilometres and a population of 75,000, and the smallest is Farafra Oasis, which had a population of less than 2,500 until recent development. The other oases are between these two in size and each has differing features. Generally, the areas are devoted to agriculture, with little else as an economic basis for life. A major exception is the Bahariya Oasis where iron ore is mined. Now, also in the region of Bahariya, fossil petroleum fuels are being extracted.

All the water of the oases comes from underground sources, where ancient rainwater has been trapped in sandstone aquifers. This is brought to the surface either by artesian pressure or by pumping. In the distant past, the area of each oasis was covered by lakes and it is the beds of the lakes that now form the oasis basins. These are flat areas of rich, clay soil; the water reaching the surface is diverted over the surrounding area to irrigate crops. There is virtually no rainfall to assist agriculture, so a delicate balance must be maintained for the continuation of life, as neither the soil nor the water is replenished. The climate is, like the surrounding desert, hot for eight months of the year and quite cool through the winter. Occasionally, freezing temperatures can be reached in January, especially at night. There is a prevailing wind, which blows from the north-north-east and, if strong enough, drives the sand of the desert with it. This sand, although forming beautiful dune fields which can protect whatever lies beneath them, is quite destructive and can cover fields, orchards and villages, cutting away at everything in its path. The other main geomorphological feature of the landscape is the stone – in most of the oases an ancient, coarse sandstone, but also there is a harder limestone in places. The limestone is derived from the Tethys Ocean which covered the area during the Cretaceous Era, some 80-plus million years ago. In some places the limestone is highly fossiliferous and forms great deposits of phosphates.

A variety of trees and plants is found in the western oases; most of them are also found in the Nile Valley. The main trees are date palms, olives, acacia (*Acacia nilotica*), tamarisk, fig, and in some places the *dōm* palm. The main commercial crops, dates and olives, are usually sold for cash to dealers, and are highly prized in Egypt. Casuarina and eucalyptus are commonly grown for timber, both imported from Australia via India in the nineteenth century. The commonest crop today is lucerne, which is everywhere grown as fodder for domesticated animals. The cereals that are grown are rice, wheat, barley, and a hot-weather crop such as sorghum. Gardens produce citrus fruits, guavas, mangoes, bananas, dates, and a variety of other fruits in smaller amounts, sufficient for the family of the gardener. Seasonal vegetables include okra, eggplants, tomatoes, beans, onions, garlic and turnips. Cultivation is done by hand, by individual farmers or small groups of villagers. This system is imposed by the irrigation regime, which is a flooding irrigation, anciently introduced by the pharaonic Egyptians. The system of irrigation, in turn, necessitates small fields with raised borders. This is the system of land use found throughout Egypt. Large-scale ploughing with big machinery cannot be accomplished effectively on such a landscape; it always requires hand finishing.

Domesticated animals are kept for meat, milk and fibre, and for transportation. They include cattle, sheep, goats, poultry, rabbits, donkeys and camels, and there are also dogs and cats (tolerated, but seldom kept as pets). The wild animals in the oases include foxes, rodents, Dorcas gazelle, and a wide variety of birds, commonly egrets and herons, doves and pigeons, sparrows and other finches, wheatears and raptors such as falcons, hawks and buzzards.

The oasis populations are composed largely of an indigenous group who are allied culturally to the Nile Valley Egyptians, but who are likely to have originated among Libyan peoples. They identify themselves first as 'oasis people', not Egyptians, and also different from nomadic desert dwellers. The great exception to this scenario is in the Siwa Oasis, where the population is Berber, a North African people. Their tongue is Berber and Arabic is a second language. Their ties are towards the west, rather than towards the Nile Valley. There are a few settled incomers in the other four oases who call themselves 'Arab' and are called 'Arab' by the oasis farmers. They derive their heritage from the Arabian Peninsula and all have tribal or family names relating to that region. There are interesting socio-economic differences between the two populations. For example, the oasis people are farmers, keeping cattle and donkeys; the Arabs do not farm and have flocks of sheep and goats and keep camels. The villages of the oases are clusters of houses built from whichever materials are to hand – in some places stone, in others mud-brick, and increasingly frequently concrete with red brick or cut limestone blocks. In the case of Siwa Oasis and parts of Dakhla Oasis, a hardened salt-crusted soil (Siwan: *karshīf*) is cut into blocks and used for building. There are also barns and sheds to keep the animals, which are brought in each night, and for the storage of harvested crops. Usually these barns are less well made than the houses and have walls of *galoose*, a packed mud, or even just straw. The villages are surrounded by the land that the villagers farm; seldom is land held that cannot be reached in time for a day's work and to return home by the evening. It is also usual for the gardens of the villagers to be clustered together and kept close to the settlement.

Water is the single most important commodity in the oases. Water distribution is carefully organized, generally by the local people. The ownership of a well is an important economic asset. In the past, well owners were the wealthiest members of the community, and they sold their water either by sharecropping or by a direct levy. Today, the government drills and owns most of the wells and sells the water at a subsidized low rate to the farmers. Occasionally, a consortium of local farmers will combine their resources and drill a well, which they then share among themselves. Virtually all the water produced is for irrigation, with only a tiny proportion taken for domestic purposes. It is now realized that the water trapped underground beneath the oases is fossil water and is not being replaced from any external source.

There is one factor in all the Saharan oases that is detrimental to farming. Since the Cretaceous Era, when the Tethys Ocean covered the whole of North Africa, there has been a deposit of salt. Salt is in the stone, the sand, the soil and the water. Flood irrigation results partly in the evaporation of water from the surface; a thin deposit of the salts in the water is then left behind as a residue, and this gradually builds up over decades and centuries. The eventual result is land that is so saline that it will not grow the required crops. The salt itself is perfectly good and is frequently gathered and eaten by the locals. The Tuareg further west, and the Danakil of the Awash Valley, have developed a major trade in salt, the result of this natural evaporation process.

THE OASES IN PREHISTORY

Although the Sahara (an Arabic word meaning 'desert') is now a vast arid region, rainless and generally apparently lifeless, it has not always been so (see Darnell, this volume). Before 8,000 years ago, with the polar ice cap covering northern Europe, rainfall in the Sahara was quite sufficient to sustain life throughout the area. Grasslands, trees and standing water in most places characterized a completely different environment, more like that of East Africa today. The bones, recovered from Neolithic sites, of various animals – elephant, buffalo, antelope, gazelle, and many other species – all attest to a savannah environment throughout the area that is now desert. The major oases at this time were inhabited at least by transient populations and often by more settled people. The oases were a good source of water, which attracted prey for those who hunted for their major source of nutrition, and enabled a human population to survive. Of course, as wild animals moved about the landscape, so humans followed. In addition, in the oases there was a source of the hard stones needed to fashion the tools required for an itinerant hunting life. *Aegyptopithecus*, who roamed the Fayum area during the Oligocene Era, was possibly the earliest human ancestor in the Egyptian region. Much later in the Dakhla Oasis, a succession of occupations in the second half of the Pleistocene Era suggest a landscape that was well watered and so covered by vegetation that early humans would have had little difficulty in making a livelihood. The stones needed for tools – chert, hard sandstone, quartzite and others – were also to be found in the neighbourhood. The earliest tools discovered to date are Upper Acheulean bifaces, and over the succeeding millennia the elaboration and increasing sophistication of stone tools (often called 'flints') ultimately resulted in fine projectile heads and tools for very specific purposes, such as drills, and ground stone pieces, which characterize the Neolithic lithic assemblage in the eastern Sahara.

The landscape of the second half of the Pleistocene was well watered. This is attested by the large number of spring mounds, which largely formed under water. In fact, in the Dakhla Oasis there were palaeo-lakes reaching levels of 175 metres above sea level. These lakes, often as deep as 35 metres, and dated between 350,000 and 150,000 years ago, have associated Mesolithic Age occupations and scattered faunal remains of what would have been a savannah environment around the margins. The lakes were fed by groundwater from artesian springs and sometimes overland flow from the escarpment. This latter would have allowed the persistence of bodies of freshwater even during the driest periods. People would have camped beside the lakes, where they could obtain fish, seeds, fruits and roots, and reeds for shelters. They would have hunted a wide variety of savannah game, such as buffalo, warthog, hartebeest, elephant, antelope, gazelle and zebra, and fish and aquatic animals such as hippopotamus.

After about 100,000 years ago, the eastern Sahara became drier and some of the large oases shrank. This was not the case with the Dakhla Oasis, where it is possible to continue to trace human activity until the end of the Pleistocene, 10,000 years ago. During this time, the 'Sheikh Mabruk' group made its appearance, producing rather crudely fashioned chipped stone tools and apparently living in rather poor and somewhat dry conditions. An earlier population had broken up into smaller and more mobile groups in order to adapt to harder times. It is known that grasses were in the area, but perhaps only in the vicinity of water sources. The 'Sheikh Mabruk' people would have had to stay close to the springs in order to have access to water and to hunt the game that came to drink.

About 12,000 years ago, the ice sheets in Europe began to retreat northwards. With this retreat, monsoon rains followed into the Sahara and the region once again became moister and warmer. Large game returned, attracted by the more plentiful water and vegetation. Human populations also expanded. By this time, tool making and several other industries had become more developed. People began to make pottery and constructed more permanent buildings. This was part of the so-called Neolithic Revolution that occurred between 12,000 and 6,500 years ago in the eastern Sahara.

In the Dakhla Oasis, there was a rich and complex fauna, with elephant, buffalo, ostrich, hippopotamus, zebra, antelope, gazelle, hare, fox and various birds and reptiles. The ecosystem suggested by this faunal variety included water, forage and shade. Humans, of course, were present as attested by the many habitation sites scattered throughout the area. There must have been some rainfall to water the grasslands which, in turn, must have been sufficient to support grazing animals, such as zebra and antelope. There must also have been trees, to offer midday shade as well as food for browsing animals such as elephants. There would have been standing water to provide wallow for buffaloes and, of course, springs to feed the system. The trees would probably have been predominantly acacia, date and tamarisk, and would have provided fuel for fires. All in all, the landscape would have been somewhat similar to that of the East African savannah today.

Another source of environmental information is found in the butchering areas of campsites. At certain times, bones were broken up into small pieces, as if to be boiled and the succulent marrow extracted. Other camps have larger bones which were probably roasted, or where the meat was eaten uncooked. There are also the remains of what must have been domesticated animals, principally goats, mixed among the bones of hunted animals. This indicates domestication and herding, and a move away from a purely hunting economy to one that also included tame animals as a protein source. Of course, milk and blood would have been exploited as well as meat. Several researchers have also identified or speculated on a similar faunal group for this period in the Siwa Oasis, Wadi el-Bakht, Nabta Playa and other locations. Herding is an economy quite distinct from hunting and implies a somewhat more settled population, although transhumance following grazing lands is an important factor. There are aggregation sites for periodical gatherings where initial agricultural practices were discovered and developed.

Additional environmental information is found in the rock art in which animals often are depicted (Winkler 1938–9). Depending upon the geographical location of the petroglyphs, they can be carved, cut, hammered or painted. Among the species identified are ostrich, goose (or duck), a large cat, elephant, zebra, pig, gazelle, oryx, long-horned cattle, goat and giraffe. These serve to confirm the finds of the remains of the animals in the butchering and hearth sites. In fact, there are no petroglyphs of animals that do not fit into the model landscape we have outlined. They are a pictorial record of what people saw in their landscape.

One interesting aspect of the rock art studies leads to consideration of the religion of such a primitive society. Suggestive are the many engravings of scenes that include tethered and led giraffes, and females (perhaps priestesses or goddesses) dressed in very elaborate costumes. Mostly, other human figures are rather sketchily rendered. While the giraffe is the most commonly depicted animal, their remains have never yet been found in the many butchering sites of the region. To be domesticated successfully, such a wild animal must either have been born in captivity or captured as a baby and kept in the presence of people. It is not impossible that the giraffe was regarded as a sacred animal.

Studies of climatic history suggest that the Holocene in the eastern Sahara was characterized by alternating wet and dry phases, with the wet phases lasting two or three times as long as the dry phases. By about 6,500 years ago the desertification of the surrounding Sahara areas was almost complete, as the climate became increasingly arid. It seems, from recent studies of pollen, that the savannah grassland and woodlands extended right across the region, from the southern Sudan to the Mediterranean coast, up to 6,000 years ago, and that a scrubbier grass and acacia landscape persisted for another 2,500 years, as the area became drier. It was during this period of drying that people began to settle in permanent habitation sites. The expanding desert together with the shrinking oases resulted in decreasing space for wild animals and a reduction of the land bridges to more fertile areas south of the Sahara. Trapped animals were soon hunted to extinction so reliance on domesticates became the survival pattern. At the same time, there is an increase in the number of grindstones on sites, as grasses and other cereals became more important in the diet.

The inhabitants of the western oases at this time are termed 'Middle Neolithic' or the 'Bedouin Microlithic' in the Kharga Oasis, and 'Fayum A', 'Masara', 'Bashendi' and 'Sheikh Muftah' in the Dakhla Oasis and Farafra Oasis. The comparative evidence suggests a blossoming of settlement in the western oases during a period of many centuries around 6,000 years ago. Dwellings are represented by circles of stones and slabs; tools become increasingly specialized; grinding equipment is normally present; hearths yield both botanical and faunal materials, the residue of foods harvested and processed; ceramics appear both for cooking and for storage. People had been forced to abandon older nomadic hunting and gathering economies because water was no longer available everywhere. Being obliged to live in more confined spaces, with more restricted wild food sources, people turned to animal husbandry and agriculture. All these major changes, which occurred over a period of time, were the result of environmental change: desertification was driving people to adapt to new conditions.

THE OASES IN PHARAONIC AND ROMAN TIMES

After the major environmental change during the Neolithic came an event of enormous importance to the oases. This was the arrival of the pharaonic Egyptians, who had adapted well to the changed environment in the Nile Valley. Their culture posed a dominant threat and had a lasting effect on the local landscape. The history of the oases themselves became confused with that of various Libyan tribes, referred to by the Egyptians as *Tjehenu* and *Tjemehu*, separate groups of people whose geographical existence is poorly understood, perhaps because they were more transhumant in their desert lives. There are references from the Nile Valley to people living west of the Nile, but no exact locations are given. The 'Libyan' tribes themselves have not left us such inscriptions as might prove helpful. That these westerners were a threat, however supposed or real, is undoubted from the references to them in Egyptian texts as a people who tried to enter the western delta from time to time (Kitchen 1990). These incursions were probably the result of periods of drought in the desert area and, particularly, in the northern oases. However, no Egyptian sites or monuments exist in Siwa, Bahariya or Farafra, from the Old Kingdom, the Middle Kingdom or the New Kingdom, although these periods are all attested in the Dakhla Oasis. We must rely instead on Egyptian references to Libyan peoples for evidence of activity in the region. These are sufficiently plentiful to indicate continuous attempts at incursive settlement in the oases. This, in turn, must mean that there was a constant and sufficient water source in each oasis to support agriculture, pastoral activities and, indeed, life itself. The general picture that emerges from this rather sparse information is one of an environment similar to that of today. Wherever a spring flowed over the surrounding landscape, vegetation grew. This would feed domesticated animals.

The Egyptians had developed a system of water control in the Nile Valley early in the Dynastic Period. It involved the creation of small fields with raised edges, interconnected so that water could be introduced by gravity and passed on to the succeeding fields. This irrigation by controlled flooding was introduced into the oases during the Old Kingdom, and remains the system in use today. We know from archaeological evidence that the Egyptians came to the Dakhla Oasis in the Early Dynastic Period. By the late 5th Dynasty, settlement was possible as they found the landscape similar to their Nile Valley homeland. The land was relatively flat, there was no appreciable rainfall, the water sources were underground and were brought to the surface by artesian pressure, and the climate was basically the same as that to which they were accustomed. The one major difference was that the water supply was constant throughout the year and did not need to be trapped and stored as the Nile inundation dictated.

The fact of the modern oasis landscape having the field and irrigation systems that originated in pharaonic Egypt is a strong historical tie between the two areas. The deserts had ensured the isolation of the various oases, but the great pull of a culturally dominant power acted as a magnet, perhaps strongest during the Roman Period. It was then that the great Roman trading empire demanded cereals, wine and oil from Egypt and the oases were areas able to provide these commodities; the wines of the 'southern oasis' were particularly prized. There is one document that details the crops and commodities that were paid and put into storage at the ancient town of Kellis as payments of rents due to an absentee landlord (Bagnall 1997). At least a portion of the payments would probably have been destined for the Roman market, but it should be noted that wheat and barley were registered in tons every year. Other crops were also deposited in good quantities. The whole document gives a vivid picture of the lively farming economy of an oasis of the Roman Period. But it was doomed when the Roman Empire began to disintegrate and the demand for produce dwindled. There was a decline in population numbers as people moved back to their families in the Nile Valley and it seems that the early Christian Period was one of relative impoverishment in the Western Desert. An additional factor may have been a gradual impoverishment of the land as the result of too much irrigation producing a level of salinity in the soil that would no longer sustain the intensive farming of earlier times.

It was not until the twentieth century AD that the agricultural basis of the oases was firmly re-established, with the introduction of more modern methods and technology and, in particular, the use of chemical fertilizers. Cropping is now at a level greater than subsistence and the oasis farmers are once again able to produce and sell a surplus. The crops are little different from what they were centuries ago.

So, the oases today are quite similar to how they were in the past, although sealed roads and electricity have wrought major changes. Nonetheless, underlying the modern aspects, there is still a character similar to that of pharaonic times. It is through consideration of the landscape, in particular, that one can gain insights into the lives both of the ancient Egyptian inhabitants and of the desert dwellers of the Western Desert oases.

NOTE

1 The accounts by many scholars of their studies in the natural sciences, archaeology and anthropology in the Dakhla Oasis will be found in Bowen and Hope 2003 and Churcher and Mills 1999. References to individuals' chapters and essays are not given in the text; fuller bibliographic references will be found in Churcher and Mills 1999: 245–50, as well as at the end of each paper.

CHAPTER FIVE

URBAN LIFE

———— ·◆· ————

Nadine Moeller

The urban milieu in ancient Egypt shaped the lives of many Egyptians and can be considered as a reflection of the society's structure. This chapter will explore the major elements of towns and their development over time. The dry climate, which characterizes North Africa, facilitates a very good preservation of organic material and mud-bricks, the principal building material used for secular structures. The resulting rich archaeological evidence can be further complemented by artistic and textual records. Within the last 20 years much new data from excavations of various settlement sites have emerged, shedding fresh light on urban life, which forms a crucial element of our understanding of ancient Egyptian culture and society.

ENVIRONMENTAL SETTING

Several factors have to be considered before looking at the actual archaeological evidence, in order to understand the setting and difficulties related to the study of urbanism in ancient Egypt. Egyptian civilization developed in the Nile Valley where the annual Nile flood played a prominent role in the local economy since the agricultural fields were enriched with fertile Nile mud on an annual basis. Therefore, any place chosen for settlement had to be safe from flooding. Nowadays this phenomenon does not exist any more because the flood cycle has been stopped with the completion of the High Dam at Aswan in 1970.

At the beginning of the Naqada I Period, settlements were founded along the desert edge or near *wadis*, an environment that was favourable because of generally wetter climatic conditions and stronger, more erratic floods. This climatic optimum (also called the Neolithic Wet Phase) occurred from the middle of the seventh to the middle of the fourth millennium BC. The first use of mud-brick has been attested at the site of Maadi during Naqada I and might be a technique imported from Palestine (Midant-Reynes 2003: 245). The earliest known larger conglomeration showing urban characteristics such as high population density, social stratification and parts of the population involved in non-agricultural activities, developed between the end of the Naqada I and the beginning of the Naqada II Periods at

Kom el-Ahmar (Adams 1995: 29–39). This is one of the few sites where the beginnings of urbanism can be traced without break until the Dynastic Period.

The end of the Neolithic Wet Phase, which was characterized by a shift to drier climatic conditions, led to an important change in the location of settlements. From the Old Kingdom onwards, towns were founded on higher ground within the flood plain, often using natural levees in the vicinity of the river. The Nile Valley is a convex river flood plain where the lowest land lies furthest away from the river channel near the margins of the valley (Butzer 1976: 16). Mud-brick was used as the main building material, well adapted to the hot climate and allowing frequent changes and rebuilding. This, as well as waste deposits around the habitation areas, created artificial mounds, so-called *tells*, which grew to considerable heights forming a typical feature within the landscape of the Nile Valley and the delta (Figure 5.1). Modern agriculture and *sebakh*-digging have destroyed much of these ancient mounds. At the turn of the nineteenth century they were quarried away in order to use the rich soil from the mud-bricks and organic waste deposits as fertilizer for fields. Numerous sites are also covered by rapidly expanding modern settlements, for example Luxor, where the remains of the ancient city lie underneath contemporary buildings and are thus almost inaccessible. Rescue archaeology, which is a legal obligation in most parts of Europe, has only started recently in Egypt. A new project initiated by the Swiss Institute for Egyptian Archaeology and Architecture has started rescue

Figure 5.1 Tell Edfu, the former provincial capital of the 2nd Upper Egyptian nome
(photo R. Bussmann).

excavations uncovering parts of ancient Syene (Aswan) (von Pilgrim *et al.* 2004). Other reasons for the loss of settlement sites are environmental changes such as river movement, which can be observed at several locations, for example at Elkab where the south-western corner of the settlement has vanished, or at Memphis, where the city's position changed over the centuries. Further problems in locating and excavating urban sites are related to dune movement and thick sediment deposits. The pyramid town at Dahshur has been located by a drill core survey, revealing that the remains currently lie 6–6.5 metres below the present surface and thus make any excavation a very labour-intensive project (Alcxanian and Seidlmayer 2002). In the delta, archaeological fieldwork is often hindered by the high groundwater level.

SETTLEMENT TYPES

Urban sites can be divided into two main types, 'naturally' grown towns which developed over a very long time, and royal foundations which were founded to serve a specific purpose. Both types show quite distinctive differences in their setting and layout, but also have many common features, providing a glimpse of urban life and the structure of society in ancient Egypt. Towns founded by royal initiatives usually provide accommodation and facilities for the personnel maintaining the royal mortuary cult or tombs. Other purposes include settlements as a means of internal colonization, elaborate workers' installations for the exploitation of raw materials or large building projects, frontier fortifications, and the foundations of new towns on conquered territory. These sites were supposed to function long-term but they certainly never did to the same extent as naturally grown towns. The pre-planned layout was often rapidly transformed by the inhabitants to fit their needs. The early Middle Kingdom town at Tell el-Dab'a and the New Kingdom workmen's village at Amarna are typical examples where such transformations can be observed (Čzerný 1999; Spence 2004b: 137–9).

Royal foundations are often situated along the desert edge, near the mortuary complex to which they were connected. The earliest evidence of town planning dates back to the Old Kingdom when accommodation for temple personnel was added near the mortuary temples, and housing was provided for workers involved in royal building projects. Much evidence for such sites comes from Giza. It is, of course, not always possible to classify these places as urban sites since they were often only used as temporary lodgings for priests who performed their duties on a rota basis, thus excluding whole families and supporting only a small selection of people. However, there is evidence in the Old Kingdom for so-called pyramid towns, which had the capacity to accommodate entire families and further members of the household, including a wide range of staff employed to maintain the cult and carry out related work. Although many of these sites have been covered by thick layers of alluvium, the recently excavated site at Giza (Figure 5.2) is an excellent example of such a complex but short-lived town (Lehner 2002). The period characterized by the height of town planning was undoubtedly the Middle Kingdom. The most famous town is Kahun, near the modern village of el-Lahun at the entrance to the Fayum depression, which was discovered by Petrie in 1889 (Petrie 1891: pl. XIV). This settlement was founded with the purpose of providing permanent accommodation for the personnel attached to the mortuary temple of Senusret II. The strict grid layout of this town

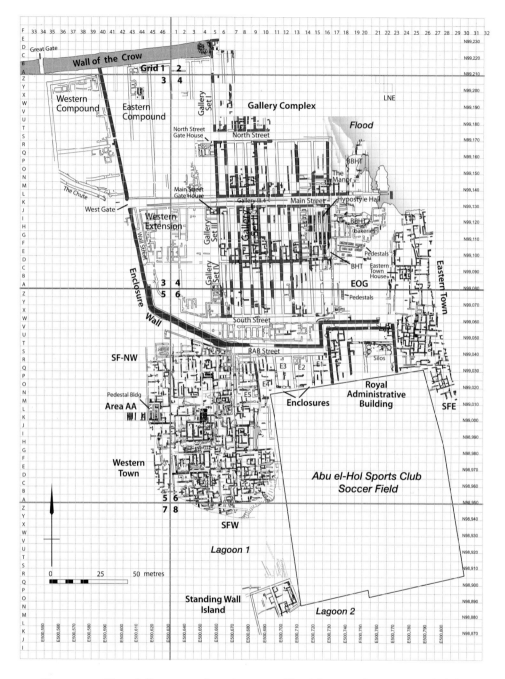

Figure 5.2 The 4th Dynasty workmen's town at Giza (after M. Lehner in *Journal of the American Research Center in Egypt*, 39 (2002): fig. 2).

has been the subject of many investigations concerning domestic architecture; studies have also looked at its population, which seems to have been divided into an elite occupying elaborate villa-type houses, and the majority of the population, living in small, simple buildings. A later addition to the town containing only very small houses was added to the west, thus dividing the town into two zones which were strictly separated from each other by an internal wall. A very similar site has been found at Abydos-South, connected to the maintenance of the funerary cult of Senusret III (Wegner 2001). After the Middle Kingdom, town planning seems to have become architecturally less rigorously regulated by the state, although royal foundations continued to be established. A well-studied site is Amarna, a newly founded capital at the end of the 18th Dynasty. Being clearly a planned settlement in its origin, it left much space for individual development of private housing, in contrast to earlier periods where often a very rigid layout was followed, ignoring the natural landscape. It is also interesting to note that the large elite houses at Amarna stood next to very small ones, so that a strict separation of living quarters for the rich and the poor, as has been observed for Kahun, cannot be identified.

Urban centres that developed 'naturally' are often situated at strategic and economically important places. The town of Elephantine is located on an island in the First Cataract region, an area which for much of ancient Egyptian history formed the southern border of the country. It thus occupied a strategic as well as a potent economic position, playing a major role in military and trade expeditions to Nubia. Furthermore, its hinterland provided easy access to stone quarries, including different types of granite and grandiorite for monuments, statues and stone vessels. The access to trade routes and raw materials is one of the common denominators influencing the development of settlements into urban centres. In some cases a long history of important religious cults, for example at Abydos and Heliopolis, or other ideological aspects would have attracted a larger population, too.

A relatively problematic topic is the capital of ancient Egypt, which would have formed the largest urban centre. The location of the capital changed throughout Egyptian history and sites including Memphis, Thebes, Amarna, Qantir (Per-Ramesses), Saïs, etc., have to be considered. Amarna is one of the exceptions, not only because it was the shortest-lived capital of ancient Egypt, but also because it is one of the best-studied urban sites. From Memphis we have surprisingly little information because much of the city has been destroyed by changes in the course of the river, and by human activity. Other sites such as Qantir have never been fully excavated, but here a recent magnetometer survey combined with partial excavation provided evidence for a large city with palaces and industrial quarters (Pusch *et al.* 1999).

URBAN WALLING

An essential element characterizing ancient cities is the existence of an enclosure wall (Figure 5.3). The practice of walling started in the early third millennium BC. Town walls not only provided protection from, and deterrence to, possible enemies, but also shaped life within the town. Streets and houses are often aligned to the town walls since the latter were more permanent features within the settlement than most other constructions. Buildings also frequently used these walls as backing since it was an easy way to gain stability. Such general alignments and orientations

Figure 5.3 Elkab: the Late Period town walls (photo D. Farout).

recognizable in Egyptian towns have been interpreted as signs of strict planning. This is certainly exaggerated because human nature in general is characterized by an innate sense of structure and proportion. Practical reasons, such as the use of buildings already standing to align new buildings, should be considered instead (Kemp 2005 [1989b]: 196).

Elephantine is one of the earliest walled settlements, a feature that developed from a 1st Dynasty fortress on the island. The enclosure walls were gradually enlarged and finally surrounded the entire settlement by the 2nd Dynasty. At Tell Edfu a sequence of different town walls is still visible today, dating from the Old Kingdom to Byzantine times. It has not, so far, been possible to determine whether they were the product of a local initiative taken by the town administration or a state project. The noticeable standardization of the architecture might be an indication that town walls were a centrally organized building project rather than merely a locally developed scheme. The uniformity of styles in architecture and material culture is typical for most of the pharaonic period, and suggests strong influence and control exercised by the central government; this only seems to have changed in favour of local diversity during periods of political instability. We have little information so far about the actual organization and decision making associated with such projects.

Enclosure walls served a variety of functions. Protection against real or anticipated threats certainly played an important role, but the walls are also likely to have functioned as status symbols, distinguishing urban centres from the rural hinterland.

It seems obvious that the 8 metre-thick walls around the settlement of Elephantine, dating to the 2nd Dynasty, were intended to create a stronghold at Egypt's southern border with Lower Nubia. A text of the Second Intermediate Period reports an attack on the town of Elkab carried out by Nubian groups (Davies 2003a: 6). Were such raids a common phenomenon? It is difficult to say since this specific event at Elkab took place at a time when Egypt was politically less strong. However, there are also tomb paintings which show sophisticated siege engines designed for attacking walled sites (Schulman 1964).

Strikingly lacking is the evidence for city enclosures dating to the New Kingdom. Was this a period when town walls were no longer built? This question is not easy to answer, but it does not seem to be a matter related to poor preservation of archaeological remains; rather, it suggests some changes in urban life. One observation that can be made is the construction of massive walls around large temple complexes, which made them resemble fortresses. The walls often stood very high and had crenellations on the top and buttresses on the outside. The costs of such walls must have been considerable. In the New Kingdom, temples became very powerful institutions and in Thebes (modern Luxor) almost every king of this period erected a huge temple complex called a 'house of millions of years' on the West Bank. These temples not only included cult buildings but also large magazines and accommodation for a sizeable population involved in the administration of the institution, as well as a royal palace. It has to be emphasized, though, that enclosure walls were an

Figure 5.4   Medinet Habu: fortified entrance to temple complex (photo N. Moeller).

important component of temples during all periods of ancient Egyptian history. One of the best-preserved examples is Medinet Habu, built under Ramesses III (Figure 5.4). A large mud-brick enclosure wall surrounded this temple, making it look like an urban centre rather than a cult complex. It is, however, difficult to explain the function of these temple enclosure walls as defensive because, at the same time, towns and palaces, for example at Deir el-Ballas and Malkata, were not surrounded by walls. At Amarna, similarly unwalled, patrols were permanently stationed in the cliffs overlooking the city. A complex system of pathways for these guards has been identified, indicating the way in which security issues were handled (Fenwick 2004). Was there no external danger, so that the erection of walls (except around temples, where they had a mainly religious meaning) was regarded as unnecessary? Or is it possible that instead of surrounding the whole city with enclosure walls, temples acted as fortresses, guarding the most valuable assets of the town and functioning as a stronghold in times of threat? For most of the New Kingdom, there were no direct threats to the heartland of Egypt, a situation that changed at the end of the 20th Dynasty.

TEMPLES

The centre of an urban site, and often its most prominent feature, was the temple. It was usually dedicated to the local town god, and in some cases other cults of national importance were added. Depending on the size and importance of the settlement, several temples and sanctuaries could exist within one urban centre. In the third millennium BC temples were rather small buildings made of mud-brick with some stone elements, while from the Middle Kingdom onwards they show a more uniform layout, being built mainly of stone. The temple remains from Tell Ibrahim Awad in the eastern delta provide a good example of such a development (Eigner 2000). In order to restrict access and separate this sacred world from the rest of the town, temples were surrounded by an enclosure wall, clearly delineating the holy precinct. Temples played an important role in the local economy and were used as a mean of display and power by the central government, which would dedicate statues, rebuild and add temple buildings. Furthermore, large endowments, which were exempt from tax, were given to temples in order to make them autonomous institutions. During the New Kingdom, especially, they were the biggest landowners in Egypt; temple building activity was the main element of official building programmes, and can be clearly identified within towns. The principal temple of a town usually remained in exactly the same place from its earliest foundation until the nationwide closure of Egyptian temples under the emperor Theodisus I in the late fourth century AD. Temples were often enlarged and rebuilt, and smaller sanctuaries added in their vicinity, generally without taking existing habitation into account. At Edfu, a large area was cleared down to the bedrock for the Ptolemaic temple, destroying the ancient town centre around it. The mud-brick enclosure wall of the new temple was clearly built into the surviving *tell*. With few exceptions, Egyptian temples were built on the natural ground surface and thus occupied a lower position than the settlements, which constantly grew in height around them (Figure 5.5). This typical Egyptian tradition stands in marked contrast to other early civilizations in the eastern Mediterranean and Near East, where the temple stood on an acropolis high above the surrounding town. The temples in the towns of Ugarit and Ebla (northern Syria) as well as the acropolis at Athens are good examples of this tradition.

In addition to the main temple of a town, smaller sanctuaries seem to have been part of the general layout of urban sites, too. An example is the famous Middle Kingdom sanctuary at Elephantine dedicated to Heqaib, where numerous mayors and high officials erected their stelae and statues. Heqaib was a governor during the 6th Dynasty who became a local saint after his death. A short distance to the east, another building has been identified as the *ka*-chapel dedicated to the High Priest of Khnum, Sobekemsaf (von Pilgrim 1996a: 149–58). This evidence from Elephantine does not stand in isolation. At Tell Edfu, traces of a small sanctuary have been found about 100 metres east of the main temple of Horus (Moeller 2005b: 35–6); and at Zawiyet Sultan in Middle Egypt, a small temple platform made of stone has been identified in the southern part of the town which probably dates to the Ptolemaic Period (Moeller 2005a: fig. 1). For the prosperity of a town, temples and sanctuaries were an essential factor since much specialized work was involved in their construction and maintenance, providing employment for a large number of people who, in return, needed to be supported with agricultural produce and raw materials.

Figure 5.5 The temple of Edfu with the *tell* in the background showing clearly that the temple lies much lower than the town. Other examples of the same phenomenon can be seen at Buto, Heracleopolis and Kom Ombo (photo D. Farout).

TOWN ADMINISTRATION

Certain areas within a town were reserved for buildings and installations which were principally used by official institutions. There was usually a governor's palace for the nomarch or mayor, as well as buildings for storage and supply which functioned as redistribution centres. A governor's palace has been identified in the south-eastern part of the town at Elephantine (Kaiser *et al.* 1999: 85–90). Much of the walls has been lost due to *sebakh*-digging and only the western façade is still preserved. Nonetheless, some spectacular finds have been made here, such as two small wooden shrines that were stored in a room that had fallen into disuse. Votive objects proved that this had been the home of Heqaib whose first, small cult place was probably located within this building. After his death, the palace remained the mansion of the governor until the early Middle Kingdom. The large number of discarded seal-impressions provides evidence for the administrative activity that took place here. A bakery was attached at its northern side (Raue 2005); built during the First Intermediate Period, it remained in use for the same period as the palace. Six wooden columns, of which three were still fully preserved, have been excavated among huge amounts of ash which had accumulated over time as it was deposited on the floor and around the building.

A large, late Middle Kingdom building which functioned as a storage institution was situated at the north-western side of the town. Its size of about 400 square metres and the lack of any of the usual household installations such as grinding stones, ovens, etc., made it clear that this building was used for administrative purposes and did not belong to a private household. A square tower with a central pillar, probably to support two storeys, stood in its south-eastern corner (von Pilgrim 1996b: 231–4). A large peristyle courtyard formed the centre of the building and in the surrounding rooms numerous storage installations can be distinguished: square and round sunken silos made of mud-brick, and rectangular cellars with vaulted roofs (von Pilgrim 1996b: 85–97, figs 25–7). Organic remains indicate that the silos as well as the cellars were used to store grain. Loose grain would have been placed in the silos while sacks filled with grain were stored in the cellars. Among the demolition debris of the building, a large number of undecorated mud-jar stoppers have been found which would have been used to seal further commodities. Such buildings must have been a typical feature of urban centres. Comparable structures have also been discovered at Tell Edfu consisting of three sandstone column bases belonging to a columned hall that dates to the end of the 12th Dynasty or early 13th Dynasty (Moeller 2005b: 42–6). The anticipated size of the building, as well as its architectural layout excludes private use and indicates that this hall belonged to an official institution. During the 17th Dynasty the area was transformed into a large silo court (Figure 5.6). In total the remains of eight round silos have been found; the largest two have diameters of 5.5 and 6.5 metres, respectively, making them the largest silos excavated so far within a town centre. A thick layer of white ash lies above these structures, indicating industrial activity in a later phase of occupation. Thus, at least from the Middle Kingdom onwards this area of the town was used by the town's administration and not for private housing.

Another example of administrative institutions within urban centres comes from the late Old Kingdom governor's palace at Ayn Asil in the Dakhla Oasis. Here, a

Figure 5.6   Administrative centre of Tell Edfu showing large silos of the 17th Dynasty
(photo N. Moeller).

combination of elements is found in close proximity: the palace not only included private and official accommodation, but also a group of *ka*-chapels for the cult of the governors (Soukiassian *et al.* 2002). Additionally, three rows of two-storey magazines covering a surface area of 298 square metres were attached to the building, as well as a large bakery. This palace must have been the administrative centre for the whole oasis and was certainly part of a larger town.

INDUSTRIAL AREAS

Archaeological evidence shows that industrial quarters were another regular component of urban centres. The evidence for industrial activity often comes from marginal areas of the settlement, but there are also examples where such activity was located more centrally. At Ayn Asil, the remains of a pottery workshop have been discovered lying west of the town and governor's palace. Four successive workshops have been identified dating from the 6th Dynasty to the First Intermediate Period. The workshops consisted of 24 up-draft kilns and included not only workspace and related facilities but also living quarters (Soukiassian *et al.* 1990). Several circular features, which have been identified as kilns belonging to an industrial area used for faience production, have been discovered at Abydos (Adams 1998). Their beginnings can be traced back to the Old Kingdom and they remained in use until the Middle Kingdom. This industrial area was situated along the margin of the settlement area and, as the site expanded, it was shifted westwards to a previously abandoned settlement area.

Much data for the existence of elaborate industrial quarters forming part of a large urban centre come from the Ramesside capital Per-Ramesses (modern Qantir) in the delta. A large metal production area has been discovered here, dating to the late 18th and early 19th Dynasties (Pusch 1990). Copper, tin and bronze were produced in large quantities for the manufacture of a wide range of objects. Parts of this town quarter underwent a transformation during the reign of Ramesses II into a large garrison for chariots, for which metal objects such as weapons and chariot equipment were produced. Evidence for the manufacture of glass has also been discovered. This is of great significance because it is the earliest evidence in Egypt for the primary production of glass from raw materials (Pusch 1999a: 111–20).

PRIVATE HOUSES

During all periods of ancient Egyptian history until modern times, dried mud-brick was the main building material for domestic architecture. This is not surprising, since mud-bricks are easy to produce and well-adapted to the hot and dry climate. They contain as their main component Nile mud, which was mixed with various other materials in different quantities as temper: chopped straw, ash, crushed sherds and sometimes even small fragments of chips from stone working (Kemp 2000a: 82). These additions helped to limit the cracking of bricks during the drying process. Roofs of buildings were either flat or vaulted. Flat roofs were made of wooden beams covered with mud-bricks or plant material with a mud layer on top. Sometimes plaster was added to create nice smooth surfaces for ceilings or roof-terraces. Vaulted roofs were also constructed of mud-bricks and could span larger distances (usually around 5 metres) while flat roofs could span no more than 3.5 metres without the additional support of columns (Kemp 2000a: 93).

The layout of houses can be divided into various types according to the architecture and internal arrangement of living units. A common type of layout is characterized by a tripartite plan, consisting of vestibule, central hall and smaller private rooms behind it (von Pilgrim 1996a: fig. 4). The entrance from the street led into the vestibule which prevented further views of the house interior, a common feature in the Near East. The total number of rooms within a house depended on the overall size of the building. Examples of buildings range from those with only two rooms to the complex layout of the large Kahun houses which combine many different elements. The essential characteristic, however, is the main living room occupying the central part of the building. In the second major house type, this feature is replaced by a central courtyard which occupies up to one third of the total area of the building and has further units arranged around it (von Pilgrim 1996b: 198). How is it possible to distinguish a courtyard from a roofed room in the archaeological record where evidence for roofing is often not well documented or preserved? The general rule here is that large, central living units with a width of more than 4 metres are difficult to roof without the use of columns as additional support. For smaller rooms, traces of pillars or columns can be helpful; often only the bases are preserved while the actual columns have long since disappeared. Column bases can be made of stone or mud-brick and are easily visible in the archaeological record.

Since wood was a precious material in Egypt, columns themselves were generally reused after the building had fallen out of use.

It is interesting to note that in a typical provincial town such as Elephantine, little evidence has been discovered for rooms serving a single purpose (von Pilgrim 1996a: 261–3). Rather, most rooms were multi-functional. The first room was usually a vestibule where people coming in from the street would enter. An oven was often situated in a second room behind the entrance; the actual oven installations have frequently disappeared but the walls show traces of blackening by fire; thick, compact ash layers deposited on the floor together with numerous fragments of bread moulds provide evidence for food preparation. The central room or hall was the largest room in the building and usually contained one or two pairs of columns. They seem not only to have had a practical function as roof supports but also to have formed an element of the interior design and possibly acted as status symbols. Halls have yielded traces of a wide variety of activities, such as food preparation, eating, sleeping and working. Smaller additional rooms lying behind the main hall were

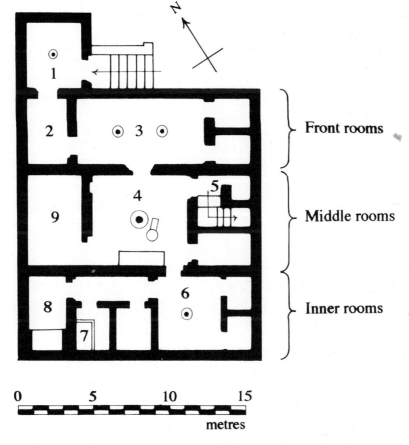

Figure 5.7 Plan of a large Amarna house following a tripartite layout. Key: 1. porch; 2. antechamber; 3. outer broad hall; 4. central hall; 5. stairs; 6. inner hall; 7. bathroom; 8. bedroom; 9. second broad hall (after K. Spence 2004b: fig. 1).

also multifunctional. At one of the houses there is evidence for such a rear room being used as an animal shed, implying that the animals (sheep and goats) had to be led through the house in order to be stabled (von Pilgrim 1996a: 262).

In elite accommodation, the single use of rooms is more common. For example, bathrooms and bedrooms were part of the larger villas at Amarna (Figure 5.7). These houses were built in enclosed compounds which also included a large open courtyard with further side rooms attached for workshops or storage, as well as animal sheds and circular granaries. The house of the sculptor Thutmose is one of the best-known examples of such a villa. The large mansions at Kahun also show some luxury elements such as large gardens, sometimes surrounded by columns, and magazine buildings and further living units for staff and other members of the household. These elite houses were thus lived in by a large number of people, not just the core family and relatives as seems to have been the case at Elephantine.

Archaeological remains generally provide evidence only for the design of the ground floor and rarely indicate what the three-dimensional layout would have been like. However, tomb paintings such as that of Djehutynefer at Thebes (TT104), which shows a three-storey building, indicate that multi-storey buildings must have existed in ancient Egypt (Figure 5.8). Unfortunately, the interpretation of this depiction has

Figure 5.8 House of Djehutynefer (after Davies, MMS 1/2, fig. 1).

been much disputed and its various interpretations range from a single-storey to a two- or three-storey building. This confusion is mainly due to the conventions of ancient Egyptian art, where several viewpoints are usually included in one illustration. However, in combination with archaeological evidence from Amarna, there is now sufficient proof that two-storey buildings were a common feature among the large villas and the small houses in the workmen's village (Figure 5.9). Even three-storey houses can be considered as feasible constructions and were probably quite common

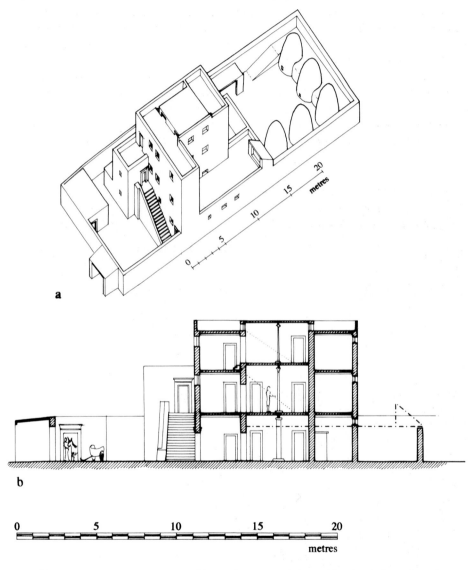

Figure 5.9   (a) Reconstruction of house P47.24 at Amarna (the size and number of windows are tentative); (b) north–south section through the house, looking east (after Spence 2004b: fig. 14).

in densely built urban centres such as Thebes (Spence 2004b: 151). Numerous column bases and painted plaster fragments which had fallen from upper floors have been identified in the archaeological record, as well as staircases leading up to the first floor. It has been suggested that the upper floor levels would have been devoted primarily to private accommodation such as women's quarters, while the ground floor was used for workshops and a multitude of other activities (Spence 2004b: 150–1). This multi-functionality has already been observed for the houses at Elephantine but, there, the evidence for upper floors has been relatively meagre. Only four houses of tripartite layout seem to have had staircases, while the larger houses with courtyards did not apparently have an upper storey at all (von Pilgrim 1996a: 256). This is striking because space was relatively restricted on the island, so it would have been in the interest of the inhabitants to construct multi-storey buildings. It remains questionable, however, to what extent the inhabitants really felt such a lack of space. The excavators observed that abandoned houses and open ground which had been formerly occupied by buildings were not immediately resettled and rebuilt, but usually left undeveloped for a period of time. It is possible that legal issues hindered quick rebuilding, but the open space was not left entirely unused. It served to keep animals and was used as space for short-term storage, mud-brick production, collective cooking and/or rubbish disposal (von Pilgrim 1996a: 254). Was this a way to ensure that some community space was available for the inhabitants? So far, there is little evidence for market places within urban centres although market scenes are known from tomb paintings. This aspect of urban life still remains largely obscure. Markets could also have taken place outside towns and need not have been a typical urban feature. The currently available evidence is still based on a few selected sites, and future work might help to answer such questions more precisely.

PART II

INSTITUTIONS

———·◆·———

CHAPTER SIX

THE MONARCHY

———·◆·———

Aidan Dodson

As has been so frequently stated that it verges on cliché, the king stood at the pinnacle of the pyramid that was Egyptian society. In theory at least, the whole of Egypt belonged to him in trust from the gods. In temples, he was the sole officiant, all officials in the state were appointed by him and all land was ultimately leased from him. In addition, his was the role of maintaining the security of Egypt and holding back the forces of chaos – especially in the form of foreigners. Thus, the status and standing of the monarchy was fundamental to the health of the country, and periods of national decline almost always went hand-in-hand with problems in the functioning of the monarchy – although the polarity of cause and effect in such cases can be a matter for debate.

ROYAL POWER

The king's formal status derived from his being an incarnation of Horus, made explicit in the first element of his five-fold titulary. During the first three dynasties this was his principal appellation, but later the king was usually known by the prenomen, a name associating him with the sun god Ra and enclosed in a cartouche. A cartouche was also used to enclose the king's birth name. The two remaining names, the Nebty and the Golden Falcon, were not usually employed independently. The designation of 'Pharaoh' derives from the Egyptian *per-aa*, 'great house' (i.e. the Palace), which began to be used to designate the king during the New Kingdom.

It was as the intermediary between humans and the realm of the divine that the king loomed large in temples great and small. In practice, the cult was delegated to the local priesthood, but the royal status, together with the king's role as the ultimate provider of resources, meant that the temples were important conduits of control. This was particularly important in view of the major economic role of temples, as the landlords or actual cultivators of much of Egypt's agricultural land. Much has been written about the temples as an alternate power base in potential opposition to the kingship, but it is important to recognize how far the temples depended on the king for their resources – what the king could give he could also take away.

Figure 6.1   Perhaps the essence of divine kingship: the diorite statue of the 4th Dynasty King Khafra from Giza (Cairo Museum CG 14) (photo A. Dodson).

A more direct exercise of power was through the civil administration. The king stood at the centre of a great network of officials, through which the state was run (for its configuration in the Thutmoside Period, see Bryan 2006). His own personal staff would sometimes undertake specific duties, such as the running of commissions for some special purpose, but there was a clear administrative structure that is detectable for much of Egyptian history.

Except in the very earliest times, the senior official was the Vizier (*taity zab tjaty*, later simply *tjaty*), roughly equating to a modern Prime Minister. Our best data for the functioning of this office comes from the 18th Dynasty, which also saw the post split between northern and southern incumbents. A number of southern office-holders included in their tombs a text known as the 'Duties of the Vizier', which sets out the key functions of the post. From these inscriptions, it may be seen that the Vizier was effectively the king's deputy for administrative matters, as well as Chief Justice. His power seems to have diminished from late in the 20th Dynasty as the rule of southern Egypt became far more focused on the military-sacerdotal institution of the High Priesthood of Amun, although the office continued to exist. Little is known about those who held the northern Vizierate.

Below the Vizier, the administration split into specialized departments, whose relative roles and ramifications varied over time, but broadly covered public works, finance, grain storage and agriculture. During the Old Kingdom, the Overseer of Works was often also Vizier, but during the New Kingdom it was a distinct post, with subordinate posts covering specific areas or institutions. Similarly, the other departments had both national and local officials responsible for various sub-divisions, at least nominally appointed by the king.

Alongside the king's ultimate responsibility for civil administration lay his military role. Theologically based on the aforementioned royal role as Egypt's guardian in the never-ending battle against the forces of chaos, the violent side of kingship is frequently invoked on the monuments. From perhaps the very earliest pharaonic monument, the Narmer Palette, down to temple façades of Roman times, the king is shown grasping the enemy by the hair, his other arm raised to smash the enemy's skull with a mace. This motif was repeated throughout the country, usually in places of prominence, and clearly promulgated what was felt to be a key concept that underlay the role of the king.

While it is likely that, as in most pre-modern societies, the king cemented his role as warlord through leading military campaigns in the field, it is only with the New Kingdom that we have direct accounts of the king fighting with his armies. In particular the inscriptions of Thutmose III and Ramesses II give a clear picture of the king as commander-in-chief, supported by a team of advisors. It is interesting that it is from the same period that we find royal princes bearing military titles for the first time since the 4th Dynasty (q.v., below). Coupled with the evidence for Egypt possessing for the first time substantial standing armed forces, it indicates a concept of explicit militarism that is not seemingly a prominent feature during earlier times – except, perhaps, during times of troubles such as the First Intermediate Period. The militarism of the New Kingdom has been generally – and quite possibly rightly – linked with the impact of the Hyksos episode, which made clear the need for a definitive shift in the military status of Egypt if the country were to cope in the new environment of the Late Bronze Age Levant.

Figure 6.2 The coercive role of the king is made explicit in the classic 'smiting' scenes that are found from the dawn of Egyptian history down to Roman times. This is Thutmose III, seen on the Seventh Pylon at Karnak (photo A. Dodson).

The standing of the military in the royal entourage of the New Kingdom is made explicit by the fact that Amenhotep III was the son-in-law of a senior chariotry officer, Yuya, while the three successors of Tutankhamun, Ay, Horemheb and Ramesses I, were all army officers by background.

THE ROYAL SUCCESSION

The mechanism by which a pharaoh came to power has been the subject of much debate over the past two centuries, but in spite of assorted exotic proposals (cf. below and Dodson and Hilton 2004: 14–18), it now seems quite clear that in practical terms a new king should be the senior son of his predecessor. This was theologically reinforced by the notion that on the occasion of the conception of the king-to-be the chief god became incarnate in the king's earthly father. The full version of this myth (with Amun as the divine father) was set out in a number of New Kingdom temples, in particular the Luxor temple of Amenhotep III and Hatshepsut's Deir el-Bahri sanctuary; with Ra as the god concerned, it is also implied in the Westcar Papyrus.

That there was a formal nomination of the heir is indicated by a number of texts, in particular the pseudo-autobiographies of Thutmose III, Hatshepsut and Ramesses II. In the second case we read:

There was a sitting of the king himself in the audience hall, while the people were on their bellies in the court. His Majesty said before them: 'This is my daughter, Hatshepsut-Khnemetamun, who lives: I have appointed her as my successor upon my throne; assuredly it is she who will sit upon my wonderful seat. She will command the people in every place in the palace; she will command you and you will proclaim her word, you will be united at her command'.

Although it is almost certain that Hatshepsut was never actually proclaimed heir, the fact that she felt able to present herself in this way indicates that such a presentation of the heir was a normal occurrence.

As for how the child was selected for such a proclamation, there is no explicit statement anywhere. However, the concept of the eldest son succeeding to the offices of his father was deeply embedded in Egyptian thought and theology, and all indications are that the crown prince was ideally the eldest son. Where a king had multiple wives, any offspring of the King's Great Wife (q.v.) appear to have outranked those of lesser consorts. This is supported by the distinction, which is seen by the latter part of the New Kingdom, between the *za-nisut-semsu*, the heir to the throne, and the (possibly multiple) *za-nisut-tepy*, the first(-born) son of the king.

When an heir to the throne died prematurely, his status passed to the next-senior brother. This was the case even if the deceased heir, himself, had children. The key point appears to have been that a son of the ruling king always had priority over anyone else in the royal succession.

There was, however, always the possibility that there was no surviving son of the king at the end of a reign. Child mortality was such that even in the cosseted environment of the royal family many young princes did not reach adulthood. Whether there was ever an instance when a daughter might have been considered as a potential successor in the absence of a surviving son is a highly moot point. Manetho claims that during the reign of the third king of the 2nd Dynasty, Binothris or Biophis (probably the historical Ninetjer) 'it was decided that women might hold the kingly office'. However, female kings are rare, with the alleged first such lady, the 6th/8th Dynasty 'Nitokris', probably the result of a scribal misunderstanding (Ryholt 2000).

Of the known female pharaohs, the New Kingdom Hatshepsut and Tawosret both obtained the throne after a period acting as regent for an under-age king, and certainly not through being a designated heir (whatever Hatshepsut might have said in the retrospective quoted above!). The obscurity of Neferneferuaten (almost certainly the former Nefertiti, wife of Akhenaten, although other candidates have been posited: see Dodson and Hilton 2004: 150, 285 n. 111) makes her case difficult to assess, although there was almost certainly a male heir in the form of Tutankhaten.

However, at the end of the 12th Dynasty we have the case of Neferuptah, daughter of Amenemhat III, who was only the second woman to use a cartouche – yet was never the wife of a king – and was buried in a manner superior to any other female of the period (Farag and Iskander 1971). Given that Neferuptah's sister(?), Sobekneferu, became the last king of the dynasty, after the reign of the possibly non-royal Amenemhat IV (cf. Ryholt 1997: 209–12), it is possible that Neferuptah had been elevated to Crown Princess by her sonless father, but was cheated of a crown by her own premature death.

Figure 6.3 The first certain female king, Sobekneferu (Louvre Museum E 27135) (photo A. Dodson).

In the absence of an heir of the blood-royal, the default mechanism is likely to have been the public nomination of the heir that formed part of the regular succession system. As to who would be the nominee in such a case, it is likely that a grandchild of the king would probably be the first choice, with more distant relations following. Beyond this, the example of Ramesses I (formerly the General and Vizier Paramessu) suggests that a proven public servant was preferred.

There were, of course, 'irregular' successions, following a *coup d'état* or the sudden death of a king. Here, the legal default mode seems to have been that the person who carried out the late king's funeral was his rightful successor. Such a mode seems to have been embedded in the myth of Osiris and Horus, whereby the latter buried – and avenged – his father before taking his place as ruler on earth while Osiris became king of the dead. This legal concept seems to lie behind the unique scene in the burial chamber of Tutankhamun, where his Osirian mummy receives the last rites from his successor, Ay.

In some circumstances, the political situation, for example civil war, made even this problematic. For example, Sethnakhte came to the throne by overthrowing his predecessor, Tawosret. Together with her erstwhile ward, Siptah, she was written out of history and their reigns condemned as 'empty years' dominated by a Syrian upstart, with the new king divinely appointed to restore order.

The theological status of such a king of non-royal antecedents was clearly somewhat tricky, particularly if his patently non-divine father might still be alive. A number of such situations are known, in particular during the 13th Dynasty. The fathers of the king were at this time referred to as 'God's Father' (*it-netjer*), as had also been the case during the First Intermediate Period. The title is problematic, however, as, certainly during the New Kingdom, it also had wider meanings. Then, it was applied to royal parents-in-law and to some royal tutors. It was also a simple priestly title, although in the latter case it was generally written using a different orthography.

THE KING'S WIFE

Until fairly recently it was held by many scholars that the king's marriage was also a significant factor in his succession. A number of monarchs are known to have married their full- or half-blood sisters, a phenomenon found from at least the Old Kingdom down to the end of Ptolemaic times. By invoking a theory popular in anthropology in the late nineteenth century that the earliest rulers of primitive societies were women ('primitive matriarchy'), a scheme was developed that stated that the actual right to the throne passed down the female line, mother to daughter, and that the pharaoh held office only by virtue of marrying the 'Great Heiress' – his full- or half-sister. This theory rapidly gained uncritical acceptance within Egyptology and beyond, and until the last third of the twentieth century was generally regarded as established fact.

However, more recent work has shown that the whole concept was a chimaera, with the vast majority of kings' spouses being of non-royal birth, even when the kings had sisters living. Furthermore, it should be emphasized that the 'divine birth' scenes are focused wholly on the divinity of the king-to-be as the basis for his right to the throne. No divine engendering of a sister or betrothal to such a sibling is involved: the clear message is that pharaoh is pharaoh by virtue of his father –

not his wife. This is also the case with the divine prototype of the pharaoh, Horus succeeding his father Osiris: Horus is clearly king by virtue of his paternity; indeed, no wife of Horus is even mentioned in the myth.

The world of the divine does, however, provide the prototype for espousing one's siblings – Geb and Nut; Shu and Tefnut; Osiris and Isis; Seth and Nephthys. This certainly provided a justification for brother–sister marriages among the pharaohs, but the intermittent occurrence of such unions indicates that there was no feeling of compulsion in this. Indeed, we have to admit that there seems to be no pattern to suggest why some kings married one or more sisters, while others did not. There are some periods where there are more examples than others (e.g. around the beginning of the 18th Dynasty), but these examples do not seem to illuminate the problem.

There are also some examples where a king's daughter held wifely titles during the reign of her father. However, it is unclear in these cases whether a physical relationship was involved, or whether the lady was simply fulfilling the ritual or political role, generally after her mother's death. In no case do we have an unequivocal child of a father/daughter union to make this clear.

The role of the wife of the king was certainly very significant, both politically and theologically, where she fulfilled the female aspect of the duality that pervaded so many aspects of the Egyptians' conceptualization of the world. Study of the institution of the king's spouse is complicated, however, by the fact that most kings had multiple bed partners, and by the variety of titles employed prior to the latter part of the Middle Kingdom (Dodson and Hilton 2004: 26–32).

The situation during the Early Dynastic Period is particularly unclear. However, the title 'Great of Sceptre' (*weret hetes*) appeared at the very end of the 3rd Dynasty, and then became a key designation for a royal wife. It fell out of use in the Middle Kingdom, before experiencing a limited revival in Saite times, along with other ancient and obsolescent designations.

Other titles that were used during the Old Kingdom include 'She who sees Horus and Seth' (*maa Hor Setekh*), 'Companion of Horus' (*tiset Hor*), 'She who is United to the Two Ladies' (*zema nebty*) and 'Follower of Horus' (*khet Hor*). It is notable that most of these titles focus on Horus; the link between the god and the king was particularly close in the earliest times.

This title-mix underwent major changes in the Middle Kingdom. One fairly typical string of the later 12th Dynasty reads: 'Noble (*iryt-pat*), King's Wife, whom he loves (*hemet-nisut meretef*), United with the White Crown (*khenemet nefer-hedjet*).'

The title *hemet-nisut* first appeared at the beginning of the Old Kingdom and henceforth became the core designator of a royal spouse; it seems to have been applicable to all recognized consorts of the king. *Iryt-pat* was initially found in queenly titles under Pepy II, and was then used down to the Late Period. It (and its male equivalent, *iry-pat*) designated membership of the highest level of society, the *pat*, which seems to indicate the intimates of the king. It was thus a logical status to be held by a queen – but did *not* have any implications as to hereditary rights to the throne, as some have held on the basis of the common, but rather misleading, translation 'Hereditary Princess'.

The *khenemet nefer-hedjet* title is found from the late 12th Dynasty until the earlier part of the 18th, and refers to the relationship of the lady with one of the two principal crowns of Egypt. Conventionally, the White Crown is regarded as the crown of Upper Egypt, and the Red that of Lower Egypt, but it is clear that north/south was not the only duality involved. In contexts such as this title, the distinction between the two crowns should not be regarded as necessarily geographical. Rather, the White Crown can be associated with the eternal aspect of Egyptian kingship, and the Red with its earthly manifestations, the *khenemet nefer-hedjet* title thus linked the royal wife into the overall 'mythic prototype' of the monarch.

Around the same time that the *khenemet nefer-hedjet* title appears, we also find the title 'King's Great Wife' (*hemet-nisut-weret*). The implications of the 'Great Wife' title are fairly clear, in that it designated the first lady of the land, a status made particularly likely in view of the fact that the first known 'Great Wife', Mertseger, wife of Senusret III, was also the first person other than a king to use a cartouche. The title continued in use into the Ptolemaic Period.

Although initially there was only one Great Wife at a time, from the latter part of the 18th Dynasty onwards there were occasions when multiple holders of the title existed simultaneously, the best-known examples being Nefertari and Isetneferet under Ramesses II. After their deaths, the latter king raised two daughters of Nefertari and one of Isetneferet to the rank, as well as bestowing it on the Hittite princess whom he had married.

A Great Wife in the New Kingdom could hold a very extensive list of titles, but many were simply evocations of her beauty, 'political' significance being restricted, apart from her 'Great Wife' title, to 'Lady of the Two Lands' (*nebet-tawy*), 'Mistress of the Two Lands' (*henut-tawy*) and 'Mistress of Upper Egypt and Lower Egypt' (*henut Shemau Ta-mehu*). Their relative importance is indicated by the fact that when space in an inscription was limited, the title King's Great Wife took precedence, followed by Lady of the Two Lands; the latter was simply a feminization of the kingly tag, Lord of the Two Lands, used since the Old Kingdom.

The structure of the titulary established during the New Kingdom remained broadly standard for the remainder of Egyptian dynastic history, although during the 26th Dynasty there was some revival of archaic titles such as 'Great of Sceptre'. Final modifications to the scheme took place under the Ptolemies, and the range of titles was rapidly reduced after Cleopatra I, wife of Ptolemy V. The co-rulership held by many Ptolemaic queens is shown by the new title, 'Ruler' (*heqat*) used by Arsinoe II and most of her successors, down to Cleopatra VII herself. An office that was often held by the Great Wife during the New Kingdom, but was not formally linked with it, was God's Wife of Amun (*hemet-netjer en Amun*). First bestowed upon Ahhotep, wife of Taa II, this designated a female counterpart to the High Priest of Amun, and seems to have been a mechanism to place a member of the royal family into the management of the most powerful of Egypt's religious cults. As such, it clearly provided an important enhancement of a Great Wife's power. However, in some cases it was held by a royal daughter who was not married to a king, and from the end of the 20th Dynasty onwards it was a wholly separate office, held by an unmarried woman who was usually the eldest daughter of a king. By the end of the Third Intermediate Period succession to the office of God's Wife was based on formal adoption, and soon afterwards the God's Wife became undisputed head of the Amun cult, to the exclusion of any male High Priest.

A King's Wife (Great or otherwise) would aspire to the dignity of King's Mother (*mut-nisut*), a title that could also, of course, be open to the mother of a usurper.

Figure 6.4   Karomama B, King's Great Wife of the 22nd Dynasty Osorkon II, on a slab from Bubastis (Tell Basta) (British Museum EA 1077) (photo A. Dodson).

Figure 6.5 Ahmose I offers to his grandmother, the *hemet-nisut*, *mut-nisut*, Tetisheri on her cenotaph-stela from Abydos (Egyptian Museum, Cairo CG 34002) (photo A. Dodson).

Such a lady was naturally an important figure at the court of her son, and in some cases could be retrospectively raised from being a simple *hemet-nisut* to being a *hemet-nisut-weret*, for example the mothers of Thutmose III and IV.

THE ROYAL OFFSPRING

The role and status of a king's sons is a complex issue (Dodson and Hilton 2004: 32–4). During the 4th Dynasty, which is the earliest period for which we have evidence, they held high offices in the civil administration, including the highest of all, the Vizierate. Yet at the end of the dynasty, the tenure of government offices by royal sons dropped off rapidly, never to reappear. During the next millennium, sons

85

of the king are but rarely attested, and it is not until the 18th Dynasty that much is known about them.

We owe our knowledge of many of these individuals solely to the tombs of their tutors. However, others are known as a result of princes once more taking office – but, crucially, only in the clergy and the army, to the exclusion of the civil government. In particular, the senior priesthoods of Ptah at Memphis and Ra at Heliopolis were granted to princes from at least the reign of Amenhotep II onwards. Interestingly, the pivotal priesthood of Amun at Thebes was not held by princes until the Third Intermediate Period.

Royal sons were being granted military ranks, up to and including Generalissimo (*imy-ra mesha wer*), at least as early as the reign of Thutmose I. This fitted well with the highly militaristic nature of the pharaonic regime during much of the New Kingdom (cf. above), with the sons actually depicted in the battle-reliefs of Ramesses II and III. Some of Ramesses III's sons held an apparently more senior title still, First Generalissimo of His Person (*imy-ra mesha wer tepy en hemef*); others were simply 'Generals' (*imy-ra mesha*). Yet other Ramesside princes were Masters of Horse (*imy-ra sesmet*), implying command over the chariotry.

A major question is how far these military posts reflected active service, or whether they were merely sinecures. Certainly, the sons of Ramesses II were depicted taking part in his campaigns, as were sons of Merenptah; some may have pursued a genuine military career, while others merely enjoyed the trappings of military status. In any case, there is evidence that princes were given military training as part of their education, the future Amenhotep II being shown receiving instruction in archery in the tomb of his tutor, Min (Theban Tomb 109).

Ramesses II and III also introduced the representation of their offspring *in extenso* within their temples, great processions of sons and daughters adorning the walls. Previously, illustrations of offspring were rare on public monuments, and depictions were normally restricted to a few senior daughters – frequently unnamed. This fundamental shake-up in the public face of the royal family – arguably the first appearance of the concept of a 'royal family', rather than simply the king and his offspring – must clearly have had some significance. A clue may lie in the plebeian origins of the Ramesside royal family, in contrast to the outgoing royal house, who (at least in theory) could trace their lineage back into the Second Intermediate Period. Against such a background, the royalty of the new family might need to be stressed, particularly into the next generation. It is in this context that we should probably see scenes of the king officiating alongside his Crown Prince – a motif wholly unknown prior to the reign of Seti I.

The status and role of royal daughters presents a number of issues (Dodson and Hilton 2004: 34–5). Apart from the aforementioned office of God's Wife of Amun, and some subsidiary sacerdotal roles as 'Chantresses' (*heset khenu*), there are no specific offices that were generally held by royal daughters. During the late Old Kingdom and again in the Third Intermediate Period, there were examples of princesses marrying commoners, but there is very little evidence from other periods, leaving open the question of whether any protocols governed the marriage of members of the royal family. There is a similar lack of data on the marriage of royal sons, although we know that one son of Ramesses II, Simontju, married the daughter of a Syrian ship-captain.

Figure 6.6 The elder surviving sons of Ramesses III shown at Medinet Habu. They include the future Ramesses IV, VI and VIII (photo A. Dodson).

Figure 6.7   Some of the younger daughters of Ramesses II, as shown at the Seti I temple at Abydos: Meryetmihapi; Meryetyotes B; Nubmiunu; Henutsekhemu and Henutpahuro[. . .] (photo A. Dodson).

THE ROYAL COURT

An Egyptian official possessed a string of titles. Some denoted actual administrative functions (cf. above, p. 77), but others were more to do with indicating his standing at the royal court – in many cases the closeness of his relationship with the king. Although the significance of some titles changed over time, in certain cases fairly fundamentally, examples of ranking titles include 'Sole Companion' (*semer-waty*), 'Fanbearer on the Right hand of the King' (*tjay-khu her imenty-nisut*) and the aforementioned *iry-pat* (see p. 82). Such titles were particularly elaborate during the Old Kingdom, when vast strings could be possessed by the most senior officials (cf. Baer 1960).

Aside from these various members of the national administration whose attendance on the king was linked both by their administrative function and their rank as courtiers, there were myriad other individuals whose attachment was to the king as an individual, rather than as head of state. At one end of the spectrum this included personal servants and attendants of the king and members of the royal family; at the other, it included persons such as the Royal Cup-Bearers who during the Ramesside Period seem on occasion to have acted as the king's 'trouble-shooters', and in some cases later rose to high governmental office (Schulman 1986).

Between these two extremes there were various officials, for example the High Steward of the King, responsible for the king's personal estates; and individuals attached to the harems (Haslauer 2001) that were found in a number of locations, including Memphis and Medinet Gurob, near the mouth of the Fayum. These were institutions concerned with the private affairs of the royal family, communities centred on royal women and children that could function as units separate from the main

Figure 6.8 The consummate courtier: the Steward of the God's
Wife of Amun, Neferura (daughter of Hatshepsut), Senenmut;
from Karnak (British Museum EA 174) (photo A. Dodson).

royal palace. While pre-New Kingdom evidence is equivocal, from the beginning of that period we find titles clearly belonging to the administrators of the harems. Apart from providing for members of the royal family, these institutions also acted as industrial centres for the production of linen. A further function seems to have been the education of royal children. Individuals who later bore the title 'Child of the Kap' (*khered en kap*) may have been those who had shared the royal princes' education. Some may have been foster-siblings, their mothers having acted as royal wet-nurses. Others receiving instruction may have been the sons of the pharaoh's foreign vassals, who were sent to Egypt for education, indoctrination – and to act as hostages to ensure their fathers' good behaviour. Clearly such individuals would have been well placed to obtain influential posts in the government or at court, if their playmates grew up to become king.

CHAPTER SEVEN

THE ADMINISTRATION

————·◆·————

Karen Exell and Christopher Naunton

INTRODUCTION

Primary evidence for the administration of Egypt is in such short supply that the study of the institutions and offices involved relies to a certain extent on analogy, often using models drawn from modern concepts, offices and institutions, which at best distort the picture available to us, and at worst are entirely misleading. Analogy can, in turn, lead to assumption: 'if, as evidence suggests, the situation was *x* in the *y* period, we can assume, in the absence of evidence to the contrary, that this was also the case during the *z* period.' It is not possible, however, to write about 'the administration in Egypt' without taking into consideration the degree to which the political, environmental or economic situation within the country altered, as this significantly affected the way in which Egypt was governed. This chapter deals in detail with the period of the New Kingdom and succeeding centuries, as a means of illustrating the ways in which the situation changed, and also that these changes are not always immediately apparent in the sources available to us.

Where necessary, the titles given to Egyptian officials, one of the major sources for administrative information at any given period (Strudwick 1985; Pardey 2001; Quirke 2001a), are provided in transcription. The offices held by individuals working within the administration do not have direct modern equivalents, but their titles are nonetheless translated using modern words and phrases. Most of these have become conventions in Egyptology, ensuring some degree of consistency in the literature, but it should be borne in mind that they do not imply direct equivalency with modern titles. The title *haty-a en niut*, for example, is normally translated as 'mayor of the City', although clearly the 'mayor' of ancient Egyptian Thebes would have had different responsibilities from the current mayor of London or New York! A title such as overseer of works (*imy-ra kat*) may have continually evolved in authority and semantic meaning, so that at different periods the title-holder may have had a different status and function. The other major sources for the administration are elite tombs, private (non-royal) monuments such as statues and stelae (Janssen 1979; Strudwick 1985), both of which inform us of the careers and activities of high-ranking government officials, and papyri and ostraca, the majority from temple archives, which record aspects of local administration (Janssen 1979; Quirke 1990a, 2001a; Pardey 2001). The discussion will attempt to assess the validity of the traditional sources and other methods for ascertaining who, at any one period, had real authority in the administration of Egypt.

The principal function of administration is the control and organization of surplus wealth, in other words, the management of the economy. Surplus wealth in ancient Egypt took the form of agricultural surplus, allowing craft specialization and the production of elite goods. Bureaucratic structures were created to manage the surplus wealth, which maintained the court of the king at the centre of the ancient state, and was fed back into the wider population in the form of 'wages'. The economy in ancient Egypt can be defined as redistributive (Janssen 1975a: 183; Quirke 1990a).

The Egyptian administration therefore encompasses the kingship and the redistribution of wealth, which are linked both ideologically and in economic practice. A discussion of the administration of Egypt must touch on the role of the king, and the ideology of divine kingship. The king's ideological role was as intermediary between the people and the gods. He maintained *maat* ('order') by offering the produce of Egypt to the gods via the temples, which functioned as machines to maintain the universe. The morning ritual in the temples mirrored the creation of the first time (*sep tepy*), when Egypt emerged from the waters of chaos, the opposite of *maat*. The general populace was excluded from this cult function of temples; people experienced the temples as economic and administrative centres. The produce that came into the temples as offerings to the gods was redistributed to temple employees and local government officials as 'wages'.

The traditional hierarchy placed the king at the head of the government, the symbolic and actual focus of all economic and military activity. His first minister, the *tjaty*, traditionally translated as 'vizier', was in charge of overseeing the different areas of government activity: royal building works, the army, temples and foreign lands. The *major* institutions were headed by individual officials: the overseer of works (*imy-ra kat*), the army general (*imy-ra mesha*), the chief prophet of Amun (*hem-netjer tepy en Imen*) and the overseers of foreign lands in the Near East or king's son of Kush (Nubia; *za-nisut kash*). Below the vizier in the administrative hierarchy a number of officials stationed at the court were responsible for the products of these major institutions: the royal document scribe (*imy-ra sesh-a nisut*), the treasurer (*imy-ra per-hedj*), the sealbearer (*sedjauty-bity*) and the overseer of the granaries (*imy-ra shenuty*). The 'court' itself existed simultaneously as a fixed administrative centre located in the active state capital, and as a travelling body following the king. Below the state administration Egypt was governed by local, provincial officials, the highest official taking the title *haty-a*, traditionally translated as 'mayor' or 'nomarch'. The mayor and his officials (scribes) worked in conjunction with the local major temple to manage the grain and other resources from the surrounding agricultural land, and to maintain the local cults (Quirke 2001a).

Beyond his ideological role, the king was both a soldier (head of the army) and a priest (chief priest of all the temples). The military and priesthood, as with the kingship, cannot be excluded from a discussion of the administration. The pharaoh Horemheb (18th Dynasty) installed soldiers as priests when the temples were reopened following the Amarna Period and the reign of Akhenaten. Soldiers frequently took up priestly posts on retirement from the army. One of the characteristics of the New Kingdom administration is the hereditary nature of high-ranking titles, a number of which, from different administrative areas, could be held within one family. At one time the viziership was held by a man called Amenemope while his brother Sennefer held the position of chief prophet of Amun (Bryan 2000: 270). Such fluidity and integration between high-ranking positions indicates that these administrative areas were regarded as being part of a single administrative structure, rather than separate and distinct 'departments' which might demand separate career paths of their post-holders – a priesthood was a post rather than a vocation.

THE ADMINISTRATION OF EGYPT IN THE NEW KINGDOM

Egypt during the New Kingdom has been characterized as having a temple economy (Janssen 1979: 509), partly based on the extensive archaeological remains of religious architecture. These vast temple complexes, in particular that of Amun-Ra at Thebes, functioned both as the ideological centre for the kingship, and as major economic centres. Such dual functions illustrate the impossibility of separating 'church' and 'state' – anachronistic and inaccurate terms in this context – when analysing political and economic structures in ancient Egypt (Janssen 1979: 509; Kemp 1989b: 193). The temple economy might, in fact, have existed at earlier periods but the archaeological evidence is lacking for large religious structures at earlier state centres such as Heliopolis and Memphis.

The New Kingdom temples were surrounded by enclosures holding extensive granaries that stored the region's grain. The provincial temples took in the grain from the surrounding region (temple and royal lands) for redistribution in the form of wages to those connected with the state or temple. Those benefiting included regional state officials, individuals enjoying priestly privileges, whether full- or part-time, workers on the temple and royal lands, military units stationed in the vicinity, and individuals involved in royal building projects. During the New Kingdom royal mortuary temples (temples built for the cult of the reigning king) at Thebes were said to be situated in the 'domain of Amun' (Haring 2001), indicating the ideological and economic link of the king/state to the major state temple located on the East Bank at Thebes, rather than a subordination of the royal mortuary cult to that of Amun. Papyrus Harris I records massive donations by Ramesses III to his mortuary temple, Medinet Habu, 'in the domain of Amun'. Traditionally, interpretations of the papyrus have read the donations as an indication of the ceding of royal lands, and therefore income, to the Amun priesthood, and unbalancing the so-called 'church/state' equilibrium. The land donations were, however, intended for the royal cult based at the royal mortuary temple, situated within the 'domain of Amun'. The temples were, in short, a branch of the government whose economic role was to pay local state employees and whose ideological function was to support the central position of the divine kingship (Kemp 1989b: 193). The king's representation throughout Egypt's temples, in the role of chief priest offering to the gods in order to maintain *maat* and the fertility of the land, had a practical manifestation in the feeding of the people from the temples.

Case study: Deir el-Medina

Sofia Häggman (2002) has demonstrated that a 'bottom-up' approach, utilizing the administrative archive of ostraca and papyri from the royal workmen's village at Deir el-Medina, can be illuminating in the study of the administration. Deir el-Medina was the settlement of the men, and their families, who constructed and decorated the royal tombs at Thebes. Häggman (2002) has analysed the data in relation to the external administration of the village, revealing the various local and state institutions, and individuals, who shared or alternated responsibility for the provisioning of the workmen. Drawing on this approach, the administration of the community at Deir el-Medina serves as a model for both the provincial administration and the associated state institutions during the New Kingdom.

Deir el-Medina stands on the west bank at Luxor (ancient Thebes), falling within the remit of the regional Theban administration. The nominal head of the community was the king who was the Lord (*neb*) of the workmen, as he was the Lord of all Egyptian society. The administrative hierarchy at Thebes was headed by the vizier as the governmental representative of the king. Below the vizier, the highest regional government official was the mayor of the City (*haty-a en niut*). Mayors were responsible for both urban areas and the surrounding agricultural and rural land. The mayor of the City oversaw royal land attached to temples (*kha ta* land), temple granaries and other financial offices in the temples, as well as heading the *qenbet* (law)-court. At certain periods a mayor of the West of the City (*haty-a en imentet niut*), that is, of

Figure 7.1 Deir el-Medina: view of the village and the Ptolemaic temple from the Western Cemetery.

the West Bank, is known (Häggman 2002: 133–5, 249–52). This post may have been instigated to administer the growing number of active mortuary temples on the West Bank at Thebes, and recurs during periods of disturbance in the mid- to late 20th Dynasty. There is evidence that the mayor of the West of the City may have been subordinate to the mayor of the City. Alongside the mayor of the City, the chief prophet of Amun maintained a parallel authority. The chief prophet of Amun was the highest authority in the administrative institution known as the 'House of Amun'. The House of Amun included the mortuary temples on the West Bank and temples as far away as Nubia. The relationship was of an administrative and cultic character but its nature is not fully understood. The House of Amun temples were not economically dependent on the mother institution. They were wealthy institutions in their own right with their own administrative structure headed by the sem-priest (*sem*). The vizier worked directly with the royal workmen at Deir el-Medina via their senior scribe (*sesh en pa kher*), unless a mayor of the West of the City, who would mediate between the two, was in post. In terms of provisioning, the workmen received their dues from the state granary and treasury, via the vizier, and additional offerings (in particular bread and beer) from the Theban temples, via the chief prophet of Amun. These latter items may have been supplied to support participation in festivals, a temple activity (Häggman 2002: 86–9).

From the mid-20th Dynasty the Theban administration underwent a number of changes. In the twenty-ninth year of Ramesses III the workmen staged the first of a series of strikes in protest at their late provisioning. Part of the response to this crisis was the increased involvement of the regional administrators, the mayor of the City and the chief prophet of Amun (Häggman 2002: 160–91). This may have been a deliberate delegation of authority by the distant northern vizier, in tandem with a need the workmen felt to appeal for assistance to a closer authority, the chief prophet of Amun. Initially the chief prophet of Amun appears in the administrative record in association with the vizier, but gradually supplants him. The chief prophet of Amun takes over the provisioning of the workmen from the House of Amun granaries.

The move from state to regional administration of the workmen's village reached its apogee at the end of the 20th Dynasty by which time the structure of the Egyptian government had fundamentally altered. This evolution, and the adaptive nature of the administrative structure, is illustrated by the activity of the King's Son of Kush, Panehsy, at this period (Häggman 2002: 200–4). Panehsy also held the title overseer of the granary. During the reign of Ramesses XI, following a command of the king, Panehsy arrived in Thebes from Nubia to assist in the grain collection, which in part supplied the royal workmen. By this stage the House of Amun was no longer involved in provisioning the necropolis, responsibility for this having returned to the overseer of the granary, but not to the distant vizier. Panehsy seems to have been summoned to fill a southern administrative imbalance, rather than, as has traditionally been thought, in his military role as king's son of Kush. An assumption of Libyan unrest and the glamour of Panehsy's high military title may have led scholars to impose a military reading on what was a purely administrative activity.

The administration changed in character and structure in relation to each individual king. Thutmose IV (18th Dynasty) shrunk the number of military titles, replacing them with bureaucrats; the rank of general is almost unknown at this period, while the rank of royal scribe, or court official (*sesh nisut*), abounds (Bryan 2000: 270).

Within the New Kingdom itself the character of the kingship and the authority of individual kings fluctuated. The 18th Dynasty saw the development of the myth of the divine birth during the reign of Hatshepsut, one of a number of legitimizing policies employed by the female pharaoh to establish her right to the throne. The myth states that the ruling pharaoh is the offspring of the god Amun, deftly linking the state god and the earthly ruler. Amenhotep III's reign represented a period of prosperity allowing ideological expansion wherein he and his court developed the ideology of a personal link between the king and the sun god, Ra. The ideology was taken to its extreme conclusion by his son, Amenhotep IV/Akhenaten. Post-Akhenaten, Egypt went through a period of crisis with no strong heir or ruler, until the establishment of a military dynasty through the appointment of Ramesses I by the former general, Horemheb, who had taken the throne at the end of the 18th Dynasty. Ramesses II, grandson of Ramesses I, is, for good reason, the best known of the Ramesside rulers (19th and 20th Dynasties). He ruled for 66/67 years, re-establishing the currency of the kingship and the authority of the king by means of monumental building projects and government or administrative reforms. One of these reforms was to allow officials higher levels of visible authority than had previously been the case; this level of authority cannot, however, be gleaned from their titles alone.

Relying on titles to inform us of the administrative structures operating in Egypt at any one time can lead to a reading of the administration as a rigid and compartmentalized bureaucracy. Such a reading can also allow an interpretation where the titles informed the activity of the individual title-holders, rather than the activity being influenced by the person of the title-holder. In practical terms, an office-holder may have carried out his official activity in the reception rooms of his home. The division of the working world into public/private or formal/informal that we understand today did not exist in the administrative sphere in Egypt. Two examples of the personalized nature of official activity, and individual authority outdistancing the remit of the titles held, can be found during the reign of Ramesses II. In the workmen's village at Deir el-Medina, during the first half of the reign, a man called Ramose held the position of senior scribe. The title conceals Ramose's aristocratic background; he occasionally used the ranking title 'royal scribe' (*sesh nisut*), indicating an association with the royal court. Ramose left hundreds of inscribed monuments, commissioned three tombs and appears in a number of tombs of Deir el-Medina workmen (Davies 1999: 79–80 and notes; Exell 2006: 161–2, 306). He is frequently depicted with the vizier Paser in these contexts. With Paser he claimed responsibility for the construction of a chapel to the cult of Ramesses II and Hathor, attached to the official Hathor temple to the north of the village. The other holders of the title senior scribe have left relatively few monuments; certainly none comes close to the monumental record of Ramose. To the south of Egypt, the King's Son of Kush, Setau, carried out a number of temple-building projects on behalf of his king (Raedler 2003). At such a distance from centralized authority we find votive stelae set up not just for the benefit of the king but also for the benefit of Setau. Setau seems to have established a network of patronage at various locations and, by doing so, to have placed himself high up in the established vertical hierarchy; in Nubia, distant from the king, his authority may have been paramount (Raedler 2003; Exell 2006: 294, 308–10). As with Ramose, other men holding this same title have not remained so visible in the archaeological record. The titles 'senior scribe' and 'king's son of Kush'

Figure 7.2 Double stela of the King's Son of Kush, Setau, at Abu Simbel, dated to year 38 of Ramesses II.

are not an index of the power and authority of these men. At different periods and dependent on both royal sanction and personal character, individuals could outstrip the authority invested in them by title. Weak individuals will have failed to rise to the challenge of their titles. Investigating the actual administration of ancient Egypt becomes a complex analysis of the authority-wielder, not the title-holders.

PROBLEMS AND METHODS: EGYPT AFTER THE NEW KINGDOM

The most significant change to have occurred in Egypt at the end of the New Kingdom was the role played by the king. At this point, the pharaoh's authority was challenged by a succession of powerful individuals in the south leading to the division of the country into two, with a line of kings based at Tanis in the delta, and a separate line of high priests ruling the south of the country from Thebes. More generally, Egypt was further divided as much of the country, and particularly the delta, was settled by migrating groups of Libyans, with their own customs and organizational structures, at the head of which was the chief. The centralized power-base was further eroded by a reduction in Egypt's economic strength, brought about by a series of low inundations at the end of the New Kingdom, and a slackening of its grip on trade throughout the Near East, resulting from the influx of hostile Mediterranean peoples into the Levantine region. With the pharaoh's influence no longer felt throughout the country, authority from region to region was transferred to local governors, and the government of Egypt effectively devolved (Redford 2004b: 101–7).

The move away from central government and the corresponding reduction in the significance of certain geographical centres, combined with a weakening of the Egyptian economy, significantly affected the scale and number of monumental building projects and the production of monuments in general. This has, in turn, had a significant effect on the archaeological evidence available for the period, which is as a result less obviously manifest than at other periods. These factors have meant that the establishment of a precise chronological framework for the centuries after the New Kingdom has proven very difficult and is still the subject of much discussion and reassessment as new evidence comes to light (Leahy 1990; Kitchen 1995 [1973]: xiv–xxxii). This was undoubtedly a period to which a single model cannot be applied to enable understanding of the means by which the country was administered. Certain documents, however, have survived, which allow us an insight into the general nature of the political situation.

The text now known as the 'Chronicle of Prince Osorkon', inscribed on a gateway in the First Court at Karnak, tells how rival political factions in the Theban area vied for supremacy in the region over a number of years (Caminos 1958). A reassessment of evidence for individuals proclaiming themselves Pharaoh has, in recent years, led scholars to posit that there was more than one line of individuals claiming the kingship of Egypt in the decades prior to the beginning of the 25th Dynasty (Leahy 1990). That this was the situation at the beginning of the 25th Dynasty itself is beyond doubt, thanks to another, fundamentally important text inscribed on the 'Victory Stela of King Piye'. Set up by this 25th Dynasty pharaoh in the temple of Amun at Gebel Barkal, in Sudanese Nubia, the stela narrates the story of Piye's military campaign to Egypt, to suppress the local rulers who had sprung up throughout the country, and to re-establish central authority, uniting the country under one ruler (Grimal 1981; 1992: 335–41). Crucially, the text describes the situation as Piye found it and shows very graphically a series of rulers, each of whom held sway in particular parts of the country, offering supplication to their new overlord. Some of these rulers enclosed their names in cartouches, declaring themselves 'pharaoh', while others were content simply to remain as local chieftains. The significance of this lies in the revelation of the extent to which the Egyptian words we understand to mean 'king', *nisut bity*, had lost their meaning by this point. They no longer implied any

Figure 7.3   Lunette of the 'Victory Stela of Piye' (after Grimal 1981: pl. V).

uniqueness, nor did those who had taken on the trappings of kingship necessarily hold any greater power or influence than others who did not, and perhaps few, if any, had much legitimate claim to kingship as this was no longer essential.

Later documents, in particular the Akkadian text of the 'Rassam Cylinder' of 671 BC which records the situation in Egypt after successful Assyrian raids on the country, confirm that local governors continued to wield authority independently throughout the 25th Dynasty (Kitchen 1973: 397; Leahy 1979: 31–9; 1999: 230–2).

THEBES IN THE 25TH DYNASTY

Differential preservation of evidence, and the likelihood that the Kushite pharaohs favoured Thebes for monumental construction, investing a certain amount of wealth in the area and in particular individuals, has meant that evidence for the Theban region has survived much better than that for any other part of the country, but enough evidence survives to suggest that the region enjoyed a degree of independence that was not entirely affected by the Kushite regime, and that this model can also be applied to the rest of the country.

Evidence for the activity of both the Kushite pharaohs and the non-royal officials is relatively abundant at Thebes. A straightforward reading of the caste of officials evident in the monumental record might suggest a situation not entirely dissimilar to that of the New Kingdom. The king (*nisut bity*), chief prophet of Amun, mayor of the City, vizier and treasurer are all present. The king it is, along with the newly significant god's wife of Amun (*hemet-netjer en Imen*), a position held by successive daughters of the pharaoh, who is shown in direct contact with the gods both in new inscriptions on the walls of existing structures and on entirely new monuments.

Titles held by less prominent individuals, but which perhaps conferred more specific responsibilities, hint at the administrative structures in place during this time. The institution surrounding the divine adoratrices of Amun, chief among whom was the God's Wife, seems to have functioned as a micro-economy in its own right, with its own granaries, priests, scribes, etc., perhaps based at Karnak or at a temple on the west bank of the Nile. Similarly, the various temples at Karnak continued to involve the population in large numbers and, therefore, were probably in control of significant portions of the economy.

Monumental building at sites such as Karnak reached heights, in terms of scale and number, not known since the New Kingdom (Arnold 1999: 43), implying a degree of concentration of wealth and/or a general revival in the country's economic fortunes. The former was, to an extent, the result of the Kushite pharaohs' particular affinity with Thebes and its patron deity, Amun. This also contributed to an upturn in the fortunes of certain high-ranking officials, some of whom are especially manifest in the archaeological record through their monumental tombs (Eigner 1984), the first to be constructed on such a scale since the New Kingdom.

On the basis of these monuments, we infer that during the 25th Dynasty there was a concentration of wealth in the hands of certain important officials. It seems probable that these officials also wielded considerable political and civil authority in the region, and this is confirmed by textual evidence suggesting that Montuemhat, in particular, was pre-eminently influential (Naunton 2004: 97, 100–2). A study of the inscriptions of these few individuals, however, shows that there is little correlation between wealth and titles held. For example, the three largest tomb complexes in el-Asasif belong, respectively, to the Chief Steward of the Divine Adoratrice of Amun (*imy-ra per wer en dwat-netjer en Imen*), Harwa; the Fourth Prophet of Amun (*hem-netjer 4 en Imen*) and Mayor of the City, Montuemhat; and the Chief Lector Priest (*hery-heb hery-tep*), Padiamenopet, each of whom seems to have risen to prominence at different times. Furthermore, the meaning of individual titles had altered significantly, and any hierarchy of offices which had previously existed had become distorted, so that the models used to understand the situation in previous periods are unhelpful in this context.

Evidence that the most prominent individuals held numerous titles simultaneously further complicates the situation. While some such titles are, perhaps, only laudatory epithets and others variants of well-known titles, it seems likely that some signalled at least notional influence, for example, over a particular priesthood or aspect of temple economy, even if the individual concerned could not possibly have devoted himself totally to the responsibilities implied by all of these titles. It also seems possible, therefore, that the accumulation of titles was a truer basis of the influence of particular individuals, and that this is the reason for the lack of correlation between individual offices and the wealth of the officials themselves.

That there were certain officials of pre-eminent importance at this time is not in doubt, though they were not necessarily the holders of titles which, in previous times, had been associated with the most influential among administrative officials. Although two holders of the office of chief prophet of Amun are known for the period, they had no real authority or influence and are known only from relatively minor monuments (Kitchen 1973: 197). Both were members of the royal family and were probably installed as a means of strengthening the Kushite association with the cult of Amun. At the same time the holders of other, supposedly lesser priestly positions are much more evident in the monumental record. At the time of Piye's invasion of Egypt in the mid–late seventh century BC, he received cooperation from a Pediamenneb-nesuttawy, possibly one and the same as the known third prophet of Amun (*hem-netjer 3 en Imen*) from this time (Grimal 1981: 170, 174). By 671 BC, as is recorded in text of the Rassam Cylinder, the Fourth Prophet of Amun and Mayor of the City, Montuemhat, had been installed (or perhaps *confirmed*) as the foremost authority in Thebes by the agents of the Assyrian ruler. He would retain this authority beyond the end of the 25th Dynasty, orchestrating the arrival of the Saite princess Nitiqret (Greek Nitocris) in Thebes to become a divine adoratrice of Amun (and heiress to the God's Wife of Amun) (Caminos 1964), which signalled the acceptance of the rule of the 26th Dynasty in the Theban region.

Montuemhat held many titles including overseer of Upper Egypt, perhaps revealing the real extent of his authority, but in inscriptions he cites far more than any other those of fourth prophet of Amun and mayor of the City. He is well known from his monumental tomb in the el-Asasif area of the Theban necropolis and a series of fine statues (Leclant 1961), and also left inscriptions of his own in the Mut enclosure at Karnak, claiming that he was responsible for the royal building programme at this time. Beyond this, however, the precise nature of Montuemhat's responsibilities and the basis of his authority are unclear. He had inherited the title mayor of the City from his father Nesptah, it having also been held by his grandfather Khaemhor. The passing of titles from one generation to the next was well established by this point,

Figure 7.4   The tomb of Montuemhat at el-Asasif (TT34).

further contributing to the difficulty in discerning specific responsibilities from the study of titles alone. Indeed, it is tempting to suggest that by this period there was in some cases no direct link between individual titles and the responsibilities of the bearer. However, in one important instance this seems not to have been the case.

Montuemhat's grandfather, another mayor of the City, also held the title of vizier, which after his death was passed to his son Pahor/Harsiese, and then to another son, Nesmin, before apparently being transferred to another family, that of Nespakashuty. This has been interpreted as the deliberate removal of the office from the Montuemhat family in order to prevent them from becoming too powerful (Bierbrier 1975: 105). This intervention could only have been brought about by the pharaoh himself, suggesting that at this stage, probably early in Taharqo's reign, the Kushites were well aware of the potential for individuals to gain independent authority. On this basis the title must have carried with it some significant responsibility; indeed, the Nespakashuty family remained prominent in the Theban region, and Nespamedou, son of Nespakashuty, was another of the local governors approved by the Assyrians, with charge of Thinis (Leahy 1979).

Complicating matters further, while there remained holders of the traditional offices of authority, a new title held by wealthy individuals emerged during the 25th Dynasty. The earliest of the very large, monumental tomb complexes of this period was built by Harwa, the Chief Steward of the Divine Adoratrice of Amun (*imy-ra per wer en dwat-netjer en Imen*) and effectively the right-hand man of the god's wife of Amun. The divine adoratrices feature very prominently in religious iconography of the newly built monuments at Karnak during this time, and it was their chief stewards whose tombs dominate the Late Period cemetery at el-Asasif. Interestingly, this position does not seem to have been hereditary. As a new position so closely associated with the Kushite royal family and royal/religious ideology, it is tempting to see this as another attempt by the Kushite kings to counter the power of the established Theban families.

None of Montuemhat's predecessors or successors, either as fourth prophet or mayor, enjoyed the same prominence, further indicating that these titles alone were not the basis of his authority. Circumstance and, in particular, a renewed concentration of wealth during the early, successful years of Kushite rule, followed by the appearance of a convenient power vacuum during the second half of the dynasty, when the country and its Kushite pharaohs suffered repeated invasion by Assyrian armies, almost certainly aided his rise.

Despite superficial similarities to the New Kingdom, the nature of the government and administration of Egypt in later periods was quite different. The titles held by the highest state officials, such as vizier, remained in use, but as the nature of the kingship itself had changed fundamentally, so did the meaning of these titles and the role of those that held them. It is not possible to speak of a 'court' for the centuries following New Kingdom. It has not yet been possible to establish with certainty the base of the 25th Dynasty pharaohs' rule, but the concept of a capital city was much altered also. Prior to the arrival of the Kushites, Egypt had had no central capital, and was administered and governed at a local level by a series of independent, local rulers. It is likely also that this remained the situation throughout Kushite overlordship. That this was the case is masked to a certain extent by the retention of certain elements of tradition such as the use of particular titles, and the

Figure 7.5   Sunk relief showing Harwa being led into the afterlife by Anubis, from his tomb at el-Asasif (TT37).

revival, inspired by Piye and his successors, of others, such as monumental construction with the king as the focus of religious iconography, apparently once again the ruler of a united Egypt.

The relationship of the pharaoh to the officials at this time is crucial to understanding the way the country was run. There was clearly an acceptance of the Kushite kings to an extent, in Thebes at least, as is shown by the prominence of their images at Karnak and elsewhere. Indeed, decorum dictated that it was only the pharaoh and the Divine Adoratrices who could be shown in association with the gods on such monuments. Several members of the royal family and other Kushites were installed in prominent, mainly priestly offices, and several members of established Theban families who rose to prominence under Kushite rule were allied by marriage to the royal house. The basis of Kushite authority, at least initially, was military. Although Egyptians from these established families appear to have continued to wield influence, this was not, perhaps, due to any inability on the part of the Kushites to strengthen further their grip. With the image of the pharaoh restored to prominence at cult centres and the temples themselves renovated, *maat* was restored, and this was perhaps the Kushites' priority, that is, to return Egypt to its proper condition, ideologically. *Maat* having been achieved, the pharaoh was perhaps content to leave the mundane business of running the country to those individuals and systems already in place: which, if true, confirms that, by this point, central authority and administration had disappeared.

CHAPTER EIGHT

THE TEMPLE PRIESTHOOD

——— .•. ———

Rosalie David

HISTORY OF THE PRIESTHOOD

The origins of the priesthood can probably be traced back to Predynastic communities, where the village chieftain performed rites for the local deity. With Egypt's development into a theocracy, the king absorbed the powers and responsibilities of the early leaders, becoming the gods' earthly representative who maintained universal order and protected the state religion. Ultimately, the king, in turn, delegated this role to the priesthood who performed the divine rituals in his name.

The priesthood has been described as 'A body of men separated from the rest of the community for the service of a god' (Hastings 1908: 293). Their duties united them into a powerful bureaucracy, and although in the earlier periods there was a less clear division between the priests and the laity, by the New Kingdom a separate priesthood was established. During the Old and Middle Kingdoms, it was customary to combine a career as a lawyer, doctor, scribe or teacher with a part-time priesthood. This was organized around a system of rotating groups (Greek: *phyles*) of priests (Roth 1991) who served at the royal funerary temples (i.e. temples attached to royal burial places, which were the location for the royal funerary cult, designed to ensure the continuation of the king's divine existence after death) in the Old Kingdom, although their role in the divine cult temples (which accommodated the resident deity's cult and provided a *locus* where the priests could perform the daily rituals) remains unclear (R. Wilkinson 2000: 90). As payment for their duties, priests received land from the temple estates and food from the god's altar at the conclusion of the daily services.

Apart from periods of temple duty, the part-time priests lived with their families in the community, and provided a powerful social link between the temple and the laity. This was particularly important since the temple cults themselves had little direct impact on people's daily religious practices, which centred around domestic gods and shrines.

However, religion and secular matters were inextricably interwoven, and the fate of the temples and their priests were firmly linked to political circumstances. Success in warfare and prosperity at home inspired kings to donate booty and gifts to the temples, thus enhancing the power of the gods and their priests. At times, this gave the clergy too much influence, enabling them to dictate royal policy.

Figure 8.1 The king performs censing as part of a temple ritual, a function usually delegated to the high priest. Based on a New Kingdom temple scene.
(© Antony E. David).

Over the centuries, the king adopted various ploys to counteract and limit this power. From the Old Kingdom onwards, leading religious offices were given at first to members of the royal family and then to the vizier (chief minister of state), to establish a centralized authority over the priesthood; in the First Intermediate Period, the nomarchs (district governors) controlled temple administration.

In the New Kingdom, major changes occurred in temple organization that introduced a clear distinction between priests and laity. Although part-time priests continued to serve in rotating *phyles*, many of the priestly offices, particularly in the large temples, now became full-time, professional posts. Increasingly, the priesthood became a separate community with less direct contact with the laity, except during the gods' festivals.

Early in the 18th Dynasty, the priesthood of Amun (Amun-Ra) reached its zenith when kings, in gratitude for their successful campaigns abroad, enriched the Temple of Karnak at Thebes (ancient Egyptian Waset; modern Luxor) with large donations of booty and prisoners-of-war. Ultimately, this gave the cult of Amun (and particularly its senior priests) unprecedented religious and political influence, which the kings were forced to confront.

For example, since the largely hereditary priesthood concentrated power in relatively few families, some rulers now consciously exercised their nominal right to select candidates to fill vacancies among the highest clergy. Also, from the reign of Thutmose IV onwards, rulers began to promote the solar cults to rival the supremacy of Amun. Most significantly, they fostered the cult of the Aten (sun's disc), which culminated in the religious upheaval engendered by the actions of Amenhotep IV/Akhenaten. In an unprecedented move, he raised the Aten to a unique status by banning all other cults, closing their temples and disbanding their priesthoods. After this brief and unsuccessful interlude, the traditional cults and the priesthood were re-established.

In the 19th Dynasty, kings resorted to other tactics to control the power of Amun at Thebes, by fostering the cults of other important deities such as Ra at Heliopolis and Ptah at Memphis (ancient Egyptian Mennufer; modern Mit Rahina). Throughout the later New Kingdom, the temples flourished and, at the great cult centres, temple personnel formed a major part of the local population. For example, in the reign of Ramesses III (20th Dynasty), the temples of Amun, Ra and Ptah at Thebes, Heliopolis (ancient Egyptian Iunu; moden Tell Hisn) and Memphis together employed nearly a hundred thousand male personnel, as well as ancillary staff.

Nevertheless, the potential power conflict between the king and priests remained unresolved, and in the 21st Dynasty, the priests of Amun achieved virtual autonomy at Thebes in exchange for supporting a line of kings who ruled from Tanis (ancient Egyptian Dja'net; modern San el-Hagar) in the delta. Although the kings retained nominal authority over the whole country, the two lines ruled simultaneously – the kings exercising power over the north while Herihor, High Priest at Thebes, ruled the south (Kees 1964).

In later dynasties, the king employed a new means of regaining control over the Amun priesthood at Thebes, by granting the office of God's Wife of Amun to the king's daughter (Robins 1983). This brought her considerable wealth and political influence, but her power was limited to the Theban area. Also, these women were obliged to remain celibate, each adopting the daughter of the next king as her successor. This ensured that the God's Wife could never establish her own dynasty at Thebes to rival the official royal line, but by holding this office, she also prevented the High Priest of Amun from gaining political control in the south.

Finally, in the Ptolemaic and Roman Periods, the status of the priests changed again although their cults continued to receive royal support and protection (Johnson 1986).

ENTRY TO THE PRIESTHOOD: ADMISSION AND INITIATION

The priests, as the king's delegates, perpetuated the gods' cults and performed the rituals to maintain the universe according to the principles established at creation.

Priests were expected to maintain high standards of personal behaviour and perform certain rites that guaranteed their physical purity and enabled them to enter the god's presence. However, the priesthood was not vocational, and its members were not required to make converts, provide inspiration and support for the laity, or initiate general intellectual debate about religion. Neither did a candidate's personal religious commitment guarantee admission to the priesthood.

To some extent, methods of entry to the priesthood varied from one period to another. Priestly offices were usually inherited as primary or secondary professions, often remaining in one family for many generations. As Herodotus states (Herodotus 1998, Book II: 37), 'when a man dies, his son is put in his place'. However, even these appointments probably had to be ratified by a council of priests and, in theory, every appointment was subject to the king's approval, although the lesser appointments were probably confirmed by the vizier.

Sometimes, for political or personal reasons, appointments were made directly through royal selection and nomination if, for example, the king wanted to reward a particular individual, or to redress the balance of power in one cult or temple by appointing a candidate from another temple or institution.

The office of priest could also be purchased. At first, this method was generally used when there was no suitable person to inherit a post. However, one study of the inheritance of titles and patterns of familial participation in a group of several hundred men and women who held priestly titles in the cult of Hathor during the Old Kingdom and First Intermediate Period shows that these titles were not generally inherited from either a parent or a spouse (Galvin 1984).

It concludes that people – particularly women – wanted to participate in the cult for political and social as well as religious reasons, and this might have prompted some to purchase the offices. Later, when this method of entry became increasingly common, a council of priests assessed the candidate who, if successful, paid a fee to purchase the office.

Little is known of the initiation ceremonies for the priesthood, although texts confirm that a *Ritual of Installation* (Sauneron 1960: 47) occurred. This might have included ritual purification and anointing before entering the temple, taking vows of obedience, and promising to maintain personal ritual purity and not to abuse the privileges of office or divulge the secrets of the priesthood. At the ceremony, the priest might have been given knowledge of the magical formulae, believed to control the natural forces of the universe.

The temple was never a place of congregational worship, and the laity had no role in its daily rituals. It was the *House of the God*, accommodating and protecting the resident deity, whose spirit resided in the cult-statue in the sanctuary. Every day, the priests performed the special rituals to ensure the god's wellbeing, and the reciprocal divine blessings which brought about the king's immortality and success in battle, and fertility and prosperity for Egypt and its people.

To enter the god's presence or handle his ritual clothing, insignia and utensils, the priests were required to attain a state of physical purity. Although there was always some variation in detail from one cult to another, basic standard regulations were established during the New Kingdom.

The priests were required to cleanse themselves before entering the temple, either in the Sacred Lake or, if none existed, in a stone basin: 'Twice a day they washed themselves in cold water, and twice every night' (Herodotus 1998, Book II: 37). They also rinsed out their mouths with natron (which occurs in natural deposits in the Wadi Natrun and at Elkab; it was used as a dehydrating agent in mummification, and for laundering clothes) to achieve inner physical purity, cut their nails and, every other day, shaved and plucked the entire head and body, as protection against vermin and fleas.

Although not a universal practice, some priests were circumcised, possibly when they commenced their official duties. The priests, although not celibate, were required to abstain from sexual intercourse in sacred places and in the period leading up to and during temple duty, when they also had to avoid those deemed physically impure, such as menstruating women. Even accidental contact could render them unfit for temple duties; similarly, pre-menopausal women could not perform rituals for part of each month. These men and women had to subject themselves to purification rituals before they could return to temple service.

The priests were also prohibited from eating certain foods during this time. The extensive list included pork, beef, mutton and lamb, pigeon, pelican, varieties of fish, beans, garlic and salt, although each prohibition probably only applied in a particular town or region where there was a close association between the god's cult-animal or sacred plant and the proscribed food. Priests were also expected not to over-indulge in alcohol.

Special clothes – clean linen garments and new sandals made from reeds or palm fibres – were also obligatory for temple service, and distinguished the priests from the laity. Generally, priests were forbidden to wear clothes and footwear made of wool or leather.

The restrictions all temple priests followed in order to attain ritual purity also applied to practitioners of magic, although the extent to which village magicians were able to fulfil all the conditions is uncertain (Pinch 1994: 77).

FUNCTIONS AND TITLES OF TEMPLE PERSONNEL

The priest was expected to be an honourable official with knowledge of the ancient texts and expertise in the rituals, although some doubtless regarded it as a means to a guaranteed income, while others engaged in fraudulent practices.

Ability to read hieroglyphs afforded the priest insight into the liturgical literature and made him conversant with medical, magical and educational texts, but, even more importantly, it gave him control over the words themselves. Hieroglyphs were not simply regarded as a written means of conveying a language; they were, themselves, potent cosmic forces, since the gods had used words to create and sustain the universe. Knowledge of the sacred writing gave the priests similar powers.

Temple organization

The size, locality and importance of a cult dictated the number of personnel employed in each temple. Throughout history, a key feature of the priesthood was the system of alternating groups of officiants who served the god in rotation. They were divided into four groups (in the Ptolemaic Period, a fifth was added) who had identical functions and number of personnel. Under its leader, each *phyle* performed the religious and ritual duties for one month and then handed the temple and its contents (which they had inventoried) to the next group. Each *phyle* worked continuously for one month, and completed three months' service each year.

In the New Kingdom, the system changed, and although part-time priests continued to play a role in the temples, they no longer exercised authority at the major cult-centres, where a full-time professional clergy, who resided within the temple precinct, was now appointed to control the temple and direct the activities of the part-time priests.

Temple personnel included priests, administrators and ancillary staff who performed a number of distinct functions. Insufficient evidence exists to identify specific titles and roles in all temples over the whole period, but it is possible to consider the broad categories.

Administrators and auxiliary personnel

The administrative staff, who varied in size and complexity in the great establishments and smaller temples, generally included senior personnel who directed the secular functions of the temple and its domain, and also artisans and general workers.

The auxiliary workers kept the temple in good repair, ensured that it was serviceable for daily use, tended the temple estates, and prepared the offerings presented to the god. Most of these were secular employees, but in some instances, when personnel performed both administrative and religious duties, they were also accorded priestly status.

The priests

Essentially, all priests were defined and separated from the rest of mankind by their initiation into the priesthood and by attaining a state of purity through the performance of special rites. In addition to those employed permanently at the temples, some priests worked outside the temple system, or combined religious duties with a secular office.

No comprehensive account has yet been discovered of the specialized categories and roles within the Egyptian priesthood. An important source of information is provided by the Christian writer Clement of Alexandria in his description of the procession of priests serving the cult of Osiris in Alexandria (Sauneron 1960: 139–40). This, and other information derived from temple inscriptions and Egyptian texts, makes it clear that temple priests fulfilled roles as ritualists and educators, and sometimes as healers.

The priest as ritualist: inside the temple

The most important duty of the temple priest was to perform the Daily Temple Ritual for the resident deity. This consisted of a morning, mid-day and evening service during which the god's statue was removed from its shrine, roused, cleansed, perfumed and dressed, and then returned to the shrine at night. At the conclusion of each service, food offered to the god was finally removed from the temple and divided among the priests as their regular payment (David 1973).

Sometimes, however, unscrupulous priests took these rations without offering them first to the god. Texts in the Temple of Edfu (Sauneron 1960: 25) exhort the priest: 'Do not hold back the supplies!', and 'One lives on the provision of the gods, but one calls provision that which leaves the altar after the Lord has been satisfied!'

In some royal and priestly mummies, there is evidence of atherosclerosis (Sandison 1962; David 1979: 30–2; David and Tapp 1991: 52). This progressive disease was uncommon in Egypt, partly because of a shorter life expectancy, but also because the diet lacked the high levels of cholesterol and saturated fats present in modern foods. However, the priests and their families, as recipients of the god's consecrated meals, enjoyed an unusual diet that contained large quantities of meat, and this presumably precipitated the disease.

Most temples had two main priestly classes – 'servants of the god' (*hem-netjer*), and 'pure priests' (*wa'ab*). The former, permitted to enter the sanctuary and have direct contact with the god's statue and possessions, included the High Priest (*hem-netjer tepy*) to whom, as the god's 'First Prophet' and the religious leader of the temple, the king delegated his ritual responsibilities. This eminent position carried great religious and political power in the New Kingdom temples where the personnel included the High Priest's delegates, the Second, Third and Fourth Prophets.

The 'pure priests' had also undergone ritual purification, and could be elevated to become 'god's servants', but generally they were lower-ranking clergy who played a secondary role in the cult. Not usually permitted access to the sanctuary, their duties often included non-ritual tasks such as carrying the god's statue in its sacred barque during the festivals, cleansing the temple with water, and supervising various groups of ancillary staff. State officials were frequently given the additional, nominal title of *wa'ab*. However, in later times, the term was often used collectively for both 'pure priests' and 'god's servants'.

Managers who directed the daily functions of the temple included an 'overseer' (*imy-ra hemu-netjer*), assisted by an 'inspector' (*sehedj hemu-netjer*) and sometimes a 'supervisor' (*imy-ra khet hemu-netjer*). As the chief temple scribe, the inspector was also responsible for the temple accounts.

In the Old and Middle Kingdoms, women also performed ritual duties in temple cults (Fischer 1989). Many women from high-ranking families held the title 'god's female servant' (*hemet-netjer*) or 'pure priestess' (*wa'abet*) during the Old Kingdom

(Lesko 1989). They usually served female deities (Hathor or, less frequently, Neith) (Galvin 1981), and since there are few examples of male priests serving these goddesses, their female counterparts probably performed the rituals carried out by male priests in other cults. There are also some examples of (mainly royal) women participating in funerary cults and cults of male gods such as Thoth or Ptah.

By the Middle Kingdom, the titles of 'god's female servant' and 'pure priestess' continued to be held respectively by the wives of high and minor officials. However, apart from the cult of Hathor (where priestesses were supervised by a male overseer), female sacerdotal titles became increasingly rare.

In the New Kingdom, women were generally excluded from the priesthood, perhaps because of the new requirement for full-time attendance to perform the rituals. Menstruation and childbirth would have denied women the opportunity to achieve the continuous state of physical purity now required to fulfil this role. From this time onwards, only very rare examples occur of women holding high priestly office.

However, women's association with the temples now continued and developed through their roles as musicians, singers and dancers. Duties associated with these posts were organized on a rota system, and could thus be fulfilled by women on a part-time basis. At Thebes and elsewhere, large numbers of women, including wives and daughters of high officials and priests (who sometimes served in the same cult) and royal necropolis workmen, held the title of 'chantress' (*shemayet*).

The women's main duty was to produce musical accompaniment for the rituals: shaking the *sistrum* (musical instrument), rattling the *menit* (bead necklace), singing hymns and dancing. They formed a musical troupe (*khener*), and could serve the cults of male and female deities (Robins 1993: 148–9). Each *khener* was led by a woman ('Great One of the Musical Troupe') whose husband was often a senior priest in the same cult; and in the most important cults, the post carried a high status. The leader's duties probably involved supervision of the troupe's training and practice, and organization of the rotas.

There were also male temple musicians; however, senior officials do not seem to have held this title, and the position apparently did not carry the same high social standing as the chantresses.

The priest as ritualist: external duties

Since the laity played no part in the regular temple rituals, festivals provided the only opportunity for wider participation in the cults of these gods. Held at different times throughout the year, festivals marked key events in the mythology of various deities and were celebrated in different ways.

During the festivals, some of the most sacred rites were held inside the temples, but much of the activity took place outside so that the laity had the opportunity to see and approach the god. The deity's portable statue was carried by the priests in its sacred barque, and this procession, accompanied by censing and singing, halted at resting stations *en route* where the priests performed various rites.

Feasting and drunkenness, in addition to expressions of great religious fervour, often occurred on these occasions. The festivals usually attracted large numbers of pilgrims, but the laity still remained observers and did not participate in the rituals. However, in addition to seeing the god's image, they now had the chance to consult

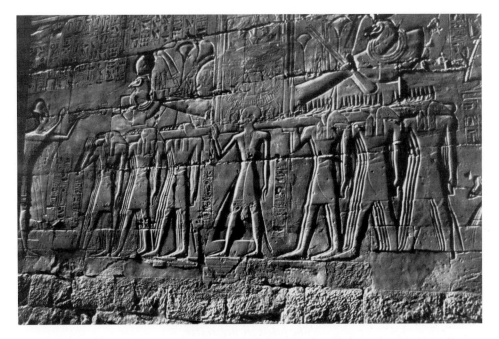

Figure 8.2 Priests carry the god's sacred barque during a festival. Temple of Amun, Karnak, New Kingdom. (© Antony E. David).

the divine oracle. Seeking the god's advice, the petitioner would approach the statue, and if he received a positive response, the priests bearing the sacred barque would interpret the divine will by moving the statue.

Oracular consultations became increasingly important in the New Kingdom, providing opportunities for the priesthood to engage with the populace. Priests also sat with local authorities on town tribunals, and when, in later periods, interrogation of the god's statue played an important role in dispensing justice, they heard, judged and interpreted the divine will in tribunals held at the temple gates.

Other priests provided an important link between the temples and the outside world. The title of lector-priest (*kheri-hebet*) was held by inspectors, overseers and scribes whose main duty was to recite the sacred formulae as part of the temple cult and funerary service. They observed the same purification rituals as other temple priests, but were not part of the temple hierarchy and probably did not perform the daily rites, perhaps officiating instead on a less regular basis. Many were attached to the House of Life, the temple scriptorium, where they read the sacred texts. Some lector-priests were also skilled in ritual magic, and it is recorded in the Westcar Papyrus that the chief lector-priest performed magic for the king. Others worked in the community, providing healing, divination and exorcism, and officiating at funerals.

Another funerary officiant, the '*Sem*-priest', also worked outside the temple hierarchy. Attired in a leopard skin, he carried out the duties originally enacted by sons for their deceased fathers in the early funerary cult, when they recited the ritual texts and performed the ceremony of 'Opening the Mouth' on the mummy or statue of the deceased, to revive and restore its life-force.

Figure 8.3 A priest lustrates mummies at a funeral service. Based on a
New Kingdom tomb scene. (© Antony E. David).

Another category of funerary priest, the '*Ka*-servant', was employed by the family
of the deceased to maintain his funerary cult. The priest made regular food offerings
at the tomb to ensure the owner's continued existence in the next world. He was
paid with land and produce from the deceased's estate and, in due course, this religious
obligation and its associated revenue were handed down to the priest's descendants.

The priest as negotiator

Priests also participated in religious and political missions. Sometimes, the king
selected priests to accompany him at religious events, such as jubilee festivals, or at
political or administrative meetings where it was necessary that the temples, as a
major employer and economic force, should be represented. Priestly delegations also
accompanied the deities when they travelled to other cult-centres for the celebration
of their festivals.

These gatherings enabled the priests to discuss, in addition to religious matters,
any common concerns such as building programmes, taxes and revenues, and economic
and political developments, and to have the opportunity to present their ideas to
the king.

The priest as educator

The Greeks visited the Egyptian temples in search of the great wisdom and learning
that they attributed to the Egyptian priesthood. A key institution in this system was
the House of Life, where the personnel undertook activities designed to provide
magical protection for the gods and the king, whose life they sought to perpetuate.
These centres were probably attached to most major temples, although some may
have been located within the temple building while others were situated nearby.
Inscriptional evidence indicates that they existed at Memphis, Abydos (ancient
Egyptian Abedju), Amarna (ancient Egyptian Akhetaten), Coptos (ancient Egyptian
Gebtu; modern Quft), Akhmim (ancient Egyptian Ipu; Classical Khemmis), Esna
(ancient Egyptian Iunyt; Classical Latopolis) and Edfu (ancient Egyptian Dbot; Classical
Apollopolis Magna).

The exact functions of the House of Life remain unclear. It may have combined
the functions of a scriptorium, temple library, university and, in some cases, medical

school. Its main purpose, however, was to foster and develop the sacred rituals that afforded protection to the gods and king.

The House of Life was a focus for discussion and development of the theology and liturgy associated with the temple's resident deity, and for preparing the sacred texts. Occasionally, scribal staff (Greek *hierogrammate*) may have been required to compose original works, but generally their duties would have involved copying earlier texts, and incorporating any corrections in the revised version. These documents included material specific to the cult and also relating to other branches of learning, such as magic, astronomy and medicine.

The act of copying the texts was never just a practical exercise, however, but drew on the wisdom and insight that resulted from the scholars' meditation and discussions. The House of Life employed priests and lay officials whose specialist knowledge and training encompassed temple liturgy, astronomy, astrology, dream interpretation, calculation of the weather, geometry, history, geography, the cults of sacred animals and, perhaps, medicine. Their shared wisdom represented the highest levels of spiritual and intellectual thought in Egypt.

The House of Life also acted as a library where the sacred scrolls were stored in narrow niches in the walls of a chamber. However, it is disputed whether it was ever used as a centre for higher education and training. Gardiner (1938b) concluded that the House of Life was a scriptorium but that it did not function as a university or school, but Strouhal (1992) has suggested that doctors might have received training there, as they did later in Alexandria and Greece.

An inscription on the back plinth of a statue belonging to Wadjhorresnet, now in the Vatican Museum, states that Darius (who ruled Egypt during the 27th Dynasty) sent him to restore a House of Life dedicated to medicine, which had fallen into decay. The text makes clear that medicine and practical teaching were the main activities of this institution.

The priest as doctor and magician

The Egyptians believed that ill health could result from obvious causes, divine retribution or unseen malignant forces exerted by enemies or the dead. Therefore, various approaches to healing were required, and these involved the interaction of priest-doctors and practitioners of magic. Methods included rational treatments, dream therapy, and the use of healing statues, holy water, spells and amulets (Ritner 1993).

During pharaonic times, the roles and functions of priests, doctors and magicians were closely linked, and at one time, a practitioner could hold several titles associated with these groups. The Ebers Papyrus (854a) confirms their parallel functions in treating patients (Nunn 1996: 113). There is no evidence that they operated as rivals; indeed, they shared many therapeutic methods, but it is not known if a patient could personally select a particular type of treatment, or if the healers usually worked together to achieve a diagnosis and cure.

There is no extant account of how doctors and practitioners of magic were trained. In many instances, the role of medical practitioner was probably hereditary; the son perhaps received parental instruction as part of a long apprenticeship, before undergoing further training, including a scribal education, in the House of Life. Again, practitioners of magic may have followed family tradition, or perhaps selected children were segregated from the community, and specially trained to develop their psychic and ritual capabilities.

Medical practitioners included the *sunu* and the 'Priests of Sekhmet'. As lay physicians, the *sunu* engaged in practical medicine and magic, sometimes working in palaces, the army, work-sites and cemeteries. Some belonged to a temple priesthood, and others, as professional magicians, were priests of Heka or Serqet. Knowledge gained through the scribal training received by some *sunu* may have formed the basis for their role as healers.

The 'Priests of Sekhmet' (*wa'abu Sekhmet*) were temple personnel. They worshipped Sekhmet, a lioness-deity who could bring disease, to placate the goddess and thus prevent illness. With the exception of eye diseases (the responsibility of the priests of Amun, Douaou and Horus), the Sekhmet priests provided specialized treatment for many illnesses. The aforementioned Ebers Papyrus (854a), the Edwin Smith Papyrus (Case 1, gloss A), and graffiti at Hatnub all indicate that Sekhmet priests and the *sunu* shared similar practices, and combined conventional and magical systems (von Känel 1984). Some Sekhmet priests held titles associated with magic, and they may also have acted as veterinary surgeons for sacrificial and cult animals (Ghalioungui 1983).

In some temples, such as Memphis, Dendera (ancient Egyptian Iunet; Classical Tentyris) and Deir el-Bahri, which had a reputation for healing, priests played special roles. Treatment included immersion in sacred water, or incubation (temple sleep) when the deity visited the patient in a dream and recommended a cure. Immersion and preparation for incubation took place in sanatoria attached to the temples although, to date, archaeology has revealed only one example – in the enclosure of the Temple of Dendera. Here, patients were totally immersed or bathed their limbs in water from the Sacred Lake, which had acquired curative properties from passing over inscriptions on 'healing statues'.

In the temple at Deir el-Bahri, the walls of a chamber built in the Ptolemaic Period to accommodate the cult of two deified human healers (Imhotep, later identified as the Greek god of medicine, and Amenhotep son of Hapu) are inscribed with graffiti, left by the many invalids who visited the sanctuary until the second century AD. However, it is unclear if they actually received any medical treatment here; possibly, they simply hoped that their faith and prayers would bring about a cure.

Ritual cleansing with water and therapeutic dream therapy were also practised in Asklepion sanctuaries at Epidaurus, Kos and Pergamum (Edelstein and Edelstein 1945). Archaeological evidence for these practices in Egypt apparently does not pre-date the Ptolemaic Period, but some inscriptional evidence, such as the stela of Qenherkhepsef (19th Dynasty) from Deir el-Medina, indicates that this kind of healing occurred earlier in Egypt (Quirke 1992).

The 'seers' (*rekhet*), women attributed with the power to diagnose sickness in children because they were in contact with the dead, may have served in the temples where they could be consulted about an individual's fate. Generally, there is a lack of evidence about the role of women in temple healing, but although they did not perhaps actively participate in the rituals, they may have enacted the role of the goddess who delivered speeches and sacred songs to the patients.

Some practitioners of magic who had the title *sau* (derived from the verb 'to protect') may have included midwives (who trained in the House of Life at Sais (ancient Egyptian Zau; modern San el-Hagar) and female practitioners in the smaller communities who gave magical protection to pregnant women and children. The title was also used by people who manufactured protective amulets.

Professional magicians also held the titles of 'Priest of Heka' (the god of magic), and *kherep Serqet* ('one who has power over Serqet'), whose duty was to propitiate Serqet, the scorpion goddess, and thus gain protection against venomous reptiles and insects.

An important papyrus in the Brooklyn Museum (Sauneron 1989) preserves a practitioner's manual for the treatment of snake-bites. Although it contains some magical spells, the papyrus deals mainly with conventional treatments, organized in a logical manner. It provides unprecedented evidence that snake-bites were treated with rational medicine by the Priests of Serqet, thus demonstrating that the *sunu* were not the only practitioners who used conventional treatments.

In the pharaonic period, most magicians were probably associated with the temples, perhaps employed in the House of Life as specialists in ritual magic and healing, but some may have practised independently, outside the temple system and, in smaller communities, the magician probably replaced the doctor as the local healer.

Eventually, when the priesthood became a predominantly hereditary system, magicians became a separate group. By the Roman Period, many no longer had any association with the temples, but performed secular magic for payment.

FINAL YEARS OF THE PRIESTHOOD

Because the hereditary priests promoted the myth that the Ptolemies, as the gods' representatives, were the legitimate pharaohs, these kings maintained the priesthood, granting them fiscal benefits, rights and immunities, and initiated temple building and restoration programmes. In turn, the priests preserved some elements of the indigenous Egyptian culture.

However, under the Romans, the temples lost their religious and fiscal privileges, and were administered instead by a secular authority based in Alexandria. Finally, a decree issued by Emperor Theodosius, recognizing Christianity as Egypt's official religion, closed the temples in AD 384.

This heralded the end of the priesthood but, even as it declined, the priests' wisdom and learning were praised by Classical writers. Porphyrius (IV: 6–8) described the priest as a person whose simple, austere life made him temperate and modest; his high intellectual ability, constantly stimulated by contact with his god, was directed towards meditation, studying theology and acquiring knowledge. Not everyone would have lived up to these exacting standards, but, after three thousand years, evidently a clear concept still existed that the ideal priest should be a man of learning and integrity.

CHAPTER NINE

THE ARMY

————— •◆• —————

Anthony Spalinger

The past decade has seen a resuscitation of scholarly interest concerning the military arm of pharaonic Egypt (Gnirs 1996; Cavillier 2001; Spalinger 2005). Some general surveys have been produced, but they lack the exactitude of modern scientific research (Partridge 2002). The following study, though in summary format, nonetheless adds to recent studies and draws some new perspectives on the issue of Egypt's military. This reinvigoration of a perennial topic has brought with it a deeper understanding of the cultural aspects of the warrior class as well as a more fundamental perception of the archaeological implication of war logistics. The emphasis upon the Egyptian New Kingdom, nonetheless, remains strong, if only due to the wealth of textual (inscriptional and literary) information still extant and the accompanying artistic depictions. Yet one must turn back to the Second Intermediate Period in order to see the fundamental substructure of the war machine of the Egyptian empire, a foundation that owed its importance to new technology and a new ideological framework (Cavillier 2001).

The period of Hyksos domination in Egypt, traditionally placed at the end of the 13th Dynasty and running through to the reign of Ahmose, first king of the 18th Dynasty, remains a very controversial and complicated subject (Oren 1997; Ryholt 1997: 295–310). Among all of the chronological and historical uncertainties, one of the more difficult remains that of the arrival of the horse and chariot in Egypt. Not surprisingly, the origins of the words for the new modes of warfare, encompassing war material (for example, armour, swords and chariots), are either Semitic or cannot be identified.

Although it took some time for the development of a military caste of elite chariot warriors to rise within the social sphere of the Nile Valley, there is no doubt that a transformation of the state, including its king, was the outcome. In particular, we can note the new ideological flavour of the 18th Dynasty monarchs. Repeatedly, they went to war. Campaigns became part and parcel of their normal activity. When young, princes were fully integrated within the Egyptian army, learning the special crafts of charioteer warfare and being inculcated with the ideology of an expanding Egyptian state. At the same time, these men were closely associated with their non-royal compatriots, officers within the army, whose backgrounds reflected the importance of their families at home.

Because horsemanship and driving war vehicles were now a desideratum for any future pharaoh, so too was the ability to lead men and to organize, both tactically and strategically, the manoeuvres necessary to propagate this new ideal. But there was yet another embedded feature of kingship: pharaohs were now skilled archers. Their 'sporting activities' were no longer limited to hunting or fishing but now included archery, handling of horses and chariots, spear/javelin throwing, oarsmanship and the like. How much the presence of foreign specialists within Egypt aided the Egyptians to advance on their own with these new technologies is another matter. The switch from copper to arsenical bronze was accomplished in the 12th Dynasty but the introduction of 'true' bronze for use in axes, to take a case in point, was later (Davies 1987: 96–101). It is possible that the frequent numbers of Canaanites (or Syrians) who resided in Egypt in the late Middle Kingdom helped to prepare a basis of reception for the acquisition of these new military items (Sparks 2004).

In the time of the Hyksos, one type of small horse was imported into the eastern delta (Decker 1965: 35–59; Spalinger 2005: 8–15). The exact date cannot be determined with accuracy, despite the on-going excavation at the Hyksos capital, Avaris (Tell el-Dab'a). Coming from Western Asia, equids had been domesticated for a long time in the steppe regions of southern Russia, and slowly but surely this art moved into the Near East. Along with the horses came chariots, vehicles that at first were small and clumsy, having two wheels that were solid. Later, changes in technology as well as technique meant that by c.1800 BC lightweight chariots with two wheels (each having four spokes), and drawn by two horses, became the norm (Littauer and Crouwel 1979). With them came a whole group of military men, the charioteers, who were to form the higher level of military society (Gnirs 1996: 17–34).

These changes can be observed by the end of the 17th Dynasty. At that time, the southern state of Thebes, controlling approximately 40 per cent of the length of Egypt, was at war with the north (the Hyksos) and the south (Nubians). The 'mutually hostile state' of Egypt's relations with the Nubians is nowhere better seen than in the evidence from the tomb of Sobeknakht of Elkab (Davies 2003a). Earlier written evidence allows us to picture an encapsulated Theban state, beset by enemies to the north and the south, but one that was able to press forward owing to its theological-political foundations (Vernus 1982; 1989a). Indeed, at this time the native southern Egyptian concept of 'victorious Thebes' became overpowering (Helck 1968: 119–20; Aufrère 2001a). True, the personalized concept of the capital of a native Egyptian state, in this case Thebes of the 17th Dynasty rulers, goes back to earlier divided times, specifically to the First Intermediate Period (Franke 1990; Morenz 2005). But in the Second Intermediate Period there was an added factor, namely the foreign occupation of Egypt. From the south, Nubians penetrated downstream, while in the north a foreign-based dynasty held power over the entire delta as well as central Egypt, ultimately controlling Middle Egypt up to Cusae. The galvanization of any political strength could only come from an amalgam of a new theological-political basis as well as the new military forms of warfare used by the Hyksos themselves.

Because of its relatively limited extent, Thebes at the beginning of the 17th Dynasty was forced to develop a new military arm, based on a large number of its young men who could use horses and chariots, but who also had to be inculcated with a messianic feeling of nationalism (Ryholt 1997: 181–3, 301–10). That there was no simple, single cause-and-effect relationship among all the developments in military technology is clear (Shaw 2001). For example, a large number of military men, the so-called 'king's sons', proliferate in the epigraphic record at this time (Schmitz 1976; Quirke 2004a). They were personally connected to the pharaoh, not by physical birth but, rather, through social and economic dependence. Equally, the administrative set-up of the Theban state reveals that some key cities and nomes possessed garrisons and military commandants, in addition to the expected civilian mayors. It is clear that this kingdom operated in a high state of military preparedness. Yet it still retained the naval orientation of earlier times. The royal flotilla was the basis of the army, and despite the gradual increase in importance of the chariotry, the old elite of marines formed the backbone of the Theban military (Berlev 1967).

The advantages that the Thebans had over their foes in the north and the south are hard to determine. Over time, they had organized a centralized state which, owing to its geographical limitations, could be easily run on a military basis. Yet practical considerations are never the only factor determining social cohesion and success. As noted above, the kingdom was set within a theological concept that placed the city of Thebes and its god Amun at the core. The Amun theology was linked with the warrior aspect of the monarch and thus his kingdom. 'Victorious Thebes' was not merely an image: it was as much a personification as an extension of the will of pharaoh and of the Theban godhead, Amun (Assmann 1992a). This feeling, one that can be seen later in private inscriptions (such as that of the naval man Ahmose Son of Abana), indicates that Thebes was 'our land'. In other words, a strong and cohesive ideological force was engendered that was able to provide this state, earlier beset by foes, with a *raison d'être* for military opposition and expansion. We must remember that Thebes could rightfully claim to be Egyptian in leadership and history, and by now Amun had become, theologically, the father of the warrior-king.

This nationalistic aspect of late Second Intermediate Period Egypt is well illustrated in King Kamose's wars against the Hyksos and also from later accounts that cover this era of foreign occupation (Habachi 1972a; Smith and Smith 1976). Kamose's royal account, composed on two stelae by his chancellor Nehy, keenly reveals the cultural bias against Apophis, the Pharaoh's enemy. The Hyksos ruler is always called an 'Asiatic'. The dichotomy between him and the son of Amun, 'Kamose-the-Brave', is a theme that runs throughout the inscriptions. Both of them were set up within the religious precinct of Karnak. All that the god wished came to pass, the result being Kamose's victory celebration upon his return to the capital. The purpose of the narrative account was not to describe the war in a classically narrative manner. Instead, there are various literary strands from different sources that enter into the composition. For example, we learn of a previous conflict between the Thebans and the Nubians. The remarkably swift move north by means of the royal fleet is never explained, and on the basis of a later story, Apophis and Sekenenra, it is assumed that the warfare recounted here is actually a continuance of recent conflict of Thebes versus the north (Wente 1973). But the collective memory of the entire Hyksos episode, in conjunction with the final wars of 'expulsion', was purposely kept in mind by the rulers of Thebes for some time, and indeed propagated to and by the elite (Redford 1970; Assmann 1992b, 1997). It is worthwhile to note that a later ruler of Egypt, Hatshepsut of the mid-18th Dynasty, still felt it effective to refer to Egypt's 'occupation' by the Hyksos, in order to bolster her propaganda (Allen 2002b).

This persistent attitude of extreme hostility is the major aspect of both Kamose's official war record and that of the soldier-sailor Ahmose son of Abana (Lichtheim 1976: 12 15). Both place emphasis upon the direct moves against the Hyksos citadel at Avaris. Kamose has his narrative interrupted by a letter from the Hyksos ruler to his Nubian counterpart, promising an alliance, and uses the event to show to the elite of Egypt how dastardly were his opponents' plans to crush the Thebans from two directions, the south and the north. Ahmose son of Abana, on the other hand, is keen to demonstrate his ability on the field, but likewise places emphasis upon the trapped nature of the foe while proclaiming his role in terms that are overtly nationalistic and xenophobic.

But there is additional information that can be brought into the equation. After Kamose died, he was followed by Ahmose, possibly his younger cousin (Bennett 1995: 42–4). The wars in the delta still continued. We lack any narrative, literary record of war from this time, even though Ahmose published an important document, the Tempest Stela, in which the Hyksos' control over the land was associated with a recent storm (Wiener and Allen 1998). The manifestation of 'the great god', clearly Amun, is placed at the forefront of the literary account. Ahmose, with his troops on both sides of him (note the military setting of the king) and the council to the rear, inspects his territories and later restores cult centres and ritual activities that had ceased. A new interpretation of the monument has placed emphasis upon possible unrest caused by the ongoing wars in the north with the Hyksos, and there is little doubt, when one examines the chronology, that the final conquest of the Hyksos capital took at least ten to 15 years of warfare. Evidently, the king's presumed success was won after a long and hard-fought struggle (Spalinger 2005: 22–4, 31 note 36). The so-called Tempest Stela is significant in this context as it appears to indicate that the king's presence away from his capital, Thebes, at least in his opening years, was considered to be a problem. The account of the 'catastrophe' was theologically interpreted as 'a manifestation of Amun's desire that Ahmose return to Thebes' (Wiener and Allen 1998: 18). Unfortunately, the extent of the damage to the inscription, as well as the difficulty in separating metaphors from their core literal meanings, hinder our understanding of this important composition.

We are fortunate to possess a series of fragments from Ahmose's religious complex at Abydos. There, in limestone, was carved a series of narrative scenes in which the king's final move against the Hyksos fortress at Avaris was depicted. In addition, the presence of the royal fleet reveals the enduring necessity at that time for the use of the marine-based army system for campaigns within the Nile Valley. After all, travel by water was considerably more effective in time and expense than travel by land. Because the Nile served as the umbilical cord for transportation and communication, he who had control of Egypt's only river possessed the kingdom. Thus the traditional nature of Egyptian warfare had been ship-based, and Ahmose, in his war reliefs, indicates that this system was still in place (Harvey 1998, 2004; Spalinger 2005: 19–23). Elsewhere, the king deports himself in a chariot, shooting his arrow from his massive bow, a scene that was to be the fundamental iconic base of all Egyptian visual narratives of war (Heinz 2001). The helpless opponents flee away from the superhuman king and his army. What distinguishes these pictures from later ones is the presence of

Ahmose's fleet. Because subsequent wars of the New Kingdom were concentrated in lands to the north, south or west, such visual narratives selected the natural means of fighting: with horses and chariots, and accompanying footsoldiers and charioteers. All of the later images of power reverberate through these reliefs. The mimetic restructuring of the king no longer placed him solely, or even mainly, within cultic roles at home, but now located the ruler far away from the capital and engaging a perennial foe. The fact that Ahmose's enemy was an Asiatic helped him to no small degree in redrawing the cultural boundaries of his nascent dynasty. Most certainly, with the fall of Avaris, the way was open for a consolidation of Egyptian trade routes and mercantile centres on the southern coast of Palestine.

It is thought-provoking to analyse the events surrounding the earlier seizure of the crucial site of Sile (Tjaru). Recent excavations have thrown welcome light on this matter, but the key point is that this fortress in the north-eastern delta served as the entrance and the exit of merchants, armies and tribes alike (Morris 2005: 46–7, 56–60). Sile, probably the second most important base of Hyksos control, fell to Ahmose *before* the capital itself. Located at Tell el-Hebua, it seems to have been significant from the Second Intermediate Period on, and bears witness to the intimate economic relations that the Hyksos had with their neighbours in Palestine. We can assume that the king's troops used the numerous canals and small waterways in order to advance swiftly upon the citadel. The decisive battle, nonetheless, had to be fought outside the walls, in what was to become the standard means of military warfare: the king or his troops advance inland; they engage their opponents in the field outside a city or fortress; the fighting is chariot-based, and when the defending side loses, the city surrenders. This was the ideal system of Egyptian military conflict, one that occurs again and again in their pictorial reports carved on temple walls (Gaballa 1976).

The process of expansion by means of war rapidly became a principal *raison d'être* of the re-unified Egyptian kingdom. The old conflict with Nubia never ceased, and we find not only Kamose but also his immediate successors (Ahmose, Amenhotep I and Thutmose I) pushing their fleet and army considerably upstream. To some degree, this was conceived as a reconquest of lost provinces that Egypt once held, in particular the territory between the First and Second Cataracts. That region, named Wawat, was soon to be completely incorporated into the Egyptian economy. Buhen at the Second Cataract was quickly established as the administrative focus of Egypt's imperialistic desires. In similar fashion, the island of Sai at the Second Cataract was converted into yet another fortress-town. This practice is known only from the southern zone of Egypt's control (Morris 2005: 112–13). Asia appears to have been another matter, probably because the logistics of political and military domination were more complex.

Under the first two rulers of the 18th Dynasty there is little evidence that the Egyptians were able to control Palestine. The need to develop a larger fighting force, composed of elite charioteers, was not at the core of the difficulty: distance and isolation were. Thus it was somewhat troublesome for King Ahmose to capture the southern Palestinian city of Sharuhen (Spalinger 2005: 34 note 31); sieges are notoriously the result of an army's incapacity to effect a swift battlefield decision. Within Egypt proper, troops and supplies could be quickly dispatched to problematic regions with little fear of interruption, and this was also the case in Nubia. In

Western Asia, on the other hand, there were no rivers that could provide such logistical support except for the faraway Euphrates in eastern Syria. Thus a different system of logistics had to be developed, one based on the active support of local cities, reinforced by key military bases. This took time.

This key difference between Asia and Nubia explains the seemingly rapid takeover of Lower Nubia (the province of Wawat) by the time of the death of Thutmose I, as well as territory south to the Third Cataract. This king even moved his flotilla far beyond the Fourth Cataract, and his exploits indicate just how effective the Egyptian logistical system was (Davies 2004). We must not assume that such an extensive voyage and the submission or defeat of the locals at the extreme limits of the known universe implies that Egypt could hold such territory. Superior military technology – in particular better bronze weapons, chariots and horses – could overwhelm the locals. In addition, the Nile was a perfect artery for expansion. Nonetheless – and the Nubian work projects of Amenhotep I and Thutmose I prove this – two key problems came to the fore. In order for Egyptian imperialism to be maintained, supply bases as well as military garrisons were needed: hence, the development of an 18th Dynasty fortress system, coupled with permanent occupation. At the same time, once the distances east and west of the Nile broadened, severe constraints were placed on Egyptian political and military control.

One reason why Middle Kingdom control over Nubia was more limited than that of the New Kingdom lies in the lower technological level at that time (O'Connor 1993; O'Connor and Reid 2003). In the 12th Dynasty, Egypt could *move* beyond the Second Cataract, as attested by campaigns against the Kingdom of Kerma. But Egypt could not *control* lands further south; hence, the major building projects of the 12th Dynasty in the Second Cataract region. This is not to deny that in the early New Kingdom major crises occurred in Nubia. One well-known case was the eruption of rebellion at the time of Thutmose I's death (Gabolde 2004). The severity of the disturbance indicates that 'pacification' did not automatically mean control.

The first century or so of the New Kingdom may be said to have provided the bases of military and political domination over Palestine and Nubia. Equally, this period witnessed the gradual development of the Egyptian army with a more complex system of administration. By the reign of Thutmose III, the chariot divisions with their leaders had come to the fore in the military (Gnirs 1996: 12–17, 31–4). 'Field marshals' of non-royal blood ran the officer class. The gradual transformation of a marine-oriented army to a land-based one entailed the establishment of a new and increasingly important career path. The military had become a powerful corporation in its own right, and with the king leading it in person, the ethos of the army and the concept of kingship had altered (Spalinger 2005: 70–80). Now, the rulers of Egypt were expected to engage in wars, to show their virility in the field, to bring back prisoners as proof of success, and to return thanks and captives to the godhead, Amun. In fact, it seems that every campaign began in the temple of Amun where a 'speech oracle' (Schenke 1960) took place during which Amun promised victory to his son, the living king. The trip to foreign and distant lands commenced from, and returned to, the religious centre of Thebes.

All kings, including Hatshepsut, were obliged to perform military deeds. Begun as a nationalistic reaction against the internally divided nature of the home country, war now assumed a permanent aspect of society that embraced all key members, not just the king and his officers. The temples included age-old ritual smiting scenes on their walls, updated to reflect the circumstance of Asiatic and Nubian prisoners. The king comported himself in a militaristic manner, whether through his manly acts of archery and horsemanship in war or peace, or within a temple bequeathing captives to workhouses, if not death (Hornung 1982a). If the influence of the newly won empire led to independence of action and confidence in strength, it also meant that the kingdom had now become one of the superpowers of the day (Redford 1995).

The independent reign of Thutmose III is traditionally seen as the apogee of the 18th Dynasty's military might and success. If so, and his published war record attempted to prove this, it was obtained only after many decades of continual warfare (Redford 2003; Cavillier 2003). There are two major divisions within the military reports of Thutmose III, although both were considered to belong together. The first covers the momentous campaign of the king to the central Palestinian city of Megiddo. That narration, detailed and historically sober, focuses upon the background to the war as well as the heroic deeds of the monarch. These two aspects permeate the composition. We learn that the north Syrian city of Kadesh was an active supporter of the resistance, undoubtedly hoping to deflect pharaonic strength away from itself. It is also evident from the official report that this opposition to Egyptian control had come about because of Egypt's seemingly unopposed success at an earlier time. Even though we do not know precisely the depth of Egyptian control in Asia, it is clear that if Thutmose I was able to fight on the Upper Euphrates, none of the small city-states of Palestine and Syria was able, on its own, to resist Egypt effectively. Some have even argued that Palestine was devastated by the Egyptians in the early 18th Dynasty, a hypothesis that still needs clear proof (Spalinger 2005: 65–6 note 7 and 96–7). If so, the opposition of the Palestinian cities with support from Syria makes further sense.

These shows of armed resistance received support from the Syrian kingdom of Mitanni. Earlier, under Thutmose I, Egypt had engaged in war with Mitanni without, however, being able to achieve a decisive victory, since Mitannian power was equal to Egypt's. Mitanni stood close to the Lebanon and maintained indirect control over central and south-eastern Syria. Any forays of Egypt into its heartland met with stiff opposition. So it is not surprising to find Mitanni actively championing a major revolt in Palestine against Egyptian control. Significantly, the subsequent northern wars of Thutmose III – Nubia had ceased to be a thorn in the side of Egypt by now – were directed inland and across Syria to the heartland of Mitanni. But before Thutmose could press his army so deep into Asia, he had to crush the rebellion at Megiddo.

In his later campaigns, all of which preoccupied him up to his forty-second regnal year, Thutmose III moved troops and war material north, through the age-old trade routes of the Via Maris on the coast, or the King's Highway in the central valley of Palestine and Syria. Furthermore, the Egyptians secured the harbours of the Lebanon, used the ports as staging bases, and campaigned inland against Kadesh and eventually Mitanni. This intense fighting ought to indicate that neither mere heroism nor personal satisfaction was at the heart of the matter. Although the economic implications of Egypt's hegemony over Asia are still murky, it can be argued that Egypt had become reliant upon the region for long-range trade as well as the possible importation of horses and chariots, the power force always needed for any army at this time.

Egypt's desire to maintain control of the Levantine ports further highlights its indirect economic influence over the eastern Mediterranean. Indeed, the recent argument that the port of Perunefer, Egyptian for 'good departure', was located at Avaris/Tell el-Dab'a, emphasizes even more the need that the Egyptians had for an aggressive marine policy (Bietak 2005). Finally, all of this control could only be maintained by some type of policing, a point that has been investigated in detail from the voluminous data revealed in the Amarna Letters (Pintore 1973; Na'aman 1975; Liverani 1990, 1994; Bryce 2003).

By the end of the reign of Thutmose III, a rigorous policy of garrisons had come to exist in Asia. Though small in number, such troops served as a 'civil guard' necessary to aid and support small wars. Local princes were closely watched and often deposed if they attempted to shake off Egyptian control. One new fortress in the Lebanon is known from the reign of Thutmose III (Morris 2005: 213). By this time, the personal involvement of the king was no longer significant. In the subsequent reign of Amenhotep II, for example, the king fought in person only twice, although a third war is known to have occurred when he was regent with his father. Thutmose IV went abroad once, to Nubia. The role of the various Egyptian 'commissioners' and garrison soldiers was locally based. Their duty was to keep the peace and not actively to upset any urban power, city or kingdom. Local troops would have been busy in their attempt to repel local marauders, especially the tribes circulating around the borders of eastern and southern Palestine (known to the Egyptians as 'Shasu') (Giveon 1971; Ward 1972). This persisted into the following dynasty, as the various Late Egyptian Miscellanies reveal (Moers 2001; Spalinger 2005: 267–9). The international correspondence of the Amarna Letters, dated to the reign of Amenhotep IV, reveals similarly parochial, though extremely bothersome, concerns.

The development of Egypt's New Kingdom Empire brought with it a host of complex social developments, such as the sudden increase in Semitic loan words associated with the contemporary military, and trips abroad to Asia (Hoch 1994: 472–3). The rapid increase in international correspondence supplemented the regularity of Egypt's bellicose activities (Cohen and Westbrook 2000), and the regular iconic representations of foreign peoples remained a set pattern in the artistic relief work of the warrior pharaohs (Hall 1986).

After the numerous wars of Thutmose III in Asia, a sudden decrease in campaigns may be noted. The Egyptian war machine developed into a corporate body in which many soldiers spent most of their lives (Gnirs 1996: 41–91). The military had become a career-oriented institution with the chariotry at its core. Through war, Egypt not only came to partake at a rapid rate in international relations, but also reflected on the peoples and cultures of the 'outside' (Loprieno 2001).

The concept of Egyptian kingship was similarly affected. The 'king as hero' was a major theme of the day, and one that lived without cosmological interpretations. Indeed, some have even claimed that there were liturgical ceremonies involving the ceremonial execution of foreigners. It is furthermore presumed that these public events took place when the pharaohs presented awards to their high officials (Schulman 1988). Kings now wished to be portrayed in their chariots, even when they hunted wild game, lions or bulls. The pharaoh trampled down the enemy and consigned the foreigner to the opprobrium of the 'other' (Assmann 1992a).

Under Amenhotep III and IV (Akhenaten), the Egyptians began to contend with a revived Hittite empire in the north; while, in the south, Nubian revolts proved a persistent irritation (Helck 1980a). The country also faced a series of internal difficulties that often rendered it incapable of mustering the energies to meet external threats. Problems associated with the dynastic lineage were common during the late 18th and early 19th Dynasties, and two kings, Horemheb and Ramesses I, rose to power without being directly related to the ruling house. There is little doubt that both men owed their success, at least in part, to their connections with the military. The two had previously been generals, and then viziers. Indeed, the former appears to have been keenly associated with campaigns and diplomacy in the northern territories as well as in the south (Martin 1989). The presumed dominance of the Egyptian war machine in determining the nature of Egyptian kingship has been a major theme in Egyptological literature (Helck 1939, 1981). The connection between kingship and the army was a regular facet of the New Kingdom and even of the late 17th Dynasty (Redford 1995; Murnane 1995b).

It has often been claimed that the Ramesside kings of the 19th and 20th Dynasties were forced to campaign at an accelerated pace in comparison to the preceding era. It is true that the conflict between Egypt and the Hittites occupied much of their time, and, later, defensive wars became a norm. On the other hand, the early campaigns of Seti I can be seen as a continuation of the earlier jockeying for power in Syria under Tutankhamun and Horemheb. The thrust of Seti's military exploits was centred around the Syrian city-state of Kadesh, located on the River Orontes. Seti followed a strategic policy similar to that of Thutmose III. First, he reinforced the Levantine coast in order to supply war material for an expected overland march into Syria. He then moved north in order to confront a Hittite counter-attack. In his fourth campaign – following the order of the Karnak reliefs – he struck against a Hittite commander in open battle. The pictorial evidence indicates a typical mêlée of chariots, and if we can believe the visual account, the Egyptians won. Yet this apparent success must be placed in perspective: the Egyptian king had to revisit the area once more, if only to deal with the recalcitrant citadel of Kadesh.

Such evidence from the Egyptian side, few in words but detailed in pictures, forms the basis of our historical reconstruction of the opening decade or so of the 19th Dynasty. As such, this differs considerably from the literary war records that earlier New Kingdom rulers left for posterity. Also suggestive of a cultural turn that elevated war deeds, both royal and private, was the increasing series of complaints preserved in the official scribal accounts of the Ramesside Period, notably the Late Egyptian Miscellanies, many of which contain artificial literary attacks on the military class (Caminos 1954; Moers 2001; Jäger 2004; Spalinger 2005: 267–70). It is readily evident that an intellectual crisis had occurred some time earlier, during which the officials or bureaucrats of the pharaonic state felt themselves under pressure from the career-oriented military men and their apparent success, at least in achieving personal fame on the battlefield. In retaliation, the officials singled out for ridicule both the presumed luckless infantryman and the elite charioteer. Irrespective of the contemporary validity of these remarks, all of which are as sarcastic as they are vituperative, it remains the case that a cleavage had occurred within certain upper segments of New Kingdom society; the rapid growth in importance of Egypt's military lay at the heart of this division.

After the inconclusive Battle of Kadesh, in the fifth year of Ramesses II's reign, the Egyptians and Hittites jockeyed for position in Syria for a further decade, but to no avail. Both parties were faced with other military and political difficulties. The Egyptians had problems in Palestine, and it was probably at this time that Egypt reorganized its northern empire (Gnirs 1996: 159–91). Elsewhere, the Libyans were becoming more aggressive (O'Connor 1990; Kitchen 1990), and Ramesses II began to construct a series of defensive fortresses on his western border (Morris 2005: 611–45). The Libyans were numerous, and if their weaponry was not technologically of the first rank, they could depend upon their allies, the seafaring peoples of the eastern Mediterranean (Manassa 2003). Contemporary accounts suggest that Libyans had begun settling in the delta, and conflicts with Egypt were to continue into the succeeding 20th Dynasty.

From the mid-19th to the early 20th Dynasty, the Egyptian army had as its main purposes the maintenance of the Asiatic possessions and control of Nubia. After years of warfare in Syria, the war machine had geared down; its job was now to keep the peace by containing the recalcitrant tribespeople of Jordan and the Sinai. To the south, the Nubian provinces were controlled by a static system of military garrisons and an effective bureaucratic organization (Kitchen 1977). But the military would be incapable of dealing with a different type of threat, invasion by peoples who did not follow the expected mode of warfare.

If the reign of Ramesses III is to be seen as the final act in the Egyptian army's effective offensive capability, then it performed admirably (Grandet 1993: 161–216). By this time, the institution of the army had become even more differentiated than before. A gradually increasing dependence upon mercenaries can be observed. Nubians, who had been members of the Egyptian war machine since the Old Kingdom, were now merely one part of a multi-ethnic institution. Various Sea Peoples, in particular the Peleshet (to be equated with the later Philistines) as well as Sherden, operated as crack troops (Oren 2000). Often the latter are depicted fighting directly at the portals of Asiatic cities or in the front line of the infantry.

From the scenes in the temple of Medinet Habu we can reconstruct the continual warfare that Egypt faced in the opening decade of Ramesses III's reign, culminating with the battle against the Sea Peoples. Despite the Egyptian victory, the economic stability of international commercial relations was broken, with the result that Ramesses III and his immediate successors had to pull their garrisons back home. No longer did Egyptian armies fight in Asia. Rather, it appears that the *internal* situation demanded stability that a forceful military could accomplish.

The rulers after Ramesses III were beset by hosts of difficulties among which we can single out the ongoing infiltration of Libyans into the western delta and further south. At the same time there was a growing division between the ruling classes of Upper and Lower Egypt, and it comes as no surprise to find the High Priests of Amun, at Thebes in the south, becoming 'barons' in their own right. This is shown in the title 'generalissimo' which such individuals as Herihor, the High Priest of Amun in Karnak at the end of the 20th Dynasty, successfully claimed for themselves (Gnirs 1996: 193–211; Janssen-Wilkeln 1999, 2001; Spalinger 2005: 269–71). External relations were similarly troubled and a revolt in Nubia, led by the viceroy, illustrated the inability of any king to control his southern territories. Within Egypt, the natural inclination of many of the elite army men, especially the Libyans, was to deal with local problems. Thus we see an increasing parochialism on the part of the army (Spalinger 2005: 271). Any analysis of post-20th Dynasty military life must deal with the rise of these new clan-oriented westerners, an issue that would take us beyond the confines of this presentation.

PART III

ECONOMIES

CHAPTER TEN

AGRICULTURE AND ANIMAL HUSBANDRY

————·◆·————

Douglas Brewer

The earliest undisputed evidence for an agricultural way of life in Egypt comes from the delta site of Merimda and sites in the Fayum and dates to just before 5000 BC, approximately 2,000 years later than the origins of agriculture in south-west Asia. Currently, there are no generally accepted explanations as to exactly how or why domesticates entered Egypt, nor how a settled agricultural lifestyle became established and spread throughout the Nile Valley. Explanatory models of peoples migrating into the valley as well as hypotheses involving the diffusion of ideas or goods (rather than human populations) have adherents, and environmental deterioration, population pressure and technological innovation have been proposed as catalysts for the adoption of agriculture in Egypt. Regardless of the mechanics of introduction, the speed at which domesticates and agricultural practices spread throughout the Nile Valley reflects the rapid cultural transformation that occurred at this time, and all scholars agree that the development of agriculture substantially changed the character of Egypt, its landscape and its people.

THE REGIME OF THE NILE

In order to understand how the ancient Egyptian agricultural system worked, one must examine the unique natural features of the Nile Valley (Hume 1925; Said 1962). To the naked eye, the Nile Valley looks virtually flat. From Aswan to the Mediterranean Sea it slopes, on average, only about 8 centimetres per kilometre, while from the river's edge to the desert margin it averages 12 centimetres per kilometre in slope. Viewed in cross-section, the river's plain is thus slightly convex in shape. This convex topography was created by the deposition of silts from annual inundations, with deposits near the river creating natural levees that slope downward to the desert margin. In certain areas along the Nile's western bank one can still see a series of ridges running parallel to the river. These ancient levees, abandoned as the Nile gradually shifted to the east, were used as natural dikes to hold and divert floodwaters for agricultural purposes.

The convex topography of the Nile Valley lent itself to the creation of a series of basins which, in ancient times, filled annually with floodwaters. These basins, of which approximately 130 have been identified, were the reservoirs for Egypt's irrigation system. Today the basins are almost totally obscured by modern development, but in pharaonic times they were a predominant feature of the valley, ranging in size from small ponds to 1,600 hectare lakes, and in depth from 0.5 to 2 metres (Hume 1925; Hurst 1952; Said 1962). These basins served as the initial sites of Neolithic cultivation, for after the floodwaters had receded, seed merely had to be dispersed over the wet mud, trodden into the moist soil and harvested when ripe.

This form of agriculture continued with few modifications throughout the pharaonic era and was dependent on the Nile and its annual flood. Each year, summer monsoon rains in Ethiopia sent water cascading down the Blue Nile. In June this influx of floodwater could be detected in Aswan and by mid-August in the delta. The river would remain at flood height for 40–60 days and then begin to recede. This annual phenomenon was responsible for Egypt's fertility, because with the floodwaters came also 110 million tons of sediment, washed down from the Ethiopian highlands (Bowman and Rogan 1999). This sediment settled over the land so uniformly that nineteenth-century travellers noted that the flat basins drained so completely that no pools were left (Hume 1925; Hurst 1952).

The floodwater irrigated the land and the sediment enriched the soil, but the floods were subject to variation. Floods that were as little as 50 centimetres lower than ideal would not extend to all the cultivable fields, and harvests would suffer, while floods that were 50 centimetres higher than ideal would remain too long on the fields and shorten the growing season. Additionally, unusually high floods might damage dikes and even threaten villages.

From ancient times onwards, Nilometers were used to gauge the height of the flood. These markers were positioned along the Nile and were calibrated to measure poor, good and excessive flood heights. Although current evidence does not indicate that the Egyptians transformed the Nilometer readings into useful measures for predicting crop yields, they most certainly understood the implications of a normal, low or high flood and prepared accordingly.

Hurst (1952) published a comprehensive and very useful study of Nile floods. He based his work on historically recorded Nilometer readings (AD 622–1522) and twentieth-century records of Nile water discharge. Both sets of data resulted in normal distribution curves (bell curves), indicating that high floods were as common as low floods during both the twentieth century and historic times.

Hurst also demonstrated the existence of certain multi-decadal periods of time that were dominated by higher or lower than average floods. For example, particularly high flood levels were recorded from AD 1869 to 1898 while from AD 1899 to 1942 floods were particularly low. Considerable variation existed, however, even within these groupings. During the period of low floods (1899–1942) ten were considered high and two dangerously high. In addition, flood heights did not appear to be predictive of the following year's flood: during the period of recorded high floods (1869–1898), the highest and lowest floods occurred in successive years with a difference of 2.75 metres in peak height. All attempts by Hurst to define cyclical or modal patterning of flood heights failed.

Shifts in flood height existed in ancient times as well. The excessive floods of the late Middle Kingdom, the low floods of the First Intermediate Period, and the declining flood heights of the Predynastic to Early Dynastic Periods serve as examples. In short, all evidence suggests that the river behaves today as in the past, with an even likelihood of high and low floods. Given this premise, supplemented by information collected from the historic period, some insights into Egypt's ancient agricultural past are possible.

The ancient Egyptians used earth and stone barrages and dams to regulate the flood and direct irrigation waters. Given this level of technology, an amazingly narrow range of floods could be considered acceptable for maintaining good crop yields. Based on historic documents, a high flood (measured at Aswan) and a low flood differed by as little as 66 centimetres. Floods just 50 centimetres higher than average were dangerous to dikes and the future crop. Floods in consecutive years measuring a difference of 2.75 metres, as was recorded in the nineteenth century, would have wreaked havoc across the ancient Egyptian countryside, destroying levees, fields and even villages. Yet the Nile's most obvious characteristic is not its variability, but its tendency to remain within a tightly defined average flood height over most years (e.g. 92.83 metres above sea level for AD 1866–1898). Averaged over time, roughly seven to eight normal floods would occur in every ten. Consequently, it was the remarkable consistency of Nile floods that provided ancient Egyptians with the opportunity for tremendous agricultural production (Willcocks and Craig 1913; Hurst 1952; Hurst *et al.* 1963).

THE BASIN IRRIGATION SYSTEM

Egypt's irrigation system was not, as many believe, designed to increase the amount of acreage under cultivation; rather, it was merely a means of water control, regulating the naturally available water so that it saturated the basin soils to the extent necessary for productive agriculture. When the river reached the requisite height, the levee dikes were opened and the basins filled. Water was held in the basins for 40 to 60 days and was then released back into the Nile or into the next basin downstream. Once the water had left the fields, no more water was added until the next flood. All crop growth was thus dependent on this single influx of moisture (Beaumont 1993).

The development of the basin system probably followed a simple scenario of expansion. Originally, Neolithic farmers merely waited for the water to recede and the land to dry to the appropriate moisture level to plant their crop. With a little augmentation of the natural levees, however, early farmers could enhance their yield. By closing the natural spill channels that returned the floodwater to the Nile, they could hold the water in the basins longer and ensure the proper planting conditions. With the passage of time, the basins between the old abandoned levees running parallel to the Nile were subdivided by artificial levees running perpendicular to the river, thereby creating a chequerboard pattern of fields. Further, by creating small channels and dikes between the artificial levees, they could direct excess water to the next plot or basin – an action of particular importance when floods were inadequate. Rather than leaving a basin unwatered, those areas not reached by a low flood could be at least partially prepared for cultivation by receiving second-hand water from nearby basins.

THE EGYPTIAN FARM

From a variety of sources, the basic outlines of an ancient Egyptian farm can be sketched. Inheritance played an important role in matters concerning the availability of land and its cultivation. Through generations of inheritance, sales, leases and other divisions, the typical Egyptian farm evolved into a composite of plots scattered across the countryside. This land could be worked by the owner, but was more commonly leased or worked by contracted labourers. Inheritance also played a role in who received leases to temple- or other government-controlled lands, and there is even some indication (e.g. Wilbour Papyrus) that field labourers held some rights to work given plots of land, even if that plot was rented or sold to another party. To what extent this practice prevailed over private, government and temple lands is not fully understood (Gardiner 1948; Menu 1970, 1982; see also Eyre 1994; J. Manning 1999; Katary 1999).

Though the scattered nature of farm plots may seem, at first glance, to be an awkward and inefficient system, likely resulting in organizational mishaps from bureaucratic levels down to cultivator, it did make long-term evolutionary sense. If a landowner's holdings were contiguous, a natural disaster such as a high or low flood would affect the crop equally, but if plots were separated across the landscape they would be affected differentially, and the owner could be assured of at least some holdings falling within the range of decent crop production.

It has been estimated that individual labourers could cultivate about 7.5 *aroura* (*aroura* = 52 × 52 m) of land (Janssen 1986: 355). Field workers were sometimes the owner or lessor, but more often were hired hands. How crops were divided between owner, lessor and cultivator is not clear, and the arrangements may never have been standardized by region or era. During the Saite Period and, most likely, the New Kingdom, taxes and rent were a pre-assessed quantity (not a percentage) of the harvest. Based on nineteenth-century production figures, an *aroura* of land produced about ten *khar* (760 litres) of grain. One *khar*, or about one tenth of an average annual yield, was assessed for taxes, which were usually, though not always, paid by the landowner (Donker van Heel 1998: note 13). Another *khar* was saved for seed, in some cases the responsibility of the owner, in others, the renter. During Greco-Roman times the government was responsible for supplying seed to at least some farms and problems continually arose with late arrival of seed rations (Gardiner 1941). The farmer and lessor or field owner apparently split the proceeds (eight *khar* or roughly 80 per cent of an average crop), but the cultivator still had to pay the workers if he or his family did not perform the labour. After expenses, the lessor and lessee/cultivator each probably took home a quarter to a third of an average crop (Brewer *et al.* 1994; Brewer and Teeter 1999).

Egyptian farmers practised both intensive and extensive agriculture. Extensive agriculture requires little work except for planting and harvesting. Egypt's vast grain fields are an example of extensive agriculture. The most intensive form of agriculture, often referred to as horticulture, is characterized by the investment of a great deal of labour in a relatively small area, such as in fruit or vegetable gardening.

Throughout the pharaonic era, ancient Egyptians relied on winter crops, especially cereals, followed in importance by legumes and flax. The principal cereals of Egypt were barley and emmer wheat. (Durum wheat and more intensive summer crops were introduced during Greco-Roman times.) Evidence for barley being the dominant grain during Old and Middle Kingdom times is supported by the common phrase 'barley and emmer'. Interestingly the reverse expression, 'emmer and barley', was used during the New Kingdom and the 25th Dynasty, suggesting a reversal of their importance (Gardiner 1941; Dixon 1969).

Although a number of words were used to refer to Egyptian grains, the word *ankhet*, derived from the verb 'to live', expressed its significance. The production of wheat and barley went beyond sustenance. In a society without money, wealth and commodity prices were expressed in measures of grain. In a very real sense, the lowly farmers of Egypt grew the country's wealth; the entire economic health of the nation depended upon their success.

Wheat and barley are short-season, early maturing grains with high yield potential. Wheat and, to a greater degree, barley can tolerate high temperatures as long as humidity levels remain low. Egypt was, therefore, a perfect environment for their cultivation and became an envied granary throughout the ancient world.

Preparations for the ancient planting season began in late October or early November before the water had completely drained from the basins. Irrigation works were repaired or dredged and property boundaries reassessed before fields were readied for planting. Tomb paintings depict in detail how the grain was grown and harvested. For some crops, the land would be broken up using a simple plough but in most cases the seed was scattered over the fresh mud and trodden into the ground by droves of herd animals. When the crop ripened, government inspectors came with measuring lines to set the taxes. In late April or early May the crop would be harvested with sickles and carried in baskets or nets to the threshing floor (Figure 10.1). Oxen or donkeys threshed the grain while men with wooden pitchforks added fresh heads from nearby stacks. Winnowers separated the grain from the chaff by tossing it in the air with wooden scoops. Samples of the cleaned grain were inspected, and the rest was tallied and sent to a granary to be divided into shares (National Geographic 1978; Beaumont 1993).

Barley and wheat were the main components of two Egyptian staples, bread and beer. Bread and beer were made using similar ingredients, and excavations at Predynastic Hierakonpolis suggest that bakeries and breweries were located adjacent to one another. In making both, the grain was coarsely ground and then mixed with water; yeast was added and the dough kneaded and left to rise. If it was to be made into bread, the dough was baked. If beer was the objective, the dough was lightly baked and placed in a vat. Moist crushed wheat, or perhaps a little already fermented beer, was added and the concoction left to ferment. Ancient Egyptian beer was a nourishing grog with a variable but small amount of alcohol (Lucas 1962; Brewer *et al.* 1994).

Each major agricultural civilization developed not only its staple cereals but also its companion legume. In ancient Egypt, lentils were an important complementary crop to wheat and barley. Like wheat and barley, lentils were not indigenous to Egypt and likely came from the Near East (Zohary 1972; Zohary and Hopf 1973). The earliest remains of lentils come from Neolithic Merimda and el-Omari. Lentils were also found in the underground stores of Djoser's pyramid (*c*.2680 BC) (Lauer *et al.* 1951).

Although yields were low compared to wheat and barley (50 to 150 kg/ha) lentils stand out as one of the most nutritious legumes, containing 20 to 25 per cent protein,

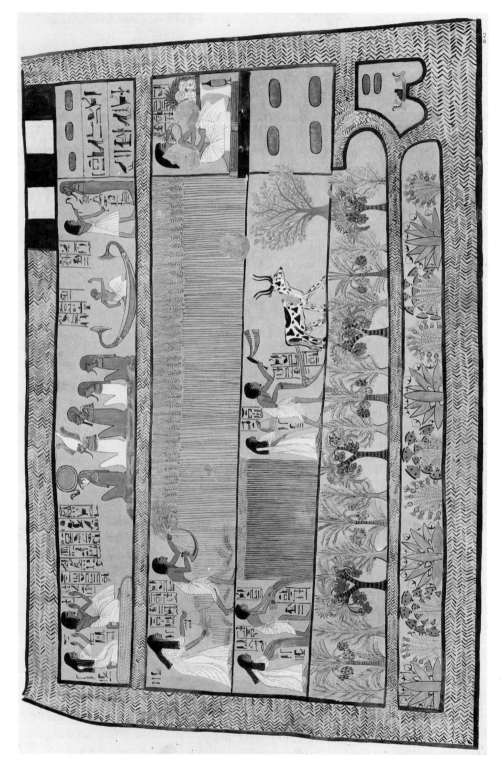

Figure 10.1 Harvesting grain and pulling ripened flax. Tomb of Sennedjem, Deir el-Medina, 19th Dynasty. Image courtesy of the Metropolitan Museum of Art.

which is near the level for lean meat (Barulina 1930). In addition, lentils also provided a number of amino acids not found in cereals. Thus the common Egyptian meal of bread and beer (cereals) augmented by lentils, a few green vegetables and a little fish, fowl and occasionally red meat held the potential for a well-balanced diet.

Egypt also produced flax, a fibrous grass that provided Egyptians with the raw material needed for the production of linen and linseed oil. The seeds offered an added bonus in that once the oil had been extracted the residue made excellent cattle feed. Like the cereal grains, flax was an annual, best planted in late October or early November and harvested in April. Soil preparation was more involved than for cereals as the ground was ploughed twice in preparation for planting, rather than once (or not at all) as for cereals. As a cultivar, flax can quickly adapt to varying conditions of soil and temperature, but the cool, moist winter climate of the delta was ideal, particularly for the early stages of plant growth (December to March), and the later dry spring assured timely plant and seed formation (el-Kilany 1939; Legget 1945; Durrant 1976). To harvest flax for linen, the plant was pulled rather than cut, because cutting the stalk could stain the fibres and reduce its value for making white cloth. The earlier in the season the stalks were pulled, the finer the linen.

HORTICULTURE

Although fruit and vegetable gardening was common in Egypt, it constituted one of the more labour-intensive forms of food production. Vegetables and fruits require considerably more water than cereals or legumes; thus gardens and orchards were generally close to a water source, and the water was hand-carried from the source to the garden. Watering a garden in Old and Middle Kingdom times was done by carrying pairs of water jars suspended from a rod that hung across the shoulder. Even after the advent of a mechanical lifting device, the *shaduf*, during New Kingdom times, water still needed to be manually hauled and distributed throughout the garden plots.

Although many vegetables and fruits grown in Egypt were introduced during Greco-Roman times, Egyptian garden plots, even as early as the Old Kingdom, produced an array of vegetables including melons, curbits, garlic, onions, leeks, radishes, lettuces and herbs (Table 10.1). Unfortunately, most of our data come solely from textual and pictorial evidence. Vegetables are difficult to identify archaeologically because they lack stones or seeds, but we do know that gardens were generally planted in small rectangular plots, and archaeological evidence suggests they were subdivided into neat one-cubit-square (45 to 52 cm) beds. Gardens were meticulously cared for, weeded, watered and harvested to provide food as well as cash crops for the farmer.

Grapes, dates and figs comprise the oldest group of cultivated fruits in Egypt. The earliest evidence for grapes in Egypt comes from Neolithic el-Omari where pips of imported, presumably wild, raisins have been recovered. Evidence for cultivated grapes dates to the 1st Dynasty, when written records distinctly specify wine and grape vines, and a wine jar was recovered from the tomb of King Den. Small carbonized pips of grapes have been found in 1st Dynasty tombs at Abydos and Naqada, and a rich find of wine jars as well as fragments of raisins were discovered in the Step Pyramid (3rd Dynasty). By the 5th Dynasty, grape vines and wine production were common tomb motifs, and written records imply that some vineyards produced

Table 10.1 Egyptian domesticates and their approximate date of agricultural production*

	Neolithic	Predy-nastic	Early Dynastic	Old Kingdom	Middle Kingdom	New Kingdom	Late Period	Greek/Roman
Sorghum/Millet					X			
Olive						X		
Caster			X					
Safflower						X		
Carob					X			
Jujube (Christ Thorn)			X					
Persea				X				
Pomegranate					X			
Watermelon				X				
Chate Melon					X			
Leek (kurrat)				X				
Garlic		X?						
Onion			X?					
Pea	X							
Faba Bean				X				
Chickpea						X		
Lettuce				X				
Celery								X
Radish								X
Swine	X							
Donkey	X							
Horse						X		
Camel							X	
Cat	X							
Dog	X							
Goose						X		
Chicken								X
Honey bee			X					

Note: * Table does not refer to earliest evidence, but to earliest example/estimate of incorporation into Egyptian agriculture.

considerable amounts of wine. One vineyard, for example, is said to have produced 1,200 jars of good wine and 50 jars of medium wine in a single year (Lauer *et al.* 1951; Zohary and Spiegel-Roy 1975; Darby *et al.* 1977 plus references; Zohary 1987).

A number of Old, Middle and New Kingdom scenes depict Egyptian wine production. In ancient Egypt, as in other hot, dry climates, grapes were grown 1.5 to 2 metres off the ground, in order to decrease the reflection of the sun's heat and allow breezes to keep the fruit as cool as possible. After picking, the grapes were placed in large vats where they were crushed by treading. The Egyptians then placed the skins in a cloth bag and twisted the bag to squeeze out any remaining juice. Due to naturally occurring yeast on the grape skins and the hot environment, fermentation began almost immediately and progressed rapidly to create a thin, watery wine. Finished wine went into jars sealed with reed and clay stoppers. Like modern labels, markings on the jar bore the name and location of the estate, the vineyard, the vintner's name, the date and an assessment of quality.

The colour and type of Egyptian grapes is uncertain, but given Egypt's hot climate, low acid (sweet) grapes probably predominated and would have resulted in a sweet rather than dry wine. Tomb paintings depict pink, green, white, red and blue grapes, and New Kingdom scenes show a dark red wine pouring out of the vats (Lutz 1922). One third-century BC text refers to an Egyptian 'white wine', while a 'black wine' is noted in Old Kingdom texts, but some scholars suggest these descriptions represent geographic origin, not wine colour (Budge 1898; Kees 1961; Darby *et al.* 1977).

Although grape vines and wine held a special place in Egyptian life, palm trees were probably a more common sight across the Egyptian landscape. The most distinctive were the date palms (Figure 10.2), which reached heights of 20 metres. Egypt's high temperatures and low humidity are particularly conducive to date production, which can reach as high as 100 kilograms of dates per tree. But a bountiful harvest requires a steady water supply, which in Egypt means irrigation or hand-watering.

Because Egypt had a less arid climate from late Palaeolithic to Early Dynastic times, it is very likely that isolated populations of wild date palms existed near sources of water. (Wild date stones have been recovered from Egypt dating as early as the sixth millennium BC.) It was not until the Middle Kingdom, however, that dates became common cultivars. Date palms in Egypt flower from February to March. Egyptians working with early cultivated dates must have been confused when only some of the flowering trees produced fruit, but they soon learned that only the female trees produce and could be cloned by vegetative propagation. To maximize fruit production,

Figure 10.2   Fruit-bearing date (left) and doum (right) palms from the tomb of Sennedjem (from Brewer *et al.* 1994: fig. 5.2).

Egyptians also practised artificial pollination, a method introduced during the Middle Kingdom which probably accounts for the rise in date production and general popularity of dates at that time. Pollination was likely accomplished by attaching or waving male flowers over the female tree, as was done during historic times.

Dates are rich in carbohydrates and proteins. The flesh of a dry ripe date is about 75 per cent sugar and will provide about 3,152 calories per kilogram. Dates are also a good source of iron and provide moderate amounts of calcium, copper, magnesium, sulphur and vitamins A, B1 and B2. In addition to its fruit, the palm trunk was valued for its wood, the fronds for weaving and the fibrous bark for rope (Täckholm and Drar 1950; Nixon 1951).

The doum palm was cultivated in Egypt also, and evidence of its use dates to Badarian times. The doum fruit varies greatly in size depending on growing conditions, but with plentiful water the palm produces large, apple-shaped fruits that provide a nourishing, ginger-sweet pulp. Although the ancient Egyptians made use of doum fruit (particularly to flavour cakes) and the stones for making buttons, beads and rings, it seems that the doum palm's wood was its most valuable asset as it is a denser wood than the date palm's (Täckholm and Drar 1950; Manniche 1989).

In addition to palms, two types of figs were cultivated in Egypt: the true fig and the sycamore fig. For both trees, only the female produces fruit and, in the wild, relies on a particular species of wasp to aid in pollination. Under cultivation, propagation is vegetative, with the farmer choosing from only the most prodigious trees to replant and expand the orchard (Zohary and Spiegel-Roy 1975). The domestic forms of both figs are believed to have been introduced to Egypt from the east (the true fig) and from the south (the sycamore fig).

Although archaeological remains are not numerous, the true fig must have been relatively common because a number of texts refer to the cultivation of figs and the great quantities of fruit that were produced. Metjen, a 3rd Dynasty noble, reportedly planted figs alongside his house. Figs are also mentioned in the Pyramid Texts, and Ramesses III claimed to have offered 15,500 measures of figs to Amun-Ra (Storey 1976; Darby *et al.* 1977).

The sycamore fig was probably the more common of the two Egyptian figs and its cultivation was almost exclusive to Egypt. Early evidence for sycamore figs dates to Neolithic el-Omari, and baskets of fruit have been found in tombs as offerings as well as depicted on tomb walls (Galil *et al.* 1976; Brewer *et al.* 1994 plus references).

ANIMAL HUSBANDRY

Agriculture in its broadest sense includes the rearing of animals as well as plants. Egyptians relied on many domestic animals for food as well as wealth: cattle, sheep, goat, pig and fowl dominate the spectrum of domestic species depicted in scenes from the Old Kingdom to the New Kingdom. Most impressive are literary references to the size of these flocks and herds, particularly temple herds, which numbered in the hundreds of thousands of animals.

Cattle seem to have had a special significance in Egypt throughout its long history. As early as the Late Palaeolithic (*c.*16,000 BC), graves of some males were marked with the horns of the giant wild aurochs, the progenitor of domestic cattle (Wendorf 1968). During Early Dynastic times a similar practice can be found in royal tombs.

Most intriguing is tomb 3504 at Saqqara in which a series of bull heads was shaped from earth and aligned along a bench (Emery 1954). Royal iconography of the time also depicted the bull as an important symbol of strength and virility. The vast herds held during the later periods suggest that cattle, as in some sub-Saharan cultures, were a measure of personal worth and status.

Several types of Egyptian cattle have been identified from the iconographic evidence: a heavily muscled long-horned type; a short-horned type; a hornless type and the zebu (Brahma) type (Figure 10.3). If the ancient artistic representations do indeed accurately depict cattle, these types differ enough that they might be considered separate breeds (Brewer *et al.* 1994). The long-horned variety known from Neolithic times is depicted as tall and lean with everted, lyre- or crescent-shaped horns, and resembles the indigenous wild aurochs. The hornless breed, known from the Old Kingdom, was referred to as 'fancy', which suggests some degree of uniqueness, but does not seem to have been rare. Unlike other cattle, however, they are never pictured as draught animals. The short-horned type is known from the 5th Dynasty, but was apparently uncommon until near the beginning of the New Kingdom. The zebu, or Brahma type, was a New Kingdom introduction to Egypt.

The earliest evidence for the use of cattle as a provider of milk comes, in fact, from Egypt (and Mesopotamia) and dates to the fourth millennium BC (Brewer *et al.* 1994). Given the type of grasses and feed available for Egypt's herds, however, milk production would have been quite poor. Ethnographic studies of cattle in

Figure 10.3   Egyptian longhorn, shorthorn and hornless (fancy) cattle
(from Brewer *et al.* 1994: fig. 7.3).

similar environments suggest that only 12 to 20 per cent of the cows would have produced milk at any one time, and the amount of milk available for human consumption would vary seasonally from 0.2 to 1 litre per day per cow (Deshler 1965). Milk production could have been increased by improving forage and offering supplements such as bread dough – a recorded, but expensive practice probably limited to a small minority of the herd population. Because cattle were generally expensive to maintain, due to their greater water and forage needs relative to other herd animals, their products (meat and milk) were generally restricted to the upper classes and to offerings at temples and shrines.

Sheep and goats are much more cost efficient than cattle and less demanding in their needs. Sheep are grazing ungulates originally adapted to hilly grasslands. A good food source for sheep would have been the stubble left over from cereal harvests. Given the small size and scattered nature of individual farm plots, ancient Egyptians, like modern herders, probably kept grazing flocks small (two to ten individuals) to best utilize fields for forage. Iconographic evidence indicates that two breeds of sheep were present in Egypt: a hairy, thin-tailed type with twisted horns, and a shorter type with a fatter tail and recurved horns found from Middle Kingdom times onwards. Goats complement sheep and cattle because they are browsers and do not compete for the same foods, preferring thorny underbrush and trees to grasses. Goats are indigenous to mountainous areas and, because of their adaptability to harsh environments, are able to thrive under extremely arid or humid conditions. Two types of goats existed in Egypt. The first, known from the Old Kingdom, was long-legged and shorthaired with a long, straight nose and scimitar horns. Near the end of the Second Intermediate Period, a second type of goat, with corkscrew-shaped horns, is pictured. It is likely, though not certain, that this type entered with the Asiatic herders of the period (Brewer *et al.* 1994).

Wild pigs are native to Europe, Asia and North Africa, and pig bones have been recovered from Egyptian sites from Palaeolithic times onwards. The date of the first appearance of domestic swine in Egypt is uncertain, but given the pig's limited use as a herd animal, it is unlikely that the pig was domesticated before the establishment of permanent settlements. The pig joins the cat, donkey and cattle as possible indigenous African domesticates. Its remains have been recovered from many Lower Egyptian Predynastic sites and are a good indication that swine were raised for food during Neolithic times. Regardless of the timing of its introduction, the domesticated pig filled an open niche by eating what cattle, sheep and goats did not. Their ability to range freely or be confined to sty offered a unique advantage over other domesticates, particularly in densely populated areas.

Egyptian palaces, villas and even modest peasant dwellings contained poultry yards and aviaries (Figure 10.4). Old Kingdom reliefs depict some of the earliest attempts to tame and raise birds, though it is likely that, for many species, domestication was not completely successful and new specimens were captured during yearly migrations. Of the more than 70 species known from Egyptian art and writings, only greylag and white-fronted geese appear fully domesticated, but other species of geese as well as ducks, cranes, pigeons, ibis and possibly chickens were kept and bred with at least some success. Penned birds were fed with scattered grain; some cranes and geese were hand- or force-fed, probably to fatten them or enlarge their livers for *foie gras*, a delicacy documented from the Roman Period.

Figure 10.4 A poultry yard from the 5th Dynasty tomb of Ti at Saqqara
(after Houlihan 1986: fig. 73).

Herding and cultivation strategies

Like the farm labourer tending his crops, it was the herdsmen's responsibility to
ensure the wellbeing of the herds by protecting them from the elements and thieves,
and providing a plentiful and balanced diet. Extrapolating from soil types, the entire
Nile Valley and many parts of the Eastern and Western Desert could hold moisture
long enough to offer pasturage. Grasses, however, lose important minerals and proteins
as the warm dry season ensues. Additionally, because Egyptian herds were large,
overgrazing was most certainly a problem. The best means of ensuring healthy herds
during the dry season was to relocate the cattle to better pasture. For the ancient
Egyptians, this meant driving the herds north to the delta and to the shores of Lake
Fayum. Although these drives crossed hundreds of kilometres and undoubtedly proved
to be hard on both cattle and herdsmen, studies of modern non-mechanized herders
indicate that productivity – in terms of weight gain, calving rate and general health
– is actually enhanced by drives.

   In studying land/water relationships, cultural geographers have found an interesting
correlation between planting and herding. Modern agriculturalists, explicitly or
implicitly using risk analysis, divide their land based on its crop-producing reliability.
If an area of land produces a good crop a high percentage of the time, then it is
reserved for cultivation, but if a section of land produces a good crop only 30 per
cent or less of the time, it is more likely to be reserved for pasturage. Land in Egypt
ranges from 0 to near 95 per cent probability for successful cultivation, so a mixed

strategy would have been the best approach to balancing farming and herding. Abundant evidence suggests that this is precisely the type of system the ancient Egyptians employed (Brewer *et al.* 1994).

Egyptian agriculturalists originally farmed near the natural levees of the Nile and pastured herd animals near the desert borders. Though technological advances allowed additional areas to come under cultivation, plenty of pasturage could still be found throughout the pharaonic period in areas not receiving enough annual floodwater to cultivate, in fallow farm plots, or in uninhabited regions of the delta.

DISCUSSION AND CONCLUSIONS

Egypt's ability to produce mass quantities of agricultural goods is well founded. The land was fertile and the agricultural cycle well-adapted to herding and cereal agriculture. To provide a better understanding of Egypt's agricultural productivity, hypothetical production statistics can be computed based on Butzer's (1976) figures of available cultivable land and textual evidence of ancient land use (Table 10.2). It should be kept in mind that these figures are for illustrative purposes only, as not all cultivable land was sown with grain every season, nor would all lands produce at peak levels. Nevertheless, the figures do reflect productivity potential.

Using data from the Ptolemaic village of Kerkeosiris, nome infrastructure accounted for approximately 5 per cent of the surface area (1.5 per cent villages, 3.5 per cent dikes, roads, etc.), and of the land that remained for cultivation approximately one-third lay fallow (usually due to a bad flood), leaving roughly two-thirds of the available land actually cultivated (Grenfell *et al.* 1902: 60; Verhoogt 1998). At Kerkeosiris, half of the cultivated land was sown with grain and the remainder was cultivated with lentils and other vegetable crops.

Given these rough figures of available land, ancient Egypt's tremendous agricultural potential can be approximated. Current Food and Agricultural Organization (FAO) guidelines state that a healthy diet must consist of a proper mixture of protein and carbohydrates. With regard to cereals approximately 400 grams a day are needed to maintain proper health. The present FAO protein standard is 37–46 grams per day (depending on body weight, climate and quality of protein), with a suggested total calorific intake of 2,000–2,800 kilocalories per person.

Table 10.2 Agricultural production levels based on available cultivatable land

Date (bc)	Cultivated land (km²)	Yield (khar)	Population
150	16,926	61,837,448	4,782,000
1250	13,888	50,738,419	2,862,000
1800	11,439	41,791,242	1,931,000
2500	10,602	38,733,346	1,589,000
3000	9,362	34,204,130	816,000
4000	9,982	36,468,238	323,000

Notes
76 litres = 1 *khar* (Kemp 1989b: 309)
1 litre dry grain = 772.5 grams (Sinclair pers. comm.)

As shown in Table 10.2, ancient Egypt's potential grain production allowed for up to 45 times the FAO allotment of cereals (18,160 grams a day per person) during Predynastic times and even during Egypt's most populous period offered nearly five times (2,078 grams a day per person) the recommended daily intake. Even if only half the cultivable land was planted with grain, as at Kerkeosiris, production still ranged from 2.2 to 2.5 times the recommended daily allowance. With the potential to produce massive surpluses well beyond the needs of its own population, it is easy to understand why Egypt was considered the breadbasket of the ancient world.

Egyptians should also have had little problem meeting the calorific standards set by the FAO. Roughly 400 grams of cereal supplies 1,600 kilocalories and 56 grams of protein, though cereals do lack certain necessary amino acids, so a little animal protein or complementary plant protein would be needed to round out the Egyptian diet. This, however, could be achieved easily by eating lentils and modest amounts of fish, fowl or red meats.

There are, however, some deficiencies in a diet dominated by cereals. Vitamin B deficiency is a common malady for those relying too heavily on cereals. Iron and calcium deficiencies would also be a concern for the Egyptians, particularly among children and women of childbearing age. Rich sources of calcium include shellfish and milk products, and green vegetables and red meats are a good source of iron, though they may not always have been available to the lower classes (Vasey 1992: 20).

Studies regarding the health of ancient Egyptians as it relates to diet are limited, but several do seem to corroborate the existence of dietary deficiencies. One sample of Predynastic, Early Dynastic and Old Kingdom Egyptians showed that, with the exception of individuals recovered from elite Old Kingdom tombs, all suffered from anaemia (Lovell, pers. comm.). This medical condition might have resulted from an iron-deficient diet, but could also be indicative of parasitic infections that were probably rampant in the ancient populations of crowded agricultural communities. Another study of Nubian skeletons, showing that osteoporosis was common among young adult females, corroborates the Egyptian data and indicates a lack of dietary calcium and iron (Armelagos *et al.* 1984). Thus, even though the Egyptians could produce mass quantities of food, certain diet-related deficiencies plagued their health. Yet these deficiencies were more a result of social stratification, poor hygiene conditions and lack of modern dietary knowledge than food production and availability, and a well-balanced diet in the form of bread and beer, lentils, a few fresh vegetables and a little meat was attainable by even those of modest means.

CHAPTER ELEVEN

CRAFT PRODUCTION AND TECHNOLOGY

——— ·◆· ———

Anna Stevens and Mark Eccleston

For much of the developed world's population today, craft production suggests a niche activity: small-scale manufacture largely divorced from industry and technological change, often directed towards the creation of luxury items. But in the pre-industrial world, and indeed in large parts of the world today, craft production can be better considered as simply the ability to work materials to shape a manufactured world. It can be viewed as a broad spectrum of activity: the manufacture of rope, the moulding of faience jewellery, the sculpting of stone blocks. While a sense of 'craftsmanship' and points of the spectrum directed towards the non-mundane are readily recognizable, so too elements of the practical and everyday are pervasive.

EVIDENCE AND APPROACHES

The study of craft production and technology in ancient Egypt is served by a relatively rich variety of sources. The end-products of manufacture form the most widespread of these: the fragments of textile, stone statues, pottery vessels and so on. Supplementary information occurs in reliefs, particularly tomb scenes from the Old Kingdom onwards, where there appears a remarkably wide range of craft activities. Also important are the three-dimensional models of craft activities included in burials during the First Intermediate Period and Middle Kingdom, the most famous group originating from the 12th Dynasty tomb of the official Meketra at Thebes. Increasingly, archaeology is supplying the by-products of manufacture and the implements that facilitated production, and not infrequently excavations have identified spaces and emplacements where craft production occurred. Inscriptions sometimes provide information through occupational titles, records of transactions, or brief descriptions accompanying craft production scenes.

No source comes free of interpretational difficulties. Representations of craft production were not intended as accurate records of practical processes and appear often to have been stylized or abbreviated. Textual references frequently lack detail, relevant information included only as secondary to the main theme, which is never craft production itself. Many of the most detailed texts date from the Roman Period, raising the question of how relevant they are for earlier periods. Archaeologists face

Figure 11.1 A scene from the tomb of the 18th Dynasty vizier Rekhmira at Thebes (TT 100) showing in the upper register the drilling of stone vessels, stringing of bead collars, and drilling of stone beads; and below, the probable curing, scraping and cutting of hides, and assemblage of finished leather goods (after Davies, N. de G. (1943) *The Tomb of Rekh-mi-Re at Thebes*, vol. II, pl. LIV, New York: Metropolitan Museum of Art).

problems of non-uniform survival of materials and the often inadequate recording of technological finds, particularly from the early days of Egyptian archaeology.

There are many gaps in our understanding of craft production in ancient Egypt. Some will undoubtedly remain. Much of the sensory aspect of production, for instance – the sounds, smells and sights – can only be imagined. In the case of industries such as leather-working, though, the processes of production themselves remain poorly understood. More work is also needed to elucidate the relationships between different industries and to position production in a broader social context. One way forward is the excavation of more raw data, particularly from workshop contexts, but undoubtedly there remains scope for existing artefacts to be reconsidered with issues of craft production in mind, and for greater application of cross-disciplinary approaches.

WORKING WITH MATERIALS

A wide variety of crafts was undertaken in Egypt, drawing upon the diverse array of raw materials available locally and in surrounding regions. Plant and animal products for leather, textiles and basketry were plentiful within Egypt, as were clay and temper for ceramics; sand, alkali and colourants for glass and faience; ores for different types of metals, and stone for masonry. While some ores, colourants and stones were in remote areas and required major state-sponsored expeditions to acquire them, they were in abundant supply for long periods of Egyptian history. These expeditions and the control of natural resources, especially in Nubia and the Levant, were a key factor in Egypt's dominant geo-political position in the East Mediterranean throughout the majority of the Bronze Age. The major raw material that Egypt lacked was good quality wood, which was obtained from the Levant throughout most of its history. Areas that Egypt did not control directly were also a source of exotic raw materials such as ivory, ostrich eggs, animal pelts, incense and ebony from further south in Africa, and rare stone such as lapis lazuli from as far away as Afghanistan.

The most prolific type of object found on excavations in Egypt is pottery, which was produced in large quantities from the Predynastic Period onwards. The Nile provided virtually unlimited supplies of silt that could be used as a raw material for producing pottery and was exploited throughout Egypt and Nubia. Marl clays were available in a much more restricted number of locations and would have required more resources to collect. The shapes of pottery vessels and the mix of clay and temper (known as fabric) used to make the pots changed throughout Egypt's history and is one of the key indicators used to date archaeological sites (Arnold and Bourriau 1993).

Other industries that used high-temperature processes included glass, faience and metalworking. These were less common than the ceramic industry in Egypt at all periods. The glass and faience industries, especially of the New Kingdom and Roman Period, have been the subject of intense recent research (Nicholson and Henderson 2000; Nenna *et al.* 2000, 2005). Due to the essentially unlimited supply of sand, the primary raw ingredient for glass and faience, it is no surprise that their production flourished, especially from the New Kingdom onwards. Amarna, Per-Ramesses, Malkata and Lisht (Nicholson 1998; Rehren *et al.* 1998; Shortland 2000; Mass *et al.* 2002) all have some evidence of glass working and new evidence from Per-Ramesses shows glass was being manufactured there from raw materials (Rehren and Pusch 2005). Metals were important to Egypt throughout its history, with large-scale expeditions sent into the Levant, Nubia and the Eastern Desert in order to secure and to mine ores for copper, gold, iron and lead (Ogden 2000). There is evidence from sites such as Timna, in the Sinai, that semi-permanent camps were set up to protect the miners and to smelt the ore into metal (Rothenberg 1972). The organization of the metalworking industry in Egypt is not well understood for any period. Large-scale workshops operated at sites such as Per-Ramesses (Rehren *et al.* 1998), but it is also likely that small-scale production within households took place during the New Kingdom at Amarna and probably at many other sites throughout Egypt's history. After the introduction of iron technology in the Late Period there would have been a blacksmith's workshop in almost every village in Egypt, producing and repairing farming tools. Understandably there has been much attention paid to the finished objects made in gold, silver and other precious metals and there is no doubt that the Egyptians led the world in this area for millennia.

Stone was particularly abundant in certain areas of Egypt and was exploited as a resource from the Predynastic Period onwards. Hard igneous rocks are available especially in Upper Egypt and in the Eastern Desert and softer rocks such as alabaster are found in the region of Luxor. A wide variety of stone types from these regions was used to produce sculpture, architectural elements and vessels throughout Egypt's history. Precious stones such as turquoise, amethyst and emerald, along with metallic ores for copper, gold and lead, were all acquired by expeditions to areas such as the Eastern Desert. Plants also provided an invaluable resource. Lengths of plant material, particularly parts of the date- and doum-palms, were manipulated into basketry and related goods; papyrus, a type of sedge, was used as a writing surface. With considerably more processing, plants also formed the basis of textiles, predominantly linen, made from flax. Where available, wood was widely exploited. From animals came skins and leather, possibly glue, and during the pharaonic period sheep's wool and goat hair, both occasionally used for textiles. Bone, horn and ivory were carved into utensils and decorative items, and ostrich eggshell was used similarly.

Pinpointing the first appearance of particular types of object or technology in the archaeological record can be useful when approaching issues such as chronology, but focusing too closely on first attestations can be misleading and unhelpful when considering broader questions of the dynamics of ancient society. Too readily, discussions of technology or industry can be reduced to those of technological advance or evolution. When assessing when, why, how and where different technologies were first used, it is important to consider that these decisions were made by people living within a society that was bound by complex social, political and economic rules that existed almost at a subconscious level of action. Long after the first attestation of metal knives in Egypt, for instance, stone blades continued in use in domestic contexts. Cost is one potential restricting factor here; another may have been simple disinterest in abandoning a tool that, for all its limitations, had stood the test of time. Adopting an overly evolutionary model of technology and the use, or not, of materials in the historical past erases the conscious decisions made by those individuals who made and used these materials.

The question of why certain technologies were not taken up by the Egyptians is, arguably, more interesting than attempts to quantify the earliest archaeological evidence for individual industries. One perplexing example is the apparent late uptake of iron smelting and smithing technology. Iron working is known to have been used in Anatolia, continental Europe and Britain from about the twelfth century BC. Iron objects are also known in Egypt from the 18th Dynasty, the most famous example being the dagger from Tutankhamun's tomb, and iron is mentioned in tribute lists from Mitanni in the Amarna Letters. It is clear from the position of iron in these lists that it was thought of as a highly prized and valuable material. The reasons why the Egyptians themselves do not seem to have taken up this technology until the Late Period will probably never be fully known. It is inconceivable that they were unaware of the technology, but there seems to have been a conscious technological choice, possibly influenced by a complex amalgam of technical, social, political and/or religious factors, not to do so.

CASE STUDY: THE INTRICACIES OF CRAFT PRODUCTION IN THE AMARNA SUBURBS

One important site for the study of craft production is Amarna, location of Egypt's capital, Akhetaten, for around 20 years (*c.*1350–1330 BC) during the late 18th Dynasty. Here lie the remains of most key elements of a major urban Egyptian settlement: palaces, temples and administrative centres, and extensive residential suburbs. Recent excavations have focused upon a patch of ground in one of the residential areas, the Main City. Over two seasons an area of some 600 square metres was examined, revealing a series of small mud-brick buildings and associated courtyards. The artefact corpus included a range of material that illustrates the important lines of enquiry into ancient craft production that archaeological research can open (Figure 11.2).

One immediate impression is how well the assemblage fits broadly with contemporary representations of craft production, such as in Figure 11.1, despite their different contexts. The working of different materials in close association conveyed so clearly in such scenes is suggested by the mixed nature of the excavated assemblage. The multi-stage nature of manufacture is reflected in items such as the glass rods (e.g. 35937 and 36481 in Figure 11.2), the end-products of a technologically complex

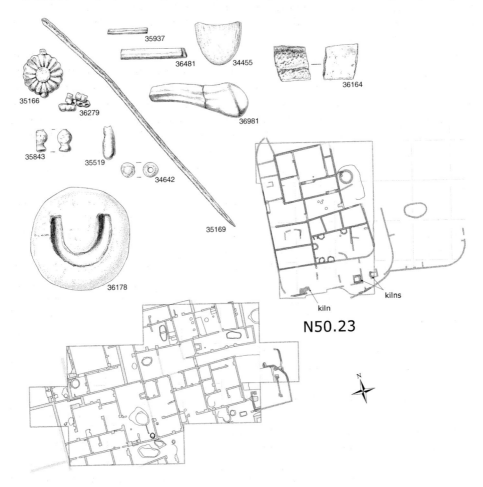

Figure 11.2 Excavation Grid 12 in the Main City at Amarna showing closely grouped domestic structures. Excavation of complex N50.23 exposed the remains of two probable kilns, a third evident when the structure was first cleared in the early twentieth century by the Deutsche Orient-Gesellschaft (the DOG plan is underlain). Finds included many fragments of glass rods, strips and bars (e.g. 35937, 36481, 34455, 36981), most seemingly intended for reworking; a small number of unfinished and misshapen glass beads and pendants (e.g. 35519); many pieces of flat faience, some shaped as rectangles and triangles (e.g. 36164); small fired clay moulds of a type used for the production of faience jewellery (e.g. 36178); faience beads fused together, presumably manufacturing errors (e.g. 36279); finished faience and glass beads, pendants and rings (e.g. 34642, 35166); various hand-held implements (e.g. 35169); and fragments of probable crucibles for the heating of metals. Objects at 1:1 (A. Boyce). Plan at 1:500 (B. Kemp and A. Stevens). Image courtesy of the Egypt Exploration Society.

process which still only represent an intermediate stage of production. Representations convey a sense of individuals working independently but in a broader co-operative environment. Something similar underlies the assemblage, the small scale of the objects necessitating individual attention, but amid a wider commonality of approach that has largely cancelled out signs of individual hands at work. The excavated material also serves as a reminder of the intimate knowledge of a material and its properties that familiarity can breed, while the presence of 'imperfect' objects begs the question of what formed an adequate product, the balance between functionality and aesthetic perfection perhaps weighted in favour of the former.

Focusing further on the objects themselves reveals something of the intricacies of manufacture; glass jewellery is an artefact group of particular interest. Two technologies are attested for the shaping of glass beads and pendants. Simple spherical forms were made by winding coils of viscous glass around a rod, but more complex shapes (e.g. 35843 in Figure 11.2) were produced by grinding down hard glass bars. Although there was clearly an awareness of the effects of heat on glass and of moulding technology as applied to faience, this shaping method recalls stonework technology. The use of glass for small delicate items was relatively new to Egypt at this time. It is possible that we are seeing here evidence of limitations in knowledge or strategy, the Amarna craftworkers adjusting to the material and transferring to it skills from a familiar technology. A finely finished product, and the compensating factor of skill, may have created the illusion of mastery of a material, although it may be that cold-worked glass was, itself, valued for its unique properties.

A second approach is to step back from the objects themselves. In doing so, we see that the buildings are, from comparison with structures elsewhere, decidedly residential. Materials such as faience and glass were being worked in what was, in essence, a domestic setting. In the north-east of the excavation area lay a house and courtyard complex (N50.23) with three mud-brick emplacements that appear to have been kilns (Figure 11.2; see also Shortland 2000: 67–70). The temperatures reached in these structures were probably adequate to fire faience and to make glass viscous enough to work. There is little in the way of comparable emplacements elsewhere across the excavation area, although a concentration of glazing debris was found in a probable kiln some 100 metres away (Peet and Woolley 1923: 19, pl. I; Shortland 2000: 67–8). In the context of this neighbourhood these kilns must have served important roles. The presence of houses at both complexes suggests that they were not openly communal facilities, but just how closely access to them was controlled by the house occupiers is unknowable. These individuals might, in turn, have been serving the officials who owned larger houses dotted across the Amarna suburbs, and who could have provided an important point of contact with broader networks through which materials were sourced and worked goods redistributed.

The question of the ultimate destination of the objects is a crucial one. It is difficult to imagine that they were being manufactured entirely for local consumption. The flat faience shapes, for instance, seem to have been used as inlays, more suited to the elaborate stone buildings of the official quarters of the city than mud-brick residences. In a sense, the Amarna suburbs appear as a vast but loosely structured factory serving the state. Through a contextualized reading of the material remains, the role of craft production in creating relationships of dependence, unbalanced yet in many ways reciprocal, between residents and across social groups, becomes tangible. The responsibility of the people in contributing to the maintenance of the city, and, by extension, of Egyptian society itself, appears here direct and visible, certainly less abstracted by layers of bureaucracy than in many societies today.

MODELS OF PRODUCTION

Remaining at Amarna, we see that the site also offers evidence for craft production of a somewhat different nature. Earlier excavations around the formal temple complexes in the heart of the city revealed scatters of manufacturing material, including debris from stone sculpting and waste from glass and/or faience production. Clusters of sculpting debris were also encountered among the residential suburbs, suggestive of sculptors' workshops, some also producing faience. In appearance, these complexes differ little from the constructions described above, although they are generally more spacious, with large courtyards. Similar complexes containing kilns and thought to have been used variously for pottery, faience and glass manufacture, have been identified elsewhere in the residential areas and fringes of the central city, in some cases lacking a house.

This range of evidence, coupled with that from tomb scenes, has prompted the proposal that craft production at the city occurred on three main levels (Kemp 1989a: 56–7): at formal institutional workshops; within 'courtyard establishments'; and in what were essentially domestic contexts. Each level is, in effect, a band in a spectrum, the individual points of which possess unique groupings of attributes in terms of setting, personnel, scale of manufacture, internal organization, and networks of procurement of materials and distribution of goods. Although only rarely does the evidence allow us to grade finely enough to identify the existence of specific points in this spectrum in ancient Egypt, models of this type provide a useful means of approaching ancient craft production (see also Bourriau *et al.* 2000: 141–2). Three of these factors – setting, people and networks – are considered further below.

SETTING

The position of state institutions as a locus of production is repeatedly evident. Tomb scenes from the Old Kingdom onwards often depict workshops under the control of state officials (Figure 11.1). Textual sources refer to spaces such as the *per-shena*, a state-controlled unit of storage and production, primarily of beer and bread, but for a period during the 18th Dynasty at least, also textiles (Kemp and Vogelsang-Eastwood 2001: 476). Such sources are often elusive on the exact location of these spaces, but some were probably attached directly to state buildings. On the ground, pottery and faience workshops have occasionally been identified in or near royal funerary complexes of the Old and Middle Kingdoms, although whether these were 'attached' workshops as such is often uncertain (Bourriau *et al.* 2000: 135–8; Nicholson and Peltenburg 2000: 180–2). Temple complexes of the New Kingdom have quite often yielded scatters of manufacturing debris from auxiliary buildings, occasionally with manufacturing emplacements, particularly for ceramic production (e.g. Jacquet 1983: 84–92, fig. 19; Spencer 1997: 59, 103; Jaritz *et al.* 2001: 148–50). The relatively unprepossessing nature of this material contrasts with the *c.*30,000 square metres of 'quasi-industrial' New Kingdom workshops excavated at Per-Ramesses, seemingly in the heart of the ancient city (see Pusch 1990, 1995). Later temple complexes at sites such as Naukratis (Petrie and Gardiner 1886: 39; Coulson and Wilkie 1986) and Tanis (Montet 1942: 105–6; Fougerousse 1946) seem to exhibit more substantial emplacements for ceramic production and metalworking, in particular, although it may be that the evidence is simply better preserved than at earlier temples.

Manufacturing spaces that are not associated physically with state institutions, and lack an overriding domestic element, are best represented at Amarna, although others are known, such as an Old Kingdom to early Middle Kingdom faience workshop at Abydos (Nicholson and Peltenburg 2000: 180–1). It is possible that some of the craft production scenes in tombs show activity in such spaces, and it may be that workshops under state control were not always located at state buildings. Craftworkers can also be identified in texts as belonging to a *per djet*, or 'personal estate'. Moving deeper into the domestic realm, craft activity is occasionally represented in scenes of houses of the upper classes (Figure 11.3) and is evident in the archaeological record of houses representing a broader socio-economic spectrum (e.g. Kemp and Vogelsang-Eastwood 2001: 307–404). Weaving, basketry and the production of hand-made pottery seem to have been particularly suited to the domestic environment. It is also worth noting the scope for activity in communal spaces such as streets, riverbanks and rural areas, and at procurement sites. The low attestation of such activity in the surviving sources, with the exception of stone-quarrying and ore-mining sites (and see Kemp and Vogelsang-Eastwood 2001: 323 for a rare attestation of street-space usage), almost certainly under-represents its spread in antiquity.

While a distinction can be drawn between spaces intended for manufacture, and 'multi-purpose' areas, the same underlying factors dictated the locating of such areas: control of output, access to raw materials and supplementary industries, proximity to the final market, and the nature of the manufacturing processes themselves. To what extent was segregation of manufacture from other aspects of life also important? The natural tendency is to propose greater segregation in formal contexts with multi-functionalism and improvisation prevailing elsewhere, but the evidence is less clear-cut. In temple complexes, a degree of segregation is suggested by the clustering of storage and manufacturing spaces around the central temple building, but surely greater division of space was possible. Practicality, proximity to the final market, and perhaps control of personnel and output, seem to have been prioritized. A sense of shifting priorities vis-à-vis the provision of workspace during the life history of a single complex is provided at the Old Kingdom mortuary temple of Khentkaus at Abusir, where a small pottery workshop appears to have been established in an internal courtyard to supply the temple cult, but not until sometime after the foundation of the temple (Verner 1992; see also Bourriau *et al.* 2000: 137–8). In high-status domestic contexts, spatial division of activities is suggested in sources such as the representation of the house of Djehutynefer within his tomb at Thebes (Figure 11.3), where scenes of weaving and spinning occupy the ground floor alongside general domestic activities, the house owner and his wife represented in the upper storeys. Yet there is no means of determining here whether this division, if indeed reflecting reality, was simply a product of freedom of space or dictated by broader social decorum. It is unlikely that spatial segregation was as readily maintained in smaller houses, although the possibility of the temporal division of activities remains.

Figure 11.3 View of the interior of the house of the 18th Dynasty official Djehutynefer from his tomb at Thebes (TT 104). On the lowest floor appear five figures preparing yarn (the largest is certainly female) and three figures working at vertical looms. For the exact processes represented, see Kemp and Vogelsang-Eastwood (2001): 78–9, 408, 410 figs 3.17 and 10.3 (after Shedid, A.G. (1988) *Stil der Grabmalereien in der Zeit Amenophis' II. Untersucht an den Thebanischen Gräbern Nr. 104 und Nr. 80*, pl. 27, Mainz: von Zabern). The artist's grid lines of the original are here removed.
Image courtesy of the Deutsches Archäologisches Institut.

In any case, craft production must have been an important factor in shaping the urban environment, and experiences of it. The devotion of large areas of central land to craft manufacture (along with food production and storage) at cities such as Amarna and Per-Ramesses may have counteracted the grandeur of the surrounding religious and ceremonial complexes – although as statements of productivity harnessed by the state these areas were probably impressive in their own right. The locating of high-temperature industries on the outskirts of settlements is a repeating, although not ubiquitous, feature. Pollution, access to water and prevailing winds, and, perhaps, undesirable social aspects of such industries, can be pinpointed as contributing factors here (see Bourriau *et al.* 2000: 137–8, fig. 5.2; Frood 2003: 38), although it is not clear if the locating of such spaces was a result of formalized proscription or, rather, of underlying social codes and neighbourhood-level decisions.

The latter appear to have dictated growth in the Amarna suburbs and with it the intermingling of production-related and residential areas. Slight clusters of tool and implement types and manufacturing debris can be recognized among the archaeological record here, slender but tantalizing evidence of occupational 'quarters' (see Shaw 2004: 21–3). Similar occupational clustering is hinted at in a New Kingdom papyrus (P. BM 10068) which lists households in a settlement named Maiunehes in western Thebes. Households engaged in like activities are sometimes listed consecutively, possibly reflecting their physical relationships (Kemp 1989b: 306–8; Shaw 2004: 18 20). If such quarters indeed existed, occupation, including craft production, appears as one of these background elements shaping urban space. Such quarters would have been important elements in the 'mental map' of a city shared by its residents.

PEOPLE

It is only in relatively recent times that modern society has become obsessed, at all social strata, with the consumption of material culture that has a built-in redundancy and obsolescence. In all periods of antiquity in Egypt there would have been some sense that everyone, apart from the very upper echelons of society, was a craftsperson. The vast majority of the population relied upon farming for their livelihood and would have needed the skills either to make or repair tools and general household objects. We can assume that the skills needed for different types of craft production would often have been passed on to young children via extended family members within the context of the household or small workshop environment. They would have been developed and honed over many years of watching, feeling, hearing and repeating the same action until it became a subconscious action that was performed with ease and dexterity.

As the evidence from Amarna has shown, the household could often be the site of production for a number of industries, possibly including those such as faience production. Previous scholarship on household industry often ascribes traditional 'women's work' such as textiles, basketry, non wheel-made pottery and other such tasks to the household, and 'men's work' such as mass production of pottery, glass, faience, metalworking, stone carving and so on to factories or larger workshops. This dichotomy also holds true for some discussions on craft specialization, where specialized production of pottery, for example, is seen as the domain of men within large workshops, with women not being involved at all outside of household production. While the majority of textual and artistic evidence supports the case that there were clear divisions of labour for certain industries, care should be taken when attempting to apply this premise to all strata of society and for all professions. In villages composed primarily of subsistence farmers, for instance, it would not be surprising to expect that women and children played a more prominent role in many types of craft production normally associated with men.

The social position of craftspeople was often quite low within a community. The most frequently quoted source for this in Egypt is the Middle Kingdom *Satire of the Trades* where a variety of trades are compared unfavourably to that of the scribe (Lichtheim 1975: 184–92). Most are described as dirty, smelly, hot and uncomfortable in some way, which is undoubtedly a true reflection of what they were like. The evidence suggests that protective clothing for industries such as glassmaking and metalworking was non-existent, with the risk of injury high. Most crafts, especially those such as basketry and textiles, require constant repetitive action and the people involved in them would have led very hard and uncomfortable lives if they plied their craft full time. Textual evidence suggests that certain industries were broken up into at least three hierarchical levels, some of which, such as faience (Nicholson 1998: 55–6) were under the direct control of the state. At the top was the 'overseer of workmen' (*imy-ra iru*), who would have had a much easier life than the workmen under him and may not even have been proficient in the skills of the craft being overseen. Titular evidence, primarily from Old Kingdom tombs, suggests that these people were drawn from the upper echelons of society. The person in charge of a team of workers was known as the 'chief workman' (*hery iru*) and would probably have served a similar role as a foreman or master craftsman of today. In some instances, it seems that this position could be passed from father to son (McDowell 1999: 129–30). The lowest position was that of the general 'workman' (*iru*), who would have been responsible for the day-to-day production of objects within the workshop.

The question of slave labour in Egypt is one that causes some debate and a certain amount of misconception based on outdated ideas. Part of the problem in understanding slave labour is the difficulty of differentiating the words used in texts to describe different types of bonded workers (Meskell 2002: 105). Although a large proportion of the population would have worked in some form of bonded agricultural labour throughout Egypt's history, the role that actual slaves played in Egyptian industry is far less certain. There are certainly examples of skilled slaves within households being used for particular professions, such as the textile industry (Kemp and Vogelsang-Eastwood 2001: 310) and of female servants provided by the state to work in houses at Deir el-Medina, although whether their duties extended to craft production is unclear (Meskell 2002: 106). The extent to which skilled foreign slaves played a role in Egyptian industry is less certain. Although the presence of skilled foreign workers within royal workshops would not be surprising, any direct involvement outside of the elite sphere is highly unlikely. The presence of foreign workers in Egypt, and the knowledge they imported, is sometimes suggested as the source of innovation in Egyptian technology. A case in point is the development of the glass industry in the 18th Dynasty, with the arrival from Syria of skilled workers, or slaves, often quoted as the impetus for the development of glass technology in Egypt at this time. In the end, though, such theories remain difficult to prove satisfactorily.

NETWORKS

The organization of major workshops fell within the bounds of the state administrative system. The titles of officials and workers are well known, as are some of the most famous high officials from the Old Kingdom onwards. State-sponsored military expeditions for raw materials were carried out under the auspices of the king, often into the desert regions beyond the Nile Valley and further afield into areas outside Egypt's area of direct control. Access to certain raw materials was crucial to Egypt's wealth and power, and production of high-status objects made with exotic raw materials put Egypt at the heart of trading networks throughout the Mediterranean, Africa and the Near East for large parts of its history. To understand Egypt's position within these networks it is important to be able to differentiate between where objects were made and where they were later used or consumed. Scientific analysis of both organic and inorganic materials has allowed major advances in this area of study, especially in the past 20 years.

There were varying levels of production in Egypt throughout its history for all types of objects and materials. Much of the population would have been working on a barter economy, even after the introduction of coinage, so there was almost endless scope for the exchange of objects, many of which could have been produced by individuals in time outside their primary occupation. We can only speculate on the mechanics of this at lower levels of society where there are few or no archaeological or textual records surviving, but at well-documented sites such as Deir el-Medina, where there was a high concentration of skilled workers, it is possible to begin to understand these processes. Here we see the example of a carpenter named Meryra making a wooden statue for someone called Ruty, in exchange for goods of equal value. The quality of the workmanship is brought into question and the dispute settled through official channels (Meskell 2004: 103–4). Similar exchanges probably took place all over Egypt every day for thousands of years, lost to us now due to their invisibility in the archaeological record. On a somewhat higher level than personal transactions among craftsmen, it was also possible for officials to commission a piece of art specifically for the king, particularly on special occasions such as his jubilee festival (Aldred 1969).

Securing access to suitable raw materials was essential for any type of production. For some crafts, such as basketry and ceramic production, this was relatively straightforward and would usually have required little or no input from the state. When rarer materials such as ivory, pigments such as cobalt, precious stones and metals were used, the direct involvement of the central administration in controlling procurement, workshops and the distribution of the finished products can generally be assumed. It was access to these exotic raw materials that allowed the royal workshops to produce the many *objets d'art* that Egypt is renowned for, and to ensure their high status within society by restricting their control, even at the highest levels of society.

Specialized production of objects in a specific and repeated manner is one way that individual community groups could have expressed their group identity, and is also the basis of typological studies. For example, it is possible to differentiate an amphora produced in the Nile Valley from one produced in the Levant or the Oases on the basis of shape, size and the clay used. If decoration, in particular, is also considered there is the potential to investigate how this might relate to group identity, although in most cases its meaning, probably immediately apparent to someone viewing it at the time, is completely lost to us now. Some regions or sites became famous for particular types of products. Where this occurs it is also possible to discuss concepts such as site specialization. Returning to the glass industry of the New Kingdom, for example, blue glass was the prime glass product at Amarna in the 18th Dynasty, while red glass was the prime product at Per-Ramesses during the 19th and 20th Dynasties. It is possible to argue the case for site specialization at both these centres. The reasons behind this are potentially very complex and could relate to factors now invisible in the material record, including easier access to specific raw materials, changes in fashion or trends, experimentation or changes in production technology.

When craftspeople were working with materials that have similar properties and traits it might be expected that several different industries worked in conjunction and shared adjacent workshop space. Although it might not be immediately obvious, a detailed knowledge of the properties of ceramics is essential for the metalworking, glass and faience industries, for instance. Without the ability to select suitable clays and tempers that produce a refractory ceramic capable of withstanding extremely high temperatures, it is impossible to smelt metallic ores and produce glass and faience from raw materials. Leather production and butchery provide a case of overlapping interest in raw materials, the by-products of one industry forming the essential raw materials of the other (Driel-Murray 2000). It would make a lot of sense to locate these ostensibly different activities within close proximity of one another. Woodworking and ivory carving, similarly, are two different professions that share skills and require a similar set of tools, and could again have been located together (Gale *et al.* 2000). Archaeological investigation of workshop contexts within Egypt should take these ideas into account when attempting to identify the specific activities that took place within them. In return, archaeology almost certainly has much more to offer on the subject of shared workspace and overlapping industries than has yet been realized.

CRAFTING IDEAS

In studying craft production we are studying more than just manufacturing processes. Craft production formed a channel for the moulding of ideas into shapes, the end-products remaining as expressions of the society in which they were created. Often the manipulation of idea into form was probably undertaken subconsciously, although on occasion there was probably greater awareness of this process. The manufacture of 'ritual' objects, for instance, offered the chance to imbue an item with symbolism through the selection of appropriate decoration and material, and make it 'effective' through ritual actions; so, elements of the Opening of the Mouth ceremony could be incorporated into the manufacture of statues (see Lorton 1999: 153). The funerary stela of a Middle Kingdom artist named Iritisen expounds his knowledge of magic and success as a craftsman (Barta 1970). The text implies that the two attributes are associated, which would make sense in a context where the quality of a product was measured both by aesthetic presentation and symbolic effectiveness, and may allude to Iritisen's skill in making ideas take shape.

One overriding feature of the material culture of ancient Egypt when viewed from a distance is a sense of continuity and, with it, stylistic conformity, following frameworks of expression established early in history. The standardized treatment of the human form, particularly in two-dimensional representational art, is probably the most explicit example, but continuity of form can also be found among items such as certain pottery vessels and hand-modelled figurines. There is little sense of plurality of traditions or individual expression although there do appear 'anomalies', particularly among items often, but not always, associated with the non-elite. What does this indicate, broadly, of the society responsible for this output? On the one hand, it seems to imply a relatively rigid framework for the production of a 'court style', with control over the output of high-end craftspeople. This may extend beyond control of aesthetic principles to governance of the ways in which ideas about the world were presented and accessed. The knowledge to unlock the system of encoded symbols employed by artists such as Iritisen, it is often argued, was restricted largely to the elite. Such conditions fit a model of a totalitarian society wherein power and knowledge are held by a few who seek to maintain the status quo (e.g. Bianchi 1998), although such rigid interpretations almost inevitably leave loose ends when applied to the distant past: when symbols appear in 'lower-class' contexts do they indicate imitation or understanding?

It can be assumed that there was greater scope for the direct manipulation of the output of craftworkers in contexts where craft production formed a distinct enterprise than when it was undertaken as an action embedded more deeply in, and indistinguishable from, everyday life. Longevity of style found among items of everyday use might indicate a sense of rigidity not so much formally prescribed, but stemming from accepted 'ways of doing things'. Anomalies, on the other hand, suggest scope for flexibility in material expression; they may have their origin in regional traditions, more widespread background 'folk culture', or individual spontaneity and improvisation. When indigenous in origin they seem unlikely to reflect drastically alternative ideas about the world and society – a true Egyptian counterculture – but lifestyles in which emphasis was placed on ideas different from those in court society. It is easy to relate rigidity in material expression to the longevity and relative stability of Egyptian society but this background flexibility was probably just as important for accommodating everyday concerns, and changing ideas relating to these. In any attempt to read the material output of a society – ancient or modern – as an expression of that society, it is crucial to look beyond the conditions of its ultimate use to those of its creation, and craft production in all its aspects.

ACKNOWLEDGEMENTS

The authors wish to thank the Egypt Exploration Society for permission to discuss unpublished results of the excavations at Grid 12 at Amarna, and Barry Kemp for his feedback on a draft of this chapter and assistance in preparing Figure 11.2.

CHAPTER TWELVE

LABOUR

———— .◆. ————

Kathlyn M. Cooney

The concept of labour cannot be extracted from the larger economic systems of which it was a part, so, accordingly, methods of workforce organization can actually tell us a great deal about the Egyptian economy. Labour organization for ancient Egyptian state institutions suggests the existence of a massive redistributive system that some scholars believe allowed only limited private-sector trade, either because the state did not allow market activities, or because society was too primitive and constricted to understand market activities (Janssen 1975b; Gutgesell 1989; Eichler 1992; Bleiberg 1996). On the other hand, evidence for labour organization in a private-sector context suggests a mixed economy including *both* market-driven systems as well as state redistribution and taxation (Kemp 1989b; Eyre 1998, 1999; Warburton 2003). Labour organization in ancient Egypt was nuanced, as was the economic system of which labour was a part. State redistribution economies and private-sector market economies need not be mutually exclusive. The state and private-sector systems co-existed, each depending on the other to distribute goods and services using different methods and conduits. In the simplest terms, state institutions relied on the taxation of goods and corvée labour, so that they could then redistribute these resources into centrally controlled state work projects. The private sector, based on privately owned lands throughout Egypt, produced the main bulk of taxable resources – in the form of both consumables and people. Labour organization in ancient Egypt was not monolithic, but flexible.

The surviving evidence for labour and craftsmanship in ancient Egypt is quite varied. Egyptologists must combine textual, art historical and archaeological materials to understand different categories of work specialization and organization. Understanding Egyptian labour systems is very much a multidisciplinary problem, as well as a problem of generalities versus specifics. The wealth of data can, nonetheless, be condensed into trends that run from the Old Kingdom to the Late Period, if one classifies labour in terms of: (1) the division of labour between skilled and unskilled workers, (2) the division between forced and unforced labour systems, and (3) labour's relation to the state (temple, king and various local government institutions).

The ancient Egyptians perceived a clear distinction between skilled and unskilled workers in terms of social place and labour structure. The social system valued artisanship and craft abilities, often passed from father to son, and so a skilled state craftsman, such as a stone sculptor or goldsmith, was afforded more freedoms and leeway, even within his institutional workshop system. Skilled state craftsmen could also enter the private sector, taking on short-term commissions for their own gain. On the other hand, an unskilled state worker, such as the mover of stone blocks or a water carrier, was given very few freedoms and no luxuries. His wages were very low, often in the form of just enough bread and beer to get him through the day. If he left his place of work, punishment was severe. Farmers, fishermen and herdsmen, although very capable in their work, had no craft skills, and thus ranked quite low on the Egyptian social scale. Peasants were severely taxed by local state officials, paid high rents if they were tenant farmers, and their farm yields amounted to bare subsistence levels year after year, even during optimal Nile conditions (Figure 12.1). These economic circumstances effectively tied most peasants to the land. The peasant could also be called up by the state to serve as a conscripted labourer. The private sector farmer would then enter the militaristic structure of the government-funded workforce. The lines that Egyptologists draw between state and private economic systems are continually blurred, resisting strict categorization. The solution is to search for a nuanced and flexible labour system model.

The Egyptians also drew a distinction, although not always a clear one, between forced and unforced labour. Forced labour can be categorized in relation to the state, and when performed for government institutions it is generally called corvée or conscript labour. This form of labour most commonly occurred during limited seasonal

Figure 12.1 Scene of harvest in the tomb of Paheri at Elkab (photo K. Cooney).

work periods, after which time peasants were allowed to go home, assuming they were able to complete their service unscathed by disease or work-related injuries. Forced labour in the private sector is better categorized as slavery, although textual documentation for slavery in Dynastic Egypt is quite limited, making a real definition of the institution practically impossible. Nonetheless, through debt or capture in warfare, some persons physically belonged to other private individuals and served their masters in households and at their place of work – even if that place was a temple or government office. State elements (such as temples or the king himself) might have owned slaves, using them in the palace, on farms or in harsher conditions at a mine, but our written evidence suggests that the vast bulk of slaves were owned by private individuals. (For summary evidence about the private ownership of slaves, see Allam 2001.)

To discuss labour systems within larger economic models, it is useful to categorize work according to its relationship to the state. Labour attached to the state was structured quite differently from labour that was privately funded. State labour was formally directed, strictly hierarchical and carefully archived; the activities and movements of state labourers were monitored and controlled according to a militaristic model. Private-sector labour, on the other hand, was set up much more informally, usually on the village market level. Workers supported by the private sector did not always have a clear hierarchical system to follow. They were not part of a formal work crew. There was no military order, usually only a master or customer to obey. Furthermore, non-state labour was rarely archived, resulting in a lack of textual documentation for this significant part of the Egyptian economy.

Driven by necessity and efficiency, the Egyptians combined numerous systems of organizing work, including private-sector labour production that was, for the most part, unattached from the state; labour systems fully attached to the state; and labour systems semi-attached to the state (Earle 1981; Clark and Parry 1990). Within all of these categories, there are further divisions – between skilled and unskilled workers, or between free and forced labourers. Until recently, most Egyptologists have focused on labour that was fully attached to the state, such as quarrying/mining monopolies and institutionalized craft workshops – mostly because the vast majority of documentation comes from the state institutions and its legion of scribal bureaucrats. The disorganized and scattered private sector has only produced a smattering of records.

Labour categorization – skilled and unskilled, free and forced, as well as state and private-sector – enables an understanding of a flexible and nuanced labour system functioning within complementary structures of the private-sector economy and the state system of taxation and redistribution. The Egyptian economy was not based on mere subsistence. The Nile Valley and its workforce provided a surplus to support one of the first multi-tiered complex civilizations in history. Agricultural surplus, prosperity and leisure allowed the construction of massive monuments – state temples, royal tombs and numerous private building projects. The Nile Valley was so fruitful that, on average, an estimated 200,000 peasants would have been able to produce the grain to feed 3 million individuals each year (Miller 1991; Warburton 2003: 201). This grain surplus allowed increased complexity: a centralized bureaucracy, taxation by the state, a wealthy upper class, increased craft specialization and the growth of conspicuous consumption by the Egyptian elite. The grain surplus thus allowed a culture of construction in Egypt – of display through palace embellishment, of piety through temple building, and of assiduous preparation for the afterlife through the creation of tombs and funerary art. This culture of materialism encouraged increased employment of Egyptian craftsmen, labourers, conscripted workers and slaves – all working within a mixed economy of market trade and state redistribution.

This discussion of ancient Egyptian labour is not meant to be a thorough, chronological description of labour practice and organization. Instead, it focuses on the varied and nuanced ways that labour could be organized through time, locale and society, using a selection of examples. The Middle Kingdom archive of the gentleman farmer Heqanakht and the New Kingdom funerary arts market in the Theban region exemplify the private-sector labour systems. Old Kingdom pyramid building, Middle Kingdom quarrying expeditions, and New Kingdom tomb building and decoration in the Valley of the Kings exemplify the state labour systems. Discussion of scribal/bureaucratic labour and soldiery is excluded here.

UNATTACHED LABOUR SYSTEMS

The household and village were the basis of the Egyptian market economy. Private-sector economic systems were first developed in villages throughout Egypt – long before a multi-tiered and centralized bureaucracy came into being. Many craftsmen and labourers would have functioned in this market economy as unattached workers, meaning they would have had no formal connections to any state labour organization. These unattached labourers rarely appear in the ancient textual documentation, which is hardly surprising. The state kept careful records, but lower-level labourers and their patrons, mostly illiterate, kept no records and were not formally organized beyond the household or village level. Pictorial scenes provide circumstantial evidence for village production and trade: trading scenes from Old Kingdom and New Kingdom tomb walls suggest that the wares of craftsmen were sold locally at market places near the riverbank (Eyre 1987a: 31–2; Kemp 1989b: 255). Despite the lack of documentation, it is clear that peasants throughout Egypt farmed privately owned lands or rental plots, and that they paid taxes. Farming villages almost certainly supported a small number of unattached craftsmen who made simple utilitarian items. Unattached craftsmen would have made the most basic necessities for the Egyptian peasantry, including simple furniture, reed skiffs, rudimentary farming and fishing equipment and tools, coarse linen clothing, basic footwear, basketry, pottery and matting, all sold at very low prices.

Throughout ancient Egyptian history, most basic necessities were probably made by private-sector, unattached labour, even though the evidence for it is scarce. As prices from the New Kingdom village of Deir el-Medina suggest (Janssen 1975b), costs for such items were very low and probably paid in surplus grain and other commodities. Although some Egyptologists claim that most of the Egyptian economy was centrally controlled for redistribution of state wares (Gutgesell 1989; Bleiberg 1995), there is no evidence that low-cost, everyday items were produced by state workshops and then distributed/sold to the population (Warburton 2003). Even the state-supplied craftsmen's village of Deir el-Medina produced and traded a large amount of basic necessities. Egyptian farm villages, which were not given supplies by the state, had to support their own unattached and possibly itinerant craftsmen who would supply them with pots, baskets, sandals and other necessities.

The home was another centre of unattached labour activity, usually undertaken by women and older children, who ground grain, made bread and beer, fetched water, cared for small children and did the onerous task of cleaning the laundry. Household production of coarse linens for clothing and bedding often fell to the women. Pictorial representations of linen preparation and weaving in Old and Middle Kingdom tombs usually show females at work. Deir el-Medina texts of the Ramesside Period prove that women produced linens at home, probably providing additional household income (Eyre 1987b: 200–1). These women had no connections to a state weaving workshop or to a large, elite household installation. They had no state training. Many Deir el-Medina texts with prices for different types of linens (Janssen 1975b) indicate that a Deir el-Medina household could add to its income through weaving work with no constraints from the state sector.

Unattached labour and craftwork were also connected to larger households. Heqanakht, a priest and official of the Middle Kingdom, carefully managed his modest lands and the workers farming them, and we have a number of letters and documents testifying to the economic organization and investments of his private property (Allen 2002a). Heqanakht sold linens woven in his own household for additional income, which he used to rent more farmland. Heqanakht organized his labour force and wage payments without any state instruction. In one letter he lists how many sacks of grain are paid to each member of his household and then tells them not to complain because times are hard: 'Lest (any of) you get angry about this, look, the whole household is just like my children, and everything is mine to allocate. Half of life is better than death in full' (Allen 2002a: 16–17). Many Egyptian workers were connected to independent private households, and they were at the mercy of their master, the landholder, as well as the current economic situation. Heqanakht, as the head of this mini economy, kept accounts of salaries, yields of land, debts and all manner of private economic information concerning the labour taking place in his household. The state only stepped in to tax the independent landholder. Heqanakht's archive is a testament to the Egyptian household and how it was run as a business, leasing land for profit, running small weaving installations for profit and paying out salaries for a number of male and female employees whom he hired and fired, depending on social and economic conditions. It is likely that more such archives were created, but little information of this depth has survived on the farming household level.

FULLY ATTACHED STATE LABOUR SYSTEMS

Throughout Egypt, private landowners organized their holdings and paid taxes to the Egyptian state. This private economic base provided the tax and corvée labour revenues for massive state-funded and organized projects (Kemp 1989b), including building pyramids and sprawling temple complexes, palace construction and embellishment, long-distance trading ventures, gold mining expeditions in the eastern deserts and Nubia, quarrying expeditions within Egypt and in adjacent deserts, large canal building projects to drain marshland and create arable farmland, as well as hundreds of master-quality workshops churning out everything from jewellery to sculpture. All of these large state-run projects required funds and labour, both acquired and structured through a stable and centralized bureaucracy of scribal officials.

The state depended on many types of labour – skilled and unskilled, as well as conscripted and free – and workers were paid a wage according to their skill level and social status. Skilled craftsmen made up a much smaller percentage of the overall state labour force and were paid a wage above subsistence level, indicating a higher social value. Unskilled and conscripted labour made up the bulk of the state labour force and had a very low value, with wages that provided a meagre subsistence for the workers themselves and perhaps a few family members. Skilled craftsmen often functioned within workshop systems attached to palaces or temples (Figure 12.2). The coveted position of state craftsman was hereditary; skilled workers trained their sons and relatives, hoping they would also receive a place in the workshop. Skilled craftsmen had some social mobility: they could climb the workshop hierarchy from apprenticeship to full-time membership to leadership positions. Unskilled workers did not have such opportunities; they hauled, fetched and carried, without any real chance of moving up their limited social ladder.

Most unskilled state labourers were conscripted – that is, they were drafted into service. These men were not slaves; slavery was, for the most part, a private-sector form of forced labour. Conscript workers, in contrast, were not owned by individuals, but were, instead, required to perform intermittent labour as a duty to the state. Conscript labour was essentially a form of taxation by government officials. The Egyptian state had a large pool of individuals from which to conscript labour: the majority of the ancient Egyptian population was composed of peasants (Caminos 1997) who worked private lands. Conscription might have occurred seasonally, when the Nile inundation made farm work impossible, or during the growing seasons when fewer workers were needed.

Information about the organization of labour conscription is not plentiful, but we do have some details in the textual record. A 12th Dynasty letter from the servant of the estate Senebni details how officials called up people for service in his area:

Figure 12.2 Carpenter's workshop in the tomb of Rekhmira at Thebes (photo K. Cooney).

the mayor sent me . . . to muster the labour force, having charged me . . . saying, 'As for any persons whom you may find missing among them, you are to write to the steward Horemsaf about them.' I . . . have sent a list of missing persons in writing to the pyramid town.

(Wente 1990: 76)

As this text makes clear, conscript recruitment usually happened at the local level: high officials called on mayors who then called on small town and village leaders to gather the available men. We know that recruitment by over-zealous officials became such a problem for certain settlements linked with the state, particularly for peasants working palace and temple lands, that exemption decrees were issued by the king to release certain populations, who were essentially already in state employ, from being called into corvée service (Helck 1975: 226–30). The corvée system was often unfair and harsh, and many ineligible men were called into service despite their complaints (Wente 1990: 74).

Once in service, the penalty for desertion was ruthless. A Middle Kingdom papyrus now in the Brooklyn Museum informs us that officials imprisoned the deserter's family until the return of the offender. Deserters were often assigned to permanent labour service if they were found (Hayes 1955; Kemp 1989b). State taxation and conscription duties were often abused by government officials, especially in difficult economic times. Many desperate people tried to extract themselves from corvée labour and taxation by fleeing to the Sinai or the oases. In the Late and Ptolemaic Periods, there is evidence that high numbers of the population opted out of the harsh farmer's existence of debt and conscription. These runaways chose to abandon the farm, to move from place to place, to join a mob of raiders or become pastoral nomads, resulting in too many fallow fields (Caminos 1997).

Conscript labour, a state-run endeavour, often occurred on a massive scale. The best-documented and most impressive conscript-supported projects were quarrying expeditions. Such large, state-run labour projects often followed the model of army or navy organization, because this was the easiest system for organizing such large numbers of people. Stone workers were organized into large crews for the starboard and port sides, which were further divided into smaller gangs. Quarrying expeditions in the Old and Middle Kingdoms were sometimes led by a general of the army, but at other times by a temple treasurer (Eyre 1987a: 10–11). There was no official office for expeditions; rather, the Egyptians organized these forays using a variety of different officials and offices. At no time did the Egyptians institute a firm system for quarrying expeditions even though stone extraction was performed by a centrally conscripted state labour force. Instead, the state structured each expedition differently, depending on the task at hand and the human resources available at the time. Old Kingdom quarrying expeditions included personnel ranging from 300 to more than 2,000 labourers, recruited by various officials and local governors from many places throughout the countryside (Eyre 1987a: 14–19).

Middle Kingdom quarrying expeditions sometimes included tens of thousands of workers (Kemp 1989b: 129). One massive group sent in the thirty-eighth year of Senusret I to the Wadi Hammamat quarries in the Eastern Desert included 18,630 workers. Preserved bureaucratic documents reveal that the expedition was led by a royal herald named Ameni who was served by 80 officials, including crew leaders,

20 mayors from around Egypt, craft leaders including two overseers of stone masons, two state treasurers and eight official scribes. The support staff was much larger and included 30 hunters, 60 bird catchers, 20 brewers, 20 millers, 20 butchers and 60 sandal-makers, all to supply a contingent of almost 20,000 men (Eggebrecht 1980: 66). Also sent along were soldiers and police of various ranks to protect the expedition and, perhaps more importantly, to keep the workers in line.

The skilled workforce on this Middle Kingdom quarrying expedition consisted of hundreds of stone masons and craftsmen. The unskilled workforce, on the other hand, made up the bulk of the team with 17,000 conscripted men. All were paid according to the hierarchy of their position. The bulk of the unskilled workforce received ten loaves of bread and one-third of a jar of beer daily, which, given the amount of work, was likely a bare subsistence wage that was consumed at the worksite. The support staff of bakers and brewers received 15 loaves of bread and almost one full jar of beer a day. The skilled craftsmen received 20 loaves of bread a day. Scribes, lower-level bureaucrats and army officers are said to have received 30 loaves a day. The treasurers and mid-level bureaucrats got 50 loaves, mayors and crew leaders 100 loaves. The leader, the herald Ameni, received 200 loaves of bread every day, the highest amount. These wages are clearly measures of each man's economic worth and social status. It is unlikely that the high officials on this expedition consumed this much bread in a day; the bread loaf was essentially a measure of grain. Each man probably consumed about ten loaves a day, the wage of the conscripted labourers. Additional 'loaves' amounted to additional payment once the expedition returned home. In other words, these amounts represent wage amounts, some of which was paid upon return from the desert, rather than rations that were consumed on the expedition (Kemp 1989b: 125–7). In the end, we understand that skilled craftsmen received double the subsistence wage, that high officials, such as mayors, received ten times the subsistence wage, and the expedition leader, 20 times.

A later New Kingdom expedition to the Wadi Hammamat in the third year of Ramesses IV included over 8,000 men, with 150 skilled craftsmen. Many of these unskilled workers were recruited from the army, a new form of labour conscription during the New Kingdom when Egypt poured resources into protecting its imperial interests. This expedition was under the leadership of a temple official – the High Priest of Amun from Thebes – and was quite costly in terms of human life with 900 dead (Eyre 1987b: 181–2), giving the average workman about a one in ten chance of perishing on the job, not to mention the unrecorded, but presumably high, chance of workplace injuries. New Kingdom gold mining expeditions were even more costly than quarrying expeditions, with a casualty rate as high as 50 per cent (Eyre 1987b: 182), but this rough figure simply stresses that for the ancient Egyptians, labour was cheap. Losses were recorded, and vacancies were filled. Some expeditions were subject to attacks by the local population, especially during unstable times.

Formally organized, fully attached state labour systems, such as quarrying expeditions, often leave a trace in the textual record. However, we have almost no written information about one of Egypt's largest state construction projects – the Giza pyramids of the Old Kingdom. Most of the evidence for the state workforce at the pyramids is archaeological, and scholars have counted the blocks and made various calculations, trying to arrive at the labour requirements for these massive constructions. Most agree that there are 2.3 million blocks (6.5 million tons of limestone) in the

Great Pyramid of Khufu. These blocks would have been laid down during the 23 years of Khufu's reign. Using these numbers, it has been estimated that the labour force had to place about 340 blocks each day, that is 34 blocks every hour, or one every two minutes, suggesting a labour force in the tens of thousands at the pyramid site itself (Lehner 1997: 224), not to mention an additional and substantial workforce at the quarry site from which the blocks came.

Scraps of textual evidence from Giza and other pyramid sites indicate that a labour force of this size was militarily organized into different subsections, each with a leader. The Giza pyramids were probably built by multiple crews of 2,000 men, which were subdivided into two gangs of 1,000 men, each with a name connecting them to the ruling king, such as 'Friends of Khufu' or 'Drunkards of Menkaura'. Archaeological and textual material from other pyramid sites tells us that each gang was divided into five *phyles* of 200 men. These *phyles* of 200 were further separated into ten divisions with 20 men each (Lehner 1997: 224–5). Such a hierarchical system followed military organization, and each man was accountable to multiple leaders: his division leader, his *phyle* leader, his gang leader, his crew leader and, finally, the upper officials of the building programme.

The men who built the pyramids of the Old Kingdom and the Middle Kingdom were not slaves. Essentially there were three types of workers at a pyramid site: (1) well-paid officials controlling the work; (2) reasonably well-paid craftsmen who focused on skilled craft work and who worked full-time; and (3) seasonal corvée workers, drafted into service from their farms. The full-time skilled workers included permanent stone cutters and masons, and they lived in workers' huts near the construction site (Lehner 2002; Hawass 2006). We know very little about how the tens of thousands of unskilled workmen were drafted into service, but officials, priests, local governors and mayors seem to have pulled poor peasants from villages throughout the country, at least according to marks found on the casing stones of Middle Kingdom pyramids (Arnold 1990). These recruits would have found themselves temporarily locked into a formally organized system which they could only escape with severe penalties, but in which they were probably encouraged to compete with other divisions and *phyles* for small rewards, and for which they were paid a subsistence wage.

Not all state labour took place on such a massive scale. The state also employed a number of highly skilled artisans, attached to small palace and temple workshops throughout the land as free workers. The state workshops created a system of hereditary job placement, apprenticeship and craft specialization that allowed efficient production of high-quality, high-value objects for use in the palace, temple and tomb. State craftsmen produced hard stone sculpture, metal objects, carpentry, jewellery, linen, glass, faience, ritual and temple implements, funerary arts and all manner of crafts such as pottery, leatherwork and basketry. Our most illuminating administrative documents come from the New Kingdom village of Deir el-Medina, an artisans' settlement in the western Theban desert, housing the highly skilled stone-cutters, draughtsmen and scribes who built and decorated the tombs of the king and his family members (Figure 12.3).

These craftsmen have left us an unmatched archive with which to study labour in ancient Egypt: thousands of letters, legal records and administrative texts preserved on papyri, limestone flakes and pottery sherds, all recording close details of daily life and work (Černý 1973; Valbelle 1985). The skilled Deir el-Medina craftsmen were

Figure 12.3 The village of Deir el-Medina (photo K. Cooney).

formally organized, and their livelihood was attached to the state. These men were trained in their craft by their fathers and relatives, making their positions largely hereditary. They were not corvée workers; rather, their positions afforded them a high social position encouraging competition for jobs, often resulting in bribery of the hiring officials, and even threats and harm to fellow craftsmen. They lived in a claustrophobic village of about 70 houses, tightly squeezed into a desert valley, surrounded by a wall, and protected by a permanent police force. The Deir el-Medina craftsmen were fully supplied by a state-paid support staff that brought in water, grain payments, foodstuffs such as oil, vegetables, fish and honey, as well as work supplies, including chisels, plaster, pigments, lamps and wicks.

The number of craftsmen in the work crew fluctuated between about 32 and 60 men, depending on how much work was required on the king's tomb. The beginning of a new king's reign was a time for rejoicing in the village of Deir el-Medina because it meant work for more men, increased rewards and quick payment, rather than the slow pay to which the crew was often accustomed. The new king would want to make good progress on his tomb in the Valley of the Kings before his own unforeseen death, and he often added craftsmen to the crew so that he could finish a grand tomb in time for his burial. At one point, at the beginning of the reign of Ramesses IV, the numbers of the crew were raised to 120 men, an unprecedented workforce in the village. It is quite likely that the ascension of a new king to the throne in the Old and Middle Kingdoms also created increased demand for skilled craftsmen, meaning work for men who might otherwise have been idle.

At the end of a given reign, when the king's tomb and the tombs of his queens and sons had already been completed, there was not enough work to justify a large crew at Deir el-Medina. In some cases, craftsmen were 'let go' and sent outside of the village for much lower-paying wage labour as part of the service staff. The service staff were full-time, free state workers, but they were only paid a subsistence wage for themselves and a few family members. One such job-cut took place in the reign of Ramesses VI: 'The vizier spoke thus: "Let these sixty men stay here as your gang, all your choice, and let the rest be brought outside. Order them to become supply staff who will carry for you" ' (McDowell 1999: 231). When there was not enough demand for high-quality craftwork, skilled workers were fired from their high-paying positions as state artisans and relegated to low-paid unskilled jobs on the service staff. Even though the Deir el-Medina village was a state workshop, government officials did not micro-manage; they left the craftsmen to deal with this staff reduction on their own, choosing who would go and who would stay. One can imagine the frantic political networking and bribery that would have ensued after such an announcement, each family trying to ensure itself a position in the crew and struggling to avoid a new life of hard work and bare subsistence wages as a member of the supply staff outside the craftsmen's village.

Even though the workforce was small, the Deir el-Medina crew still used a naval system to organize themselves, in the fashion of formally organized state labour. They divided themselves into port and starboard sides. Each side of the crew included a foreman, a scribe of the tomb, two or three deputies, chisel bearers, draughtsmen and multiple craftsmen without a specialized title. Their work and attendance were carefully monitored by the scribe of the tomb. The Deir el-Medina craftsmen's official boss was the vizier, resident at eastern Thebes, and we have evidence of close correspondence between Deir el-Medina scribes and the office of the vizier.

The Deir el-Medina crew worked a ten-day week, and they usually took a two-day weekend, in addition to numerous festival days. The average Deir el-Medina craftsman was paid a wage of five-and-a-half sacks (about 415 litres) of emmer wheat and barley a month from different state sources, including the vizier's office and temples in the area (Kemp 1989b). The overseers and scribes each received seven-and-a-half sacks (about 560 litres) of grain a month. Every Deir el-Medina craftsmen received wages that were far above subsistence levels, enough to feed at least two nuclear families for a month. Deir el-Medina craftsmen were quite wealthy in comparison to the general peasantry, investing large amounts in animals, garden plots as well as in their tombs and funerary goods. The state also provided monthly supplies of fish, beans, oils and other foodstuffs. Still, the wages did not always arrive on time, and the Deir el-Medina workforce sometimes felt it necessary to strike and demonstrate for the delivery of their wages:

> The gang passed the walls, saying, 'We are hungry!' . . . And they called out to the Mayor of Thebes as he was passing by. He sent Nefer . . . to them, saying, 'Look, I will give you these 30 sacks of emmer to be a means of life.'
>
> (McDowell 1999: 236)

The ability to stop work and plead for fair wages testifies to the social value of the skilled craftsmen in Egypt. They were not punished by any government officials for demonstrating, as far as we can tell, and many of their attempts to be paid were partially successful, even during lean economic times.

The Deir el-Medina archive of textual material tells us a huge amount about skilled workshop labour, but it also provides information about the unskilled labour force connected to a given workshop, in particular the staff who provided water and other services for the Deir el-Medina workers. Laundry was picked up from each family by the service staff, cleaned at the riverbank and returned to the desert community. Water was especially difficult for the service staff to bring into the workmen's valley. The state assigned about six men at a time to act as water carriers, and they often rented donkeys at a loss, to save themselves from carrying heavy jars of water, indicating that these state labourers were able to make choices about how to do their work. Unfortunately, many water carriers worked themselves into an insurmountable state of debt to other individuals, renting donkeys from the Deir el-Medina craftsmen and others for which their subsistence wages of one to one-and-a-half sacks of grain a month (75 to 112 litres) could not pay.

On the whole, the village of Deir el-Medina, which housed a permanent state workshop attached to the office of the vizier, was able to run work and life affairs as the villagers wished – as long as they functioned within the accepted formalized system and kept up with their work in the Valley of the Kings. They worked according to a formal naval model. They kept an official roll of attendance. They requested work supplies when required, and they communicated freely with the office of the vizier.

SEMI-ATTACHED LABOUR SYSTEMS

In order to provide themselves with a more stable economic existence, the Deir el-Medina craftsmen also acted as businessmen on their own account by taking on well-paid commissions for furniture, coffins and other craft goods. Private household production, such as coffin decoration or linen weaving, was a significant addition to Deir el-Medina household income, allowing villagers to save for their own tomb and funerary goods.

Deir el-Medina craftsmen used their reputation as state-employed artisans to earn a substantial additional income in the private sector, decorating funerary art and furniture for the wealthy Theban elite and for fellow villagers. This additional work by the Deir el-Medina state craftsmen falls into another category of labour organization; it was performed by state craftsmen for wealthy commissioners, but in the private sector. When working in the private sector for their own gain, they functioned as semi-attached state craftsmen. High-paying commissions were only available via their reputation as royal craftsmen. Working as semi-attached craftsmen, they could retain their connections with the vizier and the Egyptian scribal elite (Cooney 2006).

Deir el-Medina workers could earn much more in the private sector, but they owed all their additional commissions to their position as state artisans because they used connections with elite commissioners and other craftsmen to receive and complete tasks. Carpenters who specialized in building wooden objects, such as coffins, worked informally with draughtsmen who specialized in painting. Hundreds of Deir el-Medina texts tell us that workmen received payment for their private-sector work. Sometimes the payment came from other artisans, who bought the partially finished piece before completing and selling it to the commissioner.

When working in the private sector for additional income, village hierarchy was important, but it was only followed if expedient. Craftsmen of different specializations organized themselves into small informal groups so that they could take on commissions for furniture and funerary arts (Figure 12.4). Carpenters almost always worked with wood construction, while draughtsmen and scribes always painted – even in the private sector. It was easier for the craftsmen to rely on an informal workshop system for private ventures, rather than striking out as independent entrepreneurs with the attendant financial risk (Cooney 2006).

Our best evidence for semi-attached labour by state craftsmen comes from Deir el-Medina, but other skilled state workers, attached to other workshops, could be hired by wealthy private individuals. Hiring skilled, state craftsmen as semi-independent contractors for arts production was costly and only accessible to the Egyptian elite population with connections to palace and temple workshops. The vast majority of the Egyptian population lived on subsistence wages and thus could not afford craftwork; only the elite scribal class could sustain the private-sector production of state-employed craftsmen. In the Old Kingdom, elite tomb owners hired state artisans to build and decorate their privately funded mastaba tombs (Eyre 1987a: 25–8). In some cases, the wealthy commissioner records on the mastaba interior that these craftsmen were generously remunerated in a variety of commodities from the tomb owner's own private sources (Drenkhahn 1976: 141; Roth 1994). Much later, in the Third Intermediate Period, there is also evidence for state craftsmen selling their work in the private sector; a Theban text records the private purchase

(a)   (b)

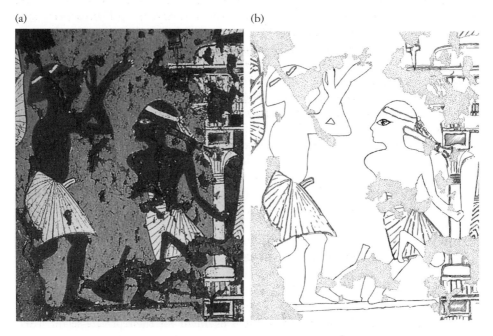

Figure 12.4   Craftsmen at work in the tomb of Ipuy at Deir el-Medina.
(a) Photo K. Cooney; (b) line drawing J. Etherington.

of a complete set of *shabti* funerary figurines from a highly placed member of a temple workshop, in this case the 'Chief Modeller of Amulets in the Temple of Amun' named Pedikhons (Edwards 1971). Throughout Egyptian history, even though the state was responsible for creating and organizing workshops, and for training and acquiring materials for state projects, wealthy individuals in the private sector were able to hire these skilled state artisans on contract. The state, therefore, indirectly supplied the labour base for high-level elite arts commissions and made possible the emergence of conspicuous consumption.

SLAVERY, PRISONERS AND THE FRINGES OF SOCIETY

Ancient Egypt was not a slave-based economy, but a peasant-based economy, and it was not until the Graeco-Roman Period that slavery had a greater impact. From the Middle Kingdom onwards, slavery became a visible part of the Egyptian economy. Although the concept is inconsistently labelled and undefined by the ancient Egyptians, slaves were essentially trapped elements of the population – often prisoners of war given to soldiers after a campaign, foreigners acquired through intensified trade or even Egyptian peasant debtors (Allam 2001). Slavery was hereditary, and, for the most part, a private-sector institution and a private-sector form of forced labour. Slaves were primarily owned by individuals, families and households, although some evidence shows slaves attached to palaces and temples. Even the craftsmen households at Deir el-Medina included slave women to help with the daily chores. These slaves could be understood as part of the craftsmen's wages, and the craftsmen sold shares of their slaves' work to other villagers. Slaves were probably not paid an actual wage, but given food to eat during the day. Their treatment depended very much on their masters, but they might have had some legal rights (Loprieno 1997; Allam 2001).

Prisoners, another trapped element of society, were often forced into labour. Prison labourers were unfree state workers, given a ration of bare subsistence, if that. The mines in the Eastern Desert and Nubia were notorious for their hard conditions, and they were often staffed by the ostracized of Egyptian society – criminals and the imprisoned and conscripted local Nubian population. It is likely that the daily bread and water rations for these people were below subsistence.

THE ECONOMIC CONTEXT OF LABOUR

These fluid and nuanced methods of labour organization and control can tell us a tremendous amount about the mixed economic systems of ancient Egypt. Skilled state workers often laboured in the private sector for their own gain. Private-sector peasants were often conscripted into attached state labour. The Egyptians maintained a balance between private-sector activity, at the village level, and formal state organization, including conscription, taxation and large state monopolies. Rigorous state organization was only practical for large labour projects, such as the extraction of gold and stone, and large building complexes. State labour organization was based on the redistribution of the taxes collected from private land owners and the peasantry. These grain taxes were funnelled into palace and temple treasuries, administered by a vast bureaucracy, and coordinated by king and vizier to institute state projects. An informally organized private-sector economy and labour force worked alongside the formally organized state workforce. The private-sector economy was essential during times of political decentralization, and it was this private sector that ultimately supported state projects with its tax revenue.

CHAPTER THIRTEEN

STATE AND PRIVATE ENTERPRISE

——— •◆• ———

Edward Bleiberg

Scholars still debate the nature of, and connections between, state and private enterprise in ancient Egypt. While many researchers have regarded the state and its associated temples as the major focus of economic activity in Egypt, increasingly others have come to treat the individual household as the more significant unit of analysis. Perhaps the future of Egyptian economic history lies in understanding how, or even whether, state and private enterprise connected to each other in different historical periods.

THE SOURCES AND THEIR FUNCTION

Much of the difficulty in creating a modern understanding of Egyptian economic history starts with the Egyptians' own records of economic activity. These sources are usefully divided into two categories, the ceremonial and the administrative (Bleiberg 1996: 115–25; Haring 1997; 2004: 24). The ceremonial sources include royal and private inscriptions on the walls of temples and tombs as well as some texts written on papyrus. These sources are useful for determining the ideology behind Egyptian statements about economic issues. Administrative texts could be recorded on papyrus or on potsherds or flakes of limestone, both called ostraca (singular: ostracon). These texts comprise actual bureaucratic documents that include records of the reception and disbursement of commodities at institutions such as the royal palace or at a temple. They also include accounts of privately conducted exchanges. Some scholars have made use of images of economic activities in tombs. These sources are just as difficult to interpret as written sources because they are imprecise, lending themselves to more than one possible interpretation. Yet they are also valuable for revealing activities not documented in texts. Scholars have, for example, examined representations of fruit markets which have left no documentation in the written record. Finally archaeological evidence can also be useful in providing further context for economic activities, especially long-distance trade.

Ceremonial sources

Ceremonial sources include scenes in tombs and temples depicting the delivery of taxes, gifts or other groups of commodities. They, moreover, comprise texts that describe feasts, offerings from kings to gods, and private endowments in temples. All of these sources are useful in establishing the official ideology behind the Egyptian economy. Some scenes in Old Kingdom tombs depict the delivery of goods to private tomb owners from royal estates. They underline the Egyptian belief that everything belonged to, and derived from, the king. Festival calendars were also ceremonial. Kings commissioned their carving on the walls of temples during the New Kingdom and later. These texts record goods received in the temple and then redistributed to the people on festival days. Yet these documents appear to be successive copies of each other rather than reports of objective fact. For example, the festival calendar found in the Ramesseum, built by Ramesses II, was reproduced with minor alterations in the festival calendar found at Medinet Habu, built by Ramesses III. This fact has suggested to scholars that the details of the inscriptions cannot be understood literally. For the modern observer, such calendars only provide evidence for the framework of temple administration, not the day-to-day details of administering a festival.

Administrative sources

Administrative sources are among the oldest documents known from ancient Egypt. They include seals or ink inscriptions on jars, and ivory tags attached to goods. Such records are preserved as early as the 1st Dynasty (Kaplony 1963, 1968, 1973). A 5th Dynasty papyrus from the funerary temple of King Neferirkara-Kakai is the oldest known administrative document on papyrus (Posener-Kriéger 1976).

The Middle Kingdom is better documented. A group of 12th Dynasty papyri excavated at Lahun in the late nineteenth century reveals economic data both in a pyramid town and at the funerary temple of Senusret II during the subsequent reigns of Senusret III and Amenemhat III (Collier and Quirke 2002, 2004). Papyrus Boulaq 18, dating to a few weeks into the reign of the 13th Dynasty king Sobekhotep II, records administrative practices at the royal palace (Scharff 1922).

While the documents from the earlier period are examples of bookkeeping, some documents preserved from the New Kingdom provide a variety of economic data including bookkeeping, but also criminal trials, civil litigation over property, and exchanges of goods between private individuals (McDowell 1999). Other administrative documents provide information on the actual administration of agricultural property (Gardiner 1941–8). Each of these documents provides evidence from a specific and particular time and place. It is often unclear whether the situation described in the document is typical for ancient Egypt and thus a good example to use in forming broader generalizations about the economy. For this reason, scholars have turned to a variety of economic models to explain the ancient Egyptian economy.

ANALYSING THE SOURCES ACCORDING TO MODERN ECONOMIC THEORIES

Scholars have taken at least two approaches to analysing the ancient Egyptian economy with modern economic theories. The substantive approach, derived from the work of Karl Polanyi, focuses on the way the economy operates within the culture as a whole. The rationalist approach, based on modern concepts of the market economy, relies on universal laws that would be true throughout history and across cultures.

Neither approach has successfully answered all of scholars' questions about the state and private economy in ancient Egypt.

Redistribution

Karl Polanyi and his followers (Janssen 1975a; Polanyi 1977; Müller-Wollermann 1985; Eichler 1992; Bleiberg 1996) assert that economic processes are not independent of the culture and universal, but, rather, are embedded in the social and political context in which the economy exists. Polanyi described such traditional economies with three patterns for pre-market economies. He called these patterns redistribution, reciprocity and exchange. Many scholars of ancient Egypt, like those who study other ancient Near Eastern cultures, have used redistribution as a model for interpreting the ceremonial inscriptions found in Egypt. In sum, they find evidence from the ceremonial inscriptions that Egyptian ideology posited that the king owned everything in Egypt. All goods were thus gathered at central collecting points in the temples and were redistributed to the Egyptian population on the basis of rank. This description fits well with Polanyi's redistribution model.

New Kingdom documents such as Hatshepsut's Punt reliefs, Thutmose III's annals and the Great Harris Papyrus are excellent examples of relief, inscriptions and papyri that support the idea that Egyptian ideology fits well with Polanyi's pattern of redistribution and the way the economy is embedded in Egyptian culture. Hatshepsut, for example, sent an expedition to the land of Punt to obtain incense for the cult of the god Amun (Bleiberg 1995: 1378). According to the inscriptions, she sent the expedition in response to Amun's direct command. She never cites purely economic motivations for her actions. There is no sense in the texts or relief of the economic realities of the import/export trade. In fact, she never fully explains how she was able to pay the people of Punt for the products they gave to Amun. Rather, Amun's and the king's prestige in the greater world at large is the point of the narrative. Yet, here the state acts for the good of the temples. It is a perfect example of the way the Egyptians described the royal monopoly on foreign trade.

Thutmose III's annals prove a similar point. In the narrative portion of the text, the king repeatedly explains that he has gone to war at the command of the god Amun and that the king's success is highly dependent on Amun's support. The inscription is also filled with long lists of goods that foreigners conveyed to the king and to Amun as a result of these wars (Bleiberg 1981). Egypt's defeated enemies transfer goods to the king under several rubrics including words that mean tax and gifts (Bleiberg 1981). Here again, the narrative emphasizes the king's and the god's prestige in the world rather than, for example, the economics of capital formation in the temples based on the large quantities of goods now brought to their storerooms. It also illustrates the centralized storage of these goods which are brought from foreign countries and deposited in the temples or in the palace.

The Great Harris Papyrus records gifts that Ramesses III gave to the temples of Ra of Heliopolis, Ptah of Memphis and Amun of Karnak (Grandet 1994–9). It illustrates both the centralized collection of goods and the distribution from royal to divine institutions. The text confirms the ideology that kings act for the gods and return both goods and services for the gods' use in recognition of royal success in the world. Although the text expresses economic ideas, it does not consider the realities of land tenure for the large tracts of land that the gods now own or the means of production for the goods promised to the gods.

Finally, the festival calendars found in both the Ramesseum and Medinet Habu describe distribution of large amounts of food and drink to the general population during festivals (Haring 1997). Here, the large quantities of goods collected for the god by the state are redistributed on a regular basis to the people. Yet even the elaborate lists of the goods redistributed are not generally considered to contain concrete information about Egyptian practices as they are intended to reflect Egyptian ideas about the proper use of the gods' treasure.

It is thus clear that the texts considered through the lens of Polanyi's theories lead to a good description of Egyptian ideology rather than analysis of economic reality. Ceremonial documents omit concepts such as the actual status of temple fields and cultivators and land lessors, trading the surplus production of the temples, the exact motives behind hoarding precious metals, and many other economic questions. They do, however, emphasize the importance of prestige issues, religious ideology and even a sort of sociology for understanding economic actions in ancient Egypt. They are an excellent illustration of the meaning of embeddedness of the economy in a specific culture.

Private economic activity

In contrast to those scholars who have attempted to understand the Egyptian economy through the lens of Polanyi's models, others have interpreted the data using the general principles of economic rationalism, derived from the modern market economy (Römer 1989; Warburton 1997; Eyre 1998; Wilke 2000). These scholars view Egyptian economic activity as business, operating on the principles of the modern market economy. For example, Eyre (1998: 174) regards the market stalls depicted in both Old Kingdom and New Kingdom tombs as businesses with capital investment and accumulation of capital rather than opportunistic trade in excess consumables, the explanation preferred by those who see the Egyptian economy as basically a redistribution system. Furthermore, those who wove cloth are understood as real capitalists who both accumulated capital and could reinvest it.

The Old Kingdom tomb of Niankhkhnum and Khnumhotep at Saqqara (Moussa and Altenmüller 1977: fig. 10 pl. 240), the tomb of Fetekta at Abusir (Verner 1994: 89–92), the tomb of Ankhmahor at Saqqara (Badawy 1978: pls 32–4) and the reliefs decorating the Unas causeway at Saqqara depict both men and women at 'market stands' offering vegetables, fruits, fish, cloth and other commodities in small pottery vessels. In addition, men offer services such as hair cutting, seal making and sandal making. From these scenes, some scholars have drawn the conclusion that Egyptian towns had stable markets for fish, fruit and vegetables, located near craftsmen who, at least in the tomb of Ty at Saqqara, appear to be itinerant because they carry everything in bags (Eyre 1998: 176).

New Kingdom tomb paintings depict similar scenes. Paintings in the Ramesside tombs of Ipuy (Davies 1927: pls 30, 34), Kenamun (Davies and Faulkner: 1947) and Khaemhet (Wreszinski 1923: 199–200) portray men unloading barges of grain into baskets tended by women at the riverbank. Women offer fish, loaves, fruit, beer and wine. Some scholars understand these exchanges as the sailor's means of getting food. They could perhaps be spending their rations of grain which constitute their salaries.

All these scenes share their location on the riverbank, the source of the idea that the quay was the market place (Janssen 1980). This role derived from the Nile's function as the major transportation artery for Egypt. Notably, nearly all temples had direct access to the quay and it is impossible to prove either that these market stalls were or were not somehow associated with the temples. Furthermore, these scenes provide no information on how customers would have paid for their purchases in a moneyless economy. The only information that is preserved for Egypt concerning barter does not seem to be related to these scenes. As Eyre has observed (1998: 178), there are too many gaps in our knowledge to understand what relationship this material might have with the demonstrably private barter transactions found in the Deir el-Medina texts. Moreover, not enough information remains from antiquity to allow scholars to discuss the existence of private craftsmen totally independent of the temple or royal economies. Whether they sometimes worked part-time and privately for themselves we simply do not know.

Eyre has also drawn a distinction between those who operated market stalls and the principal individuals involved in the transactions recorded in numerous contemporaneous documents from Deir el-Medina. The most famous of these documents, often used to illustrate the nature of private Egyptian barter transactions, is Papyrus Cairo 65739. The document records court proceedings brought by a woman named Bakmut against a woman named Irynefer arising from the sale of a female slave (Gardiner 1935c; Bleiberg 1995: 1377; Eyre 1998: 178). Essentially, Bakmut makes the claim that some of her goods were used in the barter to obtain the slave and thus Irynefer should not have sold the slave without Bakmut's participation. Irynefer wants to demonstrate in court that she used only her own goods to obtain the slave and thus she was the sole owner.

In the introduction to this document, Irynefer states that she had woven cloth for seven years before she bought the slave. Cloth, indeed, is one of the main commodities Irynefer lists in this document which she claims to have used to barter for the slave, in addition to metal vessels, beaten metal and honey. For Eyre (1998: 179), the document demonstrates that Irynefer had used cloth weaving as a means of building her savings to obtain a slave. Cloth production became a means of increasing her personal wealth.

Eyre also adduces other examples of cloth as a source of private wealth. In the letters of Heqanakht, dating to the early 12th Dynasty, the author uses the profits of a cloth sale to rent land. Part of this land is then used to grow flax. Another Heqanakht letter deals with giving a woman flax to spin into thread for him. The letters seem to document small-scale manufacture of cloth, from obtaining land for growing flax, spinning the flax into thread, perhaps weaving the cloth, and finally selling it so that the process can be repeated with land rental. Heqanakht seems to be in the cloth business as well as being a subsistence farmer (Eyre 1998: 180). Thus, for Eyre, the widespread evidence of centralized weaving does not negate the possibility of privately manufactured cloth in ancient Egypt. Yet there is no way to be certain that Heqanakht's activities do not represent outsourcing by the large, centralized weaving establishment. The relationship cannot be established either way.

The same criticism could be brought to the evidence from Papyrus Brooklyn 35.1453A,B (Eyre 1998: 181). This document contains a ship's log. The papyrus records lists of men both collecting and distributing materials that relate both to yarn spinning and honey. Again, institutional connections in this text can neither be demonstrated nor disallowed. The women do, however, give their production back to the ship using the Egyptian term *bak*. Although the root meaning of the word is 'work', in ceremonial texts it is clearly a technical term referring to goods sent to a temple (Bleiberg 1988). It is not clear if the women are selling retail or if they are somehow outsourcing for a central establishment that is associated with a temple. The ship's logs might represent the distribution that local manufacturers depended on for widespread use of their goods; yet, it is difficult to imagine, without any evidence, that local manufacturers had national distribution networks unrelated to royal or divine institutions. These transactions might well be part of the temple economy. There is no way to determine with certainty whether this document describes commerce or taxes.

Thus for Eyre (1998: 185), the redistributive economy has little effect on anyone except the elite who are directly a part of it. Ordinary people, in this view, are taxed, but they do not benefit in a regular way from redistribution. The household, in this view, becomes the most important unit of production rather than the temple or the royal government.

ECONOMY WITHOUT MODELS

Even though scholars have mostly derived the ideology of the ancient Egyptian economy from the ceremonial texts, others have also used these documents to examine specifically the administration of the institutions called the Temples of Millions of Years. The ceremonial texts still allow analysis of important administrative terms. One case is the meaning of the phrase 'Temple (*hut*) of Millions of Years in the domain (*per*) of Amun'.

Haring (1997) has used the ceremonial and administrative texts from the Ramesseum and Medinet Habu to study the economic basis for these institutions. Both of these temples were located on the western bank of the Nile opposite modern Luxor and Karnak. Haring argues that these temples operated independently and were not integrated into the larger administrative structure called the domain of Amun. He argues on the basis of the texts that there is no overall pattern of economic relations among these temples of millions of years, the temple of Amun in Karnak and the royal palace. He finds that each of these institutions operates independently. Haring thinks the connection is religious but not administrative because there would be no advantage in making it administrative for any of the parties involved. The expression 'in the domain of Amun' is thus only ceremonial and not really administrative. This again is a question of ideology versus administration and this is a good example of where this concept helps scholars disentangle the two categories.

TAX AND TRADE BEFORE COINAGE

Among the most important differences between ancient and modern economies is the use of coinage as money. The Egyptians were unaware of coinage until late in their history. The earliest Egyptian document to calculate a tax in money, Papyrus Berlin 3048, dates to the Third Intermediate Period (Muhs 2005: 3). Before importing this Greek invention, the Egyptians had developed several methods of calculating taxes in the state sphere, salaries for state workers and conscripts, and prices in private exchanges.

From earliest times the royal government conducted an inventory of Egypt's wealth, presumably to set taxation goals. Wealth was counted primarily in terms of the number of cattle, but there is evidence for counts of land, other objects of value, and people (Wilkinson 1999: 220–1). The Palermo Stone refers to biennial cattle counts as early as the 2nd Dynasty, and also a count of 'gold and the fields'. The 6th Dynasty tomb biography of Weni refers to a count of 'everything which can be counted', probably including people for conscription (Lichtheim 1975: 21).

The local governors, called nomarchs, were responsible for delivering taxes to the central government. The nomarch Ameny of the Gazelle Nome (Beni Hasan) who lived in the late 11th or early 12th Dynasty succinctly described the process in his tomb biography:

> I spent the years as Lord of the Oryx nome with all dues for the king's house being in my charge. I gave gang-overseers to the domains of the herdsmen of the Oryx nome and 3000 oxen as their yoke-oxen. I was praised for it in the king's house in every year of the cattle tax. I delivered all their dues to the king's house and there was no shortage against me in any bureau of his.
>
> (Lichtheim 1988: 138–9)

Residents of Old Kingdom pyramid towns – where workers who administered the work of the pyramid complexes lived – were exempted from many taxes as well as conscription. A series of royal decrees found at Dahshur, Giza and Coptos all exempt various classes of priests and other workers at the royal funeral monuments from paying specific kinds of taxes and from conscription for other kinds of work (Goedicke 1967). These exemptions must have been an incentive to remain at work in the pyramid towns, though why such an incentive was needed is not clear. Perhaps kings wanted to insure against removal of those charged with maintaining the funeral cult which was to keep them alive forever in the next world. Exemption from the cattle levy is notably absent from those exemption decrees, however. This absence may point to the importance of this particular type of levy for maintaining the central government during the Old Kingdom.

In addition to cattle, the other largest tax was paid by farmers in grain. During the New Kingdom, Papyrus Wilbour shows that grain was taxed at the rate of one and a half *khar* (76.88 litres = 20.31 US gallons = 16.91 British gallons) of grain per *aroura* (two-thirds of an acre = 2.67 km^2) (Katary 1999: 65). Tomb paintings show tax assessors both measuring the standing grain in the field, and collecting and recording large baskets of grain for shipment to centralized storehouses (James 1985: 126).

All taxes before the first millennium BC, it is clear, were collected in kind. Private sales were also conducted by barter for goods, with the use of a unit of exchange rather than actual coinage. In the New Kingdom this unit was one *deben* (approximately 91 grams) of copper which could be divided into ten *kitĕ*. A *kitĕ*, or one-tenth of a *deben*, was a common measurement for more valuable metals such as silver and gold.

In Papyrus Cairo 65739, the document described above, Irynefer lists 24 separate items that she used to trade for a slave girl. The agreed value of the slave girl was first determined in *deben* and *kitě*. Then each of the items which Irynefer offered in exchange was appraised at a value in *deben* and *kitě*. The total value of the 24 items in Irynefer's list was determined then to be equal to the value of the slave girl in *deben* and *kitě*. No actual *deben* and *kitě* were traded in this transaction. These measurements represent only the agreed value of each of the items which were part of the exchange.

The Egyptians computed salaries in units of bread and beer, the two staples of an ancient Egyptian diet. They never seem to use *deben* and *kitě* in calculations of salary. It seems likely that the lower salaries, which were close to subsistence level, were paid by giving bread and beer to employees or conscripts. To ensure uniformity, each loaf of bread was baked from a standard recipe, using equal amounts of ingredients. Thus, each loaf had a standard nutritional value.

Standardization was assured through a system called *pefsu* in ancient Egyptian, which can be translated as 'baking value'. *Pefsu* could also be used to ensure that a predictable number of loaves would be baked from a known amount of grain. The baking value was based on the number of loaves produced from a measure of grain. The higher the value, that is, the more loaves from one measure, then the smaller the loaves, or the weaker the beer, or the smaller the jars. Most wage lists seem to assume that a standard *pefsu* value has been used in baking and brewing (Bleiberg 1995: 1379).

Standardization could also be assured through the use of tokens or tallies. From the Middle Kingdom fortress of Uronarti in Nubia, tallies have been discovered in the shape of a standard loaf of bread. Presumably this tally could be used to check that a worker's wages in bread loaves were all the same size. Beer jars were also presumably a roughly standard size (Bleiberg 1995: 1380).

The standard basic wage was ten loaves of bread plus one-third to two full jugs of beer per day. This was the amount paid to the lowest-paid staff members. Other workers were paid in multiples of this standard wage varying from twice as much to 50 times the standard wage for top earners (Bleiberg 1995: 1380).

Various methods could be used for calculating wages. One ship's crew received half the ration of the captain. In another case the highest paid official received 38⅓ loaves while the lowest paid worker received 1⅓ loaves.

In another example from the Middle Kingdom, it appears that the staff of the temple of Wepwawet in Asyut received a commission on all the goods which came to the temple. The staff was paid by the 'temple day'. This unit was defined thus:

> As for a temple day, it is 1/360 part of a year. Now, you shall divide everything which enters this temple – bread, beer, and meat – by way of the daily rate. That is, it is going to be 1/360 of the bread, the beer, and of everything which enters this temple for (any) one of these temple days which I have given you.
>
> (quoted in Kemp 1989b: 126)

In this temple the regular staff received 2/360 of the total revenue of the temple, while the chief priest received 4/360.

In another case from the Middle Kingdom, describing the wages of an expedition leader, the chief of the expedition received 500 loaves per day. Clearly, large sums like this were not paid out in actual loaves of bread or jars of beer. It seems highly unlikely that an expedition leader could actually take his ever increasing number of loaves of bread, growing from 500 to 1,000 to 1,500 in three days, to 15,000 loaves of bread after a month, with him on an extended trip into the desert. It also seems impossible that he could eat this much, even with a large family and servants. Therefore, it seems possible that 500 loaves of bread is actually a unit for measuring out commodities, approximating our idea of a unit of money. It must have been possible to save also and draw against an account of bread and beer owed (Bleiberg 1995: 1380).

During the Late Period, coinage imported from Greece began to play a role in the Egyptian economy. At first, the state began to collect some taxes in silver during the Third Intermediate Period. Customs duties on goods from outside Egypt might also have been paid in coinage (Muhs 2005: 4). Increasing trade with Greece in the Saite Period was a possible stimulus for the use of coinage in exchanges. But even at this point, use of coins was most likely limited to elites. During the Saite through to the Persian periods, coins are found only in hoards (Muhs 2005: 5). Isolated coins, suggesting more widespread circulation, occur only in the fourth century BC. Before the arrival of the Ptolemies, the hoards of silver coins suggest that they were valued as bullion rather than money. Although the Persians minted coins in Egypt in imitation of Greek coinage, it was only after the arrival of the Ptolemies that small denomination coins seem to have been used in actual transactions.

The absence of money except as a unit of exchange in classical pharaonic society is an excellent example of the basic differences between ancient and modern economies. This absence suggests one of the reasons why many Egyptologists have reservations about applying modern economic principles to analysing ancient practices.

ORGANIZATION OF LABOUR

Labour (see also Cooney, this volume) was provided to the government through a system of conscription which may have originated in prehistory. Conscription was the chief source of labour for construction projects, maintenance of the irrigation system, agricultural work on crown administered lands and expeditions outside Egypt for raw materials. To some extent, this labour was organized by the *phyle* system. During the Old Kingdom, this system divided at least some Egyptians into five groups of workers. Each group had a name: The Great Phyle, The Eastern Phyle, The Green Phyle, The Little Phyle and The Perfection Phyle. Each *phyle* name probably made reference to its protective deity. In the Middle Kingdom there were only four *phyle*s, each known by number. The numbers might refer to the season of the year when the *phyle* served (Roth 1991). The evidence for *phyle*s in the New Kingdom is much less specific. A different system of gangs, as seen at Deir el-Medina, may indicate a reorganization of the labour force at this time.

Workers were initiated into a *phyle*, possibly at puberty. Each *phyle* did government service for a specific amount of time each year. The amount of time seems to have varied with the kind of labour performed. Many of the *phyle* rotations seem to have been monthly. During this period, workers received rations and lodgings, possibly generous enough to help support their families for part of the year.

CONCLUSION

The data currently available for analysing the state and private economy of ancient Egypt leave many gaps in our knowledge. Although ceremonial texts inform scholars about the ideology behind the Egyptian economy, administrative texts reveal details of specific times and places, and private sales contracts, legal proceedings, private letters and wills offer details of private economic life, it is nearly impossible to tie these elements together into a coherent pattern.

A major obstacle in constructing a coherent picture of the relationship between the state and private economy is the fact that the relationship was probably ubiquitous. Because the relationship was widespread, with many points of contact, the texts do not mention connections that would have been obvious to the ancients. Thus any connection between the activities described in the ship's log in Papyrus Brooklyn 35.1453A,B and the state remain unacknowledged, perhaps because they would have been obvious to an Egyptian. Such ancient assumptions would be true also of market place scenes in tombs. Since the ancients knew what these scenes represented, it was unnecessary to explain them. Thus, modern observers can make automatic assumptions about the nature of these market stalls' connections with the state, or independence from central control, based on modern prejudices. Only additional information, as yet undiscovered or unanalysed, will allow scholars to construct a firmer foundation for our knowledge of the state and private economies.

CHAPTER FOURTEEN

LAND TENURE AND TAXATION

——— ·◆· ———

Sally L.D. Katary

The Egyptian pharaoh exercised in theory absolute rights of ownership over the lands and resources of Egypt as both the living Horus and the ruler of a centrally planned and organized state. He was entitled to bestow lavish gifts of land and property on those institutions, settlements and individuals he favoured. At the same time, the king was equally justified in demanding that the recipients of his largesse recompense the state in the form of duties or imposts of various kinds on land and property. These 'taxes' might include a share in the produce of the land, cattle and other livestock from herds throughout Egypt, as well as human labour for state projects. Since the king regularly apportioned the land of Egypt for individuals and institutions, which in turn produced revenues of all kinds for the state, it was a mutually beneficial relationship.

At Egypt's unification *c.*3100 BC, traditional village communities were absorbed into a central administration capable of providing economic and political stability to a land newly at peace and poised for economic expansion. The overwhelming importance of agriculture as the backbone of Egypt's economy led to the strategic organization of Egypt's land wealth in the Early Dynastic Period to exploit these resources most efficiently. By the 3rd Dynasty, royal foundations that derived their *raison d'être* from the ideology of divine kingship exercised the lead role in land management as the primary agricultural producers and, therefore, as sources of royal revenue (Figure 14.1). Royal farming estates were well established by the reign of Sneferu, one regnal year alone of this king occasioning the establishment of 35 estates 'with people' and 122 cattle-farms (Malek 1986: 68). By the mid-5th Dynasty, the great proliferation of royal cult temples capable of supporting large numbers of officials gave these temples a central place in the administration of the state economy. On occasion, donations of arable land ranging from two to more than 1,704 *arouras* (1 *aroura* = 52 m × 52 m, 0.27 ha or 0.66 acres) were made by pharaoh to the great foundations (Malek 1986: 79).

Appointment to even a nominal temple office gave an individual the right to share in the land and resources of the temple *ex officio*. The *khentiu-she*, smallholders with cult responsibilities who resided in the royal pyramid cities, benefited from the royal foundations in having the right personally to cultivate their land with freedom from

Figure 14.1 Estates providing income for the royal cult, from the pyramid temple of Sneferu at Dahshur (from Kemp 1989b: fig. 40).

corvée by royal decree (Eyre 1987a: 35–6; 1994: 111–12). Many such holdings developed into profitable estates as in the case of Pepinakht-Heqaib, the 6th Dynasty governor of Aswan. Large-scale landholders likely used ordinary peasants (*meret*) to cultivate their extensive holdings. The great estates thus became the basis of wealth in the Old Kingdom and their landholders, men of outstanding wealth and authority.

Private ownership of land in the Old Kingdom was likely limited after the transformation of the village economies (Malek 1986: 79). However, the desire for the personal disposal of landed property was eventually realized when gifts of land made by the king, first to his family and eventually to more distant favoured officials, were secured for the family by the establishment of permanent mortuary endowments. Children shared in the produce of the lands that composed the endowment in return for their services in carrying out the responsibilities of the funerary cult. Offices came to be inherited from father to son and this hereditary job tenure brought with it the right to all acquired property. These foundations often formed the centre of a profitable agricultural operation. Rights and privileges were, however, subject to withdrawal as old foundations were dissolved and new beneficiaries named. This might happen at a change of dynasty or when major changes in the organization of the government occurred as at the end of the Old Kingdom (Kees 1961: 63–4). Land under neither institutional authority nor private ownership fell into the category of 'Crown land' under the administration of the Royal Residence, its income available to the state (Malek 1986: 79).

With a centralized government established in the capital at Memphis, a national system of taxation was required to finance the lifestyle of the king and his court as well as the monumental building activities and other projects that reflected royal power and authority. The first organized system of revenue collection dates to the end of the Predynastic Period before the unification of Egypt when written records first occur in the form of inscribed dockets or labels and incised pottery vessels. These have been found in the Abydos tomb of King 'Ka' and likely denote the contents of storage vessels as tax paid into the treasury under royal authority as signified by the royal *serekh* (Wilkinson 1999: 57–8). From the Early Dynastic Period comes evidence of inscribed labels of bone, wood or ivory, private stelae from Saqqara and Abydos from the 1st Dynasty, as well as inscribed vessels of 2nd Dynasty date. The careers of prominent senior officials in the period from the 1st to the late 3rd Dynasty throw the most light upon landholding and the revenues derived from vast agricultural estates. The autobiographical tomb inscription of Metjen, controller of vast estates throughout the delta under Djoser, is a good example. This earliest of tomb autobiographies describes the career path of an ambitious government administrator in terms of offices he held, estates controlled and personal wealth acquired (Wilkinson 1999: 144–7).

The Palermo Stone (Figure 14.2), a double-sided black basalt stela, supplemented by smaller fragments, dating to no earlier than the end of the 5th Dynasty, is all that remains of the earliest royal annals, reaching back to the reigns of semi-mythical rulers of Predynastic date (Redford 1986: 88–90; Wilkinson 2000a). As a record of noteworthy events in the reigns of individual kings almost to the end of the 5th Dynasty, the details of the Palermo Stone proliferate as the document approaches its final entry. Among the principal events commemorated in the horizontal rows of rectangular compartments that mark the individual regnal years is the biennial 'Following of Horus' (*shemsu-Hor*) (Kees 1961: 102–3; Helck 1972a; Wilkinson 1999: 142, 220–1). This royal tour along the Nile reflects the preoccupation of the central administration with the documentation of the economic wealth of the land as measured in herds of cattle and small livestock, the extent and productivity of arable fields, resources in precious metals, and human population.

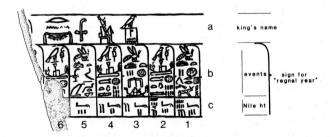

Figure 14.2   The Palermo Stone (from Kemp 1989b: fig. 5).

The 'Following of Horus' included a biennial cattle census (*tjenut*) as early as the 2nd Dynasty, later supplemented by a 'census of gold and fields' and other taxable resources. From as early as the reign of Djer onwards, such censuses were supplemented by regular notations of the height of the annual Nile inundation, likely occasioned by a realization that the flood levels necessary for Egypt's economic survival were declining (Butzer 1976: 28). These data were used to determine the tax levied on arable fields.

As early as the Predynastic Period, responsibility for the collection, storage, processing and redistribution of all kinds of state revenues was assigned to the Treasury (Figure 14.3), an institution composed of an elite cadre of literate administrators, supervised by a chancellor (*khetemu-bity*) under the authority of the vizier (*tjaty*). The variety of names given to this institution, the Treasury of Upper Egypt (*per-hedj*, 'The White House'), the Treasury of Lower Egypt (*per-desher*, 'The Red House') and, eventually, 'The Two White Houses' (*perwy-hedj*), may attest its Predynastic origins in separate kingdoms of Upper and Lower Egypt. More important, however, the binary structure of the Treasury acknowledges that Upper and Lower Egypt were too physically different for their needs to be well served by a collection system that did not recognize this difference (Wilkinson 1999: 125–7).

Produce from the fields was sent to the *per-shena*, a storage facility for foodstuffs intended for distribution to dependent government employees and as donations to temples and funerary institutions, cementing relationships between the Crown and local institutions. The storage of surplus grain reflects the wisdom of experience in providing a hedge against inadequate harvests in years to come (O'Connor 1972: 99). Moreover, surplus grain and manufactured goods could be used by the central government for foreign trade (Trigger 1983: 59). While government granaries are not actually attested until the 3rd Dynasty, they no doubt existed under the Treasury long before that (Wilkinson 1999: 128). Closely connected with the *per-shena* was the *per-heri-wedjeb*, or 'house of largesse', a sub-department of the Treasury responsible for the redistribution of revenues in kind to the privileged elite as well as to the state-supported cult temples of Egypt (Gardiner 1938a: 85–9; Malek 1986: 35; Warburton 1997: 72). The Treasury also saw to the manufacture of secondary products, ranging from wine and beer to meat, bread and oils for the provisioning of the Memphite court. The tomb inscriptions of the overseer of the Treasury (*imy-ra per-hedj*) Pehernefer from the late 3rd Dynasty contribute valuable details concerning this vital Treasury function (Junker 1939; Wilkinson 1999: 129–31).

Tax revenues financed lavish royal building programmes, royal residences and harems, as well as work in the quarries and military posts dependent upon government support to maintain border security and trade routes. Increasing financial demands upon temples and funerary endowments led these institutions to demand exemption from specific kinds of tax obligations and the arbitrary seizure of their property and personnel (Hayes 1946; Goedicke 1967; Helck 1975). However, charters of immunity were primarily intended to protect temples and funerary foundations from exploitation by unauthorized officials and persons of wealth and influence. Pharaoh himself never relinquished the right to make financial demands upon these institutions as is suggested, for example, in the absence of an exemption from the cattle levy.

The oldest charter of immunity is the 4th Dynasty Exemption Decree of Shepseskaf issued for the benefit of the estate and staff of the pyramid of Menkaura (Sethe 1903:

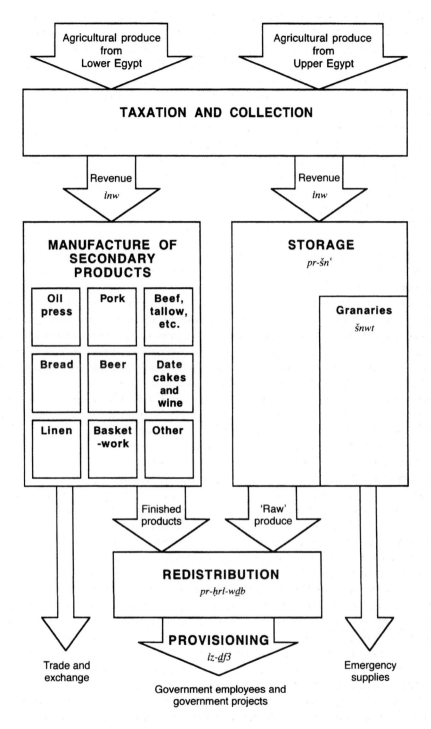

Figure 14.3 The workings of the Treasury in the Early Dynastic Period (from Wilkinson 1999: fig. 4.3).

160). The 5th Dynasty Decree of Neferirkara extended royal protection to staff and employees of the Temple of Osiris at Abydos (Sethe 1903: 170–2). Pepi I enacted a similar decree to protect the pyramid towns that supplied labour and income to the service of Sneferu's two Dahshur pyramids (Sethe 1903: 209–13) from demands for any work (*kat*) for the Palace, from any tax (*medjed*) for any department of the royal residence, and to prevent villagers from being arbitrarily seized.

In removing productive agricultural land from the tax base and excusing temple personnel from labour on government projects, charters of immunity may have damaged the financial stability of the Old Kingdom. However, how much land was actually exempted from taxation or how much revenue loss these exemptions entailed cannot be determined. Exemption decrees certainly did not eliminate all the financial obligations of the landowning institutions to the central government (Kanawati 1977: 72). Revenues denied the Treasury would likely not have been sufficient to rescue the Old Kingdom government from eventual financial insolvency.

From the late 5th Dynasty until the end of the 6th Dynasty, the central government made efforts to deal with challenges to its tax-collecting mandate (Kanawati 1980: 128–9). Behind Merenra's appointment of nomarchs or district governors over the provinces (nomes) was likely the intention to increase both agricultural productivity and government revenues. The creation of the office of the vizier of Upper Egypt at Abydos may be similarly interpreted. The need to counter the overwhelming dominance of the offices of vizier and overseer of Upper Egypt by power-hungry royal relations precipitated Pepi II's abolition of the independent office of the overseer of Upper Egypt and led to the subordination of the tax-collecting activities of Upper Egyptian nobles to the direct control of the southern vizier. Thus, despite the move towards administrative decentralization that elevated nomarchs to increasingly greater prominence and privilege, economic reforms preserved the financial control of the central government over the capital and provinces until the combined effects of excessive expenditures, inadequate inundations and provincial independence brought the Old Kingdom to the edge of the abyss.

The authorities did not take kindly to officials who were delinquent, derelict or dishonest in carrying out their tax-collecting responsibilities. Depicted in the Saqqara mastaba of the 6th Dynasty vizier Khentika are five nomarchs brought before the vizier on charges of corruption or dereliction in the remission of tax revenues (James and Apted 1953: pl. IX). Three of the men lie prostrate before Khentika; two others are lashed to posts as attendants wielding batons beat the offenders. Thus, even the privileged of the society could not take their obligations lightly. Moreover, Khentika's tomb is not singular. Centuries later in the Theban tomb-chapel of Menna, a Treasury official under Thutmose IV, there are scenes where both peasant and well-to-do tax evaders face the vizier for judgement (James 1985: 84–5).

During the Middle Kingdom much revenue came from cultivated lands designated *khebsu* or 'ploughlands', Crown agricultural units created and managed by government administrative departments (*waret*) and likely cultivated by corvée labour (Hayes 1955: 27–9). Workers were divided into five (Old Kingdom) and later four (Middle Kingdom) teams or *phyles* that rotated in completing their government service, the men paid in rations and lodging that would have accommodated their families (Roth 1991). Reorganization of the *phyle* system probably occurred during the New Kingdom.

Other fields were in the charge of smallholders called *nedjesu* whose precise relation-ship to the land is unknown. Some Middle Kingdom smallholders were relatively independent. Correspondence of the mortuary-priest and farmer Heqanakht with his son regarding the operation of the family's main landholding reveals that in the early Middle Kingdom a landholder might cultivate his holdings himself or rent his land to others (James 1962; Baer 1963). It is possible that Heqanakht inherited his landholdings, received them as remuneration for services rendered, purchased them, received them in payment of a debt or from a combination of sources. He may even have leased some of the land. His claim to the property was no doubt based upon his payment of taxes due on the land. As long as taxes were remitted, the landowner could do with the land as he wished (James 1985: 242–3; Eyre 1994: 111).

A Middle Kingdom tax assessor's journal from Haraga in the Fayum affords a glimpse into methods of tax recording on agricultural land at that time. Tax assessors under the authority of the royal treasurer measured and recorded details of the fields and registered the tenants or landowners. The timing of the activities to the second month of the inundation suggests that some kind of fixed tax was involved (Smither 1941). Over the next millennium, scenes in Theban tombs, notably the tomb of Menna, depict the measurement of cultivated fields by surveyors as scribes calculate the yield. Especially informative is the mid-18th Dynasty tomb of Paheri, mayor of Elkab, where the inspection of the fields of his own estate is detailed (James 1985: 106–12, 119–30). The vast panorama of agricultural activities depicted reflects a preoccupation with the effective management of the land and the distribution of its produce.

Even though Egypt possessed a favourable environment for agriculture, there were times when monsoon rains over Ethiopia brought about lower Nile levels than usual with serious consequences for the ancient Egyptian economy. In his tomb inscription, Khety I, nomarch of Asyut during the First Intermediate Period, claims responsi-bility for rebuilding or enlarging a canal 10 metres wide and providing irrigation to drought-afflicted areas, thus developing a water management system (Griffith 1889: pl. 15; Brunner 1937: 11–12, 64–7; Butzer 1976: 51–6; James 1985: 115–16; Lichtheim 1988: 26–9). He also claims to have remitted taxes imposed under his predecessors and to have stockpiled grain for his people's benefit. At Beni Hasan, the tomb autobiography of Amenemhet (Ameny), nomarch of the Oryx Nome under Senusret I, describes Ameny as the saviour of his people during 'years of hunger' occasioned by poor floods (Newberry 1893: pl. VIII; James 1985: 113; Lichtheim 1988: 135–41). As nomarch, Ameny had responsibility for the collection of all dues (*baku*) owing to the king's house, including the cattle levy and taxes levied on grain. He claims that he preserved his nome in times of famine and paid his dues to the government through wise policies of land management that did not discriminate between rich and poor.

Other contemporary documents detail the pain and suffering that peasants endured when they attempted to evade or desert their term of compulsory labour for state projects: tilling the fields, digging and repairing irrigation channels, labouring on construction projects and manning expeditions abroad to obtain raw materials. Papyrus Brooklyn 35.1446, a late Middle Kingdom document, describes the fate of 80 residents of Upper Egypt who fled their corvée obligations in the reign of Amenemhat III (Hayes 1955; Quirke 1990a: 127–54). Their abandonment of their responsibilities resulted in indefinite terms of compulsory labour as felons on government-owned lands and the conscription of their family members as well. There was no escaping the burden of corvée for the vast majority of the Egyptian population, but periodic reviews of punishments meted out to offenders offered hope of relief.

During the New Kingdom, the temples provided the infrastructure necessary to channel the wealth of the country efficiently to qualified recipients, serving both as collection centres for taxes from all sectors of the economy and also as the direct beneficiaries of tax revenues. Revenues of taxes maintained temples and foundations and their staffs, and also provided offerings for their altars, livestock for sacrifice, clothing for temple statues and assorted cult paraphernalia. Military garrisons and foreign settlements where prisoners of war and mercenaries lived were supplied by the general levy (*heter*) as were quarry-workers and the workmen of the Royal Necropolis. The general levy also supported the royal palaces and harems. Provisioning was accomplished by a complex, well-coordinated bureaucracy with ties to the Treasury of Pharaoh and Granary of Pharaoh under the vizier's authority.

The administration of the general levy on provincial towns and villages is documented in the inscriptions of the Theban tomb-chapel of Rekhmira, vizier of Upper Egypt under Thutmose III and Amenhotep II (James 1985: 59–69; van den Boorn 1988). The inscriptions detail the nature and extent of Rekhmira's responsibilities as vizier as well as providing an understanding of the underlying ethical principles of New Kingdom administration. Rekhmira is depicted executing the functions of the office of vizier with an accompanying text outlining the duties of the vizier in the format of a practical handbook. Among these duties are the collection and receipt of taxes from the hands of various administrators (Figure 14.4), including overseers of the treasury, who reported on the state of the economy in every government department. Where there was a shortfall in revenues generated by the general levy for such expenses of state as military campaigns, the equipping of garrisons or even construction of pharaoh's tomb, the vizier was authorized to impose special interim levies.

From the beginning of the New Kingdom, pharaohs awarded individuals of high achievement lands and slaves in recognition of their service to the state. Over his lifetime, Ahmose son of Abana was rewarded with extensive estates, including one of 60 *arouras*, as 'favours' of the king (Sethe 1905: 6.7–9). Since such estates were often widely dispersed geographically, cultivation required the services of extra-familial labour, slaves or local cultivators. Shares in the estate would pass down in the family of these citizen farmers, generation to generation, and strengthen the bond between the state and the heirs as beneficiaries of loyalty rewards, setting a land tenure pattern for the New Kingdom (Eyre 1994: 114–15).

Following the Amarna Period at the end of the 18th Dynasty, royal authority was reasserted in the form of the Edict of Horemheb. A stela at the Karnak temple of Amun sets out the reforms of the military pharaoh Horemheb, issued to curtail the abuse of authority in both the central and local governments that occurred during the Atenist revolution of Akhenaten. They make it clear that the government would no longer brook the unlawful seizure of tax revenues by unscrupulous officials and soldiers occasioned by the pervasive lawlessness of the times (Pflüger 1946; Helck 1955a; Kruchten 1981). The central government reasserted its right to demand the payment of taxes in goods and services for the support of the government and its enterprises and put violators of the Edict clearly in defiance of the law. However,

Figure 14.4　Receiving payments in kind, from the tomb of
Rekhmira at Thebes (from Kemp 1989b: fig. 80).

Horemheb's decrees were essentially ad hoc responses intended to correct the worst of the abuses rather than a systematic overhaul of the legal system. The primary concern was with protecting the interests of the state and re-establishing the age-old institutional framework for regular revenue collection that depended heavily on the temples and their staffs in the absence of a codified system governing revenue collection (Théodoridès 1971; Kemp 1989b: 235–6).

Despite the reforms of Horemheb, the abuse of authority continued in the Ramesside 19th Dynasty. Seti I issued a charter of immunity to define the rights and safeguard the employees and property of his temple of Osiris at Abydos from unauthorized seizure (Griffith 1927; Edgerton 1947; Gardiner 1952). Temple cargo ships laden with revenues in gold or other products from Nubia intended for the temple foundation in Abydos were easy targets for unscrupulous officials. The dire warnings of the Nauri Decree, carved on a cliff at Nauri just north of the Third Cataract, threaten harsh punishments to any commander, scribe or inspector of the Nile fortresses tempted personally to appropriate shipments.

The Great Harris Papyrus (Papyrus Harris I) provides an indication of the wealth of the temples of Amun, Ra, Ptah and smaller, less well-known temples, including a total of 1,071,780 *arouras* (295,007.44 ha), equivalent to 13 to 18 per cent of the available cultivable land (Erichsen 1933; Schaedel 1936; Kees 1961: 66–7, 209–10; Grandet 1994–9; Haring 1997: 174–9; Warburton 1997: 303–9). While it was once assumed that Papyrus Harris I was Ramesses III's confirmation of the total landholdings of Egyptian temples, it is likely that these properties constitute the new donations made by the king personally, specifically for the benefit of his own mortuary temple at Medinet Habu (Haring 1997: 174–9, 188–91). For this interpretation to be feasible, the lands of royal funerary foundations would have returned to the Crown at the death of their founder for potential redistribution or reassignment to new foundations as the current ruler saw fit (Schaedel 1936: 48; Kees 1961: 66–7). While Papyrus Harris I cannot be used to confirm the statement of Diodorus (I, 21.73) that the temples of Egypt possessed one-third of Egypt's land, the continuous reassignment of cultivable land through royal gift to select foundations is evidence of the continued pre-eminence of the temples of Egypt as landowners (Kees 1961: 67).

The Wilbour Papyrus, an enumeration of assessed plots of agricultural land in Middle Egypt under the charge of temples and secular institutions in year 4 of Ramesses V, provides evidence of a harvest tax (*shemu*) payable on small plots of privately held land as well as large institutionally cultivated estates (Gardiner 1941–8; Faulkner 1952; Menu 1970; Janssen 1986; Katary 1989; Haring 1997: 283–326; Warburton 1997: 309–12). Smallholders of myriad occupations and titles ascribed plots in apportioning domains, most frequently three or five *arouras* in size, paid dues on their crop calculated on only a tiny portion of the area of their plot, usually consisting of *qayet* or ordinary arable land, at a fixed rate of 1½ sacks per *aroura*. Plots of five *arouras* were large enough to support a family of some eight persons. By contrast, larger tracts of cultivated land in non-apportioning domains worked by field-labourers (*ihuty*) under the authority of institutional staff (*ihuty* as 'agent of the fisc') incurred a tax of 30 per cent of the harvest where the yield was calculated as five sacks per *aroura* of normal arable land, the remaining 70 per cent returned as wages to support the cultivators (also *ihuty*). Tracts of institutionally cultivated 'fresh land' (*nekheb*) and 'elevated land' (*tjeni*) were assessed at 10 and 7½ sacks per *aroura*, respectively. Also detailed in Wilbour are holdings of Crown land (*kha-ta* or *khato*-land of pharaoh), located upon the domains of institutions, supervised by institutional staff in the role of 'agent of the fisc' and cultivated by field-labourers.

In addition to providing valuable details of the land assessment, the Wilbour Papyrus describes an agrarian regime in which temples and secular institutions administered cultivable land as agents of the state rather than as competitors undermining state authority. Debate as to whether the *shemu* of these fields should be interpreted as taxes payable to the state or as rents accruing to institutions is moot in light of the fact that institutional landholdings cannot be distinguished from state property. The granaries of temples functioned as subunits of the state granary. The institutions named in the Wilbour Papyrus comprised, in effect, a specialized unit of the government with a mandate to administer, cultivate and collect grain revenues.

The Turin Taxation Papyrus, from year 12 of Ramesses XI, further illustrates the interconnectedness of landowning institutions and the state (Gardiner 1948: xiii–xiv, 35–44; 1941). Here the scribe of the necropolis Dhutmose sets out to collect grain revenues (*shemu*) owing to the government by various institutions and individuals for use as payment of wages for the necropolis workmen at Deir el-Medina (Warburton

1997: 311–13). The receipt of the grain by the mayor of the City and the chantresses of Amun and the storage of the same in Theban granaries (Figure 14.5) reveals the overlap between civil and religious authorities. Other Ramesside texts detailing the collection and transportation of grain revenues for the state, such as Papyrus Amiens and its other half Papyrus Baldwin, Papyrus Louvre 3171, the Griffith and Louvre fragments and Papyrus British Museum 10447, confirm the picture of a closely interwoven network of bureaucrats and agencies engaged in revenue collection, transportation and redistribution (Gardiner 1941, 1948; Gasse 1988; Janssen 2004).

The difficulties faced by a farmer (*ihuty*) in meeting his tax assessment come to life in a collection of model letters used in the training of scribes. Among the Late Egyptian Miscellanies are a number of compositions where the burden of taxation borne by cultivators is dramatically described (Gardiner 1937; Caminos 1954). Papyrus Anastasi V (15, 6 ff.) describes the plight of the hapless farmer when the tax-collector

Figure 14.5   The granaries of the Ramesseum (from Kemp 1989b: pl.6).

195

arrives to collect the harvest-tax (*shemu*). Unable to hand over the tax, the farmer is beaten and thrown into a well. His wife is bound, his children fettered and his neighbours abandon him to his misery. This dire portrait of the overburdened farmer is certainly exaggerated in order to glorify the privileged status of the scribe since, as the letter writer goes on to remind the reader, 'he who works in writing is not taxed; he has no dues (*shayet*) to pay'. Devoid of the exaggeration demanded by the genre of the letters, the hapless farmer appears to be independent and relatively free of outside interference (Eyre 1994: 110).

Taxpayer's rage permeates a letter from Meron, Mayor of Elephantine, to the Chief Taxing Master Menmaatranakht (around the reign of Ramesses XI) (Gardiner 1951). In Papyrus Valençay I, Meron vents his outrage about grain taxes he is said to owe on a plot of land for which he denies responsibility. Meron claims that the liability for taxes rests with 'private persons' or 'freemen' (*nemehu*) 'who pay gold to the Treasury of Pharaoh'. He maintains that were this land his responsibility, this grain would be justifiably exacted (*shedi*) from him. Meron's complaints are not without parallel. In the model letter Papyrus Bologna 1094 5, 8–7, 1, a prophet of the House of Seth complains about 'the excessive money' he had been ordered to pay on both the *khato*-land of Pharaoh he administers and the holdings of his own temple, declaring, 'It is not my due tax (*heter*) at all!' And further, in Papyrus Anastasi V (27, 3–7), a retainer bemoans, 'It is I whom you have found to penalize (*saha*) among the entire body of taxpayers (?) (*shet*).' Complaints, denials and outright evasion were strategies well known to the New Kingdom revenue collector.

Meron maintains that smallholders called *nemehu* were the guilty parties and that these *nemehu* made regular payments directly to the Treasury of Pharaoh as would be the case with independent 'owners' with tax liability, regardless of who actually cultivated the land. The Treasury of Pharaoh is also mentioned as the recipient of taxes on landed wealth in the Memphite tomb-chapel of Mes in the colourful story of litigation concerning a land grant made by King Ahmose to Mes's ancestor, the ship-master Neshi, as a reward for valour in the war against the Hyksos (Gardiner 1905; Gaballa 1977). The estate, the exact size of which is not known, was handed down generation to generation until the reign of Horemheb when three rival branches of the family contested rights of trusteeship over it. The inscription confirms the New Kingdom custom of pharaohs awarding plots for cultivation to veterans, a custom that continued throughout the Ramesside Period on the evidence of the Wilbour Papyrus where military men hold small plots as virtual private property. According to the Inscription of Mes, documentation of the payment of taxes by smallholders was kept in the record offices of the Treasury of Pharaoh and the Granary of Pharaoh in the national capital. It was to these offices that one appealed to contest rights of ownership. Neshi's property is described as his 'share' (*peseshet*) or 'division', the same terminology that occurs in the Wilbour Papyrus in the headings of paragraphs that list the plots of individual smallholders on 'apportioning domains' (*remenyt pesh*) of temples and secular institutions.

Complex terminology used to specify various levies demanded by the state on individuals, groups, institutions and towns for unnamed beneficiaries occurs in fragmentary tax lists on the verso of the Royal Canon of Turin from the reign of Ramesses II (Gardiner 1959: pls 5–9; Helck 1972a; Janssen 1975a: 173–7). *Baku*, 'work', for example, applied to taxes in kind on the non-agricultural products of fishermen, natron-workers and mat-makers. *Tep-djeret* 'head-hand' may have denoted a tax obligation of lesser officials such as controllers, deputies and Medjay (police). *Shedyt* seems to have denoted the 'exaction' of a tax levy, whereas *shayet*, 'dues', occurs in such expressions as 'dues of the staff', 'the precise exaction' and 'his yearly dues: 1 cow'. The term *heter/heteri* occurs in such phrases as 'exact levy' and 'the levy that is upon them'. The use of *heter/heteri* in this context is different from the use of *heter/heteri* in documents from the village of necropolis workmen at Deir el-Medina where the term signifies deliveries of the workmen's wages rather than dues paid out by them. The flexibility of the terminology shows that levies paid to the state might become the income of its dependants (Janssen 1975a: 176).

Also relevant is the Ramesside Bilgai Stela from the delta concerning the estate of a chapel dedicated to Amun of Usermaatra-setepenra (Ramesses II) where a Commander of the Fortress of the Sea declares that he is 'an officer advantageous to his lord, paying (his) harvest-tax (*shemu*) in full and (his) dues (*shayet*) in full' (Gardiner 1912). The immense satisfaction the official derived from his accomplishment is clear from his boast: 'Great was my excess of *shemu* and *shayet* (paid), ten times greater than my [annual] levy (*heteri*) of *shemu* and *shayet*.'

The tomb biography of Amenhotep, the high priest of Amun whom Ramesses IX lavishly rewarded for his faithful service according to the famous reward scene in the Karnak temple of Amun, is also a valuable source of information on taxes (Lefèbvre 1929: pl. II; Černý 1975: 628–9). Amenhotep's tomb biography proclaims that harvest-tax (*shemu*), dues (*shayet*) and labour (*baku*) of the people of the house of Amun-Ra, King of the Gods, were under his authority (Warburton 1997: 321–2). Amenhotep's tax-collecting authority derives from both his rank as high priest of the largest landowning institution and his membership of one of the most powerful ecclesiastical families of the day, a family that exerted supreme authority over the finances of the temple of Amun and of the pharaoh himself in monopolizing the offices of Steward of Amun and Chief Taxing Master. Thus, while high priests continued to wield immense authority as the administrative heads of vast estates, one whose family members occupied the top financial offices of the state had the inside track to vast power and the acquisition of great personal wealth.

The frequency of the occurrence of the term *baku* for a person's 'work' or 'labour' in the New Kingdom indicates that the corvée continued to play an important role in the economy. The Nauri Decree mentions the payments of honey and wine as the '*baku* of my people'. The term *beh* in the Nauri Decree denotes compulsory labour for cultivating and harvesting fields, the work of weavers of a state institution, as well as quarry workers and construction labourers (Helck 1955b: 1374.9; 1958: 1962.15). The word *beret* in Nauri may also denote corvée labour. It also occurs in Papyrus Anastasi II (8, 2) where a stablemaster's maidservant is made to serve in the *beryt* 'hired gang' (?) (Caminos 1954: 55 (8, 2)). A reference later in the text to the work of a stablemaster's retainer in Troia (modern Turah) may be an allusion to the quarrying activities of conscriptees.

Foreign lands conquered by Egypt contributed to the general levy in paying *inu*, 'tribute' or '(obligatory) gift' or even 'additions'. Ineni, architect of Thutmose I, describes the '*inu* of all foreign lands' that was the annual levy (*heter*) the pharaoh exacted on behalf of the temple of Amun (Sethe 1905: 70.4–6). Hatshepsut refers to the labour of foreign lands as their annual levy for the House of Amun (Sethe

1905: 331.14–16). As more and more foreign territory came under Egypt's dominion during the empire-building of the New Kingdom, tribute in kind or labour increased exponentially. Once they were part of the Empire, foreign lands and settlements shared the responsibility of Egyptian towns and provinces to contribute to the annual levy as directed by their local authorities (Redford 1972: 150; Bleiberg 1996). From Asiatic Retenu in the east to Nubia in the south, tribute poured into Egypt, bringing silver, gold, lapis lazuli, precious stones, chariots, horses, cattle and small game as well as people to provide labour.

In the fifth year of his reign, the Libyan pharaoh Shoshenq I was required to adjudicate a heated dispute concerning land and water rights in the Dakhla Oasis where the evidence of land-registers going back about 80 years was called into account (Gardiner 1933; Edwards 1982: 548; Kitchen 1986 [1973]: §247). The inscription suggests that the owner of a well enjoyed title to the land it flooded, and affirms the private ownership of the land and water at issue. Another stela of Shoshenq I celebrates the king's intervention in the affairs of the temple of Herishef in Heracleopolis when he learned from Nimlot, his son and army-commander, that the customary tribute for the daily ox-offering from the towns and villages of Heracleopolis had been neglected (Redford 1972: 153–4; Edwards 1982: 542–3; Kitchen 1986 [1973]: §247). Shoshenq restored the 'levy [*tep en heter*] throughout the year, (now) and forever', dedicating 365 oxen and praising Nimlot's own donation of 60 oxen. The king's generosity may reflect awareness of Heracleopolis's significance as a locus of potential political discontent (Myśliwiec 2000: 47–8; Edwards 1982: 543). The resemblance of Shoshenq's financial scheme to that of Solomon suggests that Solomon used the Egyptian system as a template for the administration of institutions of the Hebrew kingdom based upon familiarity with Egyptian administrative practices (Redford 1972: 153–6).

A jubilee inscription from year 22 of Osorkon II, inscribed on the portal of his new court in the temple of Bastet at Bubastis in Lower Egypt, appears to give tax-exempt status to Thebes and her people in gratitude to Amun for this auspicious occasion (Naville 1892). The inscription suggests continuity in government fiscal policy exempting the temples of Egypt from tax going back to Amenhotep III (Naville 1892: 4; Grimal 1992: 325). However, the overwhelming resemblance of the text to a jubilee inscription from Amenhotep III's temple at Soleb in Nubia renders the historical significance of the Bubastis inscription suspect (Kitchen 1986 [1973]: §280).

Over the 21st to 24th Dynasties, Libyans became entrenched in the western delta, the oases of the Western Desert and the zone of agricultural land between Memphis and Heracleopolis, undergoing Egyptianization and contributing to a cosmopolitan society in the north (Taylor 2000: 339–41). Evidence of agricultural activity in the south is gleaned from Papyrus Reinhardt, a cadastral survey of 21st or 22nd Dynasty date relating to fields of the Amun temple of Thebes in the tenth nome of Upper Egypt in the hands of various functionaries (*ihet*) or cultivated by corvée labour (*ihet-beh* or *beh*) (Vleeming 1993). Other papyri of proximate date relating to fields of the Domain of Amun at Karnak specify *khato*-land, donated land (*henek*) and *nemeh*-fields cultivated in a landholding regime similar, perhaps, to that described in the Wilbour Papyrus (Gasse 1988; Katary 2006). Donation stelae of the 22nd and 23rd Dynasties detail agricultural lands granted to temples as wealth-producing endowments for funerary cults and also testify to newly undertaken agricultural enterprises in the delta, the base of Libyan power (Taylor 2000: 351).

The 25th Dynasty Victory Stela of Pi(ye) at Gebel Barkal in Kush recounts his successful invasion and conquest of Egypt in the face of insurrection by a northern coalition (Gardiner 1935a; Lichtheim 1980a: 66–84; Grimal 1981; 1992: 335–9). The royal decree provides the speech of allegiance by Peftjawybast, the Libyan ruler of Heracleopolis, according to which Heracleopolis would contribute to the general annual levy to supply the house (*aryt*) of Pi(ye). Thus, the maintenance of royal residences by the general annual levy continued into the Third Intermediate Period under foreign rulers.

The reign of Taharqo witnessed the restoration of the New Kingdom temple of Kawa in Nubia to its former grandeur as well as the building of a new temple to Amun (Macadam 1949, 1955). Taharqo assigned the wives of the chieftains of Lower Egypt to service in the great temple. By bringing Libyan and other Lower Egyptian captives into the service of his Nubian temples, Taharqo demonstrated victory over the rebellious delta princes who continued to agitate against Kushite control of Lower Egypt (Arkell 1961: 132; James 1991: 697).

Just as Pi(ye) levied a tax on Heracleopolis to supply victuals for his own house and harems, so too did Psamtik I, founder of the 26th Dynasty, requisition produce of occupied foreign territory to support his court according to the Louvre Stela from year 52 (Redford 1972: 149). This practice has its precedent in two passages in the Edict of Horemheb concerning similar levies on goods and services for royal residences (Helck 1958: 2144.10–11, 2146.5–10). Moreover, the late 19th Dynasty Gurob Fragments refer to fish requisitioned (*heter*) from a local official for the Harem of Mi-wer (Gardiner 1948: 15).

According to a great stela found at Karnak, Nitocris, daughter of Psamtik I, was adopted in year 9 by the Kushite God's Wife of Amun Shepenwepet II and her successor Amenirdis II as their rightful heir in a great diplomatic coup celebrating the recognition of Psamtik's suzerainty over Thebes and the reunification of Upper and Lower Egypt (Caminos 1964). The Adoption Stela of Nitocris details the wealth lavished upon the future God's Wife, including food offerings from delta temples and the temple at Karnak and the royal endowment of 2,230.21 acres of cultivable fields in seven nomes in the northern part of Upper Egypt and four nomes of Lower Egypt (James 1991: 709; Myśliwiec 2000: 112–16). By putting so much land at his daughter's disposal, Psamtik I made certain that she would outshine any previous God's Wife of Amun in the vastness of her wealth.

Further evidence of the Saite donation of sizeable estates to temples comes from the Mit Rahina Stela of Apries which celebrates a substantial tax-free perpetual endowment to the temple of Ptah at Memphis consisting of an estate with cultivable lands, serfs (*meret*) tied to the land, cattle and produce (Gunn 1927; Lloyd 1983: 302, 315). While the Crown continued to supply real estate and the labour, the priesthoods remained privileged landowners of no less importance. Members of the military, largely descended from Libyan mercenaries and appearing frequently as smallholders in the Wilbour Papyrus, constituted the third major class of free landowners during the Late Period as also in the Ptolemaic Period when Greek sources refer to them as *machimoi* (warriors) (Lloyd 1983: 301, 309–10, 327–8; Katary 1999).

The level of prosperity achieved under Saite rulers was recalled by Herodotus (II.177.1) when he commented on the high productivity of the land as a result of sound Egyptian agricultural practices. Of course, the occurrence of high Niles played no small role in this prosperity.

An inscription from Naukratis has been interpreted as commemorating Nectanebo I's imposition of a 10 per cent tax on goods both imported into Naukratis and produced there for the benefit of the temple of the Saite goddess Neith to whom the founder of the 30th Dynasty attributed his success (Gunn 1943; Braun 1982: 41; Lloyd 1983: 294, 329). Naukratis was the delta port city selected by the Saite pharaoh Amasis for the amalgamation of the trading activities of wealthy Greek and Carian merchants, granting the city the privileged status of a chartered city which, in turn, would respect the authority of pharaoh (Braun 1982: 37–43; Grimal 1992: 363). Nectanebo I's tax applied to all Aegean imports entering Egypt through Naukratis, including gold, silver, timber and worked wood products. The temple of Neith, however, may in fact have received only one-tenth of the proceeds of whatever the tax was (Lichtheim 1980a: 87, 89 n. 10). Ptolemaic rulers put into effect a 10 per cent levy according to the Famine Stela from the Island of Sehel, at the First Cataract (Barguet 1953; Kees 1961: 320–1). This inscription claims that after a seven-year famine, Djoser in thanks gave Khnum of Elephantine a gift of a large Nubian estate with an income derived from the taxes levied on its harvests, fisheries, cattle herds and natural resources. Shrewd priests of the temple of Khnum created this fiction to safeguard their interests against priests of Isis of Philae who had come to have patronage over the same territory.

The donation of tax-free estates to temples under the Saites continued into the Persian Period as indicated by the Petition of Petiese where it is made clear that Amun's temple at Teudzoi (el-Hiba) received extensive royal landholdings, the priests granted income and often land-allotments on temple estates (Griffith 1909; Lloyd 1983: 302, 307–9). Thus temple estates remained an important component of the agricultural economy without necessarily contributing to state coffers. However, there was no lack of royal interference in the financial affairs of temples, such as that of Nectanebo I's son Teos, who, in order to underwrite his support of a satraps' revolt against Artaxerxes II and subdue Syria, foolishly imposed heavy taxes (Myśliwiec 2000: 169).

The annual land leases that proliferate from Saite to Ptolemaic times detail the land tenure of smallholders of middle social status, such as soldiers, scribes, priests and women, who possessed plots from one to ten *arouras* situated on temple holdings or cult endowment land, recalling land tenure in the Wilbour Papyrus (Lloyd 1983: 309–10; Eyre 1994: 129–30; Katary 2000, 2001). Lessors used the services of lessees of similar middle social status in sub-contract arrangements where materials and labour were provided by the tenant who paid the lessor with a share of the harvest. Registers of the harvest tax were concerned with identifying the party bearing tax liability.

When Alexander conquered Egypt in 332 BC, Cleomenes of Naukratis exercised authority as 'administrator' (*dioiketes*) to force the priesthoods to pay double taxes, and maintained a ruthless ironclad monopoly over grain exports to the Aegean (Turner 1984: 122–3). When Ptolemy I assumed rule of Egypt after Alexander's death, he delegated administrative authority to Greeks and Macedonians but retained fiscal and bureaucratic aspects of ancient Egyptian agriculture, including land surveys and crop schedules (Crawford 1971: 139). Native Egyptian peasants continued in their traditional roles as cultivators and providers of corvée labour. While land reclamation under the early Ptolemies trebled the cultivable land in the Fayum, and experimentation with crops sown and land management followed, endemic structural problems in the Ptolemaic regime led to a failure to sustain the early level of economic development (Thompson 1984: 365–9; 1999a, 1999b; Manning 2003: 232).

The Egyptian countryside remained a complex mosaic of different classes of land to which variable rates of taxation applied. New patterns of landholding notable in the Fayum depression, which included gift-estates to wealthy Greeks and the settling of Greek soldiers as *cleruchs* on the land, coexisted with the pharaonic tradition of small-scale landholding on temple lands, notable in the Theban area, with the right to pass these holdings down in families. Nevertheless, there was no development of a formal state system of private ownership or the means to enforce it: a structural problem of the Ptolemaic state. Temples retained their privileges and status in land management but the Ptolemies exercised supervision over their finances (J. Manning 1999: 100–1). Over time, the Ptolemies struggled to find tenants for the cultivable land available and were obliged to adopt strategies of land grants, auction and tax reduction to keep land under cultivation: a situation of rural poverty amid a possible surplus of cultivable land. While the central coordination of locally organized economies allowed the flourishing of local government under the management of local elites, it would be the Romans who would open a new chapter in the history of Egyptian land tenure by guaranteeing private ownership in law (Manning 2003: 226–34; Thompson 1984: 369–70).

PART IV

SOCIETIES

CHAPTER FIFTEEN

GENDER AND SEXUALITY

T.G. Wilfong

The study of gender and sexuality is essential for an understanding of ancient Egyptian society, but these subjects have been slow to enter the mainstream of Egyptological research, and such work that has been done has, for the most part, been of the most basic, descriptive kind. But gender and sexuality are interrelated aspects of ancient Egyptian society that richly repay the application of the wide body of theoretical methodologies that have grown up in the wider study of these areas.

GENDER

'Gender' is often used and understood as a synonym for 'sex' in the biological sense or used euphemistically for 'women'; both biological sex and women are important parts of what makes up gender, but they are not the only components. Gender can be defined, in its most basic sense, as the set of social constructions relating to, arising from and imposed upon biological sex. The study of this wider category of gender first appeared as a direct development of feminist research devoted to restoring women to a history from which they had often been excluded. Feminist historians quickly came to realize that this was not necessarily enough: women needed to be considered within a larger context of gendered relations and roles, and the basic category of 'women' itself could be simplistic and reductive, as its meaning constantly shifted and adapted in response to social, cultural and even biological factors. A central moment in gender studies came with the publication of feminist historian Joan Scott's 'Gender: a useful category of historical analysis' in 1986; the priorities that this essay outlines have proven extremely prescient in terms of the concerns of scholarship on gender today. Scott already envisioned gender as part of a larger group of factors (including class or status, race or ethnicity, and age) essential for historians in any field. Although scholarship on gender has gone far beyond the programme outlined in Scott's article, it remains deeply indebted to Scott's insights and foresights; it should be essential reading and rereading for those who study gender in ancient Egypt.

Ancient Egypt was a highly gendered society: the Egyptians presented themselves in text and image in very specifically gendered ways, and the material culture of ancient Egypt reveals a complex system of gendered divisions. The very language that the Egyptians spoke and wrote was heavily gendered, with masculine and feminine substantives, pronouns and markers in a wide range of forms. The texts that the Egyptians wrote provide much of the important evidence for gender, helped by the language and writing systems' gender-specific nature, and even by apparent gendered differences in language use (as in, e.g., Sweeney 1998). The visual representations that the Egyptians made of themselves are gendered in a variety of ways: the physical details of biological sex, but also cultural gender markers (clothing, hairstyle, accessories, attributes of gendered occupations), a gendered code for skin colour (generally dark reddish brown for men, yellow or light brown for women) and a status-based size coding that often reflects gender as well. The archaeological record reveals complex and subtle gendered differences in the material culture – gendered artefacts, practices and spaces, as well as the physical remains of the ancient Egyptians themselves, which show a wealth of detail about the impact of gendered differences on health and burial practice (for the latter, see, e.g., Meskell 1999). This wide array of evidence for gender in ancient Egypt, though, is frequently ambiguous and often hard to interpret as a whole; it has been more common to focus on a single area of investigation: women in ancient Egypt. The central work in this regard remains Gay Robins's *Women in Ancient Egypt* (1993), founded on the pioneering work of earlier scholars, and carried further in the years since its first publication by a wider range of Egyptologists.

Women

The study of women in ancient Egypt is an appropriate place to begin any wider investigation of gender: as far back as Herodotus, ancient Greek and Roman historians commented on the position of women in Egypt as unusual and different from the situation in their own worlds, and characteristic of ancient Egyptian society. Compared to the other contemporary Mediterranean civilizations, women did occupy a uniquely visible and autonomous position in Egypt, and this was considered a distinctive characteristic of Egypt even in ancient times. As a result, there has tended to be much generalization about, and idealization of, women's position in ancient Egypt, especially in the more popular literature. A detailed examination of the Egyptian evidence, though, reveals a decidedly mixed picture of women's status and roles, which varied widely by status and individual circumstance, and changed over time.

Ancient Egypt was, at its core, a male-dominated society; women were excluded from its administration and its rule in all but the most exceptional circumstances. Royal women attained their status by a relationship (mother, wife, sister, daughter) to a king, and the few women who managed to rule as king did so (at least initially) as regent to a young son or brother and almost certainly with the support of senior (male) members of the royal court. The best-known example of a woman who ruled as king is, of course, Hatshepsut, the daughter and widow of kings who ruled as regent for her stepson Thutmose III in the 18th Dynasty. The visual and textual representations of Hatshepsut give an idea of the exceptional nature of her position as king: the varying representations of her with female or male body and attributes, the confused (or deliberately complex) use of male and female referents in texts, the role of her daughter Neferura in fulfilling some of the traditional duties of the King's

Figure 15.1 Gilded plaster and inlaid funerary mask fragment of indefinite gender, first century BC–first century AD (Kelsey Museum of Archaeology, University of Michigan KM 4651).

Great Wife, all attest to the challenges Hatshepsut faced in fitting her rule into a male paradigm. Similar challenges were faced and addressed in similar ways nearly 1,500 years later by Cleopatra VII, who acted as regent for her brothers and son successively; her rule was further complicated, however, by the volatile international political situation of her time.

Royal and elite women could, and did, occupy other official positions of power, in addition to whatever unofficial influences they were able to exert. The office of God's Wife of Amun, for example, instituted in the early New Kingdom, gave great resources and influence to its holder and increased in power through the Third Intermediate Period (Graefe 1981). Elite women occupied formal priestly offices in earlier periods, but by the New Kingdom women's participation in temple cult had been channelled into the positions of 'musician' to a particular god or goddess, a title held by many elite women well into the Late Period (Onstine 2005). The interpretation of apparent scribal titles held by a few elite women in both the Middle Kingdom and Late Period, however, is subject to some debate. In general, the end of the New Kingdom seems to mark a transitional period in the status of elite women in Egypt (and probably, at least to a lesser extent, women in general); women become less closely identified with husbands or male relatives, especially in funerary contexts.

Elite women are, of course, the best-documented women of ancient Egypt but are, in many ways, the least representative. The majority of women in ancient Egypt at all levels of society had, as primary duties, the administration of a household, however humble, and the care of children. But many women also worked within and outside the home in a variety of endeavours, the most common being farming. In earlier periods, women are associated with textile production, although this is a profession that shifts to men by the New Kingdom. Conversely, in the New Kingdom, we find women participating actively in riverbank markets as sellers and traders of commodities made in the home (Eyre 1998). Women also worked in a variety of service occupations, and often served as slaves.

Whatever their status, women in ancient Egypt shared some common roles and expectations. Most ancient Egyptian women were expected to marry and have children. Motherhood was an archetypal role for women, with the strong precedent and model of the goddess Isis as a guide and an aid. Much Egyptian medicine and magic was related, directly or indirectly, to facilitating motherhood in some way. Marriage was a core gendered relationship in the lives of almost all ancient Egyptians; women and men of all levels of Egyptian society were expected to marry. However, marriage itself was a relatively informal relationship that might be best described as cohabitation with intent to reproduce, and was documented mostly by contracts to secure property or ensure support of women (especially in Demotic documents of the later periods). Parents were often involved in initiating and facilitating marriages, which tended to take place within local class and occupational groups, but both men and women could have input in their own choice of partner. Women had a number of property and inheritance rights in the context of marriage. Divorce was, at least in the periods for which we have good documentation, relatively easy and common, and its frequency could lead to a complex set of relationships from successive marriages. In spite of the relative informality of marriage and ease of divorce, the married household was a central social unit in ancient Egypt. There were women who lived independently of these expectations of marriage and motherhood, but they were rare.

The wide range of material from the Ramesside Period workers' village of Deir el-Medina provides a useful picture of how widely women's status and roles could vary across different bodies of evidence in a specific period and context (this material is surveyed in Toivari-Viitala 2001). Documentary texts show women in a great variety of active roles in the community in spite of their relative lack of status within the official workers' hierarchy and administration. Women bought, sold, transacted business, owned property and disposed of it on their own or through male relatives. They provided crucial support services to the official endeavour of the village (building the royal tomb), while also participating in the thriving unofficial economy of the town. Although barred from priestly office, women held the office of 'musician' dedicated to a particular deity, and also seem to have performed less official magical duties as 'wise women' (McDowell 1999: 114–15). Within the family, women raised children and administered the activities of the house, but also had some say in the composition of these household units by their choices in marriage and divorce. But these same documents also show some fundamental inequalities in women's positions in the village; women were excluded from the official ranks of the scribes and artisans, and had no direct say in the administration of the village, no direct role in the legal settlement of disputes. Although possessing theoretical autonomy, women were, in fact, constrained by the social order, as seen in the letters relating to cases of adultery and other social disruptions. The documents also show women to have been subject to violence and rape at the hands of men, with ambiguous systems of protection and recourse. Both textual and archaeological evidence show women's property concentrated in practical items for home use, more often passed on by will rather than taken to the grave; women's burials tend to contain fewer grave goods than men's (Meskell 1998b). Literary texts circulating at Deir el-Medina likewise highlight these contradictions of women's status and roles. A number of the surviving stories show women in a decidedly misogynistic light – either scheming and deceitful or passive and maladroit. The wisdom literature – instructions to elite men – reaffirms a system in which women are considered either as good wives or bad influences; the instructions sometimes recommend respect for women, but bear underlying assumptions of women's untrustworthiness. Contrast with these texts the love songs that survive from Deir el-Medina and celebrate women, love and desire. Although some of these can be seen as objectifying women into idealized (and unthreatening) erotic abstractions, a number of the love poems are remarkable for their specificity and approach to women as equal partners in relationships. Indeed, some of the poems are written in women's voices and speak of women's desires in such a way as to suggest to some scholars that they might have been written by women. Taken together, the literature in circulation (and presumably read aloud to a wider audience than those who could read) at Deir el-Medina reveals a popular culture rife with mixed messages about, and to, women, which fit with their mixed position in Deir el-Medina society, revealed by the evidence of their everyday lives.

Given the high status and position that some Egyptian women occupied relative to women in other ancient cultures, it is easy to project modern attitudes and aspirations onto the women of ancient Egypt. Recent popular writing on the subject, in particular, seems to want ancient Egyptian women to be just like 'us', to reflect modern western ideals and aspirations for the equality and importance of women. But we must guard against this tendency, because it can lead to distortion of the evidence. The majority of women that we know from Egyptian sources are elites, and most of these high elites; they are exceptional in many ways, and it is impossible to generalize about women's lives as a whole from the lives of elite women. Egyptian literature, especially in later periods, sometimes shows a strain of misogyny that is hard to reconcile with the status of women reflected in, for example, documentary sources. In addition to the New Kingdom literary texts already mentioned, one finds in Demotic literature an ongoing emphasis on the dichotomy of 'good' and 'bad' women: one might note the female characters in Setna I or, even more explicitly, the tales of 'good' and 'bad' women in the recently published Petese Stories in the Carlsberg Papyri (Ryholt 2005). The archaeological record shows examples of violence against women that fit modern profiles for domestic abuse as well as profound inequities in the burials of women and men. In spite of women's unique position there, ancient Egypt was still, very much, a male-dominated society.

Men

As a result of the entirely necessary attempts to retrieve hitherto neglected evidence for the lives of women from the textual, archaeological and representational records, the roles of men, maleness and masculinities in ancient Egypt have gone relatively unexamined. One could, of course, justifiably argue that much of past Egyptology was, in effect, a study of ancient Egyptian men, but the treatment of 'men' as a problematized category that is important for a wider understanding of gender in Egyptian society remains to be accomplished. In recent years, the study of men within a wider context of gender studies has come to some prominence (usually under the rubric of 'masculinity studies'), but this approach is not without its potential pitfalls. Concentration on 'men' as a gendered category can be a problematic issue; some feminist scholars have been wary of the newer field of 'masculinity studies' as having at least the potential to undo decades of progress in feminist scholarship and reinforce outmoded masculinist paradigms. There is, however, an emerging body of theoretical literature on issues relating to men from a gendered perspective that addresses these concerns and makes it clear that masculinity studies has great potential. Given the predominance of men in many aspects of ancient Egyptian life, masculinity studies has much to offer the study of gender in ancient Egypt.

There were many privileges and advantages of being a man in ancient Egyptian society; indeed, the category of 'man' was largely a normative one in ancient Egypt – men and men's concerns dominated Egyptian culture and were largely assumed to be the norm. But men's positions in Egyptian society were subject to a wide range of instabilities and anxieties: economic class, social position, ethnicity and other factors could affect any man's situation. Men were subject to gendered constraints and expectations in Egyptian society just as complex as those for women: there were things that men did and did not do that reflected and affected Egyptian concepts of maleness and masculinity. The gendered expectations for kings (to rule, to father a male heir to succeed, to play the roles of both Osiris and Horus) might differ in the specifics from those of his officials, his scribes and his farmers, but there were certain common elements throughout. Men at all economic levels were expected to marry, beget children and support a family; men were expected to fill their roles and positions in society, to carry out certain duties, as their fathers did before them.

Again, the example of Deir el-Medina is instructive. The community was administered, run and guarded by men to facilitate the work of men on the royal tombs. Men headed household units, supported families and possessed more resources than women; men had family tombs built for themselves in which they, again, dominated their 'house of eternity'. The majority of the extensive textual material at Deir el-Medina was written by men for men, and shows the community to mirror the male-dominated society of Egypt as a whole. But some of the Deir el-Medina material suggests the instabilities of men's positions as well. Documents of criminal cases contain accusations against men that reflect specifically male issues in the community, such as the charges against the foreman Paneb in Papyrus Salt 124 that include assault, theft and rape. The literature from the community that shows women in negative ways may do so in reflection of male anxieties about their relationships to women. Even the so-called Turin Erotic Papyrus (Omlin 1973), containing scenes of men having sex with women, might at first glance seem to glorify the sexual prowess of men, but also may be satirizing and critiquing men's behaviour. The extensive dream book from Deir el-Medina in Papyrus Chester Beatty III is an extraordinary catalogue of specifically male dreams that could reveal a wealth of male anxieties and aspirations (Szpakowska 2003).

Other genders

A superficial survey of the evidence might appear to show gender in ancient Egypt as a fixed dichotomy of male and female, but in fact the situation was much more complicated. Although gender categories in general usually followed along the lines of biological sex (itself not always so clear-cut), there was some latitude for movement between them. Thus, in the New Kingdom Tale of the Two Brothers, Bata cuts off his own penis and later tells his wife 'I am a woman just like you.' This single sentence is an extraordinary statement on Egyptian understandings of gender, the implications of which remain to be fully explored. Later sources in Coptic tell of comparable transformations of women into men; in the story of Hilaria, this process first involves superficial changes through cross-dressing, but the physical pressures of ascetic practice later affect physical changes (reduction of breasts and cessation of menstruation) that allow Hilaria to be seen as male by her fellow monks (Wilfong 1998). Otherwise stably gendered individuals will sometimes show incongruous markers, such as the occasional representations of the goddess Mut with an erect penis. But further, separate intermediate or 'third' gender categories also did exist in ancient Egyptian thought. Eunuchs, of course, were present in Egypt, as they were in cultures throughout the ancient Near East and Mediterranean, where they occupied a separate gender category. But eunuchs never held the special position in Egyptian society that they did elsewhere, although their real position in Egypt is becoming clearer thanks to recent research (Vittmann 2000: 167–73, with a distinction of eunuchs and castrates). The later periods, of course, saw the introduction of the Classical conception of the dual-sexed hermaphrodite into Egypt (Wilfong 1997: 87–9). But the Egyptians, themselves, had their own unique 'third' gender categories that are only now beginning to be identified and understood; Mark DePauw (2003) has identified a number of instances of apparent intermediate or ambiguous gender groups that will repay further study.

In looking for evidence for gender in ancient Egypt, it is easy to miss instances in which gender is ambiguous or altogether absent, although such cases do occur. The highly gendered Egyptian language, in fact, contains elements that are not grammatically gendered (the first person singular and plural pronouns, for example), although many such elements of 'common' gender can, in fact, be gendered in the writing with suitable male and female determinatives. Conversely, although representations of humans in ancient Egypt are almost always graphically gendered through details of body and costume, there is a significant subset of material that is deliberately ungendered. The New Kingdom anthropoid 'ancestor busts' from Deir el-Medina contain good examples of this, entirely understandable in that they served as stand-ins for deceased relatives both male and female. Burials of the dead are sometimes subject to gendered ambiguities or confusions (e.g. mismatched sex of coffins and bodies), although it is hard to know how many of these are the result of carelessness rather than intention. Funerary representations of the dead in an idealized state, particularly those of anthropoid coffins, often also show no signs of gender. The gender of the dead for much of ancient Egyptian history is subject to ambiguities of various kinds; although the dead participate in gendered activities and are frequently shown as gendered in two-dimensional art, the ambiguous three-dimensional figures and the wide reference to all dead by way of a male god's name (Osiris) may reflect some ambivalence that is as yet poorly understood. It is only in the later Ptolemaic and Roman Periods that the dead are referred to by gendered titles as 'Osiris' or 'Hathor', and certainly in these later periods the dead become more explicitly gendered and gender plays a greater part in their afterlife transformation than before (Riggs 2005: 41–94).

SEXUALITY

Modern understandings of sexuality are largely related to gender, although there is considerable debate whether this is equally the case in other times and other cultures. Much of the current study of sexuality is founded on work done on ancient Greek and Roman sources, specifically the central work of Michel Foucault, his multi-volume *Histoire de la sexualité* (1976–84), from which much current work on sexuality has arisen. As much of the theoretical literature is careful to reinforce, perhaps the greatest pitfall in the study of sexuality in the ancient world is to project modern attitudes and ideas onto the past. The majority of historians of sexuality argue, following Foucault, that sexuality is socially constructed rather than innate and that modern categories of sexuality as a marker of identity (heterosexual, homosexual, bisexual, etc.) did not exist in the ancient world. There is, however, some disagreement over whether there were comparable ancient categories of identity based on sexuality, particularly as related to gender. In any case, historians of sexuality and Egyptologists are a long way from a complete understanding of the construction of sexuality in ancient Egypt.

The study of sexuality in ancient Egypt is still at a relatively early stage, and much of the effort in this area until very recently has been devoted to attempts to identify and understand basic sources. This is a task complicated both by earlier Egyptologists' tendencies to suppress, veil or alter sexual imagery and material, and the frequently ambiguous or allusive nature of the sources themselves. The landmark

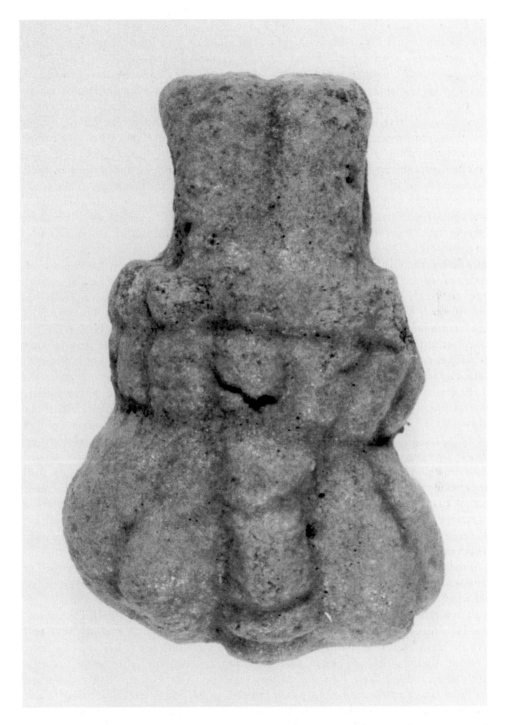

Figure 15.2 Faience phallic amulet from Karanis, University of Michigan excavations 1933, first–third centuries AD (Kelsey Museum of Archaeology, University of Michigan KM 24160). Reproduction approximately three times actual size.

works in this area for the pharaonic period were J.A. Omlin's (1973) publication of the so-called Turin Erotic Papyrus and Lise Manniche's groundbreaking survey *Sexual Life in Ancient Egypt* (1987), both of which exposed Egyptologists to a wealth of material hitherto uncollected. Dominic Montserrat's *Sex and Society in Graeco-Roman Egypt* (1996) carried this task further chronologically, but is an important source of theoretical approaches for earlier periods as well. In the past decade, a number of Egyptologists have begun to carry the work on sexuality in ancient Egypt further by concentrating on detailed analysis of specific bodies of evidence through the lens of modern theoretical approaches to sexuality.

The Egyptians themselves did not articulate the nature or limitations of their understandings of sexuality in a single source, and part of the challenge in the study of sexuality in ancient Egypt is bringing together very disparate and often highly ambiguous material. Our knowledge of the boundaries of Egyptian sexuality come largely from larger listings of prohibitive or negative statements, such as those found in the so-called 'Negative Confessions' of the Egyptian *Book of the Dead* (chapter 125). Most often couched in terms of male sexual behaviour, such texts are, for the modern historian of sexuality, frustratingly non-specific – general denials of sexual 'misbehaviour', with adultery and homosexual intercourse being the few behaviours that are routinely specified. Sexual taboos in a religious context, such as the listings of the 'abominations' of a particular god or the interdiction on sexual activity on a given day, can provide more detail, but are less widely applicable. So, rather than looking to such negative evidence, it might be more profitable to examine the kinds of sexual relations represented in Egyptian texts and art.

The most frequently represented kinds of sexual activity and relations, both explicitly and implicitly, in the Egyptian evidence are procreative. Certainly one ideal, if not always stated, result of sexual activity in ancient Egypt was the production of children as heirs and supporters of their parents. This ideal, procreative sexual relationship would take place within the context of a married relationship. Disruptions to married relationships through adultery were frowned upon, although adultery was punished more often through the social pressures and ostracism found in the documentary record than the murder of adulterers found in various literary texts. Adultery was a concern because of its potential to produce illegitimate succession and also its disruption to the household unit, by extension a disruption of *maat* itself; adultery was frequently associated with crime in documentary sources (Eyre 1984).

Procreative sexuality also became, by extension, a symbol or promoter of further fertility, and sexual images in ancient Egypt often held as much (if not more) emphasis on a generalized fertility as on specific acts of procreation. An elaborate and allusive visual vocabulary developed to symbolize and promote fertility in such contexts as tomb paintings and the decoration of houses (such as those at Deir el-Medina), and a wide range of textual sources promote or otherwise address fertility in some way. Fertility figures, whole or partial images of humans that emphasize sexual features, are common throughout Egyptian history (e.g. such offerings to Hathor described in Pinch 1993 or the numerous phallic figures in Manniche 1987), although their specific functions are not always understood.

Sex for pleasure could and did, in the Egyptian world-view, often overlap with procreative sex. In the absence of specific reference to sexual pleasure, as in the New Kingdom love poetry, it is not always possible to know if a specific text or image celebrates the pleasures of sex rather than (or in addition to) its procreative or fertility aspect. The so-called Turin Erotic Papyrus (Omlin 1973) is a good example of this ambiguity: does it celebrate the pleasures of sex, is it a work of pornography or eroticism, does it satirize on a general or specific level, or does it serve more than one function? Sexual activity before marriage was not stigmatized but was clearly not envisaged for reproduction; there was no emphasis on preserving virginity in ancient Egypt, but at least an implicit trend towards women avoiding motherhood before marriage (Johnson 2003). Egyptian sources describe or allude to a wide range of sexual activities that are not procreative, and Egyptians on occasions practised (or attempted to practise) contraception and abortion. These things suggest that the Egyptians were very much open to the possibilities and pleasures of non-reproductive sexual relations.

Modern theorists on sexuality in the classical world place a great amount of emphasis on the idea of sexual relations as asymmetrical relationships of power, and one can certainly see this in ancient Egypt, especially in relation to the gods. A good example can be seen in the Middle and New Kingdom accounts of the older god Seth's attempted or successful sexual penetration of the younger god Horus to show his domination, in the course of their long struggle over succession to the throne of Osiris. Seth's intentions are highlighted in the New Kingdom version by the trick played upon him; the scene before the gods in which the seed of each god is summoned is designed to demonstrate which god has successfully penetrated, and thus dominated, the other. Seth's career in these and other sources illustrates to some extent the paradigm of the historians of classical sexuality, whereby a free, adult male can sexually dominate anyone lower in status: women, younger males, slaves, etc. Indeed, most historians of ancient sexuality see power as a central factor in the choice of sexual object rather than any kind of gendered preference or orientation. While this may have been true for the ancient Egyptian gods, it is less clear that it applied to mortals as well; the sexuality of free, adult males in ancient Egypt seems to have been less wide-ranging than in classical Greece or Rome. Or do the various denials of heterosexual adultery and homosexual intercourse in the *Book of the Dead* suggest similar possibilities, but expressly prohibited ones?

Homosexual relations between men are noted in a variety of (mostly literary) contexts, always in a disapproving way, but these also indicate that such relationships did exist in ancient Egypt; Richard Parkinson's (1995) study of Middle Egyptian literary texts is the most significant recent work in this area. Whether the Egyptians had a concept analogous to what we know as 'homosexuality' remains unclear; the general consensus is that they did not, but later Coptic evidence suggests that there may have been some such category of behaviour if not identity (Wilfong 2002). Homosexual acts are prohibited in the *Book of the Dead*, and frowned upon in other sources, but homosexual relationships are occasionally represented. Perhaps the best example is the Middle Egyptian story of the affair between King Neferkara and his general Sisenet (the latter a man who, notably, did not have a wife). The story is far from approving of this relationship, which is kept secret, and it is likely that the king would have terminated it in the lost ending; still, it remains a rare representation of an ongoing relationship between two men. Other evidence is more ambiguous, and attempts to find homosexual relations between historical figures (Akhenaten and Smenkhara, Niankhkhnum and Khnumhotep) through purely representational evidence have not found wide scholarly acceptance. Apart from rare instances of negative confessions from the *Book of the Dead* adapted for female owners, there is very little evidence for sexual relations between women in the pharaonic period, although there is much relevant material from Egypt in the periods following (Wilfong 2002).

Certain kinds of sexuality were not, as far as can be determined, explicitly prohibited among the Egyptians, and were expressly attributed to the Egyptians by Classical authors. Close-kin sexual relations within the context of marriage, especially between brother and sister, were persistently associated with ancient Egypt throughout its history. Egyptian kings, of course, married sisters, half-sisters and, less commonly, daughters in certain periods as a means of keeping wealth and power within their family as well as in emulation of divine precedent. The early generations of Egyptian gods, of course, were forced to rely on brother–sister relations for the production of successive generations of gods (Osiris and Isis even while still in the womb, for which see Quack 2004), and the triad of Osiris, Isis and Horus was especially influential as a royal precedent. Although the terms 'brother' and 'sister' had relatively wide use in certain periods as terms of endearment for lovers or as designations for husband and wife, close-kin marriage does not seem to have been common outside the royal family in the pharaonic period. The Roman Period in Egypt, however, saw a veritable explosion of close-kin marriage, including many full brother–sister marriages, that can be verified from census documents: as many as a quarter of the households in the Fayum contained close-kin married couples at one point (e.g. Scheidel 1995). These figures are far beyond anything comparable found in human history and the reason for this unparalleled extent of close-kin marriages in Roman Egypt is unclear, although there was certainly some connection to the importance, however limited and symbolic it may have been, of close-kin marriage in the pharaonic period.

The instances of bestiality and necrophilia described as practices of certain Egyptians by Classical authors (in contexts religious and funerary, respectively) are not documented in the Egyptian evidence, but there are some allusions in Egyptian texts to the ideas of sex with animals and the dead. Legal documents of the New Kingdom and Third Intermediate Period often contain clauses that threaten violators of the agreement (and, occasionally, their families) with rape by a male donkey, an animal associated with the god Seth and thus with sexual prowess and transgression. Sexual activity among animals, themselves, is occasionally shown in representations of daily life in tombs, doubtless both as a feature of farm life but also as a symbol of fertility. Occasional visual and textual representations of animals having sex are given a humorous slant, as in the British Museum satirical papyrus BM 10016/1 (Russman 2001: 167–9). And although actual sexual activity between living and dead is unattested in Egyptian evidence, the sexuality of the dead themselves is frequently alluded to, if poorly understood. Funerary literature of different periods envisages the dead as sexual beings, and the post-mortem fertility of the dead is a matter of some interest, not only in the texts promising fecundity in the afterlife and in allusive tomb images (e.g. O'Connor 1996), but also in the sometimes sexualized treatment of the dead body, especially in the later periods when sexual features of mummies are emphasized. And the dead can initiate sexual situations with the living through their materialized spirits, the most spectacular instance being detailed in the Setna I story, where the spirit Tabubu arouses the priest Setna (although the relationship is apparently not consummated). The sexual attentions of the dead were of less concern to the Egyptians, though, than sexual assault by demons; certain magical texts offered protection from, among other things, demonic rape through the ears.

Clearly, much work, both in terms of identification of further pertinent sources and analysis of this material, remains to be done on sexuality in ancient Egypt. It is likely that much 'new' data is already available but its relevance for the subject of sexuality has yet to be identified. Both gender and sexuality will provide rich and challenging areas of research for a wide variety of Egyptological researchers.

CHAPTER SIXTEEN

ETHNICITY AND CULTURE

———•◆•———

Stuart Tyson Smith

> You set every man in his place. . .
> Their tongues differ in speech,
> Their characters likewise;
> Their skins are distinct,
> For you distinguished the peoples.
> (Akhenaten, *Great Hymn to the Aten*
> (Lichtheim 1976: 131–2))

Ethnic identities are defined through real or perceived commonalities of culture, history and language. Some doubt that ethnicity even existed in the past but argue instead that ethnicity is linked closely to the dynamics of European colonialism and the nationalist movements of the nineteenth century (Kohn 1944; Handler 1988; Banks 1996: 123–31); but the ancient Egyptians present us with a surprisingly modern construction of ethnic stereotypes as distinctive traditions, bounded in space and time, and, as the quote above illustrates, combining a common ancestry (skin colour), shared culture (character) and language (speech). Almost a thousand years later Herodotus defined the Greek *ethnos* in strikingly similar terms as 'the kinship of all Greeks in blood and speech, and the shrines of the gods and the sacrifices that we have in common, and the likeness of our way of life' (Rawlinson 1964: vol. VI, 44). Renfrew (1996) points out that this focus on genetic, linguistic and cultural foundations for ethnicity corresponds to the modern definitions that stress a common territory, descent (or a myth of origins), language, culture and beliefs (especially religion). In this essentialist construction, ethnic identity is monolithic and bounded, immutable and self-defined. Ethnicity does not, however, exist in isolation, but is juxtaposed with the ethnic 'other', who are often presented in a negative light. Ethnic affiliations are deployed in both positive and negative contexts, for example, in recent history being used to justify discrimination in the American South, but also to create ethnic solidarity in the civil rights movement that ultimately ended formal segregation. Four basic ethnic groups, one Egyptian and three 'others', were incorporated into the New Kingdom solar theology, each depicted with distinctive costumes, hairstyles, facial features and skin colour (Figure 16.1). In Egyptian ideology, negative ethnic stereotypes of foreigners helped define a positive Egyptian identity.

This chapter examines the ethnic dynamics of ancient Egyptian culture, ranging from the ideological depictions of the ethnic 'other' in monumental art and state documents to subtle expressions of ethnic identity left by ordinary individuals in the

Figure 16.1   Map showing the four main ethnic groups from Egyptian ideology and sites mentioned in the text.

archaeological record. First, I will consider the important and sometimes counter-intuitive insights that anthropological research provides about the nature of ethnicity, which is less primordial and more flexible than one would think, considering the way in which ethnicity is constructed by us today and the ancient Egyptians thousands of years ago. In the light of this discussion, I will use Loprieno's distinction between a foreigner *topos* and *mimesis* in Egyptian literature to contrast the creation and deployment of ethnic stereotypes in the state ideology with the more nuanced and fluid depiction of ethnicity in more prosaic texts and personal monuments. I will conclude with two case studies from Egyptian-controlled Nubia to illustrate the insights that archaeology can provide into the day-to-day cultural dynamics of ethnicity on Egypt's southern frontier.

THE ANTHROPOLOGY OF ETHNICITY

Ethnic identity is a powerful phenomenon. It is powerful both at the affective level, where it touches us in ways mysterious and frequently unconscious, and at the level of strategy, where we constantly manipulate it.

(Royce 1982: 1)

Today, ethnicity and race are nearly synonymous in common usage, and as a result, both Egyptologists and other scholars have attempted to match ancient Egyptian ethnic characterizations to modern racial categories. For example, Nubians are often referred to as 'blacks', and the generic term *nehesi* is often translated as 'black' or in earlier texts 'negro' (e.g. Breasted 1906a: 296; Redford 2004b). It is important, however, to keep in mind that they are *not* the same concept. Unlike ethnicity, race *is* a modern construct, founded on the misguided biological/evolutionary notion that there are distinct sub-species of humans, based upon the physical characteristics of each group. Far from being absolute, however, phenotypic traits such as skin colour, hair and nose shape are distributed in clines, or continuously varying distributions of traits inconsistent with distinctive racial categories (Keita and Kittles 1997; Visweswaran 1998). Egyptian depictions of the different ethnic groups actually reflect this distribution (*contra* Sarich and Miele 2004), with Nubians dark (black), Egyptians intermediate (red), and Libyans and Asiatics lighter skinned (yellow) (see Figure 16.1). The construction of race as an absolute, biological category led to extremes of discrimination in the American South that we do not see in Egypt or even among ancient Mediterranean peoples in general (Snowden 1983). Nubians such as the Royal Fanbearer Maiherpri or Asiatics such as Vizier Aper-El could achieve high social and political positions in spite of their lineage and the negative ideological ethnic stereotypes discussed below.

Archaeologists and historians also tend to conflate the general concepts of culture and ethnic group (Hides 1996; Díaz-Andreu 1996; Perry and Paynter 1999). This view relies upon the essentialist assumption that ethnic groups are bounded and uniform with a set of shared beliefs handed down in a continuous tradition (Jones 1996). This essentialist view is not unexpected, since people inevitably construct ethnic identities in ways that emphasize immutable, primordial attachments and shared cultural practices. Yet, on closer inspection, the seemingly immutable characteristics of ethnicity are surprisingly mutable and socially contingent (Glazer and Moynihan 1963; Royce 1982). Ethnic groups are subjectively constructed, derived by actors who determine their own ethnicity, regardless of the objective 'reality' of their cultural similarities or differences (Graves-Brown 1996). For example, Barth (1969) observed that Pathans founded their ethnic identity upon a narrow selection of social elements, not broadly shared cultural features.

Most importantly, ethnic identities are constructed through a consciousness of difference with reference to the specific cultural practices of ethnic 'others'. As a result, competition and conflict sharpens ethnic polarization (Spicer 1962; Isajew 1974; Hodder 1979; Royce 1982; Comaroff and Comaroff 1992; Jones 1997). For example, Herodotus reflects a Greek consciousness of both community and superiority (Daugé 1981; Díaz-Andreu 1996). Ancient Egyptian and Near Eastern ideology created and manipulated a positive ethnic self juxtaposed with negative ethnic others in order to legitimize the power and authority of their kings (Loprieno 1988; Liverani 1990; Smith 2003). In each case, the king pacified the 'barbaric' foreigners, protecting the inner order and civilization represented by the ethnic self (Figure 16.2). A study by Robert Kurzban, John Tooby and Leda Cosmides (2001) suggests that this emphasis on difference could provide an evolutionary basis for the construction of both race and ethnicity as a by-product of coalition building by our early ancestors. Racial and ethnic stereotypes were easily undermined when the researchers replaced racial categories with an arbitrary yet visible cue correlated with group membership, such as shirt colour. This is consistent with the notion that racial/ethnic categories are socially constructed rather than having some fundamental biological basis, as some continue to suggest (again *contra* Sarich and Miele 2004). Constructions of us–them quickly trump physical differences that previously provided the basis for group identity.

THE ETHNIC *TOPOS* IN EGYPTIAN IDEOLOGY

> I am indeed like a stray bull in a strange land . . . No Asiatic makes friends with a Delta man. And what would make papyrus cleave to that mountain?
>
> (Sinuhe, 12th Dynasty (Lichtheim 1975: 227))

The self–other opposition reflected in this quote from the *Tale of Sinuhe* plays a central role in ancient Egyptian constructions of different ethnic groups. Antonio Loprieno (1988) makes a distinction between *topos* and *mimesis* in the depiction of foreigners in Egyptian literature that provides a useful lens for us to examine ancient Egypt's ethnic dynamics. The foreigner *topos* represents an idealized view of the world, which serves a rhetorical, not necessarily a literal end. When tied to power relations, the features selected to define the ethnic other are often negative and subordinating such as, in ancient Egypt, the insertion of 'wretched' before any mention of Kush (Nubia, Figure 16.2) or Retjenu (Levant). The celebratory ideology found in Egyptian monuments and texts constructed an ethnic 'other' by creating an ethnic *topos* juxtaposing civilized Egyptians with barbaric foreigners. Several literary themes characterize the derogatory ethnic stereotype of the foreigner *topos*, reflecting the strong self–other opposition of ethnicity in Egyptian ideology.

Figure 16.2 'Wretched' Kush from the base of a statue of Ramesses II at Luxor Temple.

In a military context, foreigners were sneaky cowards, instantly defeated by the king if they fought at all (Liverani 1990). Thus, the Middle Kingdom boundary stela of Senusret III, set up at Semna just south of the Second Cataract, reads:

Since the Nubian listens to the word of mouth,
To answer him is to make him retreat.
Attack him, he will turn his back,
Retreat, he will start attacking.
They are not people one respects,
They are wretches, craven-hearted.
(Lichtheim 1975: 119)

The *Instruction for King Merikara* adopts a similar theme for the Asiatic:

Lo the miserable Asiatic . . .
He fights since the time of Horus,
Not conquering nor being conquered,
He does not announce the day of combat,
Like a thief who darts about a group . . .
The Asiatic is a crocodile on its shore,
It snatches from a lonely road,
It cannot seize from a populous town.
(Lichtheim 1975: 103–4)

This *topos* was materialized in scenes depicting the king in battle (Figure 16.3). As Liverani (1990) points out, the larger than life depiction of the ruler backed up by neat rows of troops contrasts with the disorderly mob of easily defeated, fleeing foreigners. Defeated enemies appear as bound prisoners led to Amun, sometimes to be executed, or residing beneath Pharaoh's throne – a common motif realized on royal statuary. The imagery in all of these scenes reflects the dress and appearance of the ethnic foreigner *topos*. Nubians and Libyans appear in a consistent stereotype. The standard Asiatic stereotype, a Canaanite, was sometimes expanded to include specific ethnic varieties, as on the throne base of Ramesses II at Abu Simbel (Figure 16.4). This diversity reflects the real cultural complexities of Western Asia compared to Nubia and Libya, a manifestation of the way real cultural and physical features are selected and abstracted to form ethnic stereotypes even today.

Whenever the king made a public appearance, he was surrounded by images of the ethnic 'other' that emphasized his role as defender of *maat* and enemy of *isfet*, namely the *topical* foreign enemies of Egypt (Loprieno 1988; Smith 2003). This motif linked his earthly battles to the larger cosmological struggle between the sun-god Ra and his evil nemesis, the snake-god Apophis (Assmann 1990). Scenes of Akhenaten at the Window of Appearances from tombs at Amarna and Thebes and the actual Window at Medinet Habu tap into this ideological message by juxtaposing the king with imagery emphasizing the defeat and pacification of ethnic foreigners (Figure 16.5). At Medinet Habu, the king literally stands upon foreign prisoners, whose heads poke out beneath his feet. Objects from the tomb of Tutankhamun show that this imagery followed the king everywhere, playing on the theme of trampling as a

Figure 16.3   Chaotic mass of *topical* Nubians massacred by Tutankhamun
and his soldiers, from a painted box found in his tomb.

means of defeating Egypt's ethnic enemies through sympathetic magic (Ritner 1993).
So Tutankhamun's royal footstools had representations of *topical* Asiatics and Nubians
upon which the king could rest the royal feet (Figure 16.6), and bound prisoners
shown on the soles of a pair of the king's sandals allowed him to trample his enemies
with each step he took (Figure 16.7). Several walking staves had stereotypical figures
of ethnic Asiatics and Nubians along the curved part (Figure 16.8), often mistakenly
identified as the handle (most notably in the new Tutankhamun exhibit, Hawass
2005: 188; also Shaw 2000a: 320). Carter's field notes and an examination of the
walking stick itself clearly show that the curved images of bound prisoners were
actually the base, so that the king could grind his enemies into the dust as he walked.

The ethnic *topos* goes even further: foreigners are not people (*remetj*) at all (Loprieno
1988: 26–9). In the *Admonitions of Ipuwer*, everything in Egypt is topsy-turvy, the
poor man is rich, a former master serves the servant, and 'foreigners have become
people everywhere. . . There are no people anywhere' (Lichtheim 1975: 151–2). In
the passage above, Merikara compares Asiatics to crocodiles, which lurk in the shallows
before unexpectedly attacking stray animals or people. The *Prophecy of Neferti* is even
more explicit, comparing Asiatic immigrants with a flock of rapacious birds descending
on the delta (Lichtheim 1975: 141). At end of the New Kingdom *Instruction of Ani*,
the student complains that no one could possibly learn everything Ani presents to
him. Ani replies that

Figure 16.4 A variety of *topical* Asiatics sit beneath a colossal statue of Ramesses II at Abu Simbel.

The monkey carries the stick,
Though its mother did not carry it.
The goose returns from the pond,
When one comes to shut it in the yard.
One teaches the Nubian to speak Egyptian,
The Syrian and other strangers too.
Say: 'I shall do like all the beasts,'
Listen and learn what they do.
    (Lichtheim 1976: 144, emphasis added)

The famous painted box from Tutankhamun's tomb reflects a similar sensibility. The two sides present a typical scene of the king in his chariot defeating a hopelessly disorganized mob of Nubians and Asiatics, respectively (Figure 16.3). This imagery,

Figure 16.5 Akhenaten hands out gold and other goods at the rewards ceremony in the Tomb of Meryra II at Amarna. Below him are depictions of bound Asiatics and Nubians, symbolizing his pacification of *isfet* (chaos) to the north and south. A group of foreigners representing the four *topical* ethnic groups participates in the event (after Davies 1905: pl. XXXIII).

Figure 16.6 Footstool from the tomb of Tutankhamun with a
Nubian between two *topical* Asiatics.

however, is juxtaposed with hunts of wild animals on the top of the box (Gardiner 1962a). In spite of the more recreational nature of these scenes, the king wears the blue battle crown, the personnel involved are exactly the same military detachments that appear in battle, and the epithets for both battle and hunt speak of Tutankhamun as blazing in the sun like Ra. This passage provides an explicit connection between foreigners and wild animals, linking their destruction to the role of Ra and the king in destroying disorder (*isfet*).

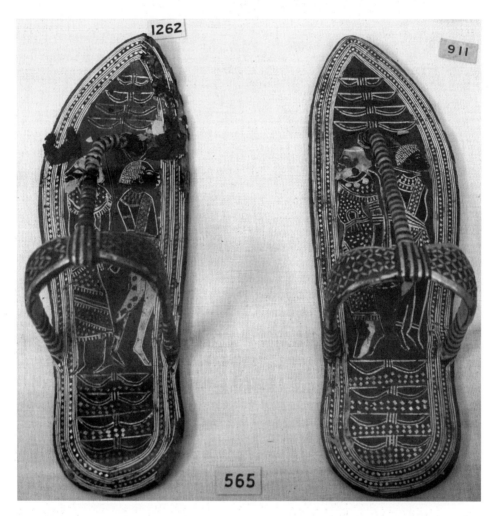

Figure 16.7   A pair of Tutankhamun's sandals, each with images of a Nubian and Asiatic along with nine bows representing the traditional enemies of Egypt.

Figure 16.8   Two of Tutankhamun's walking sticks with images of Nubians on the
crook-like bottom. Although Nubians predominate, other sticks have images
of Asiatics.

ETHNIC *MIMESIS* IN EGYPTIAN CULTURE

I won his [the Ruler of Retjenu's] heart and he loved me, for he recognized my valor. He set me at the head of his children, for he saw the strength of my arms.

(*Sinuhe*, 12th Dynasty (Lichtheim 1975: 227))

It is tempting to take the foreigner *topos* at face value. After all, the textual and artistic evidence for Egyptian constructions of ethnicity appear to provide an authoritative insight into the ancient mind that archaeology could never hope to match, but of course these sources represent only the narrow view of the state. Based upon the ethnic *topos* of Nubians as a poorly organized culture without the fortified cities that became part of the Asiatic *topos*, Egyptologists have and tend still to underestimate the complexity and power of the Nubian Kerma culture (*c.* 2400–1500 BC) which was an urban civilization itself from at least the end of the Old Kingdom to its destruction at the beginning of the New Kingdom (O'Connor 1993). The scale and elaboration of the Second Cataract forts puzzled early scholars so much that Adams (1977) suggested they were an expression of hyper-monumentality akin to the pyramids of Giza. Archaeological excavations at Kerma, however, have shown that this civilization was highly complex with a large, fortified capital. Kerma clearly posed a serious potential threat to Egypt from at least the Middle Kingdom onwards (Bonnet *et al.* 1990), in contrast to the Egyptian ethnic *topos* of Nubians as poorly organized and incapable of serious resistance to Egyptian hegemony. The mention of raids penetrating deep into Egypt in a recently discovered inscription in the tomb of the 17th Dynasty governor Sobeknakht at Elkab in southern Egypt confirms that the ancient Egyptians themselves recognized just how serious the Nubian threat was at the height of Kerma's power during the Second Intermediate Period (Davies 2003b).

To Loprieno (1988), this kind of text reflects the foreigner *mimesis* – a more realistic portrait of foreigners encountered in daily life. For example, Sinuhe interacts with Asiatics who are real people, not just abstract ethnic stereotypes. He even 'goes native' and effectively becomes an Asiatic, so much so that the king's children do not recognize him at first upon his homecoming. Whether or not he actually existed, Sinuhe's ability to shift identities shows us that the ancient Egyptian author recognized the mutability of ethnic identity, and the instrumental manipulation of ethnicity that Sinuhe uses in order to insinuate himself into the court of Ammunenshe, as the quote above illustrates. The previous quote expresses the opposite sentiment, and, ironically, it is the king's appeal to Sinuhe's primordial ethnic identity as an Egyptian that brings him back to the Egyptian court. Egyptian artists creating private monuments also acknowledged the ambiguities and complex nature of ethnic identity. Loprieno (1988: 35–9) points out that the funerary stelae of Nubian mercenaries who settled at Gebelein during the First Intermediate Period depict them as Egyptian in every way, except for their facial features and skin tone, which follow the Nubian ethnic *topos*. In a similar way, the later *Book of the Dead* from the New Kingdom tomb of Nubian soldier and confidant of the king, Maiherpri (Figure 16.9), depicts him as a member of the highest Egyptian elite except for his Nubian physiognomy (Daressy 1902). Wives of Nebhetepra Mentuhotep II, the first Middle Kingdom ruler, are shown with dark skin and have names indicating Nubian ancestry. Ahmose Nefertari,

Figure 16.9   Maiherpri from his 18th Dynasty copy of the *Book of the Dead*.
Only his physiognomy and hairstyle match the Nubian *topos*, and the latter
also appears on Egyptian soldiers (cf. Figure 16.3).

a founding figure of the New Kingdom venerated long after her death, is shown
with dark skin in contrast to the other rulers shown with her, clearly an indication
of her Nubian ancestry (Figure 16.10). In a similar vein, the Asiatic Aper-El rose to
the rank of vizier during the New Kingdom, while keeping his Canaanite name
(Zivie 1990). Egyptians even found things to admire and emulate in foreign cultures.
Asiatic deities such as Reshep were incorporated into the ancient Egyptian pantheon
during the New Kingdom, and the ram imagery of Amun and Ra was possibly
borrowed from Nubia at the same time. Egyptian military equipment and imagery
were also particularly influenced by Nubia during the New Kingdom, including the
tightly curled, cropped hairstyle and leather loincloth (e.g. the hairstyle of the Egyptian
soldier in Figure 16.3). The Egyptian hieroglyphic determinative for soldier has an
ostrich feather in his hair and carries a bow, two iconic features of the Nubian ethnic
topos (Gardiner 1957: 443).

Although these more prosaic sources help balance the ideologically charged
celebratory texts and representations of the Egyptian state, only archaeology can
provide any indication of ethnic dynamics for the great mass of ancient Egyptians.
Colonial frontiers provide an interesting location for the examination of ethnic
dynamics, since ethnicity is often heightened in situations where cultures come into
contact and conflict, such as the Egyptian occupation of, and interactions with, Libya,
Syria-Palestine and Nubia. Archaeologists have generally assumed that ethnicity

Figure 16.10 Ahmose Nefertari and her son Amenhotep I as venerated royal ancestors in the 20th Dynasty tomb of Inherkhau (TT359).

should appear as a distinctive material assemblage, reflecting ethnicity's primordial attachments. Ethnic groups, however, have proven elusive in the archaeological record, causing some archaeologists to despair of ever identifying ethnicity. There is, however, an emerging consensus among anthropologists and sociologists that we should not expect to find absolute and bounded ethnic groups (Graves-Brown 1996). Instead, ethnic identities are situational and overlapping, constructed and negotiated by individuals in specific situations. As a result, attempts to correlate ethnic groups directly with archaeological cultures are misguided, relying on the assumption that material correlates should match an essentialist view of ethnicity. If ethnicity is situational and contingent, then we can expect a considerable degree of archaeological variability in the expression of ethnic identity, and overlapping rather than mutually exclusive material culture distributions (Hodder 1982; Wiessner 1983; Eriksen 1992; Jones 1996; Hall 1997; Smith 2003).

At first glance, Egyptian colonists in Nubia apparently forged a society identical to the Egyptian core, unlike the northern empire in Syria-Palestine (Trigger 1976; Kemp 1978; Adams 1984; Higginbotham 2000). The fortress at Askut is no exception. Built in the late 12th Dynasty, this small fortified settlement was occupied continuously through the initial period of Egyptian colonization in the Middle Kingdom, through Nubian control in the Second Intermediate Period, down to the end of the New Kingdom empire in the 20th Dynasty (Smith 1995). As is the case elsewhere in Lower Nubia, Askut's whitewashed walls would have provided materialization of Egyptian dominance, and probably of Egyptian ethnicity as well. The community's houses and a small chapel also signalled the inhabitants' Egyptian identity (Smith 2003). Like the other forts, Egyptian-style artefacts dominate the material assemblage. As a result, Egyptologists have emphasized the emulative character of these settlements, characterizing them as a transplant of Egyptian culture through colonization and/or as a complete assimilative acculturation of native groups.

Recent archaeological studies of frontier communities, however, caution against equating the overall percentage of native versus colonial artefacts with cultural and ethnic groups, instead calling for a nuanced analysis that focuses on different components of the archaeological assemblage (Yoffee and Kamp 1980; Stanish 1989; Aldenderfer and Stanish 1993; Lightfoot and Martinez 1995; Stein 1999). For Askut, I will focus specifically on two social contexts, culinary practices through the domestic ceramic assemblage, and religion through ritual objects, namely figurines.

Culinary practices vary both between and within cultures as a marker of status (Goody 1982), and several archaeologists emphasize the importance of cuisine in the construction of social identities, including ethnicity (Yoffee and Kamp 1980; Santley *et al.* 1987; Stanish 1989; Lightfoot and Martinez 1995; Burmeister 2000; Bunimovitz and Faust 2001). Pottery can provide an archaeological proxy for culinary practices, since it was the primary medium for food preparation and consumption. Nubian and Egyptian pottery differs dramatically in manufacture and decoration, so it is easy to separate even body sherds along cultural lines. As is the case at the other forts, Nubian pottery appears consistently at Askut, but overall in small numbers. When broken down into sub-assemblages, however, an interesting pattern emerges (Figure 16.11). The percentage of high-quality Nubian serving pottery fluctuates, starting very low in the Middle Kingdom, when the fort system was established, increasing substantially in the Second Intermediate Period, when Nubians controlled the area, and declining sharply in the New Kingdom, correlating with a new colonial policy of assimilation (Smith 2003). Storage vessels show a similar distribution. The prominence of Nubian fine wares during the Second Intermediate Period may reflect an instrumental assertion of ethnic ties demonstrating links between the former colonial community and their new Kerma overlords through display during feasting, perhaps driven by the men who helped manage the lucrative trade in luxuries. This might correspond to Goody's (1982: 151–2) notion that the elements of culinary practices that connect to larger political systems tend to be more changeable in order to meet political contingencies.

By contrast, Nubian cooking pots are drastically over-represented at Askut, starting at nearly half of the cooking sub-assemblage, growing to two-thirds in the Second Intermediate Period, and dominating during the New Kingdom. This pattern is more akin to the late Middle Kingdom increase from 20–40 per cent in Levantine Middle Bronze Age pottery at the Hyksos capital at Avaris (Tell el-Dab'a), when Syro-Palestinians came to dominate the site (Bietak 1997a). Preliminary results of residue analysis using gas chromatography with mass spectrometry imply that different Egyptian and Nubian cuisines also existed at Askut. If we suppose, as Egyptian historical sources indicate, that women did most of the cooking, then Nubian women transformed colonial culinary practices by maintaining their own ethnic cuisine. Goody also observes that those culinary practices without external entanglements

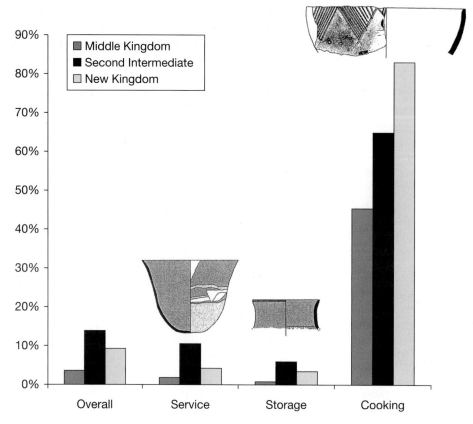

Figure 16.11   Frequency of Nubian pottery at Askut in the Middle Kingdom, Second Intermediate Period, and New Kingdom.

tend to be more conservative, and the prominence of Nubian cooking pots and cuisine at Askut may reflect the less overt influence of Nubian women on the community's culinary practices. The fact that the proportion of Nubian cooking pots, and presumably Nubian cuisine, increases steadily over time, however, implies that this is more than just a passive retention of a Nubian *habitus*, but, instead, an active assertion of Nubian ethnic identity that eventually came to dominate this particular social context. Although rooted in the *habitus*, culinary practices play an important role in engendering and negotiating social identities (Wood 1995). In a similar colonial context, native women in Spanish Saint Augustine used local pottery and maintained native culinary practices (Deagan 1983). Lightfoot and Martinez (1995) argue that native women in California's Russian colony at Fort Ross used cuisine and the organization of domestic space to assert their native identity. Culinary and burial practices allowed slaves on southern plantations to maintain a separate ethnic identity, and cuisine continues to play a key role in African-American ethnicity (McKee 1999: 235). Thus, Nubian women within Egyptian colonial communities such as Askut might have used culinary practices to provide an ethnic counterpoint against Egyptian political and cultural hegemony.

Nubian religious influence was also centred in the household at Askut (Smith 2003). Although a small formal temple akin to those found at Deir el-Medina was built during the New Kingdom, Nubian-style fertility figurines represent around half of the human figurines found at the site (Figure 16.12). An increasing proportion of the cow figurines may reflect the Nubian religious emphasis on cattle, although the shapes are simple and also appear in Egypt. The statuette of a seated pregnant woman in classic Nubian style was found adjacent to a typically Egyptian household shrine that was continuously used from the Second Intermediate Period to the middle of the New Kingdom. As well as cooking, women were particularly concerned with

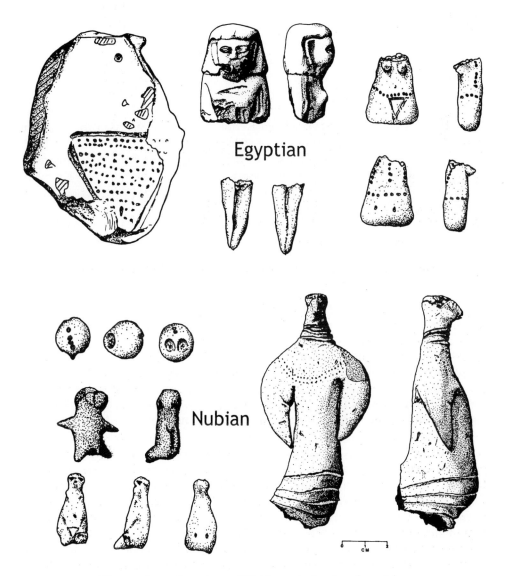

Figure 16.12 Egyptian and Nubian style figurines from Askut.

fertility magic and household religion (Robins 1993; Pinch 1993, 1994). This pattern may reflect a transculturation (Ortiz 1940; Deagan 1998), or blending of Nubian elements into an Egyptian ritual setting. This subtle influence contrasts dramatically with the strong Asiatic religious imprint at Avaris (Tell el-Dabʿa) during the late Middle Kingdom and especially Second Intermediate Period, when massive temples provide the largest Middle Bronze Age religious structures in the Levant (Bietak 1997a).

Funerals and burial practice demonstrate primordial ancestral and territorial ties, key elements in the construction of ethnicity (Santley *et al.* 1987). It is no coincidence that cemeteries in Bosnia and Kosovo were targeted in campaigns of ethnic cleansing (Chapman 1994). Middle Bronze Age Asiatic-style burials at Avaris (Tell el-Dabʿa) correlate with the rising influence of Asiatics at the site during the transition from the Middle Kingdom to the Second Intermediate Period, when the Hyksos controlled a large area of Egypt. During the New Kingdom, Nubian burial practice seems to disappear, reflecting a combination of renewed colonization and a deliberate policy of cultural/ethnic assimilation (Smith 1997a). Located at the headwaters of the Third Cataract of the Nile, the ancient Egyptian New Kingdom colonial cemetery at Tombos lies only ten kilometres from Kerma, the former capital of the kingdom of Kush. Thutmose I carved a number of stelae to commemorate his defeat of Kush at the beginning of the 18th Dynasty. Preliminary evidence from three seasons of excavation indicates that the cemeteries there were used from the early New Kingdom to the Nubian 25th Dynasty at the end of the Third Intermediate Period (Smith 2003; in press).

Apart from small amounts of Nubian pottery, funerary architecture and grave goods reflect Egyptian burial practice. An elite area contained perhaps ten large pyramid tombs of a type popular with high-level bureaucrats during the New Kingdom (Figure 16.13; Badawy 1968). Like the massive fortresses of Upper Nubia, these impressive structures would provide a materialization of Egyptian control. One of these tombs even had funerary cones dedicated to Siamun and his wife Weren, a type of decoration only rarely found outside Thebes. Only one other tomb in Nubia had them, at the provincial capital of Aniba (Steindorff 1935; Ryan 1988). As an Overseer of Foreign Lands, Siamun would have played a prominent role in the colonial administration, regulating traffic across this internal border and, perhaps, assembling the annual tribute of gold, cattle, slaves, ivory and other precious goods from the conquered kingdom of Kush. In a nearby middle-class cemetery, remains of decorated and inscribed coffins, evidence for mummification, and specialized items such as *shabti* figurines reflect an Egyptian belief system (S. Smith 1992). The use of vaulted subterranean chambers as family crypts also reflects Egyptian practice. Objects of daily life – including personal items such as cosmetic equipment, a boomerang for hunting birds, furniture, including remains of a folding seat, and an almost entirely Egyptian ceramic assemblage – demonstrate its overwhelmingly Egyptian cultural orientation. Luxuries such as a rare Mycenaean juglet attest to the prosperity of the community (Smith 2003).

During the second season of excavation, however, we found burials of four women in Nubian style (Figure 16.14), flexed and oriented with the head to the east as

Figure 16.13 Small private pyramid from Deir el-Medina (Thebes). Similar tombs appear at the major New Kingdom colonial sites in both Lower and Upper Nubia.

opposed to the position of the Egyptian burials that lay above and around them, extended (i.e. mummified) on their back with the head to the west. Similar burials were found in the cemetery associated with the New Kingdom temple-town of Soleb (Schiff Giorgini *et al.* 1965). Looters had moved one of the Tombos burials into an unusual position in order to steal valuable jewellery (Smith 2003), but missed a set of Egyptian amulets dedicated to the dwarf god Bes, who protected the household from both physical and spiritual dangers (R. Wilkinson 2003: 102). A Kerma-style cup was placed at the head of another set of two Nubian burials (Figure 16.14), but apart from the cup and a couple of shell beads, the grave goods associated with all four burials were Egyptian. Nubian pottery from the pyramid's courtyard, however, may reflect the introduction of Nubian cuisine into the funeral feast (Smith 2003). Funerals provide opportunities for the dead to make a final assertion of identity, but also allow for an active re-assertion or re-negotiation of their offspring's and relatives' social position and identity (Hodder 1982; Morris 1987; Metcalf and Huntington 1991; Meskell 1994). Egyptian (and presumably also Nubian) funerals were public events. Even though their grave goods were not particularly Nubian, the burial of women in Nubian style at Tombos would make a dramatic assertion of ethnic identity set against the very Egyptian monumentality of the elite cemetery's pyramids.

Figure 16.14 Nubian-style flexed burials of two women from the Unit 7 chamber tomb at Tombos.

CONCLUSIONS

> I would like to know what (use) is my strength with a Prince in Avaris and another in Kush, and I sit united with an Asiatic and a Nubian, each man with his slice of this Egypt, sharing the land with me?
>
> (Kamose, 17th Dynasty (Gardiner 1916))

Perry and Paynter (1999: 306–7) attribute the tendency for archaeologists and historians to think of ethnic groups as distinctly bounded and exclusive, to the very nature of ethnic identities, which are inevitably constructed in essentialist terms that obscure the actual complexity and contextual, gendered nature of ethnicity in frontier communities such as Askut and Tombos. The key thing to understand about ethnicity is that although people construct ethnic identities as an essential quality ascribed at birth and immutable, in fact ethnicity is socially contingent and can shift depending on the social and economic interests of individual actors. This has profound implications for the archaeological and historical search for ethnicity, which is often an ultimately futile hunt for neatly bounded units that can be linked to ethnic groups. Instead, we should abandon an overly normative view of ethnicity and look carefully at different social contexts; and we should expect inconsistencies, since ethnic identities can shift in different situations. This means that we need to think as much, if not more, in terms of individual actors than group dynamics in order to get at ethnicity.

Egyptian ideology provides us with a clearly instrumental construction of ethnicity that we should be cautious about conflating with widespread cultural beliefs. From the 1st Dynasty to the Ptolemaic Period, literary and artistic representations of the ethnic 'other' in the foreigner *topos* reflect the orthodoxy of the king's topical role as subduer of the traditional enemies of Egypt (Figure 16.15) who threaten *maat*, the eternal order of things, because they embody *isfet*, the chaotic disorder that threatens to unravel the world. On the other hand, evidence from more private contexts reflects a *mimetical* viewpoint in the broader society, depicting foreigners as real people within an Egyptian cultural framework. In contrast to state art, private tombs often represent a more realistic view of foreigners, especially when an acculturated immigrant to Egypt owns the tomb. Similarly, Egyptianized Nubian princes of Egypt's New Kingdom empire in Lower Nubia, such as Djehutyhotep of Tehkhet and Hekanefer of Miam (Aniba), are shown as Egyptian officials in their tombs, which have the same repertoire of scenes and assemblage of grave goods as a typical elite tomb in Egypt (Simpson 1963b; Säve-Söderbergh and Troy 1991). Only their genealogies point to their Nubian origins. At the same time, the foreigner *topos* required that those same princes appear with all the trappings of the Nubian ethnic stereotype while bearing the 'tribute' (*inu*) of Wawat and Kush (Lower and Upper Nubia, respectively). A New Kingdom letter from the vizier to a Nubian prince describes this event:

> Think about the day when the tribute is sent, and you are brought into the presence [of the king] under the Window [of Appearances], the Nobles to either side in front of his Majesty, the Princes and the Envoys of every foreign land standing, looking at the tribute ... tall *Terek*-people in their garments, with

Figure 16.15 Ptolemy XIII executes prisoners in front of the god Horus on the main entrance pylon of Edfu temple in a *topos* that goes back to the 1st Dynasty.

fans of gold, high (feathered?) hairstyles, and their jewellery of ivory, and numerous Nubians of all kinds.

(author's translation, after Gardiner 1937)

The ethnic stereotypes from this text provide a good match to the pictorial representations of Nubians in the tribute scenes and on Egyptian monuments. Carefully orchestrated events like this one would reach a large audience, both of elites and commoners. They provided a dramatic performance of the foreigner *topos* that demonstrated the king's command over people from far-off lands wearing exotic costumes and bearing exotic and valuable gifts. Hekanefer and the other Nubian princes were of little ideological value as Egyptians, but played a key legitimizing role in promulgating the image of Pharaoh as taming the earthly forces of *isfet* when they appeared in a Nubian guise (Smith 1997b; *contra* Kemp 1997). The fact that they had to appear as Nubians during the event demonstrates how an instrumental deployment of ethnicity can result in dramatic shifts in ethnic identity in different social contexts.

We can see this dynamic playing out in more subtle ways in the day-to-day interactions reflected in the archaeological record. Even though at first glance both Askut and Tombos seem to represent the kind of imperial frontier cultural conservatism discussed by Kopytoff (1999), we can see the appearance of both Egyptian and Nubian cultural features as an active social practice, an assertion of ethnic identity by different actors in different social contexts. In settings such as Egypt's Nubian frontier, assimilative acculturation models over-simplify cultural interactions by emphasizing the transmission of core cultures to peripheral societies with little consideration for individual agency (Lightfoot and Martinez 1995). Individual men and women played a role in cultural and ethnic dynamics that transformed colonial society into a dynamic social field for negotiating cultural differences, producing an ethnic hybrid at places such as Askut, Tombos and Avaris.

CHAPTER SEVENTEEN

LOCAL IDENTITIES

—— •◆• ——

Fredrik Hagen

One of the most striking features of the civilization of ancient Egypt is the seemingly homogeneous nature of much of its cultural output. However, research has shown that beneath this superficial likeness there existed, at all times, a range of local variations. These local traditions are found in all types of material and they, along with a range of textual sources, relate to the largely unexplored subject of ancient Egyptian local identities. This chapter looks at different ways in which the question of local identity can be approached, as well as ancient expressions of social identity at a local level.

Modern identities are recognized as complex social constructs, and ancient ones are unlikely to have been any less so, but the relevant material from Egypt is fragmentary and frequently problematic. According to sociologists, the concept of social identity is:

> based on the assumption that society is structured hierarchically into different social groups that stand in power and status relations to one another, [and that] social categories provide members with a social identity; a definition of who one is and a description and evaluation of what this entails . . . [it is] that part of the self-concept that derives from group membership.
>
> (Hogg and Vaughan 2002: 401)

These group-structures may vary from community to community in form and function, but they are a fundamental part of all human interaction. Mapping out these structures is difficult even in modern societies, where such relations can be observed in person and interviews conducted with individuals involved in the social processes, but in the case of an ancient culture such as that of Egypt the difficulty is greater and the resources available more limited.

For the purpose of this chapter, 'local identity' is defined as group interaction where the geographical context is central: an ancient Egyptian's identification with a social group with strong links to a specific area, such as his village or nome, and the ways in which this influences interaction with both his fellow group members and members of other groups. The issue of national identity is not treated here, nor issues related to ethnic, professional or family identity, although strictly speaking these issues can never be entirely separated: every individual is simultaneously a member of a number of different groups (national/ethnic groups, regional groups, professional groups, family groups, etc.), all of which form part of that individual's social identity.

There are two types of evidence, broadly speaking, that are related to the concept of local identity in ancient Egypt. The first is that of variations in material culture, and the second consists of textual material where the ancient Egyptians express aspects of local identity. The former category is, in some ways, the more problematic, because how variations in material culture relate to abstract social constructs such as local identity is frequently unclear. It is not possible, or even desirable, to list every type of variation or tradition as reflected in the material record in a chapter such as this: the following discussion has to be restricted to a limited number of examples.

To Egyptologists, the most readily accessible expressions of local identity often relate, for reasons of survival of the evidence, to funerary practices. Studies of mortuary material from various contemporaneous sites can be compared to reveal local traditions and customs from the earliest periods of Egyptian history. In the Predynastic Period, for example, the traditional view has been to differentiate between two main regional pottery traditions in the funerary record, Naqada and Maadi/Buto, the former appearing to replace the latter towards the beginning of the Early Dynastic Period, but within these regional traditions local variations are observable (Wilkinson 1999: 35). Similarly, variations in the types and number of grave goods, as well as the orientation of graves in cemeteries of the period, may be an expression of local traditions relating to religious belief and ritual (Grajetzki 2003: 1–6). Studies of pottery from both funerary and settlement contexts have shown that local traditions were prevalent throughout Egyptian history, but also that in certain periods specific vessels display a remarkable homogeneity, both in the Nile Valley itself and in the oases of the Western Desert. Interestingly, these periods seem to be characterized by a strong royal administration and political stability, although the underlying reason for this homogeneity remains unknown: it may have been an increase in trade using centrally produced pottery, or perhaps restrictions governing the production of it (Bourriau *et al.* 2000: 138–40). Pottery, because of its distribution in both temporal and geographical terms, offers a way to map and evaluate local practices in a broader context, although the process of evaluation can be problematic. A change in material culture may reflect a change in the technology used to produce the objects, as well as a change in the functions of the pottery itself, but how such changes relate to issues of social identity is a complex and, perhaps, unanswerable question.

Other funerary materials that display regional variations include coffins, where local production practices are observable from the First Intermediate Period onwards. These variations are traditionally classified into two traditions, one Upper Egyptian (Asyut, Akhmim, Thebes, Gebelein, el-Mo'alla) and one Lower Egyptian (Memphis, Beni Hasan, el-Bersha, Meir), but there is a range of local variations attested within these broader traditions. Middle Kingdom Theban coffins, for example, frequently display domestic scenes as part of the decoration, and contemporary coffins from Akhmim are characterized by the painting of the offering list on the east side of the coffin, next to the standard eye-panel. One of the most distinctive local styles is the so-called *rishi* coffin from Thebes, dated to the Second Intermediate Period and the New Kingdom, where the outside of the anthropoid case is decorated with a pair of wings. The transmission of the religious texts associated with coffins and burials also exhibits local variations, both in distribution and in form. The Coffin Texts, found on coffins from at least the First Intermediate Period onwards, are first attested in Upper Egypt, and only make their appearance in Lower Egypt after the unification at the end of the First Intermediate Period; the northern tradition was, instead, characterized by its use of the Pyramid Texts. Local traditions are also reflected in the way some Coffin Text 'spells' are only attested in certain geographical areas: the group CT 229, 236–7, 239, 241, 644 and 932 occur only in the southern part of Upper Egypt, and CT 289–90, 293–5, 297–300, 473–4, 576–8 occur only on coffins from el-Bersha. Scholars have noted how patterns in the local use of these religious texts show a preference for those related to deities known to have been associated with the corresponding geographical areas, and this raises the question to what degree local gods and religious practices formed part of ancient Egyptian local identity (Willems 1988: 247–9).

From the Early Dynastic Period onwards there is evidence for gods being associated with localities in the form of inscriptions mentioning 'the god of the city' (*netjer niut*, Schlichting 1984: 1250). Cities could, in fact, be spoken of in terms of their principal deity, such as 'City of Amun' (Thebes), 'City of Thoth' (Hermopolis) and 'City of Ptah' (Memphis), and gods were given corresponding epithets such as 'Lord of Thebes' (Amun), 'Lord of Hermopolis' (Thoth) and 'Mistress of Dendera' (Hathor). Local gods could also be named after their towns, as with the heron god Djebauti, named after Djebau (Buto), or the vulture goddess Nekhbet, named after the ancient town of Nekheb (Elkab). These local deities occasionally rose in prominence to become part of national ideology, as in the case of the aforementioned Nekhbet who came to represent Upper Egypt in the titulary of Egyptian kings, together with the cobra goddess Wadjit of Lower Egypt (Assmann 2001: 17–27). One of the most direct expressions of the way in which ancient Egyptians saw their local gods as part of their identity is found in the religious literature of the New Kingdom, in *Book of the Dead* Spell 183, which emphasizes the bond between individual, place of origin and the local god:

> I have come today from the city of my god: Memphis. It is truly the most beautiful of all the nomes in this land. Its god is the lord of Maat, the lord of food, rich in costly things. All lands come to it, Upper Egypt sails downstream to it, Lower Egypt with sail and oar, to make it festive every day, as its god has commanded. No one who dwells in it says 'Would that I had!' Blessed is he who does right (*maat*) for the god therein!
>
> (*Book of the Dead* 183)

Here, the speaker identifies himself by naming his god's hometown (Memphis), and in doing so also identifies his god as Ptah (Memphis being the 'City of Ptah'). He goes on to describe the positive qualities of both the god and the city, praising its material wealth and its position as a cultural centre. The opening lines of the text echo the autobiographical texts of the Old Kingdom onwards, where the deceased asserts his ethical behaviour in relation to his geographical context: 'I have come from my city, I have descended from my nome . . . having done what is right (*maat*) therein' (Janssen 1946: 38, 42, 59–60, 82–3).

A common theme in these texts is the responsibility of the local elite to take care of their nome or town: 'I am one who looked after my town', 'I am one who made (my) city live with grain', 'I was one loved by his city', 'I was one loved by his lord and praised by his city' (Janssen 1946: 64–5, 88, 96, 100, 114). The 6th Dynasty nomarch, Qar, in an autobiography that draws heavily on the established formulae of the genre, states that:

> I have come from my city . . . I gave bread to the hungry and clothes to the naked whom I found in this nome . . . I was the one who buried every man of this nome who had no son, with cloth from my own estate.
>
> (el-Khadagry 2002: 206)

This emphasis on the social roots linking an individual to his hometown finds its fullest expression in the autobiographies of local rulers in periods characterized by a weak or non-existent central administration, such as the First Intermediate Period. The autobiographical stela of the town treasurer Iti, of ancient Imyotru in the Theban nome (near modern Gebelein), expands on the common theme of 'giving bread to the hungry one':

> The Royal Treasurer and Sole Companion, Iti, says:
>
> 'I am an excellent citizen who acts with his arm, a great pillar of the nome of Thebes, a well-regarded individual in the South. I made Imyotru live through difficult years, when four hundred men suffered therefrom. I did not take the daughter of a man, I did not take his field . . . I supplied barley to Iuni (Armant) and Hefat (el-Mo'alla) after Imyotru (Gebelein) had been provided for, while the Theban nome [went north] and south. I never let Imyotru go north and south to another nome (in search of barley) . . .'
>
> (Lange and Schäfer 1902: 2)

The historical reality behind such statements remains problematic due to the formulaic nature of autobiographical inscriptions, but Iti's claims nonetheless illustrate a sense of belonging to, and moral responsibility towards, his hometown. In terms of social identity theory, he displays loyalty to, and responsibility for, his in-group members. This is initially at the expense of out-group members (the neighbouring people of Iuni and Hefat), but these are eventually provided for – once his hometown has received what it needs.

The formulaic claims of having looked after and been loved by one's hometown survive in autobiographies well into the Late Period: 'I am a man who is good in his town. I rescued its inhabitants from the very great turmoil when it happened in the whole land'; 'I suppressed crime in Tawer, I guarded Tawer for its lord, I protected all its people'; 'I was one beloved of his city, praised by his nome, and kind-hearted to his towns'; 'I was one unique and excellent, great in his town . . . I sought what was useful for my town in my time'; 'I nourished the poor of my town' (Lichtheim 1980a: 16, 19, 26, 35, 39).

The above examples are all from compositions and inscriptions that belong to formal textual registers, each governed by concerns about audience, purpose and unwritten rules for what should (and what should not) be expressed – what Egyptologists often call 'rules of decorum' – and this makes their interpretation difficult. The example from the *Book of the Dead* is problematic as a source for local identity because as a material object it has a very specific role to play: as part of a magical formula it need not reflect social reality. Autobiographies were likewise influenced by what were, at any given time, thought to be socially acceptable subjects to address. The increased emphasis on looking after local people in elite autobiographies during times of a weak central administration is less likely to reflect a genuine shift in the concern of the officials in question than a shift in the regulations that governed their expression, despite attempts by some scholars to read these texts as objective historical accounts.

Less formalized texts such as private letters, although invariably governed by their own 'rules of decorum', echo the sentiments expressed in the quotations above. In New Kingdom letters, the highly stylized greeting formulae include well-wishes where regional gods are called upon to safeguard the letter's recipient, and the gods of other geographical areas are implored to bring the addressee back safely:

> I say every day to Amun-Ra, king of the gods, Mut, Khonsu, and all the gods of Thebes, Pra-Harakhti when he rises and sets, to Amun-united-with-eternity together with his Ennead, Amun of the Throne(s) of the Two Lands, while I am standing in your courtyard daily, to give you life, prosperity and health, a long lifetime and a good old age, and many favours before the General, your lord; and may Amun bring you back sound, and may I fill my embrace with you when you have returned alive, prospering, and healthy, and may they [i.e. the gods] save you from arrows, stones, spears and every danger which there is in that land in which you are, and that the gods of that land bring you back down to Egypt, and may they hand you over to Amun of the Throne(s) of the Two Lands, your lord.
>
> (Janssen 1991: 12)

When the sender was from another area where other gods were prominent, the formula changed correspondingly. An example from Elephantine calls upon the local city gods Khnum, Satet and Anuket (Wente 1990: 130–1); letters from Deir el-Medina regularly call upon the patron god of that village, the deified Amenhotep I (Wente 1990: 135–6, 150, 160, 179); and occasionally letter writers will ask the recipients to pray to local gods on their behalf: 'Call upon Amun United-With-Eternity and every god of my village to keep me safe with my lord' (Wente 1990: 185). Despite their formulaic nature, examples such as these reflect individuals' attachment to local gods and the part which that relationship plays in the composition of their local identity (Baines 2001b). Archaeologically, local variations in cult practices, both in terms of the physical setting and the focus of worship, are most obvious in periods before state-imposed architectural ideals and cult organization, in the 'Pre-formal' phase of Egyptian temple building (up to and including the early parts of the Middle Kingdom). Sites such as Elephantine, Hierakonpolis, Abydos, Tell Ibrahim Awad, Coptos and Medamud provide an archaeological context for the worship of local city-gods (Kemp 2005 [1989b]: 112–35), or more accurately for the local and semi-popular worship of deities strongly associated with the area (some 'city-gods' were worshipped far from 'their' cities from an early point of Egyptian history, as shown by Hornung 1996 [1982b]: 70–2). Examples of truly local cults, whose focus were 'deities' not worshipped elsewhere, include those of the deceased governors of 'Ain Asil in the Dakhla Oasis, as well as that of Heqaib at Elephantine (Kemp 2005 [1989b]: 197, 201) – comparable perhaps to the cult of the deceased king Amenhotep I and queen Nefertari among the villagers of Deir el-Medina at Thebes.

In the literature of ancient Egypt social and local identity is thematicized on both a regional and a national level. *The Story of the Eloquent Peasant* sees the protagonist leave the safety of his village in order to sell his goods in more central areas, when he is obstructed by a corrupt noble who seeks to appropriate the peasant's goods and donkeys. In *The Story of the Shipwrecked Sailor* the protagonist is washed up alone on an island while on a royal expedition. Following his encounter with a giant mythological snake, who assures him that his rescue is imminent, he swears that he will thank the god responsible with offerings, 'as should be done for a god who loves men in a far-off land which men do not know' (*Shipwrecked Sailor* 148–9): this echoes the concerns expressed in the letter formulae discussed above. The danger of travelling, of leaving behind a familiar socio-geographical environment, is by no means the *leitmotif* of these stories, but rather the conceptual background against which they unfold, and in doing so they reveal, indirectly, related attitudes and concerns. *The Story of Sinuhe* sheds some light on similar issues. In this story, when the protagonist is explaining his state of confusion, he describes it on two occasions as being 'like the nature of a dream, like a Delta dweller seeing himself in Elephantine, a man of the Delta marshes in Southern Egypt' (Koch 1990: 29, 67). Implied here is the potential disorientating effect of finding oneself outside a known socio-geographical context, and the recognition that even within the borders of Egypt the differences in language and social mores could be significant.

The wisdom instructions (Egyptian *sebayt*) – the most widely copied genre of literary texts in ancient Egypt – are compositions that claim to teach wisdom and correct behaviour. These frequently focus on the importance of group membership and interaction with members of other groups, and the geographical context is often emphasized. *The Instruction of Ptahhotep* advises the reader to take a wife who is 'known to her city' (*Ptahhotep* 500b), and *The Instruction of Ani* cautions 'Beware of a woman who is a stranger, one not known in her town' (16.13), highlighting the way in which the reputation of an individual serves as a landmark in a social landscape. This is not restricted to women. *Ptahhotep* addresses the assumed male reader (Ptahhotep's son) with advice on how to behave 'in a city which is known to you' (*Ptahhotep* 431), and many of its maxims are concerned with maintaining a social status and a good reputation: 'Do not sate only your own mouth when with your people' (*Ptahhotep* 165); 'Do not be greedy towards your people' (*Ptahhotep* 318); 'Satisfy your friends with what comes to you' (*Ptahhotep* 339); 'Know your friends and you will prosper; do not be mean to your friends' (*Ptahhotep* 489–90). One who does not conform to, or maintain, the mores of the local community is said to be 'an enemy to the town' (*The Instruction of Amenemope* 8.5). In *The Prohibitions*, a didactic composition known only from the village of Deir el-Medina, the concern with maintaining social bonds within a local community is emphasized in a similar way:

> You should not ignore your neighbours (on) the day of their need, and they will surround you in [your moment of need]. You should not celebrate your festival without your neighbours, and they will surround you, mourning, on the day of burial . . . You should not be hard-headed in fighting with your neighbours.
>
> (McDowell 1999: 143)

Perhaps the most explicit text in terms of the emphasis on local identity and the ties between an individual and his village is the Demotic instruction of Papyrus Insinger. Chapter 22 of this composition, under the heading 'The teaching not to abandon the place in which you live', is concerned with the local geographical context of everyday life. Here, too, religion and the idea of a local god looking after his people is central: 'The god who is in the city is the one by whose command are the death and life of his people' (Papyrus Insinger 28.4; translation by Lichtheim 1980a: 186–213); 'The godly (man) who is far from his town, his worth is not better known than that of another' (28.6); 'The impious man who leaves the way of his town, its gods are the ones who hate him' (28.10); 'He who is distant while his prayer is distant, his gods are distant from him' (28.15). Not all the advice relates to the religious context supplied by an individual's hometown, and social concerns are also central: 'respect the people of your town' (8.2), 'Do not let your son marry a woman from another town, lest he be taken from you' (15.15). The latter example hints at the prominent role family ties played in local communities, attested in detail in the material from Deir el-Medina where family life and friendships can be reconstructed from letters and informal communications between the villagers (McDowell 1999: 28–52).

The Instruction of Amenemope warns 'Do not say "Find a powerful superior for me. A man in your town has injured me" ' (22.1–2), which draws attention to another aspect of local identity which has left little or no trace in the archaeological record: that of law and the enforcement of law at a local level. A central concern here is access to justice, and the composition of the bodies or institutions involved in dispensing it. All but the most serious cases were brought before a local court (Egyptian *qenbet*) consisting of local officials, none of whom was a professional judge in the modern sense of the word (Eyre 2005). In such circumstances the social relationships in a village took centre stage in a way that may seem alien to modern judicial practices, and the wisdom instructions' emphasis on building up and retaining a positive reputation in one's local town reflects this. In this judicial setting, social identity becomes more than an abstract concept, it becomes social capital: 'Do not go to court in order to falsify your words . . . tell the truth before the official, lest he lay a hand on you. If another day you come before him, he will incline to all you say' (*Amenemope* 20.7–17). A fictional representation of the difficulties involved in the judicial process when conducted outside an individual's local frame of reference is found in *The Eloquent Peasant*. After the protagonist's initial approach to the High Steward Rensi to complain about Nemtynakht and his trickery, the reaction from the officials surrounding him is that 'Surely it's only a peasant of his (Nemtynakht) who has run off to someone else . . . is there really reason to punish this Nemtynakht for a little natron and a little salt?' (B1 75–79). Individuals with political authority at a local level were expected to judge cases as and when they appeared, the ideal being to 'cause two contestants to go out content' (Kloth 2002: 91–3) – to see that justice was done, certainly, but also to maintain the social equilibrium in a local community by making sure both parties would accept the judgement.

A more romanticized expression of themes related to local identity is found in the New Kingdom compositions known as 'Praise of Cities'. These poems are attested for many of the major cities of the Ramesside Period, including Thebes, Memphis, Hermopolis and Per-Ramesses (Lichtheim 1980b), and in them the authors express a longing for, and pride in, their hometown:

> See, my heart has slipped away,
> it is hurrying to the place it knows,
> it is travelling upstream to see Memphis.
> But I sit (at home)
> and wait for my heart,
> to tell me about the condition of Memphis.
> No task succeeds any more in my hands,
> my heart has departed from its place.
> Come to me, Ptah,
> and take me to Memphis.
> Let me see you as desired;
> I am awake, but my heart sleeps.
> My heart is not in my body,
> and all my limbs are seized by evil.
> My eye is weary from seeing,
> my ear does not hear,
> my voice is raw,
> and all my words are garbled.
> Be gracious to me and let me recuperate.
> (Caminos 1954: 150–2)

> See, I do not wish to leave Thebes;
> I have been taken against my will.
> I will dance when I sail north,
> when Thebes is with me again,
> and the domain of Amun is all around me.
> . . .
> Bring me into your city, Amun,
> for I love it.
> I love your city more than bread and beer, Amun,
> more than clothing and ointments.
> The soil of your place is dearer to me
> than the unguents of a foreign land.
> (Posener 1977: 391)

> What do they say to themselves
> in their hearts every day,
> those who are far from Thebes?
> They spend the day

dreaming of its name, (saying)
'If only its light were ours!'
. . .

The bread which is in it is more tasty
than cakes made of goose fat.
Its [water] is sweeter than honey;
one drinks of it to drunkenness.
Behold, this is how one lives in Thebes!
The heaven has doubled (fresh) wind for it.
(McDowell 1999: 158)

The latter example is particularly interesting because unlike most literary manuscripts from ancient Egypt it has a known provenance. It comes from the village of Deir el-Medina, just outside Thebes, and the copyist is one Amennakhte son of Ipuy, an historic individual known to have lived in the village. Although the village lies a short distance away, it is Thebes as the local administrative centre that is the focus for the poem cited above. Similarly, in the tomb of Neferhotep (TT 216) at the same village, the deceased proclaims: 'How happy is he who lives in Thebes, spending (time) in this great place!' (Kitchen 1975–89: vol. III, 592, 5–6). To read these poems as expressions of local identity is not entirely unproblematic, because we know little about their social context and transmission. They occur on ostraca, papyri and even as graffiti on tomb walls, but only for a limited time (during the New Kingdom). What instigated the emergence of the genre, and why it subsequently disappeared, is unknown, and there need not be a direct correlation between the rise and fall of a literary genre and a supposed historical phenomenon such as an increased awareness of local identity. Although the poetic genre of 'Praise of Cities' disappears, the sentiments they express are echoed in later autobiographies, such as that of Harsiese, from the Late Period: 'You were born in the city of Thebes, as one who belonged to the following of Osiris. Its homes nourished you as a child, its walls received your old age' (Otto 1954: 144).

Occasionally ancient Egyptian writings display another aspect of local identity: that of language and language variation. The nature of the hieroglyphic writing system does not allow for the recovery of regional dialects in texts, so for most of Egyptian history the issue of local linguistic identity remains inaccessible. Only in Coptic, the later stage of the Egyptian language where the Greek alphabet (plus six or seven signs derived from Demotic) was used to write Egyptian, is there evidence for dialects such as Sahidic, Bohairic, Akhmimic, Lycopolitan and Fayyumic (Loprieno 1995: 8, 41). However, there is no reason to believe that there was less linguistic variety in earlier periods, and scholars have even asserted the existence of sociolects (Loprieno 1996b: 519). There are few indirect references to regional dialects, but in the *Satirical Letter of Hori* from the New Kingdom the scribe describes his correspondent's letter-writing style as 'so confused when heard that no interpreter can understand them [i.e. the words]. They are like a Delta man's conversation with a man of Elephantine' (Wente 1990: 109). Despite our inability to extract regional dialects from the hieroglyphic writing system (including the cursive Hieratic and Demotic derived from it), it does reveal, from the New Kingdom and onwards, variations in palaeography typical of certain geographical areas (Möller 1909: 2–3;

Satzinger 1977: 1188). These variations reflect a northern tradition centred around Memphis, and a southern tradition primarily represented by the Theban area. The difference becomes more pronounced in later periods, to the extent where scholars talk of two different types of writing, 'Abnormal Hieratic' in Upper and Middle Egypt and 'Early Demotic' in Lower Egypt, although eventually the former merged with Demotic (el-Aguizy 1998: 238).

As can be seen from the examples discussed above, the evidence that relates to ancient Egyptian 'local identity' is at once both fragmentary and extensive. It is extensive in the sense that local variations are attested for most types of material remains, but interpretation is frequently hindered by our lack of understanding of the socio-historical context. It is fragmentary in the sense that the attitudes and ideals associated with an abstract social concept such as local identity do not, by their nature, leave much trace in the archaeological record. The material that does survive paints a picture of a society where individuals were keenly aware of both their own group memberships and those of others, as well as the duties, privileges and responsibilities connected with them.

CHAPTER EIGHTEEN

MORALITY AND ETHICS

——— ·◆· ———

Boyo G. Ockinga

THE FOUNDATION OF ANCIENT EGYPTIAN ETHICAL VALUES

In Ancient Egypt, the foundation upon which ethical values rest is the principle of *maat*, a concept that embraces what we would call justice but which is much broader, signifying the divine order of the cosmos established at creation. It is personified as the goddess Maat, held to be the daughter of the creator, the sun god Ra. Maat's role in creation is expressed in chapter 80 of the Coffin Texts (*c.*2000 BC) where Tefnut, the daughter of Atum, is identified with *maat*, the principle of cosmic order, who, together with Shu, the principle of cosmic 'life', fills the universe (Faulkner 1973: 83–7; Junge 2003: 87–8). *Maat* is, therefore, one of the fundamental principles of the cosmos, present from the beginning, like the personification of Wisdom in the later Biblical tradition (*Wisdom of Solomon* 7, 22; 7, 25; 8, 4; 9, 9). This concept of creation and the role of *maat* has also been likened to that found in Plato's *Timaeus* (30a–b), where the creator demiurge forms a cosmos governed by reason by replacing disorder with order (Junge 2003: 88).

The theological treatise transmitted in the Coffin Texts lays the ethical foundation of society in the past, at the beginning of the cosmos. The recognition of *maat*'s great antiquity is found in another early composition of a different genre, a teaching. The *Instruction of Ptahhotep* states: 'Great is *maat*, enduring its effectiveness; it has not been disturbed since the time of Osiris. One punishes the one who transgresses against the laws; it is something that the rapacious do not comprehend' (Lichtheim 1975: 64).

The 'time of Osiris' is located in the mythical past when the gods ruled on earth as the predecessors of the later historical kings, and the reign of the god Osiris appears in a king list of the time of Ramesses II (Gardiner 1959: pl. 1). The 'disturbance' refers to the murder of Osiris by his brother Seth and the latter's usurpation of the throne. Eventually *maat* was restored when Horus, the son and rightful heir of Osiris, was installed on the throne of his father. The text explains why *maat* has not been disturbed since then, for anyone who breaks the law is punished and does not have the opportunity to disrupt, something that 'the rapacious' do not appreciate and therefore suffer punishment. We see here a link between *maat* and the law, indicating that the law enshrines *maat*, i.e. that ethical values are to be found in the provisions of the law, which, in Egypt, is promulgated by the king.

The origins of *maat* thus lie in what is called the 'time of god', a period in distant antiquity often referred to as a benchmark against which the present is measured (Luft 1978: 155 ff.). A related concept is the *sep tepy*, 'the first occasion', which refers to the creator god's first appearance as the rising sun; it was the aim of every king to restore things to how they had been at the *sep tepy*. The authority of the past is enshrined in Egyptian thinking and is frequently found in the Wisdom tradition. The sage Ptahhotep requests of the king that he be allowed to train an assistant: '"I will tell him the words of the hearers, the counsels of the forebears, who aforetimes listened to the gods." . . . Then the majesty of this god (the king) said, "Educate him in the words of the forbears!" ' (Lichtheim 1975: 63).

The *Instruction for King Merikara* (*c.*2000 BC) also holds up the past as a model and urges that one imitate the ancestors:

> *Maat* comes to him (the wise) sieved, like the counsels of the saying of the forebears. Imitate your fathers, your forebears . . . Behold, their words are preserved in the writings. Unroll them, that you may read and imitate the knowledgeable; for skill is created through learning.
>
> (Lichtheim 1975: 99)

In Ancient Egypt it was the purpose of the wisdom tradition to identify the order that governed society and to give guidance on how to live a life in harmony with the order of society through practical advice on how to behave in specific situations, rather than theoretical treatises on the principles of *maat*.

The phraseology of early biographical texts, attested from the 5th Dynasty onwards, assumes a set of values that are generally accepted and that would have reflected this order; one of the stock phrases of these texts is the assurance that the speaker was one who conformed to the norms and expectations of society: 'I am one who did what all people praise' (Janssen 1946: F143); 'One who does what his lord praised, who does what his father praised' (Janssen 1946: F144–5); 'I did what the great desire and the small praise' (Petrie 1909: pl. II; Janssen 1946: F127).

Biographical texts also provide an insight into these values as found, for example, on the false door of Neferseshemra (6th Dynasty):

> 'I have come from my city, I have come down from my province,
> having done *maat* for its lord, having satisfied him with what he desires,
> having spoken *maat* and done *maat*,
> having said what is good and repeated what is good,
> having seized a good moment, I desiring good therein for people,
> having judged two people so that they are satisfied,
> having rescued the weak from the hand of one stronger than he when I could;
> having given the hungry bread, <the naked> clothing and a landing to the
>   boatless,
> having buried the one without a son, having made a boat for one without a
>   boat;
> having respected (my) father and been kind to (my) mother;
> having raised their children.' So he says, his good name being Sheshi.
>
> (Sethe 1903: 198.13–199.8; Lichtheim 1975: 17)

A Marxist interpretation of the concept of *maat* as a construct of the ruling class to control the masses is made unlikely in view of statements such as 'I am one who did what all people praise', and 'I did what the great desire and the small praise', which suggest that the values referred to were generally accepted. As Friedrich Junge states, for someone from within the system there is no reason for seeing in the concept of *maat* a control mechanism; for an ancient Egyptian, the structure of the world is not the product of an intellectual model, it is undeniably a product of the creation – the world just happens to be like that (Junge 2003: 87–8).

HISTORICAL DEVELOPMENTS IN THE ROLE OF *MAAT*

In the Old Kingdom the view prevailed that those who transgressed against *maat* and did not uphold and live by the values of society would, without fail, suffer the consequences. This view is reflected in the passage from the sage Ptahhotep quoted above (Lichtheim 1975: 64). The last clause of the passage suggests that 'the rapacious', who transgress against *maat* and suffer the consequences, do so out of ignorance; if they understood what penalty their acts would incur they would behave differently. *Maat* was the force that unified society and the state, personified in the king who held a pivotal position in ensuring that it was upheld and that transgressors were punished (Assmann 1990: 51 f.). His role is expressed in the Pyramid Texts, the oldest body of religious literature from Ancient Egypt: 'Heaven is at peace, the earth rejoices, for they have heard that he (the king) has put *maat* [in the place of wrong]' (Faulkner 1969: Spells 1775–6). When Neferseshemra speaks of 'having done *maat* for its lord, having satisfied him with what he desires' it is the king to whom he refers. The king also rewarded good behaviour and in the earlier periods the traditional funerary offering formula 'an offering that the king gives' would have been literally true: whether one received the requisite funerary offerings thus depended upon one's behaviour in this life (Assmann 1990: 244). This is why the traditional autobiographies, such as that of Neferseshemra, which assure the reader of the speaker's good character and behaviour, are found in funerary contexts. Recognition of the connection between this life and the next can be discerned in an 11th Dynasty text from Thebes: 'I did what the great desire and the small praise from a desire that (I) remain in life on earth (and) the necropolis' (Petrie 1909: pl. II; Janssen 1946: F127). The eloquent peasant expresses it more poetically:

> But *Maat* will be for eternity, to the netherworld it goes down in the hand of the one who does it. He is buried, the land being united with him, his name not having been erased on earth; he is remembered because of goodness.
>
> (Parkinson 1997: 73)

To the end of the Old Kingdom, the biographical texts emphasize that people lived their lives in conformity with the values accepted by society – people claim they did what the people praise, i.e. their behaviour was in harmony with the values and expectations of society. Although these values are ultimately of divine origin and sanction, there is no indication that the gods are directly involved in upholding them; the inevitable consequence of transgressing against *maat* – the norms and structures of society – is punishment, meted out by the king through his officials.

Following the breakdown of the centralized state at the end of the Old Kingdom, with the social upheaval and disruption of royal authority that accompanied it, we find an interesting modification to the phraseology of the biographical texts. As earlier, people still claim to have done what the people praise, i.e. to have behaved according to the norms accepted by society, enshrined in the concept of *maat* and upheld by the king: for example, the provincial governor Amenemhat says he was 'one who did what the great praise' (Sethe 1935: 19.15; Janssen 1946: F149). But one now frequently finds that the gods are also mentioned: 'One who did what people desire and the gods praise' (*Siut* IV: 62; Janssen 1946: F126); or the gods appear as the sole arbiters of what is correct behaviour: 'I have come from my city and descended from my province having done what my god praises and what all my gods praise' (Sethe 1935: 4.12–14; Janssen 1946: F148); Hapdjefa is one 'who does what all the gods of Asyut praise' (Sethe 1935: 64.13; Janssen 1946: F150). We see here a more direct involvement of the gods in the affairs of society: in contrast to the concept of *maat* as the intermediary between god and humankind, governing the behaviour of society, regulated by the king (Assmann 1990: 51 ff.) and being 'what the people praise', the gods are now directly involved in determining correct behaviour.

This more direct link between *maat* and the gods can also be seen in the Middle Kingdom Wisdom tradition. In the *Eloquent Peasant*, a work set in the 9th/10th Dynasties (*c.*2165–2040 BC), the peasant urges in his eighth petition: 'Do *maat* for the lord of *maat*' (Lichtheim 1975: 181), where 'lord' refers to the god rather than the king. He also claims that his statements about *maat* 'have issued from the mouth of Ra himself' (Lichtheim 1975: 181). The Middle Kingdom *Prophecy of Neferti* describes the disorder into which the land has fallen, including the break-up of the unified state, and attributes it to the sun-god Ra having withdrawn from mankind, i.e. *maat* is dependent on the god (P 51; Lichtheim 1975: 142 f.). The same view is found in another Middle Kingdom text, the *Admonitions of Ipuwer*, where the question is posed, 'Where is he (the god) today? Is he asleep?' (Lichtheim 1975: 160). The more direct involvement of the deity in the affairs of humankind is reflected in the position of the king who is less an independent authority and more the agent of god on earth; the *Instruction for King Merikara* states, 'for them (humankind) he (the creator god) predestined rulers, to lift up the back of the weak' (Lichtheim 1975: 106). The kings of the period are at pains to emphasize that their deeds are in agreement with the commands of the god, in other words the king acts in accordance with divine decree rather than simply on his own authority; Senusret I says: 'He (the sun-god Ra) begat me to do what should be done for him, to accomplish what he commands to do. He appointed me shepherd of this land, knowing him who would herd it for him' (Lichtheim 1975: 116).

Thus, with the failure of the institutions of society, enshrined in the king, at the end of the Old Kingdom, one turns to a higher authority, the deity, as guarantor of *maat*. Experience showed all too plainly that in this life those who lived according to *maat* did not always prosper and that those who ignored it often did – a situation that was in direct contrast with the old Wisdom tradition, according to which those who transgressed against *maat* were automatically doomed to failure. Now, punishment for wrong behaviour is transferred to the deity and the ultimate judgement of behaviour takes place not in this life but in the court of the netherworld, as expressed in the *Instruction for King Merikara*:

> The Court that judges the wretch, you know they are not lenient; on the day of judging the miserable, in the hour of doing their task. It is painful when the accuser has knowledge! Do not trust in length of years, they view a lifetime in an hour! When a man remains over after death, his deeds are set beside him as treasure, and being yonder lasts forever. A fool is he who does what they reprove!
>
> (Lichtheim 1975: 101)

Similar sentiments are expressed five centuries later on the mid-18th Dynasty stela of Baki (lines 3–4):

> I rejoice in speaking *maat*, knowing that it is beneficial for the one who does it on earth, from the beginning to death. It is an effective bastion for the one who speaks it (on) that day of arriving at the court that judges the distressed, discerns characters, exterminates the sinful and destroys his *ba*.
>
> (Varille 1954; Lichtheim 1992: 129)

Thus the realization of mortality influenced Egyptian ethical thinking; in this context, Jan Assmann's observation on the outcome of the struggle between Horus and Seth is illuminating:

> The claims of the physically stronger remained convincing only so long as the deities imagined themselves to be immortal. When they are reminded of their mortality, they, Seth included, immediately return to the principle of *maat*, which alone makes it possible to overcome death.
>
> (Assmann 2001: 140–1)

In the words of the eloquent peasant, '*Maat* will be for eternity, to the netherworld it goes down in the hand of the one who does it' (Parkinson 1997: 73).

In the Ramesside Period, in the context of the rise of personal piety, we encounter for the first time texts that speak of the direct intervention of a god in a person's earthly life, meting out punishment for wrongdoing. The texts do not go into detail about the misdemeanours committed, but they all involve the deity – swearing falsely by Ptah (stela of Neferabu, BM 589; Simpson 2003: 287–8); transgressing against the Peak of the West (stela of Neferabu, Turin N50058; Simpson 2003: 286–7); injuring a cow from the herd of the god Amun (stela of Nebra, Berlin 20377; Simpson 2003: 284–6). These texts document a significant development in the concept of *maat*. Until this time, *maat* had been the mediating principle between god and humankind and one's fate and fortune, ultimately decided in the next life, depended on how one measured up to its standards. Here, we have the recognition of a direct transgression against the deity with punishment inflicted directly by the deity in this life. We also find the view expressed that all people are totally dependent on the unfathomable, inscrutable will of god (Brunner 1963); one can no longer assume that one will do well in this life if one adheres to the principles of *maat*; in the words of the *Instruction of Amenemope*, a text that is heavily influenced by personal piety:

'Indeed, you do not know the plans of god' (22,5; 23,8); 'Man is clay and straw, the god is his builder. He tears down, he builds up daily; he makes a thousand poor by his will, he makes a thousand men into chiefs' (24,13–17; Lichtheim 1976: 146–63).

However, to conclude that *maat* has no role to play in this world (Assmann 1990: 254), and that the price paid for the new attitude of self-centred personal piety was a breakdown in social cohesion, leading to corruption and insecurity (Assmann 1989: 80; 1990: 265 f.), goes too far. Although we have more evidence for corruption in this period (see below), it is clear that *maat* still has a role to play. Amenemope states: '*Maat* is a great gift of god, he gives it to whom he pleases' (22,5); but *maat* does not operate automatically; one cannot assume, as did the old Wisdom tradition, that one would inevitably prosper if one always acted according to *maat*; god's will is inscrutable and overrules all. What is important in life is not one's fortune but one's relationship with god, in particular when one leaves this life: 'Happy is he who reaches the hereafter when he is safe in the hand of god' (*Amenemope* 24,13–17). To be safe in the hand of god implies having lived a life pleasing to god, but there is also the recognition that perfection cannot be achieved: 'man is ever in his failure'; 'there is no perfection before the god' (*Amenemope* 19,15 and 22; Lichtheim 1976: 157, 158).

That personal piety, which emphasizes the relationship of the individual with god, does not have to come at the expense of social cohesion is aptly illustrated by the autobiographical text of Anhurmose, high priest of Onuris in Thinis in the reign of Merenptah (19th Dynasty), in which his devotion to god is clearly expressed, yet where we also find an extensive exposé of social and ethical values:

> (34) I was upright of heart, without inclining to a sinful thing,
> I was a silent one, perfect of character, patient, . . .
> (35) who associated with him who had nothing.
> I was glad of the quiet-natured, who hated one of fiery speech;
> (36) I was one who expelled wrongdoing and [drove out] sorrow,
> who paid attention to the voice of the widow.
> I rescued the drowning, gave sustenance [to those who] were lacking.
> I was a protector (37) of the weak, who aided the widow robbed of her
>   possessions.
> I was a father to the [father]less, a mother who rescued the little ones;
> I was a nurse to his (38) clientele, who placed them upon a goodly path;
> I was a shepherd to his [people], who protected them from all misfortune;
> I was captain of his dependents, (39) attentive, caring about their concerns;
> I rejoiced in truth (*maat*) . . .
> I was the confidant of the humble . . .
> (40) I was one who paid attention to the poor, who did what he said.
> I rejoiced at justice; to hear falsehood is an abomination!
> (41) I did justice on earth as many times as there are hairs on the head;
> I was justified in all my situations on the day of reckoning . . . (42) . . .
> I was one beloved of the commoners,
> who made joyful the hearts of the people (43) because of matters;
> I was generous to him who had nothing, reviving the weary-hearted;
> I wept at a case of misfortune and cared for him who was (44) downcast;

I was attentive to the cry of the orphaned girl, doing all that she desired;
I lifted up the child burdened by sorrow, put an end to [his misfortune]
    (45) and wiped away his tears;
I cast sorrow to the ground for the woman who poured forth cries of grief
    ... (48) ...
I anointed the widow who had nothing and gave clothing to the naked;
I separated two quarrellers so that they went (49) in peace;
I pacified two brothers who were arguing and drove out their anger with
    my words.
I drove distress out of the hearts of the people and made glad the heart
    (50) of the sad.
I protected the poor stripling until the day of his flying off came;
I raised the downcast ...
I [gave support] (51) to the poor woman so as to warm her limbs by the
    fire;
I was a possessor of sustenance, who poured out provisions, who satisfied
    him who wished to eat.

                                 (Ockinga and al-Masri 1988: 31–47)

Rather than seeing personal piety as a movement that contributed to the breakdown of the old system of *maat* we should see in it a response to the failure of the old system. It had become clear that living a life determined by *maat* did not always lead to worldly success, but as we have seen, this did not result in an abandonment of the ethical standards *maat* enshrined; what changed was the argument in favour of adhering to these standards, which now is that they are the will of god, to whom success in this life is subordinated. To stand in the right relationship with god is what matters because at the final judgement, where *maat* still has a central role, the mortal – 'ever in his failure', for whom 'there is no perfection before the god', to quote Amenemope – is dependent on god's mercy.

THE JUDGEMENT OF THE DEAD

Next to the traditional biographical inscriptions and the writings of the Wisdom tradition, the Teachings and Instructions, the classic and widely known ancient Egyptian text that deals with the judgement in the netherworld gives us an insight into the ethics of the ancient Egyptians. The text forms Chapter 125 of the *Book of the Dead*; in the introductory section the deceased address the gods before whom they are to be judged:

Behold, I have come before you,
there being no sin of mine,
there being no trespass of mine,
there being no evil of mine,
there being no accuser of mine,
there being none against whom I have done anything,
(for) I live from *maat* and I am nourished by *maat*.
I have done what people say and that which pleases the gods;

I have satisfied god with what he desires;
I have given bread to the hungry and water to the thirsty,
clothing to the naked and a ferry to the boatless;
I have given divine offerings to the gods and funerary offerings to the spirits.

(Budge 1898: 260, line 12 ff.)

We note here echoes of the phraseology of the biographical texts; what follows, a list of misdemeanours the deceased denies having committed, complements the autobiographical texts, which make positive statements about the good deeds of the deceased. Two lists of wrongs the deceased denies having committed follow, the second the actual 'Declaration of Innocence' (the so-called Negative Confession), an address to the 42 divine judges, in which the deceased denies having committed 42 'sins'. The wrongs listed are all ones of commission; there are none of omission. Some are of a general nature, denying having done evil or wrong or having sinned; the rest are very specific. The order of the 'sins' is random although one can discern various categories:

- *Crimes against god*: 'I have not depleted the loaves of the gods', 'I have not stolen the cakes of the dead', 'I have not stopped a god in his procession', 'I have not stolen a god's property', 'I have not attacked and reviled a god', 'I have not cursed a god';
- *Fraud*: 'I have not diminished the *aroura* (field measure)', 'I have not added to the weight of the balance', 'I have not falsified the plummet of the scales', 'I have not held back (irrigation) water in its season', 'I have not trimmed the measure';
- *Criminal acts*: 'I have not killed', 'I have not ordered to kill', 'I have not stolen';
- *Exploitation of the weak*: 'I have not mistreated cattle', 'I have not robbed the poor', 'I have not taken milk from the mouth of children', 'I have not maligned a servant to his master', 'I have not extorted'; 'I have not caused fear';
- *Moral and social failings*: 'I have not coveted', 'I have not cheated', 'I have not told lies', 'I have not spied', 'I have not prattled', 'I have not committed adultery', 'I have not quarrelled', 'I have not been false', 'I have not had a hasty heart', 'I have not made trouble', 'I have not wanted more than I had';
- *Character failings*: 'I have not made many words', 'I have not been haughty', 'I have not been boastful', 'I have not sulked', 'I have not raised my voice'.

(Lichtheim 1976: 124–7).

The following address to the gods assures them that the deceased is pure, 'I live on *maat*, I feed on *maat*', and repeats the statements found in the traditional biographical texts 'I have done what people speak of, what the gods are pleased with; I have contented a god with what he wishes' (Lichtheim 1976: 128–9).

Chapter 125 of the *Book of the Dead* should be read in association with Chapter 30, the text inscribed on heart scarabs:

Heart of my mother! Heart of my (stages of) development, do not witness against me, do not oppose me in the court, do not show enmity against me in the presence of the keeper of the balance (Thoth). . . . Do not make my name odious

259

to the courtiers (of the god). . . . Do not think of sin next to the god, in the presence of the great god, lord of the West [i.e. the other world].

(Budge 1898: 96; Lichtheim 1976: 121)

Here the heart is addressed and adjured not to speak out against the deceased in the court of the netherworld. Texts such as these are often thought to illustrate the ancient Egyptians' attempt to ensure their afterlife by means of magic, even if this involved circumventing justice. Yet the tale of Setne Khaemwas and Si-Osire (Lichtheim 1980a: 138–42) illustrates the recognition that it is not funerary rituals and equipment that ensure a blessed afterlife but the outcome of the judgement before Osiris. In the tale, a rich man who is buried with all the funerary trappings is condemned to eternal torment whereas a poor man buried in a hole in the ground wrapped only in a mat receives a place of honour. At the judgement the good deeds of the poor man are found more numerous than his misdeeds in relation to his lifespan and in relation to his luck on earth. With the rich man the situation was the reverse. Setne Khaemwas was a son of Ramesses II; although the Demotic text dates to the Roman Period and may have been influenced by Hellenistic ideas, some of the central concepts can be traced to pharaonic times. In particular, this can be demonstrated for the weight given to a person's lifespan and fortune on earth in the judgement process. In the illustrations to Chapter 125 of the *Book of the Dead* from the 19th Dynasty onwards, showing the weighing of the heart, these two concepts appear associated iconographically with the balance, in the form of three deities concerned with an individual's fate – Meskhenet, personifying the birthstool, Shai, personifying 'fate', and Renenet, who personifies the course of an individual's life and personal development. Thus, at least as early as the 19th Dynasty, a person's lifespan and fortune were taken into consideration at the judgement (Seeber 1976: 83–8). Earlier texts make statements suggesting that one's fate in the afterlife depended on one's attitude to *maat*: in the Middle Kingdom *Tale of the Eloquent Peasant* we read: 'But Maat will be for eternity, to the netherworld it goes down in the hand of the one who does it.' The contemporary *Instruction for King Merikara* makes it very clear that the judges in the netherworld cannot be fooled (see above p. 256). Rather than interpreting the 'Declaration of Innocence' and the text of the heart scarab as cynical attempts at circumventing justice, it is probably more appropriate to understand them in the context of the central principle of the presumption of innocence enshrined in Common Law – it was the task of the divine tribunal to establish guilt or innocence and, as the sources attest, the ancient Egyptians believed that it did so.

THE ANTITHESIS OF *MAAT*

Chapter 125 of the *Book of the Dead* emphasizes *maat*; the judgement takes place in the 'Hall of the two *maat*s' – duality expresses completeness. In one of the 42 declarations the deceased also states 'I have not been deaf to *Maat*'. There is no single term that encompasses the negative as comprehensively as *maat* does the positive. *Isfet*, commonly translated 'sin', is the most frequently encountered. Already in the *Pyramid Texts* it appears as the antonym of *maat* (Faulkner 1969: §256). At the end of the Middle Kingdom we read in the *Complaints of Khakheperra-sonb*, '*Maat* has been cast out while *isfet* is in the council chamber' (Lichtheim 1975: 147). At his accession the king re-established *maat* in the land; in the words of his Restoration Decree, Tutankhamun 'drove out *isfet* throughout the Two Lands (Egypt), *maat* being established in its place' (Pritchard 1969: 251). *Isfet* encompasses words as well as deeds: 'There was not *isfet* which came from my mouth, no evil thing which my arms did' (Lichtheim 1988: 72). Another antonym of *maat* in its specific sense 'truth' is *gereg* 'falsehood, lie', which is also related to *isfet*. In Chapter 126 of the *Book of the Dead* the baboons who sit at the prow of the barque of the sun-god Ra are 'those who present *maat* to the Lord-to-the-Limit (sun-god), who judge between the weak and the strong . . . who live from *maat*, whose food is *maat*, whose hearts are free of lies (*gereg*), their abomination being sin (*isfet*)' (Budge 1898: 269). Although *isfet* can mean 'sin' in a general sense, the concept of 'sinfulness' as a definition of the basic human condition, forming a barrier between humankind and the gods, is not found. The closest one comes to such a view is a statement on the stele of Nebra (*c.*1250 BC): 'Just as a servant is wont to commit sin, so the lord (deity) is wont to forgive' (Simpson 2003: 286). It is recognized that to err is human, but the reference is still to individual acts rather than a general condition. In theory, it was possible to live a life without sin in accordance with *maat* and, as we have seen, it was the aim of the instructions and teachings to help one achieve this.

MAAT AND REALITY

As is only to be expected, reality and the high ethical standards we find expressed in the ancient sources did not always coincide. The denials of having committed various wrongs are a clear indication that people did, in fact, at times behave in this way. The denials are, at times, so unrealistic that one is tempted to interpret them as hypocrisy; for example, the following, on a statue of the general and later king Horemheb: 'I am a just one of god since being on earth, I satisfy him with *maat* every day. I have shunned wrongdoing before him, I never [did evil] since my birth' (Lichtheim 1976: 101). But the ancient Egyptians, the writers of such words and those to whom they were addressed, would doubtless have been only too aware that such standards are unattainable. They should, therefore, be interpreted as affirmations of ethical values universally acknowledged by society, as ethical standards that the writers accepted and with which they identified. Since, in Nebra's words, mortals are wont to commit sin, reality looked rather different.

Occasionally, we catch a glimpse of this reality. The *Tale of the Eloquent Peasant* (Lichtheim 1975: 169–84; Parkinson 1997: 54–88) is all about the attempts of the peasant to have wrongs committed by a corrupt official righted. In the contemporary *Instruction for King Merikara* we have indirect evidence for abuse of power by royal officials. The writer advises the future king:

> Make great your officials, that they keep your laws; he whose house is rich is not partial and a propertied man is one who does not lack. A poor man does not speak justly; one who says 'Would that I had!' is not upright. He is partial towards him whom he likes, favouring him who rewards [i.e. bribes] him.
>
> (Lichtheim 1975: 100)

The problem of partiality on the part of officials is one that the king's *Instructions to the Vizier* are aware of. In this text, best preserved in the tomb of the 18th Dynasty vizier Rekhmira in Thebes, the king urges: 'Regard one whom you know like one whom you do not know, one close to yourself like one far from your house' (Lichtheim 1976: 23). However, the text is aware of the danger of taking this too far, quoting the example of the vizier Akhtoy (early Middle Kingdom):

> Avoid what was said of the vizier Akhtoy, that he denied his own people for the sake of others for fear of being falsely called [partial]. If one of them appealed a judgement, that he had planned to do to him, he persisted in denying him, but that is excess of justice.
>
> (Lichtheim 1976: 22–3)

In the New Kingdom our sources are more plentiful. Letters (Wente 1990) and documents from Deir el-Medina, the village of workmen who built the tombs of the kings (McDowell 1990), illustrate the human weaknesses of the ancient Egyptians. In the school writings of the Ramesside Period referring to dishonest judges, Amun-Ra is 'The vizier of the poor. He does not take bribes from the guilty, he does not speak to the witness, he does not look at him who promises (i.e. offers a bribe)' (Lichtheim 1976: 111). A papyrus of the late 19th Dynasty records a long list of misdemeanours committed by a chief of workmen at Deir el-Medina – he is accused of having obtained his office by bribing the vizier, and a later vizier, who punished him for other wrongs, was himself dismissed by the king (Černý 1929: 256). A papyrus of the mid-20th Dynasty provides evidence for charges of misconduct and large-scale embezzlement levelled against personnel, including a priest, of the temple of Khnum at Elephantine (Peet 1924).

CHAPTER NINETEEN

LAW

———— ·◆· ————

Schafik Allam

By the early third millennium BC, Egyptian society had become consolidated: a centralized state was achieved with Pharaoh as its head; a highly developed administration was then created.

THE CONCEPT OF *MAAT*

In order to understand law in this society, it is important to realize that the ideology of the time was a religiously determined whole. A society shaped by religion, as Egypt was, saw every aspect of the world as being under the sway of divine power which established and maintained order. Hence, among the Egyptians there arose a religious concept central to the appreciation of the social order with its inherent rules. It was called *maat* – mythologically personified and anthropomorphically represented as a goddess of order, harmony, truth and justice. This goddess embraced not only the cosmic order, but also the entire realm of terrestrial life where human affairs take place. Thus Maat became the divinity to whom everyone was responsible for his deeds. The concept of *maat* manifestly touched upon morality and ethics; in fact, the entire order of society was bound up with this doctrine (Helck 1980b; Teeter 2001; Ockinga, this volume).

This was crucial for the Egyptian concept of monarchy, because the king, as son of the gods, had the task of defending *maat* in the world (Goebs, this volume). By virtue of his insight into the essence of *maat*, the king knew what was right for society. Accordingly the king was called upon to maintain and, eventually, restore order – and consequently issue appropriate laws. Thus, in Egypt, official legislation comprised not divinely revealed statutes, as in Judaism and Islam, but laws which the king issued as needed.

Not only the king but all instruments of the state took *maat* as their ruling principle, as the goal and duty of their activity. *Maat* was, in other words, the embodiment of just administration: bureaucracy and judiciary were responsible for *maat*, and thus for maintaining just order. This is illustrated by a trial record which, after giving the date of the proceedings, begins with the words: 'May the court proceed according to the precepts of Maat' (Allam 1973a: 212). Ultimately, it was the task of all people to live in accord with *maat*. After death each person was still held accountable, for life continued after death in a heavenly realm, provided that one passed the other-worldly judgement. Vindication was determined there by just behaviour during one's life on earth.

From all this it appears that law (rules regulating the behaviour of members of society) was tied up with a religious world-view. *Maat* symbolized an ideal order, for which all people had to strive; moreover, *maat* governed all human activity as well, establishing an ethical framework for every deed.

Maat subordinated the social order to a broad concept of equity. As the Egyptians strongly valued peace, they held this doctrine in highest regard, and generally possessed a well-developed sense of justice. So, very early on, the taking of law into one's own hands (self-help) lost any validity. To the Egyptian way of thinking, the only admissible means of defending disputed rights was due process in court. Moreover, Egyptians, given their sense of justice and social responsibility, were inclined to advocate not only their own rights but also others'. One trial record, for example, shows a father who took his own son to court, because the son had committed adultery. From another trial record we infer that a workman brought his co-worker to law for stealing tools from state property. In both cases it fell to a third party to bring the offence before the court (Allam 1973a: 301 and 217–19, respectively). Already then, we have in Egypt cases of 'volunteer prosecutors'.[1]

It is not our intention here to portray legal usage in pharaonic Egypt as a pristine ideal. Whether in some golden age the idea of justice in society was perfectly realized is an academic question. The judicial practices of the ancient Egyptians already suggest, among other aspects, transgressions and litigations in practically every area of daily life.

RELIGION AND LAW

There are further connections between religion and law in pharaonic Egypt. Indeed, religion was always significant in the legal relations between people. This close relationship, even interdependence, between religion and law manifests itself in one especially noteworthy consequence: since the gods were regarded as source and guardian of established order, they could be consulted for a proper decision in doubtful cases. Thus, alongside the usual legal process, the Egyptians also employed divine judgement, placing the omniscience of a divinity at the service of judicial proceedings. This practice was based on the belief that the gods championed the cause of justice.

Today we are well informed about the trial procedures of the Egyptians, thanks to the corpus of texts preserved from the settlement of Deir el-Medina in western Thebes. Among the inhabitants, as in any community, there were various conflicts and breaches of the law. A local court, composed of local dignitaries, sat regularly to judge such matters. Two distinct types of trial procedure are attested. Normally, the court exercised full civil and penal jurisdiction. On certain occasions, a god was also summoned, who then, as supreme judge, proclaimed the decision in a given case.

The documentation reveals many trials in which, remarkably, the divine judge settled disputes not arbitrarily, but on juridical grounds. For example, in a suit over a house the god is said to have awarded the house to a man on the basis of a royal regulation. A royal ordinance, therefore, served in this case as the legal basis for the judgement. Other records suggest the application of the current law of succession before the divine court. In such cases the divine judge seems to have exercised no discretionary power; he was apparently bound by the ordinary norms of succession (Allam 1973b: 81–2).

In general then, the divine judgement process reflected the normal, secular procedure. The essential difference appears to be that the judicial decision, according to Egyptian belief, was proclaimed not by a man, but by a god who commanded what was appropriate for the case at hand. Why was the god consulted at all? It seems that the local court sometimes had judgement pronounced by an authoritative god, in the expectation that the defeated party would submit to divine will. This application of divine judgement fell into disuse shortly after the Ramesside Period.

PRIVATE PIOUS FOUNDATIONS

A basic development during the course of Egyptian history was the emergence of law separate from religion, in other words its secularization. But this did not always mean the simple profaning of legal usages: in some cases the emergence of truly legal concepts derived its impulse from religion itself. A good example is the creation of private pious foundations (Allam 2003: 42–5; forthcoming a).

A prominent motif in Egyptian tomb decoration is the bringing of offerings for the deceased. Egyptians were always concerned about their sustenance in the hereafter, because they expected to have a life after death much like earthly existence. So they resorted to magic and ritual in the hope of securing sustenance for themselves in the afterlife; nevertheless, they also depended upon the actual delivery of food and drink at the tomb. Egyptians had a strong sense of this obligation and trusted in the loyalty of their family and survivors. There must have been cases, however, where this piety diminished, thus giving rise to doubts as to whether an individual would be properly provided for after death. Gradually it became common to make arrangements during one's own lifetime for continuing services after death, enlisting the assistance of family members and even outsiders. An individual would then bequeath to these people fields or revenues, obliging them to present mortuary offerings and celebrate the required services. Should these people for any reason fail to meet their obligations, others were to take their place, fulfilling the prescribed duties and receiving the same compensation. With mortuary services thus provided for from generation to generation, the endower was secure forever.

In this way, the pious foundation set up by the individual came into being, as a permanently established juridical mechanism. As the religious and ethical injunction to care for the dead lost its force, a legal obligation was created in its place.[2] The founder sought, furthermore, to protect himself against a possible neglect of his endowed intent. He did so in quite a practical fashion, by enlisting the local temple, as represented by its priesthood. Thus the continuing reliability of mortuary offerings was secured by their incorporation into the temple service, whose constancy was guaranteed as a matter of course. Texts from Old Kingdom times onwards testify that Egyptians increasingly entrusted their mortuary rites to priests.

From later texts we learn that, in some cases, the king was designated as the ultimate beneficiary of the foundation. This is illustrated by the inscription of a high official who established a pious foundation for his king (Amenhotep III) in the temple at Memphis. He furnished it with, among other things, fields, serfs and cattle. The king, for his part, ordered the priesthood to perform the same services for the endower's statue. The piety and loyalty of the endower to his king might thus have played a role in his establishing the foundation. The legal historian, however, would recognize in the incorporation of the king an additional means of security for the survival of the foundation. Having placed the foundation under the charge of the king and priests, the endower could be assured that state and temple would guarantee the longevity of his foundation. Hence a legal form, such as that of the foundation, was not monolithic in character; rather, it was conditioned by human aspiration in connection with practical needs.

We can thus see how a juridical obligation (the private foundation, in this instance) came into existence, and how for the first time in history the Egyptians developed it into an institution that kept on growing through the centuries and, having taken on sophisticated forms, continued well into modern times (Allam, forthcoming a).

Law thus asserted its autonomy as early as the age of the pyramids, while the role of religion in legal matters began to diminish. From this point on it was not religion which determined the legal standing of a matter, but rather the juridical mechanism, which became authoritative, even in the religious sphere. Actually, the force of law even found expression in religious belief. For example, in the mythological conflict between Horus and Seth, the gods themselves had to appear before a court in order to resolve their dispute (Allam 1992). In a similar vein, the judgement of the dead took place before a special court, and occupied a prominent place in Egyptian belief (Helck 1980a; Quirke 2001b).

THE EXECUTION OF JUDGEMENTS

Research on the documentation from Deir el-Medina has provided valuable information about the legal system in this workmen's community; as regards the judicial practices, the execution of judgements deserves special attention. In the past, scholars were in the dark about this procedure, since all that was known was that a court usually pronounced at the end of a trial the formula '(Party) A is right; (party) B is (proved) wrong'. Inadequate understanding gave rise to all sorts of hypotheses, and scholars thought that Egyptian courts never really put any judgement into effect. But now, with the material from Deir el-Medina, we are able to shed new light on this aspect of ancient Egyptian procedure (Allam 1973b: 98–106; cf. 1985: 71–7 and 2004: 42–5).

Several records demonstrate that the local court was an institution which not only issued judgements, but also carried them out. For example, a text tells of a lawsuit between a woman and a scribe about a garment. The court adjudged the scribe right, whereas the woman was to blame; the text also discloses that the garment was given to the scribe right away. In another example, a conflict over the landed property of a woman was judged by the court, which declared the woman in the right. The text adds that she was given the property in question. In yet another trial, where a scribe confronted a painter, we are informed that the first was found in the right and the other in the wrong. Moreover, the court punished the painter with a thrashing and condemned him to hard labour (in a quarry). Many records confirm that such corporal punishments were actually carried out. Other measures of coercion could be taken as well: in one case the court ordered two workmen to apprehend a man by putting him in fetters.

In some trials there was also the threat of confiscation of the losing party's property. In such cases the court would set a time limit, giving the debtor the opportunity to avoid proceedings against him by making a payment or other kind of recompense. If a debtor was in a position to fulfil his obligations but tried to evade them, the court could order one of its staff to seize items of the debtor's property. In one law suit, the court decided against a debtor; he then promised under oath to pay his creditor. The text adds, moreover, that the court appointed a workman to supervise the debtor, in other words to ensure the settlement of the debt. Other texts confirm this practice. In one letter, the sender relates to his correspondent that the court-bailiff arrived and took a garment.

Numerous minutes tell us that the plaintiff asked purely for the payment due to him in accordance with the agreed transaction. We know, however, of several cases in which the defeated party at court had to pay an amount significantly higher than the sum owed to the plaintiff (Allam 2005). The requirement that the debtor pay more than the original amount of his debt was issued by the court, especially when the defendant unsuccessfully contested the plaintiff's claims. In one law suit, the plaintiff took an oath affirming that his adversary had not yet settled his debts; the latter was then beaten. The text also mentions that one of the two men made a confession a few days later; no doubt this man was the adversary, who had possibly contested his creditor's claims in court. Consequently he was liable to a heavy penalty: he had received goods worth two units of silver but had to pay back goods to a value of roughly four-and-a-half units. In another trial, not only was the debtor required to pay his debt increased by a considerable fine, but also to take an oath whereby he affirmed the transfer of the seized property in favour of his creditor – thus approving of all the proceedings by which the dispute was settled.

CIVIL AND CRIMINAL LAW

The texts considered thus far seem to indicate an empirically based law, founded upon facts currently experienced. But in the documentation from Deir el-Medina, which has greatly enriched our knowledge, there is also evidence of some initial steps towards dogmatic thinking.

For the inhabitants, the only acceptable way to settle disputes was by trial before the court. Composed of local dignitaries, the court presided over cases that would be classified today as both civil and criminal. In other words, the court was called upon to pass judgement not only on disputed rights between individuals, but also on offences such as theft, adultery, defamation, assault, etc. Equally, the court could act as an executory power with various means of coercion: it could exercise the power of sequestration in respect of a debtor's property, and of physical punishment against a wrong-doer.

The surviving evidence from Deir el-Medina reveals that some trials ended with the swearing of an oath by the losing party at the order of the court. In civil cases the defendant swore to meet his obligation to the opponent as soon as possible, whereas in criminal cases he promised to cease his illegal conduct in the future. In many trials, however, the court was not content with such a simple promise. The defendant was, therefore, required formally to accept a penalty of corporal punishment, to be inflicted if his promise was not kept.

Looking carefully at the penalties, we can see a distinction with respect to criminal offences. In civil cases the losing party promised to pay his debt, or incur a thrashing (typically 100 blows). For criminal offenders, however, more severe corporal punishment was the norm. In a slander trial, for example, the proscribed penalty for a repeat offence was mutilation of the nose and ears. This punishment, as well as impalement, could be imposed as the penalty against a person convicted of disturbing the repose of the dead. In another trial for a similar offence, the penalty comprised an application of the bastinado and the inflicting of five open wounds. As to the penalty for adultery, it was mutilation of the nose and ears, and exile to Nubia, or exile combined with hard labour.

Thus the court seems to have distinguished between civil disputes among citizens, on the one hand, and criminal offences on the other. Such a distinction must reflect an emerging awareness that certain transgressions offended the entire community and should, therefore, be punished more severely by the law (Allam 1978). By all appearances, therefore, the distinction between criminal cases and civil disputes seems, as far as this author is aware, to have occurred for the first time in history in pharaonic Egypt.

JURISPRUDENCE

To judge from the surviving texts, the Egyptians apparently had no concept of jurisprudence as a discipline; theoretical deliberation as the basis of substantive law is not attested for pharaonic times. Yet a papyrus has come to light which proves that the consideration of legal questions in isolation, as well as the abstract elaboration of legal norms, was not unknown to the Egyptians. The papyrus comes from Hermopolis (el-Ashmunein) and can be dated to the early third century BC. The *recto* of this unique papyrus, containing 305 preserved lines of demotic script, has an unusual subject: theoretical legal discussion, divided into approximately 200 articles grouped into four sections (Allam 1986; Stadler 2004).

The first section deals with tenant farming arrangements and disputes between the tenant farmer and the lessor. One article provides a good example:

> If a person takes a field on lease in order to cultivate it, and the lessor gives him seed-corn, but the field receives no water due to (drought) in the year in question, they should not oblige him to render the harvest [i.e. payment]. Ordinarily they require (only) that he return the seed-corn.
>
> (col. II, 10–11)

The text also contains contract formulae which served as templates, and the arrangements to be made, for example, by the purchaser of a house in order to protect his interests against an unfair seller. Rental agreements for various types of buildings are also discussed, as well as litigation arising from non-payment of rent. The papyrus treats in detail one particular marriage settlement, under which the woman ceded to her husband a considerable amount of capital; he, in turn, guaranteed her an endowment. The concern here is not with the general pattern of marriage contracts, but with the disputes that could arise between father-in-law and husband when such contracts were not honoured.

There follow cases concerning real estate, for example, when an individual built a house on a plot of land and the title to the land was later claimed by someone else. The text describes the procedures to be applied in order to settle the conflict (col. VI, 3–11). Next, the text treats various disputes among neighbours. The following example is typical:

> If a man brings action against (another) man, saying 'He has opened the entrance of his house (facing) my plot', and if it is the case that the defendant has no claim to the (neighbouring plot), then ordinarily they seal the entrance completely.
> (col. VIII, 19–20)

The final paragraphs in the papyrus deal with the law of succession – especially the position of the 'eldest son' in disputed cases – as well as various actions regarding inheritance.

From other contemporary documents, we know that all the questions treated in the text are cases reflecting issues common in everyday life. The text also mentions procedures for the assessment of evidence, on the basis of which the judge had to decide a given case. The types of admissible evidence (such as oaths, entries in the official register, judicial inspection, etc.) are also known from other contemporary texts. The papyrus thus gives a useful overview of law in Egypt in the early Hellenistic period. Incidentally, the text contains no mention of corporal punishment, with the sole exception of a bastinado in the case of someone who erected a building without waiting for official approval.[3] By looking more closely at the text, it appears that it discusses only questions concerning private property, omitting matters of criminal law. Evidently the author was mainly interested in the property rights of the individual.

With this intent, the author classified formulations in sections according to subject. So, leases of arable land are dealt with in one section, problems of inheritance in a second, litigation between neighbours in a third, and so on – along with appropriate subdivisions. No doubt the arrangement of the material betrays an author who knew very well how to treat legal questions systematically, even if his arrangement does not entirely correspond to ours today.

In order to discuss the topics, the author conceived theoretical disputes and situations, designed for guidance in the judgement of any number of actual cases. He made use, too, of a repertoire of stock definitions – for example, paraphrases for our designations 'plaintiff', 'defendant', etc. The author also made use of abstract classification, developing, for instance, the notion 'thing' (*neket*), just as later a Roman jurist used the concept *res*.

From all this, we can deduce that the author was a true jurisprudent. For modern scholars this conclusion is highly significant for the study of legal history. Earlier it was doubted whether there were scholars in ancient Egypt who could be qualified as jurists in the strict sense of the word. Today their existence is undisputed.

The aforementioned law book was obviously not confined to local use. We have proof – in the form of two papyrus fragments from Oxyrhynchus (el-Bahnasa), corresponding fairly closely to certain passages in the text – that a Greek translation existed, too. This Greek papyrus appears to have been written in the second half of the second century AD. The translation, however, was probably made at the beginning of the Hellenistic era. This means that both the Greek translation and the original demotic law book are to be attributed to the same period. However, the Greek version is not a literal translation. It must, therefore, have been made on the basis of a different demotic original. There were, then, several copies of the demotic law book in existence at the same time. Hence we may assume that towards the onset of the Hellenistic era several such law books existed, circulating throughout the country.

This assumption is confirmed by another demotic papyrus, a theoretical treatment in précis form about the certification of a legal transaction, along with the eventual submission of documents to the contracting parties (Lippert 2003). According to the papyrus, certain contractual relations between private individuals are meant to be regulated through documentation. After the event the two parties enter eventually into conflict: one asserts that, although he has made the expected payment, he has not received from the other party the document necessary to establish his credit. This papyrus might have been composed towards the end of the third century BC. In addition, another demotic papyrus – from Tebtynis (Umm el-Baragat) and assigned to the time between the late Hellenistic period and early Roman rule – has close affinities to the law book from Hermopolis.

Thus, there appear to have existed a number of Egyptian law books, of varied topics, stemming from a variety of times and places (Chauveau 1991; Tait 1991; Lippert 2004a, 2004b). We might venture the hypothesis that all these texts descended from a single original; the archetype would have ultimately derived from the time of the Persian ruler Darius I. This hypothesis, appealing as it is, is not wholly tenable, however, because apart from one historical report (*vide infra*), no conclusive evidence is forthcoming from the Persian Period.

Returning to the law book from Hermopolis, and looking closely at some of its formulations, such as dating formulae, we can detect archaic or archaizing elements. Harvest time, for example, is mentioned several times in the text. But the harvest time cited here (May–June) does not correspond to that of the calendar in use during the third century BC, when the text was transcribed. At that time a fluctuating calendar was in use. The harvest time mentioned in the papyrus corresponds rather to the calendar of the eighth century BC. Consequently we may assume that the relevant paragraphs were taken from a much older manuscript, reflecting the conditions of the eighth century BC (Pestman 1983: 17–18). Several other features of the text also lead to the same conclusion. Thus, the Hermopolis law book contains portions of a variety of texts from different periods, all having been reworked probably by a jurist of the early third century BC.

Since the author proceeds *inter alia* from earlier sources, without saying so explicitly, he might well have reworked laws of earlier kings and used them as the basis of his own decisions. Several papyri show that laws from pharaonic times were still valid in early Hellenistic times. The policies of the Ptolemies point likewise in this direction: they promulgated many regulations concerning administration and finances, but as long as their interests were not threatened, they allowed the Egyptian population to continue living according to the old accepted pharaonic rules.

In all the aforementioned demotic papyri, Egyptian jurists treated legal material systematically; they clearly followed a relevant principle of organization, with thorough-going subdivisions in each category. We can detect here a deepening of juristic thought, the point of departure for law as a rigorous scientific discipline: here began genuine jurisprudence.

EGYPTIAN LAW UNDER GREEK AND ROMAN RULE

As for Egypt under Greek and Roman rule, the country underwent major reforms in many respects. Yet, the Ptolemaic bureaucracy was, to some extent, the direct continuation of the pharaonic one, especially at the local level. Equally, the population continued to live more or less by its traditional legal principles, largely inherited from the past, since neither the Ptolemies nor the Romans were willing to interfere in such matters, as long as their own interests were safeguarded.

During the pharaonic Late Period, the judicial apparatus must have been reorganized. Indeed, as early as the reign of Psamtik I, new idioms ('the judges' and 'judgement house') were standardized in demotic documents, indicating that the administrative reforms enforced by the king must have called *inter alia* for major modification of the judiciary. Furthermore, the documentation, though revealing the responsibilities of the new courts, betrays no sign of any administrative activity on the part of the courts. These were, then, wholly devoted to jurisdiction; this professionalization might have culminated in a separation of administrative and judicial powers.

When the Ptolemies arrived, new law-courts were created for non-Egyptian residents. As to the native judicial apparatus, however, the picture does not seem to have changed; we can reasonably conclude that the Egyptian population continued to seek legal redress before its own courts (henceforth termed *laokritai* in Greek documents), just as it had before (Allam 1991). At court sessions in pharaonic times there was always an official – simply called 'scribe' – who worked with the judges. This official introduced cases and took actions in concert with the judges, thus forming a link between the central government and the local judiciary. Under the Ptolemies, too, we can recognize the same official discharging the same functions at law-courts, but with the Greek designation *eisagogeus*, even in demotic documents (Allam, forthcoming b).

A similar situation is found concerning the official land-registers. From the beginning of pharaonic civilization, the administration was diligent in keeping records of agricultural land, which contributed grain and other products to the royal granaries and treasury. Hence, royal land-archives were maintained by the government. In time, these archives began to be consulted for reasons other than taxation – for instance, when disputes arose over private land rights. In such situations the law-court, seeking a proof beyond reasonable doubt, could have recourse to the archives. Such archives existed in the Ramesside capital (Per-Ramesses) and even in the remote Dakhla Oasis.

In the Hellenistic period, Greek documents describe an instrument called *katagraphé* – pointing likewise to an official land-register recording private possessions of land. During the Roman era, too, there existed such a register in every city, but labelled *bibliothéké enktéseon*; it enhanced the publicity of rights connected with private land possessions, so that the purchaser of a piece of land, for example, could search the archives and be assured that no third party's right would obstruct his acquisition. From these facts, we can conclude that neither the Hellenistic instrument nor the

Roman land-archives was an innovation (indeed, a counterpart of the pharaonic institution existed neither in Greece nor in Rome), the underlying concept having already been practised in pharaonic Egypt for at least a millennium. Rather, the Ptolemies and Romans merely introduced some changes to improve efficiency (Allam 1994, 2006).

These examples suffice to demonstrate that commonly used Greek terms can easily blur our view. They should not be taken at face value as indicators of true innovations introduced in Egypt.

HISTORIOGRAPHICAL

Classical authors write respectfully of law and justice among the ancient Egyptians. For instance, Diodorus Siculus (I, 94–5) speaks of six pharaohs (Mnevis, Sasychis, Sesoosis, Bocchoris, Amasis and Darius) who were great legislators (cf. Menu 2005). We know, moreover, that several Greek law-makers (Solon for certain, perhaps also Plato, and many others) travelled to Egypt in order to study *inter alia* Egyptian law. The Persian king Darius I, especially, is said to have held Egyptian law in high regard and to have occupied himself with it extensively. According to one later, demotic papyrus, dated to the late third century BC, Darius ordered his satrap in Egypt to assemble the savants so that they might collect all that was known of Egyptian law before the Persian conquest; these savants, having worked for 16 years, produced a codification written in demotic, with a version in Aramaic (Bresciani 1996).

In conclusion, it seems that the history of law, which was to play itself out over the course of millennia in the Mediterranean basin, began in pharaonic Egypt.

NOTES

1 The idea of enabling the volunteer to accuse the wrong-doer in court was introduced later in Athens by Solon for all citizens in connection with certain crimes.
2 Foundation is meant here in the broader sense: an institution designed by human objective with, as its appointed purpose, the fulfilment of an enduring goal. Two things are necessary to achieve the goal: a lucrative property, which the endower cedes from his property; and a lasting, i.e. renewable, personal association which will be responsible for administration of the foundation's aims.
3 The thrashing was effectively applied in civil and penal trials alike.

PART V

IDEOLOGIES

——•◆•——

CHAPTER TWENTY

KINGSHIP

——.•.——

Katja Goebs

At the latest with the unification of the state under the rule of a single king around 3000 BC, Egyptian theologians developed a sophisticated ideology of kingship that portrayed the pharaoh as the link between the spheres of men and gods (Baines 1995b: 95–7, 115; Dreyer and Ziegler 2002). This ideology justified his (officially) unchallenged rule at the head of the centralized state, and aided in its smooth functioning. Accordingly, various strategies were developed to express and reinforce this status, including royal dress and regalia, iconography, myths, rituals and propagandistic texts.

RULING WITH *MAAT*

In his capacity as an essentially 'divine' being, the Egyptian king enjoyed many prerogatives, but he also had obligations: to the gods, who – according to Egyptian belief – had 'created' him and 'given him the office of kingship', to the court and elite who accepted him as their ruler and in many cases were instrumental in bringing him to power (for example, when several royal sons were vying for the kingship, or when the previous ruler had no male heir), and to the general population, whose work sustained the country and its government. Explicit reference to these three domains can be found in a piece of wisdom literature generally dated to the early Middle Kingdom, the *Instruction for King Merikara*. Composed in the aftermath of the social changes brought about by the First Intermediate Period, the ideology of kingship reflected in this text had clearly undergone some important developments compared to earlier periods. However, this text is the most 'pragmatic' surviving treatise on the office of kingship, and reflects a tripartite view of the social world (outside of the kingship) that is attested throughout Egyptian history. In it, the deceased father of Merikara instructs him on the proper conduct of the royal office, and includes the following recommendations:

Make your monuments last through love of you!
Make the cor[vée workers] whom the city has gathered have plenty –
They will thank God for this bounty . . . and pray to [the Gods] for your health.
Respect the officials! Make your people well! . . .

275

Make your great ones great, so that they will enact your laws!
Someone wealthy of house cannot be partial . . .

Do Truth so that you may endure on earth!

Make [many] monuments for God;
This makes the name of him who does it live.
A man should do what is good for his soul:
Performing the monthly service, putting on white sandals [i.e. ritual dress],
Joining the temple estate, keeping confidential the mysteries,
Entering into the sanctuary, eating bread from the temple!
. . .
God knows the man who acts for Him . . .

(Parkinson 1997: 218–21)

All three levels of obligation – to the general populace, the elite and the gods – can be subsumed under the ideological notion of 'Ruling with *maat*', which is also explicit in this text (Assmann 1995a [1990]: 200–12). This concept is attested as early as the mid-2nd Dynasty, in the Horus name of its sixth king, Sekhemib-perenmaat – 'Horus strongwilled, who comes forth for [i.e. champions] Maat' (Wilkinson 1999: 202).

Maat is a term that has been translated in various ways (see Ockinga, this volume): it is most commonly rendered 'justice' or 'righteousness', but in the context of exercising the kingship it relates first and foremost to the maintenance of the cosmic equilibrium, which included the social and political spheres (Assmann 1995a [1990]: 219; Baines 1995a: 12). The cosmic dimension of *maat* is expressively conveyed in its mythical embodiment as a solar daughter and 'Eye' (that is, disc) of the sun god (Assmann 1995a [1990]: 160).

When, according to myth, the creator Atum brought about the 'first occasion' (*sep tepy*) of sunrise, he set into motion the cyclical equilibrium of the Egyptian cosmos, with its eternal sequence of interchanging day and night, of the waxing and waning of the moon and the months, of the agricultural seasons – dependent on the flooding and receding of the Nile – and of the reigns of kings, who counted their regnal years from the date of their own accession to the throne (Derchain 1975/76; Assmann 1995a [1990]: 174–95). This last practice points to the underlying idea that each new rule represented a 're-creation' of the status quo, and relates to a dogma of kingship that demanded of the office holder a continuous struggle against the threats to the existing order. Thus, the king would repel *isfet*, 'chaos, disorder, the untoward' (Derchain 1965: 24–8; Assmann 1995a [1990]: 213–22), which, depending on the context, could be mythically embodied in either the snake-demon Apophis, who threatened the course of the solar barque across the sky, the god Seth and his 'gang' of followers, who – among other things – stood for the illegitimate assumption of rule, or simply all the 'enemies of Egypt', internal or external. In defeating *isfet*, the king would maintain *maat* on a variety of levels, including the sphere of everyday life, where it affected the 'correct' way of life according to societal norms, social solidarity and – for the king – responsible government.

Accordingly, one of the most prominent artistic motifs in Egyptian royal iconography from the earliest periods onwards – predating even the time of the supposed unifier of the country – is the representation of the king smiting his enemies (Figure 20.1), generally with a stone mace, a motif that remained part of the royal iconographic repertoire until the very last days of pharaonic culture (Hall 1986).

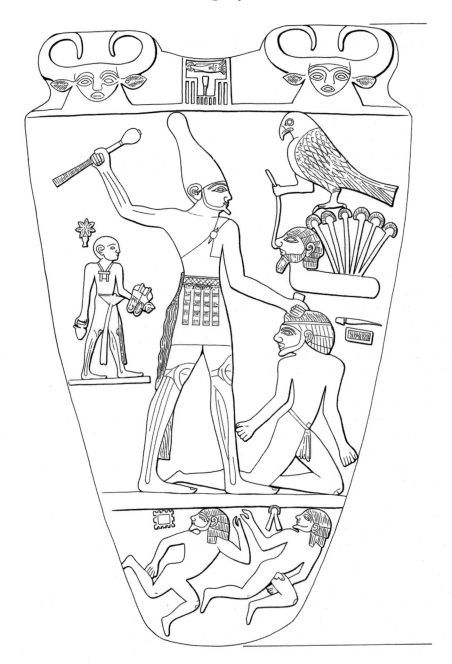

Figure 20.1   Narmer, wearing the White Crown of Upper Egypt, smites a captive enemy, from the Narmer Palette, 1st Dynasty (Egyptian Museum, Cairo JE 32169/CG 14716) (from Kemp 1989b: fig. 12).

A theological treatise first attested in the New Kingdom, but potentially going back to the Middle Kingdom, states that the king was placed on earth by the solar creator expressly in order to maintain *maat* and defeat *isfet*: 'Ra has placed King NN on the earth of the living for ever and eternity, judging the people, satisfying the gods, bringing about Maat, and defeating Isfet' (Assmann 1970: 22; English translation in Assmann 1995b: 19–21).

Accordingly, *maat* was under threat whenever a king died, and every ruler had to re-found its order, which also involved the ritual re-unification of the Two Lands (Millet 1990) (Figure 20.2). On the late Old Kingdom Palermo Stone, a ceremony

Figure 20.2 Symbolic expression of the 'unification of the Two Lands' on the throne-base of a statue of Senusret I from his mortuary temple at Lisht, 12th Dynasty (Egyptian Museum, Cairo JE 31139/CG 414). The gods Horus (left) and Seth (right), as representatives of the 'Two Lands', tie the heraldic plants of Upper and Lower Egypt, the 'lily' and papyrus, to the Egyptian hieroglyph *sema*, meaning 'to unite'. The group is topped by the birth name of Senusret I, and can be read as 'Senusret is the uniter of the Two Lands' (from Kemp 1989b: fig. 6).

of 'uniting Upper and Lower Egypt' appears at the beginning of every new reign (von Beckerath 1997: 14–15 with fig. 3). Representations and accounts of the king's battles against Egypt's external enemies – involving the iconography of smiting discussed above – were placed on the outer walls of temples, where they would serve a dual purpose: they reinforced to the general population the image and myth of the pharaoh as preserver of *maat* and Egypt, and represented, at the same time, a symbolic protective shield against all threats to the order of the cosmos – an image of which every Egyptian temple represented (Bell 1997: 132–3; most expressly in the Greco-Roman Periods. Finnestad 1985; 1997: 203 26).

While the origin of the smiting motif may be sought in actual historical battles, the image quickly became canonized. Many new rulers went to battle at the onset of their reign, but even the ones who did not were represented in the pose of smiting the enemies of Egypt and *maat*. To the Egyptian, eternally recurring ritual truth superseded an – unpredictable and unique – historical one (Hornung 1966; 1992: 147–64). The most famous illustration of this world-view can be found in the Egyptian accounts of the battle of Kadesh against the Hittites, from which the Egyptian army, led by Ramesses II, narrowly emerged intact (Murnane 1995b: 208–15; Silverman 1995: 51–2). We know from the diplomatic correspondence kept in the Hittite archives of the time that the conflict ended – after many years – in a truce. However, the pictorial Egyptian sources in particular present their pharaoh as victorious and divine, just as the ideology of kingship by *maat* demanded.

A further ritual guarantee of the maintenance of *maat* is attested from the First Intermediate Period onwards, when the concept of 'Raising *maat* to the Great God, the Lord of Heaven' appears in texts. From the later 18th Dynasty onwards, this is expressed iconographically in the king offering a figure of its embodying goddess to the gods (Teeter 1997). Even later, and most prominently in the Ramesside Period, the king would offer his own name (usually) containing the element '*maat*' to the head of the pantheon (Teeter 1997: 34).

THE KING AND THE GODS

In addition to the ideological implications, the practice of offering *maat* underlines the reciprocal nature of the relationship between king and gods. While text and images inform us that the gods 'bestow' the kingship upon the reigning pharaoh, 'placing' him on the 'throne of Horus of the living', conferring 'the entire world' to his hands and/or setting the foreign countries under his feet, the king repays this favour and prerogative by showing himself to be a responsible ruler who governs 'with' or 'in' *maat*, symbolically represented by the figure of the deified concept that he offers to the gods in his role of performer of their cults (see below).

This closely intertwined relationship of king and gods could be expressed in a number of other ways. Most poignantly, it finds illustration in the iconographic motif of king and god embracing (Figure 20.3), or engaged in similar poses of affectionate interaction.

Innumerable representations throughout the temples of Egypt depict the king in this pose, or holding hands with a deity. Where the theme is specifically the relationship with goddesses, he may be seated on the deity's lap, or nursing from her breast

Figure 20.3   Senusret I embraces Amun-Ra, from the White Chapel in the temple of Karnak, 12th Dynasty (photo P. Brand).

(Leclant 1960). In most scenes, moreover, the deity extends the hieroglyphic sign for 'life' (*ankh*) to the nose of the king.

These iconographic motifs reflect an important topic in the ideology of Egyptian kingship, which was also one of the foundations of the centralized state: the divine descent of the Egyptian ruler and his being fashioned in the gods' image, or as their 'likeness' (Hornung 1982b: 138–9; Silverman 1991: 65–6). The latter is made explicit in texts at least from the early Middle Kingdom onwards – for example, in the *Instruction of Amenemhat*[1] – and found a particularly poignant expression in Tutankhamun's birth name, which literally translates as 'Living image of Amun'.

Horus on earth

In addition to having been placed on the throne by the gods, and being their descendant, the Egyptian king was believed to be the embodiment of divine power on earth – an ideology that seems to have been formulated by Upper Egyptian rulers some time during the Naqada II period (Wilkinson 1999: 33–4). Some Egyptian king-lists, such as the Royal Canon of Turin, place a generation of gods before the first human kings of Egypt. They are succeeded by a group of 'spirits' (the Predynastic rulers), followed by the legendary Meni/Menes (Baines 1995a: 14–15; von Beckerath 1997: 20). As far as the fragmentary papyrus can be reconstructed, it appears that it is the falcon god Horus (of Hierakonpolis) who was thought to have been the last divine king on earth (Gardiner 1959: pl. I). This corresponds to the Heliopolitan myth of creation, where the creator god set in motion the conception of a divine line of kings, ending with Horus, the son of Isis and Osiris (Lesko 1991: 90–4). With the ascent of Horus to the throne, his father Osiris became the deceased god-king of the Netherworld.

From the earliest periods, the Egyptian king was identified with this falcon-god, and thus with the last divine ruler on earth. This is evident from the oldest of Egyptian royal titles – attested already in the late Predynastic Period – the Horus name (Quirke 1990b: 22–3; Wilkinson 1999: 201–3). This title – adopted upon accession – was written within a so-called *serekh*, a hieroglyph of the palace façade constructed in the niche-architecture typical of the late Pre- and Early Dynastic Periods, and surmounted by a squatting falcon, symbol and embodiment of Horus (Barta 1990; Figure 20.9). In this way, the title also alluded to the fact that the king was 'hidden' in (and thus represented by) the palace, just as the gods were hidden in their temples (Hornung 1982b: 139). The modern term used for the Egyptian king – Pharaoh – derives from the Egyptian title *per-aa*, literally 'Great House/Estate', in other words 'Palace'. The palace separated the ruler from the people – in the same way that a flagpole demarcated the sacred, and thus segregated and inaccessible, area of temples, and evolved into the Egyptian hieroglyph for 'god', *netjer* (Baines 1995b: 122–3).

The identity of the king and Horus could be expressed in various ways. Among the most striking are items of feathered dress – an actual example survives from the tomb of Tutankhamun (Egyptian Museum Cairo JE 62627; see, e.g., Saleh and Sourouzian 1986: 191) – and depictions of the ruler as half falcon, half man (Figure 20.4). Representations of the king with a falcon either squatting on the back of his throne, or attached to the back of his head/crown in a protective gesture (spread wings) seem to relate to the personal protection of the king by this god. Texts, moreover,

Figure 20.4 An 18th Dynasty king as a falcon (Louvre E 5351)
(Réunion des Musées Nationaux/Art Resource, NY).

inform us that the king was sitting on the 'throne of Horus of the living', and one of the epithets used to refer to the incumbent to the throne was 'falcon in the nest'.

THE FIVE-FOLD TITULARY – ASPECTS OF KINGSHIP

The king's Horus name was soon augmented by other royal titles that reflected his relationship with the gods. The first to appear was the *nisut-bity* title (Quirke 1990b: 23–4; Wilkinson 1999: 205–7). This expressed the other central element of Egyptian royal ideology, its duality. The first use of this title dates to the middle of the 1st Dynasty, in the reign of Den, whose 'accession' (*khat nisut bity*) is recorded on the Palermo Stone. The title literally translates as 'He of the sedge and the bee' and thus refers explicitly to the dual nature of the kingship, first and foremost over the two geographical units of Upper and Lower Egypt. It is thus that Greek texts translate this title, and Egyptian sources, too, attest to such a geographical significance. Egyptology has traditionally translated it in the same way, as 'King of Upper and Lower Egypt', but the vaguer 'Dual King' has become fashionable in recent years, since other 'dual' royal aspects, such as a human/divine nature, can also be included under such a translation. *Nisut* was also the generic term used to refer to the king in texts (the Egyptian word for the office of kingship, *nesyt*, is derived from it), while *bity* alone was more prominent in administrative contexts.

From the late 3rd Dynasty onwards, the *nisut-bity* title appeared enclosed in a ring, the so-called cartouche (cf. Figure 20.2), as was the later 'Son of Ra' name (see below). The cartouche's Egyptian designation, *shen*, expresses its protective function, while its form of a never-ending circle (or oval) reflects a symbolism of everlastingness.

With the advent of the *nisut-bity* title, which was prefixed to the king's throne name (or *prenomen*), his role in 'binding together' (the two halves of) Egypt and the cosmos moved into the centre of Egyptian royal ideology. The title was of great political and theological significance, as changes to the *nisut-bity* name of certain rulers attest. Thus Mentuhotep II changed his name from Nebhepetra to Sematawy, 'Uniter of the Two Lands', after the recentralization of the state in the middle of the 11th Dynasty (Gestermann 1987). Most *nisut-bity* names were compounded with the element Ra, attesting to the importance of the sun god for kingship and state.

Another expression of the king's dual nature, firmly attested from the reign of Semerkhet (second half of the 1st Dynasty) onwards,[2] was the *nebty* title, 'The Two Ladies' – a reference to the king's protection by, and descent from, the two goddesses embodied in the Double Crown of the Egyptian ruler, the vulture Nekhbet of Elkab and the serpent Wadjit of Buto (Baines 1995b: 127; Wilkinson 1999: 203–5). Moreover, the latter was symbolically present in the uraeus serpent adorning the king's forehead. In texts the king could appear as the son of these deities, and images showed him nursed by them.

A further, if much later, important step in the development of the full titulary was taken with Djedefra's (early 4th Dynasty) assumption of the *sa-Ra*, 'Son of Ra' title, which was prefixed to the birth-name (or *nomen*) of the ruler (Quirke 1990b: 25). With it, the king's divine descent from the (theologically increasingly important) solar and creator god became firmly entrenched in Egyptian royal ideology. According to Egyptian patrilineal conventions of inheritance, he was thus a legitimate ruler.

However, it has been argued that we may also see a first step away from the image of the fully divine king, to one whose divinity was, in its explicit dependence on the gods, limited (Hornung 1982b: 141–2, 191–2). This circumscribed divinity of the king may also have found expression in a further common epithet, *netjer nefer*, 'the perfect(ed) god' (Silverman 1991: 65; Baines 1995a: 9), which may imply a (ritually) 'acquired divinity'.

Be that as it may, the significance of the sun god Ra for Egyptian royal ideology is omnipresent in the sources from this time onwards: not only was the king believed to be his son, he was also his 'representative' (*sety*) on earth – an epithet he shared with gods such as the lunar Thoth (as the night time ruler of the sky), and the creator and patron of craftsmen Ptah (Goebs, in press: chapters 2.1.1; 4). The king's rule was said to be 'like that of Ra, forever', and his crowns were those 'of Ra on the first occasion (of creation)'. These formulaic statements were retained throughout Egyptian history, even when, from the Middle Kingdom onwards, Amun(-Ra) emerged as the new head of the pantheon and, later, 'king of gods', and the ruler's legitimacy increasingly derived from him.

Finally, under Djedefra's successor Khafra, a further title became an established part of the titulary, which remains obscure to this day: the (Horus of) Gold Name (*Hor nebu*) (Wilkinson 1999: 207–8). The gold sign, without the Horus falcon, had appeared in conjunction with royal names from the time of Djer onwards (as seen on the Palermo Stone). The title may bear some relationship with the early cultic centre of the god Seth, Nebu/Ombos, and some scholars maintain that the squatting Horus falcon on top of the sign for Ombos expressed the final victory of Horus over Seth. Others have suggested that it emphasizes the divine nature of the king, since the flesh of gods was believed to be golden (Quirke 1990b: 11).

MYTHS OF KINGSHIP

Several of the royal titles discussed above make references to gods of Egyptian myth with whom the king wished to associate himself. As stated, these mythical associations, representing the ruler as son, representative and embodiment of gods on earth, served to legitimize his claim to the throne.

Thus, besides being the Son of (Amun-)Ra, the king's identification with Horus made him at the same time the son of Osiris and Isis, and the competitor of his uncle Seth, who was also contending for the throne. Snippets of this myth are attested from the Pyramid Texts onwards, but the fullest account is found on the Ramesside Papyrus Chester-Beatty I, which has Horus and Seth battling over their claim to the throne in various ways and guises, until Horus finally triumphs in the court of the Lord of All (Griffiths 1960; Broze 1996). While one meaning of this myth is clearly the victory of *maat* over *isfet*, with Seth representing the latter, a subsidiary significance is the emphasis on legitimate patrilinear succession. Several accessions to the throne by royal brothers are attested throughout Egyptian history, but the preferred means of inheritance was from father to son, as the myth of Horus and Seth makes emphatically clear: Seth is tricked by Isis into saying 'Shall one give the cattle (here symbolizing the inheritance of the kingship) to the stranger while the man's son is here?' (e.g. Lichtheim 1976: 217).

The *Contendings of Horus and Seth* further serves to illustrate the fate of the deceased king, who was identified with Osiris (among other gods) from the Pyramid Texts onwards. Osiris became the ruler of the Netherworld – the myth accords him a full royal titulary – and judge of the dead. As such he would – most explicitly from the New Kingdom onwards – merge with the sun god Ra when the latter entered the Netherworld at sunset, and thus be cyclically, and eternally, reborn (Hornung 1982b: 93–5).

This solar-osirian concept finds expression in both the funerary architecture and literature of Egypt: the pyramids, preferred funerary monuments of kings in the Old and Middle Kingdoms, are commonly accepted to represent replicas of the primeval mound, the location of the first sunrise out of the aquatic pre-creation universe, and 'stairways' to the heavens, as some of the texts found in the pyramids from the late 5th Dynasty onwards suggest (e.g. Lehner 1997: 34–5). Boat-burials found near several pyramids relate to the deceased king's wish to remain mobile in the afterlife, just as the sun and stellar gods journey across the heavens in boats. The rock-cut tombs of the New Kingdom with their descending corridors represent the path of the setting sun into the Netherworld, to the place where the union with Osiris took place every night. The numerous Underworld Books ornamenting their walls attest to this belief (Hornung 1990b).

Unsurprisingly, new steps in the mythical ideology of kingship were often taken by rulers whose claim to the throne was not undisputed. The most famous myth of royal legitimization is that of the Divine Birth, which, in its canonized form, is first attested under Hatshepsut of the 18th Dynasty (Brunner 1964; Silverman 1995: 70; Assmann 2004). It is obvious that this pharaoh, both by virtue of her gender and her transcending the role assigned to her by state and tradition – as regent for her nephew Thutmose III – had a particular need to emphasize the legitimacy of her claim to the throne. Images and texts relating to the conception of the ruling king by Amun-Ra, king of gods, and the queen of the predecessor are recorded on the walls of Hatshepsut's funerary temple at Deir el-Bahri and became an established part of the royal dogma from this time onwards (Figure 20.5). However, as stated, virtually all pharaohs, from the Old Kingdom onwards, found textual and iconographic means of representing themselves as 'bodily sons' of the gods. A narrative surrounding the divine conception of the first three kings of the 5th Dynasty by Ra and his high priest's wife appears already in the late Middle Kingdom (Papyrus Westcar = Papyrus Berlin 3033; for a translation see Parkinson 1997: 116–19), and may have been written to legitimize the succession of rulers in the mid-13th Dynasty.

Even the 'monotheist' Akhenaten, while aiming to abandon all myths in favour of a single divine concept of the Aten, still mobilized some very old mythical constellations in order to enhance his claim to the throne. He declared himself the sole son of his god, and his *ka* and representative on earth (Silverman 1995: 74–9), while presenting himself – in both text and image – as Shu, the firstborn son of the Heliopolitan creator god Atum. Certain representations indicate that his queen, Nefertiti, could be equated with Shu's twin sister Tefnut/Maat. In this way, the Amarna monarchs associated themselves with a generation of gods far older than the traditional royal deities.

THE RITUAL KING

A further 'myth' of kingship can be discerned in the representation of the reigning monarch as the sole performer of all cults throughout the land, which was also

Figure 20.5 The god Amun-Ra and queen Mutemwiya conceive king
Amenhotep III in a scene from his divine birth cycle at Luxor Temple
(from Kemp 1989b: fig. 70).

expressed in his epithet *neb iry (i)khet*, 'lord of performing the rituals'. In reality, the rituals would have been performed by priests, and references in documents such as the above-cited Papyrus Westcar, which emphasizes the fact that 'His Majesty [king Nebka of the 3rd Dynasty] *himself* did the performance of the rite', suggest that this was a rather exceptional occurrence. Kingship ideology, however, made the ruler the mediator between gods and men, and as such he was represented as performing the rituals for the gods on the walls of all temples (Traunecker 2002). In return for his services and the maintenance of *maat*, the gods confirmed the king in his office and presented him with a long and prosperous reign. This reciprocal ritual relationship between king and gods has been labelled with the Latin phrase *do ut des* ('I give so that you may give') by Egyptologists.

As stated, ritual was of paramount importance for the Egyptian world-view and its guarantor, the king. In ritual, the world became ordered, knowable and controllable. Moreover, it allowed its human actors to assume the roles of gods, and the priests to assume the role of the king. As his titles suggest, the king essentially fulfilled the role of the creator and king of gods, (Amun-)Ra, on earth, while being – at the same time – Horus, his descendant. Hence, many of the rituals attested from Egypt concern the maintenance and renewal of the cosmos.

Rituals of victory, for example, are closely related to the iconographic motif of the king smiting his enemies, discussed above (Serrano 2002: 79–91). In them, the pharaoh symbolically destroyed the forces of chaos, who could appear in the form of human enemies (but might be represented by simple pots of red clay that would be broken), hippopotami (as in part of the myth of Horus enacted annually in the temple of Edfu) or other wild animals, such as wild bulls, lions or other game. Ritual hunts, in particular, provided a good basis for emphasizing the king's physical strength, and – from the mid-18th Dynasty – this aspect of the royal persona became increasingly important (Redford 1995: 157–84). Thus, Amenhotep II informs us at length about his physical exploits in the areas of sport and warfare, claiming to have rowed at the stern of a boat with 200 men for 'three miles . . . without interrupting his stroke', and to have shot arrows from his moving chariot at four targets of copper in succession, 'so that it [each arrow] came out of it [each target] and dropped to the ground' (Lichtheim 1976: 42).

A further prominent set of rituals decorating the walls of temples and ritual objects relates to the foundation of temples or other institutions (e.g. Wilkinson 1999: 222, 305–6; Gundlach 2001: 368). Every foundation was equated with the moment of the first solar creation (Reymond 1969), and the king assumed the role of the creator god in this context. Early examples of such, and related rituals, appear already on late Predynastic monuments such as the Scorpion macehead (Figure 20.6).

A third set of rituals, finally, represented the king as facilitating the cyclical renewal of the cosmos. Examples of these include the celebrations surrounding the ritual death and resurrection of Osiris at Abydos (Schäfer 1904), the raising of the *djed*-pillar, and the festival of Sokar (Gaballa and Kitchen 1969; Graindorge-Héreil 1994; Wilkinson 1999: 301–2).

In addition to perpetuating the link between king and gods, other important rituals established and defined the relationship between the king and his subjects, and – in particular – the elite. The Palermo Stone records both royal visits to cultic installations, as well as the *shemes-Hor*, 'the following of Horus', which occurred every

Figure 20.6 'King Scorpion' ritually founds, or opens, what is believed to be an irrigation canal, Scorpion macehead, late Predynastic Period (Ashmolean Museum, Oxford E 3632).

two years and is generally believed to have been a royal tour through the kingdom for the purpose of inspection, tax-collection, and – potentially – the exercising of judicial authority (Baines 1995b: 126; Wilkinson 1999: 220–1).

The famous Middle Kingdom tale of the courtier Sinuhe, who fled Egypt to live in Syria but was welcomed back to the Egyptian court at the end of his life, provides some insight into the procedures at court during a royal audience. In this tale, Sinuhe is received at the palace portals, guided to the audience chamber, and has to prostrate himself in front of the enthroned Senusret I, whom the text calls a 'god'. Having been raised up, the queen and royal princesses, in performing a ritual 'pacification' of the – potentially enraged – king, function as intermediaries between king and courtier (Parkinson 1997: 40–1), much as, in temple reliefs, goddesses are often shown as facilitators in the interaction between god and king.

Many of the best surviving representations relating to the architecture of, and life in, Egyptian royal palaces date to the Amarna Period. One of the frequently depicted themes is the appearance of the king to the people/elite at a so-called 'window of appearance', which, ornamented with friezes of fiery uraeus-snakes, underscored the radiantly divine appearance of the king in his regalia. On these occasions he could reward deserving members of the administration or army with symbolic and other gifts – the so-called 'gold of honour' is particularly well attested (e.g. Ertman 1972; Kemp 1989b: 287–9) (Figure 20.7).

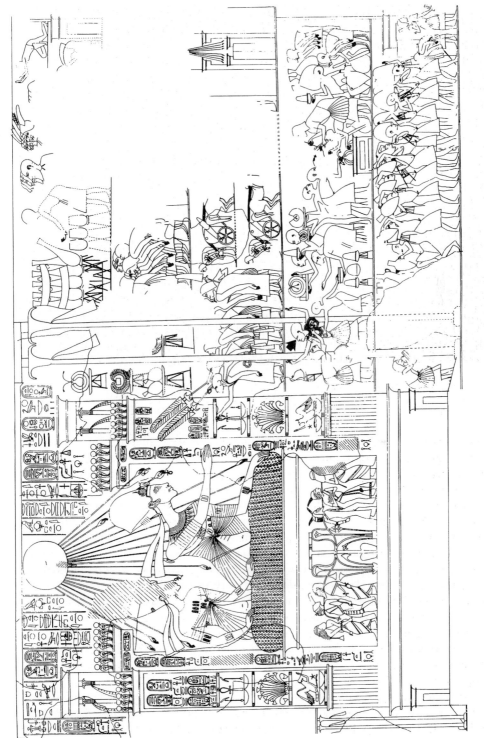

Figure 20.7 Akhenaten at the 'window of appearance' in one of his palaces bestows the gold of honour on a loyal official (from Kemp 1989b: fig. 92).

On these occasions, the king could also receive foreign delegations and be presented with prisoners of war (Bleiberg 1984; Gordon 2001: 547). They would – ritually – acclaim the Egyptian king and accept his superiority over all other rulers, and a number of prisoners of war could be 'sacrificed' in honour of the gods at certain times. The practice is in line with the official view of non-Egyptians as the eternal enemy and antithesis of the Egyptian world order, which had to be eternally subdued by the ruling king. The contemporary diplomatic correspondence, by contrast, often tells a very different story (examples in Moran 1992).

Rituals of accession and royal paraphernalia

The rituals most significant for the office holder himself were those that related to his accession to the throne. As stated, royal ideology held that the king was both conceived and crowned by the head of the pantheon. Already in the Coffin Texts, the 'ornaments of Geb', and thus of kingship, are presented to Horus by the solar creator Atum. Key scenes of the coronation ritual are found on the walls of all Egyptian temples, but the exact sequence of events remains unknown to this day. Papyrus Brooklyn 47.218.50, dating to the fifth or fourth century BC, describes a ritual for the confirmation of the kingship on the occasion of the New Year's celebrations, and we can assume that the rituals surrounding the actual accession to the throne would have been similar (J.-C. Goyon 1974). The steps attested are the following: waking, leaving the palace, purification, entering the temple, coronation, royal induction, nursing by goddesses, enthronement and announcing the titulary.

It is yet again Hatshepsut who has left us the most explicit description of her coronation, in a sequence of scenes on the outside walls of her 'Red Chapel' in the temple at Karnak (Figure 20.8) (Lacau and Chevrier 1977).

It remains disputed to this day if the actual ritual coronation would have involved priests in the role of the crowning deities, and if there were, indeed, as many steps as Hatshepsut depicts. The only 'historical' account of a coronation appears on the Rosetta Stone and dates to the Ptolemaic Period (196 BC). There, Ptolemy V is simply said to have worn the Double Crown of Upper and Lower Egypt (see below) during his ceremonies of accession: 'His Majesty appeared in glory in it in Hatkaptah [Memphis] when every ritual of the royal installation in the temple was performed for him after he had assumed his supreme office. . .' (after Quirke and Andrews 1988: 21).

The only crowns bestowed in the above-cited Papyrus Brooklyn 47.218.50 are the *seshed*-band and the *wereret*, and the Double Crown which is said to be represented here by a white *shesep*-band (J.-C. Goyon 1974: 55). However, the multiplicity of Egyptian crowns is borne out by the iconographic record, and relates to the multi-part character of the royal titulary: the king, like the sun god, united in himself a variety of aspects. Thus Thutmose III asserts in his coronation inscription: 'I was elevated in dignity because of the crowns, which are on his [Ra's] head; his uraeus was fixed on my head . . . he has fixed my crowns (for me) and assembled my royal names for me' (Sethe 1905: 160.1–3).

In receiving the various crowns, the king underwent a process of deification during which he was externally likened to Ra (Goebs, in press). This transformation was enhanced by the assumption of other multicoloured, and in particular golden and

Figure 20.8 Hatshepsut, wearing the oldest attested royal dress – a pleated *shendyt*-kilt with bull's tail and a broad collar – is crowned by Amun-Ra with a combination of the *nemes*-headdress and the *Atef*-crown. The accompanying text refers to the latter as the '*atefu*-crown of Amun-Ra'. The numerous uraei adorning the crown imbue it, and its wearer, with fiery luminosity (photo P. Brand).

silver, paraphernalia, such as collars, bracelets, anklets, staffs and sceptres, that made him appear as the radiant 'god' that kingship ideology professed him to be. In addition, the height of many of the Egyptian crowns pointed toward the heavenly or divine. In Hatshepsut's coronation, one text describes her crown as 'piercing the sky'. Adornment with the fiery uraeus, embodying the solar eye, as well as with solar or stellar discs, whose number proliferated from the later New Kingdom onwards, added yet more fiery radiance (Figure 20.8).

The sequence of crowns bestowed on Hatshepsut in her Red Chapel comprises (some blocks are destroyed) the *nemes* ; the white or golden *khat* or *afnet* ; the Blue Crown and cap (*khepresh*); the *ibes*-wig and *seshed*-headband with uraeus ; the Red Crown (*deshret, net, mekhus, bit(it)*); the White Crown (*hedjet; shemas;* in some contexts *wereret*) (Figure 20.9); the Double Crown (*pa-sekhemty; pshent; wereret*); the *atef* and *hemhem* ; the *henu* , a combination of the Amun-crown base surmounted by a pair of falcon or ostrich feathers, and (usually) augmented by a pair of ram's horns and a solar disc (here standing in for the missing Double Feather Crown (*shuty*)); and an otherwise unknown headdress, the Crown of Atum (see Goebs 2001 for brief descriptions of the individual crowns and their symbolism).

As stated, the multiplicity of Egyptian crowns relates to the many aspects of Egyptian kingship, of which the various crowns and other regalia were symbols. In particular, from the early New Kingdom onwards, combinations of crowns became more and more popular, with increasing numbers of ornaments — uraei, discs, horns — being added. All of these elements functioned as 'hieroglyphs' that could be combined into 'iconographic sentences', to be read by the viewer of the royal person or image. This interpretation is supported by several cases of royal representations with headdresses that have been altered posthumously.

The *sed*-festival

A further festival of utmost importance for the kingship was the jubilee celebrated after 30 years of rule, and thereafter every three years — the *sed*-festival (Hornung and Staehelin 1974; Wilkinson 1999: 212–15). Its earliest attestations date to the early 1st Dynasty (Serrano 2002: 42–78, esp. 77). The festival represented a renewal of royal potency and a reaffirmation of the king's divine descent and legitimacy. Some of the ceremonies surrounding this occasion emphasized the physical strength of the king, who had to run around markers that symbolized Egypt/the created world (Figure 20.9) (actual examples survive in the funerary complex of Djoser's Step Pyramid), and drive cattle. The fact that royal rule had to be ritually re-asserted entails the possibility of a 'loss' of divinity and divine favour, and raises the question of how divine the Egyptian king really was.

KING OR GOD?

The multiplicity of Egyptian crowns, and the elaborate rituals associated with their assumption, suggest that the king's coronation was of utmost importance, and represented a rite of passage during which he was transformed into a divine being (Goebs, in press, esp. chapter 4). A certain 'degree' of divinity was claimed by incumbents when they alluded to having been 'kings in the egg', that is, from birth, and the same ideology was expressed in the myth of the divine birth. However, the fully fledged 'divine' king only emerged after his accession, attesting to a perceived distinction between the 'person' of the king (*hem*) and his office, as expressed by the five-fold titulary and other epithets (Silverman 1995: 65). A particularly important role seems to have been played by the assumption of the royal *ka*. A person's *ka*, which has been translated as both 'double' and 'life-force', was created at the same time as the human body. In the case of the king, it could be carried behind him in the form of a human-headed and crowned standard during public appearances. From the time of Amenhotep III, Luxor Temple was the place where the new ruler merged with the *ka* of his royal ancestors during the Opet-festival (Bell 1985; 1997: 137–45). This, and all other ceremonies of deifying the king, can be interpreted as a means of uniting the concepts of a mortal and a divine ruler in one person (brief summaries by Silverman 1991: 58–72; Baines 1995a: 4–5; Traunecker 2002: 145).

However, it appears that the divinity of the king, however elaborately expressed in text and iconography, was still limited, as the above-cited epithet *netjer-nefer* implies. An actual cult of living kings, modelled on that of the gods, only appeared in the 18th Dynasty and employed its own iconography, which included the

Figure 20.9 Djoser – his Horus name, Netjeri-khet, is inscribed in the *serekh* or 'palace façade' in front of his White Crown – during his ritual *sed*-festival runs around an area delimited by two sets of markers. The ritual served to confirm his territorial claim to Egypt (from Kemp 1989b: fig. 20).

so-called horn of Amun, a curved ram's horn fixed at the side of the ruler's head(dress), and full solar or lunar discs which could, at times, appear to 'hover' above the king's head (Bell 1985: 266–9) (Figure 20.10).

In summary, it is clear that the ideology of divine kingship was one of the prime motivating factors of the centralized Egyptian state. We can state with relative confidence that Egyptians participated in the gigantic royal building projects – of

Figure 20.10 Amenhotep III venerates his own, deified, self in the temple at Soleb in Nubia. The deified king sports a *nemes*-headdress surmounted by a lunar disc and the ram's horn of Amun, and is carrying the *ankh* and *was*-sceptre characteristic of deities (after Wildung, D. (1977) *Egyptian Saints. Deification in Pharaonic Egypt*, fig. 4, New York: New York University Press).

tombs, temples and other structures – not only because they were forced to do so by an authoritative state apparatus, but because they truly believed that they were supporting the representative of the sun god on earth in maintaining the cosmic equilibrium, *maat*. As stated, this concept also entailed the preservation of the social hierarchy, in which the king, royal family and a relatively small and affluent elite dominated the mass of common Egyptians. Accordingly, the former groups had an obvious interest in propagating and augmenting the myths of divine kingship. The fact that the various dynasties of foreign rulers adopted Egyptian symbols and myths of the divine king serves to illustrate just how successful this system must have been.

Certainly, there were differing positions. From the Middle Kingdom, following the uprooting of social values in the First Intermediate Period, there is evidence that admits to the mortality and fallibility of the king. At the same time, authors were able to compose (sometimes rather disrespectful) stories about the actual (that is, non-ritual) lives of kings, even if these were generally fictional. A particularly striking example is the Tale of King Neferkara (probably Pepi II of the 6th Dynasty) and his homosexual relationship with one of his generals, Sasenet (Parkinson 1997: 288–89). In the aftermath of the Amarna 'revolution' and later, during the rule of various foreign dynasties in Egypt, the Egyptian elite increasingly directed their attention and expectations to the gods, and away from the now conspicuously imperfect king, in a process that is mirrored in the diminished respect shown to the Egyptian king and court in neighbouring countries (Rössler-Köhler 1991; Baines 1995a: 33–42). The famous *Tale of Wenamun* (Lichtheim 1976: 224–30), set at the end of the 20th Dynasty, bears eloquent witness to the changed situation.

Formally, however, Egypt adhered to its time-honoured ideology of kingship until the end of pharaonic history, and beyond.

NOTES

1. There, reference is made to humans as the 'living images' of the king, implying, in turn, his likeness with the gods according to the Egyptian belief that men are images of the creator-god (e.g. Parkinson 1997: 206 M I.9). The largely anthropomorphic representations of Egyptian gods – if often sporting animal heads – underscore this outward similarity.
2. Potentially as early as Aha, to judge from an ivory label from the tomb of queen Neithhotep (the mother of Aha?). See, e.g., Spencer 1993: 63 fig. 42; discussion in Wilkinson 1999: 203–4.

CHAPTER TWENTY-ONE

CREATION MYTHS

——— •◆• ———

Lucia Gahlin

Myths were constructed in order to provide explanations for the fundamentals of human existence. Creation mythology contains a range of carefully constructed metaphors, and provides a window into the ancient Egyptian mind. These myths were probably generated by the educated temple priesthoods.

The realm of the gods was, to a certain extent, envisaged to reflect that of mortals. The myths portray the antics of the deities, their displays of emotion, and the often difficult, as well as positive, relationships between them. In the creation myth of Heliopolis, for example, the earth god Geb and the sky goddess Nut become so passionately attached to each other that they have to be physically separated by Shu (the god of air) before creation can continue. So myths were also a means of animating, and making accessible, the divine world.

Several explanations as to how the universe came into being survive from ancient Egypt, associated with different important cult centres, but sharing common ground. Local deities took on the role of creator god who was self-engendered and went on to generate the other gods and goddesses before creating humans, animals and plant life. The three main cosmogonies originated in the cult centres at Memphis, Heliopolis and Hermopolis. However, it has been argued that the different creation myths did not have different local origins, but that the myth of creation with its various strands was composed as one, unified explanation, and local cults chose to emphasize and embellish different parts of the myth (Quirke 1992: 25). For example, in the temple of Horus at Edfu the image is one of a celestial falcon perching on a reed; in the temple of Khonsu at Karnak, Khonsu as creator god was a ram-headed snake who fertilized the cosmic egg; and so on.

The underlying principle is one of order (perfection and balance) established out of chaos. A state of dark primordial wateriness is used to represent chaos, out of which emerges a mound, and on it a primeval creator god, Ta-Tenen ('the land which becomes distinguishable/distinct'). The Egyptians called the emergence of this mound the 'First Time/Occasion' (*sep tepy*).

This mythological chain of events clearly reflects the annual flooding of the Nile and the subsiding of the water to reveal deposits of thick black silt that were incredibly fertile but which required the sun for growth to take place. At all times the sun was believed to be the chief source of creative energy. The rhythm of night and day shaped a belief in the sun god creating order out of dark chaos.

From the New Kingdom onwards, there is evidence for a belief in all deities being aspects of the one primeval solar being. In hymns dating to the reign of the 18th Dynasty king Amenhotep III, the sun god is set apart from the other gods. He is the supreme god, alone, far away in the sky, while the other deities are part of his creation, alongside men and animals. Akhenaten took this idea further when he attempted to abolish the pantheon, and worship only the one solar creator god, the Aten.

In creation mythology, fertility and sexuality prevail, but the Memphite explanation depends upon the creator god Ptah harnessing three abstract catalysts: Heka (divine energy, or magic), Sia (divine knowledge, or creative thought) and Hu (divine utterance, or authoritative command). The sun god also makes use of these principles in the Old Kingdom Pyramid Texts.

The oneness of the creator god tends to be contrasted with the multitude of beings that he generates from himself. His aloneness tends to be emphasized (Zandee 1992: 179). He then divides to create separate, but interdependent, elements.

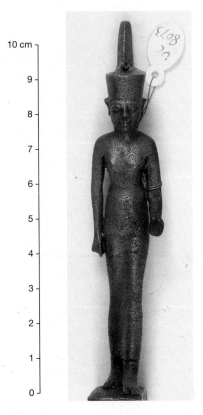

Figure 21.1 Late Period bronze figurine of Neith (Petrie Museum UC 8073).
Image courtesy and © Petrie Museum of Egyptian Archaeology, University College London.

The chief creator gods of Egypt were male, although female creators do occur in the mythology, such as Neith, 'the mother and father of all things'. She is said to have used divine words to create the universe (in some versions, she uses seven words or statements, which in a later magic text become the 'sevenfold laugh of the creator god' (Hornung 1992: 44)). Neith is credited with the invention of childbirth, and like Khnum she features in texts concerning the fashioning of newborn babies, and their animation with the breath of life. As a cow (Mehetweret, 'Great Swimmer'), she rises out of the primordial waters with the sun between her horns; and her spit (or vomit) becomes Apophis, the sun god's greatest threat.

THE CREATION MYTH OF HELIOPOLIS

According to the Creation Myth of Heliopolis (ancient Iunu, modern Tell Hisn, now located in a north-eastern suburb of Cairo), before anything existed and creation had taken place, there was darkness and endless, lifeless water (Nu or Nun). A mound of fertile silt emerges from this watery chaos. The self-engendered solar creator god

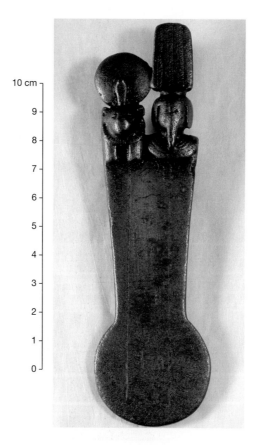

Figure 21.2 Late Period bronze counterpoise with heads of Shu and Tefnut (Petrie Museum UC 16566). Image courtesy and © Petrie Museum of Egyptian Archaeology, University College London.

Atum ('the all' or 'the complete one') appears upon the mound. He grows lonely. By masturbating, and collecting his semen in his mouth, he is able to spit out Shu (the divine personification of air) and Tefnut (the divine personification of moisture). Shu also embodies eternal cyclical time (*neheh*) while Tefnut embodies eternal linear time (*djet*) (Quirke 1992: 26).

Atum is said, in the Memphite Theology, to create the Ennead 'with his semen and his fingers'. Once a male–female pair is brought into existence, procreation takes place more conventionally. The result of Shu and Tefnut's sexual union is Geb (the earth god) and Nut (the sky goddess). Their father Shu forces them apart by lifting Nut up to her place above the earth.

According to Coffin Text 76, Shu created eight 'infinite beings' to help support Nut's body. An alternative explanation was that the sky was supported by 'four pillars of heaven'. After creation has taken place, infinite, dark and inert Nun (i.e. chaos) continues to exist above and beyond the sky, surrounding the world and supporting it. One of the recurrent fears of the ancient Egyptians was that the sky would fall

Figure 21.3 Late Period faience figurine of Nefertem (Petrie Museum UC 45396). Image courtesy and © Petrie Museum of Egyptian Archaeology, University College London.

in and they would be drowned. The subsoil water and the Nile flood were both thought to flow out from Nun. Naunet mirrored Nun and surrounded the Netherworld.

The Ennead (nine; Egyptian *pesedjet*) of Heliopolis comprised Atum ('the bull of the Ennead'), Shu, Tefnut, Geb and Nut; and the offspring of the latter two gods – Osiris, Isis, Seth and Nephthys. The number three symbolized plurality, so nine (three times three) expressed an all-encompassing totality (Hornung 1992: 45). Elsewhere the word *pesedjet* can serve as a collective noun for gods, however many.

From the end of the 18th Dynasty, the original appearance of Atum is explained using the image of a blue lotus flower (or water-lily) (*Nymphaea caerulea*) (divinely personified as the deity Nefertem), bobbing on the surface of the primordial waters. The petals open, and out rises the sun, personified as a golden child (or ram-headed deity). This first sunrise was called 'the beautiful moment'. Another symbol of the birth of the sun god was the *benu* bird (a heron by the New Kingdom), whose name means 'rising in brilliance'.

Atum is usually represented as a man wearing the double crown of Upper and Lower Egypt, although he could also be portrayed as a snake. Other animals deemed sacred to him were the lion, bull, ichneumon, lizard and dung beetle. The *t(u)m* of Atum's name can be translated 'not to be' and 'to be complete', so there are several interpretations of the god's name, most commonly 'the all'/'the complete one', but also 'he who is not yet complete'. Another scholar favours 'the undifferentiated one' (Hornung 1982b: 66), the idea being that Atum contained within himself the life-force of every other deity (male and female) yet to come into being (Hart 1990: 12). He held the title 'Lord to the Limits of the Sky', and was regarded very much as a solar deity (he was syncretized with the sun god *par excellence*, Ra, in order to form the combined deity Ra-Atum).

In one version of the myth, Ra-Atum sends his eye to find his children Shu and Tefnut who are lost in the primordial watery darkness. The eye goddess returns to find that the sun god has grown a new eye. She weeps and her tears become humankind. Another version has humans originating from the solar child's tears when he was separated from his mother. The ancient Egyptian words for 'people' and 'tear' are very similar: *remetj* and *remyt*. Deities were believed to originate from the creator god's sweat, or laughter, depending on the version of the myth.

The crocodile god Sobek (who was also believed to embody the concept of the primordial ocean) was recognized as a creator deity when he was syncretized with the sun god Ra, and was represented wearing a sun disc on his head. He too 'gave birth to all that exists' (Papyrus Bucher, Papyrus Strasbourg no. 2, II, 1).

The idea of the primeval mound emerging from the watery chaos is quite clearly an image borrowed from the natural environment. The ancient Egyptians built their settlements on the highest possible ground in order to avoid the damaging inundation. When the Greek historian Strabo visited Egypt during the reign of the Roman emperor Augustus, he commented that as a result of the annual flood:

> the whole country is under water and becomes a lake, except the settlements and those are situated on natural hills or on artificial mounds and contain cities of considerable size and villages which, even when viewed from afar, resemble islands.
>
> (Strabo, *Geography* 17.1.4)

The focal point of the cult temple at Heliopolis would have been the sacred *benben* stone (mentioned in Pyramid Text 600) which probably symbolized the primordial mound, although it has also been interpreted as Atum's petrified semen (Frankfort 1948: 380 n. 26). It stood in the *Hwt-Benben* ('Mansion of the *benben*'). Frankfort refers to an area of the temple of Heliopolis called 'The High Sand' which he presumes symbolized the primordial mound; this then leaves the *benben* free to be interpreted as the first drop of Atum's semen that fell into Nun before he went on to bear Shu and Tefnut (Frankfort 1948). According to Frankfort, a late inscription in the temple of Khonsu plays with the words *hnn t* ('seed'), *hnn* ('to beget'), *hnhn* ('to flow out') (Frankfort 1948: 380, n. 26); but Quirke (1992: 27) argues that the word *benben* derives from *weben* ('to shine').

The Ennead of the Heliopolitan myth occurs for the first time in the Pyramid Texts of the Old Kingdom: PT 527, 'Taking his phallus in his grip and ejaculating through it to give birth to the twins Shu and Tefnut'; PT 600, Atum is described as the god who 'spluttered/sneezed (*yshsh*) out Shu and spat out (*tef*) Tefnut' (note the similar sounds of the verbs and the names of the respective deities). This account is also given in the Coffin Texts: CT 80, Shu claims of Atum, 'He conceived me in his nose', and CT 81, 'He has born me from his nose'; CT 77, 'I am this soul of Shu which Atum poured out with his hand, when he created orgasm. Sperm fell into his mouth. He spat me out as Shu together with Tefnut, who came forth after me'. The same imagery occurs in the Book of Overthrowing Apophis (28, 22–9, 2) where the sun god says: 'They [the primeval gods] came forth from myself, after I had copulated with my grasp. My desire came forth by my hand, my sperm fell into my mouth'; and in the early third century BC Papyrus Bremner-Rhind (BM), 'I sneezed out Shu . . . I spat out Tefnut'.

The goddess Hathor in her aspect of *djeritef*, 'his hand', is likely to have personified Atum's hand in his act of masturbation at that early stage of creation. Atum's hand had functioned as a vulva in the absence of a female element. The goddesses Nut, Isis, Meskhenet and Mut might also be described as 'hand of the god' (*djeret netjer*). A symbol of this 'androgynous procreation' (Zandee 1992: 181) was the *bulti*-fish (*Tilapia nilotica*), the female of which takes the eggs and sperm into its mouth and eventually spits out the young fish.

The triad of Atum, Shu and Tefnut is significant; there is reference to the time when Atum 'became three' (Coffin Texts II, 39c–e). His *ka* ('vital power') is present in his two children (Pyramid Texts 1652a–1653a). During the reign of Akhenaten, the iconography of the king, his queen Nefertiti and the Aten reflects that of Shu, Tefnut and Atum.

Shu (probably meaning 'empty'/'dry') was the divine personification of air and sunlight, and although he was thought to bring the sun to life each morning and to protect it against the serpent demon Apophis in the Netherworld, he was often associated with the lunar deities Thoth and Khonsu. He was represented in human form with an ostrich feather on his head, or with the head of a lion, and it was in this guise that he was referred to as an 'Eye of Ra', and was worshipped at Leontopolis (Tell el-Muqdam) in the delta.

Tefnut was the divine personification of moisture. There is a reference in the Pyramid Texts to her being the atmosphere of the underworld. Tying in with the imagery of duality, where her brother-consort Shu was associated with sunlight, she

Figure 21.4 Late Period faience amulet of Shu (Petrie Museum UC 52649). Image courtesy and © Petrie Museum of Egyptian Archaeology, University College London.

was associated with the moon. Like Shu, she might be regarded as an 'Eye of Ra', and as such was represented with a lioness head (and was worshipped at Leontopolis). She could also appear in the form of a rearing cobra, when she was identified with the uraeus on the front of the royal headdress.

Once Atum has sparked off the process of creation, the myth hinges on the existence of male–female partnerships, and sexual intercourse is the catalyst for continued creation. It is interesting that the divine personification of earth (Geb) is male and not the female idea found in other cultures. It is also noteworthy that the procreative couples all have brother–sister relationships, thereby providing a divine prototype for childbearing marriages within the royal family.

Geb was the divine personification of the earth, and as such was a god of fertility. He was sometimes coloured green and was visualized with plants growing out of him. He was often depicted reclining beneath the arched body of his sister-consort, the sky goddess Nut. He was always represented in human form, sometimes with an erect penis. He occasionally wore the Red Crown of Lower Egypt, but more often had a goose (the hieroglyph used to write his name) on his head (his daughter Isis could be described as the 'egg of the goose').

Nut was the divine personification of the sky. The darkness at night was explained by Nut swallowing the sun in the evening and giving birth to it at dawn, so it had spent the night hours travelling through her body. This image was depicted on the ceiling of tombs and on the underside of coffin and sarcophagus lids, expressing the belief that Nut divinely personified the burial place, and as the sun was born from her each morning, so the deceased might be reborn from her into the Afterlife. She was usually represented as a woman arching over the earth, but could also be represented as a cow.

THE CREATION MYTH OF HERMOPOLIS

The Creation Myth of Hermopolis Magna (ancient Khemnu ('Eight Town'), modern el-Ashmunein, in Middle Egypt) begins by concentrating on the physical elements that are necessary for creation to take place. The fundamental factors are arranged in four male–female aspects of the dark chaos of the primeval ocean: primordial water (Nun and Naunet); air or hidden power (Amun and Amaunet); darkness (Kuk and Kauket); and formlessness or infinity (Huh and Hauhet). These divine personifications of the basic elements of the cosmos are referred to as the Ogdoad (eight). The four male gods are all frog-headed, and the four goddesses are snake-headed. The eight elements interact to create a burst of energy, allowing creation to take place. Texts refer to them as 'the fathers and mothers who made the light' or 'the waters that made the light'.

In one version of the myth a primeval mound of earth described as the Isle of Flames (probably a reference to the first sunrise) rises up out of the primordial water, and the sun god is born on it. The Macedonian Period inscription in the tomb of the High Priest of Thoth at Hermopolis, Petosiris, at Tuna el-Gebel refers to Thoth, in the form of an ibis, placing a cosmic egg on the mound of earth. The egg cracks, hatching the sun which rises up into the sky.

Four of the Ogdoad are mentioned in the Pyramid Texts – Nun and Naunet; Amun and Amaunet (PT 301) – but the earliest known version of the full myth dates to the Middle Kingdom Coffin Texts (CT 76). All eight deities appear, although Amun appears as Tenem, closely linked to the Ennead. The numbers four and eight were both considered magically significant by the ancient Egyptians, and both were associated with totality.

The claim was that the Ogdoad had been necessary for the creation of the primordial mound (i.e. the Ogdoad had existed before the Ennead). However CT 76 describes Shu as having created the Ogdoad, thereby giving Atum and the Heliopolitan creation myth primacy: 'I am Shu, father of the gods . . . I am the one who begot the Huh gods again as Huh, Nun, Tenem, Kuk.'

Elsewhere, in representations of the sun god coming into being, the eight primordial deities mentioned in this myth can be depicted as baboons in the posture of greeting the rising sun. This is a fine example of the ancient Egyptians' incorporation of the natural world into the iconography of their religious belief system. At dawn baboons sit up on their rear legs with their front paws raised, in order to warm their undersides in the morning rays of the sun. This upright posture with arms and hands raised in front of the face was adopted as the posture of adoration by humans before the gods.

Amun (literally 'the hidden one'/'the one who conceals himself') may appear in this myth as an element of the primordial chaos, but by the Middle Kingdom he had achieved the position of 'King of the Gods' (early 12th Dynasty inscription in the jubilee chapel of King Senusret I at Karnak). His national significance was due

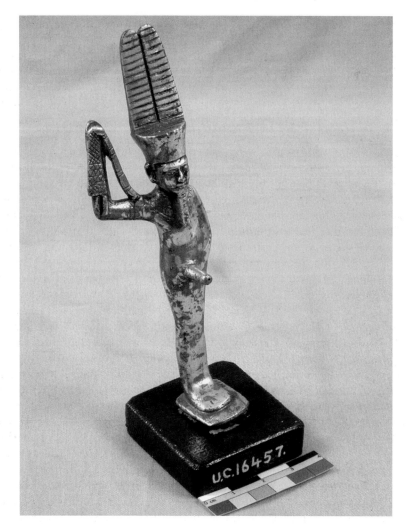

Figure 21.5 26th Dynasty silver figurine of Amun-Min (Petrie Museum UC 16457).
Image courtesy and © Petrie Museum of Egyptian Archaeology, University College London.

to the emergence of local Theban rulers at the beginning of the Middle and New
Kingdoms who were successful in reuniting and ruling the whole of Egypt after a
period of disruption. He was syncretized with the ancient sun god of Heliopolis, Ra,
to become Amun-Ra. He was also combined with the ithyphallic fertility god Min,
to form the god Amun-Min or Amun Kamutef (literally 'bull of his mother', i.e. he
impregnated his mother and so provided the sperm for his own existence). One of
his epithets was 'mysterious of form' but he was usually represented in human form
wearing a tall double-plumed headdress. He could also be envisaged as a ram (*Ovis
platyra*) with horns curving inwards close to his head.

During the New Kingdom the Theban priesthood of Amun elevated their deity
to the position of supreme creator god *par excellence*. Hymns were composed emphasizing

that he transcended all other deities, and that, as his name implied, he was beyond knowing. A fine example of such a hymn occurs on the 19th Dynasty Papyrus Leiden I 350, in which he is described as the 'Great Honker/Cackler', a primeval goose responsible for the cosmic egg from which the sun would hatch. The 'Great Honker' epithet is a reference to the noise Amun makes in the silence as the catalyst for the emergence of the primordial mound (i.e. sound waves are the dynamism for creation).

Papyrus Leiden I 350 also describes Amun (in his syncretized state with Ra) as 'the father of fathers, the mother of mothers' (V, 2–4). He is also said to have 'given birth to the primeval gods' (Papyrus Neschons = Papyrus Cairo 58032, I, 2). As with the other self-engendered creator gods, the word used is that of childbirth, *mes*.

So Amun becomes the Ogdoad and then Ta-tenen (the primordial mound at the time of creation); the sun god; the Ennead of Heliopolis; and all the other deities. An inscription in the temple of Hibis in the Kharga Oasis reads: '[he] rests in thousands and thousands of gods, who came forth from him' (Davies 1953: pl. 33, 25–6). In fact, all gods are regarded as aspects of Amun. But the three main gods that make up Amun are Ra (his face), Ptah (his body) and Amun (his secret self).

In the hymns, Amun is 'the most Unique One who gave birth to gods and men' (Papyrus Berlin 3049 XVI, 2). In this respect, he is identified with Khnum 'who models (*qed*) men, who gives birth to (*mes*) the gods', the ram-headed creator god of Esna in Upper Egypt. He creates the universe by modelling the other gods, humankind (both Egyptians and all those who speak other languages), animals, birds, fish, reptiles and plants out of clay on his potter's wheel. He pays particular attention to the moulding of the human body, getting the blood to flow over the bones and stretching the skin over the body. He takes special care with the installation of the respiratory and digestive systems, the vertebrae and the reproductive organs. He animates the body with the breath of life. He ensures the continuation of the human race by keeping an eye on conception and labour. This myth appears in inscriptions on the walls of the Graeco-Roman temple at Esna in Upper Egypt. At Esna, the syncretized Khnum-Ra is equated with the primeval god Ptah-Tatenen.

In the myth of the divine birth of the ruler, Khnum models the ruler and his or her *ka* on his potter's wheel (Hatshepsut at Deir el-Bahri and Amenhotep III at Luxor temple). This 'divine birth' is the result of the sexual union of the queen mother and the god Amun.

Khnum was an ancient deity represented as a man with the head of a ram, or in entirely ram form. The type of ram used to portray him was the earliest one to be domesticated in Egypt – *Ovis longipes* – which had curly horns extending horizontally from the head. The ram is commonly a symbol of procreativity. The ancient Egyptian for 'ram' was *ba*, which was also the word for a concept akin to our 'personality' (possibly those non-physical attributes which make any one human being unique, or perhaps the moral essence of a person's motivation and movement). It may well then have been a result of ancient Egyptian word play that Khnum came to be regarded as the *ba* of the sun god Ra, and so this deity was represented with a ram's head while passing through the Netherworld in his solar barque.

Connected with his capacity as a creator god was his role as patron deity of potters, and his association with the fertile soil, the annual inundation and the Nile cataracts. He was worshipped as 'Lord of the Cataract' on the island of Elephantine, at the First Cataract at the southern border of Egypt; and was believed to control the caverns of Hapi, the divine personification of the flooding Nile, and, in so doing, was regarded as a benefactor by the people of Egypt.

In fact, Hapi himself appears as a primeval god in the Coffin Texts. CT 320 states 'I am Hapi, foremost of births, who made what is, and brought into being what is not'. He claims to have come into being before vulvas and the primeval deities existed.

THE CREATION MYTH OF MEMPHIS

Ptah is the self-engendered creator god of Memphis who is referred to as the 'father of the gods from whom all life emerged'. He is linked with Atum of Heliopolis. He brings the universe into being by conceiving all aspects of it in his heart, and then by speaking his thoughts out loud. The similarity with the *logos* doctrine of St John's Gospel has been noted. First Ptah creates the other gods and goddesses (including Atum), and then towns with shrines in which to house them. He provides wood,

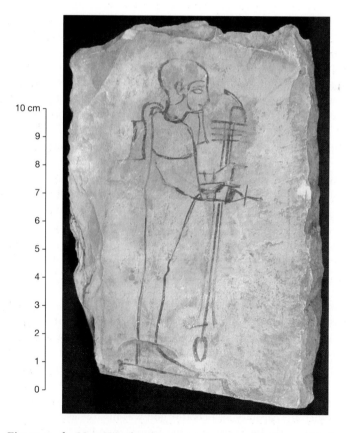

Figure 21.6   New Kingdom limestone ostracon with figure of Ptah (Petrie Museum UC 33195). Image courtesy and © Petrie Museum of Egyptian Archaeology, University College London.

clay and stone statues to act as bodies for the spirits or divine power (*ka*) of the deities, and offerings to be made to them forever. He brings everything into being by declaring their names. He creates the moral and social order (*maat*), including the concept of religion and how it was to be practised by the people of Egypt; and crafts, such as sculpture.

The 'Memphite Theology' has survived inscribed on a rectangular slab of black granite (92 × 137 cm) (British Museum 498). The inscription was commissioned by the 25th Dynasty king Shabaqo who ordered it to be set up in the temple of Ptah at Memphis. It was retrieved from the village of Mit Rahina which built up over the ruins of the ancient temple. The introduction explains that the king ordered the story to be copied on to stone because the original was written on a material which was becoming very worm-eaten (presumably papyrus or leather), and thus difficult to read. Unfortunately, the slab itself became difficult to read owing to its reuse as a lower grindstone. The central depression and radiating grooves are the result of this reuse. It was originally thought that the style of language used in the inscription was typical of the Old Kingdom. It is now generally agreed that the original was probably composed in the 19th Dynasty (Allen 1988: 43), but that it was deliberately archaized in order to endow it with greater authority.

Ptah was the chief deity of the city of Memphis which had been founded as the administrative capital of Egypt at the beginning of the 1st Dynasty. He was represented in human, semi-mummified form, wearing a skull cap and holding a staff that combined the *was*-sceptre of power, the *djed*-pillar of stability and the *ankh*-sign for life. From the Middle Kingdom onwards he was depicted with a straight beard.

Ptah was clearly regarded as a master craftsman as early as the Old Kingdom. In the Coffin Texts, as well as in later Ramesside texts, he is deemed responsible for crafting gods and the sun, and for the ripening of the vegetation. He was patron deity of craftsmen; and the High Priest of his cult at Memphis held the title 'Overseer of Craftsmen'.

The ancient Egyptians were not aware of the function of the brain, and instead identified the heart as the seat of wisdom and emotion. The idea of thinking with one's heart appears often; as does the naming of something in order to give it a life force. In the Memphite creation myth the initial concept of a god coupled with the uttering of his or her name causes its vital force (*ka*) to come into being. This then requires a vessel in which to reside. The vessel is a statue which can then act as the icon or focus of the particular cult. The 'Opening of the Mouth' ceremony was performed on statues of gods and kings destined for the shrines and temples, as well as on mummified bodies prior to burial; ritual instruments were held up to the mouth and nose of the statue or dead body in order to ignite the senses and breathe life into the 'vessels' for the *kas*. In fact, Ptah was credited with having invented this particular ritual.

The supremacy of Ptah is emphasized by the claim that the Heliopolitan myth has the myth of Ptah as its foundation, and that Atum acts as the heart and tongue of Ptah. Two of the forms Ptah is said to take are 'Ptah-Nun, the father who begot Atum', and 'Ptah-Naunet, the mother who bore Atum'. From the reign of Ramesses II, Ptah merges with the god Ta-tenen ('the Risen Land'). The Memphite Theology describes him as 'Ta-tenen, who gave birth to the gods and from whom everything came forth'.

A creation myth dating to the Graeco-Roman Period establishes Ptah once again as the original creator, within the context of the creation myth of Hermopolis. It is Ptah who brings the Ogdoad into being by not only conceiving of them, but also fashioning eggs, and fertilizing the primeval marsh with his seed. He then causes the union of the Ogdoad to become one – the creator god Amun.

TEMPLES AS SYMBOLS OF CREATION

The temples of Egypt were designed to reflect the universe at the time of creation. They were frequently identified as the horizon of the god. The foundation of a temple was a re-enactment of creation. Every temple was believed to stand on the primordial mound, and the names of cities reflected these cult centres. Memphis was, for example, called 'The divine emerging primeval island' and Thebes was 'The island emerging in Nun which first came into being when all other places were still in obscurity'.

Some of the earliest temples featured a mound of sand which is thought to have symbolized the primordial mound. As already mentioned, the ancient cult temple of Heliopolis had its *benben* stone, and perhaps the obelisks erected here and at cult centres elsewhere in Egypt might have had the same association.

Every temple had a sacred lake that appears to have symbolized the primordial waters, so the purification of the priests each day mirrored that of the sun as it passed through the waters of Nun at the end of each night. On his victory stela (Cairo Museum 48862), the 25th Dynasty king Piye is said to visit the temple at Heliopolis and wash his face in 'the river of Nun', as the sun god did.

The undulating mud-brick walls surrounding some sacred precincts have been interpreted as the waters of chaos lapping at the edges of the mound of creation. They were built in curved courses (pan bedding) resulting in a wavy effect. Anyone passing through the wall was symbolically purified in the waters of Nun.

Inside the enclosure wall, the temple buildings evoked a marshland, with pillars and walls decorated with a variety of plant life; the columns of colonnades and hypostyle halls had papyriform and lotiform capitals. Stars painted on the ceilings imitated the night skies. The gentle rise in floor level from the entrance of the temple to the inner sanctuary (using ramps and steps), with the shrine on a raised plinth, resulted in the cult statue standing as if the creator god, on top of the primordial mound. So every deity in his or her temple throughout the land was the creator god within that temple context.

KINGSHIP AND CREATION

Another architectural design that has been interpreted as mirroring the primordial mound is the pyramid, both in its stepped and smooth-sided forms. Frankfort links the transition to smooth-sided pyramids in the 4th Dynasty to the Heliopolitan *benben* (Frankfort 1948: 153).

The Pyramid Texts trace the king's birth back to the time of the primordial creator god. He is said to have been born from the self-impregnated sun god Ra or Atum; or even from Nun. An inscription in Theban Tomb 49 reads 'The king was born in

Nun before heaven and earth came into being'. The Memphite Theology united the king with Ptah.

The verb 'to appear on the throne'/'to appear in glory' (*kha*) is also the word for 'to rise' of the sun. It is written with the hieroglyphic sign of the sun rising over the primeval mound. The king's throne was reached by steps and sometimes a double stairway; this was perhaps an identification with the primordial mound for which the hieroglyphic sign was a single or double staircase.

The king appears to play the role of creator god on earth. In this capacity he is able to make use of Heka, Sia and IIu, and was primarily responsible for the maintenance of order.

CREATION AND RENEWAL

Some books of the Underworld, on the walls of New Kingdom royal tombs, seem to imply that the creator god would eventually grow weary and return to the chaos until it was time for a new universe to be created. In fact, sunset was, to a certain extent, regarded as the end of the world, when the sun god entered dark chaos. But, of course, the sun rose each morning, thereby ensuring the ordered universe was recreated. Thus each sunrise could be called *sep tepy* ('the First Time').

A renewal of creation also took place annually on New Year's Day, *wepet renpet*, 'the opening of the year' ('that which rejuvenates itself'), and less frequently, with the accession of a new king. The hymn to the Creator God in the First Intermediate Period/Middle Kingdom *Instruction for Merikara* states: 'The world was created, and it is continually maintained, for the sake of humankind.' But, some sources reveal that, as well as being a creator, the sun god was a destroyer, prone to devouring all living things.

A concept of the end of time when the sun will shine no more, and sky and earth will be reunited, is in keeping with the importance of symmetry to the ancient Egyptians – a beginning and end characterized their conception of the world (Hornung 1992: 49).

ACKNOWLEDGEMENTS

I would like to thank the Petrie Museum of Egyptian Archaeology for all the photographs. Please visit their website (www.petrie.ucl.ac.uk) for further information on the objects.

CHAPTER TWENTY-TWO

TEMPLE CULTS

———•◆•———

Emily Teeter

Temples were the setting for the performance of a wide variety of cult actions that provided the basic structure of ancient Egyptian religion and the means of communication between the divine and profane realms. Most cult actions took the form of offering rituals in which the king is shown giving the god(s) food, drink, flowers, incense or other gifts.

The performance of temple cult rituals served several essential functions. Most importantly, they were believed to maintain the cosmic and earthly order. This order of the universe was personified as the goddess and concept known as *maat*. Maat controlled the many eternal cycles of the universe, such as the rising and setting of the sun and the life-giving inundation of the Nile. The Egyptians viewed their world as a place of predictable and repeating patterns, whose unending rhythm, which was dependent upon *maat*, created a sense of safety and security. The temple cults, which were performed at defined intervals, were essential for preserving the balance of *maat* against the ever-threatening forces of chaos (*isfet*). Indeed, as indicated by Papyrus Berlin 3055 (22nd Dynasty), every offering was equated with *maat*: 'that which you (the god) eat is *maat*, your beverage is *maat*, your bread is *maat*, your beer is *maat*, the incense that you inhale is *maat*' (Moret 1902: 142).

Temple rituals also served to demonstrate the legitimacy of the king, for all cult actions were done in his name, and, with few exceptions, it is the king who is shown in the act of offering to the gods. This royal prerogative was a vivid reminder of the role of the king as the intermediary between the divine and profane spheres, and it also served to differentiate the king from his mortal subjects. The endless scenes of the king offering food or flowers or incense to the god(s) that decorated the walls of temples were intended to display the power and authority of the state by demonstrating the relationship of the king to the gods and the king's ability to maintain the balance of *maat*.

The importance of temple cult actions is evident in their longevity. Offerings to the god(s) can be documented through all periods of ancient Egyptian history. Many of the specific rituals were unchanged for millennia, a reflection of the deeply conservative nature of the Egyptians. This permanence of ritual actions reflects the

Egyptians' love and desire for repetition – of creating yet another unbroken cycle of action and liturgy that reinforced and protected the natural rhythms of the universe.

The distinctive architectural form of temples evolved to accommodate cult activities. A succession of hallways was provided for the transit of divine processions. The vast open courts were places where, on certain occasions, the public could assemble to participate, at least passively, in the temple cult. Much of the overall area of temples was devoted to storerooms where the sacred furniture and the goods for offerings were stored.

The main focus of temple cults was the maintenance of the god who, in the form of the cult statue, dwelled in the sanctuary of the temple (Figure 22.1). Because deities were patterned upon humans, they were believed to have the same fundamental requirements – food, drink and clothes – all of which were satisfied through offering rituals. The statue was not considered to be the deity itself, but, rather, it was a repository or receptacle for the power (*ba*) of the god. The statue was considered to be the deity's physical or revealed form (*ka*). As related in a text from Edfu, 'the god rests in his shrine after his *ba* has united with the image of his *ka*' (Alliot 1949: 23 in Lorton 1999: 193). The Memphite theology further explains that Ptah created the

Figure 22.1 Reconstruction of the sanctuary of Luxor Temple. The double doors of the naos are open, revealing the cult statue. Illustration by Jean-Claude Golvin, courtesy of J.-C. Golvin and Editions A. and J. Picard.

gods 'having placed [them] in their shrines, the gods entered into their bodies [i.e. the *ka* statue] made of every kind of wood, every kind of stone . . . having united the gods [i.e. the cult statue] with their *ba*'.

The ability of the cult statue to be imbued with the *ba* energy of the god was dependent upon the statue being prepared through the 'Opening of the Mouth' ritual, the actions and recitations of which symbolically awakened the senses of the statue enabling it to hear, breathe and see. Texts indicate that this ritual was performed in the workshop before the statue was transferred to the temple.

The *ba*-power of the deity was omnipresent, and it could reside in numerous statues simultaneously, each one considered to be equally charged with the divine *ba*. It is not clear if once the statue was enlivened, the *ba* stayed with the statue overnight. A text from Edfu relates that the god Horus 'sleeps in Edfu daily', and that the god Ra 'sleeps in it [the Edfu nome] until dawn' (Lorton 1999: 196–7). However, other texts from Edfu imply that the *ba* of the god came and went from the statue each day with the rising and setting sun: 'His [Ra] two eyes are fixed upon his cult statue; his living *ba* comes from heaven and rests upon his statue every day' (Žabkar 1968: 40); and 'The people worship your [the god's] *ka* (while) your *ba* in heaven joins your image' (Alliot 1954: 553–4 in Lorton 1999: 197).

Information about the appearance of cult statues comes from texts that describe them as being composed, at least partially, of precious material. A cult statue commissioned by Ramesses VI is described as:

> of good *nib*-wood and persea wood, the torso coloured and all of its limbs of faience like real jasper, and his kilt hammered (?) yellow gold; its crown of lapis lazuli, adorned with serpents of every colour; the uraeus on his head of six-fold alloy inlaid with real stones; its sandals of six-fold alloy.
>
> (P. Turin 1879 in McDowell 1999: 95)

The Tutankhamun Restoration Stela describes a new statue that the king commissioned for the Karnak temple as: 'His holy image being of electrum, lapis lazuli, turquoise, and every precious stone' (Murnane 1995a: 213). On a stela in the hypostyle hall at Karnak, the statue of the god is described as being made of 'gold from [the booty] of his majesty's prowess, out of the revenues of all the foreign lands'.

There are a few examples of statues that can, with some probability, be identified as cult images. One is a solid silver image of a falcon covered with gold foil, inlaid with glass and semi-precious stones. It is 42 centimetres tall and weighs 16.5 kilograms (Figure 22.2). The materials echo texts that describe the gods as having bones of silver, skin of gold and eyebrows of lapis lazuli. One can get an idea of the size of other cult statues from the shrine, or naoi, that enclosed them in the temple sanctuary. There is considerable variation in the interior space of these shrines, ranging from 75 to 143 centimetres (Roeder 1914), indicating that most of the cult statues were under (human) life-size. However, most reliefs of kings before shrines show the deity more or less the same height as the king (Figure 22.3).

Temple cults can broadly be divided into four types: the daily offering cult of the god(s); temple cults of the living or deceased king; cult activities associated with festivals; and cults of private individuals.

Figure 22.2 19th Dynasty (?) silver and gold statue of a falcon god that
may have been a cult statue. Image courtesy of the Miho Museum, Tokyo.

Figure 22.3 Ramesses III offers incense and a libation to Ptah who stands in his shrine (20th Dynasty, from Medinet Habu). The open leaf of the shrine's door is positioned behind the incense pot that the king offers. Image courtesy of the Oriental Institute of the University of Chicago.

THE DAILY OFFERING CULT

The daily offering cult consisted of a series of actions that were performed to care for the god in the temple's sanctuary. Various sources confirm that the daily offering service was enacted three times a day, mimicking the timing for breakfast, lunch and dinner.[1] Several texts refer to offerings being provided specifically as 'meals' for the god (Pyramid Texts Utterance 273.4; Epigraphic Survey 1941: pl. 138 col. 45; Haring 1997: 47).

There is very detailed documentation of this ritual both in text and representation. Long sequences of individual ritual actions, although their exact sequence is not always understood (e.g. Blackman 1919 (1998); Helck 1976; David 1981; Osing 1999, for discussions of the probable sequence of ritual actions shown on the walls), are shown in the temple of Seti I at Abydos, the hypostyle hall at the temple of Amun at Karnak, and the temple of Horus at Edfu. Written documentation of the daily offering cult is also rich, the most complete being Papyrus Berlin 3055 (22nd Dynasty) which records the full liturgy and accompanying actions for Amun, and Papyrus Berlin 3014 and 3053, for the goddess Mut. Temple walls are also covered with inventory lists of what was required for the daily services (Nelson and Hölscher 1934: 42–63; Haring 1997: 39–51, 399–410).

The daily offering ritual involved much more than just meeting the physical needs of the god, for each of the priestly actions was equated with mythological events. For example, drawing back the bolts of the shrine's door was equated with pulling the fingers of Seth from the eye of Horus, and red cloth that was offered was equated with the eye of Ra.

In depictions and descriptions of the daily offering service, the officiant is, with few exceptions, the king,[2] emphasizing his semi-divine status and his role as the intermediary between mankind and the gods. In actuality, the ritual was enacted by various levels of priests (*wab*s, lectors and god's fathers)[3] who acted in the name of the king. These men (for there is no record of female priests serving in this role) were ritually purified by washing, which gave them authorization to enter the sacred areas of the temple. Brief hieroglyphic texts on doorjambs specify the level of purity (for example, 'twice' or 'four times') required for entrance. According to Papyrus Berlin 3055, the newly purified priest introduced himself to the god by declaring 'It is the king who sends me'. He then began a series of rituals.

The morning ritual was the most elaborate of the three daily enactments. As the sun rose, the chief priest washed his body with water, made purifications with incense and washed his mouth with natron in a room of the temple called the *per-duat* 'the House of the Morning' (Blackman 1918 (1998): 197). As related in one text: 'There were performed for him [the priest] all the ceremonies that are performed for a king'; hence, through purification, the priest temporarily became a true royal surrogate. Then, he joined the company of other priests, a divine chorus and temple attendants who assembled the sacred objects, implements and food offerings that were required. Holding a candle, the chief priest entered the sanctuary intoning 'Awake in peace! May your awakening be peaceful!' (Meeks and Favard Meeks 1996: 127). He then started a series of cult actions, each of which was accompanied by a set recitation. He broke the clay seals on the double doors of the naos, drew back the bolt and opened the doors to expose the statue of the god. This opening of the shrine's doors was referred to as 'Opening the Sight' of the god (Moret 1902: 49–56; Lohwasser 1991:

28–33). The act served as a mythical allusion to giving birth, the rising of the sun alluding to life anew, and the double doors being equated with the vulva of Nut. The priest then 'kissed the ground', prostrating himself before the god. After several repetitions of adoring the god and purification with incense, he poured clean white sand on the floor of the sanctuary. He then recited the 'Spell for Laying Hands upon the God' (i.e. he removed the statue from the shrine, placing it upon the sand) (Moret 1902: 167–70). He began the toilet of the god by removing the deity's clothing, which was probably a simple linen wrapping,[4] and wiping away unguents applied the previous day. After further purification with natron, the statue was presented with white, green and red cloth that symbolized the uraeus, fertility and the blood of Isis, respectively.[5] The god was then dressed in the 'great cloth' (some sort of linen garment), and was adorned with a broad collar, sceptres, anklets, bracelets; and, in the case of Amun, the tall plumes associated with that god were affixed to his head.

Toilet complete, the deity was presented with trays of food offerings and jars of wine and beer (Figure 22.4). After an unspecified interval allowed for the god to 'consume' the meal, the food was removed. Finally, after more purification with incense, the priest, grasping a *hdn*-plant, backed away from the shrine, sweeping away his own footprints, a ritual action that was also believed to repel evil from the god's shrine (Nelson 1949).

There is a lack of agreement among scholars about what actions were performed during the noon and evening rituals,[6] other than that the morning ritual was the most elaborate, as reflected by the Pyramid Text that relates 'their big ones are for his morning meal; their middle-sized ones are for his evening meal; their little ones are for his night meal', implying that food may have been offered three times daily.

Figure 22.4 Ramesses IV offering a tray of food and sacrificed cattle to Khonsu in the Temple of Khonsu, Luxor, 20th Dynasty (photo E. Teeter).

Sauneron (1980 [1960]: 88), however, suggested that the midday service did not involve food offerings, but, rather, was composed of presenting water and incense before the closed shrine and offering to the 'secondary gods [and] the deified sovereigns worshipped in the temple', while the evening actions were 'roughly, a repetition of the first service of the day, except that the sanctuary remained shut and all the ceremonies took place in the side chapels around the [sanctuary]'. Quirke (1992: 75) refers to the evening events thus: 'the reverse service would be performed, and the image returned behind the bolted doors of the shrine for the night, to rest until the next morning when the cycle would be repeated'.

The daily offering cult continued to be performed in the Amarna Period, but it was modified to suit the new theology. Since the deity of Akhenaten, the Aten, had no corporeal form, the ritual was modified, eliminating acts such as the morning toilet and the presentation of fabric, for there was no cult statue. The dark sanctuary of the god was replaced by the light-filled courtyards of the Aten temples. Rather than presenting food offerings to the god's statue, hundreds of offering tables arrayed in the sunlight were heaped with provisions (Figure 22.5).

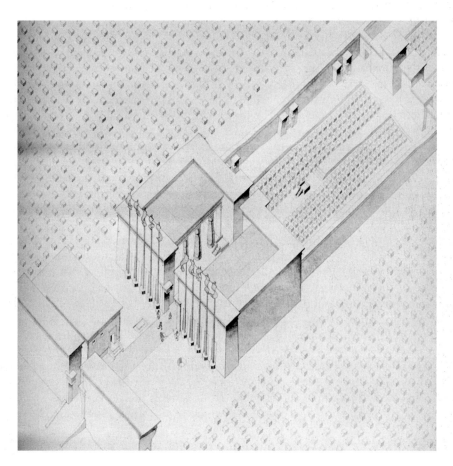

Figure 22.5 Offering tables in the Per-hai temple at Amarna located in the sun to enable the rays of the Aten to 'consume' the offerings (from Pendlebury 1951: pl. VIa).

The identity and number of the participants also changed. Rather than a single main officiant – a priest in the guise of the king – Akhenaten and Nefertiti together consecrate piles of offerings. What had previously been a private and hidden ritual was replaced by a more public one, attended by the royal daughters who stand nearby and shake sistra, by ladies-in-waiting, dwarfs and onlookers who adore the royal family as they offer to the Aten (Davies 1905: pls v, xii).

At Thebes, the daily offering ritual that was enacted in the temples on the east bank was also performed in the royal ('mortuary') temples on the west bank. A text at Medinet Habu, the mortuary temple of Ramesses III, relates

> I [Ramesses III] have established for you [Amun] a divine offering of the daily requirement . . . I have [given] attention to your statue in the morning. The Ennead which is in my temple is in festival every day. I made your fixed portion festive with bread and beer. Cattle and desert animals are slaughtered in your slaughterhouse . . . .
>
> (Epigraphic Survey 1941: pl. 138 cols 32–3; Haring 1997: 44–5)

TEMPLE CULT OF THE KING

In all periods, offering rituals in the temples were enacted in the name of the king, but in the same context, the king was also the recipient of offerings. The royal (also called mortuary) temples or 'Mansions of Millions of Years' (Haeny 1997; Haring 1997: 20–4, 419–25, plus references), at Thebes and elsewhere, were establishments for the celebration of the cult of the king. During his lifetime and after his death, offerings were made to him, just as they were to the gods in other temples. A text from Medinet Habu relates there were two statues of the king in that temple who were the 'co-recipients' of offerings (Epigraphic Survey 1941: pl. 138 col. 50; Haring 1997: 46). Some Theban mortuary temples had an emplacement for a false door of the king's deceased father, while others had a more elaborate temple-within-a-temple located to the south of the main structure, where the deceased king and his father were worshipped (Hölscher 1941: 29–31).

Some of the cults of individual kings were celebrated for years, or even millennia, after their death. An official in the reign of Ay prayed that he might 'smell the incense of the offerings when there is a gathering(?) in the temple of [Thutmose III]' who died 150 years earlier, and there are references to the cult of Thutmose I in the late 20th Dynasty – some 500 years after that king's death (Nelson and Hölscher 1934: 45–6; Haring 1997: 394).

Upon death, the king joined the ranks of all his predecessors to form a constellation of deceased ancestors. This cult of deceased kings was celebrated by leaving food offerings before lists of cartouches, as in the 'Hall of Ancestors' in the temple of Seti I at Abydos (Porter and Moss 1927–99: vol. 6, 24–5), or before representations of the kings, as in the Temple of Thutmose III at Karnak (Porter and Moss 1927–99: vol. 2, 111–12; Andreu *et al.* 1997: 114–15) where 61 former kings were honoured.

FESTIVAL CULTS

Another category of temple cult was associated with the many festivals that dotted the Egyptian calendar. Each festival had a set 'script' of actions and recitations.

Festivals were celebrated very frequently. In the reign of Thutmose III, 54 festival days (of the 365-day year) were commemorated, while in the reign of Ramesses III the count rose to 60 (Kemp 1989b: 206). Some occurred at frequent intervals, such as the Decade Festival which was celebrated every ten days. Others, such as the New Kingdom Festival of Opet, Feast of the Valley and Festival of Min, were celebrated only once a year.

Festivals were opportunities for direct or indirect public participation in temple cults, for in the course of most festivals, the god(s) left the confines of the sanctuary and travelled around the perimeter of his or her own temple, or moved from one temple to another. In preparation for procession, the divine statue was removed from the naos in the sanctuary and placed in a wooden carrying shrine. These shrines could be very elaborate. One, commissioned by Thutmose I for Osiris at Abydos, is described as being made of silver, gold, lapis lazuli, black copper and 'every splendid stone' (Breasted 1906b: 38). The shrine was placed on a ceremonial boat that was supported on a series of transverse poles. These poles lay upon two long carrying poles that rested upon the shoulders of a double file of priests. As the sacred boats increased in size, the king boasted of the increased number of carrying poles required. Tutankhamun claimed that he increased the carrying poles for the image of Amun to 13, when 'the noble god had formerly been upon only eleven', and those which supported the statue of Ptah were increased from nine to 11 (Murnane 1995b: 213). The processional boat was splendid. Thutmose I commissioned one 'of new cedar of the best of the terraces [of Lebanon], its bow and stern being made of electrum' (Breasted 1906b: 39). The identity of the god concealed within was indicated by a representation of the deity on the bow and stern.

During the course of processions, the community gathered to adore the deity through song, dance and prayer. Periodically, the boat bearing the god would temporarily rest in kiosks and shrines along the route, allowing the community to see the god (or at least the shrine), and to place oracles before it.

Festivals also served to link temples. During Opet, Amun of Karnak travelled to his 'Southern Harem' at Luxor Temple. During the Decade Festival, Amun of Karnak crossed the river to Medinet Habu, and in the course of the Beautiful Feast of the Valley, the boats of Amun and the king crossed the river and received offerings at the royal temples of Hatshepsut, Seti I, Ramesses II and Ramesses III. When crossing the river, the processional boat was placed on a larger ship called the *Userhat*, 'Mighty of Prow', a magnificent river barge whose golden topsides were painted with scenes of the king making pious offerings, and whose deck was decorated with sphinxes, obelisks and statues of the king (Altenmüller 1975: 250; Murnane 1979: 18).

The major festivals of the principal Theban gods (Amun, Mut and Khonsu) included a boat for a statue of the king, emphasizing his role as both donor and officiant of the cult and also celebrating his union with the deities. A text at Medinet Habu relates 'Whenever you [Amun] appear in my temple he [the image of the king] follows you' (Epigraphic Survey 1941: pl. 138 col. 38; Haring 1997: 45–6). The culminating rituals of the annual Opet Festival were held in Luxor Temple. The reliefs in the southern part of that structure depict a series of offering rituals that resulted in the deification of the living king (Bell 1997). Other festivals incorporated ritual actions, such as releasing four geese or doves for Min (Murnane 1980: 38–9), or shooting arrows at targets and throwing balls at the four cardinal points performed during the Decade Festival (Cooney 2000: 29).

TEMPLE CULTS OF NON-ROYAL INDIVIDUALS

Although individuals had limited access to the temples, they could participate passively in the cult by establishing a statue of themselves in the temple. Most commonly, such statues were made of stone or bronze. They were of various sizes, from votives to nearly life-size. They were placed in temple hypostyle halls and courts where they could serve as eternal 'doubles' of the individual, allowing him or her eternally to absorb the offerings and prayers that were enacted in the temple, much like the lists of deceased kings were served by offerings. Although this practice was very common in the New Kingdom and later, it is attested as early as the 4th Dynasty in the tomb of Metjen (Rizzo 2004: 512). The son of Shemau, an 8th Dynasty official, commented on the practice: 'Your [his father's] statues, your offerings tables . . . which are in any temple or temple precinct' (Robins 2001a: 40). According to the inscriptions on the statues, some were gifts from the king. Others were apparently unrelated to royal favour, but were certainly commissioned by, and intended to commemorate, elite members of the community. The popularity of the statue cult in temples is demonstrated by the 'Karnak Cachette' discovered in 1903, which consisted of statues that were cleared out of the temple in the early Ptolemaic Period and given an honourable burial to the south of the hypostyle hall. The cachette contained an astounding 17,000 statues and ritual objects, in addition to approximately 750 stone statues, many of which were of individuals rather than deities or members of the royal family (Traunecker and Golvin 1984: 171).

ECONOMIC IMPORTANCE OF TEMPLE CULTS

Whether for the daily ritual or for the annual festivals, rituals of purification with incense and the offering of food, drink and other objects were the primary actions that made up temple rituals. Much ceremony and opulence surrounded these offerings. Ramesses III claimed 'His Majesty has ordered that a divine offering be established anew for (my) father Amunrasonter on his great offering table of silver (called) "Great of Provisions" ' (Epigraphic Survey 1936: pl. 108 col. 6; Haring 1997: 89–90). Other texts refer to great jar stands of gold and silver upon which offerings were deposited (Nelson and Hölscher 1934: 42–3).

A clearer idea of the economic impact and importance of temple cults can be gained from texts that state the amount of food required for the daily service(s), especially since it was, at least in theory, enacted in each temple in the land. Offering lists at Karnak specify the following requirement for the daily offerings: 21 sacks of grain (a sack being 76.88 litres (Haring 1997: 418)), six fowl, two or three measures of wine, 14 baskets of fruit, four (or more) baskets of incense, four *hin*-measures of honey, two of fat, ten bunches and ten baskets of flowers, and 100 bundles of vegetables (Haring 1997: 410). The silver and gold offering stands that Ramesses III placed in the forecourt of his small temple at Karnak were laden daily with 36 loaves of bread of specified weights, 20 gold jars of beer, four baskets of incense and four of fruit 'as the daily allowance'. A block recovered from the Ninth Pylon at Karnak relates that the daily offering for Ra consisted of 377 loaves of various types of bread, and 34 jugs of beer, as well as specified amounts of fruit, vegetables, milk, pigeons and incense (Murnane 1995b: 33–4). An offering list of Ramesses III at the Karnak temple enumerates that 20 sacks of grain were offered daily, making 7,300 sacks (561,244 litres) per year (Haring 1997: 91).

A massive infrastructure was required to provide for the needs of the temple cults for they were major consumers of produce, birds, fabric, incense and flowers. Ramesses III proclaimed that he caused 'things to exist which are removed from the land, barley . . . like [sand of] the shores, in order to provide for the altars of the gods' (Haring 1997: 89). An ostracon dating to the reign of Ramesses II states that the domain of Amun in the northern region of Egypt had 8,760 cultivators, each producing 200 sacks of barley; [number lost] of cowherds, each in charge of 500 animals; 13,080 goat herders; 22,530 fowl keepers, each in charge of 34,230 birds; 3,920 donkey drivers, each with 870 donkeys; and 13,227 mule drivers, each with 551 mules, as well as fishermen (Kitchen 1999b: 235–8).

The temple grain and herds were raised on vast tracts of land located throughout Egypt. The produce from these farms was apportioned to specific temples. In many instances, the source of the produce was far away from its ultimate destination, another indication of the sophistication of the Egyptian temple cult's offering distribution system. Ramesses III recounted:

> I built farms in your name in the Beloved Land [i.e. Egypt] and in the country of Nubia as well as in the country of Asia. I charged them with their produce as a yearly requirement [i.e. annual tax]. All towns whatsoever are brought together with their goods (*inu*) in order to send them to your *ka* . . . I collected for you herds of all kinds of animals, fields, gardens and high grounds, *iuef-neri* [an unknown topographical term] grounds and marshes. The birds that descend in the swamps are slaughtered in order to make your offerings festive with nourishment and game. I filled your workshop with the spoil of my force. Your granary is overflowing with grain. Your treasuries are spitting out gold and silver. Things of all lands are entering it.
>
> (Epigraphic Survey 1941: pl. 138 cols 40–8; Haring 1997: 47)

The supplies for the temple cult could also be derived from foreign conquest. Ramesses III claimed:

> I filled it [the temple treasury] and I completed it with my victories which I accomplished in every country with my great force. Its treasuries contain gold, silver, all types of linen, incense, oil, and honey, like the sand of the shore.
>
> (Epigraphic Survey 1932: pl. 107; Haring 1997: 49, 51)

Barry Kemp has likened the temples in Western Thebes to ancient 'reserve banks' because of the immense amount of grain – which was the standard means of economic exchange – they stored. The granaries at Medinet Habu are calculated to have held 56,972 sacks of grain, while those at the Ramesseum held 214,906 (Kemp 1989b: 195; Haring 1997: 118 and n. 1 for slightly different numbers). The Ramesseum stores have been calculated to be capable of supporting 3,400 families for an entire year (Kemp 1989b: 195). Although an individual temple 'owned' tracts of land throughout Egypt, the temples were economically linked, at least in Thebes, and the supplies of one temple were often transferred to another. For example, offering lists at Karnak indicate that some of the provisions for the daily offering ritual at that temple were supplied by the royal temple of Ramesses III at Medinet Habu, a total of 7,756¼ sacks a year going from the granary of the west to the east;[7] while in the Theban tombs of Ineni and Puyemra, the incense for the 'royal' temples on the west is shown being weighed out in the Karnak temple (Haring 1997: 135–6, 207–8; Ineni: Porter and Moss 1927–99: vol. I/I, 159 (4); Dziobek 1992: 39–40; Puyemra: Davies 1922: 92–6, pl. xl; Porter and Moss 1927–99: vol. I/I, 72 (6)).

The vast land holdings, and the staff to herd the animals and to grow the grain, were protected by royal decrees, such as one of Seti I at Nauri that exempted the staff or the lands from being diverted to other purposes.

SIGNIFICANCE OF TEMPLE CULTS TO THE PUBLIC

Although the temple rituals revolved around the king and the god, in real terms they had practical significance for individuals of the temple staff, and in the community as a whole. The food offerings presented to the god were called 'reversion offerings' (*wedjebu hetep*), meaning that after the god had 'consumed' the food, it reverted to the temple staff as part of their wages. This custom is known from the late Old Kingdom (funerary papyri of Neferirkara) and it continued until the end of the Ptolemaic Period, as indicated by the Canopus Decree. The important role that reversion offerings played in feeding others than the god may explain why burnt offerings, although known in Egypt, were not a significant part of temple ritual – for the food was to be consumed by priests and their dependants. So, too, the very human qualities of the god – their needs were patterned upon those of humans – stressed eating and drinking rather than having to resort to the more abstract 'inhaling' fumes of immolated offerings.

Nothing is known about the amount of time required for the god to be sated – but the fact that the offerings included freshly slaughtered fowl and beef suggests that the food did not linger for an extended period of time.

The quantity of reversion offerings received by any priest was apparently determined by several different formulae. According to the texts of Hapdjefa, a Middle Kingdom nomarch of Asyut, the amount of reversion offerings that he received was based, not on the total offerings for a specific day, but upon a percentage of the annual offerings, which presumably helped equalize larger amounts of offerings used during festival days. Since he worked as a priest 27 days of the year, he was allowed a quantity equal to the total offerings for 360 (days of the year) divided by 27.[8] A priest of Hathor in the Old Kingdom received one-tenth of 'all that enters the temple' (Blackman 1918 (1998): 132). To get a more concrete idea of what was received, an overseer of the temple of Senusret II at Lahun was granted 16 loaves of bread and 25 jars of beer daily (Haring 1997: 11), certainly a considerable amount of food that would have fed a large household leaving surplus to barter for other goods.

Temple cults also affected individuals who were not directly connected with the temples, for people could receive reversion offerings in exchange for making donations to the temple, much like an annuity. An individual's portion of the reversion offerings could be directed to their own funerary cult, or the offerings could be used as food during their lifetime (Haring 1997: 7–12, 142–55). The Middle Kingdom endowment by Hapdjefa consisted of contracts which stipulated that in exchange for granting land and produce from his fields to the temple, offerings from the same temple would be placed before his memorial statues (Haring 1997: 8). Neferperet, who served in the army of Thutmose III, was rewarded with a small flock of animals, a certain quantity of whose milk and offspring were designated to be used for offerings in the temple cult. Although the flock itself belonged to the temple, Neferperet and his family were charged with their care and, in exchange, they were allowed to retain a portion of their output (Kemp 1989b: 191; Haring 1997: 145–7). In another endowment from the reign of Amenhotep III, the donor, the chief steward Amenhotep, donated land, serfs and animals as offerings for a temple. In return, a portion of the offerings used in the temple cult was directed to his tomb (Haring 1997: 10). A text on an offering table of a doorkeeper of Amun of the Temple of the Hearing Ear at Karnak relates the same practice of diverting temple offerings for private use: 'All that comes forth on the table (?) of the lords of eternity [i.e. the gods], as good and pure things for the *ka* of the Osiris, the *wab*-priest . . . Nia' (Habachi 1972c: 74). These arrangements that diverted the flow of offerings from the temple to private hands were usually made by the permission of the king, and were formalized by an *imyt-per* document (Logan 2000).

Apparently there were abuses of reversion offerings. The endowment text of the steward Amenhotep warned:

> Listen you *wab*-priests, lector priests and god's servants . . . His Majesty has given to you bread, beer, meat, cakes and all good things in order to nourish you in his temple of United-with-Ptah, with the daily requirement of every day. Do not be greedy for my offering bread which my own (?) god ordered for me (?) in order to pour water for me at my tomb.
>
> (Haring 1997: 11)

Another text from Edfu warns priests not to remove the divine food offerings prematurely:

> Do not go freely to steal his [the god's] things. Beware, moreover, of foolish thoughts. One lives by the food of the gods, and 'food' is called that which comes forth from the offering-table(s) *after* the god has been satisfied with it.
>
> (Haring 1997: 11)

PUBLIC AWARENESS OF THE TEMPLE CULT

How much did the community know about the cult actions that were enacted in the temple? There is considerable evidence to suggest that in the Dynastic period, there was little sense of mystery about the nature of temple rituals. The majority of the priests who worked within the temple were part-time employees who returned to their other occupation(s) in the months they rotated off duty (see further in Haring 1997: 3–5, 222–4). Although the lower-level priests would not have had access to the sanctuary, it seems very likely that they were familiar with the ongoing activities. The general public had even more restricted access, but they were allowed into parts of the temple whose walls were covered with reliefs that showed the rituals performed within the more sacred, private areas (Teeter 1997: 4–5). For example, the hypostyle hall at Karnak, whose walls are decorated with scenes of the daily offering service was – as indicated by texts on its architraves – 'a place where the common people praise the name of His Majesty' (Nims 1954: 80; Kitchen 1975–89: vol. 2, 559.7–9), and 'the place where Amun is made manifest to the people' (Nims 1965: 93), indicating that the public was allowed into this area, at least on certain occasions.

In conclusion, temple cults were an absolutely fundamental part of ancient Egyptian religion and culture. The ritual actions performed in the temple were thought to safeguard the universe through the maintenance of *maat*. The cult actions expressed the relationship of the king and the gods, and their economic impact, through the innumerable sacks of grain, baskets of incense, fabric, cult statues and other temple furniture, provided an important component of the economy. But, perhaps most important, the constant repetition of ancient rituals provided constancy, and a rhythmic pattern of life and belief that sustained the faith of the population.

NOTES

1 See P. Turin 1879 for 'three offerings are conducted for them [the statues] daily. . . his statue receiving incense and libations for its god's offering' (McDowell 1999: 95); Pyramid Text Utterance 273.4: 'Their big ones are for his morning meal; their middle-sized ones are for his evening meal; their little ones are for his night meal'; P. Sallier: 'the priest performs the service . . . three (times daily)' (Caminos 1954: 318); 'its [the rooms leading to the sanctuary] double doors open on the hall of offerings in order to worship Ra three times daily' (Alliot 1949: 102 in Lorton 1999: 145).

2 Queens and individuals of quasi-royal status, such as the God's Wives of Amun of the Third Intermediate and Late Periods, may be shown enacting typically royal rituals such as the presentation of Maat (Teeter 1997: 13), but it is difficult to determine if isolated scenes, such as offering incense, may be a reference to them carrying out fuller cult duties such as a daily offering ritual.

3 See the invocation 'Listen you *wab* priests, lector priests, and gods' servants' (Epigraphic Survey 1941: pl. 138 col. 31, and Haring 1997: 11); and '[I say to] you, divine fathers of this temple, *wab*-priests, ritual priests, dwellers in the hand of the hand-[priests], all the lay priests of the temple' (after Breasted 1906b: 39 (Abydos Stela of Thutmose I)).

4 See the statues of divinities enclosed in shrines from the tomb of Tutankhamun which, when discovered, were wrapped in short lengths of linen much like a cloak (Reeves 1990: 130). Sauneron (1980 [1960]: 85–6) states, 'In practice, the divine clothing was not renewed every day; it was done at the solemn services which took place once or twice a week. But daily the symbolic offering of the four strips of material took place.'

5 Some versions indicate four colours of cloth. See Sauneron (1980 [1960]: 85–6).

6 Heiden (2003: 312) commented 'Any written or pictorial reference for ritual clothing, bodily purification, as well as the provision of divine insignia on the cult statue by the priest is lacking . . . As a result, it is possible to speculate that treatment of the cult statue was never really carried out by the priest'. However, the economic documents that record amounts of food and other objects used in the rituals make his suggestion very unlikely.

7 This cooperation between what are often today perceived as 'festival temples' as opposed to 'mortuary temples' suggests that their purposes were not so very different. See Haring (1997: 68, 94, 207–10, 383–8).

8 The distribution according to temple day was the practice in the Middle Kingdom. It was not followed in the New Kingdom but again became the practice in the Ptolemaic Period (Haring 1997: 8).

CHAPTER TWENTY-THREE

PRIVATE RELIGION

——•◆•——

Lucia Gahlin

Private religion is a term used to describe the religious beliefs and practices of an individual outside the framework of the state or organized religion. By its very nature, the evidence is less likely to have survived than that for state religion and, when it has, it may well be difficult to interpret correctly. Little survives regarding private religion prior to the New Kingdom, and the extent to which we can assume similarities pre-1550 BC is always questionable.

Private religion would have taken place in the household, at shrines, by the graveside, in the outer, more accessible parts of temple buildings, or other locations with or without a perceived sacred value. The emphasis was on the personal relationship between an individual and the divine.

This chapter interprets 'private religion' as religion that took place outside the temples, and which did not relate to the calendar of festivals of these establishments. Consequently it does not address practices associated with the temples such as oracular consultation (for which we have evidence from the New Kingdom onwards). This chapter will also avoid private funerary beliefs and practices, as this aspect of Egyptian religion is covered elsewhere (Ikram, this volume).

Private religion corresponds to beliefs and related actions which ensure the continued existence and well-being of an individual, and his or her family (living, dead and future). Letters surviving from the late Ramesside Period often contain the affirmation 'I am well/alive; tomorrow is in the hands of the gods' (Baines 1991: 195; Quirke 1992: 134). Those in need sought an explanation in the divine. This is well documented in the New Kingdom 'penitential hymns' from Deir el-Medina, for example a hymn on a limestone stela dedicated to Ptah by Neferabu (British Museum 589), in which the artist regards the cause of his inability to see (perhaps an eye infection) as a punishment by the god for having sworn a false oath.

Private religion was not an alternative to state religion, nor was it regarded as unorthodox, but it was a crucial aspect of the religious lives of the people. Like the rituals in the temples, private rituals utilized sorcery or enchantments (*akhu*), and magic (*heka*), interpreted as the catalyst or energy required for creation to take place. Neither *akhu* nor *heka* was intrinsically good or bad, but could be channelled either way, although during the pharaonic period antisocial or unacceptable magic appears to have been less common and tended to be attributed to foreigners, or directed against them (as in the use of execration (or curse) texts). The sources from the West Theban New Kingdom village of Deir el-Medina reveal that most magic performed was defensive, and was used against dangerous animals (especially snakes and scorpions), demons and deceased individuals.

An individual might be born with enhanced *heka* (for example, a dwarf) or might go through a phase when he/she was believed to possess *heka*, for example during lactation. The milk of a mother who had given birth to a male child was considered particularly efficacious medically/magically (the two were not distinct).

Designated members of the local community might act as a channel between an individual and the divine world. The titles and equipment of some of these practitioners have survived. There were the *sau* (from the word for 'protection' and also 'amulet' (*sa*)) which can be translated 'protection-maker' (Pinch 2004: 100) (midwives might also be designated *sau*). There was also the *rekhet* ('knowing one' or 'wise woman') who appears to have been a medium between the living and the spirit world. Her mediation was sought to explain a *bau*, 'manifestation of a god', a supernatural encounter compared to death on Berlin Stela 20377.8 (Borghouts 1994: 129). Finally there were the *hery seshta* ('Chief of Mysteries/Secrets') and *kherep Serqet* ('one who has power over the scorpion goddess') who was clearly a scorpion (and snake) charmer and someone who could treat bites and stings. This latter title might be held by someone also bearing the title *sunu* ('doctor'). So there were members of society operating outside the temples who were believed to facilitate people's interaction with the divine, or spirit, world. The lector priest might have played a similar role as mediator between the temple and the local community.

A Second Intermediate Period cache of paraphernalia, presumably belonging to a 'Chief of Mysteries', was discovered in a tomb under the Ramesseum on the west bank at Thebes. It included a box with the title *hery seshta* inscribed on the lid; a bronze wand in the form of a snake; a wooden figure wearing a Bes mask and holding metal snakes; and spell papyri. Snake-shaped wands (usually of bronze) may have been representations of the cobra-form goddess Weret Hekau ('Great of Magic'). Depictions of the divine personification of magic, Heka, show him holding two crossed snakes, and wooden and ivory figures masked like the protective spirit-deities Bes and Beset have survived, holding metal snake wands. In the Old Testament Book of Exodus, the magicians attending Pharaoh perform the miracle of turning their wands into serpents.

Another type of wand to survive is the so-called apotropaic wand (about 150 are known, dating mainly to the First Intermediate Period and Middle Kingdom). They can be of calcite, faience and ebony, but are mainly of hippopotamus ivory. Perhaps the association with the hippopotamus goddess Taweret is deliberate. The wands are decorated with a selection of magical images (including snake-breathing lions and human-headed winged snakes), protective *sa* and *wedjat*-eye amulets, and deities such as the god of chaos and infertility Seth, and the apotropaic household deities, Bes and Taweret, who are often shown wielding knives threateningly. When inscribed, the brief inscriptions are concerned with protection ('by night and by day'), nearly always of women and children, against any perceived threat to their existence (such as demons, ghosts and sorcerers), particularly at times of birth and early childhood. The precise ritual use of the wands is unknown.

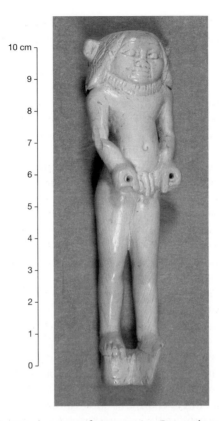

Figure 23.1 Middle Kingdom ivory figure wearing Bes mask, and perhaps originally holding metal snakes (Petrie Museum UC 16069). Image courtesy and © Petrie Museum of Egyptian Archaeology, University College London.

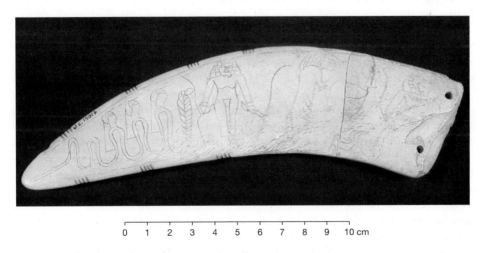

Figure 23.2 Middle Kingdom hippopotamus ivory apotropaic wand (Petrie Museum UC 15917). Image courtesy and © Petrie Museum of Egyptian Archaeology, University College London.

Further 'weapons in a magical defence system for the vulnerable' (Pinch 2004: 100) were the magic rods that have survived from the Middle Kingdom and Second Intermediate Period. Glazed steatite examples display representations of animals such as frogs, turtles, baboons, crocodiles and felines, in addition to lamps and amuletic symbols such as the *sa* symbols and *wedjat* eyes. Originally these rods would also have had miniature models of animals attached to them. Again it is not certain exactly how these rods would have been used, but they presumably served to dominate those animals depicted on them, and turn their power into a protective rather than a malignant force.

There were always the 'poor man's' alternatives to these rather elaborate items; the magical texts include spells that refer to the brandishing of a stick or a branch, particularly in the commanding of spirits and demons; or a spell might be recited over a drawing, for example of deities (Isis, Ra and Horus) on the hand of someone bitten by a snake. The erasure of the drawing by licking was a crucial part of the ritual (for example, in the 19th Dynasty Turin Papyrus *Isis and the Sun God's Secret Name*).

Magico-medical texts survive from the late third millennium BC through to the fifth century AD. They combine the use of remedies (to be taken internally, applied externally or administered by fumigation) with spells to be recited as part of magical rituals incorporating amulets and other such devices. The texts use three words: *shesau* (prognoses, diagnoses and prescribed treatments); *pekheret* (prescription, i.e. list of ingredients and recipes for medicaments); and *ru* (spells or incantations). All three were combined in one cure (Quirke 1992: 111). Various of the ingredients used in the remedies had clear ritual or magical significance, but would have also had a certain medicinal value, for example honey, which modern studies have proved can be used to treat surgical wounds, ulcers and burns successfully. In the 19th Dynasty Papyrus Leiden I, 348, the first of the spells to cure burns is to be recited over a dressing of honey. Honey was also believed to ward off evil spirits. This seems to correspond to the idea that demons and the disaffected dead inhabited an inverted world; consequently their mouths were where their anuses should be, and so they fed on human faeces (Coffin Texts 205, 206), and were repelled by honey (Papyrus Berlin 3027).

The ancient Egyptians might consult a 'Calendar of Lucky and Unlucky Days' in order to determine the most propitious day for performing a ritual. The best-known is the 'Cairo Calendar' which was penned in the 19th Dynasty, but appears to have had its origins in the Middle Kingdom. Many of the days were linked to mythological happenings. Further guidance was offered by 'Dream Books' which listed a series of possible dreams and what dreaming them foretold about the future. One such papyrus dream book was owned by the 19th Dynasty scribe Qenherkhepeshef who was in charge of the administration at Deir el-Medina. It advises the use of protective spells upon waking from a nightmare. As with the Cairo Calendar, the style of the language suggests a Middle Kingdom original. Deities might appear in dreams to aid healing or offer guidance. In the first millennium BC the practice of incubation became popular whereby people went to sleep (and dream) in temple *sanatoria*. Perhaps the earliest known reference to this practice is to be found on a 19th Dynasty stela dedicated to Hathor by the same Qenherkhepeshef (British Museum EA 278).

As already noted, two of the deities that featured in private religion were the protective deities Bes and Taweret. They were closely linked to the vulnerable periods in the life of the household, such as childbirth. Bes had a close association with

Figure 23.3 New Kingdom limestone ostracon with drawing of Bes (Petrie Museum UC 33198). Image courtesy and © Petrie Museum of Egyptian Archaeology, University College London.

music, dance and drunkenness, all of which had a role in private religion. These deities appear as tattoos; in amuletic form; on stelae, head-rests, beds and other household goods; and painted on the interior walls of houses.

Other amulets were also used as protective devices in the lives of the ancient Egyptians. These included the *sa* and *tit* hieroglyphic signs. Threaded on linen thread, amulets would probably have been knotted together. The process of untying the knots would have formed part of the process of prophylactic magic.

The basis of many spells and ritual objects was sympathetic magic, to ensure, for example, the transfer of pain during birth. Spell 28 of Papyrus Leiden I, 348 stresses 'Hathor, the Lady of Dendera is the one giving birth', thus magically removing this burden from the woman struggling through her labour at that precise moment. The concept underlying the vessels in the form of pregnant and lactating women may well have been one of sympathetic magic. The pregnant women vessels are thought to have contained oil, perhaps to massage on the stomach to reduce the appearance of stretch marks and ease the birth. Marks on the pots have been interpreted as tampons to prevent miscarriage. It was hoped perhaps that the pregnant woman would avoid miscarriage by association with the pot and oil. In the case of the lactating women pots, perhaps any liquid placed in the vessel would become woman's milk by sympathetic magic (especially if it was then poured out through the nipple of one breast).

Figure 23.4   Amarna Period faience amulet of Taweret (Petrie Museum UC 1207). Image courtesy and © Petrie Museum of Egyptian Archaeology, University College London.

Another principle of Egyptian magic was the creative potency of the image and the written word. Spells might be written on, or said over, a variety of ritual objects including birthing bricks, which were divinely personified as the goddess Meskhenet. Another type of ritual object, probably erected in the outer, more accessible areas of temple complexes, was the *cippus* of Horus, which dates from *c.*1400 BC to the second century AD. The belief was that water poured over these stelae would become imbued with the potency of the spells and imagery inscribed on them (the child Horus overcoming various creatures), and could either be drunk or applied as a cure or preventative against scorpion bites and other ills. Rainwater, itself, was believed to have healing properties. It is listed in Papyrus Ebers 77 in a prescription for, among other ailments, problems with the leg. The fact that the central images on *cippi* have sometimes almost been rubbed away suggests that access to the magic could also derive from touch. A fine example of such a stela, which also has a myth concerning healing a scorpion sting inscribed on it (*Isis and the Seven Scorpions*), is the so-called Metternich Stela in the Metropolitan Museum of Art in New York.

Votive offerings were a point of contact between an individual and the divine. These offerings might be placed in a variety of contexts. Votive offerings to Hathor have been particularly well studied (Pinch 1993). Of 768 female figurines with known archaeological provenances, 220 came from tombs, 227 from domestic contexts and 321 from temple contexts (Pinch 1993). Some lie on a model bed, breastfeeding

10 cm
9
8
7
6
5
4
3
2
1
0

Figure 23.5 Ptolemaic Period green shale *cippus* of Horus (Petrie Museum UC 2341). Image courtesy and © Petrie Museum of Egyptian Archaeology, University College London.

a young child, others have a child modelled on the hip or back, and others are inscribed with a request for a child (for example, on Louvre E800, a plea for 'the birth of a child to Tita').

Private religion in the household focused on placating the spirits of previous generations and managing fertility cults to ensure the next generation. Stability in this life was only possible if the ancestors were appeased and the production of children was successful. Ritual objects have been found in domestic contexts, suggesting private fertility cults. The objects include fertility figurines, model beds (some with breastfeeding women lying on them), stelae, figurines of deities and amulets. A group of votive material discovered in an 18th Dynasty house at Amarna (N49.21) included a stela with a depiction of a woman and child worshipping Taweret, two broken female figurines and two model beds.

331

10 cm
9
8
7
6
5
4
3
2
1
0

Figure 23.6 Second Intermediate Period (?) pottery female figurine
(Petrie Museum UC 43280). Image courtesy and © Petrie Museum of
Egyptian Archaeology, University College London.

From the New Kingdom onwards, a spell in the form of a divine decree ('oracular amuletic decree') might be written on papyrus and placed in a cylindrical case, worn around the neck. One such decree in the Turin Museum, probably dating to the 22nd Dynasty, may be difficult to interpret fully but the gist is clear: 'We shall fill her womb with male and female children, we shall save her from a Horus birth (?), from miscarrying (?), (and) from giving birth to twins'.

The archaeologist working at Deir el-Medina for much of the first half of the twentieth century AD found a rectangular mud-brick 'box-bed' structure (originally plastered and painted or whitewashed) in the corner of the front (first) room in 28 of the 68 houses he excavated (Bruyère 1939). There is now conclusive evidence for such beds in about 53 per cent of the houses (Meskell 1998a: 222). (Comparable fixtures have been found in the walled village at Amarna, in Main Street House 3 and Long Wall Street House 10.) They are Ramesside in date and their platforms are 1.7 metres long, 80 centimetres wide and 75 centimetres high; three or four steps lead up to a partially or fully enclosed structure (Friedman 1994: 97). Their purpose is debatable but it has been suggested that this was where the women of the household gave birth, or at least first nursed their newborn children. It has also been suggested that these structures would have provided a certain degree of privacy for sexual intercourse; other scholars argue that the platforms served as shrines (Uphill 1988: 25), or merely as seats (Hobson 1990). Perhaps most likely is a multi-purpose use for the 'box-bed' (Friedman 1994: 111). In at least two of the houses (NE15 and SW6) the structure has an associated cupboard which may well have had a cultic function, perhaps housing a stela, statue or 'ancestor bust' (see below). A fixture in front of the 'box-bed' in Long Wall Street House 10 in the village at Amarna has been interpreted as an altar (Kemp in Meskell 2002: 116). The assumed connection with birth derives from the remains of painted decoration, which was found on some of these structures: painted scenes that include parts of figures of Bes; a dancing female flute player with a Bes tattoo on her thigh and foliage around her; a marsh scene with a figure that has been understood as both a child and Bes; and the lower part of a kneeling naked woman, with the same plant and a servant girl.

Within a household context, and particularly at the time of pregnancy, birth and confinement, the image of Bes was important and usually served a protective or apotropaic role. But at least one scholar has interpreted the painted figures of Bes on the sides of some of these 'beds' as a means of protecting sleepers rather than women in childbirth or confinement (Romano 1990).

A parallel for the woman with the Bes tattoo is the female figure on a blue faience bowl dating to the 18th or 19th Dynasty, now in the Leiden Museum. It is also useful to note the image of Taweret, or possibly Ipy (another mother goddess and 'lady of magical protection') in the pubic region of a so-called 'paddle doll' in the British Museum (EA 23071). The positioning of such tattoos is very specific (close to the genital region) and the nature of the deities is such that they may well correspond to one or more of a number of related concepts: successful childbirth; protection from gynaecological disorders or venereal diseases; ensured fertility; increased eroticism.

Returning to the wall paintings, they can usefully be compared with the so-called 'Wochenlaube' ostraca (dating mainly to the 19th and 20th Dynasties): post-partum scenes that tend to be characterized by the presence of vegetation, and more specifically a convolvulus-like plant. These sources indicate the possible erection of a temporary shelter in which birth, and the ensuing confinement period, might have taken place. In spell 33 of P. Leiden I, 348, the woman addresses Hathor directly with the words, 'Come to me Hathor, my mistress, in my fine pavilion, in this happy hour'.

The confinement period was followed by celebration, another important aspect of private religion. Following Ruddedet's (the new mother's) 'cleansing' in Papyrus Westcar (Papyrus Berlin 3033): 'She said to her maid, "Has the house been made ready?" She said, "It is ready with everything good except beer jugs".' Once the lack of alcohol has been remedied, 'Then his [the husband Rawoser's] heart was happy beyond everything, and they sat down to a day of feasting' (Lichtheim 1975: 220–1). Alcohol consumption was a prerequisite of celebration, and was important in marking social integration. It was also linked with ideas about pacification (as exemplified by the New Kingdom myth *The Destruction of Mankind*).

An important aspect of ancestor worship was the pacification of the ancestors. The need was felt to appease the spirits of the dead, to keep them on one's side and to stop them becoming angry and causing trouble. Egyptian families commemorated their dead relatives on special occasions such as the annual 'Beautiful Festival of the Wadi' when they visited the tombs of their relatives and ate a meal with them. But more private were the rituals that took place on a daily basis in the household. 'Calendars of Lucky and Unlucky Days' designate certain days as being suitable for 'pacifying your *akhu* [the family ancestors]', and several texts specify that the ancestors must be pacified 'in the home' (e.g. Papyrus Sallier IV). So, Egyptian families would have performed rituals to appease the powerful spirits of their dead relatives, very likely at shrines in niches in the main (second) living rooms of their houses, with stelae and anthropoid busts as the focus of the ancestor cult. The *akhu iqeru* ('effective spirits') that these represented were the intermediaries between the living members of the household and the spirit world – the dead and the gods – particularly in the areas of disease, child mortality and legal grievances (Friedman 1985: 97).

At Deir el-Medina, it appears that while the first living room was associated with women and fertility, the second was the one associated with men and ancestor cults (Meskell 2002: 110–21). The main feature of these second rooms, together with a niche shrine or 'cultic cupboard', was a low mud-brick divan. Altars and false doors have also been found in these rooms. Perhaps these doors allowed contact with the spirits of ancestors (Meskell 1998a: 231); some had dedications to the patron deities of the village, Amenhotep I and his mother Ahmose-Nefertari. The use of red paint (a colour often used in magic) on the floors, door jambs and lintels has been interpreted as ensuring protection and ritual potency (Meskell 2002: 119).

About 150 'ancestor busts' or '*akh iqer* bust statues' (Friedman 1985) have been found throughout Egypt, mostly in a domestic context, especially at Deir el-Medina (about 75 examples). They are made of clay, sandstone, faience, wood or limestone, and range in height from just over one centimetre to 28 centimetres. Five are double busts. The main characteristics of the busts are a human head of indeterminate sex on a rounded support or base which resembles shoulders below the neck (but there is no modelling of the human chest); the presence of a collar, sometimes with pendant lotus blossoms and buds painted on the front, or a broad collar (*wesekh*); and a tripartite wig covering the scalp (a few are bareheaded). The busts are rarely inscribed. The suggestion that these busts were housed in niche shrines in the houses (even if they were not actually found in them) has been generally accepted, but one scholar argues that few of the busts can be connected with houses with absolute certainty (Keith-Bennett 1981). It is pointed out that the representation of such busts in scenes of the Underworld and vignettes of the *Book of the Dead* (in funeral processions and piles of funerary offerings) suggests a function other than (or at least in addition to) ancestral and votive functions.

Between 50 and 60 stelae have been found at Deir el-Medina (mostly dating to the 19th Dynasty and usually less than 25 centimetres in height), showing mostly male, and a few female, dead of the community identified as 'able/excellent/perfect/ effective spirits of Ra' (*akh iqer en Ra*). These were *akhu* who were believed to be wise, free from wrongdoing, and at one with Osiris and Ra (*Book of the Dead* chapter

Figure 23.7   New Kingdom (?) wooden 'ancestor bust' (Petrie Museum UC 16550).
Image courtesy and © Petrie Museum of Egyptian Archaeology, University
College London.

64). The villagers of Deir el-Medina seem to have appealed to these ancestors (probably fairly recently deceased and known to the supplicants) to ensure the continuity of the family line, and to act as intermediaries for them in the divine realm. The Deir el-Medina evidence is the fullest, but several more stelae are known from elsewhere in the Theban region, and from Abydos, Memphis, and Aniba in Nubia. The dedicatee tends to be depicted smelling a lotus blossom, seated before an offering table. He or she is often shown holding a cloth, sceptre or *ankh*-sign. The offerings are interpreted as an offering of the house-cult. The stela was obviously a point of contact established between living and deceased relatives, through prayers, supplications and offerings. But, like the busts, the archaeological contexts suggest that these stelae were not exclusive to domestic use, and clearly also served votive and funerary purposes; their portable size would have allowed the same stela to be used in more than one context (Friedman 1994: 112–14).

Like the gods, the dead were held responsible for problems and solutions in the lives of the living. By dying and passing on into the Afterlife, an individual was believed to come closer to, and hopefully prove influential in, the divine world. About 20 letters survive addressed to deceased individuals (especially spouses and fathers).

Figure 23.8 First Intermediate Period pottery dish with a 'letter to the dead' in hieratic (Petrie Museum UC 16244). Image courtesy and © Petrie Museum of Egyptian Archaeology, University College London.

They tend to be written on pottery or linen, and range in date from 3100 to 1200 BC. They might have been placed near the body at the time of the funeral, or when a tomb was reopened for later burials. They are usually concerned with legal matters, such as rights of inheritance, and infertility. One example is in the Petrie Museum of Egyptian Archaeology (UC 16244). It is written in hieratic on a pottery dish, found in tomb Y84 in cemetery Y at Diospolis Parva, and dates to the First Intermediate Period. It is a letter to a dead man Nefersekhi probably from his widow, whose daughter is being defrauded of her share of the inheritance. An Old Kingdom letter written on a vessel (in the Haskell Oriental Museum of Chicago) is an attempt by a daughter to petition her dead father for a 'healthy male child'. The emphasis is on the deceased being an *akh iqer*. In each case, the vessel might well have held an offering to the deceased. Presumably a corresponding oral practice existed.

So the dead could prove useful; but they could also cause problems. The Egyptians feared the unsettled dead (such as women who had died without producing a child, or those who had not been buried properly) who were believed to be able to cause all kinds of distress, including illness. The shadow of a dead person was regarded as a potential source of harm to the medicine prepared by a doctor. Oracular amuletic decrees and the fourth/third century BC Brooklyn Magical Papyrus mention female ghosts as a common source of danger to nursing mothers and young children. The New Kingdom *Instructions of Ani* claim that all misfortunes are the fault of the dead ('the spirit (*akh*)'). It is little wonder that the Egyptians were keen to ensure that the spirits of their ancestors were placated.

Underpinning the Egyptian religious belief system was the fundamental importance of *maat*, a concept of order. *Maat* was central to the accepted code of behaviour and the distinction between right and wrong, which, in turn, ensured harmony within ancient Egyptian society. The body of 'instructive literature' that has survived from ancient Egypt provides an insight into correct (i.e. socially acceptable) behaviour which was clearly bound up with religion. For example, maxim 7 of the Old Kingdom *Instruction of Ptahhotep* advises on good table manners, and ends: 'Thus eating is under the counsel of god.' Ultimately, behaviour and morality during life were judged by the gods after death (in the 'Weighing of the Heart', *Book of the Dead* Chapter 125).

Private rituals were concerned with the maintenance of order in the daily lives of individuals, households and communities. A trauma, such as a loss, illness or disaster, was perhaps interpreted as a manifestation of chaos or disorder (Baines 1991: 125). The ancient sources make it clear that the maintenance of purity on a personal and household level was crucial in ensuring that *maat* was successfully maintained.

The life of the individual and household, and thus private religion, revolved around the human life cycle, stages of which were deemed impure, so purification rituals were essential within the household for re-establishing purity – in the same way that order was constantly being re-established or restored. Those human states regarded as socially or ritually impure were, at the same time, central to the social acceptance of the individual by the local community, and by society at large. The transitional stages that punctuate the human life cycle were thought to be times when the human body became vulnerable to outside influence, usually of a harmful nature. The Brooklyn Magical Papyrus is a treatise on the protection of pregnant women against misfortune and, more specifically, harmful spirits or demons. Personified death appears in the magico-medical texts as a constant unseen threat. A spell in one such document, the 12th Dynasty Ramesseum Papyrus no. IV, aims to combat the dangerous attempts by 'death' to have sexual intercourse with a pregnant woman: 'You shall not have sexual intercourse [with this woman] . . . . You shall not associate with her; you shall not do to her anything bad or evil.' Taweret, the household goddess particularly associated with protection during childbirth, was also said to command demons (Louvre statue E a 35478, 2) and to be capable of bringing about death (Louvre statue E 25479); an inscription on a statue in the Aberdeen Anthropological Museum (no. 1422) reads 'life and death are in her grasp'.

The mysteries of the menstrual cycle, the taboo of bodily fluids (especially female blood), and the fear that the pollutive blood might attract demons and entry by negative influences into the human body via open orifices (in this case the vagina), resulted in worries concerning insecurity, and the need for women to undergo rituals of purification following menstruation, in order to ensure their social acceptance and place in the ordered framework of society. The ancient Egyptian word for menstruation and 'to menstruate' is *hesmen*, the same as that for the verb 'to purify oneself', and also the term for the purifying agent natron. In the demotic tale of Setne-

Khaemwese and Naneferkaptah (Setne I), Ahwere reveals her pregnancy by announcing the absence of her menstruation: 'When my time of purification came, I made no purification' (III, 7).

Purification following childbirth is referred to in Papyrus Westcar: 'Ruddedet cleansed herself in a cleansing of fourteen days.' Parallels for this practice can be found elsewhere. A similar Hebrew tradition is outlined in Leviticus, which states that a woman is unclean for seven days after giving birth to a son (as after her menstruation) and must then undergo a period of purification lasting 33 days before she is ceremonially purified (or two weeks and then 66 days if she has had a daughter). Papyrus Westcar stipulates that newborn babies were washed immediately after birth: the goddesses performing the roles of midwives 'washed him, having cut his naval cord'. A religious text accompanying a scene on the south exterior wall of the offering chamber of the *mammisi* at Edfu reads: 'It is the Lady of Dendera who appears with her two children to purify her limbs after giving birth.' Similar post-partum rituals may well be depicted in the so-called 'Wochenlaube' scenes in which a woman might be shown attended by servants holding items such as bowls and mirrors; and on the scenes painted on the 'box-beds' found at Deir el-Medina and the workmen's village at Amarna.

Taweret might bear the epithet 'Taweret of water', 'Lady of pure water' or 'the purifier' (*pa wab*). Fragments of purification basins inscribed with the goddess's name have been found in Chapel 1213 at Deir el-Medina. One limestone fragment (British Museum no. 28) reads 'an offering which the king gives to Taweret, the Purifier'; in return for which he hopes the goddess will 'grant life, prosperity and health to the *ka* of Aan [possibly Chief of Works] in the Place of Truth'. It has been suggested that Taweret's epithet, 'she who removes the water', might be reference to amniotic fluid rather than to purification (Turin Stela N. 50057). Purification rites certainly appear central to the cult of Taweret. The documentary evidence from Deir el-Medina reveals that men might be absent from work for associated ritual purposes. On one particular day five or six men are said to 'make themselves pure for Taweret', a ritual that might have been linked to the menstruation or parturition of a female member of the family. The list of feasts on the recto of Ostracon Michaelides 48 includes 'The purification of his daughter'. There is also reference to solitary retreats by men to the Theban desert mountain, involving purification and fasting under the invocation of Taweret.

In the fifth century BC Herodotus (1998, Book II) commented that the Egyptians were circumcised, as they 'preferred purity above fresh air'. The 25th Dynasty Victory Stela of Piye (Cairo Museum 48862) explains that three local Egyptian rulers were not granted an audience with the Kushite king because they were 'uncircumcised and ate fish', in contrast to Namart, the prince of Hermopolis, who was allowed entry as he was 'pure and did not eat fish'. A clear parallel is thus being drawn between circumcision and purity.

In the magical texts, such as the Demotic Magical Papyrus of London and Leiden (Papyrus British Museum 10070 and Papyrus Leiden 383, two fragments of the same manuscript, dating to the beginning of the third century BC), it is made clear that a state of purity is deemed necessary for the efficacy of the particular spell or ritual: 'If it be that you do not apply (?) purity to it, it does not succeed; its chief matter is purity.' Apparently the most crucial element of this correct state (it is the only specified requisite) is an abstinence from sexual intercourse: 'You must lie down on green reeds, being pure from a woman' (seemingly for three days beforehand). It was also considered highly beneficial to include a young boy in the ritual; so, the presence of a virgin was considered ideal.

Infant mortality was so high that when a child was born there would have been a keen interest in whether or not (s)he would survive through the vulnerable early years. Various recorded tests and observations and 'Calendars of Lucky and Unlucky Days' indicate a belief in fate or destiny. Shay was a personification of 'destiny', while Thoth was said to record a child's lifespan and destiny on the birth bricks: 'That hour that was written on thy delivery stone must come.' The Seven Hathors were thought to hover invisibly over the newborn child, and pronounce the manner of his/her death (e.g. in the New Kingdom *Tale of the Doomed Prince*). There was also a belief in 'fortune' (*renenet*) or 'the god who is in' which could allay an adverse destiny (Baines 1991: 125). It was thought that a good or bad omen could be foretold by the sounds emitted by the mother and child at birth. For example, if a newly born baby uttered '*ny*' it would live, but if '*embi*' it would die (Papyrus Ebers 838).

The importance of the name as a component of a person's identity is clear. Magic could only be performed if the relevant names were known (e.g. *Isis and the Sun God's Secret Name*); to know someone's name made it possible to demonize that person and exercise control over him/her. The names given to children at birth reflect a number of popular religious beliefs: the concept of portent; a celebration of the festivals of particular deities; and the consultation of oracles during pregnancy. However, as today, names often became hereditary within a family, and so the original reason for a particular name would be lost with time. Many names incorporate the word *netjer* ('(the) god'). Others relate to specific deities, and call upon their divine protection for the benefit of the child; or they extol the virtue of a particularly deity. The importance laid on the name given to a child at birth is exemplified by the fact that criminals might be deemed unworthy of their birth names, and so might be given new ones. This practice of name-changing appears most commonly when the original name contained that of a deity or was said to have been chosen by the mother. Sometimes a proper name appears to correspond to an important (and possibly life-changing) occurrence in that person's life; again the emphasis is usually on an encounter with a particular deity. For example, the name of the man kneeling before a statue of Amun, on stela British Museum 23077 from Deir el-Medina, translates as 'I have seen Amun'.

The beliefs and practices discussed in this chapter helped the ancient Egyptians understand, and respond to, the traumatic (and joyous) events in their lives.

ACKNOWLEDGEMENTS

I would like to thank the Petrie Museum of Egyptian Archaeology for all the photographs. Please visit their website (www.petrie.ucl.ac.uk) for further information on the objects.

CHAPTER TWENTY-FOUR

AFTERLIFE BELIEFS AND BURIAL CUSTOMS

—·•·—

Salima Ikram

A fundamental aspect of ancient Egyptian religion was a belief in the afterlife (Ikram 2003). This belief was a basic component of religion from the Predynastic to the Roman Period. The Egyptians' vision of the afterlife, however, evolved throughout their history. As there are no surviving religious texts that outline the earliest beliefs of the hereafter, much of our reconstruction of these belief systems comes through archaeological material, and is also extrapolated from textual and physical evidence deriving primarily from the New Kingdom.

It is apparent that although all levels of society might have shared the same belief systems, social stratification remained even after death. Kings, who were divine beings, had an afterlife different from that of their subjects. Non-royals shared a similar afterlife, but the ways of achieving this varied depending on wealth. However, it seems that regardless of the relative opulence or poverty of a burial, if the individual had lived in *maat* (truth), the right prayers had been recited and the correct rituals enacted, this afterlife was available to all. The only real barrier to achieving an afterlife was to be buried outside Egypt: the Egyptians believed that in order to be reborn, they needed to be interred in Egypt. If they died abroad, their families went to great lengths to bring their bodies back for burial so that the proper funerary rituals could be carried out and they could be buried in their native land, and thus enabled to reach the afterworld.

After death, the souls of non-royals were thought to travel to an eternal life in a place that was an enhanced and improved version of the land of Egypt. The location of this land varied over time: it could be subterranean or celestial. It was known as the 'Field of Iaru (Reeds)', and was under the rulership of the god Osiris, the most important funerary deity. Here the deceased lived as a 'justified one', or *maa kheru* ('true of voice'), with the approbation of the gods.

A royal afterlife was more complicated and tied to the fact that kings were divine. After death, kings would become *akhu*, divine spirits, and united with the stars. They would have a manifold existence in the hereafter. On the one hand, they would travel with the sun god Ra in his barque through the sky, defeating demons and enemies, to be triumphantly reborn the next day. This cycle would continue throughout eternity, emphasizing that even in death kings had a responsibility to help the gods

340

maintain order within the cosmos. On the other hand, they also held a place in the heavens as eternal stars. They also managed to enjoy a royally opulent hereafter.

THE MYTH OF OSIRIS

Central to Egyptian funerary beliefs lay the myth of Osiris, god of the dead and ruler of the afterworld. Osiris judged the dead and decided if they had lived 'justified' lives and were to live eternally in the Fields of Iaru, or whether they should be destroyed and die. In Egyptian mythology he was the first mummy and the first being to be resurrected. Osiris is typically shown as a mummiform individual, his arms crossed over his chest, and his hands grasping a crook and a flail. His bandaged body is painted white, while his flesh is coloured black or green, colours symbolic of rebirth and resurrection in ancient Egypt, as they were associated with the fertile black silt of the Nile floods and the resulting green of the plants.

The myth of Osiris is not preserved fully in any Egyptian text. The most complete version is that of Plutarch, a Greek historian. Doubtless this is a Hellenized version, but it outlines the crux of the story: during the Golden Age, Osiris was the first divine king of Egypt, ruling with his queen and sister-wife Isis. His brother Seth, together with Seth's sister-wife Nephthys, also formed part of the court. Predictably, Seth became jealous of Osiris's power and plotted to overthrow him so that he could take the throne. He planned a banquet at which he would present a rich gift, a wooden casket, covered with gold and encrusted with semi-precious stones, to whomever it fit. Seth had taken the precaution of making it precisely to Osiris's measurements. When Osiris lay down in the box, Seth and his 72 cohorts slammed down the lid, sealed it with molten metal, and hurled it into the Nile, making the box the prototype for the coffin. Seth then usurped the throne of Egypt.

Osiris's casket was carried by the Nile into the Mediterranean Sea, and to Byblos in modern Lebanon. There it lodged in a tree. Isis, mourning her husband's fate, went in search of him, and finally found him there. According to some legends, her tears are the source of the Nile's inundation. Isis brought Osiris back to Egypt, but Seth found him again and cut him into several pieces which he scattered throughout Egypt. The number of pieces depends on the version of the tale, although 14 is the most common variation.

Once again Isis went in search of Osiris. She successfully gathered together all but one crucial body-part; a fish had eaten Osiris's penis. She made a false one out of mud, and then, after restoring his body, magically breathed life into it (the first resurrection of the first mummy). Isis then turned herself into a bird, specifically a black kite, and mated with her husband. Frequently Isis and Nephthys are portrayed as kites, flanking the bier of the deceased, just as they guarded the bier and mourned the death of Osiris.

As a result of her brief union with her husband, Isis became pregnant, and retreated to the marshes of the delta until she gave birth to her son, Horus. Horus grew to manhood here, guarded and sustained by his mother and the goddess Hathor. When he reached maturity, Horus emerged from hiding and engaged Seth in a series of dramatic contests for the crown of Egypt, which he ultimately won. These are recounted in the myth cycle entitled *The Contendings of Horus and Seth* (Lichtheim 1976: 214–23).

After Horus's victory, he was crowned king of Egypt, while Osiris became king of the dead and of the underworld. Thus, living kings were identified with/as Horus, and dead ones with Osiris. Seth was granted dominion over the deserts and fringes of Egypt. Horus and Osiris were designated lords of order and *maat*, while Seth was lord of chaos and disorder.

Osiris's cult centre was located at Abydos, allegedly the place where his head had been buried, and a gateway to the afterworld. Many Early Dynastic rulers were buried here, with a royal presence continuing through the New Kingdom and later. As Osiris's chief burial place, as well as a major royal cemetery, Abydos became a centre for pilgrimage from the late Old Kingdom onwards. Egyptians flocked there from all over the country, leaving votive offerings and stelae throughout the site. A pilgrimage to Abydos became a pivotal part of Egyptian funerary beliefs, and, in addition to actual pilgrimage, it was also featured in tombs, in both two- and three-dimensional representations. The mummy was shown being transported to Abydos on a bier so that Osiris would bless the deceased and send the soul on to the after-world through the gateway (a break in the cliffs) located at Abydos. As the Middle Kingdom progressed, the deceased became increasingly closely identified with Osiris to the extent that any dead person took the epithet 'Osiris N(ame of deceased)'; in earlier times the term was restricted to royalty. As Osiris, the deceased would follow the same path as the god had, being reborn to live eternally.

ASPECTS OF THE INDIVIDUAL

According to Egyptian belief, all people consisted not only of the physical body, but of different component parts which, when taken together, comprised the entire individual. These parts were: *ren*, the name; *sehwat* the shadow; *ka*, the double or life-force; *ba*, the personality or soul; and *akh*, the spirit. The royal *akh* was more potent than that of a non-royal person, as it contained a spark (or more) of divinity. A major part of Egyptian funerary religion was devoted to ensuring the survival not only of the body, but also of all of these components. The name was important to identify the person, both in this life and the next, but the *ka*, *ba* and *akh* were most important in terms of the individual's eternal survival.

Of these different aspects of the individual, the *akh* is the most difficult to understand as it is complex and esoteric, and not clearly defined in any Egyptian text. The *akh* is thought to result from a union of the *ba* and the *ka*. It only emerged after death, and was the manifestation of a successful resurrection from an ephemeral to an eternal being. Thus, the *akh* was the deceased transfigured into an immutable being of light, frequently associated with the stars. Not everyone became an *akh*, as people who had lived lives that were not in harmony with *maat* would be annihilated. However, all funerary texts and rituals were directed toward a successful afterlife, and the creation of the *akh*.

The *ka* and the *ba* depended partly on the physical body for their continuing survival and well-being. The *ka* was created simultaneously, twin-like, with the body (by the god Khnum), and continued through life and into death. It was the force that animated the individual and continued to exist throughout eternity. After death, it required the same sustenance that the body had had in life, and could use the mummy, as well as two- or three-dimensional representations of the deceased, as vehicles to gain nourishment. Its area of activity and power seems to have been restricted to the tomb and its chapel.

The *ba* was the travelling form of the spirit, depicted as a human-headed bird, often with arms as well as wings. It was most active after death, although certain texts imply that the *ba* was present during an individual's lifetime, although restricted in its movements (Žabkar 1968). It could be released to travel during life when the person was asleep (a state considered akin to death), in dream-travel. The *ba* could travel in this world, in the afterworld, or even with the sun god in his sacred barque. Despite its mobility, the *ba*, like the *ka*, had to return to the body of the deceased in order to be reunited with its physical anchor; otherwise the deceased could not be re-animated and used as a link to the earth, or benefit from the offerings provided for the deceased. It was this need to preserve the body that gave rise to the science of mummification, as the mummified body provided the eternal home for these aspects of an individual's being.

MUMMIFICATION

A mummy is the artificially preserved body of a human or an animal. Mummies were produced from perhaps as early as the late Naqada II Period until the Christian era, in an effort to preserve the earthly body for the use of the *ka* and the *ba*. The ancient Egyptian word for mummy is *sah*; the modern English word, mummy, is derived from the Arabic words for wax and bitumen, *muum* and *mumia*, thence mummy. The Arabs who first came upon mummies thought that bitumen was responsible for their dark colour. Bitumen is a black, pitch-like substance occurring naturally in Persia and in the area of the Dead and Red Seas. It was sporadically used in mummification from the late New Kingdom onwards.

Although the origins of mummification are shrouded in mystery, Egyptologists posit that the idea arose when naturally preserved Predynastic burials were exposed by accident, thus giving the Egyptians the idea of artificially preserving their dead so that the bodies could be used in the afterlife. Perhaps the naturally desiccated bodies of animals found in the desert also contributed to the idea of mummification. Until recently, it was thought that mummification started during the Dynastic Period, but recent evidence from the sites of Adaima and Hierakonpolis suggests a Naqada II Period origin (Ikram and Dodson 1998: 113).

The main objective of mummification was the preservation of the body through desiccation (Ikram and Dodson 1998: 103 ff.). This was achieved in Egypt using natron, or *netjery*, divine salt. Natron is a mixture of sodium bicarbonate, sodium carbonate, sodium sulphate and sodium chloride, which occurs naturally in Egypt, most commonly in the Wadi Natrun some 64 kilometres north-west of Cairo. It both desiccates and de-fats. Although common salt (sodium chloride) was also used in economical burials, natron remained the preferred desiccant up to and including the Christian Period.

Mummification changed throughout Egyptian history. The 'classic' (New Kingdom) method, which took 70 days, was carried out in the following way. First, the brain was removed and discarded, as its function was unknown to the ancient Egyptians. This was generally achieved by breaking the ethmoid bone with a sharp metal tool that was inserted through the left nostril, providing access to the cranium. The tool was then used to slash and chop at the brain, thus breaking it up so that it could be extracted via the nostril using a hooked implement. Melted resin was then poured into the cranial cavity through the nostril, which would be stopped with a linen plug. This served to coat and disinfect the cranial cavity, thus preventing bacterial infestation. The viscera were then removed by a cut in the left flank. These would be washed and treated separately in the same manner as the corpse, after which they were wrapped, placed in containers called canopic jars, and buried with the mummy.

The heart remained inside the body, as the Egyptians believed that it housed the soul or essence of the individual. It was a key organ in resurrection as it was weighed against the feather of truth or *maat* before the soul continued its journey to the afterworld (see below). It is because of the importance of the heart that the Egyptians favoured the left side of the body.

After desiccation, the body cavity was washed with water and wine, dried with linen cloth/towels, and then immersed, inside and out, in dry natron, traditionally for a period of 40 days. The natron extracted the water, leaving the body in a leather-like state. After desiccation, the body would be removed from the natron. In the subsequent 30 days, it was oiled to return some flexibility to the limbs, further anointed with unguents, resins and spices, and then wrapped in bandages to make it ready for burial. Several caches of embalming materials have been found that have helped identify the materials used during mummification.

During the course of anointing and wrapping, prayers and spells were recited to the accompaniment of rituals and the burning of incense. A priest in the guise of the jackal-headed god, Anubis, lord of mummification, officiated. Wrapping was a very important process as the bandages and spells provided both a physical and metaphysical layer of protection for the body. Amulets were interspersed with the wrappings at key positions on the body for its protection and to provide assistance in the journey to the hereafter (Andrews 1994).

THE FUNERAL

After embalming, the mummy was ready for the funeral and its perilous voyage to the hereafter. The elaborateness of the funeral depended on the wealth of the deceased. The central focus of the procession was the encoffined body which was transported on a sled, or carried by bearers, to the tomb. Mourners, both professionals and family members, surrounded the coffin, ululating and crying. Priests waving incense directly preceded the coffin, and two women, possibly priestesses, in the guise of the goddesses Isis and Nephthys, flanked the coffin and possibly led the mourners. Offering bearers carried grave-goods to the tomb, both preceding and following the coffin. These included furniture, jewels, clothes, toiletries, food, drink and other material goods. The *tekhenu*, a peculiar object that was included in funerary processions from the Middle Kingdom onwards, often followed the coffin. Initially the *tekhenu* was shown as a wrapped figure crouched in the foetal position, with only the head visible. In the New Kingdom it was shown as a featureless wrapped bundle, occasionally with the head or arm showing. Its precise function is unknown. Funerary dancers, called *Muu* dancers, sporting tall headdresses, sometimes participated in the procession. They played an obscure part in the final rituals as their dancing was supposed to help support the deceased's soul in the afterlife.

While grave-goods were deposited within the tomb's burial chamber(s), the mummy remained outside for the final rites. The most important ritual for resurrection occurred at the tomb entrance. The rite, called the 'opening of the mouth' ceremony (*wepet-ra*), was crucial to transform the deceased into an *akh*. The main celebrant was the funerary *sem*-priest, identified by the leopard skin that was a mark of his office. The priest was a clergy-member or the heir of the deceased. Participating in the funeral was an important responsibility of the heir, and by acting appropriately he might be insured of his inheritance. Other funerary priests also participated in the ritual, particularly lector-priests who read prayers throughout the ceremony, thus ensuring the safety of the deceased at this crucial moment. The opening of the mouth was carried out using tools and implements that were used at the birth of a child, such as the *pesesh-kef* knife (Roth 1992) that was used to cut the umbilical cord. An adze, or a foreleg of an ox, was also important in the re-animation ritual. The implements were used to touch the chest, eyes, nose, mouth and ears of the mummy, accompanied by the chanting of special prayers, thus returning the five senses to the body.

The funeral culminated in a feast where the re-animated mummy presided over the ancient Egyptian equivalent of a wake. Presumably many of the food offerings brought for the deceased were consumed then, with a share being consecrated for the deceased and placed in the tomb. Then the corpse was placed in the burial chamber filled with funerary goods, to the accompaniment of prayers. Friends and relatives would bid their final farewells, sometimes placing flower garlands on top of the mummy and the coffin.

Additional funerary rites were also carried out, involving special offerings and burials of objects. In the Old Kingdom some of these were buried in a secondary 'false' shallow shaft, generally found in the southern half of the mastaba (Rzeuska 2006). Part of the shaft-filling ritual involved the placement of offerings when the shaft was half-filled; offerings were then placed either on top of the fill or in a niche (e.g. the burial of Hetepheres, mother of the 4th Dynasty king Khufu).

In the New Kingdom and later, 'corn mummies' or Osiris beds were placed in the tomb or its courtyard as part of a funerary ritual. The former are small coffins shaped like the figure of the god Osiris containing bundles of grain that were wrapped in the shape of an ithyphallic Osiris figure, symbolizing the resurrection of the deceased (Raven 1982). The latter are Osiris-shaped wooden trays that were filled with earth and planted with grain. The grain would germinate in the tomb, indicating the rebirth of the deceased as Osiris.

A particularly dramatic funerary ritual that occurred in the Ramesside Period and is certainly attested in texts of the Old Kingdom was 'breaking the red pots' (*sedj deshrewt*), involving the smashing of red pottery. The symbolism of this is unclear – possibly it changed over time. Scholars have variously suggested that the pots used in the funerary rites were smashed so they would not be desecrated by further use, rendering the pots harmless and non-magical, symbolizing the destruction of Sethian forces (van Dijk 1993). In modern Egypt, pot-breaking rituals occur generally when one does not want someone to return; perhaps in antiquity this rite also helped to keep the spirit of the deceased safely and peacefully in the afterworld.

THE ROAD TO RESURRECTION

After the interment, the soul of the deceased began its perilous journey to the afterworld. (Evidence for this comes from the New Kingdom and is extrapolated for earlier periods.) The dog/jackal-headed god, Anubis, guided the deceased along this route after presiding at the mummification ceremonies.

Slightly different funerary beliefs held sway during the different epochs of Egyptian history. The majority of evidence that we have comes from the Middle and New Kingdoms and is derived from funerary texts inscribed on coffins, tombs and papyri (Hornung 1999 [1990a]). A clearer picture for royalty is available for the Old Kingdom, in addition to subsequent periods, due to the Pyramid Texts, texts inscribed in the burial chambers of pyramids starting at the end of the 5th Dynasty (*c.*2350 BC) and continuing until the end of the Old Kingdom.

In general, the deceased had to answer a series of questions posed by various gods and demi-gods, and to pass tests involving spitting serpents, fiery lakes and other terrifying things, before arriving in the judgement hall of Osiris. Several gods would help and protect the deceased along the way. The most significant were Isis and Nephthys, sisters of Osiris who are shown mourning the deceased. During the funeral, priestesses took on their personae and positioned themselves at the head and foot of the coffin (which also had images of these goddesses painted upon it). Other goddesses that helped to protect the deceased were Neith and Selqet. The former was a war-goddess, and the latter was associated with scorpions, considered as one who cured and made people breathe again.

These four goddesses were also directly associated with the mummy as they, together with four demi-gods, were responsible for the protection of the viscera and appear in this connection on coffins and canopic chests. The companion demi-gods are known collectively as the 'Four Sons of Horus'. These were originally shown with human heads, but, from the Middle to the New Kingdom, became more individual. Imseti, protector of the liver, paired with Isis, is shown as a man. The baboon-headed Hapy was in charge of the lungs and was associated with Nephthys. Duamutef was canid-headed, and protected the stomach; he was associated with Neith. Qebehsenuef was hawk-headed, and cared for the intestines; he was associated with Selqet. These demi-gods appear on canopic jars, coffins, sarcophagi and other funerary equipment, and also helped protect the deceased en route to the afterlife.

When the deceased arrived safely in the hall of judgement, the heart – which was the repository of the soul, essence and personality of the deceased – was weighed against the feather of *maat* or truth. The god of recording and writing, Thoth, related the deceased's history and took note of his fate. If the heart and the feather were balanced, the deceased could enter the blessed Fields of Iaru to live eternally. If the heart was heavier than the feather, the soul would be consumed by the monster Ammut and disappear forever. Ammut was a terrifying creature with a crocodile head, the foreparts of a lion, and the body and hindquarters of a hippopotamus.

If the deceased succeeded in attaining eternal life, Horus or Anubis would escort him there to live eternally with his *ka*, *ba* and *akh*. As insurance for a safe passage, the Egyptians placed amuletic heart scarabs over the heart of the mummy. These were large scarabs inscribed with spells (especially Spells 30, 30B, 26, 27 and 29B from the *Book of the Dead*) that would provide the correct answer to any question posed by the different gods on the journey to the hall of judgement and during the heart-weighing ceremony.

Other forms of insurance to guarantee a successful rebirth were funerary texts; these can be described as guidebooks of spells that helped the deceased navigate through the afterworld. The earliest examples are the Pyramid Texts, originally inscribed exclusively in the burial chambers of kings' and queens' pyramids. There are a total of some 800 spells, although only selections were used in the different pyramids (Faulkner 1969). These spells helped the king or queen ascend heavenward to become one with the gods. There are three types of spells: protective spells to ward off dangerous creatures; spells for safe travel; and a set of incantations associated with the execution of funerary rituals, such as the opening of the mouth. The texts were organized in the tomb for the convenience of the dead king, with the first spells to be used facing the king, and the others following sequentially (Allen 1994). In the Old Kingdom there is no known equivalent set of spells for non-royals.

In the Middle Kingdom and later (particularly the Late Period), however, the use of some of the Pyramid Texts was, to some extent, usurped by the elite, and abandoned by royalty. It is unknown which, if any, texts were employed by royalty during the Middle Kingdom.

The elite gained another set of funerary texts in the Middle Kingdom: the Coffin Texts that were inscribed on the interior of the wooden coffins of the elite as well as on mummy masks, tomb walls and even on papyri (Faulkner 1973–8). Coffin Texts are clearly rooted in the Pyramid Texts and are probably a manifestation of the usurpation of royal privileges that was a result of the turmoil of the First Intermediate Period. Coffin Texts guarantee everyone (not just royals) an afterlife associated with Osiris, and comprise at least 1,187 spells, often with accompanying vignettes. Unlike the Pyramid Texts, they emphasize a reunion with loved ones in the hereafter. Portions of these spells are actually maps, with passwords and keys to overcome the various difficulties on the path to the afterworld, including gaining victory over Apophis, a monstrous serpent who was the arch-enemy of the sun god Ra. Ra was the most important Egyptian god and the quintessential symbol of rebirth and resurrection, dying in the west, and born again in the east. Traditionally, the dead king accompanied Ra in his solar barque, battling Apophis and other enemies to ensure the beginning of a new day. It was because of Ra that, traditionally, Egyptian tombs were located on the west bank of the Nile (*imenti*, also used as a word for the afterworld) where the sun set, their doors facing the rising sun.

The most famous Egyptian funerary texts were composed during the New Kingdom, or just before. The best known of these is the lavishly illustrated *Book of the Dead*, more correctly the *Book of Coming Forth by Day*, with the first exemplar found in the coffin of Queen Mentuhotep of the early 17th Dynasty (Allen 1974; Faulkner *et al.* 1994–8). These texts continued in use, sporadically, until the Roman Period. The *Book of the Dead* was a shorter text than its predecessors, consisting of some 200 spells, many of which originate from the Pyramid and Coffin Texts. The spells were designed to provision, protect and guide the deceased to the afterworld in the Fields of *Iaru* (Reeds). Spells from this collection were inscribed on tomb walls, coffins, papyri, mummy cloths, amulets (e.g. heart scarabs) and *shabti* figurines that were designed to serve the dead and work in their stead for eternity (Stewart 1995).

Unlike the Coffin Texts, which emphasize the reunion with one's family, the focus in the New Kingdom books is on the regeneration of the individual after a successful judgement in the hall of Osiris. A significant element is the 'negative confession' in which the deceased provides a list of all the evil deeds that he had eschewed, such as lying, bearing false witness, robbing, cheating, killing, etc. The scene of the weighing of the heart is a very important vignette.

Several other afterworld books date to the New Kingdom and later (Hornung 1999 [1990a]). New Kingdom royal burials in the Valley of the Kings (and a very limited number of elite burials that emulated them) were inscribed with standardized texts that describe the geography of the hereafter, and relate the path of the sun god on his barque through the netherworld during the 12 hours of the night, culminating in his successful rebirth in the morning. The most significant of these underworld books are the *Book of the Amduat* (or the *Book of What is in the Underworld*) and the *Book of Gates* (named for the large gates that guarded each hour of the day and night). These books are frequently oriented in the tomb so that they start in the west and end in the east, thus imitating the path of the sun god's barque on its route to rebirth. The elite usurped these texts in the Third Intermediate Period; at that time, the *Book of Coming Forth by Day* became extensively used in royal burials.

At the end of the 18th Dynasty a new set of funerary texts evolved: the 'Books of the Sky' (Hornung 1999). The sun god, although still important, is here joined in importance by Nut, the sky goddess, indicative of a celestial afterlife. The sun's route through the sky (depicted as Nut's body) is emphasized, with its rebirth the following day. The *Book of Nut*, the *Book of the Night* and the *Book of the Day* are some of these celestial books, with the last being unusual in that it describes the diurnal path of the sun instead of the usual nocturnal voyage.

Additional funerary texts were composed during the course of Egyptian history. Some of these appear primarily as inscriptions in royal tombs, such as the *Litany of Ra* and the *Book of the Heavenly Cow*, both of which lack illustration (Hornung 1999 [1990a]). Ultimately, the elite usurped most of these funerary texts.

THE IMPORTANCE OF THE TOMB

In addition to the funerary texts and the amulets surrounding the mummy that served to convey the dead safely to the afterworld, the tomb itself was significant in the deceased's voyage between the temporal and the eternal realms. A tomb consisted of two parts: the substructure where the deceased was buried and which was sealed, and the superstructure that included the decorated tomb-chapel, accessible to priests and visitors. Thus, a tomb was not only a place for the eternal protection of the body, but was a vehicle for the survival of the name and reputation of the deceased. It served as the main cult place where the *ka* and *ba* could access offerings and transit between this world and the next.

A perfect tomb was designed so that its architecture and decoration (together with its contents) would help transport the deceased between this world and the next, to enjoy a successful and full afterlife (Kamrin 1999; Dodson and Ikram 2008). On a very obvious level, images and texts recreate the cosmos, and show the tomb owner enjoying an ideal afterlife that was similar to an earthly existence, but better.

Scenes showing food production, hunting, fishing, banquets, festivals, as well as events relating to the deceased's profession(s) are frequently featured in tombs. Images of royalty and divinity are also present, but are more common in the New Kingdom than in preceding periods (Harpur 1987; Manniche 1987; Hartwig 2004; Dodson and Ikram 2007). On a more metaphysical and metaphorical level these images also worked as spells and allusions to religious texts that protected the deceased and ensured a successful and safe resurrection (Dodson and Ikram 2007).

Actual prayers providing for, and safeguarding, the deceased were also inscribed on tomb walls, with the earliest and most significant one being the *hetep-di-nisut* formula, translated as 'a gift (or boon) that the king gives'. These formulae are found inscribed on lintels, false doors and offering tables, and all start with the same phrase, though from the 5th Dynasty onward gods such as Anubis and Osiris are also mentioned in this offering formula. Perhaps originally the king did literally provide for the deceased, although in later times this was a convention rather than the reality. The text then continues with a list of offerings, with the standard being a thousand of bread, a thousand of beer, oxen, fowl, linen, natron, and all things good and pure to be given to the deceased, followed by his name. Even if the tomb was robbed, formulae such as this would ensure the sustenance of the deceased's soul in the hereafter.

One of the most important parts of a tomb was the false door. This stone doorway was inscribed with an offering formula or list, together with the name and titles of the deceased. It was fronted by an offering table, and was generally located directly over the burial chamber. This was the focal point of a tomb, where the spirit could move between the land of the living and the land of the dead, hear prayers and access offerings. In some instances, statues were associated with false doors and also played a key role in the cult of the dead.

Naturally, the poor could not afford the same type of tomb as members of the elite. However, their ideal of eternity probably did not differ from that of the wealthy. Presumably, they would try to achieve the best afterlife that they could within the economic constraints that bound them. False doors and offering stelae, together with prayers and actual offerings, would have to provide them with the mechanics to transit between the two worlds and to sustain the soul of the dead.

INTERACTION BETWEEN THE LIVING AND THE DEAD

After the burial, the deceased was sustained not only by the prayers and images inscribed on the tomb walls and on the funerary papyri, but also by an active mortuary cult. For the wealthy, the responsibility lay with funerary priests and family, while the poor would probably rely exclusively on family members or perhaps shared priests. Mortuary cults provisioned the tomb on a daily basis, and were endowed with land by the deceased during his/her lifetime.

The mortuary priest provided the deceased's *ka* with food, drink, incense, oils and linens, and prayed regularly at the tomb-chapel. Presumably, offerings would be consecrated to the deceased and then taken away by the funerary priests as payment for their services. Texts from some tombs (such as that of Hapdjefa at Asyut) minutely detail the sources for the provisioning of his cult, and the payment of the funerary

349

priest. Some burnt offerings might be made, but there is little literary or physical evidence for this. Additionally, the priest would be responsible for the upkeep and security of the tomb. On feast days family members would visit the tomb and add their prayers and offerings to those of the priest(s). Offering/cult places were generally located within the chapel at the site of statues or false doors, but were also sometimes situated on the exterior of the chapel for easy access.

Ultimately, it is probable that the funerary endowment would vanish, through diversion to the benefit either of the deceased's descendants or of others, due to the extinction of the family line. This was why the decorations and inscriptions of the tomb were so important: they magically provided for the *ka* even when physical offerings were no longer available. Inscriptions carved on tombs adjure visitors to call the deceased by name and recite the offering formula for his *ka*, thus providing him with sustenance. Prior to the 6th Dynasty the dead sometimes threatened the living with unpleasantness should they *not* pray as they passed the tomb. However, by the end of the 6th Dynasty, the dead even promised positive intercession with the gods if visitors recited the requisite prayers.

Beyond the celebration of the funerary cult, the recitation of the *hetep-di-nisut* formula when passing a tomb, and visiting family graves (as is done in Egypt today), the living had other methods of interaction with the deceased. Ancestor cults – manifested by statues in the shape of mummiform torsos erected at tombs and in household shrines – were also celebrated (see Gahlin, 'Private religion', this volume). The living could also pray to the dead – either at the cemeteries, or before these statues – to intercede on their behalf in the realm of the supernatural. Letters to the dead were another means of communication (Gardiner and Sethe 1928). These letters were written on papyri, linen or pottery bowls. The bowls were inscribed with a request or question from the living, and filled with offerings in order to appease or bribe the dead spirit to comply with the request. The dead spirit, or *akh*, could intervene directly on behalf of the living, and could also act as an intercessor in the divine realm, enlisting the help of Osiris and other gods.

The dead could also be unquiet and unruly, especially if they had died prematurely or by violence. They might reappear as ghosts or malign spirits (*mut*) that spread chaos and misery among the living, in contrast to the blessed dead (*hesy*) (Ritner 1993). As some letters to the dead attest, these spirits had to be appeased and put to rest to restore *maat*.

CURSES

The Egyptians believed in protecting their tombs both by physical and metaphysical means. Although the former were more common than the latter, they were equally ineffectual against looters. Indeed, there are a very limited number of tombs that are inscribed with what might be interpreted as 'curses'. Some from the Old Kingdom (primarily from the 6th Dynasty, e.g. the tombs of Hesi and Khentika at Saqqara) threaten anyone who enters the tomb in an impure state or after eating abominable things, rather than any potential thieves. The tomb-chapel was like a temple, and thus visitors had to be ritually pure to enter. The violator is menaced by the judgement of the council of the gods and physical punishment by the tomb owner. Other 'curses' are more violent and threaten the *ba* of the interloper with attacks by serpents, scorpions, crocodiles and hippopotami (such as those found in the tomb of Petety and his wife at Giza). As time progressed, these curses became fiercer, and more concerned with the desecration of the tomb and its contents. An inscription at Tefibi's tomb at Asyut (First Intermediate Period) states that if anyone destroys the tomb, or the images therein, his son will not inherit, no funerary ceremonies will be carried out, and there will be no offerings and libations for him in the afterworld. It should be noted that no curses have ever been found in any royal tomb.

PART VI

AESTHETICS

CHAPTER TWENTY-FIVE

ART

—⋅◆⋅—

Gay Robins

INTRODUCTION

The ancient Egyptians had no term corresponding to the modern Western abstract notion of 'art', although there were words for different items, such as statues, stelae, coffins and so on, which we today regard as belonging to the category of ancient Egyptian art. It is convenient, however, for modern scholars to use the term 'art' to describe the visual as opposed to purely textual material that has come down to us from ancient Egypt (Baines 1994). Like all art, ancient Egyptian art derived its original meaning from its cultural context. It was deeply embedded in the Egyptian world-view, which both shaped the range of subject matter and the images shown, and was at the same time expressed by these images. Thus, although, as modern viewers, we can appreciate Egyptian art for perceived aesthetic qualities and supply our own meanings and criticism, if we wish to understand what it meant to the original patrons, artists and viewers, then it is necessary to try to comprehend the cultural context that gave rise to it and within which it functioned (Robins 1997; Hartwig 2001).

For the ancient Egyptians, the created, ordered world inhabited by deities, transfigured dead and humanity was brought into being by the creator god in the midst of the unformed, chaotic primordial waters that continued to surround and interpenetrate the universe even after its creation. At the same time, the first sunrise occurred and every sunrise thereafter was a repetition of creation. The order brought into being with creation was expressed by the concept of *maat*, personified as the goddess Maat. The created world also included chaotic elements, represented by the god Seth, and there was a continual battle to maintain *maat* and subdue chaos (*isfet*). Seth caused the chaos of death by the murder of his brother Osiris, but order was restored when Isis, the sister-consort of Osiris, brought her brother back to life to become ruler of the *duat*, the realm of the dead, and conceived and gave birth to his son, Horus, who became the divine embodiment of kingship.

The death and resurrection of Osiris provided a divine model for the Egyptians that gave them hope that they too would be resurrected and given new life after death. This hope for an afterlife was further supported by the many examples of cyclical renewal the Egyptians experienced in the world about them, especially the daily cycle of the sun, the monthly lunar cycle and the annual cycle of the Nile. Thus, the Egyptians' seemingly overwhelming preoccupation with death arose from their desire to make a successful transformation into the new life that they believed existed beyond death.

The living inhabited a world that was constantly threatened not only by death, but also by the many vicissitudes of life: disease, accidental harm and misfortune. These were caused by invisible manifestations of deities, demons and the dead, and ritual texts, actions and images were used to harness other potent forces from the same invisible realm to protect individuals and bring about their well-being. Much effort concentrated on fertility, conception, safe birth and successful child-rearing in order to ensure the continuity of the family.

A pivotal role within the cosmos was played by the king. While alive, he was the manifestation of Horus on earth and thus holder of the divine office of kingship. Although he was a human being, because he embodied this divine aspect of kingship, he was able to mediate between humanity and the potentially dangerous realm of the divine. He was specifically said to have been placed by Ra, the sun god and creator, 'in the land of the living for all time, judging humanity, satisfying the gods, bringing order (*maat*) into being and destroying chaos (*isfet*). He gives offerings to the gods and funerary offerings to the transfigured dead' (Baines 1995a). The ordered world of Egypt represented *maat*, while the deserts and foreign lands beyond were chaotic places. Thus, the king could pursue the battle against *isfet* by hunting the chaotic animals of the desert and subduing foreign lands and their inhabitants.

This understanding of the cosmos shaped the concerns and subject matter of ancient Egyptian art which, in consequence, focused on the interaction of the king with the cosmic world of the gods; the king's own cosmic role in maintaining order and destroying chaos; the legitimation of the king's role, on which the functioning structure of the universe depended; the well-being of the transfigured dead through the proper provisions made for their burial and on-going funerary cult; and the survival of the living by ensuring the continuity of the family and providing protection and healing against misfortune, disease and physical harm. Visual material, most commonly in the form of wall scenes, statues, stelae, coffins, illustrated papyri, jewellery, amulets and other personal items, was therefore located within temples, tombs, palaces, houses and on the individual body.

Within temples, where the king and priests performed the ritual cult for the gods and access was highly restricted, wall decoration dealt with the relationship between the king and deities, legitimation of kingship, temple ritual and the role of the king as priest. The more public exterior areas showed the king as enforcer of *maat* (cf. Figure 16.15). In tombs, the images on the walls and on stelae, coffins and funerary papyri were concerned with the successful transition of the deceased into the after-life, but also displayed the high status of the deceased owners, memorialized them for future generations, and showed the performance of the offering cult, necessary for the owners' continued existence (Hartwig 2004).

Statues were produced for specific settings in temples or tombs, where they played a vital role in temple or funerary ritual (Robins 2001a). Most statues were places where a non-physical entity, such as a deity, the royal *ka*-spirit of the king or the *ka*-spirits of the dead, could manifest itself in this world, once the image had undergone the opening of the mouth ritual that enabled it to function ritually. The most important item in any temple was the cult statue, made of precious materials (cf. Figure 22.2) and kept in the most sacred and protected part of the temple (Robins 2005). Many other images of deities were also dedicated by the king within temples, and statues of the king were also placed there, so that the king could have a perpetual presence in all temples throughout Egypt – wherever he actually was.

In tombs, statues of elite officials and their wives provided a place that could be inhabited by the *ka*-spirit of the deceased owner, in order to receive offerings brought by the living. High-ranking officials also placed statues of themselves within temple precincts, where they allowed the owner to be perpetually in the deity's presence (cf. Figure 6.8). Other votive offerings, consisting of images of deities and items associated with deities, were presented at temples and shrines by donors to establish a link with the deity to whom they were dedicated (Pinch 1982, 1993).

In palaces, which provided the setting for the king's ritual appearance as the image of the sun god on earth, when he illumined the world, just as the sun god illumined the world at dawn, the decoration referred to the newly awakened dawn world and to the subjection of chaotic forces (O'Connor 1991). Houses provided a location for ritual activities relating to the well-being of the family. Since the Egyptians believed that the dead had the power to intervene in the lives of the living for good or ill, the cult was directed in part toward deceased ancestors, through images called ancestor busts (cf. Figure 23.7) and stelae of deceased individuals (Demarée 1983; Friedman 1994). Large numbers of small figurines found in domestic contexts showing nude women alone or with children attest to another major concern: the fertility and thus continuity of the family (Pinch 1983). Items used in the household, such as mirrors and cosmetic objects, often carried images relating to well-being and fertility, which protected the individual user from misfortune and harm, as did articles of jewellery and amulets (Andrews 1994; Romano 1995). Such objects often ended up in tombs, after having been used in life, since their reference to fertility and birth could also aid in the rebirth of the owner into the next life (Robins 1996).

PATRONS, AUDIENCE AND ARTISTS

In modern Western society, we have developed the idea that art is for general viewing and appreciation, to be visited in museums and art galleries and available through mass reproduction. In ancient Egypt, art was far more restricted. Since its primary purpose was to fulfil a particular, usually ritual, function, rather than to be viewed, many items were placed in restricted or inaccessible locations, such as the interior of temples or sealed burial chambers, where the only audience would be the gods and the dead. Patrons and living viewers were the king and the elite – that is, the literate male officials who staffed the government bureaucracy and their families – who together probably formed no more than 5 per cent of the population. Although the quality of art produced varied, with the best being made for the king and his high officials, and the less accomplished for individuals of lower standing, there is little that can be attributed to the sphere of the non-elite (Pinch 1982: 140).

Artists, who as far as we know were all male, were part of the elite. Although the names of a number of artists survive, few works can be attributed to individuals (Bogoslovsky 1980; Keller 1981, 1991, 2001; Davies 2001a). Artists were organized in temple or royal workshops and operated in teams (Drenkhahn 1976, 1995; Eaton-Krauss 2001). However, these teams would work under a 'master', whose vision, within the strict parameters set by tradition and function, would be realized in individual works of art. The best-known group are the artists who decorated the 19th and 20th Dynasty royal tombs in the Valley of the Kings (Hornung 1990b). They lived in a government settlement on the west bank at Thebes, now called Deir el-Medina (cf. Figure 12.3), and have left, in addition to their artistic production, a large amount of textual material relating to their daily lives and the organization of their work (Valbelle 1985; McDowell 1999; Andreu 2002).

THREE-DIMENSIONAL REPRESENTATION

Statues and statuettes of formal figures – that is, deities, the king and the elite – were usually made of stone, wood or metal (Kozloff *et al.* 1992; Robins 2001a). They vary in size from very small to colossal, but share a limited set of poses – standing, seated and kneeling – and a characteristic known as frontality, which means that the head and body face forward and do not twist or turn. This may be partly due to their context either within a niche or shrine, whose only opening is to the front, or against a flat, architectural element, such as a pillar, and also to their function as a focus for ritual performance, so that they face the person carrying out the ritual in front of them.

Informal figures in the round are often incorporated into mirror handles and elaborate cosmetic items. They are generic rather than representing specific individuals, and do not have the ritual function of formal images. Because of their function as straight handles, figures incorporated into mirrors usually display frontality, but where they appear as servants carrying cosmetic pots or trays, their bodies often twist and turn in space to accommodate the weight of the object they carry.

Formal stone statues began as a rectangular block of stone slightly larger than the desired size of the finished object. Front and back views of the image were sketched out on the front and back of the block, while two profile images were drawn on the sides. Sculptors then cut away the stone on all four sides and the top around the sketched outline until they achieved the rough shape of the statue. As they cut the original sketches away with the stone, they would re-mark important levels and points with lines or dots of paint. Once they had the outline of the statue shaped, they could concentrate on modelling the face and body, and executing the details of costume and other items.

Soft stones, such as limestone and sandstone, could be worked with copper tools. However, such tools alone were incapable of making an impression on hard stones. These had to be worked with hammers of even harder stone, and copper or bronze tools, in conjunction with a quartz abrasive which actually did the cutting, and were then polished by rubbing with hard stones and an abrasive. Soft-stone statues were finished by smoothing, plastering and painting. There is some evidence that colour was sometimes applied to hard stone statues, but this might have been only to highlight details, since the surface of the stone was usually finished with a high polish and many stones were probably chosen for the significance of their colours (Kozloff *et al.* 1992: 125–53; Baines 2000).

Most formal stone statues recall the shape of the original block of stone, so that the resulting statues are strongly rectilinear. Furthermore, the stone was usually not cut away between the arms and the body, and between the legs in standing figures, and the legs and the seat in seated figures, and items do not protrude from the body. At the rear, statues usually have a wide, rectilinear back slab or a narrower back pillar. The fact that formal stone statues were rarely fully freed from the original stone block from which they were cut gives an impression of solidity, strength and power. While this might have been partly symbolic, it was also practical in helping to protect the statue from damage.

Wooden statues were normally made with the head, torso and legs in one piece, with the arms, front of the feet and base made separately and pegged together. In contrast to stone statues, they rarely have back pillars, and the separately carved arms not only frequently project away from the body, but they often hold separate items, such as staffs and sceptres. They were usually plastered and painted, although the paint was sometimes applied directly to good-quality coniferous wood. In some cases, the wooden statue was used as the foundation for the application of sheet gold or copper to give the appearance of a metal statue.

Metal statues were made by the lost-wax process, with larger ones utilizing a clay core to reduce the amount of metal used. They rarely have back pillars, and different parts of the statues could be cast separately and joined by pegs or mortise and tenon joints, so that they more closely resemble wooden rather than stone statues.

TWO-DIMENSIONAL REPRESENTATION

With two-dimensional images, the Egyptians had to invent a way to show the three-dimensional world on a flat surface (Robins 1986: 10–19; 1994a: 1–23; Schäfer 1986 [1919]). The system they developed made no attempt to incorporate the illusion of the third dimension, as in perspectival systems, and was thus conceptual rather than perceptual. Objects were shown in their most recognizable aspect – in profile or full-view, plan or elevation – and then combined on a single drawing surface. The human figure was a composite form (cf. Figure 20.9) made up of a profile face, a full-view eye, full-view shoulder and chest, and profile buttocks and limbs. A single nipple or breast was shown in profile on the front line of the torso. The navel was moved inside the front line of the stomach in order to render it more clearly visible. Until the late 18th Dynasty, both feet were shown from the inside (Russmann 1980). The open hand, whether empty or holding an object, is always drawn with the fingers slightly curved and the thumb on the concave side of the curve.

Formal figures are shown in the same limited range of poses found for formal statues. Informal figures representing the non-elite have a much broader range of poses, since the activities they are performing on behalf of the elite are what is important (cf. Figure 12.4). Nevertheless, their figures are, similarly, composites. Most images incorporate inscriptions in the hieroglyphic script of which each sign is a small two-dimensional image drawn according to the same principles as the larger images the text accompanies. Individual hieroglyphs can also be used meaningfully as part of a composition, as when gods give life to the king by holding out an *ankh*-hieroglyph, or a tomb owner is shown standing holding a staff in one hand and a cloth in the other, the image simply being a large version of the hieroglyph that writes the word *ser*, 'official' (Fischer 1973).

Figures and objects were combined into compositions by arranging them on the drawing surface in horizontal registers (cf. Figure 11.1). The feet of all the figures are placed on the baseline, even when horizontal overlapping of figures shows that some are to be understood as being behind others. Depth can also be indicated by vertical overlapping, with figures being placed gradually higher in the register, showing that items situated higher in a register should be understood as being behind those lower down (cf. Figure 8.2). Objects tend not to float unattached in a register, so that if they are placed above the register baseline, they are often anchored by their own internal baseline. Time may be conveyed by subject matter, such as the different seasons of the agricultural year, but it is not incorporated into the drawing system itself, for instance through direction or quality of light, or the representation of shadow. Scale was used not to indicate relative size in life, or distance from the viewer, but to mark relative importance, so the larger a figure, the higher its status (cf. Figure 20.7). Thus elite figures are larger than non-elite, and figures of the king are larger than non-royal ones. By contrast, figures of the king and deities are usually drawn on the same scale, indicating the king's divine aspect.

The use of registers gives order to the represented material. Scenes or groups of scenes are often surrounded by a framing device that further enhances the impression of order. Scenes are often balanced, one against another, and pairs of scenes that are approximately symmetrical, although never exact mirror images, are frequent (cf. Figure 20.2). The carefully ordered compositional system used by the Egyptians can be seen as a visual representation of *maat*. The notion of chaos could be incorporated into the system through the absence of order in the arrangement of figures, often achieved through the absence of register lines. However, such chaotic elements were usually contained within an ordered composition and shown under attack or already defeated (e.g. Epigraphic Survey 1986; cf. Figure 16.3).

Figures could face either right or left, but the primary orientation was to the right (Fischer 1977). On a self-contained monument, such as a funerary or votive stela, the most important figures would face right with subordinate ones facing left (Robins 1994b). On more complex monuments, other factors come into play. In temple decoration, deities are usually shown facing out from the interior of the building, while the king's figure normally faces into the temple. In tomb-chapels, figures of the owner usually look toward the entrance and figures of the living toward the interior. As small images, hieroglyphs can also be oriented to the right or left. When they refer to a particular figure, text and figure face the same direction.

The use of texts in scenes added meaning for those who could read. In addition to identifying the figures and actions depicted, texts on funerary items often contain offering formulae requesting a variety of benefits for the deceased, while votive stelae carry formulaic texts adoring the deity to whom they are dedicated. Some funerary texts are addressed to the living, suggesting that interaction was expected with the viewer. Even if the viewer could not read, the presence of hieroglyphs would impress and add status to the monument and its owner, since it implied literacy on the latter's part. Texts probably also added to the effectiveness of a monument just by their presence.

Two-dimensional painting on plaster normally began by sketching the composition in red, often on a squared grid (Robins 1994a), with corrections, which could some-times be quite extensive, being made in black (e.g. Hornung 1971: pls 27–38, 42–4,

49–59). The scene was then painted with a broad brush in flat washes of colour, normally with one pigment being prepared and applied at a time. The figures were then outlined and details added with a fine brush (Baines *et al.* 1989; Bryan 2001). Relief scenes were carved after the initial sketch had been completed, either into raised relief (cf. Figure 20.3), where the background was cut away around the figures, or into sunk relief (cf. Figure 16.2) where the figures were cut into the stone. Sunk relief was developed for use on exteriors, where bright sunlight tends to flatten raised relief, but during some periods it was used on interiors as well. After the surface was cut into relief, it was plastered and painted in the same way as flat painting.

Although formal figures of individuals might sometimes incorporate a likeness of the subject, they were less concerned with recording specific features than with producing an ideal image that reflected the status, gender and role of the subject portrayed (Spanel 1988). This was done by insignia, costume, hairstyle, jewellery, skin colour, items carried, pose and physical perfection (Robins 1999, 2001b). Images of the king, normally shown with youthful faces and vigorous bodies, are recognizable by their various crowns and sceptres, the uraeus worn on the brow, and certain items of dress (cf. Figure 20.10). Although their features were idealized to produce a fittingly regal image, individual kings often have recognizable face types that were possibly based on actual appearance (Kozloff *et al.* 1992: 125–9). Deities were also given perfect, youthful bodies and faces, and their features often reflected those of the reigning king. Elite men were also shown with an ideal, youthful image, but could in addition be represented by a more mature figure with soft muscles, paunch, rolls of fat on the chest, or lines on the face, the two images showing different life stages. Elite women, by contrast, had only one ideal image, youthful and slender, that stressed the subject's fertility and child-bearing potential.

Because figures represented a generic ideal for the category represented, identification of individual images was provided by accompanying inscriptions. By contrast, non-elite figures were rarely identified, because it was their actions – labouring on behalf of the elite in the fields, marshes, workshops or household – not who they were, that led to their depiction. Their figures are deliberately contrasted to those of the elite by their smaller scale, active poses, simple clothing or nudity, lack of jewellery, and in some cases the incorporation of physical imperfections.

MATERIALS

Egypt and the surrounding deserts were rich in materials that could be used in making art, but some items needed to be imported from further afield. Although few native Egyptian trees produced large pieces of good-quality timber, wood from the sycomore fig was used for coffins, stelae and statues. Better-quality coniferous wood, imported from Syria, was used to make high-status coffins and statuary (Gale *et al.* 2000). Copper was mined in the Eastern Desert and Sinai, and gold in the Eastern Desert and Nubia. Bronze, an alloy of copper and tin, was introduced by the Middle Kingdom, and although some tin may have been obtained from the Eastern Desert or Sinai, it was also imported. Some silver was probably obtained from the gold mines used by the Egyptians and was really an alloy of silver and gold, but purer metal with little gold content was imported (Ogden 2000).

The most important stones used to make statues were the soft stones, limestone, sandstone and steatite, and the hard stones, basalt, granite, granodiorite, greywacke, quartzite, siltstone and travertine (calcite). Gemstones, such as carnelian, jasper and amethyst, used in jewellery making and inlay on statues and other objects, were available in the Eastern Desert, and turquoise was mined in Sinai, but lapis lazuli had to be imported from the Badakhshan region of Afghanistan via Near Eastern trade routes (Aston *et al.* 2000). Egyptian faience was made from readily available materials, quartz, lime and natron or plant ash, covered with a soda-lime-silica glaze usually coloured dark blue, light blue or turquoise through the addition of copper, often obtained from malachite. It was regarded as an artificial gemstone and used to make beads, amulets, inlays, sculptures, bowls, cups, cosmetic items and a wide range of funerary items (Friedman 1998; Nicholson and Peltenburg 2000). Glass, which uses the same basic materials as faience, was not deliberately produced until the 18th Dynasty, when raw glass and the technique of manufacture were imported into Egypt from the Near East. Like faience, it was usually coloured and regarded as an artificial gemstone used to make beads, amulets, inlays, small vessels and sculptures (Cooney 1960; Riefstahl 1968; Nicholson and Henderson 2000).

Pigments were made from minerals (Lee and Quirke 2000; Colinart 2001; Heywood 2001; McCarthy 2001; Middleton and Humphrey 2001). Black was made from carbon, and white from calcium carbonate (whiting) or calcium sulphate (gypsum). A brighter white was obtained from huntite. Red and yellow pigments were commonly made from red and yellow ochre, but realgar was also used for red and orpiment for yellow. Brown pigment was obtained from ochre, but could also be produced by mixing other pigments or overpainting. A compound of quartz, lime, plant ash or natron coloured with copper was used to make an artificial pigment, Egyptian blue, and with more lime and less copper, a synthetic green pigment. Paint analysis has shown that huntite, realgar and orpiment were less common than the other pigments and were probably not used before the late Middle Kingdom; they might have been imported. Most painting was done onto dry gypsum plaster applied to the painting surface of stone, wood or mud-brick, but paint was generally applied directly onto papyrus. The pigments were ground and mixed with a binder of animal glue or plant gum for application (Newman and Halpine 2001).

THE SYMBOLISM OF COLOURS AND MATERIALS

Although colour use was based largely on a stylized version of natural colouring, colours and materials carried symbolic meaning for the Egyptians, many of which were related to the important themes of creation, cosmic renewal, order and chaos, and rebirth and regeneration (Aufrère 1991; Wilkinson 1994; Baines 2000, 2001a; Robins 2001b). White was associated with purity, but it also incorporated the notion of light, and was part of the word for 'dawn'. The same word also meant 'silver', a material with lunar associations that included the notion of renewal on the model of the moon's monthly renewal. Black was the colour of the fertile soil of Egypt and was linked to notions of fertility and regeneration. It was the colour of the underworld whose regenerative properties renewed the sun each night and whose ruler was the resurrected Osiris, who was sometimes shown with black skin to signify his underworld connection and regeneration. The underworld deity, Anubis, is shown as a black jackal, although jackals are normally sandy coloured. Black stones, such as granodiorite, were used to symbolize the regenerative properties of Osiris and his realm (Kozloff *et al.* 1992: 142).

Red was a powerful colour that could have positive or negative meaning (Pinch 2001). It was used to refer to the chaotic, hostile desert, called 'the red land', the realm of the chaotic god, Seth, but it is also the colour of the sun at its rising and setting, and so refers to the solar cycle and the regeneration of the sun. Yellow, too, referred to the sun and the regenerative solar cycle. In painting, yellow pigment was often used to represent gold, and gold as a material was closely associated with the sun god. Warm-coloured stones, such as red granite and yellow, orange, red, brown and purple quartzite, were also solar in meaning and used to refer to the regenerative solar cycle and, in royal statues, to the solar aspect of kingship.

The Egyptians seem to have seen blue, turquoise and green as shades of one colour they called *wadj* (Baines 1985). The hieroglyph for *wadj* was written with a papyrus stem and umbel, suggesting that it included the colour of growing vegetation. By extension, it carried notions of flourishing and of regeneration, based on the regenerative nature of plants that died back in the driest part of the year and sprang up again when the land was watered by the inundation. Osiris was often shown with green skin, as were faces on 26th Dynasty coffins, equating the deceased with the regenerated Osiris. The most highly prized green stone was turquoise, which ranges in colour, in our terms, from green through turquoise to light blue. It was associated with Hathor, goddess of birth and rebirth, who was called 'lady of turquoise', and the colour was also associated in sun hymns with the rising sun and thus its rebirth. Funerary items were often made of turquoise-coloured faience because of the association with rebirth (Friedman 1998).

In contrast to turquoise, the prestigious stone lapis lazuli is dark blue, a colour that was connected to the night sky, often rendered in dark blue paint with yellow stars; the primordial waters of the underworld, out of which the sun, sometimes called the 'child of lapis lazuli', was born each day; and with the hair of deities, which was said to be of lapis lazuli, and often painted blue. Because of the regenerative significance of the colour, many funerary items were made of dark blue faience (Friedman 1998).

In addition to colour, the luminosity and brilliance of a material were significant. Both faience and glass were valued for their shiny, light-reflecting surfaces, and the normal word for faience was *tjehenet* 'dazzling', which relates it to the brilliance of the sun (Friedman 1998: 15; Bianchi 1998: 24). Statuettes and other small items of steatite could be glazed to give them a similarly shiny surface (Kozloff *et al.* 1992: 198–9). Hard stone statues were usually highly polished to produce a gleaming, light-reflecting surface (cf. Figure 6.1), as were metals. Varnish was sometimes used over painting, especially on coffins, to give a glossy sheen (Serpico and White 2001). The luminous, reflective quality of these surfaces linked the objects with the scintillating light of the sun and other celestial bodies.

The very process of making art had significance. Making was a form of creation and the process of making took chaotic raw materials from outside the ordered realm of Egypt and transported them into the ordered world, at the same time imposing order upon them as they were worked into their final forms (Bianchi 1998: 22–3).

UNDERSTANDING IMAGES

In addition to the symbolism associated with colours and materials, motifs and subject matter also carried culturally constructed meaning, which would have been obvious to the intended ancient Egyptian audience but which lies outside the visual vocabulary of modern viewers (Derchain 1975a, 1975b, 1976; Robins 1990; Wilkinson 1992, 1994). For instance, in a funerary context, many motifs ultimately signify the regeneration hoped for by the deceased. The scarab beetle shown pushing the sun up over the horizon at dawn, by analogy with the dung beetle pushing its ball of dung, became a symbol of the solar cycle and the rebirth of the sun (Bianchi 2001). Its significance was enhanced by the fact that as a hieroglyph the scarab wrote the word *kheper* 'to come into being', and it is the sunrise that brings the world into being every morning after the darkness of the night. The sun god at dawn was also thought to be born each day out of a blue water lily (lotus), so that images of the flower referred to the sun's rebirth and the solar cycle that the deceased hoped to join (Germer 2001: 541). They are found in abundance in funerary contexts: held by the deceased, among piles of offerings, as part of floral bouquets offered to the deceased, and as growing plants in scenes that incorporate pools and marshes.

Papyrus reeds appeared in formal bouquets offered to the deceased, growing in scenes with marsh settings, and as an amulet in the form of a single stem and flower. The plant carried with it all the associations of the colour term *wadj*, but was also linked to Hathor, goddess of birth and rebirth, and in her cow form she was often shown with a clump of growing papyrus, even in the desert setting of the Theban necropolis. Papyrus marshes also recalled the swampy setting of the primordial waters in the midst of which the created world came into being. They are liminal areas at the edge of the ordered world of cultivated fields, and not only harbour chaotic forces in the form of the untamed wildlife, but also hold transformative potential as the site of creation, rebirth through Hathor, and regeneration through the notion of *wadj*. All these related meanings worked together to express the desire of the deceased for regeneration and rebirth in the next life.

Scenes showing the king and deities, usually found in temple contexts and royal tombs, exclude the rest of humanity, and are given a cosmic setting: the top of the scene is bounded by an elongated sky hieroglyph painted blue, while the baseline represents an elongated earth hieroglyph, so that the depicted action takes place on a cosmic stage between heaven and earth. The *ankh*-sign carried by deities symbolizes life. Life belongs to the gods who give it to the king, an act that is depicted by holding out the *ankh* towards the king's face, occasionally with a text saying that a deity 'gives life to your [the king's] nose'. To understand this gesture fully, we need to realize that there is a phrase 'the breath of life', so that life is something that is breathed. In royal tombs, the *ankh* held out to the king signifies the granting of life through rebirth after death.

The motif of foreigners represents the chaos found outside the ordered world of Egypt, and figures of foreigners being subdued or already overcome and bound were widely used to symbolize the king's ability to overcome chaos and maintain cosmic order. In the palace, figures of bound foreigners are found on the floors, steps leading up to the throne dais, the dais itself, and the king's footstool (Robins 1997: 136–7; cf. Figure 16.6). Bound and lined up in rows, they are visually subdued by having order imposed on them, while the king walks over them or rests his feet on them, a visual form of a common phrase in royal texts 'all foreign lands are under his [the king's] feet'. On the great pylon gateways fronting temples, the king is shown smiting bound foreigners with a mace or scimitar to show his effectiveness as maintainer of order, but the motif also has an apotropaic function, protecting the purity of the ordered interior of the temple from the chaotic forces that surround it (Hall 1986). In the New Kingdom, exterior temple walls sometimes also have scenes showing the king defeating foreigners in battle (Epigraphic Survey 1986). Here, the enemies are rendered chaotically without baselines with figures falling in all directions in the battle itself. In the aftermath of the battle, prisoners are shown bound and lined up in ordered registers, signifying that by their defeat, *maat* has been imposed. These scenes demonstrate how ancient Egyptian art must often be read on more than one level, for these battles commemorate actual events, show the king successfully fulfilling his cosmic role as the upholder of *maat*, and act apotropaically to protect the purity of the temple interior. How much of the meaning of any piece of ancient Egyptian art is read will depend on the knowledge of the viewer.

CHAPTER TWENTY-SIX

ARCHITECTURE

———•◆•———

Kate Spence

Ancient Egyptian monumental architecture has been famed since ancient times (Herodotus 1998: 108) and its abstracted forms, stylistic features and extensive decoration are instantly recognizable. It has been accorded a privileged position in histories of world architecture as a result of its early and widespread use of stone, its technological achievements and the scale of some of its buildings, most notably pyramids and temples (Giedion 1964). Egyptian architecture as a form of artistic expression is a worthy subject of study in its own right (e.g. Baldwin Smith 1938; Smith 1998), but the broader implications of the topic should not be underestimated. In particular, architecture forms important evidence for royal and private activity, and it provides context for the texts and art carved or painted on its walls and for objects discovered within.

It is important to recognize, however, that preservation of architecture is patchy and our record is strongly biased. Mortuary monuments were traditionally built in the desert and are consequently more often preserved than temples, palaces, institutional structures and domestic buildings which were usually constructed close to the flood plain. Such sites have frequently been destroyed by the movement of the river, the construction of later buildings or the removal of mud-brick and organic settlement debris for use as agricultural fertilizer. Structures built in southern Egypt have often survived better than those built in the delta and northern Egypt as a result of widespread urbanization and industrialization in the north. Ancient buildings recorded by early visitors (e.g. Russell 2001) have often completely disappeared: blocks were removed for reuse and limestone was burnt in kilns to produce slaked lime for use in construction, a destructive practice dating back at least to the Ptolemaic Period in Egypt. Later periods are also better represented by standing monuments than earlier ones, with a number of Egypt's most famous visitor attractions, such as the temples of Dendara, Edfu and Philae, dating mainly to the Hellenistic and Roman periods (Arnold 1999).

There are many possible ways of approaching ancient architecture and this chapter can only touch on a few. Monuments can be treated art-historically, examining style, organization and decoration in particular types of buildings alongside the emergence of new forms and motifs over time (e.g. Smith 1998; Arnold 1999). One can investigate technology and construction methods (Clarke and Engelbach 1930; Arnold 1991) or the underlying conception of space to which constructed buildings relate (Ricke 1950; Allen 1994). There are economic, social and political implications inherent in the decision to build and in the form and later use of the resulting structures (Spence 2004a; Roth 2005; Kemp 2005 [1989b]: 99–110): although these can be difficult to pinpoint in the absence of textual sources, architecture features prominently in histories of Egypt, particularly for earlier historical periods (e.g. Trigger *et al.* 1983; Shaw 2000b). Agency and the design process can also be examined, although the evidence for pursuing this line of enquiry for ancient Egypt is more limited than might be expected (Badawy 1948; Arnold 1991: 7–25; Rossi 2004: 92–179; Kemp 2005 [1989b]: 158–60). This chapter begins with a very brief treatment of the emergence of building traditions in Egypt and moves on to early monumental architecture, looking in particular at the step pyramid complex of King Netjerikhet Djoser. A discussion of the foundation ritual and evidence for the design process is followed by consideration of key themes in the architecture of tombs, temples, fortifications and domestic structures. Finally, some aspects of the design process are examined.

EARLY BUILDING IN EGYPT

The earliest evidence for built structures in Egypt is the remains of simple huts and enclosures constructed from locally available materials such as reeds, wooden poles, rough fieldstone and mud (Rizkana 1996; Wengrow 2006: 30, 78). As in other parts of the world, these structures were designed primarily to provide shelter from the elements and, perhaps, protection for livestock and demarcation of space. Mud-brick gradually came into widespread use in the Nile Valley and was used to create rectilinear structures and to line burial chambers, as both dwellings and tombs became increasingly complex in the late Predynastic Period (Spencer 1993: 34–7). Around the time of unification the incipient state recognized the potential offered by architecture for creating visual statements of its power and authority throughout the land, as well as creating structures with internal spatial differentiation within which social and ritual aspects of court life could be enacted (Wilkinson 1999: 230–60; Kemp 2005 [1989b]: 99–110).

Preserved architecture of the Early Dynastic Period is almost entirely of mud-brick although representations suggest that temporary structures of reeds, matting, wood and perhaps animal skins remained important in the construction of shrines and presumably also other structures (Kemp 2005 [1989b]: 142–54). Royal architecture of the period features massive mud-brick walls, often constructed with decorative niching known today as 'palace-façade' style (Figure 26.1; Wilkinson 1999: 230–60; Kemp 2005 [1989b]: 99–110). This is seen both on monumental mortuary enclosures associated with the royal tombs at Abydos, and also on a gateway leading into what appears to be an early palace at the site of Hierakonpolis (Kemp 2005 [1989b]: 80–3). This style of decoration derives ultimately from Mesopotamian temple architecture but seems to have been associated with the king in Egypt. It is additionally found decorating the tomb superstructures of some of the highest officials as a visual marker of close association with the royal court (Kemp 2005 [1989b]: 101). Although little of the interior of the Hierakonpolis 'palace' has been excavated, it shows

Figure 26.1 'Palace-façade': decorative niching on the mud-brick exterior
walls of Khasekhemwy's funerary enclosure at Abydos
(from Wilkinson 1999: pl. 6.2 top).

complex differentiation of space, which is also clear in the arrangements of elite tomb
interiors, thought to mimic the ordering of domestic structures, in some cases complete
with bedrooms, bathrooms and toilets (Roth 1993: 44).

THE STEP PYRAMID COMPLEX

Although the first examples of the use of stone in royal architecture are found in the
Early Dynastic Period – stone elements such as portcullises are found in the royal
tombs at Abydos (Spencer 1993: 93–5), and the Gisr el-Mudir, a massive enclosure
of the 2nd Dynasty at Saqqara, was constructed of limestone (Mathieson *et al.* 1997)
– it was in the pyramid complexes of the Old Kingdom that stone architecture really
took off. The turning point was the Step Pyramid complex of King Netjerikhet
Djoser of the 3rd Dynasty (*c.*2667–*c.*2648 BC), a hugely innovative project in terms
of scale, materials, technology and design (Firth and Quibell 1935; Lauer 1936;
Lehner 1997: 84–93).

The pyramid itself is the central feature of the complex (Figure 26.2). It is
constructed of relatively small limestone blocks laid at a slight angle to increase
stability. The lowest step on the south face has now fallen away revealing that the
pyramid had been constructed over a large rectangular mastaba ('bench-shaped') tomb,

characteristic of Egyptian burial practices at the time. The mastaba tomb had, itself, been enlarged at least three times before the decision was made to build a four-stepped pyramid over the existing structure and, so successful was the result, the pyramid was enlarged once again into its final six-stepped form (Lauer 1936: 10–26, pls 6–12; Lehner 1997: 84–7). A number of possible explanations for this pyramidal form have been put forward. It effectively differentiated the burial place of the king from the tombs of his followers and was a very visible symbol of power, dominating the landscape around the royal residence. It might also have been intended to represent the mound of creation, a prominent theme in later Egyptian religious texts: some early elite tombs featured a stepped mound of mud-brick hidden within the bench-shaped superstructure. Another possible explanation is that it symbolized a giant stairway to the sky.

Beneath the pyramid is the burial place of the king: a chamber constructed of granite at the base of a shaft 28 metres deep (Firth and Quibell 1935: 27–34, pls 10–17; Lauer 1936: 27–67, pls 15–20). Around the burial chamber ran a series of corridors. Most of these were undecorated and were probably used to store the burial goods placed in the tomb with the king; but, to the east of the burial chamber, the walls were inlaid with small faience plaques intended to replicate the appearance of matting structures. In three tiled niches, low-relief carvings of the king were found, showing him striding or running in a vigorous manner, accompanied by royal standards, symbols and hieroglyphs; it seems that these scenes were intended to represent the king reanimated after death and extending his power into the afterlife (Friedman 1995). A second tomb structure is found at the south end of the enclosure and contained a similar granite vault, this one too small to contain a body and thought perhaps to be for the king's *ka*; three further carved reliefs of the king were also found here (Firth and Quibell 1935: 54–64, pls 35–46; Lauer 1936: 49–112, pls 31–7).

The pyramid stands at the centre of a large enclosure within which are a number of courtyards and buildings that provide fascinating evidence for the experimentation involved in the transition to stone architecture (Lauer 1936). The walls and buildings reproduce the forms of traditional mud-brick and reed structures, but carved in stone to render them permanent. The technical properties of this new material were not fully understood, however, and, in the entrance hall, columns carved as bundles of reeds were not erected free-standing but were engaged to short spur walls while the hall was roofed with stone 'logs' cut with extra depth to counter the poor tensile strength of the stone (Figure 26.3). The majority of the free-standing 'buildings' in the complex are actually solid, with rubble fill supporting the stone 'roof': only narrow and short passages lead inside, winding to dead ends. Externally these structures take the form of shrines built from reeds and matting and faithfully reproduce much of the detailing of these temporary shelters. Only a few of the buildings have proper interiors, among them a small chamber (called a *serdab*) on the north side of the pyramid containing a statue of Djoser; tiny holes allow the statue to gaze out into the northern court and the sky above. The mortuary temple on the northern side of the building also has a fully functional interior presumably designed for use during the funeral and for cult activity after the king's death.

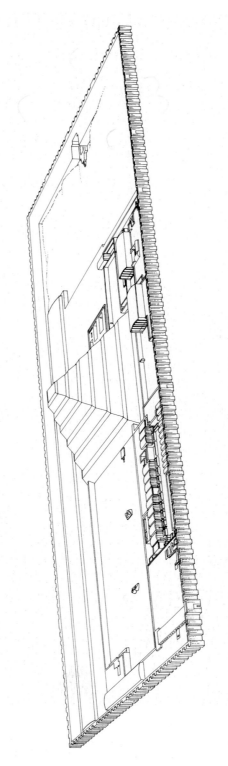

Figure 26.2 Reconstruction of Netjerikhet Djoser's step pyramid complex at Saqqara (drawing by Kate Spence after Lauer 1936: pl. IV).

Figure 26.3 Engaged columns and roof of stone 'logs' in the entrance passageway of Netjerikhet Djoser's step pyramid complex. The upper portions of the structure have been reconstructed incorporating original elements of the building (photo K. Spence).

PYRAMIDS

The pyramids at Giza are the only surviving example of the seven wonders of the ancient world. Even today, stripped of most of their gleaming white casing and surrounded by the suburbs of modern Cairo, they remain extraordinarily impressive (Figure 26.4). Pyramids were originally built only for kings and some queens, and, to date, over 90 royal pyramids have been found, all constructed in an 80-kilometre stretch of the west bank of the Nile between modern Cairo and the mouth of the Fayum – with the exception of a group of small pyramids of the early Old Kingdom which seem to have served as markers of royal authority in provincial towns (Seidlmayer 1996: 119–27). The pyramid was a burial marker and stood within a larger complex containing a temple for the mortuary cult and a much smaller 'satellite' pyramid, thought to be associated with the *ka* or 'vital force' of the deceased. Major pyramids also had a causeway and valley temple while queens' pyramids tended to cluster around those of their fathers, husbands and sons.

Although the associated temples were richly decorated, pyramids themselves usually were not. Old Kingdom pyramids (primarily those of the 6th Dynasty) had burial chambers carved with Pyramid Texts: spells intended to aid the transfiguration of the dead king and his passage to the afterlife (Faulkner 1969). These are not present in late pyramids, although at least some Middle Kingdom pyramids had decorated capstones carved from hard stones such as black granite.

Figure 26.4   The pyramids at Giza (left to right) of Menkaura, Khafra and Khufu.
The three smaller pyramids belonged to close female relations of Menkaura
(photo K. Spence).

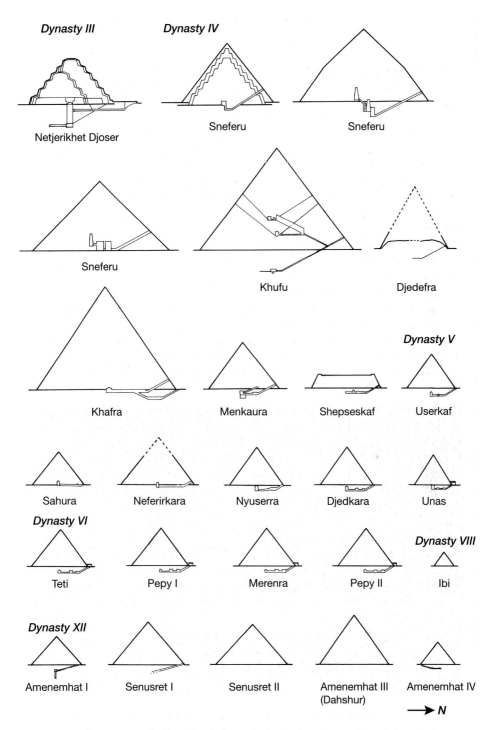

Figure 26.5 North–south sections through a selection of pyramids of the Old and Middle Kingdoms. All are drawn to the same scale (drawing by Kate Spence, adapted from Lehner 1997: 16–17).

TOMB ARCHITECTURE

Monumental tombs dominate the architectural record of the Old Kingdom. Pyramid architecture underwent significant development in the early 4th Dynasty and this points to major changes in the understanding of these structures (Figure 26.5). The most obvious of these changes was abstraction of the form of the stepped pyramid into a true pyramid. This change took place over the course of the reign of Sneferu who constructed three pyramids (Lehner 1997: 97–105; Verner 2001: 159–89): first an eight-stepped pyramid at Meidum; then a pyramid at Dahshur south which was originally intended to be a steep-sided true pyramid but which, as a result of structural instability, had its design altered twice and in its final form featured a significant change of angle on the sides (hence its modern name, the Bent Pyramid); then a rather shallow true pyramid at Dahshur north. Finally, casing was applied to the Meidum pyramid to turn that, too, into a true pyramid.

The intention of these early true pyramids seems to have been to create the tallest structure possible while retaining the true pyramid shape (Rossi 2004: 185). This is seen in the experimentation with the angles of the sides, in the location of structures in high places (such as at Giza and Abu Rawash) and also in the increasing scale of early pyramids. The 4th Dynasty pyramids were the tallest structures created in the ancient world: the Great Pyramid was 146.59 metres high and the tallest of all. The desire to build high also led to changes in construction techniques at this time. Blocks were now laid horizontally and were increasingly large: the pyramid was held together by gravity (Arnold 1991: 159–64, figs 4.88–92).

The emphasis on size was short-lived. By the late 4th Dynasty the focus of the burial complex had shifted from the pyramid as the burial marker of the king to the mortuary temple as the locus for the cult of the deceased (Stadelmann 1997: 11–15; Arnold 1997: 59–70). Pyramids rapidly decreased in scale and from the 5th Dynasty became fairly standardized with the majority of later Old Kingdom pyramids having a height of around 50 metres and a slope of 50–56 degrees (Lehner 1997: 16–17). As scale diminished, so too did the necessity of building a solid core from massive blocks, and pyramid cores were often roughly built or filled with rubble and were occasionally even constructed from mud-brick (Arnold 1991: 159–64). These cores were still cased with gleaming white limestone and, at the time of construction, would have looked identical in finish to the 4th Dynasty pyramids. However, the poor construction techniques led to the widespread destruction of these later monuments once their valuable casing stones had been removed: many are now just mounds of rubble. Pyramid construction was revived in the Middle Kingdom by the 12th Dynasty kings, apparently as a conscious attempt to invoke the glories of the Old Kingdom. In the New Kingdom, richly decorated royal tombs were excavated in the Valley of the Kings at Thebes (Reeves and Wilkinson 1996). After the New Kingdom, kings were sometimes buried within the enclosures of major temples.

Neither the pyramids nor the tombs in the Valley of the Kings were built in isolation. In the Old Kingdom the pyramid usually formed the focus of a spatial sequence leading from a Valley Temple via a long causeway to a temple adjacent to the pyramid where the mortuary cult was performed in front of statues of the deceased and the false door (a solid doorway representing the point of transition from this world to the next) (Lehner 1997: 18–19). In the New Kingdom the mortuary cult was performed in a temple built on the Theban west bank, close to, but physically separated from the tomb in the Valley of the Kings (Haeny 1997).

The majority of Egyptians were buried in simple pit tombs without superstructures. It is clear, however, that those who could afford to invest in architecture preferred to concentrate on the construction and embellishment of tombs rather than houses, which were of mud-brick and usually undecorated. Most elite tombs in Egypt can be categorized into three types (for useful summaries see Altenmüller 1998; Shedid 1998; Kampp-Seyfried 1998; Seidel 1998). Rock-cut tombs are found in all periods at sites where the cliffs of the high desert were close enough to settlements; in addition to chambers cut in the rock and burial shafts, some of these tombs had outer enclosures, causeways and other features. Mastaba ('bench-shaped') tombs were built in the Old and Middle Kingdoms, often on rather flatter sites, and were free-standing structures, originally solid but gradually acquiring internal chambers that increased in number and complexity over the course of the Old Kingdom. From the late 18th Dynasty, many tombs take the form of small temples with pylons and open courts leading to sanctuaries, and some were equipped with pyramids (Kampp-Seyfried 1998: 250–1). As in royal mortuary temples, the focus of the structure and cult activity was either on a statue of the deceased or on the false door. There is considerable variation between regions in the design of tombs and in the content and techniques of decoration, although this becomes less apparent from the New Kingdom onwards. Offerings for the funerary cult and scenes of daily life are particularly prominent in decoration.

TEMPLES

Other than the massive mortuary temples attached to pyramid complexes, we have little evidence for the construction of temples before the Middle Kingdom. Barry Kemp (2005 [1989b]: 116–35) has described the early shrines that do survive as 'preformal' as they show little of the formality of contemporary royal mortuary structures or later temples, exhibit significant variation in design and are sometimes rather small. This suggests that royal involvement in many of these projects was limited or non-existent, further implying that kings of this period were more concerned with their own cults than with those of Egypt's many gods. From the Middle Kingdom we have more evidence for royal temple construction projects, formal but still small in comparison with pyramid temples and with the cult structures of later periods (e.g. Badawy 1966: 70–89). These were rectilinear and usually constructed of mud-brick, although stone structures also survive.

During the New Kingdom there was widespread construction of stone-built temples in Egypt and Nubia (Badawy 1968: 154–371) reflecting increasing devotion to the gods among kings and a corresponding increase in the power of the temples as institutions (Kemp 2005 [1989b]: 248–60). It is these temples along with later examples that dominate the surviving record.

The temple was viewed primarily as the dwelling place of the god and was structured around a shrine containing the god's image in the form of a statue. Cult activity revolved around caring for the statue which was regularly washed, dressed and offered food and drink with ritual words spoken throughout (Shafer 1997: 22–3). The shrine was set inside an enclosure wall, usually built of mud-brick, which divided the sacred space within from the profane world outside and offered a degree of ritual and perhaps physical protection for the temple and its possessions (Shafer 1997: 5; R. Wilkinson 2000: 56–7). The creation of this sacred space was effected through foundation rituals performed by the king prior to construction (see below).

Although there were small temples such as that of Ramesses I at Abydos (Porter and Moss 1927–99: vol. VI, 28) that consisted of little more than a sanctuary and enclosure, many temples such as that at Luxor were larger and more elaborate (Figure 26.6). Additional halls and courts could be constructed in sequence in front of the sanctuary, often increasing in scale further from the shrine (Shafer 1997: 6; R. Wilkinson 2000: 54–79). These halls and courts were usually symmetrically arranged along the approach to the shrine, creating long processional routes that were used by kings and priests approaching the divine images, and also by the gods when their images travelled outside the temples in boat-shaped shrines carried on the shoulders of priests. The processional route would pass through many gateways, some built in the form of pylons which were stylized representations of the horizon, flanked with obelisks and colossal statues (R. Wilkinson 2000: 54–61). Additional small temples dedicated to other gods might be built within the enclosures of major temples.

Traditional Egyptian temples had dark interiors, lit by slots in the ceiling of the inner rooms and with torches or lamps. Spaces were often richly decorated. Ceilings were painted with stars to represent the night sky through which the king moved as he passed through the temple towards the sanctuary, his route marked out by winged sun-discs carved above each doorway: the space had cosmological associations

(a)

Figure 26.6 Luxor Temple: (a) the façade constructed by Ramesses II with statues and obelisks, one of which is still *in situ* (photo K. Spence); (b) plan of the temple showing its expansion over a number of generations (drawing by Kate Spence, adapted from Kemp 2005 [1989b]: fig. 99).

(b)

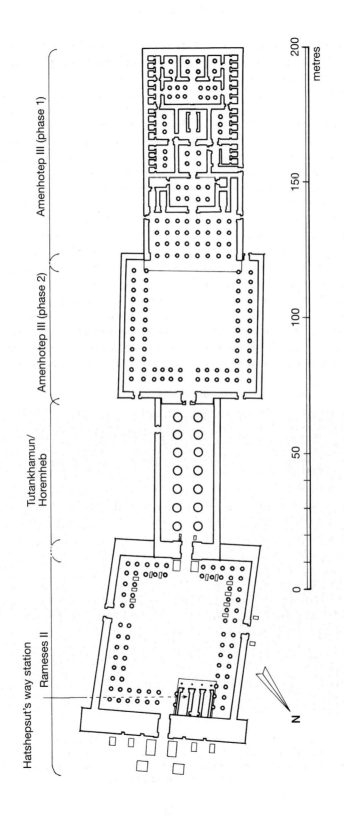

Hatshepsut's way station / Rameses II

Tutankhamun/ Horemheb

Amenhotep III (phase 2)

Amenhotep III (phase 1)

N

metres

0   50   100   150   200

and the king animated the temple space as the sun gives life to the world (Shafer 1997: 5; R. Wilkinson 2000: 76–9). Columns were often carved in the form of plants that contrast strongly with the abstracted rectilinear forms of the rest of the architecture. All available surfaces other than the floor might be further decorated in low sunk or raised painted relief. Statuary also formed an important part of temple decoration and images of the king praying and making offerings were placed in the temple, along with images of favoured courtiers and administrators. Some of the royal statues were colossal and some were also created integrally with the architecture as seen on the façade of Abu Simbel temple or in the Osiride royal statues lining porticos that were a relatively common feature of New Kingdom temple architecture.

During the Amarna Period, the focus on the cult of the visible sun led to the construction of temples that were almost entirely open, in stark contrast to the dark interiors and sanctuaries that characterized most Egyptian temples of the New Kingdom (Badawy 1968: 200–8). It is possible that the Aten temples were based on the architecture of earlier temples to the sun god Ra at Heliopolis, but too little is preserved of the latter structures to be sure. Many aspects of temple architecture remained unchanged even at Amarna, however: temples were still symmetrically arranged around a processional route and gateways were constructed in the form of pylons. Solar worship was not limited to the Amarna Period: open courts containing solar platforms or 'altars' were constructed throughout the New Kingdom within temple complexes dedicated to the worship of Amun-Ra, such as those at Deir el-Bahri, Karnak and Abu Simbel.

Some temples were built as single projects. Examples include the majority of the west bank temples at Luxor (these are actually mortuary temples but during the New Kingdom the mortuary provision for kings was reduced to subsidiary chambers within major temples dedicated to Amun-Ra (Haeny 1997)), and temples at Soleb and Abu Simbel constructed by Amenhotep III and Ramesses II, respectively. Other temples such as those at Karnak, Memphis and Philae grew over time as kings added to the work of their predecessors.

The construction of Egyptian temples continued into the Ptolemaic and Roman Periods and some of the most famous temples of all, such as Edfu, Dendera and Philae, were constructed then (Arnold 1999). Despite the fact that the architectural vocabulary used was traditional and the rulers in question were not Egyptian, temple construction remained prominent and designs were vibrant and inventive. It is during these later periods that more elaborate decorative schemes and plant columns were developed, kiosks and birth houses became more common within temple design as rituals evolved, and the idea of the temple as a microcosm of the universe reached its clearest expression (Finnestad 1997). After the last remaining cults of the Egyptian gods were shut down in the fifth and sixth centuries AD, many temples remained important religious sites with halls or courts transformed into churches and, later, mosques, a factor that contributed significantly to the preservation of some monuments.

FORTIFICATIONS

The Egyptians also produced astonishingly sophisticated military architecture and, as royal projects, these should be considered alongside other constructions initiated at court. A chain of fortresses built in Nubia in the Middle Kingdom supplies the best-known examples but contemporary structures were built in Sinai, too, and New Kingdom forts were built along the Mediterranean coast towards Libya to match existing provision in Sinai (Arnold 2003: 91–3 provides a useful summary).

The forts vary in scale and in setting. Large rectilinear structures were built on open areas of ground adjacent to the river or coast while in Nubia a second set of forts was built on rocky outcrops commanding a good view of the river (Lawrence 1965; Kemp 2005 [1989b]: 231–41). These conform closely to the local topography and were often rather smaller than the forts built on open ground. All the forts were built of mud-brick with occasional use of stone facing. They feature massive walls with buttresses, ramparts, towers, fortified gateways and water-stairs; rounded towers with openings for archers were designed to cover attack from any angle. Some fortresses have double enclosures, ditches and fortified spur-walls to provide additional protection. Although there is no doubt that these forts served defensive purposes on Egypt's borders, they also served ideological purposes, advertising the king's power and resources beyond the physical limits of his authority (Spence 2004a).

DOMESTIC ARCHITECTURE

All houses were built of mud-brick, a thermally insulating material suitable for use in arid climates (Endruweit 1994: 32–45). In the houses of the wealthy, extensive use might also be made of stone fittings such as door-frames and column bases, and of wooden columns, doors and shutters. There is great differentiation in the scale of non-royal dwellings both in planned settlements such as Kahun (Petrie 1891: 5–8, pl. 14) and in unplanned residential quarters of towns such as Amarna (Tietze 1985). While the smallest houses have only three or four tiny rooms, large dwellings feature a whole range of interior and exterior spaces of varying proportion and scale, including columned halls and porticos (e.g. Bietak 1996a). The layout of larger houses is carefully structured and is focused on the bedroom of the head of household, and on the dais within the central hall (Figure 26.7). The interior of a house is carefully screened from the outside through a tortuous entry sequence leading to the square hall which forms the centre of the house and the location of the dais. Further groups of rooms opened from this central hall as did the stair to the upper storey, where this existed. The architecture of large houses played an important role in establishing and expressing relationships between individuals of varying ranks, depending on how far and in what manner they were allowed to enter. Houses tended to be oriented towards the prevailing wind (usually north or west) to keep the interiors cool, and rooms had high ceilings with small windows set near the top of the walls to allow hot air out and light in (Endruweit 1994: 57–78, 89–119). Even elite houses seem to have had little decoration, although patterned friezes and the occasional representative painting are found.

The majority of palaces were also built of mud-brick as is clear from surviving examples at sites such as Deir el-Ballas, Tell el-Dab'a, Malkata and Amarna (Lacovara 1997: 24–41; Kemp and Weatherhead 2000). A few, such as the Theban palaces attached to mortuary temples and the Great Palace at Amarna, were built from stone, perhaps a reflection of their important ceremonial roles (Assmann 1972). The focus of the palace seems most often to have been the throne setting of the king, and palaces usually also contain an inner section within which a bedroom and bathroom of the king are located. Large and high columned halls also seem to have been a feature of Egyptian palace architecture. At Amarna, the only site where significant numbers of both palaces and houses are preserved, it seems that more variation is found in palace architecture than in houses with both axially ordered structures and those with more complex entry arrangements preserved, formal differences presumably

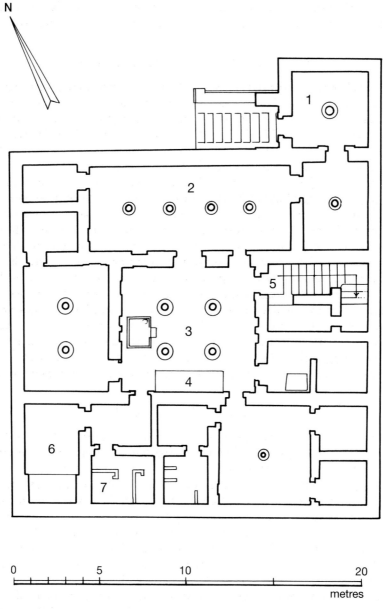

Figure 26.7 The layout of a large house at Amarna (house P.47.19). Key: 1 porch; 2 front hall; 3 central hall; 4 dais; 5 stair to upper storey; 6 bedroom; 7 bathroom (drawing by Kate Spence after Borchardt and Ricke 1980: plan 23).

reflecting the differing uses of the four major palaces preserved at the site. Palaces seem to have been extensively decorated with painted scenes considerably less formal than contemporary temple and tomb decoration. The Amarna palaces featured paintings of pond scenes and wildlife and of the royal family relaxing and handing out rewards to loyal supporters, alongside more traditional elements of royal iconography such as bound captives and heraldic plants (Kemp and Weatherhead 2000). The Tuthmoside Palace F at Tell el-Dabʿa featured bull-leaping scenes with maze backgrounds that had clearly been created by Aegean craftsmen (Bietak 2005; Steel, this volume).

THE FOUNDATION CEREMONY

Work on royal projects often began with a foundation ceremony (Weinstein 1973: 1–22; Rossi 2004: 148–73). The most complete set of texts and depictions of the ceremony dates to the Ptolemaic Period but the Palermo Stone provides a 1st Dynasty reference to the ceremony (Wilkinson 2000a: 111–13). The earliest depiction of the 'stretching of the cord' – in which the alignment of the structure was established by the king in the company of the goddess Seshat – dates to the 2nd Dynasty reign of Khasekhemwy (Engelbach 1934). Following the alignment of the structure a trench was dug into which purifying substances such as sand and natron were placed. The king also moulded the first brick for use in construction, and sometimes placed plaques or foundation deposits under the corners of the building or enclosure.

The foundation ceremony is interesting as it renders the project the concern of king and gods rather than those who actually designed or constructed it. This divine involvement plus the emphasis on purification differentiates the completed space from the world around it and makes it sacred. The whole design and construction project is collapsed into an atemporal set of ritual actions in which the king performs specific activities symbolic of creation of the whole structure. It is the importance of both the act of creation and the sacred space resulting from this act that raises architectural design above the level of mere mortals and removes it (at least in the official textual evidence) from the remit of those who actually worked on the project.

THE DESIGN PROCESS

Our understanding of the processes behind Egyptian architectural design is limited, largely as a result of the paucity of textual sources and the nature of the information provided by building texts. Where written evidence in the form of royal inscriptions survives, kings tend to present buildings as royal projects in their entirety, from inception to dedication, and usually focus on the piety of the donor and the scale of the gift, which is generally described as being bigger, grander and more costly than all previous buildings (Björkman 1971: 26–31); the involvement of 'architects' is only infrequently mentioned (Kemp 2005 [1989b]: 158–60). We have the names of individuals holding titles such as 'Overseer of Works' and 'Royal Master Builder' (Arnold 2003: 20) who were responsible for the running of projects and technical execution and probably also for design, although there is little unequivocal evidence that this was the case. Some information is provided by biographical texts which occasionally refer to specific projects, such as Ineni's involvement in the construction of the tomb of Thutmose I and in the creation of his obelisks (Breasted 1906b: 40–4);

however, these texts tend to focus on the responsibility placed on the individual rather than on the nature of the work undertaken.

The fact that information on design is not forthcoming from the textual sources should not be equated with lack of interest in spatial layout, form, decoration or aesthetic impact of projects: the buildings themselves provide clear testimony to the skill and inventiveness of the designers. Egyptian kings were fully aware of the potential impact of architecture (Spence 2004a; Kemp 2005 [1989b]: 99–110) and it is evident that those associated with building projects were often highly favoured by the kings under whom they served, suggesting that their role was recognized and valued: examples include Nefermaat and Hemiunu under Sneferu and probably Khufu, and Senenmut during the reign of Hatshepsut (Arnold 2003: 20). Two officials closely associated with architectural projects, Imhotep (reign of Djoser) and Amenhotep son of Hapu (reign of Amenhotep III), were venerated long after their deaths on account of their 'wisdom' (Wildung 1977).

Examples of drawings and models used in design survive along with further drawings and texts associated with the process of construction which display a pragmatic approach to creating a building and managing the project (Badawy 1948; Rossi 2004: 92–147). However, constructed monuments also show interest among designers in spatial ordering and use of forms, aesthetic impact and the symbolic associations of form and space.

Choosing a site: architectural planning

Egyptian designers chose sites with great care: buildings were situated with clear consideration for natural features of the landscape, such as the river or cliffs, and the existing built environment. Evidence for stellar orientation of Old Kingdom pyramids (Žába 1953) and solar orientation of some New Kingdom temples such as Karnak (Leitz 1989: 70–9) suggests that structures might also relate to broader cosmic concerns. Proximity to the projects of illustrious ancestors was also an important consideration which in some cases led to the construction of buildings on very awkward sites, good examples being the temples of Hatshepsut and Thutmose III at Deir el-Bahri which involved substantial modification of the adjacent cliff (Figure 26.8). Only at a few sites, such as Thebes and Amarna, do we see clear evidence of large-scale planning involving the construction of a number of separate but related structures, but it is likely that this is the result of the poor state of preservation of many city sites. Where city-wide planning can be identified, the emphasis seems to have been on the creation of processional routes linking a number of structures related through ceremonial use. At Thebes under Hatshepsut, building work was undertaken at a number of sites including Karnak, Luxor, Deir el-Bahri and Medinet Habu and houses were razed to construct processional routes between these structures (Roth 2005; Kemp 2005 [1989b]: 264–7). Hatshepsut also constructed way stations along the processional routes where the sacred boat-shrine of the god Amun-Ra could rest as it was carried around the city on the shoulders of priests. At Amarna, royal buildings again seem to be laid out in relation to processional routes such as the royal road (Kemp 2005 [1989b]: 284–8) but there is no evidence that any degree of control or planning was exercised over the construction of housing at the site. However, a 13th

Figure 26.8   The temples at Deir el-Bahri. To the left are the remains of the mortuary temple of Nebheptra Mentuhotep (II). Hatshepsut's mortuary temple is on the right and substantial modification of the rock-face above the temple is still clearly visible. The arrow marks the position of the rock terrace on which Thutmose III constructed a temple, wedged in between the two earlier structures (photo K. Spence).

Dynasty boundary stone found at Abydos shows that processional routes and sacred space could be protected by royal decree (Leahy 1989).

Spatial ordering

The organization of Egyptian architecture can seem strange to a modern Western audience steeped in the modernist view that each space is created for a particular activity. There certainly are spaces that have particular functions such as temple sanctuaries, burial chambers or storerooms (Arnold 1962), but many do not conform to such a model. Many spaces seem to have been intended primarily as transitional, that is, their main purpose was to lead into another space. Much of Egyptian architecture is concerned with the creation of symbolic distance between the focus of a building (such as a sanctuary or throne room) and the outside world, mediated through the individual entering and moving through the structure. This was achieved by isolating the focus of the building from the outside through the use of one or more enclosure walls and creating a route that passed through numerous gateways and a variety of spaces, often both open courts and roofed spaces. Liminal points were often emphasized through the use of gateways in the form of pylons, oversized doorways and kiosks (R. Wilkinson 2000: 54–60). The idea that a direct link could be created between this world and other spheres seems to have been prominent and is clear in the provision of false doors as points of contact with the afterlife or divine sphere in both tomb and temple architecture (Gundlach 1984). Within temple and tomb architecture, space was often laden with cosmographic associations created by the foundation ceremony and emphasized through decoration (R. Wilkinson 2000: 76–9; 1994: 60–81).

The focus on route is perhaps clearest in the architecture of pyramid complexes, where a pair of temples linked by a long causeway mediates the transition from the valley to the pyramid itself, and also in the elongated plans of major state temples such as those at Luxor and Karnak, which were often developed over several generations. However, it was also important in domestic architecture and is apparent in palaces and in the houses of the elite where distance was created between the head of household and the visitor.

Choice of forms

There is a strong tendency toward symmetry in the arrangement of elements in Egyptian architecture. Structures were carefully proportioned but this seems to have been achieved by eye or with simple ratios rather than through the use of complex mathematical formulae as is sometimes claimed (Rossi 2004: 147). Buildings display a distinctive architectural vocabulary often derived from rendering temporary forms in stone: the torus moulding and cavetto cornice are thought to derive from the structural frame and the palm frond roof of reed shelters, respectively, while the battered walls found in many buildings are similarly thought to derive from the form of early rammed earth structures. Although the unfamiliarity of these features can make buildings appear similar to the modern eye, this impression is superficial and masks real inventiveness in the formal composition of structures. Some features also had particular symbolic associations, for example temple gateways were often built in the form of a pylon which was considered a stylized representation of the horizon (Wilkinson 1994: 27–9, 36–7).

Aesthetic impact

There can be no doubt that kings intended their buildings to impress: Hatshepsut's obelisk inscriptions anticipate the awe and respect of future generations (Lichtheim 1976: 25–9). Building at a very large scale was probably the most effective way of ensuring that creations had impact (Wilkinson 1994: 38–42) and the largest pyramids of the Old Kingdom and temples of the New Kingdom onwards rank among the biggest architectural creations of the ancient world (Figure 26.9); colossal statuary and tall obelisks were prominent among building projects. There was also a competitive element involved: kings of the New Kingdom repeatedly stated that their own constructions were more impressive than those of their predecessors and, presumably, the construction of massive monuments rapidly came to be expected. The ability to mobilize and organize a large workforce was key to the erection of large structures with limited technology, and the organizational apparatus was developed early in

Figure 26.9 The colonnade hall at Luxor Temple showing the massive scale of some temple-building projects (photo K. Spence).

Egyptian history as is apparent from Djoser's pyramid, although it was only at times of strong centralized control that the resources were available for large-scale projects. However, size was not everything and some of the most beautiful monuments built by powerful kings are small: examples include Senusret I's white chapel and the Ptah temple of Thutmose III, both at Karnak.

Choice of materials was also important to a structure's aesthetic impact (Wilkinson 1994: 82–95): the intention that buildings should last eternally is frequently stated in Egyptian texts and seems to be an important factor in the decision to use stone for much monumental architecture. The use of expensive materials such as hard stone, metals and imported woods was sometimes specified by kings in their building inscriptions (Björkman 1971: 26–8). Hard stones were sought after because of their value in indicating status and command of resources, as they were hard to quarry and had to be transported long distances. Granite is also very strong and was much used for roofing pyramid burial chambers and constructing monolithic columns and obelisks. Additionally, stone was valued for symbolic connotations of colour and, in the case of hard stones, polished sheen: black granite and basalt were associated with fecundity; red stones were associated with transitional spaces, while white stones such as limestone or the translucent Egyptian alabaster were associated with light (Spence 1999). The presence of different materials within a construction also related to the cosmographic nature of the project (Aufrère 2001b) and samples of different types of material were sometimes placed in foundation deposits (Weinstein 1973: 421–2).

Mud-brick was widely used in the construction of domestic architecture and fortresses, but it was also the preferred material for constructing temple enclosure walls, maintaining symbolic associations with defence and protection derived from defensive structures. Temporary structures of reeds and matting remained in use throughout Egyptian history, the temporary nature apparently associating them with ritual purity, but it was also common to find reed architecture replicated in stone, borrowing the symbolic qualities of the temporary structure while rendering them permanent.

Monumental architecture was often richly decorated with texts and carved reliefs or paintings, adding to its impact. Some decoration was intended to embellish or complement the architectural form: this includes ceiling patterns, borders, dados and decorative friezes, and might involve working elements such as royal cartouches or heraldic emblems into friezes or bands around columns. Other decoration, usually on walls or flanking doorways, was representational. In the inner parts of temples, surfaces were usually divided up into registers and decorated with numerous scenes of the king performing rituals or offering before the gods, while in the outer parts of temples, larger scenes representing activities of the king, including smiting and battle scenes, are frequently found. Tomb decoration was often similarly divided into registers representing a variety of scenes associated with the offering cult and life of the deceased. Although we can refer to representational wall paintings and reliefs as 'decorative' in the context of architecture, and they had considerable aesthetic impact, it is also clear that these two-dimensional images were actually considered to be powerful and effective: the 'opening of the mouth' ritual was carried out on temple reliefs as well as on statues (Weinstein 1973: 424).

CONCLUSION: ON THE STATUS OF EGYPTIAN ARCHITECTURE

Although the material remains of Egyptian architecture represent over 3,000 years of human activity, the scale of the achievement is not diminished by the length of the time frame. No other ancient culture sustained such heavy investment in construction over long periods, raising questions as to why architecture features so strongly in the Egyptian record. The royal construction projects were possible as a result of social and political stability during periods of strong centralized control, a rich natural environment and a highly stratified society that provided both the manpower and the resources for projects as well as their focus (the king). Architecture was essential to expressing and maintaining relations within the social hierarchy through the demarcation and stratification of domestic space as well as the focus on impressive burial architecture and temples. For kings, there can be little doubt that architecture played an important political role, expressing very visibly the strength of Egypt and the power to command resources.

Beyond this, however, building provided the key to the king's relationship with the divine sphere which was fundamental to his effectiveness as a ruler. The architecture of royal tombs and mortuary complexes provided a means for the post-mortem transfiguration of the king and his subsequent association with the gods, while the creation or embellishment of temples provided a space within which the divine could become immanent and the king could interact with the gods. Through his creative act the king fulfilled his filial duty to the gods and sustained *maat* or 'right order' within the world, for the benefit of all Egypt. Ultimately, the architecture was more important than the kings who constructed it, as is clear from the fact that an active tradition of temple building continued into the Ptolemaic and Roman Periods when Egypt was ruled by foreign kings who rarely spoke Egyptian and, in the Roman Period, only rarely visited Egypt.

CHAPTER TWENTY-SEVEN

LITERATURE

——·◆·——

James P. Allen

Our view of ancient Egyptian culture is largely a product of its words. The modern understanding of ancient Egypt began with the recovery of its words, in Champollion's decipherment of the Rosetta Stone. Today, every university curriculum of Egyptology requires the study of at least one phase of the Egyptian language and its texts. Generations of Egyptologists have interpreted Egypt's material remains in light of its words; only in recent years has the opposite approach received equal attention.

The modern preoccupation with Egyptian texts is, in part, a reflection of ancient Egypt's own values. Few monuments or works of art were allowed to speak for themselves: most were enhanced with words, and many with texts that went beyond mere descriptive labels. Literary creations were prized more highly than material ones, as a Ramesside poem confirms:

> The learned writers since the time of the gods . . .
> their names have become fixed for eternity.
> . . .
> Tombs and tomb-estates were made for them but have dissolved,
> their personnel gone, their stela covered with dirt.
> Their tomb is forgotten but their name is pronounced from their scrolls,
> as fresh as when they were made.
>
> (Gardiner 1935d: vol. I, 38; vol. II, pl. 18)

Hieroglyphs, the medium of writing, were called *medu netjer* 'god's speech', the same term used to describe the means by which the world itself was created (Allen 1988: 45–6).

Despite the value that the Egyptians placed on writing, however, literature is largely a modern category imposed on the ancient texts. The Egyptian language had no word for 'literature'. The nearest approximation is the phrase *medet neferet*, which means something like 'fine speaking'.[1] This is often understood as the equivalent of the French *belles lettres*, but its exact meaning is uncertain. The adjective *nefer* covers a semantic range from the moral ('good') to the aesthetic ('beautiful', 'perfect') but can also mean 'fresh' or 'final' (Erman and Grapow 1926–50: vol. II, 253–62). The phrase *medet neferet* might, therefore, refer to compositions that are arbiters of morality, whose language is well-turned and eloquent, and whose ideas are both fresh and enduring – perhaps as good a definition of literature as any.

The ethical connotation is paramount in the composition known as the *Teachings of Ptahhotep*, which is entitled 'Beginning of the phrases of fine speaking that . . . Ptahhotep has said as a teaching of the ignorant to learn according to the standard of fine speaking, as something effective for the one who will hear, as something distressful for the one who is to transgress it' (Jéquier 1911: pl. 2). Ptahhotep's 'phrases of fine speaking' are meant to edify: his 'teaching' deals with ethical, moral and social behaviour. 'Fine speaking', therefore, is the verbal counterpart of the Egyptian concept of *maat*, the standard of ideal behaviour. Ptahhotep's title identifies 'fine speaking' as a 'standard' of edification, using the term *tep-heseb* (literally, 'head of counting'), which denotes a means of reckoning and is applied mostly to quantifiable referents, such as mathematical and chemical formulae, weighing and architecture (Erman and Grapow 1926–50: vol. V, 291). Conversely, the *Tale of the Eloquent Peasant* describes *maat* as 'the standard (*tep-heseb*) of hieroglyphs (*medu-netjer*)' (Parkinson 1991b: 44). Ptahhotep does go on to say that 'fine speaking is more hidden than malachite, yet it is found with maidservants at the grinding stones' (Maxim 1: Jéquier 1911: pl. 2). Although this is normally understood as a reference to eloquence rather than ethical norms, it may actually mean that even the speech of servants can be edifying: the *Tale of the Eloquent Peasant* also refers to 'the hiddenness of *maat*' (Parkinson 1991b: 31).

Edification thus seems to be the basic connotation of 'fine speaking'. In so far as that phrase defines what the Egyptians themselves would have considered literary texts, Egyptian literature consists primarily of compositions such as the two mentioned in the preceding paragraph. These belong to a genre often called 'wisdom literature' and which the Egyptians themselves termed *sebayt* 'teachings'. It is, perhaps, no accident that all the ancient authors whose names have survived are associated solely with such compositions.[2]

The modern understanding of what constitutes Egyptian literature is broader but somewhat debated. Under the rubric of 'ancient Egyptian literature', anthologies of translations have included examples from nearly every textual genre except accounts, legal texts, and reference works such as onomastica and medical or mathematical papyri (e.g. Lichtheim 1975, 1976, 1980a; Simpson 2003). This is, in part, a reflection of the fact that many of the textual features found in the teachings also appear in other genres. These include devices such as clause and sentence structure, metre, alliteration and metaphor, and an elegance of expression that bespeaks considered composition – what has been called 'poetical fashioning or the reflection thereof' (Brunner 1986: xi).

The primary organizational feature of the teachings is the structure known as *parallelismus membrorum*, found also in biblical texts and other ancient Near Eastern literature. In this device, the concept expressed in one clause or sentence is repeated, elaborated or contrasted in the following clause or sentence, a pattern in Egyptian texts that has been termed 'thought couplets' (Foster 1977):

> You should not make plans among people:
> the god will punish in kind.

For a man says 'I will live from it':
then he lacks bread because of the statement.
For a man says: 'I will be powerful':
then he says: 'My fame is my own trap'.
For a man says he will plunder another:
then he ends up giving to one he knows not.
No plan of people has ever come about:
what comes about is the god's commands.
Think only of living in peace:
what they give comes of its own accord.
>   (*Ptahhotep* Maxim 6: Jéquier 1911: pl. 3)

The same feature appears in other kinds of Egyptian texts, such as narratives and the theological compositions in praise of various gods, known as hymns (Foster 1975, 1993; Assmann 1999b), and even in biographical inscriptions:

I am wealthy, well-off with fine things:
there is nothing I am missing in all my things.
I am an owner of cattle, with many goats;
an owner of donkeys, with many sheep.
I am rich in grain, fine in clothing:
there is nothing missing from all my wealth.
>   (Stela of Mentuwoser: Sethe 1928: 79)

It has also been claimed that literary texts, both teachings and other genres, display a regular verse-metre of two to three units of stress per line, based on syntactic structure (Fecht 1963, 1964–5). In Ptahhotep's Maxim 6, cited above, for example, the lines of the first couplet each contain two metric units; those of the second, three units; and the remainder alternate between two units in the first line and three in the second. Similarly, the lines of Mentuwoser's text each have two stress units except for the penultimate, which has four. The regularity of this feature, however, and its literary significance, have been questioned (Lichtheim 1971–2).

While literary texts do display thought couplets and metre, neither feature is, itself, indicative of literature as opposed to other kinds of Egyptian texts. Both devices can be found even in more prosaic compositions, such as bureaucratic letters:

This is a communication | to the Lord
about having attention paid | to your royal servant | Wadjhau
by letting him (learn to) write | without letting him escape,
in accordance with everything good | that the Lord does, | healthy | and alive,
and having attention paid | to your house,
in accordance with everything good | that the Lord does, | healthy | and alive,
because it is the Lord | that does all good
with respect | to yours truly.[3]
>   (Griffith 1898: vol. II, pl. 35)

Here, the couplet displays merely the organizational processes of Egyptian thought, while the pattern of two to four units of stress per line seems to reflect the rhythms of the Egyptian language as a whole rather than the conscious use of a literary artifice.

Such compositions point up the difficulty of identifying formal criteria that can be used to distinguish a corpus of Egyptian literature among the mass of surviving texts. In the face of this quandary, one response has been to reject genres as modern impositions on ancient compositions (see especially Altenmüller *et al.* 1970). Literature then becomes a subjective category, its texts chosen either from a consensus that they belong to the realm of literature or from a sense that they are, if not part of that realm, at least 'literary' in style (e.g. Posener 1951, 1952). This view informs, *inter alia*, the anthologies cited above, in which the broadest possible selection of texts is included in order to represent fairly the range of 'poetical fashioning' in Egyptian compositions.

More recently, however, Egyptology has used modern literary theory to narrow the definition of ancient Egyptian literature (e.g. Kaplony 1977; Gumbrecht 1996; Loprieno 1996a; Assmann 1996, 1999a; Parkinson 2002: 22–32; Quirke 2004c: 24–8). Concepts such as fictionality and intertextuality have been brought to bear in an attempt to distinguish literature from other genres, such as funerary texts, which can have some of the same formal features. One of the earliest movements in this direction argued for a practical distinction between compositions designed for a specific purpose, such as funerary texts and hymns, and those with no such evident functional context, which can be considered literature in the narrow sense of the term (Assmann 1974). This is, in part, an argument from silence: for texts such as the teachings, neither the reason for their creation nor their intended audience is known (see Parkinson 2002: 75–81).[4] The texts themselves, however, usually supply a prologue that places them in a functional setting – for example, 'Beginning of the teaching that a man of Sile named Duauf's son Khety made for his son, named Pepy, as he was going upstream to the capital to put him in the school of writing among the foremost officials' children of the capital' (Helck 1970: vol. I, 12–16). This feature argues that lack of a functional context is no accident: 'contextual independence is the hallmark of literature in ancient Egypt' (Assmann 1999a: 4).

The existence of numerous copies of some of these texts indicates that they were used didactically, but it does not necessarily follow that they were created with that purpose in mind, as has been suggested (Assmann 1996, 1999a). It is equally possible that at least some of them were written, initially and primarily, merely for the purpose of personal expression. This rationale is explicit in the *Sayings of Khakheperra-seneb*:

> Would that I had unknown phrases, unused verses,
> as new speech not bypast, free of repetition,
> no verse of oral transmission that those before have said,
> that I might strain my belly of what is in it,
> in the relief that every speaker experiences.
>
> . . .
>
> Would that I knew, and others knew not, of what has not been repeated,
> that I might speak it and my heart might answer me,
> that I might enlighten it about my suffering,
> cast off to it the load that is on my back, the phrases of my annoyance,
> express to it my suffering because of it,
> and utter a sigh of relief from my anguish.
>
> (Gardiner 1909: pl. 17)

In such cases, the texts approach the modern experience of poetry: musings of the author committed to writing in diction that is consciously crafted. Like some modern poems – such as those of Emily Dickinson – they need not even have been written for contemporary or posthumous circulation, though they clearly became treasured once known to others.

This appreciation of literature as a genre applies primarily to texts from the classical age of Egyptian literature, the Middle Kingdom, and it encompasses not only the teachings but also related musings and prophecies, as well as stories and songs (see Parkinson 1991a: 105–22; 2002: 293–321). None of these texts is attested in documents older than the early Middle Kingdom. A number of them are set in, or attributed to authors from, the Old Kingdom or First Intermediate Period: 3rd to 4th Dynasty (the *Teaching for Kagemni*), 4th Dynasty (the *Teaching of Hordjedef*, the *Prophecy of Neferti*, the stories of Papyrus Westcar), 5th Dynasty (the *Teaching of Ptahhotep*), 6th Dynasty (the *Story of King Neferkara*, possibly also the *Story of Hay*), and 9th/10th Dynasty (the *Teaching for Merikara*, the *Story of the Eloquent Peasant*). The language in which they were composed, however, is that of the early Middle Kingdom or later; pseudo-historical attributions are an established conceit in numerous Egyptian texts.[5] As defined here and in most recent studies, therefore, Egyptian literature as a distinct genre is a relatively late phenomenon of ancient Egyptian civilization.[6]

The core of this corpus, both in the ancient sense and by modern consensus, consists of the compositions known as *sebayt* 'teachings' (Brunner 1988; Vernus 2001). Along with a few fragmentary texts, eight major teachings have survived from the Middle Kingdom: those of Hordjedef, Ptahhotep, Amenemhat I, Khety, and a Man for His Son; those for Kagemni and King Merikara; and the *Loyalist Teaching* (see Parkinson 2002: 310–19).[7] Most of these early compositions are concerned with fostering *maat* through proper behaviour, and their counsel is presented as that of a father to his son. They deal with the proper conduct of a man of station, or a king, and counsel, in particular, against rash behaviour, greed and the misuse of authority. Except for Khety and the anonymous speaker of the *Teaching of a Man for His Son*, neither of whom is titled, the father is stated to be either royal or a high official. Their advice is occasionally general: 'If you want your conduct to be good, take yourself away from all that is evil' (*Ptahhotep*: Jéquier 1911: pls 9–10); 'Do *maat* while you remain on earth' (*Merikara*: Quack 1992: 172). More often, however, it has reference to specific ethical or social situations involving a choice between two kinds of behaviour, rash and ill-considered versus calm and temperate. The paradigm in these texts is often that of the calm, 'still' man as contrasted with the garrulous, hot-tempered one:

> Speech is something like fire:
> the unconsidered response is an incendiary;
> but it is flourishing at the mouth of the still man,
> making coolness out of garrulousness.
> Calmness is effective, patience is good;
> respond to the knowledgeable, depart from the ignorant.
> 		(*Teaching of a Man for His Son*: Helck 1984: 62–3)

Of the two instructions attributed to kings, that for Merikara concerns the conduct of a just ruler, while the *Teaching of Amenemhat* warns pessimistically against placing too much trust in courtiers – the reflection of an assassination attempt on Amenemhat, which is described in the text. The teaching ascribed to Khety, also known as the *Satire of the Trades*, is the first of a sub-genre extolling the scribal profession as a means of social advancement; Khety's lack of titles is a deliberate conceit underlining the humble station of the father and son.[8] The 'Loyalist' Teaching advocates submission to the king as a means of 'living properly and conducting a lifetime in peace', a theme that also appears in the *Teaching of a Man for His Son* (Posener 1976: 17, 57; Helck 1984: 52–7).

Closely related to the teachings are some ten further works usually called discourses after the Egyptian words *medet* 'speech' or *medut* 'words' that appear in the titles of some of them (Parkinson 2002: 303–10). These include two prophecies, of Neferti and Ipuwer (the latter also known as the *Admonitions*); the discourses of Sisobek, Reniseneb and the Fowler (all entitled *medet* 'speech'); and the *Words (medut) of Khakheperra-seneb* and the *Dialogue of a Man and His Ba*. Although they are not called 'teachings', they probably belong in the same genre: the Egyptians included three of their authors in the ranks of those of the teachings (see note 2), the *Prophecy of Neferti* is a response to the king's request for *medet neferet* 'fine speaking' (Helck 1992: 9 and 13), and the *Dialogue of a Man and His Ba* contains the words 'So, come and I will teach you' in its fragmentary beginning (Parkinson 2003: 128, 130–1). To these should probably also be added the composition known as the *Eloquent Peasant*, which is a series of nine disquisitions on the nature of *maat* set in the frame of a story of injustice (Parkinson 1991b); the *Discourse of Sisobek* seems also to have had a narrative component, and, together with the *Discourse of the Fowler*, is similar in form and tone to the *Eloquent Peasant* (Parkinson 2002: 304–7).

Most of these works are different in character both from the teachings and from one another. The two prophecies, the discourses of *Sisobek* and *the Fowler*, and the *Tale of the Eloquent Peasant* all invert the frame of the teachings in casting their addresses as delivered from lowly speakers to their superiors, reflecting the adage of Ptahhotep, cited above, that 'fine speaking . . . is found with maidservants at the grinding stones'. In the *Words of Khakheperra-seneb* and the *Dialogue of a Man and His Ba*, the addressee is the speaker himself – 'my heart' in the former and 'my *ba*' in the latter. Both compositions are meditations on the difficulties of life and how to deal with them: Khakheperra-seneb seeks relief through novel 'phrases' and 'verses', which reflects the value that the Egyptians placed on their literature; the man speaking to his *ba* is attracted by death as a solution to life's sufferings, but is troubled by the uncertainties of the afterlife in 'the West'. The surviving manuscript of the *Words of Khakheperra-seneb* contains no ultimate resolution of the author's quandary; that of the *Dialogue of a Man and His Ba* ends with the practical recommendation to 'cling to life' and 'desire that you reach the West' after death (Sethe 1928: 46).

The category of Egyptian literature that resonates most with modern readers is that of tales. Apart from the *Eloquent Peasant*, these include three major works – the stories of the *Shipwrecked Sailor*, *Sinuhe* and Papyrus Westcar – and some ten or more incompletely preserved. All are told in the third person except for *Sinuhe*, which is cast in the form of a first-person autobiography such as those inscribed in elite tombs. Their themes are varied, ranging from tales of the gods (*Horus and Seth*) and the king (*Nemay*, *Ghost of Snefer*, *King Pepy and the General*) to those involving the relationship between people and the gods (*Shipwrecked Sailor*, *Herdsman*, Cairo Myth), the king

(Papyrus Lythgoe, *Sinuhe*, *House of Life*, Papyrus Westcar) and one another (*Hay*). Their styles vary as well, from highly literary, with the metre and couplets of works such as the teachings, to more prosaic narratives comparable to the 'folk tales' of many cultures.

Tales composed in the first style include the story of Sinuhe, which has been characterized as poetry (Foster 1993; Parkinson 2002), and those of the Shipwrecked Sailor, the Herdsman and the House of Life. Like the teachings and discourses, they can be regarded as the personal expression of their authors and, therefore, as literature in the same sense, regardless of whatever other purpose might have underlain their creation. They lie at one end of a literary spectrum, with the teachings at the other. The teachings convey their moral message in an openly didactic style. The discourses convey a similar message less directly, through the authors' reflections on experiences and the state of the world. The authors of the tales express similar reflections even less directly, through the eyes and thoughts of their characters. Though cast as adventures, the tales are not merely entertainment but expressions of the values of Egyptian society, such as perseverance in the face of adversity (the *Shipwrecked Sailor*) and faith in the strength and wisdom of the king (*Sinuhe*).

The function of the prose narratives in the canon of Egyptian literature is less clear, partly because they are less well preserved than their more literary relatives. The fragmentary tale of *Horus and Seth*, which dates to the early Middle Kingdom, is similar in style and content to myths that form part of the genre of contemporary funerary texts. The next clear examples of the prose style all date to the late Middle Kingdom and the Second Intermediate Period, including the tales of Papyrus Lythgoe, *Hay*, *King Pepy and the General*, the *Ghost of Snefer*, Papyrus Westcar and the Cairo Myth. Most of these reflect a tradition that probably existed alongside the more highly literary style, perhaps partly oral (see Parkinson 2002: 138–46). To the extent that they express moral values, they do so through the events that befall their characters, or in the relationship of their characters to one another, rather than through a single protagonist who serves as a vehicle for the author's own thoughts and experiences.

The classical corpus of literature also includes a few miscellaneous works that fall outside the genres of the teachings, discourses and tales. These include the compositions known as the *Sporting King* and the *Pleasures of Fishing and Fowling*, a royal eulogy, and the *Harper's Song*. All employ the metre and couplets of other literary works, although the first three are set within a narrative framework. Those three are preserved only in fragments (Parkinson 2002: 311–12) dating to the Second Intermediate Period and the New Kingdom. The *Harper's Song* also survives in two later copies, from a late 18th Dynasty tomb and a Ramesside papyrus (Müller 1899: pls 12–16; Boeser 1911–13: vol. I, pl. 6). Its prologue identifies it as 'the song that is in the tomb-enclosure of (King) Intef'. If not merely pseudo-historical, this attribution could refer either to one of the three or four Theban rulers of the 11th Dynasty, another of the 13th Dynasty or three more from the 17th Dynasty. The song's classical grammar favours one of the Middle Kingdom rulers – perhaps Intef II, who is credited with two poetic prayers on a contemporary stela (Lichtheim 1975: 94–6).

The prose narratives of the late Middle Kingdom and the Second Intermediate Period mark both the end of the classical period of ancient Egyptian literature and the beginning of its later tradition. Works from the later tradition are often included in anthologies of Egyptian literature in translation, but they have been less intensively studied than their earlier counterparts as a literary corpus *in toto*. After the last classical compositions there seems to have been a hiatus of some 200 years or more – essentially corresponding to the 18th Dynasty – before new works were added to the corpus, in the literary renaissance of the Ramesside Period (Baines 1996). Their language varies from that of the earlier literature to the contemporary idiom known as Late Egyptian, and their style ranges from classical metre and couplets to colloquial prose.

Five major teachings from the later tradition are preserved – those of Ani, Papyrus Chester Beatty IV, Amennakht, Hori and Amenemope – as well as the work known as the *Prohibitions*. All exhibit the same sort of metre and arrangement into couplets as their classical ancestors. Unlike the latter, most are called not merely *sebayt* 'teaching', but *sebayt metret*, meaning something like 'testimonial teaching', stressing the fact that they represent not merely prescriptions but also a summation of the author's practical experience in living a moral life (Vernus 2001: 12–13; Quack 2005: 94).[9] The *Teaching of Ani* is a Ramesside counterpart of the *Teaching of Ptahhotep*, with the same sort of narrative epilogue and division into thematic sections; this arrangement is further codified in the *Teaching of Amenemope*, which is divided into 30 'chapters'.[10] The *Prohibitions*, by contrast, consists of a loose collection of couplets, each beginning 'you should not' and occupying a single line in the sole surviving manuscript (Černý and Gardiner 1957: pl. 1); in this arrangement the work reflects the earlier maxims of Papyrus Ramesseum II, from the classical period (Barns 1956: pls 7–9).

The looser genre of discourses has no counterpart in the later tradition. That of the tales, however, is well represented, with some ten major compositions. These deal with some of the same themes as their classical ancestors: the doings of the gods (*Truth and Falsehood*, *Horus and Seth*, *Astarte and the Sea*) and the king (*Apophis and Seqenenra*) as well as the experiences of greater and lesser mortals (tales of the *Doomed Prince*, the *Capture of Joppa*, *Khonsuemhab and the Ghost*, the *Two Brothers*, *Wenamun* and a *Tale of Woe*). All use the earlier prose style of Papyrus Westcar and its contemporaries rather than the high literary structure of *Sinuhe*. Their language ranges from a later form of classical Middle Egyptian, known as 'traditional Egyptian' (e.g. the *Doomed Prince*), to that of the contemporary colloquial idiom (*Wenamun*).

To the genre of songs the later tradition adds a number of new Harper's Songs (Lichtheim 1945) and several cycles of love poems (Mathieu 1996). The former are composed in the style of classical literature, like their Middle Kingdom ancestor, but in 'traditional Egyptian' rather than pure Middle Egyptian. The latter also employ 'traditional Egyptian'; though arranged in couplets, they normally use a new metrical structure, with four units of stress in the first line and three in the second (Mathieu 1996: 189–215).

With the exception of the Harper's Songs, which date to the late 18th Dynasty, all of these works from the later tradition of Egyptian literature belong to the literary renaissance of the 19th to 20th Dynasties. Following the end of this era, Egyptian literature seems to have undergone a further hiatus of some 400 years before entering its final stage, in the Saite and Ptolemaic Periods.[11] The literature of this last tradition is mostly composed in the contemporary language known as Demotic. It reprises all of the earlier genres, though often in new styles and formats.

The earliest work of this final tradition, the Brooklyn Teaching, is written in hieratic rather than Demotic, though its language is closer to that of Demotic than to Late Egyptian (Jasnow 1992). Arranged for the most part in couplets, it deals with the relationship between master and servant. Reflecting their Ramesside ancestors, Demotic teachings proper are called either *sebayt* 'teaching' or *metret* 'testimonial' (Quack 2005: 94). They are represented primarily by two texts, the *Teaching of Ankh-Sheshonqi* and Papyrus Insinger (Lichtheim 1983; Quack 2005: 94–127). These follow the style of the classical text of Papyrus Ramesseum II and the Ramesside *Prohibitions*, with individual maxims arranged in single lines of text. The earlier of the two is the *Teaching of Ankh-Sheshonqi*, dating perhaps to the fourth century BC. It is a collection of maxims preceded by a narrative describing how the author, detained for a perceived offensive against the king, wrote them 'on the sherds of the jars containing mixed wine, which they would bring in to him while he was imprisoned'. The medium is a conceit reflecting the literary structure of the maxims, which are arranged both singly and in couplets or groups of three or more lines. The later text of Papyrus Insinger displays the same compositional style, but with its maxims grouped into 25 'teachings' of varying lengths.

Related to the category of teachings are a number of Demotic prophecies that reflect the classical genre of discourses (Quack 2005: 148–61). The most significant of these is the *Prophecy of the Lamb*. Similar in theme to the earlier *Prophecy of Neferti*, it predicts upheavals and the eventual conquest of Egypt by foreign forces before order is restored under a new 'founder'; the composition is reflected in Manetho's statement that 'a lamb spoke' in the reign of the 24th Dynasty king Bakenrenef (Ritner in Simpson 2003: 445–9).

Demotic secular poetry is represented primarily by the work known as the *Degenerate Harper* (Thissen 1992; Smith 2000; Quack 2005: 81–93). Composed largely in couplets, with a perceptible metre (Smith 2000: 1983), it parodies the earlier Harper's Songs with an invective against the musician himself, who is described as a glutton 'without control'.

Tales are by far the best represented (and published) genre of Demotic literature (Quack 2005: 16–80, 128–47). They are all composed in prose style and the colloquial language, and reflect some of the themes of earlier tales: primarily stories of the gods (the *Myth of the Sun's Eye* and the *Tale of the Swallow and the Sea*, the latter recalling the Ramesside tale of *Astarte and the Sea*) and royal figures (the *Tale of Amasis and the Skipper*, the Petubastis Cycle and the *Adventures of Setna Khaemwaset*). Of these, the longest and best preserved are the Setna tales, two stories recounting the fabulous adventures of Prince Khaemwaset, son of Ramesses II and a mythical figure in the Ptolemaic Period.

The history of Egyptian literature as a whole shows a process of constant reinvention within the four main genres that appear in the earliest texts: teachings, discourses, tales, and songs or poetry. Within these genres the most significant developments are the loss of the high literary tale composed in metred couplets after the Middle Kingdom, and the introduction of a new and consistent metre in the love songs of the New Kingdom.

All the works of Egyptian literature are characterized by a single trait: their lack of a functional context. Unlike their literary relatives in the realm of funerary literature, hymns and monumental inscriptions, they were evidently composed only for the purpose of expressing the thoughts of their authors.[12] Their audience – in so far as one was intended – was undoubtedly the same class of literate scribes and officials that produced them (for the Middle Kingdom, see Parkinson 1996). Their reception within that universe is reflected, in part, by their subsequent appearance as texts used for the education of scribes. This phenomenon is essentially limited to the classical texts, which appear in numerous copies from the New Kingdom to the Late Period; a number of the early compositions are known only from such copies.[13] Transmission was greatest for the teachings: with the exception of the *Teaching for Kagemni*, these works are attested in over 200 later copies.[14] Copies of works from other genres are also preserved, though more selectively and in lesser quantities.[15]

The educational function of these texts is easiest to appreciate in the case of the teachings, which not only offer models for writing and composition but also convey the moral values of Egyptian society (see Assmann 1999a: 8–9). The didactic use of the *Tale of Sinuhe* and the *Prophecy of Neferti* are less understandable; both were perhaps seen as prime examples of their respective genres.[16] Apart from education, however, it is also probable that some works owe their preservation to an appreciation of their value as literature. Texts such as the tales of *King Pepy and the General* and the *Ghost of Snefer*, the *Sporting King* and the *Pleasures of Fishing and Fowling* survive not only in schoolboys' copies but also on papyri from the New Kingdom to the Late Period (Parkinson 2002: 296, 301, 311–12), and works of Demotic literature are preserved primarily on manuscripts from libraries or private collections (Quack 2005: 13). Quotations from some of the classical works occur in compositions of the Ramesside Period (e.g. Vernus 2001: 374–6) and later (Jasnow 1999; Quack 2005: 173). These are, perhaps, the most eloquent witness to the esteem in which the ancient Egyptians held their literature and its authors:

> Those learned men who foretold what was to come,
> what came from their mouths has come about,
> found in verses,
> and written in their scrolls.
> The children of others have been given to them
> as heirs like their own children.
> . . .
> Once departed, their names would have been forgotten,
> but writing is what makes them remembered.
> (Gardiner 1935d: vol. I, 38; vol. II, pl. 19)

NOTES

1 The verbal noun *medet* 'speaking', equivalent to the infinitive of the verb *medwi* 'speak', seems to have referred originally to the act of speaking as opposed to its content *medu* 'speech' – the latter reflected, *inter alia*, in the term *djed medu* 'recitation' (literally, 'the saying of speech'), originally construed only with *medu*, not *medet*. See Erman and Grapow 1926–50: vol. II, 179–82.

2 The Ramesside poem cited above praises eight 'learned writers'. Of these, five are named within teachings attributed to them (Hordjedef, Neferti, Khety, Khakheperra-seneb and Ptahhotep); the remaining three (Imhotep, Ptahemdjehuti and Kaires) may be the putative authors of similar compositions, either anonymous or lost. A Ramesside relief (Simpson 2003: xviii–xix, fig. 6) that names 34 revered men includes at least three of the same authors (Imhotep, Kaires and Khakheperra-seneb) along with two more named in other teachings (Ipuwer and Amenemope). See Derchain 1996; Quirke 2004c: 33–6.

3 Units of stress are indicated by 'ı' in the translation. The metre ignores the phrase *ankh(u) (we)dja(u) s(enebu)* 'may he be alive, sound, and healthy', which is automatically appended to the indirect term of address *neb* 'lord' in such texts.

4 The prologue to the *Prophecy of Neferti* sets this teaching in the context of a king who wants to be 'diverted', and the stories of Papyrus Westcar are presented as told to a king by his sons (Blackman 1988; Helck 1992: 9). In both cases, however, the setting is probably an ironic conceit, designed to stress the contrast between 'entertainment' and elucidation: in the *Prophecy of Neferti*, the king who wants to be 'diverted' (Sneferu) is warned, instead, of forthcoming perils, while the Westcar stories contain both criticism of the king (Khufu) and a prediction of future kings, divinely sanctioned and not allied with Khufu's own family. The literary status of both these texts is discussed below.

5 For example, the rubrics to Spells 64 and 148 of the New Kingdom *Book of the Dead* both claim that 'This spell was found in Hermopolis . . . in the time of the Dual King Menkaura, justified, by the king's son Hordjedef', naming a king and prince of the 4th Dynasty (Naville 1886: vol. I, pl. 167; Budge 1910: vol. I, 192–3). See Vernus 2001: 17. This conceit might also underlie the inclusion of Imhotep among the authors noted in n. 2, above: the name is probably that of the 3rd Dynasty official of King Djoser revered as patron of wisdom in the Ramesside Period and later (see Parkinson 2002: 320).

6 The reasons for this phenomenon are discussed in a separate study (Allen, in preparation).

7 All of these are entitled *sebayt* 'teaching' except for the teachings for Merikara, whose title is plausibly restored as such (Helck 1977: 3), and Kagemni, whose beginning is lost.

8 Their lack of social status is also implied in the fact that Khety's son is to be enrolled 'amongst the children of officials and the foremost of the capital' (Helck 1970: vol. I, 12–16; see Brunner 1944: 9–10).

9 The *Teaching of Amenemope* is entitled 'Beginning of the instruction in (or 'from') life, the testimonial of soundness', contrasting the terms *sebayt* and *meteru* (Lange 1925: 24; Vernus 2001: 13).

10 The arrangement and some of the themes and wording of the latter work are reflected in the biblical Book of Proverbs: see Williams 1961; Vernus 2001: 306–8.

11 This gap might reflect the lack of published material from this period rather than an actual hiatus in creative composition: see Jasnow 1992: 40–1.

12 Although the intended function of the works known as hymns is assumed to have been ceremonies of worship, it is possible that some of them were composed, at least initially, to record their authors' thinking about the nature of reality and the human experience – the ancient Egyptian counterpart of Greek philosophy or medieval theology. Works from the latter spheres, however, are not generally considered as literature in the strict sense.

13 The latter include the teaching for Merikara and the teachings of Hordjedef, Amenemhat, Khety and a Man for His Son; the prophecies of Neferti and Ipuwer and the *Words of Khakheperra-seneb*; the tales of *King Pepy and the General* and the *Ghost of Snefer*; and the *Sporting King*, the *Pleasures of Fishing and Fowling* and the *Harper's Song*.

14 The number of copies for the various works are as follows: *Ptahhotep* (1), *Loyalist* (1), *Merikara* (9), *Hordjedef* (19), *Man for His Son* (50), *Amenemhat* (68), *Khety* (108). The didactic *Tale of the Eloquent Peasant* is preserved in four manuscripts from the Middle Kingdom.

15 These include the tales of Sinuhe (21 later copies) and *King Pepy and the General* (3); the prophecies of Neferti (22) and Ipuwer (1), and the *Words of Khakheperra-seneb* (1); the *Sporting King* and the *Pleasures of Fishing and Fowling* (1 each), and the *Harper's Song* (2). The *Tale of Sinuhe* is also attested in five Middle Kingdom manuscripts.

16 Some evidence for this view is provided by the text of the *Hymn to the Inundation*, preserved in 24 copies of the New Kingdom and Ramesside Period (Helck 1972b); and in the epistolary work known as *Kemit*, which survives in hundreds of copies from the Middle Kingdom and later (Parkinson 2002: 322–5). These can be seen as model texts to educate scribes in religious texts and official correspondence.

PART VII

INTERACTIONS

———•◆•———

CHAPTER TWENTY-EIGHT

EGYPT AND NUBIA

———•✦•———

Timothy Kendall

The Nile Valley south of ancient Egypt's traditional southern border at Aswan is known as Nubia.[1] The Greeks and Romans called it *Aithiopia* ('Land of Burnt Faces'), and throughout much of their history the ancient Egyptians called it variously *Ta-Seti* ('the Bow Land') or *Kush*. In recent decades, as archaeologists have more intensively explored this 'Middle Nile' region and its borderlands, they have enlarged the definition of Nubia to include all of modern Egypt south of the First Cataract and all of the modern Sudan north of the equatorial provinces, including the adjacent Sahara and eastern deserts to the Red Sea.

If an unbroken Nile historically unified Egypt, the river's meanders and cataracts tended to disunite Nubia. Archaeologists thus speak of three distinct Nubian geographic/culture zones: Lower Nubia, which extends from Aswan to the Second Cataract (the Sudanese border) and which, since 1968, has been submerged by the waters of Lake Nasser; Upper Nubia, which begins at the Second Cataract and extends upstream to the Fourth Cataract; and Southern Nubia, which extends from the headwaters of the Fourth Cataract to an as yet undefined distance beyond Khartoum (O'Connor 1993: x–xi).[2] The total river length is at least 2,000 kilometres.

Archaeological exploration of Nubia has lagged far behind that of Egypt due to its remoteness. Despite famous nineteenth-century surveys of the region's visible monuments, broad archaeological interest in Nubia was sparked in the twentieth century primarily as a response to the raising of dams at the First Cataract. When construction of the Aswan High Dam threatened Lower Nubia with permanent submersion in the early 1960s, a massive international effort was organized to record and rescue its archaeological heritage. This campaign not only produced quantities of data highlighting the region's importance as an ancient cultural sphere distinct from Egypt, it also inspired many scholars to pursue 'Nubiology' for its own sake and, from the 1970s, to pursue research into the Sudan, then still little explored archaeologically. After 35 years, their efforts have established that Lower Nubia, far from being central to Nubian history, was mainly a buffer zone between two major centres of ancient civilization, namely Egypt and the northern Sudan.

Almost annually, new archaeological finds are made in the Sudan that break down or alter long-held scholarly assumptions and force major reconsideration of the interrelationship between Egypt and its southern neighbour. Nubian history, at the moment, is a very dynamic field, and new, strikingly different treatments of the subject are being written all the time, based on their authors' own personal perspectives and/or field experience (e.g. Török 1997, 2002; Morkot 2000; Smith 2003; Edwards 2004; Redford 2004b). The text offered below is yet another version. It differs from those already published by adding data drawn from the writer's own recent work at Gebel Barkal (ancient Napata). This material, not yet fully published, is included because it provides details essential to understanding the eventual Egyptian–Nubian political/cultural symbiosis.

Between the eighth and fourth millennia BC, the climate of the Nile Valley was wetter than at present, with summer rains falling longer and farther to the north. These conditions rendered the deserts of Upper Egypt and Nubia seasonally habitable and turned wide areas into game-rich savannah. As cattle were introduced and domesticated, Mesolithic subsistence patterns of hunting, gathering and fishing were gradually subordinated to herding, which offered a more reliable food supply but required mobility in pursuit of pasture. Like the present Nilotic pastoralists of the southern Sudan, the Neolithic peoples of Upper Egypt and Nubia probably did not normally kill their animals for meat but raised them for milk and drawn blood. The herds, thus, became a 'walking larder'. The people supplemented their milk/blood diet with meat from wild game and cereals gathered wild or cultivated in small plots. As the herds multiplied, they provided food for ever larger groups and doubtless elevated in rank those with the greatest wealth in animals, a process leading to social stratification and power politics. The abundance in the deserts of rock drawings of cattle, both in Egypt and the Sudan, suggests the wide range of these ancient herders. Their dependency on cattle, which was augmented by sheep and goats, led over time to religious beliefs in which bulls and rams played important cultic roles.

In the northern Sudan, recent surveys in the deserts – along extinct Nile tributaries such as the Wadi Howar, the Wadi Muqaddam and the Wadi el-Khowi – have revealed hundreds of Neolithic sites and an ancient ecological landscape vastly different from today's (Fuller and Smith 2004; Keding 2004; Welsby and Anderson 2004: 42–8, 53–60). At present the most systematically surveyed and excavated sites are those bordering the Wadi el-Khowi, an ancient Nile channel system east of Kerma that, between about 7000 and 3000 BC, supported numerous pastoral communities. As the Nile migrated westward, many habitation sites and cemeteries on its east bank were preserved. One of the earliest is el-Barga, c.7000–5500 BC, where people were already raising and venerating cattle and using finely cut and polished coloured stones as personal ornaments (Honegger, personal communcation; Honegger 2004).

Further west on the Wadi el-Khowi, an area called Kadruka has revealed many later Neolithic settlements and cemeteries dating from about 4200 to 3800 BC. Although the settlements have suffered by deflation, the dead were buried within large mounds, still well preserved, where common graves were arranged around single rich burials. If the mounds themselves indicate advanced communal organization, the central burials appear to be those of group leaders (Figure 28.1). These individuals were buried with polished stone maceheads – implying that they were no strangers to warfare – and, occasionally, with female figurines. Bucrania were placed over their bodies, perhaps suggesting a cultic relationship between bulls and chiefs, a trend

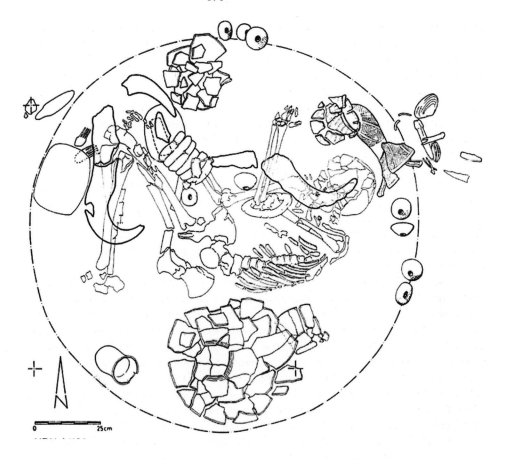

Figure 28.1 A Neolithic chieftain's grave from Kadruka, east of Kerma, Sudan, *c.*4200 BC. Surrounded by the graves of over 60 others, this man was buried with a stone palette, a polished stone female figurine, five elegant pottery vessels and nine polished stone maceheads. An ox skull was also placed over his body. Image courtesy of Jacques Reinold and the Section Française de la Direction des Antiquités du Soudan.

also observable in Egypt (Wilkinson 2003b: 99–112). In one instance a central burial was that of a female, interred with an adult male companion, providing the earliest evidence of two recurring features of ancient Nubian culture: matriarchy and human sacrifice.

At el-Ghaba, 430 kilometres south-east of Kadruka, near Shendi, Sudan, a cemetery of several hundred graves also contained burials of 'elite' men and women, interred with similar pottery, polished stone weapons and bucrania. The same patterns appear at Kadero, a large settlement of the same date sited just north of Khartoum, where some 8 per cent of the 200 graves excavated were richly furnished. The parallel burial patterns and material objects between these sites and Kadruka are also closely related to those at el-Multaga, about halfway between them, near ed-Debba, Sudan. This suggests that in the late fifth and early fourth millennia BC much of Nubia was populated by culturally kindred groups with ruling elites. The flaring-mouth beaker, typical of all these sites, is closely related to beakers found in contemporary Badarian sites in Middle Egypt, suggesting long-distance Nubian–Egyptian contacts even in the late fifth millennium BC (e.g. Holmes 1999).

Dramatic evidence of Neolithic culture has also been found in Lower Nubia in the desert about 100 kilometres west of Abu Simbel, around a dry lake bed called Nabta. Here, as at el-Barga, an occupation of early cattle herders dates from the seventh millennium BC. Another, from the late fifth millennium, included ceremonial burials of cattle, rings of megaliths marking buried, worked, bovine-shaped boulders, lines of megaliths and a 'calendar circle' of upright stones designed to predict the summer solstice about 4000 BC. Such cultural features – religious ritual involving cattle, the construction of stone monuments, and interest in measuring time – demonstrate the presence of strong political and intellectual leaders and presage by centuries some of the outstanding hallmarks of Egyptian dynastic civilization (Wendorf and Schild 2002a).

By the early fourth millennium BC, as rainfall decreased or ceased in Upper Egypt, desert pastoral zones disappeared there, and riverine agriculture gradually supplanted herding. Seasonal cattle camps became permanent settlements and these, in time, became large towns, which by 3100 BC were united under a deified king, and an Egyptian state was born. In Nubia, by contrast, summer rains still kept the deserts seasonally habitable, and since narrower flood plains there limited agriculture, the population remained smaller, more cattle-dependent and more mobile. As in Egypt, however, the most productive regions apparently coalesced into distinct polities governed by powerful rulers.

Contemporary with the later Egyptian Predynastic, distinctive cultures appeared in both Lower and Upper Nubia, suggesting the presence of two or more such polities. The northern, known as the 'A-Group', became very well known in the 1960s during the Lower Nubian rescue campaign when over 100 cemetery sites between the First and Second Cataracts were identified, exhibiting uniform burial customs and material culture. Although habitation sites were rarely found, the graves mixed high-quality local goods with a variety of Egyptian imported products, showing that these people carried on a brisk trade with Upper Egypt during the late fourth millennium BC. The scarcity of settlement sites and the small size of the cemeteries might suggest that much of its population was pastoral and mobile and dwelt near the Nile only seasonally (Gatto 2001–02). A recent study of A-Group skeletal and funerary material has shown that, as at Kadruka, cemeteries were organized around the graves of important individuals, but many of these were women (Nordström 2004 and references).

A series of large A-Group graves at Qustul, near the Second Cataract, contained quantities of both A-Group luxury products and late Predynastic Egyptian trade goods. Among the objects were two stone vessels, carved with scenes of royal figures, seated in boats and wearing the tall, knobbed 'white crown' familiar in later Egyptian art as the headdress symbolizing a pharaoh's authority over Upper Egypt or, figuratively, 'the South'. Since these vessels were of a distinctly Nubian type stone and bear the earliest known representations of kings wearing this crown, Bruce Williams proposed in 1980 that these scenes portrayed Nubian rather than Egyptian kings, that the Qustul graves belonged to an A-Group monarchy, and that Qustul, some 400 kilometres upriver from the contemporary seat of Egyptian royal power at

Hierakonpolis, was an A-Group royal capital (Williams 1986). Unfortunately, due to the flooding of the region by the Aswan Dam, these theories could never be verified. However, if they seemed radical when first proposed, subsequent research in Upper Nubia has seemed to render quite probable the possibility that one or more Nubian 'kingships' existed contemporary with Egyptian Dynasty 0.

The A-Group entity (however it is imagined) disappears archaeologically by the 1st Dynasty, an apparent victim of Egyptian military conquest. Rock inscriptions near Buhen seem to commemorate victories over Ta-Seti (Lower Nubia) by two kings of Dynasty 0. Just as the assumption of the red crown by the Egyptian ruler in the 1st Dynasty is thought to have commemorated his conquest of Lower Egypt, it is now at least plausible that his adoption of the white crown commemorated his conquest of A-Group Nubia. Although by the 1st Dynasty the Egyptians considered Ta-Seti to be their first nome or province, at least five more Egyptian wars against it are recorded between the 1st and 4th Dynasties. Ta-Seti continued to be populated by herdsmen until then, for a year date of Sneferu notes that he carried away from it '7,000 captives and 200,000 head of cattle'.

South of the Second Cataract, A-Group material culture transforms into a closely related culture known as the 'Pre-Kerma', best known from extensive settlement remains four kilometres east of Kerma, Sudan, just above the Third Cataract. The 'Pre-Kerma' site, dating from about 3200 to 2500 BC, consists of traces of many round huts, storage pits and cattle corrals, and has the appearance of a typical modern Nilotic cattle camp. Recent excavations, however, suggest that this settlement might only have been a suburb of a much larger town surrounded by defensive walls. If true, the main Pre-Kerma site might have been the seat of an important ruler, just as A-Group Qustul might have been, and as nearby Kerma was several centuries later.

A-Group and Pre-Kerma pottery, and pottery from the large cemeteries of el-Qadada (*c.*3700–3300 BC) in southern Nubia, all show common traits of style and manufacture. In all three areas, people were buried, flexed, in pits, accompanied by fine pottery, ground stone cosmetic palettes, rubbing stones, pigments and copper objects; and in all three areas, graves sometimes included female figurines – all suggesting pan-Nubian relationships. The practice of human sacrifice again manifests itself at el-Qadada.

The A-Group were unquestionably the chief suppliers of African raw materials to Egypt during the Late Predynastic Period. Once the pharaohs had eliminated them or their rulers, Egypt began trading directly with the more prosperous and populous South. It is probably no coincidence that the earliest Egyptian material yet found in Upper Nubia dates to the 3rd or 4th Dynasty and comes from Sai Island, 600 kilometres upstream from Aswan (Geus 2004a: 114; 2004b: 46–51). Textual references suggest that by the end of the 5th Dynasty (*c.*2350 BC), Egyptian traders were already travelling beyond the Third Cataract and establishing ties with local rulers.

The Egyptians occupied Lower Nubia throughout the 4th and 5th Dynasties, but by the early 6th Dynasty they withdrew under pressure from new cattle pastoralists pushing in from the deserts. With distinctive burial customs and material culture, these people are known archaeologically as the 'C-Group'. Contemporary Egyptian texts reveal that they formed three independent states or tribal regimes in Lower Nubia: Irjet, Setju and Wawat. By the end of the 6th Dynasty, only Wawat remained, suggesting that its ruler had absorbed the others and by then had created a single

Lower Nubian 'kingdom'. Since Lower Nubian rock drawings, ostensibly from the First Intermediate Period, depict figures wearing the white crown or include hieroglyphic inscriptions bearing royal names unknown in Egypt, it has been plausibly suggested that these belonged to native Nubian kings of Wawat (Morkot 2000: 47–56).

By the 6th Dynasty, the Egyptians were hiring Nubian mercenaries for their armies in large numbers. Most were said to come from Irjet, Setju and Wawat, or from Medjau and Tjemeh (the southern Eastern and Western Deserts, respectively). Still others came from an Upper Nubian land called Yam, best described in the contemporary biography of Harkhuf, an Egyptian trader who led four expeditions thither. Yam clearly lay south of the Second Cataract – probably also south of the Third – and had a 'ruler' to whom Harkhuf brought important gifts from the Egyptian king. This potentate reciprocated by returning caravans of Nubian merchandise to Egypt, defended the whole way by Yamite mercenaries (Kendall 1989).

The seat of the Yamite king is uncertain, but it was most likely Sai or Kerma. Sai is a large island in the Nile, 150 kilometres south of the Second Cataract, on which there are remains of a large Nubian town and cemetery of the third and second millennia BC. It was also the terminus of the Western Desert oasis road from Egypt, which Harkhuf is known to have taken. Kerma, 200 kilometres farther upstream, is an even more likely choice, since it was uniquely situated at the point where all southern trade routes converged. Excavations there have revealed an extensive fortified settlement, founded in the late third millennium BC, with a large, round African-style 'palace' and many objects dating from the time of Harkhuf, including fragments of calcite vessels inscribed with the names of the Egyptian kings he served.

Between the end of the Old Kingdom and the beginning of the Middle Kingdom (*c.*2134–2040 BC), political turmoil and famine in both Egypt and Nubia probably disrupted trade. During this period, while local kings asserted themselves in Lower Nubia, Yam disappeared as the main power in Upper Nubia and was replaced by a new one, called Kush, which had obviously overthrown it.

After the reunification of Egypt under the 11th and 12th Dynasties, the Egyptian kings aggressively reoccupied Lower Nubia and immediately came into conflict with Kush. To deter the latter's northward expansion, the kings built 11 heavy forts along the rapids of the Second Cataract, between Buhen and Semna. A number of Egyptian campaigns against Kush are recorded during this period, and contemporary Egyptian 'Execration Texts' (inscribed on small unbaked clay figures of bound captives that were ritually smashed to 'kill' them) name two successive 'rulers of Kush', a father and son, indicating that its monarchy was hereditary. The long period after Senusret III when Kush is not mentioned in Egyptian texts probably suggests that Egypt was experiencing such serious military reverses in Nubia that they could not be put into writing. By the 13th Dynasty, Egypt had abandoned its forts and withdrawn from Lower Nubia entirely. Stelae of Egyptian officials still living at Buhen now freely acknowledge their service to kings of Kush, and a newly discovered biographical text of a governor of Elkab records a devastating invasion of Upper Egypt by Kush in the 17th Dynasty (Davies 2003b).

The distinctive archaeological remains of Kush, even before they were identified as such, were known as the 'Kerma Culture', so named after the ancient urban complex at Kerma, Sudan, which, as is now known, was the site of the Kushite capital (Bonnet *et al.* 1990; Kendall 1997). Unfortunately, the city's original Nubian name remains unknown, for no surviving Egyptian text mentions it, and its own people were non-literate.

Kerma was probably founded as a town about 2200 BC as the result of a sudden westward shift of the Nile to its present bed, forcing the relocation of the Pre-Kerma settlement, which by then had been occupied for some seven centuries. The new city then grew steadily over the next millennium, reaching its peak of size and prosperity about 1500 BC, when it was destroyed by an Egyptian army led by Thutmose I.

In its 'Classic' phase, during the Second Intermediate Period, Kerma was a huge settlement with a walled 'royal city' at its heart. It included a temple complex at the base of an enormous, mud-brick ritual platform called the 'Deffufa', a large palace with associated warehouses, residences for elite citizens and troops, bakeries, bronze foundries, workshops, gates and streets (Figure 28.2). The earliest levels show that it was once crowded with small round huts that clustered around a much larger 'palace'

Figure 28.2 A view of the early capital of Kush at Kerma, Sudan, looking east, toward the great mud-brick ritual platform known as the 'Western Deffufa' from two palatial buildings and one of the city's streets. Image courtesy of Charles Bonnet and the Mission archéologique de l'Université de Genève à Kerma (Soudan).

of similar form. By later levels, the houses and palace had become rectilinear and were made of mud-brick, showing marked Egyptian influences. Outside the walls, a line of small chapels served the cult of Kerma's rulers, who, like the pharaohs, assumed divine status. A small stela from Buhen reveals that they also wore the white crown.

The city's cemetery contains tens of thousands of graves, and grew from north to south. This has permitted precise documentation of the evolution of the Kerma culture over a millennium. The dead were buried flexed, initially laid on cowhides, later on fine wooden beds. Accompanying them were superbly made ceramics, jewellery, clothing, weapons, food offerings, even pet dogs, flocks of sheep and sacrificed servants or family members. The graves were marked by tumuli, covered with pavements of white and black pebbles. Nobles and royalty had increasingly grandiose burials with free-standing chapels. The last Kerma rulers were buried beneath gigantic mounds, 90 metres in diameter, with huge mud-brick chapels. These kings, placed in small, treasure-filled chambers, were accompanied by dozens or hundreds of sacrificed servants; their mounds traditionally were ringed by hundreds or thousands of cattle skulls, suggesting the livestock were sent as offerings from all over the kingdom by the ruler's subject peoples (Figure 28.3) (Bonnet 2000).

Figure 28.3 Cattle skulls ringing the perimeter of the grave of an early king of Kush at Kerma, Sudan, *c.*2000–1800 BC. Image courtesy of Charles Bonnet and the Mission archéologique de l'Université de Genève à Kerma (Soudan).

In around 1580 BC, the Theban rulers of the 17th Dynasty, long threatened by Kush and bullied into vassalage by the Hyksos, sought to reclaim their independence. Intercepting news that the king of Kush had just died, Kamose invaded and successfully reoccupied Lower Nubia. His successors, Ahmose and Amenhotep I, founders of the 18th Dynasty, later pushed beyond the Second Cataract and seized Sai, where they built a new stronghold. This made it possible for Thutmose I (*c.*1500 BC) to launch troops over the Third Cataract and to attack Kerma itself. After burning the city and crippling the Kushite army, he continued up the Nile another 560 kilometres and left an inscription on the rock called Hagar el-Merwa, just below the Fifth Cataract.

Hagar el-Merwa is the farthest point known to have been reached on the Nile by any pharaoh. Thutmose's feat was later repeated by Thutmose III and perhaps Ramesses II, who added their own inscriptions to his. The rock not only bears their names but also those of many of their accompanying officials. One was a High Priest of Amun, almost certainly under Thutmose I (Davies 2001b; 2003c). This suggests that the conquest of Kush was also one of official religious discovery and that the formal introduction of the Egyptian Amun cult into Nubia began with Thutmose I (Kendall 2007).

It is Thutmose I's own inscription at the Hagar el-Merwa that features an image of the Egyptian state god Amun in novel guise as a man with ram's head. This form of the god is thought to merge a native Nubian ram deity with the Egyptian god (Kormysheva 2004: 109–33), and it became the form of the god soon identified with many Egyptian–Nubian holy sites, especially the lone butte known as Gebel Barkal, just downstream from the Fourth Cataract (Figure 28.4). The Egyptians called this hill variously 'Pure Mountain' and 'Karnak' and identified it as the Nubian mani-festation of Amun's main sanctuary at Thebes, 1,200 kilometres downstream. They

Figure 28.4 View of Gebel Barkal, near Karima, Sudan. The Egyptians identified this isolated hill just below the Fourth Cataract as a primeval Karnak and the residence of a mysterious southern form of their state god Amun. The mountain – and Napata, the city built around it – became the chief religious centre of the later kingdom of Kush (photo T. Kendall).

also advertised it – at least locally – as the older of the two Karnaks, even suggesting that it was Amun's birthplace. Here, they stated, the god dwelt hidden inside the rock as an alter-ego ('*ka*') of his Theban self and from here granted the pharaohs the kingship of Egypt (Kendall 2007).

The most striking feature of Gebel Barkal is its statuesque pinnacle, 75 metres high, which was recognized both as a natural colossus of a rearing uraeus wearing the white crown (Figure 28.5) and of a king and/or god wearing the white crown (Kendall, in press). The presence here of these powerful symbols of southern kingship allowed Egyptian propagandists to proclaim – at least for Nubian consumption – first, that Gebel Barkal was the original source of the white crown and the birthplace of Egyptian kingship and the first kings; second, that Amun of Gebel Barkal was the original grantor of Upper Egyptian kingship; and third, that all of Nubia as far south as Gebel Barkal was an extension of Upper Egypt and the Thebaid (Kendall 2002: chapter vii).

Figure 28.5 A drawing of a relief from the south wall of the great hall of Abu Simbel showing Ramesses II making offerings to 'Amun of Karnak' seated inside Gebel Barkal. The image reveals that the Egyptians imagined the mountain's pinnacle (see Figure 28.4) to be a natural statue of a uraeus wearing the white crown, which gave rise to a belief that Nubia was a part of Upper Egypt and that primeval Upper Egyptian kingship derived from Gebel Barkal. Drawing by Peter Der Manuelian.

These 'facts' neatly legitimized Egyptian rule over Nubia by 'proving' to the Nubians that their own land and kingship had always belonged to Egypt and that their god and the Egyptian Amun were the same deity. A version of this tradition – that Osiris, mythical first king of Egypt, was a Nubian – would be reported in the first century BC by Diodorus Siculus (3.2.1–3.6) (Eide *et al.* 1994–2000: vol. 2, 644–5).

Given the scant but continuous evidence for Nubian kings wearing the white crown since protohistoric times, the possibility that the Egyptians might at an early period have appropriated the crown and, later, some of the royal lore about Gebel Barkal from Nubia cannot be lightly dismissed. To what extent the Egyptians in Egypt acknowledged Gebel Barkal ('Southern Karnak') as the source of the white crown is still unknown. Certainly within Nubia itself the belief that Gebel Barkal was the true source of Egyptian kingship became widespread. It was surely this dogma that engendered the 25th Dynasty and the subsequent Egyptianizing Kushite state.

When the Egyptian kings, in the early fifteenth century BC, crushed the last Kushite resistance and incorporated Nubia, Egypt became the wealthiest, most powerful nation on earth, gaining now a monopoly over all African produce and gold, which was mined in the Nubian deserts. For the next 350 years, Egypt directly ruled Upper and Lower Nubia (called 'Kush' and 'Wawat', respectively) through an administration headed by a Viceroy ('King's Son of Kush'), whose authority was said to extend from 'Nekhen (Hierakonpolis, Upper Egypt, the traditional Egyptian seat of the white crown) to Karnak [i.e. Gebel Barkal, the southern source of the white crown]' (Davies and Gardiner 1926: 11). The Viceroy's chief duty was to collect revenue from the two provinces and to present it to the king in great annual spectacles. He also controlled a provincial army, composed largely of Kushite recruits. The children of Nubian nobles were raised at the Egyptian court, acculturated, and returned to their districts as governors of their own people, and Egyptians now settled in Nubia in great numbers, often taking Nubian spouses. Temples were built and dedicated to Amun and other deities in newly founded towns in Upper Nubia such as Napata (beside Gebel Barkal), Pnubs (Dokki Gel), founded on the ruins of Kerma, Tabo and Gem-pa-Aten (Kawa), just south of Pnubs. Between the Third and Second Cataracts, Egyptian towns and sanctuaries were built at Tombos, Sesebi, Soleb, Sedeinga, Sai and Amara, and the old cataract forts were reoccupied. In Lower Nubia, many more temples and towns were built during the reign of Ramesses II. By the 20th Dynasty, however, such energetic building programmes ceased. As Sea Peoples and Libyans threatened northern Egypt, troops were doubtless withdrawn from the South, leaving Nubia vulnerable to native insurrections. By the eleventh century BC, Nubia once again became untenable, and the pharaohs made yet another withdrawal.

The political fracturing of Egypt during the Third Intermediate Period was unprecedented. At the end of the 20th Dynasty, the pharaoh, residing in Lower Egypt, was stripped of his southern authority by the High Priest of Amun at Karnak, who took royal titles himself for ritual purposes. In view of this, one must wonder if this was a result of the king's loss of Gebel Barkal (the Nubian 'Karnak'), the perceived source of white crown authority, and of Nubia itself, Amun's southern empire, which again became independent under native rulers unknown.

During the three centuries after the New Kingdom, nearly all written and arch-aeological records for Nubia cease. The primary archaeological sites of this period are two cemeteries, both near Gebel Barkal. The first, Hillat el-Arab, is a cluster of large rock-cut tombs, without inscription, containing abundant late and post-New Kingdom material. The tombs evidently belonged to a post-colonial Kushite aristocracy. The second, el-Kurru, is a sequence of chieftains' graves, probably dating from the mid-ninth century BC, that evolve rapidly from Nubian tumuli to small, Egyptian-style pyramids. Interred here was a line of local rulers who were at first neither Egyptianized nor literate but were, by its end, thoroughly so. Becoming ardent devotees of Amun, they restored the old Egyptian temples, which had fallen into ruin, and, by authority of the god of Gebel Barkal, they proclaimed themselves kings of Egypt (Kendall 1999: 3–117, 164–76). What or who promoted their cultural and religious conversion remains undocumented, but Egyptian priests who had emigrated from Thebes may be suspected – men inimical to the 22nd Dynasty and eager to promote a rival dynasty to restore Amun's 'Upper Egyptian' empire.

By about 750 BC, the reigning member of the el-Kurru dynasty, Piankhy (variously read 'Piye'), pressed his claim to Upper Egypt and occupied it peacefully. With this move, he again united 'the two Karnaks' and restored the Nubian empire of the New Kingdom. About 732 BC, opposed by a 'rebellion' of Lower Egyptian kinglets, he successfully invaded the north and thus restored the kingship of the 'Two Lands'. By using variously the throne names of Thutmose III and Ramesses II, Piankhy identified himself as their reincarnations.

After his death in 721 BC, Piankhy was succeeded by his brother Shabaqo, who, moving from Napata to Memphis, was remembered as the founder of the 25th Dynasty – Egypt's Kushite dynasty – which included three more kings, Shabataqo (Shebitqo), Taharqo and Tanutamani, reigning until 663 BC. Remembered for their piety, the Kushite pharaohs sponsored a cultural renaissance in Egypt and exported it to their homeland. Their interest in ancient traditions even included reviving the pyramid as the proper royal tomb type – but they built their tombs only in the Sudan and always returned there for burial. If the kings wore traditional pharaonic regalia and scrupulously followed Egyptian rituals and protocol, they represented themselves as ethnically Nubian and preferred a unique skull-cap crown (Figure 28.6). This crown, it now appears, was derived from the profile of Gebel Barkal and apparently identified its wearer as the possessor of the kingship now stated by the Kushites to have been first granted by the Creator at this mountain (Figure 28.4) (Kendall 2002: chapter vii; in press: n. 63). Not surprisingly, the Kushites rebuilt the New Kingdom coronation complex at Gebel Barkal and re-enacted there the same rituals once performed by the pharaohs, whom they now claimed as their 'ancestors'.

After winning Egypt, the Kushites faced the threat of an expansionist Assyria, which they vainly attempted to oppose. After 671 BC, during the reign of Taharqo, the Assyrians attacked Egypt in almost annual campaigns. In 667 BC, they captured Memphis and the king's family, and drove him back to Napata, where he died in 664 BC. His successor Tanutamani immediately reconquered Egypt only to be driven out the following year by a renewed Assyrian assault, in which Thebes was sacked. After this disaster, Tanutamani and his successors remained in the Sudan, consolidating their empire there. Too weakened to recapture Egypt, they merely ignored the emerging Saite pharaohs of the 26th Dynasty and continued to claim, by authority of Amun of Gebel Barkal, that they were the true kings of Egypt.

In 594 BC, probably to put an end to Kushite posturing, Psamtik II dispatched an army into Nubia, which destroyed a Kushite force at Pnubs (Kerma) and went on to Napata, burning the Gebel Barkal temples and palace. Caches of deliberately destroyed statues of Kushite kings from Taharqo to Aspelta were found both at Gebel Barkal (in 1916) and at Pnubs (in 2003), providing vivid evidence of these raids (Bonnet and Valbelle 2005). The reigning king was probably Aspelta. Unfortunately, after his reign written records from Kush become very scarce, and our knowledge of events is very limited.

Figure 28.6 Portrait of a Kushite king of the 25th Dynasty, from a destroyed temple of Horus at Edfu. The unique badge of Kushite kingship was the 'cap-crown', which simulated the shape of the perceived source of their kingship: Gebel Barkal (see Figure 28.4). By this time, the Kushites claimed that Amun of Gebel Barkal granted them both Upper and Lower Egyptian kingship, prompting them to wear twin uraei. This relief was altered by followers of the Saite king Psamtik II, following his devastating raid on Kush in 594 BC. One of the uraei has been erased to indicate that Kush no longer had authority in the north (photo courtesy of Gay Robins).

Following its Egyptian hegemony, Kush endured continuously as a state in the Sudan for another millennium. The names of some 70 of its rulers are known, most preserved only from tombs. Archaeologists divide the kingdom's history into two broad cultural phases: the Napatan and Meroïtic. During the first (*c*.850–280 BC), the cultural centre of the kingdom lay in the north, at Napata, and the kings were buried in pyramids at nearby el-Kurru and Nuri. During the later (*c*.280 BC–AD 360), the cultural and political centre of the kingdom lay in the south, at Meroë, and most of the rulers were buried there, although a few chose burial at Gebel Barkal.

During the Napatan Period, Kushite culture rather slavishly followed Egyptian models in art, architecture and burial practices, and royal inscriptions were written exclusively in Egyptian. Although only four of the 18 Napatan kings after Aspelta left surviving historical inscriptions, these reveal that the kings dwelt primarily at Meroë, travelled to Gebel Barkal for their coronations, and repeated this and other ceremonies in regular visitations to the northern towns, Pnubs and Gem-pa-Aten. The kings also typically recorded their temple building projects and their campaigns against surrounding enemy tribes. Recent discoveries of a Napatan fort in the Wadi Howar and of a Napatan settlement in the central Bayuda show that Kush sometimes dominated lands far from the river (Jesse and Kuper 2004; Kendall 2006–7). On the other hand, royal records also indicate that Meroë itself was occasionally captured and occupied by enemies.

Throughout the Napatan Period, nearly all royal burials took place at Nuri, about 10 kilometres north-east of Gebel Barkal on the opposite bank. Founded by Taharqo, this cemetery was used by 19 of his successors and 54 queens to the early third century BC (Kendall, in press). The kings were interred in deep, rock-cut chambers beneath large masonry pyramids, 20 to 30 metres in height. They were buried like Egyptian royalty – mummified, laid in nested gilded mummy cases, supplied with canopic jars and hundreds of *shabti*s (model servant figures), and buried with much treasure and food offerings (Dunham 1955).

According to the Greek writer Agatharcides (quoted by Diodorus Siculus, 3.6.1–4), an oracle of Amun (presumably at Gebel Barkal) occasionally sent letters to the kings, informing them when their reigns should end and ordering them to commit suicide (Eide *et al.* 1994–2000: vol. 2, 647). This custom was reportedly followed until the reign of Ptolemy II (285–246 BC), when a king 'Ergamenes', upon receipt of his letter, went to the temple with his troops and slew the priests. Although many scholars doubt this tale, the practice of depriving kings of a natural death was so pervasive across Sudanic Africa even to the nineteenth century (Kendall 1989: 694–5) that the account must be taken seriously to some degree – especially since a king Arkamani was the first to build his pyramid at Meroë. This event also coincides with the transition to the Meroïtic Period, when there appears to be a marked break with Egyptian norms. Kushite art now begins to exhibit more African elements. The rulers show a preference for exaggerated corpulence and occasionally display their tribal scars. Females now frequently assume the throne, and local gods, unknown in the Napatan pantheon, become prominent. Hellenistic art motifs and architectural ideals are also freely borrowed and combined with Egyptian. And if rulers continue to erect pyramids, they eschew burying *shabti*s and occasionally resort to the old Nubian custom of sacrificing real servants.

The use of Egyptian written language sharply declines in the Meroïtic Period, replaced by the native Kushite tongue, called Meroïtic, which was expressed in new cursive and hieroglyphic alphabets. Although these scripts were decoded in 1911, the language has defied translation. Recent scholarship in Nilo-Saharan languages, however, has led to the discovery of Meroïtic cognate tongues, and spectacular advances in Meroïtic are shortly anticipated (Rilly 2007).

Meroë, on the east bank of the Nile between the Fifth and Sixth Cataracts, became the political capital of the kingdom in the sixth century BC. Like ancient Kerma, its centre was a walled 'royal city', containing generations of palaces. Abutting this was an Amun temple, rivalling in size that of Gebel Barkal; its sacred way was flanked by many smaller shrines. The surrounding residential areas were bordered on the east by mounds of slag, locating the city's iron smelting operations. Further east were cemeteries for commoners and nobles, and, 5 kilometres distant, raised on adjacent ridges, the towering pyramids of over 40 rulers (Grzymski 2005 and references).

The Kushite monarch presided over an empire of semi-isolated regions connected by long, inhospitable desert roads or river tracts. The northernmost was Lower Nubia, always contested with Egypt. In the third century BC Ptolemy II invaded and seized it, but by the century's end Kush had regained it. Détente later saw the rulers of both states collaborating in building or restoring Lower Nubian temples. When Rome replaced the Ptolemies, its attempt to tax the province prompted a Kushite attack on Aswan in 24 BC. In retaliation, Rome dispatched an army that attacked Napata. After this exchange, Meroë and Rome established a peace that endured until the decline of both powers, and Lower Nubia remained securely Kushite.

Meroë's Upper Nubian province was severed from Lower Nubia by the desolate Second Cataract region. Centred mainly within 'the Dongola Reach' (Third to Fourth Cataracts), it contained the kingdom's religious capital Napata and its sacred mountain, through which the Kushite kings claimed their crown and linked themselves to a mythical Nubiocentric Egyptian past. The province's other important towns were Sanam Abu Dom (opposite Napata), Pnubs (on the site of ancient Kerma) and Gem-pa-Aten (modern Kawa), all currently under excavation.

The kingdom's most fertile and populous province was 'the Island of Meroë' (between the Atbara River and Blue Nile), which was connected to Upper Nubia by a long road across the Bayuda Desert (bypassing the Fourth Cataract). This included the capital Meroë and dozens of temple towns along the east bank of the Nile and far out into the eastern Butana steppe-lands. Many of these – Dangeil (near the Fifth Cataract), Hamadab, el-Hassa, Naqa, Musawwarat es-Sufra – are all, too, under excavation.

One or more Kushite provinces existed still further south, for recent archaeological surveys, up to 222 kilometres south of Khartoum, report numerous Napatan and Meroïtic sites, all on the east bank of the White Nile (Eisa 2004: 247–9).

The causes for the decline of Kush remain mysterious; the last royal pyramid was erected at Meroë about 360 AD. Increasing desertification may have been one factor. Axumite victory inscriptions have also long suggested that Meroë fell to Axum (Ethiopia), but it may already have succumbed to another powerful neighbour, the Noba ('Nubians'), whom classical writers reported dwelt opposite Meroë on the west bank. By the fourth and fifth centuries AD, the former Kushite provinces had fragmented into separate polities, known as the Post-Meroïtic kingdoms. The only records of their existence are cemeteries of enormous burial mounds, thought to mark their power centres: Ballana, Qustul, Zuma, Tangasi, el-Hobagi and others (Adams 1977: 382–429; Lenoble 2004: 186–92, 193–203). Some of these tombs were very rich and belonged to rulers continuing Meroïtic traditions, but literacy among them had apparently ceased. Missionaries from Byzantium and Alexandria converted the region to Christianity in the sixth century AD, and when written records resume, the ancient land of Kush had been partitioned into three Christian Nubian (Noba) kingdoms (Anderson 2004: 202–8, 209–37).

In 2004, construction began on the Merowe High Dam at the Fourth Cataract, about 360 kilometres north of Khartoum. This huge hydroelectric project, scheduled for completion in 2008, will create a lake 125 kilometres long, displace up to 70,000 people, and inundate a huge, remote tract whose settlement history, until now, has been completely unknown. This project has spurred a major international archaeological salvage campaign, reminiscent of that conducted in Egypt during the 1960s. When its results are in, the history of Nubia will probably have to be radically rewritten – again (Ahmed 2004).

NOTES

1 Recent general reference works include Eide *et al.* 1994–2000; Török 1997; Wildung 1997; Morkot 2000; Smith 2003; Edwards 2004; Redford 2004b; Welsby and Anderson 2004.
2 Ongoing surveys reveal that many 'Southern Nubian' cultures continue well upstream of the confluence of the Blue and White Niles.

CHAPTER TWENTY-NINE

EGYPT AND THE LEVANT

———— ·◆· ————

Manfred Bietak

R esearch within the last two decades has shown that, from prehistoric times, Egypt was not an isolated oasis of the river Nile but had close connections with the Near East. Not only have Natufian arrow tips been found near Helwan in Lower Egypt, but at Merimda, in the western delta, the entire lithic production and population type of the earliest stratum show strong Natufian connections (Eiwanger 1984: 59–63). Moreover, the ceramic material is strongly influenced by the Palestinian Pottery Neolithic tradition. All the evidence suggests that there was a strong influx during this period, reaching the south-western delta. Immigration from Canaan can be deduced for the Chalcolithic Buto-Maadi culture from ceramic imports, local imitations and semi-subterranean dwelling types borrowed from the contemporary Chalcolithic culture of Palestine (Faltings 1998, 2002; Hartung 2001: 322–7). Trade with the Levant was the main reason for this immigration, but the relatively lush living conditions of Egypt must surely have invited immigration by the inhabitants of neighbouring arid zones. Egypt needed raw materials such as coniferous timber from the Lebanon and commodities such as olive oil and wine which turn up from the Naqada IIc period onwards as far south as Abydos (Hartung 2001, 2002).

The impact of Egypt can be felt in the late Predynastic and early 1st Dynasty in the southern Levant in a number of settlements with a high percentage of imported and locally made Egyptian pottery (Brandl 1992; Wilkinson 1999: 152–5). It has even been suggested that Egypt colonized this region for a time in order to gain control over the copper production in the Negev and the Sinai. This was discontinued during the 1st Dynasty and trading expeditions seem thereafter to have been dispatched to the Levant by sea, destined for Byblos. Towards the end of the 2nd/beginning of the 3rd Dynasty, the Sinai was depopulated (Gundlach 1994: 60–70), the local population probably deported to Egypt, and the Egyptian kings took over the exploitation of the mines.

An increasing demand for timber from Lebanon induced the early Egyptian court to build a close relationship with Byblos in particular. The temple of this harbour town was the recipient of Egyptian royal donations from the end of the 2nd Dynasty onwards (Dunand 1939: 26–7, 161–2, 200, 267–8; 1937: pls XXXVI–XXXVIII, CXXV). Egypt's influence expanded during the Old Kingdom to include other princely centres of the Levant. Trade developed favourably for both sides. Egypt exported luxury goods such as ointment and eye paint, faience jewellery, semi-precious stones, gold, toilet objects of wood, ivory, ebony and, most probably, fine linen. In turn, Egypt imported timber, pitch and resin, bitumen, olive oil and other types of oil, wine and other commodities not available in the Nile Valley.

Such foreign enterprises might have stimulated immigration of foreigners from the Levant. Egypt was in need of workers, craftsmen and soldiers; and, for its seagoing ships, it needed experienced sailors and, we can assume, shipbuilders. For the construction of such boats Egypt depended entirely on cedar wood from Lebanon. In the 5th Dynasty pyramid temple of Sahura there is a relief of a seaborne expedition to the Levant, most likely to Syria or Lebanon (Borchardt 1913: pls 12, 13). The ships brought back products of this land and, most important, sailors and their families (Figure 29.1a) (Bietak 1988). About 150 years later, a relief from the causeway of Unas shows typical Asiatic sailors on seagoing ships, while Egyptians manoeuvre river boats (Figure 29.1b) (Bietak 1988: 36). Towards the end of the Old Kingdom,

(a)

Figure 29.1a Return of the fleet of Sahura (5th Dynasty) from the northern Levantine coast with recruited Western Asiatic sailors and their families under the command of Egyptian officers. Image courtesy of the Ägyptisches Museum Berlin.

(b)

Figure 29.1b Causeway of Unas (end of the 5th Dynasty) at Saqqara with reliefs showing seagoing ships with Western Asiatic sailors under the command of Egyptian officers (photo C. Mlinar).

the expression *kepeny-* (Byblos-) ships for seagoing vessels may indicate that such boats were originally designed at Byblos (Glanville 1932: 31; for a different opinion, see Säve-Söderbergh 1946: 47–8).

The evidence for the involvement of people from the Near East in the operation of the navy and maritime commerce in the Old Kingdom leads to the conclusion that there were communities of such foreigners in Egypt. Indeed, we have onomastic evidence of Asiatics living in Egypt during that period (Fischer 1959: 264–5; 1961: 75; 1991: 63). The discovery of a series of broad-room and bent-axis temples from the late Predynastic Period to the Old Kingdom at Tell Ibrahim Awad in the northeastern delta suggests settlements of foreigners along the easternmost Nile branch (Figure 29.2) (Eigner 2000; Bietak 2003a). It might not be a coincidence that the oldest determinative for the god Osiris, in the 5th Dynasty, depicts an Asiatic (Shalomi-Hen 2006: 94). It therefore seems possible that important aspects of this delta deity originated from an Asiatic vegetation god.

Egyptian activity in the Levant was not exclusively peaceful. In tombs at Deshasha and Saqqara, sieges of Asiatic towns are shown (Piacentini 1987: Schulz 2002: 25–34). The expedition leader Weni, during the 6th Dynasty, reported a raid against a settlement beyond an area called the 'Gazelle nose', probably the Carmel ridge (Piacentini 1990: 18). This suggests that increasing disruptions at the end of the Early Bronze Age brought the relationship between the two regions to an end. The urban culture of the Levant broke down and gave way to a nomadic or semi-nomadic way of life, introduced by the Amorites. This situation anticipated the breakdown of the Egyptian Old Kingdom.

Figure 29.2 Left: temple with bent axis from Tell Ibrahim Awad, phase IIb. It seems to have originated as a broad-room temple with a central podium and two entrances (after Eigner 2000: fig. 2). Right: The original broad-room temple of Tell Ibrahim Awad, phase IIc, with the secondary installations removed. There is a cult podium in the middle of the back wall, as is usual with broad-room temples. The step against the middle of the front wall indicates the position of a central entrance, later closed (interpretation by M. Bietak of the archaeological documentation in Eigner 2000: fig. 3).

Middle Kingdom literature (*Merikara, Ipuwer*) attests to the infiltration of Asiatic populations into Egypt and the colonization of the eastern delta (Gardiner 1909: 38, 4,5–4,8; Quack 1992: 91, E 85–7). Wall paintings in the Theban tomb of general Intef (late 11th Dynasty) show a siege of a town or fortress defended by Asiatics (Jaroš-Deckert 1984: pl. 17, folding pls 1 and 3). As there were no towns or fortresses in the Levant at the time, this siege could only have taken place in the delta during the wars of unification under the 11th Dynasty king Nebhepetra Mentuhotep II. From the beginning of the 12th Dynasty we find evidence of Asiatics serving as soldiers in the Egyptian army (Hatnub: Anthes 1928: 36–7; Schenkel 1962: 84–95; Beni Hasan: Newberry 1893: pls 16, 31, 47; Posener 1971: 541). During the 12th Dynasty, Egypt's relationship with the re-established urban centres in the Levant, especially Byblos, was resumed after a long interruption. Egypt also campaigned against city-states such as Sekmem (Shechem?) under Senusret III (Porter and Moss 1927–99: vol. 5, 66), and launched seaborne expeditions against specific areas in the Levant. This is revealed by the discovery of a fragment of the annals of king Amenemhat

II (*c.* 1911–1876 BC) (Altenmüller and Moussa 1975) which shows that Egypt brought back booty and captives in great numbers from such raids, which reached as far as Cyprus.

Western Asiatic people called *aamu* can be traced in Egyptian texts from the time of Senusret II until the end of the 12th Dynasty. (The etymology is still disputed: they are known under this name from the 6th Dynasty, heralding the arrival of the Amorites at the fringes of Egypt.) The Illahun papyri indicate that many *aamu* were concentrated near the residence of the 12th Dynasty at Itj-tawy (Lisht), in closed settlements called *wenut.* Asiatics were employed mainly in low-ranking professions such as workers, doorkeepers, messengers, singers in temples or serfs on private estates (Posener 1957: 152; Luft 1992; Schneider 2003: 232–90). In the 13th Dynasty there is evidence that elite households had Western Asiatic slaves in large numbers. They were given Egyptian names and were quickly assimilated (Albright 1954; Hayes 1955; Posener 1957; Schneider 2003: 207–28). Evidence from the Sinai (Gardiner *et al.* 1952: pls XXIII, XXX, XXXVA, LI no. 163; 1955: 92 no. 85, 103 no. 95, 112 no. 110; Seyfried 1981: 188–201) indicates that people from Western Asia living in Egypt were employed as expedition specialists, some carrying weapons. Inspired by Egyptian writing, they developed for their own use the earliest alphabetic writing system, attested in the Sinai and along expedition tracks in the Western Desert (Gardiner 1962b; Darnell 2003c; Hamilton 2006; Goldwasser 2006b: 130–60).

Anticipating a potential threat, Egypt monitored Nubian tribes and the city-states of Canaan. Magic was deployed as one remedy. The names of hostile places and their leaders were written on pots or figurines which were then smashed. The lists on the earlier collection of these 'Execration Texts', dated to the reign of Senusret III, often contain several princes' names for a single toponym (Sethe 1926), while the later lists from the end of the 12th or even the 13th Dynasty contain many more toponyms with mostly one prince each (Posener 1940). It might be dangerous to read into this a consolidation of locally segmented systems; but the recently urbanized Middle Bronze Age Culture seems to have retained some tribal organization from its semi-nomadic past, which might explain the occurrence of several princes for each town in the early Execration Texts (Posener 1940: 39; 1971: 555–8). All the names are north-western Semitic.

From the Middle Kingdom onwards, male Asiatics are depicted in Egyptian art with a black or red coiffure, prominent aquiline nose and often yellow skin (Posener 1971: 22). As a lively illustration of pastoral nomads of the early Middle Bronze Age we have a representation of a caravan of smallstock breeders entering the Nile Valley in the tomb of Khnumhotep II at Beni Hasan (Figure 29.3) (Newberry 1893: pl. 31; Shedid 1994: 60–1). They are clad in woollen dresses decorated with multi-coloured ornamental patterns, kilts reaching below the knee, and overcoats wound around the shoulder, held together with a toggle pin. Women have similar ornamental wool dresses covering one shoulder. All wear leather sandals. The group is equipped with duckbill axes and socketed spears, both typical of an early phase of the Middle Bronze Age.

Egypt tried to interfere in Near Eastern politics to support its partners such as Byblos, as revealed by an autobiographical inscription from the time of Senusret III (Allen, forthcoming). Towards the late Middle Kingdom, Egypt seems to have created a network of allied city-states in the Levant. They were probably eager to

Figure 29.3   A group of nomads approaching the mayor Khnumhotep, 12th Dynasty, from a wall painting at Beni Hasan (after Prisse d'Avennes 1991: pl. II.47).

enter into a special relationship with Egypt, expecting protection against other ambitious kingdoms in the north. The prince of Byblos, the prince of Kumidi (Kamid el-Loz) in the Beqaʿ, and probably others, took the Egyptian title *haty-a*, meaning 'mayor'/'governor' (Montet 1928: 155–61; Edel 1983). At the same period, Egyptian luxury goods were sent as prestige presents to courts in the Levant (Figure 29.4). Egyptian taste and motifs influenced local arts in Syria, especially in the time of the 13th Dynasty, including glyptic art and palatial mural paintings (Scandone-Matthiae 1990; Teissier 1996; Taraqji 1999). Palestine seems not to have been in a close relationship with Egypt at that time, except perhaps Ashkelon, where numerous Egyptian seal-impressions of the late 12th and early 13th Dynasties were found in the oldest moat of the fortification system (Stager 2002). It seems that this biggest city-state of Canaan at the time, with its natural harbour, was voluntarily part of the Egyptian trading network in the Levant. The rest of Palestine, however, was ignored by the Egyptians in favour of the rich Syrian towns which were the much more attractive trading partners.

The centre of Egypt's activity in the Levant was the harbour town of Tell el-Dabʿa (Avaris), a settlement constructed at the beginning of the 12th Dynasty and completely re-settled by Canaanites from the late 12th Dynasty onwards (Bietak 1996b, 1997a, 1997b, 2001). From the cultural features, the inhabitants seem to have originated in the northern Levant, most probably from the area of Byblos – Egypt's most important partner at that time. The oldest graves of this community belonged to soldiers with their distinctive Near Eastern weaponry. They cluster around a huge domed tomb of a high official whose monumental limestone funerary statue shows him in Syrian dress with an impressive, red, mushroom-shaped coiffure (Figure 29.5b) (Bietak

Figure 29.4   Egyptian royal gifts of Amenemhat III and IV from the tombs of princes of Byblos (after Cat. Paris 1998: 72).

Figure 29.5a North Syrian *Mittelsaal* house at Tell el-Dabʿa.

1996b: fig. 17, pl. 4; Schiestl 2003: 116–27, figs 4–6, pl. 125). Nearby was a big, north-Syrian, *Mittelsaal* house (Figure 29.5a) (Bietak 1996b: figs 7, 8). Soon after-wards, local dignitaries lived in a palatial mansion of Egyptian style with an attached cemetery (Bietak 1996b: 21–30). A scarab with the title 'Prince of Retjenu' from one of the palace tombs (Figure 29.5c) (Martin 1998) suggests that this palace might have been the seat of the Prince of Retjenu (the area of Lebanon and Palestine) (Gardiner 1947: 142*–149*). Such a title would make sense only if it belonged to an Asiatic dignitary in Egyptian service, in charge of trade with the Levant. This would also explain why the 'Brother of the Prince of Retjenu' repeatedly accompanied Egyptian mining expeditions to the Sinai (Figure 29.6a) (Gardiner *et al.* 1952: pls 39, 85).

A cylinder seal manufactured in Egypt with the representation of the northern Syrian storm god Hadad/Baʿal Zephon (Figure 29.6b) (Porada 1984) might indicate that Canaanite cults had been established by the Asiatic community in the eastern Nile Delta as early as the beginning of the 13th Dynasty (Figure 29.7) (Bietak 1990).

(b)

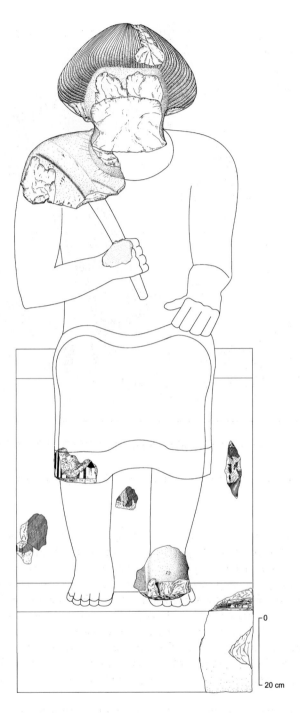

Figure 29.5b   Statue of a Canaanite dignitary, possibly the Prince of Retjenu, found at Tell el-Dabʿa (after Schiestl 2006: fig. 2).

(c)

Figure 29.5c Seal of the Prince of Retjenu, found in a tomb at Tell el-Dabʿa
(after Bietak 1991b: pl. 22a).

Asiatic burial customs – not otherwise known in Egypt – can also be observed, such
as house burials, the lack of mummification and the burial of teams of donkeys (Figure
29.8) (Forstner-Müller 2001, 2002; Schiestl 2002). From the late Middle Kingdom
onwards there is evidence of Near Eastern types of temples (Bietak 1996b: 36–41).
The oldest evidence for the toponym Avaris also dates to that time (Czerny 2001).

With the disintegration of the authority of the 13th Dynasty, the political importance of Avaris grew. It became the capital of a local kingdom (the 14th Dynasty),
which separated itself from the 13th Dynasty. One of the first kings of the 14th
Dynasty was Nehesy, who left a scattering of monuments in the eastern Nile Delta.
Seth/Baʿal, recently established as the local cult of the Asiatic enclave, became the
dynastic god. At that time, the frontier town of Tjaru at Tell el-Hebua, north-east
of Qantara, already existed as a fortified settlement of Near Easterners, like Tell el-
Dabʿa (Abd el-Maksoud 1998).

Six or seven decades later, Avaris became the capital of the 15th Dynasty, the
so-called 'Hyksos', the 'rulers of foreign countries'. From *c.*1640–1530 BC, Egypt

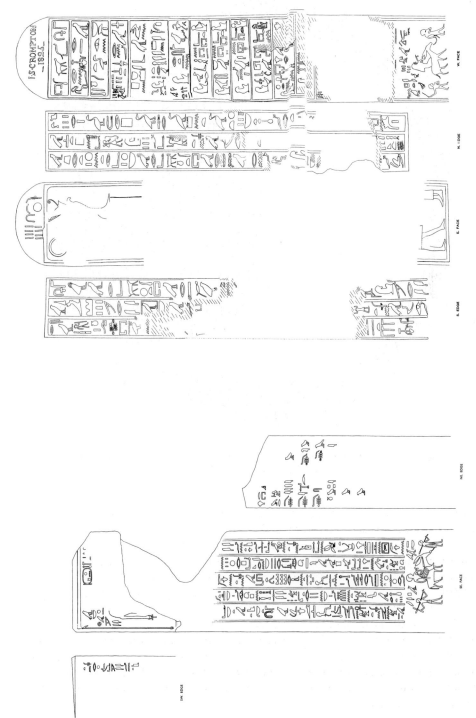

Figure 29.6a Representations of the brother of the Prince of Retjenu from stelae at Serabit el-Khadim (after Gardiner *et al.* 1952: pls 39, 85).

(b)

Figure 29.6b   Cylinder seal with a representation of the north Syrian storm god as patron of sailors (after Bietak 1990: 15, Abb. 5).

was under their rule. They seem to have originated from the same pool of people as the 14th Dynasty; a political break is not observable in the archaeological material.

Hyksos rule was based on a strong warrior class, which shows up in burials with weapons. Government seems to have been carried out via a loose system of vassals, with a 'homeland' in the eastern delta and a strong grip on Middle Egypt (Gardiner 1916; Habachi 1972a: 51–5). The 17th Dynasty in Thebes, in a nominal vassal status until the reign of the 15th Dynasty king Apepi, enjoyed a large degree of independence. It is not known how far the Hyksos controlled the central or western delta, but they definitely controlled the oasis road to the kingdom of Kush in the Sudan, with which they had built up good relations (Collin *et al.* 2000; Collin 2005).

Hyksos rule caused a rapid enlargement of Avaris to approximately 250 hectares, more than twice or even three times the size of Syrian royal towns in the Middle Bronze Age such as Ugarit, Qatna, Ebla, Byblos or Hazor. It seems that in the middle of the seventeenth century BC there was a substantial influx of population to Avaris. However, they were not recent immigrants but must have been living in Egypt for some time as their material culture was highly Egyptianized. Soon afterwards, other sites at the edge of the eastern delta were settled, such as Tell el-Yahudiya (Weinstein 1997; Holladay 2001a) which showed a typical Near Eastern rampart fortification (Naville 1893), and Tell el-Maskhuta in the Wadi Tumilat (Holladay 1997, 2001b). Other sites of this acculturated Near Eastern population have been found at Inshâs, Ghita, Farasha, Tell Kua and Tell el-Sahaba.

A blend between the Levantine Bronze Age and Egyptian cultures developed. In the sacred sphere, Near Eastern temple types were used at Tell el-Dabʿa, such as the broad-room temple and bent-axis temple, whereas the surrounding cemeteries had Egyptian-type mortuary chapels. However, they showed Near Eastern influence in some of their installations (Bomann 1991: 85–6). The altars for burnt offerings in front of the temples were obviously a result of Near Eastern tradition, especially one between oak trees which were holy to Asherah, the consort of the Canaanite god El (Bietak 1996b: 36). A house for funerary meals attached to the sacred precinct is reminiscent of ancient Near Eastern installations such as the *bêt marzeah* (Bietak 2003b: 155–9). So are the *favissa* pits with the remains of such meals in the vicinity of the altars (Müller 1996, 1998, 2001, forthcoming). Also Near Eastern may be the construction of the tomb vaults (van den Brink 1978: V, 93; Forstner-Müller 2002). Levantine amphorae were used for the burial of infants, even though Egyptian vessels

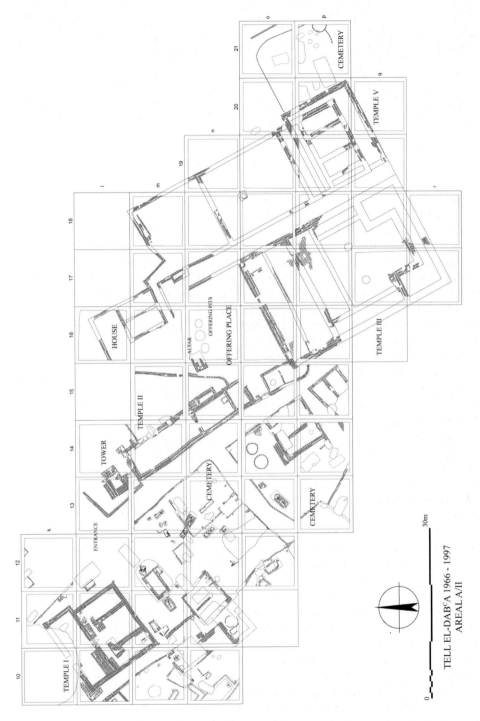

TELL EL-DABᶜA 1966 - 1997
AREA A/II

0 _____ 30m

Figure 29.7 The sacred precinct at Tell el-Dabᶜa shortly before the beginning of the Hyksos period.

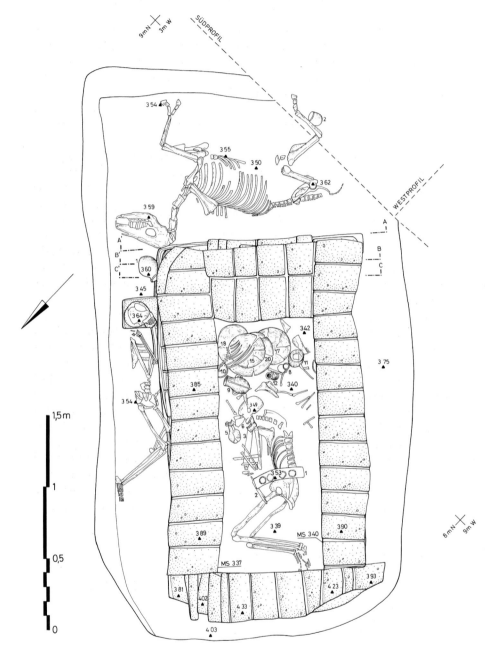

Figure 29.8 Warrior tomb with donkey burials at Tell el-Dabʿa (after Forstner-Müller 2002: 173, figs 8a–b).

would have been more resistant to breakage. In warrior burials, the weapons are exclusively Near Eastern in typology (Philip 2006). Horses and chariotry were introduced to Egypt either in the early Hyksos Period or even during the late 13th Dynasty (Boessneck and von den Driesch 1992b: 24–5).

The Hyksos and the Asiatic population which supported their rule seem to have had north-western Semitic birth names (Redford 1992: 100, 106–10; Ryholt 1997: 99–102, 126–30; Schneider 1998: 33–56), and most probably spoke such a language; some of the Hyksos adopted Egyptian throne names (Table 29.1: second, third and fifth lines). There are still difficulties in identifying and associating the names of the 15th Dynasty rulers known from monuments with the partly corrupted names of the Manethonian tradition. At present a tentative synchronization can be proposed (Table 29.1).

According to the Royal Canon of Turin, the 15th Dynasty reigned for 108 years, between 1638 and 1530 BC (Farina 1938: 56; von Beckerath 1964: 22, 135–6; 1997: 137; Ryholt 1997: 118–19). The source of their power was overseas trade with the Levant and Cyprus, especially in copper, olive oil and other commodities. We do not know exactly what brought about the downfall of the Hyksos. It is probable that the cutting off of commodities from the Sudan, especially gold and ivory, also caused disruption of trade in the eastern Mediterranean. Epidemics at Avaris might have exacerbated the situation: in the London Medical Papyrus and Papyrus Hearst, both from the early 18th Dynasty, bubonic plague is called 'the Asiatic disease' (Goedicke 1986).

During the long reign of Apepi, king Seqenenra of Thebes seems to have had difficulties with his overlord in Avaris, as indicated by the literary Papyrus Sallier I (Gardiner 1932: 85–8; Säve-Söderbergh 1953: 43–5; Goedicke 1986; Goldwasser 2006a). Interestingly, the mummy of Seqenenra shows deadly wounds inflicted by Asiatic battle-axes (Bietak and Strouhal 1974). He thus seems to have been killed in the course of an uprising; afterwards, the situation might have calmed down. Still during the reign of Apepi, Kamose, the successor of the slain king, started another uprising, attacking first the vassals of the Hyksos in Middle Egypt before finally launching an assault against Avaris with ships and troops. An envoy sent by Apepi to the king of Kush – to try to win support against Kamose – was intercepted and sent back to Avaris. Kamose erected several stelae at Karnak to commemorate these events (Habachi 1972a). Kamose died in the same year and it took a long period of years until the Thebans, under Ahmose, were once again able to marshal another

Table 29.1 Synchronization of 15th Dynasty rulers

Manetho	Monuments	Genealogy of Priests
Salitis	Seker-her (Schneider: Sikru-Haddu)	Sharek
Bnon	Meruserra Yaqub-her	
Apachnan	Seuserenra Khyan	
Iannas	Yanassi-iden	
Apophis	Aauserra Apepi	Apopi
Assis/Archles	Khamudi (Schneider: Chalmudi)	
Ahmose	Ahmes	Ahmes

assault against the suzerains of Avaris. After taking Memphis, Ahmose bypassed Avaris and cut it off from its connection to Palestine by capturing the frontier fortress of Tjaru (Tell el-Hebua) (Peet 1923: 129, n. 2). Finally Avaris was taken, apparently after a longer siege. Ahmose also besieged another stronghold of the Hyksos in Palestine with the name Sharuhen, probably Tell el-ʿAjjûl in southern Palestine (Kempinski 1974).

Avaris itself was not destroyed, but abandoned. Only the area of the temple of Seth/Baʿal Zephon – the chief god of Avaris – showed continued activity. The pharaohs of the 18th Dynasty respected its precinct, and it was only abandoned in the Amarna Period, to be rebuilt again under Tutankhamun and Horemheb. But what happened to the Hyksos rulers and their people? We do not know the fate of the last Hyksos king, Khamudi, but the Asiatic community in Egypt did not retreat to Palestine as Josephus claimed. In the layers of the early 18th Dynasty at the western edge of Avaris, the pottery shows that the ceramic production of the late Hyksos Period continued, with its blend of Levantine Bronze Age and Egyptian forms, into the reign of Thutmose III (Bietak, forthcoming). Vessels connected to wine production, such as amphorae, dipper juglets and strainers, continued to be produced in their original Bronze Age forms – perhaps a sign that viticulture remained in the hands of Canaanite prisoners of war. Also the weaponry of the 18th Dynasty was produced along Near Eastern lines. The same is true of chariots and most likely everything connected with the grooming and training of the horses. All this is a sign that a fair proportion of the Asiatic population which had supported Hyksos rule remained behind and was integrated into Egyptian society. Canaanite cults (Stadelmann 1967: 32–47, 99–110) were certainly maintained at Avaris and Peru-nefer (Collombert and Coulon 2000: 217), the major Egyptian naval stronghold in the time of Thutmose III and Amenhotep II. Other Asiatic cults, such as Baalat, Anat and Qudshu (Qadesh), are known from there in the 19th Dynasty.

It seems likely that those cults were a continuation from Hyksos Avaris, which, according to texts (Kamose second victory stela), had a big harbour. In this connection, the idea that the Egyptian port of Peru-nefer was at or near Memphis has to be refuted from a geographical point of view. Harbours for seagoing ships in the delta could only be positioned in reach of the tides, since, in the season of dryness (*shemu*), before the annual inundation in summer, the Nile was not navigable all the time. It seems also to make no sense for the Egyptians to have located a naval and military base for offensive activities in the Levant more than 150 kilometres upstream, which would have delayed any military reaction for days. The newly discovered military installations at ʿEzbet Helmy – especially a huge palace precinct of royal dimensions, covering 13 acres from the prime time of Peru-nefer (Figure 29.9) (Bietak 2005; Bietak and Forstner-Müller 2003, 2005) – now provide the hitherto missing arch-aeological evidence for such a base at Avaris (see Daressy 1928–9, 1929–31; Habachi 2001: 207). Fish remains show that the site was in antiquity in reach of the tides (Boessneck and von den Driesch 1992b: 42–3).

At the beginning of the 18th Dynasty, Egypt was not yet an imperial power. However, the traumatic experience with the Hyksos and the invasion of the Kushites during the Second Intermediate Period brought about the conviction that only the annihilation of those hostile powers would secure the Egyptian state. Ahmose re-conquered Lower Nubia after destroying the last stronghold of the Hyksos, Sharuhen

Figure 29.9 Plan of the palace precinct at Tell el-Dabʿa/ʿEzbet Helmy.

(Sethe 1905: 4). The traditionally close relationship with Byblos was probably also restored under Ahmose.

Amenhotep I (Schmitz 1978) tried to annihilate the kingdom of Kush (Bonnet 1991: 114) and seems also to have been active as far north as the kingdom of Tunip (Redford 1979), perhaps preparing the ground for an assault by his successor Thutmose I as far as the Euphrates. However, there is no record of activity in Palestine. What were the pharaohs suddenly doing in northern Syria far beyond their original realm? The southwards movement of the Hurrians (Wilhelm 1981) might provide the most likely answer. After the destruction of the powerful Amorite kingdoms of Yamkhad (Aleppo) and Babylon by the Hittites in the sixteenth century BC, and the subsequent rapid withdrawal of this new power in the Near East due to internal turmoil, the way was free for the Hurrians who originated north of the Euphrates. They created a kingdom known as Mitanni between the Euphrates and the Khabur, under an Indo-Aryan elite. Hurrians and Aryans (the Mariannu) soon infiltrated the sensitive network of city-states in Syria (Naʾaman 1994). Mitanni was thereby able to create

433

a series of client states, gradually spreading its influence southwards. As in the Middle Kingdom, Egyptian commercial and political interests were focused on the rich states of Syria, intermediaries for long-distance trade with Mesopotamia, Asia Minor and, to some extent, Cyprus. Any interference from another power was against Egyptian interests and led inevitably to conflict.

Thutmose I (Baligh 1997) campaigned in northern Syria, pushing northwards as far as the Euphrates. On his way through Syria he seems to have met little or no resistance; it was probably a show of force towards the Syrians and Mitanni. During the short reign of his successor Thutmose II, the Shôsu-Bedouin from the Syrian Desert entered the fertile plains and in the course of the following centuries became an increasingly troublesome neighbour for the Egyptians and Canaanites alike (Giveon 1971: 1, 9–10). It seems that, in Hatshepsut's 22-year reign, she gave little attention to Syria, and the Hurrian infiltration of city-states spread throughout the region. It is, perhaps, no coincidence that after the death of Hatshepsut, a coalition of 330 city-states was formed under the leadership of the princes of Tunip and Kadesh. The coalition troops were concentrated near Megiddo at the southern edge of the Jezreel plain, from where they perhaps intended to plan an attack against Egypt (Helck 1971: 118–19). The major part of Palestine, which – with the exception of the area around Sharuhen – had not been among Egypt's enemies since the Hyksos Period, was now in this coalition.

Young Thutmose III (Cline and O'Connor 2005; Dorman 2005) did not hesitate. According to his annals in the Temple of Karnak (Noth 1943; Grapow 1949; Redford 1986, 2003) he summoned an army and, marching first along the *via maris*, secured Gaza and Jaffa – an important harbour – before moving inland to the Aruna pass where he surprised the enemy coalition by appearing unexpectedly along a risky route through the Carmel mountains. He defeated the dispersed enemy and took Megiddo itself, where the princes had taken refuge, after a siege of seven months (Figure 29.10) (Nelson 1913; Faulkner 1942; Goedicke 2000; Redford 2003: 7–34, 109–10; Spalinger 2005: 83–100). All the princes, with the exception of the fugitive prince of Kadesh, had to swear an oath of allegiance to Egypt. Thutmose III left the princes in charge of their cities, but decided later to take control of their lands. The sons of the local rulers were taken hostage to Egypt to be educated in a special institution attached to the palace in order to succeed their fathers as faithful Egyptian vassals.

Numerous further campaigns were necessary to secure Canaan and Syria. To judge by the archaeological record, towns in Canaan were no longer allowed to build defensive walls. Moreover, garrisons were installed at strategically important places. Along the Syrian coast a chain of harbour towns was captured and secured with garrisons and supply bases. Thus, logistic lines were secured along the coast, with Peru-nefer as the major dockyard and provision base at home. Close ties with Crete, the major sea power at the time, might have helped Egypt to build up its navy (Vercoutter 1956; Wachsmann 1987; Matthäus 1995; Bietak and Marinatos 2003). It seems no coincidence that only in the time of Thutmose III was the designation 'Keftiu (Cretan) ship' used for a specific seagoing vessel (Säve-Söderbergh 1946: 49). All in all, one cannot but admire Thutmose III's logic in building up his military infrastructure to prepare the way for a showdown with Mitanni and the conquest of Syria.

In his thirty-third year, Thutmose III launched a campaign from his Syrian harbours, via Aleppo and Carchemish, to the Euphrates, even bringing boats with him to cross

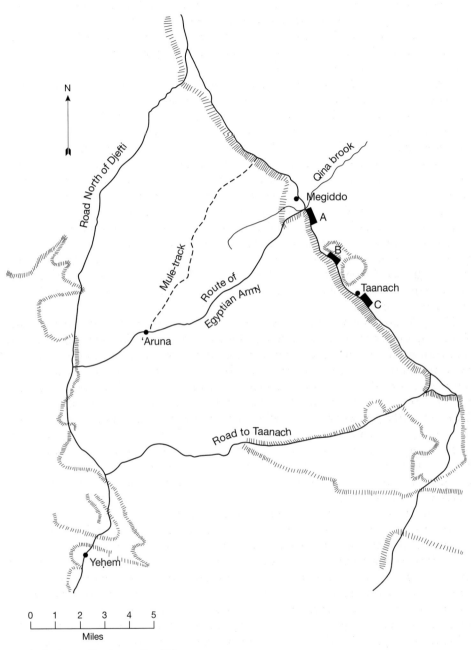

A. Syrian north wing on the 19th
B. Syrian central reserve somewhere along this road
C. Syrian south wing

Figure 29.10 The Battle of Megiddo (after Faulkner 1942: 8, map 1).

the river. The adversary did not engage in a decisive battle, but in this and following campaigns the city-states in the Orontes Valley, including the arch-enemy Kadesh, fell into the hands of the king. The area from Ugarit and Niya southward now belonged to the sphere of Egypt; but the area north-east of the Orontes stubbornly resisted conquest. These stunning feats of warfare brought Egypt great respect in the Levant until the Amarna Period. Delegations from Assur, Babylon, Cyprus and, most probably, the Hittites, brought presents and opened diplomatic contacts for years to come. Trade flourished, especially with Cyprus which was important to Egypt because of its copper production.

Amenhotep II (Der Manuelian 1987) received military training at Peru-nefer. He seems to have become obsessed with military pursuits such as rowing, archery and training chariot horses. Under his rule, Canaanite cults flourished (Stadelmann 1967: 32–6, 146–50). As king, he compared himself to Ba'al or Reshep. At Peru-nefer, we have to imagine, alongside Nubian archers, a big community of people from the Near East, working in the dockyards and in the army. Foreign emissaries, among them Mariannu from Canaan, came to Peru-nefer and were provisioned there (Golenischeff 1913: 67 f., 183 f.), showing that Palestine at this time was already heavily infiltrated by Hurrians and Aryans.

During a co-regency of three years (Redford 1965; Murnane 1977: 44–57) with his father, Amenhotep II took over military affairs. The Syrian states, under the influence of Mitanni, changed sides near the end of Thutmose III's life, but Amenhotep II was not able to restore the Egyptian realm completely. In his first campaign he was engaged in the area of Takhshi around Kadesh, personally killing seven princes and bringing their corpses back home, hanging on the prow of his ship (Helck 1955b: 1297; Klug 2002: 283, 290). In his seventh year, the king campaigned in the far north, grappling with Qatna, conquering Niya and securing Ugarit against rebellion. But the towns in the Orontes Valley north of Kadesh were lost soon afterwards. The high number of Shôsu-Bedouin among Egyptian prisoners of war suggests that they had steadily become a major problem through their incursions into Canaan (Janssen 1963; Giveon 1971: 12–15). In the Sharon plain, a Mitannian envoy was captured with a cuneiform letter tied to his neck, showing that Mitanni never tired of subversive diplomacy in the Levant. Nevertheless, Mitanni seems to have entered peace negotiations with Egypt after coming under attack from the Hittites. It seems doubtful if such a treaty was ever concluded, as Mitanni was subsequently able to defeat its adversary in the west and regain Aleppo.

Little is known about the military campaigns of Thutmose IV (Bryan 1992) in the Near East. He seems to have been active against Mitanni at the beginning of his reign. Otherwise the king seems to have regulated the enthronement of princes in the area controlled by Egypt. His son and successor, Amenhotep III (Kozloff *et al.* 1992; Schade-Busch 1992; Cabrol 2000; O'Connor and Cline 2001), probably never campaigned in the Near East. Instead, his reign was characterized by intense diplomacy, especially with Mitanni, Babylon, Hatti, Arzawa, Cyprus and the Syro-Palestinian city-states. He also concluded several diplomatic marriages, especially with two princesses of Mitanni, Gilukhepa and Tadukhepa. During his reign, Shuppiluliumash of Hatti tried to meddle in the internal politics of Mitanni and to win over client states in northern Syria. This led directly to closer ties between Mitanni and Egypt and to the second diplomatic marriage. Tushratta of Mitanni also sent to the ailing

Egyptian king, who suffered from severe caries and probably a tongue carcinoma, a statue of Ishtar of Nineveh, famous for its healing powers.

The administration of the Near Eastern possessions, about which we learn mainly from the Amarna Letters (Moran 1992), seems to have originated in the reign of Thutmose III (Mohammad 1959; Helck 1960; 1971: 247–52; Weinstein 1981: 12; Na'aman 1981; Groll 1983; Murnane 1997). According to Near Eastern tradition it was based on vassalhood. Three provinces were created, each under a *rabisu* (most probably corresponding to the Egyptian title of an 'overseer of the foreign countries'). The northernmost province was Amurru, stretching from Ugarit to south of Byblos, and inland to the Orontes. Its capital was the harbour town of Sumur, and there were other strongholds with garrisons, such as Ullaza. Inland was the province of Upe, centred on the oasis of Damascus and the Beqa' Valley, with its capital at Kumidi. The southernmost province was Canaan (including what is today Palestine) with its capital at Gaza. The task of the *rabisu* was to mediate between the city-states and secure the taxes imposed by Egypt.

Besides the seats of the *rabisu* there were strongholds such as Jaffa, Yarimuta, Sumur and Ullaza on the coast, Beth Shan in the Jordan Valley, and other places known only from texts. In addition to the royal towns, there were also towns or domains belonging to temples in Egypt, with their revenues going to their proprietors. The system worked in an indirect way, with the princes responsible for the delivery of taxes. They imposed pressure on their own people which led to local rebellion, exploited by rival factions in the local nobilities.

During the long reign of Amenhotep III, tendencies to defect can be observed in some regions. Some city-states in Palestine tried to win Babylon as a protective power, but were refused due to the good relationship between Babylon and Egypt. More serious in the long run was the formation of the kingdom of Amurru within the Egyptian province of the same name. Its troublesome ruler Abdi Ashirta was recognized by the Egyptians as a prince. Since Egypt did not want to invest in military protection, it entrusted him with the protection of the capital Sumur and the other provincial stronghold, Ullaza. This was used by Abdi Ashirta to impose his control over the other city-states of Amurru. His method was to destabilize the cities with the help of the Habiru, to murder or depose the local prince, and to take over power. For a long time he was able to reassure the Egyptians of his good intentions, but was subsequently captured and killed. Amurru remained a problematic region.

Perhaps more than in the Thutmoside Period, numerous immigrants from the Near East now came to Egypt (Helck 1971: 352–69) as envoys, merchants, sailors, soldiers, different craftsmen and professionals. Foreign technologies were introduced, such as glass-making, metallurgy and military techniques. Egypt was subject to many different influences from the Levant, which are found in diplomacy, literature, music and, of course, in manners and customs that were foreign to Egypt. It seems that many foreigners served in the army and at the court of Akhenaten, often in confidential top positions such as the vizier of Lower Egypt Aper-El, the Second Prophet of Aten Pentu, some of the commissioners in Syria, and probably also the chamberlain Tutu. Like his father before him, Akhenaten also married a princess of Mitanni. In his foreign policy, Akhenaten's endeavours are often underestimated. It was a difficult time, with the Hittites under Shuppiluliumash having grown strong again and challenging Mitanni and its clients in northern Syria. Mitanni was reduced to its core territory, and its king, Tushratta, was murdered by one of his sons. The time of this major power and ally of Egypt was over. All this encouraged the defection of Syrian client states from Egypt. For example, Aziru of Amurru, the son of Abdi Ashirta, succeeded in gaining control over one harbour after another, over Sumur and, finally, for a while, over Byblos. The pleas for help by the loyal princes in southern Syria went unanswered by Egypt at this critical time. Finally, Aziru was summoned to Egypt where he was able to exculpate himself with the help of people at court. He then returned home and soon defected to the Hittites. After some time, Ugarit in the north was also obliged to change sides.

At the same time as the Hittites attacked ʿAmqa, Akhenaten seems to have passed away. His death must have caused something like a political earthquake in Egypt and abroad. It is very likely that the major political shift in northern Syria, including the defection of Amurru, happened at this time of weakness. Horemheb (Hari 1964; Kruchten 1981; Martin 1989), initially under Tutankhamun and Ay as supreme general and later as regent, was mainly responsible for Egyptian defences and endeavours to regain lost ground. He refortified the military and naval stronghold at Tell el-Dabʿa – most probably Peru-nefer – with a formidable fortress (Bietak 2005). As a king he rebuilt the temple of Seth/Baʿal at the nearby site of Avaris as a part of a programme to restore the temples destroyed in the Amarna Period (Bietak 1985, 1990). He installed his long-time military colleague Paramesse (later Ramesses I) as his successor. The Ramesside dynasty seems to have originated in the eastern delta, probably Avaris. This brought about the installation of the god Seth of Avaris in his Asiatic guise as dynastic god of the 19th Dynasty (Montet 1933; Bietak 1990).

Seti I, son of Ramesses I, engaged in warfare in the Near East from the first year of his reign. First he had to bring a new wave of Shôsu-Bedouin in southern Canaan and northern Sinai under control (Faulkner 1947; Gaballa 1976: 100–6; Spalinger 1979; Murnane 1985; Epigraphic Survey 1986; el-Saady 1992; Kitchen 1993b; 10–26; 1996: 2–26; 1999a: 3–53). He then finished the construction of fortresses along the *via maris*, begun by Horemheb, and seems to have extended this campaign to the Jordan Valley in order to regain lost territory (Porter and Moss 1927–99: vol. 7, 380; Kitchen 1993b: 17–19, 20–1). He also took Hammath and Yenoam and was engaged in mediation among local chiefs. Later, Seti I secured the coast at Acre, Uzu and Tyre, and received the homage of the princes of Lebanon.

From his third year onwards, Seti I decided to re-establish Egypt's old possessions in Syria. He conquered Amurru and took Kadesh, where he left a victory stela (Porter and Moss 1927–99: vol. 7, 392; Kitchen 1993b: 26). Ramesses II, his son and successor, was a powerful personality who, during a reign of 67 years, left an imprint on Egyptian history like no other ruler (Desroches-Noblecourt 1976, 1996; Kitchen 1985, 1996, 1999a; Freed 1987; Bleiberg and Freed 1991; Menu 1999; James 2002). He took over from his father the residence at Qantir/Tell el-Dabʿa and re-founded it under the name of Per-Ramesses (Habachi 1954, 2001; van Seters 1966; Pusch 1999). Continuing the tradition of Avaris, Canaanite cults flourished there: the dynastic god Seth retained his character as Baʿal (Montet 1933; Kitchen 1996: 116–17, §71; 1999a: 168–72); Astarte had a temple in the east of the town.

Prepared by his father for active kingship, Ramesses II determined to restore the Egyptian domains in Syria, provoking a clash with the Hittites who summoned an enormous army from all parts of their empire. In his fifth year, Ramesses marched in anticipation with four army corps from the Beqa' Valley to Kadesh on the Orontes (Figure 29.11a) (Goedicke 1956, 1985; Faulkner 1958; Gardiner 1960; von der Way 1984; Spalinger 1985, 2005: 209–34; Kitchen 1999a: 3–54). Misguided by manipulated intelligence, Ramesses moved ahead along the Orontes Valley with only the corps of Amun, and camped west of Kadesh where he learned that he had been led into a trap (Figure 29.11b) (Kuschke 1979; Mayer and Mayer-Opificius 1994). Hidden behind the huge *tell* of the town, and perhaps behind shrubs and woods, was the entire Hittite army. Crossing the river with their chariotry at a ford south of Kadesh, the Hittites cut the corps of Ra into pieces and started to attack the camp, while the other two Egyptian units were still too far away to take part in the battle. The Egyptians were rescued from total disaster by the fact that the enemy used only its 2,500 chariots and started to plunder the Egyptian camp, and by the sudden arrival of the Na'arin (elite troops) who appeared from the coast at the rear of the Hittite army, pushing it back into the River Orontes (Schulman 1962). This seemed to have saved the day (the first of the battle) and might have looked like a victory; but the enormous Hittite infantry was still untouched. The Egyptians, with their troops still scattered, must have withdrawn, perhaps overnight. A letter from the king of the Hittites to Ramesses was perhaps a wise suggestion, offering to withdraw with the bonus of a temporary armistice. That Kadesh remained in Hittite hands, that Amurru changed again to Hittite control, and that the Hittites seemed to have moved into Upe are clear signs that this famous battle – which Ramesses celebrated, in temple reliefs and poetic texts, as a splendid victory – was, in fact, a strategic defeat.

The Battle of Kadesh encouraged unrest in Canaan, and in the following years Ramesses was kept busy consolidating northern Palestine. He also moved into Transjordan before he was able to try his luck again in Amurru in his eighth year. In the long run, this permanent state of conflict exhausted both parties and, in the twenty-first year of Ramesses II's reign, a peace treaty was concluded between the two superpowers (Langdon and Gardiner 1920; Porter and Moss 1927–99: vol. 2, 2nd edn, 132 (§492); Edel 1994; Kitchen 1996: 79–85, §64; 1999a: 136–44). The border between the two powers was not defined, but we may suppose that Amurru north of Byblos was with the Hittites, whereas Upe and Canaan stayed with Egypt. The treaty was finally cemented in the thirty-third year of Ramesses II by a marriage with the oldest daughter of the Hittite king (Kitchen 1975–89, 1999a: 146–63). In her retinue arrived numerous maids and troops who seemed to have been stationed permanently at Per-Ramesses: military workshops, found at Qantir, produced Hittite shields (Pusch 1989: 250–2; 1990: 103–4).

Although the Egyptians did not strictly follow all the terms of the peace treaty (they gave refuge to the deposed predecessor and nephew of Hattushili, Urhi-Teshub), peace and friendship were maintained until the end of the Hittite empire. Merenptah, the thirteenth son and successor of Ramesses II, even sent food aid (the earliest known in history) to the hunger-stricken Hittite kingdom (Kitchen 2003: 4, 5:3, col. 24).

The next decades were dramatic for Egypt and the whole of the eastern Mediterranean. Due to major migration of different peoples, states and communities were destroyed in western Asia Minor, Cyprus and the Aegean. Peoples were displaced and took to the sea in search of new homes; some became pirates, some offered themselves as mercenaries, causing unrest, warfare and destruction throughout Anatolia,

(a)

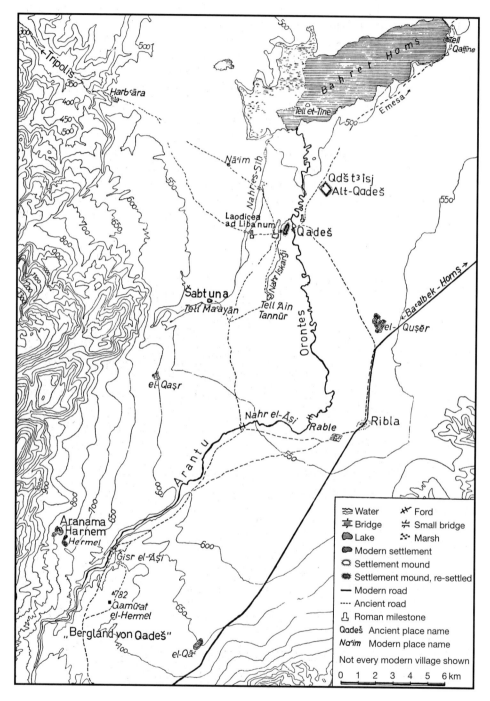

Figure 29.11a   Map of the Battle of Kadesh (after Kuschke 1979: 9, fig. 1).

the Aegean, Cyprus and the Levant (Stadelmann 1968: 160; Sandars 1985). At the same time, the Libyan tribes of the Libu and Meshwesh tried to settle in Egypt (Hölscher 1937: 61–3; Kitchen 1990: 19–24). They made common cause with the 'Sea Peoples' of the Lukka, Sherden, Akawasha, Turusha and Shekelesh, most of whom seem to have originated in western Asia Minor, and some of whom had already served as auxiliaries of the Hittites at the Battle of Kadesh.

According to the great victory inscription of Merenptah (Schulman 1987; von der Way 1992; Manassa 2003) this coalition penetrated as far as the eastern delta, threatening Per Ramesses and causing its abandonment as a royal residence. The Egyptians finally defeated the coalition in a long battle at Pi-yer, probably near Memphis; but Egypt's desperate defence against the Libyans and Sea Peoples within its own territory seems to have encouraged an uprising in Canaan. According to the so-called 'Israel Stela' from the mortuary temple of Merenptah, encounters took place in the same year (*c.*1209 BC) at Ashkelon, Gezer and Yenoam (near Lake Tiberias). For the first and also the last time, the name 'Israel' appears in this listing. As the

(b)(i)

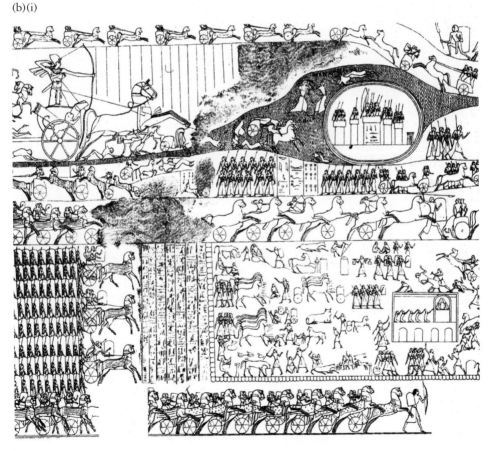

Figure 29.11b (i) Representation of the Battle at Kadesh, (ii) with the tent of the pharaoh enlarged (after James 2002: 99–102, 104–5).

(b)(ii)

hieroglyphic determinative signifies a people, not a toponym, we can conclude that Israel at this time was a still-unsettled tribe beyond Lake Tiberias in Transjordan (Engel 1979). From the same period, Shôsu-Bedouin from Edom are mentioned in Papyrus Anastasi VI (54–6) as obtaining permission from the Egyptian frontier authorities to move temporarily into the Wadi Tumilat to feed their livestock during a drought (Giveon 1971: 131–4). This example of a frontier protocol is seen as a model for the biblical sojourn of the Israelites in Egypt, but with other migrants.

In the Ramesside Period it was common for high officials to be of Near Eastern origin. At the end of the 19th Dynasty, after the reign of Seti II, there seems to have been a dispute about the succession and a chancellor with the name Bay, referred to as the Asiatic *irsu* (upstart, literally 'the one who made himself'), played a role as kingmaker and power-broker (Gardiner 1961: 282). He and the xenophobia surrounding him are taken by Old Testament scholars as a model for Joseph and the sojourn of the Israelites in Egypt (Knauf 1994: 103–6).

Papyrus Harris (Erichsen 1933) and the reliefs of the temple of Medinet Habu inform us about the mighty deeds of Ramesses III, considered the last great pharaoh of the New Kingdom (Fèvre 1992; Grandet 1993; Vandersleyen 1998). The king is shown in land and sea battles against the Sea Peoples (Porter and Moss 1927–99: vol. 2, 2nd edn, 518–20 (188, 189); Heinz 2001: 306–7), particularly the Philistines (Dothan 1989; Dothan and Dothan 1992), who tried to invade Egypt. In addition, the king had to grapple with Libyan invasions. Historical criticism (Stadelmann 1968), however, has clearly shown that while the king was engaged against the Libyans in his fifth year, Egypt lost the major part of coastal Palestine to the Philistines, the Djeker and other Sea Peoples. After helping to bring about the collapse of the Hittite empire, they started to build bridgeheads (Figure 29.12) in the later Pentapolis, at Dor and the bay of Acre, and were responsible for the destruction of Ugarit and most of the other Syrian harbour towns (Bietak 1991a, 1993; Stager 1995). It seems that some Sea Peoples had already tried to settle there and had offered their services to the Egyptians – since some of them, wearing the characteristic feather-crown, were integrated into the Egyptian army against the Libyans in the fifth year of Ramesses III. Moreover, Sea Peoples can also be discovered among the Egyptian crews during the main sea battle (below).

In the king's eighth year, the Sea Peoples made an attempt to invade Egypt by land, with heavy, ox-drawn wagons, and by sea (Nelson 1930: pls 32, 37). They were defeated in a land and a sea battle which most probably took place at the mouth of the easternmost Nile branch (Figure 29.13). (The land battle did not take place in Amurru as has often been proposed, as Stadelmann (1968) was able to demonstrate by the lack of an itinerary of the Egyptian army.) However, Egypt was only able to keep its territory in the Jordan Valley by fortifying the settlement at Beth Shan. Since the 19th Dynasty, Egypt had attempted to gain a more direct grip on the administration of Canaan. Egyptian governors with their special residences (Oren 1985) and scribes (Goldwasser 1982, 1984) were established in the important towns to govern them directly without local princes. Such endeavours were stepped up under Ramesses III. Egypt also tried to enlist spiritual support by constructing temples for Canaanite deities at Beth Shan (Rowe 1940) and Lachish (Ussishkin 2004: 215–81).

In one of his last raids, Ramesses III campaigned in the desert of Seïr, east of Jordan, against the Shôsu-Bedouin – among them probably the Proto-Israelites (Figure 29.12) (Giveon 1971: 134–7, doc. 38). It seems that some of the prisoners of war from this conflict were distributed among the temples of Egypt as slaves. It is, otherwise, too much of a coincidence that the so-called four-room house, typical for Israelite domestic buildings from the twelfth century onwards, appears in a single but clear instance at the same time in Egypt as the house of a workman in Western Thebes (Figure 29.14) (Bietak 1991b).

The Jezreel plain was held until the reign of Ramesses VI and the area south of the Wadi Gaza including Tell el-Farʿah-South a little longer. In the end, however, Egypt was forced to withdraw from the Levant completely. Having already left the

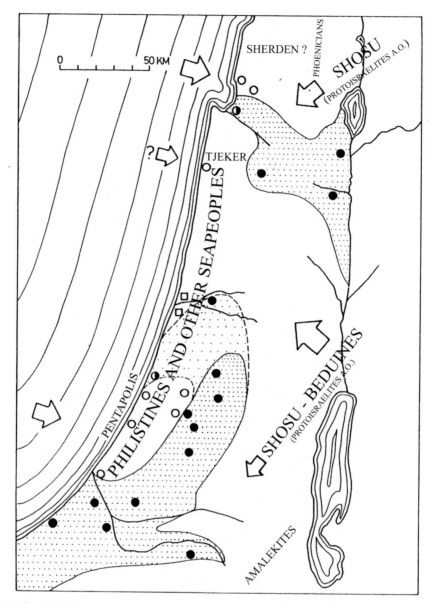

REST OF THE EGYPTIAN PROVINCE CANAᶜAN AFTER THE
NCURSION OF SEAPEOPLES UNDER THE REIGN OF RAMSES III

● DATED EGYPTIAN SITES
   OF THE 20th DYNASTY
◑ SITES OF THE 20th DYNASTY
   WITHOUT INSCRIPTIONS
⇨ EARLY BRIDGEHEADS OF
   THE SEAPEOPLES

○ TOWNS OF THE PENTAPOLIS AND DOR, AKKO, T.KEISAN
□ IMPORTANT LATER TOWNS OF THE PHILISTINES
▦ REST OF THE EGYPTIAN PROVINCE CANAᶜAN

Figure 29.12   Canaan in the first half of the 20th Dynasty, showing the settlement
of the Sea Peoples and the Shôsu-Bedouin, and Egyptian-held territory (after Bietak 1993: 295).

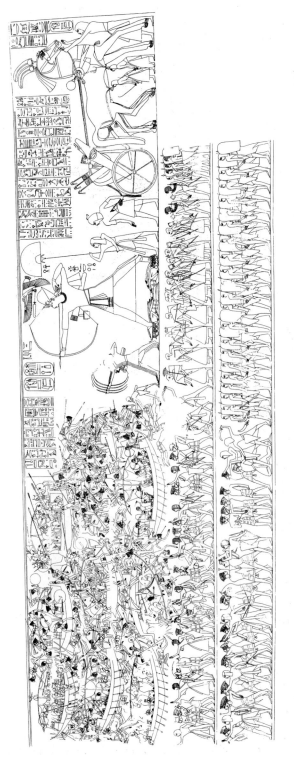

Figure 29.13 The sea battle of Ramesses III against the Sea Peoples, from the north wall of the temple of Medinet Habu (after Heinz 2001: I.18).

(i)

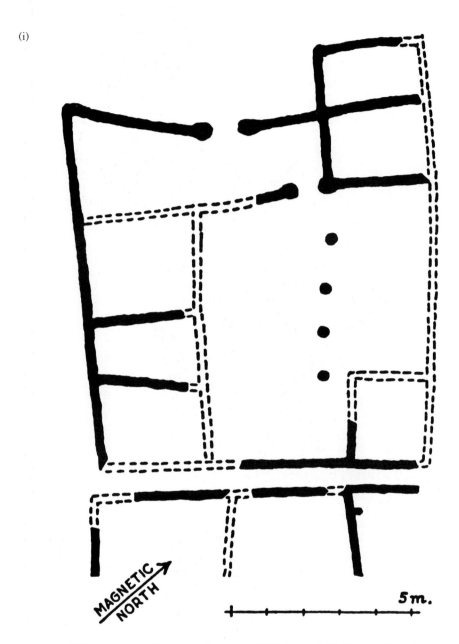

MAGNETIC NORTH

5m.

Figure 29.14 Four-room houses in (i) Thebes and (ii) Canaan, from the twelfth century BC (after Hölscher 1939: fig. 59 and Früz 1980: Abb. 1, respectively).

(ii)

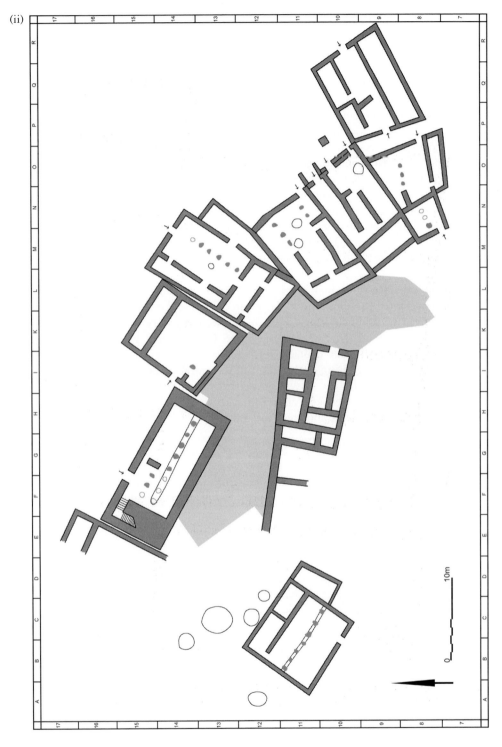

Figure 29.14 (ii)

447

coast of Canaan to the Philistines, Djeker and Sherden, it had to leave the main inland centres to the Canaanites. The northern Galilee was settled by Phoenicians, moving southwards due to unrest in their homelands, while the Shôsu took control of the Judaean highlands, before encroaching on the Canaanite centres (Giveon 1971: 236–7). Israel and the Philistine kingdoms had to compete for supremacy in Palestine. Other Shôsu such as the Edomites, the Moabites and the Ammonites were also involved and finally settled in Transjordan where they founded new kingdoms (LaBianca and Younker 1995). In Syria there was also ethnic movement. The last remaining and revived imperial power, the Assyrians under Tiglath-Pileser (1114–1076 BC), controlled Phoenicia for some time and levied tribute on harbour towns (Wiseman 1975: 461).

Egypt continued to maintain contacts with the new powers of the Levant, but it was no longer an imperial power itself. Along the Phoenician coast, it was viewed as an ordinary trading partner and even had to draw on its past prestige to be respected as such, as is shown by the story of Wenamun (Gardiner 1932; Egberts 1991, 2001; Schipper 2005). A flicker of Egypt's past glory was temporarily reignited by the raid of Shoshenq I (945–924 BC) into Palestine, but this was an act of plunder, not of conquest (cf. 1 Kings 14: 25 f.).

The Phoenician city-states flourished, giving Egypt access to trade with the Levant, Cyprus and the eastern Mediterranean. Egyptian culture and religion produced motifs that were picked up in Phoenician art, such as jewellery, ivory carving, glyptic and repoussé work on metal. In the meantime, the Greek world grew in power and prestige, enjoying even closer contacts with Egypt (Lloyd 1975: 9–60). Egypt, of course, could not stop meddling in the affairs of its new neighbours, provoking attack and foreign domination by the Assyrians, confrontation with the Babylonians and finally domination by the Persians, after which it was absorbed into the Hellenistic world of Alexander the Great and the Ptolemies.

ACKNOWLEDGEMENTS

I would like to thank Toby Wilkinson for editing this manuscript, Irene Kaplan for helping me with the bibliography and Nikky Math for producing the illustrations except where stated otherwise.

CHAPTER THIRTY

EGYPT AND MESOPOTAMIA

———·◆·———

Toby Wilkinson

INTRODUCTION

Egypt and Mesopotamia – the valley of the River Nile, and the land between the Rivers Tigris and Euphrates – were the twin cradles of civilization in the ancient Near East. The highly developed, complex societies that arose in the two areas during the fourth millennium BC dominated their respective hinterlands for much of the following four thousand years. Yet, the Egyptian and Mesopotamian heartlands were geographically remote, and the two civilizations – which, to a large extent, remained culturally distinct – came into direct contact only infrequently, when their spheres of influence intersected in the Levant.

Three major phases of interaction are apparent, each of a different character, reflecting the particular geo-political circumstances of the time. The first phase of contact took place during the second half of the fourth millennium BC, a period of growing social complexity and state formation, corresponding to the later Predynastic Period in Egypt, the Middle and Late Uruk Periods in Mesopotamia. The second phase was briefer, occupying the third quarter of the second millennium BC (the 18th Dynasty in Egypt, the Late Bronze Age in Mesopotamia and the Levant) when the Egyptian and Mesopotamian powers vied for political supremacy in the Near East. The third phase – which witnessed the final clash of the two great civilizations and their eclipse by new powers in the region – spanned the first half of the first millennium BC (the Late Period in Egypt, the Iron Age in Mesopotamia and the Levant). A detailed examination of these three periods, the underlying dynamics and the types of contact that took place – ranging from trade to military confrontation and diplomacy – reveals the complex, changing and often contradictory relationship between Egypt and Mesopotamia over the course of their long histories.

CULTURAL EXCHANGE AT THE DAWN OF HISTORY

The earliest evidence for contact of an indirect nature between Egypt and Mesopotamia is the appearance in the mid-fifth millennium BC, in both regions, of small items of

449

lapis lazuli, the precious dark-blue stone derived from sources in the Pamir Mountains of Tajikistan, the Chagai Hills on the Pakistan–Iran border and, most famously, the mines of Sar-i Sang in the Badakhshan province of Afghanistan (Delmas and Casanova 1990: 504). The pattern of lapis lazuli importation in Mesopotamia and Egypt is strikingly similar, suggesting that both regions participated in the long-distance trade networks that carried low-weight, high-value commodities across western Asia (Feldman 2001: 387).

As the process of social stratification in Upper Egypt gained momentum during the second quarter of the fourth millennium BC (the Naqada I and early Naqada II periods), the ruling elites at the sites of Naqada (ancient Nubt) and Hierakonpolis (ancient Nekhen) began to enhance their power and prestige by exploiting the gold reserves of the Eastern Desert. This gave them the means to enhance Egypt's participation in the system of international trade. At the same time, the Mesopotamian Uruk culture expanded beyond its Sumerian (southern Mesopotamian) heartland in search of high-value commodities, greatly extending the Mesopotamian sphere of influence to the north and west (Rothman 2001; Postgate and Campbell 2002). The stage was set for the first period of sustained contact between Egypt and Mesopotamia.

Initially, an intensification in trade seems to have characterized the relationship (Mark 1998). The archaeological evidence for this phenomenon comes exclusively from the Egyptian side, in the form of imports from Mesopotamia and locally produced imitations (Wilkinson 2002a). (Mineralogical analysis of the gold found in fourth millennium BC Mesopotamian contexts might yield evidence for the other side of the trading partnership.) The artefacts of Mesopotamian origin or inspiration found in Egyptian graves of the Naqada IIB–C period (*c.* 3600–3300 BC) comprise pottery vessels and seals; most of the latter have been found at the site of Naqada. The context was a period of significant socio-economic development in Upper Egypt, whereby local elites were engaged in a concerted programme of status demarcation and display. The conspicuous consumption of prestige commodities, especially exotic, imported goods, was one important means of achieving this; another was the conscious adoption and use of 'artefacts of complexity' (Postgate and Campbell 2002) which assisted the imposition of political and economic control. Cylinder seals first appeared in Upper Egypt as imports from Mesopotamia, but the usefulness of such small, portable objects in matters of economic administration, not least to record the ownership of goods, was swiftly recognized by the emerging elites. Hence, the cylinder seal was adopted into Egyptian administrative practice where it survived for many centuries.

In Late Uruk Mesopotamia, another system for recording economic information existed side-by-side with cylinder seals, in the form of clay tokens. They have been found at Uruk 'colony sites' on the Upper Euphrates, and on the nearby Amuq Plain of northern Syria, as well as in the Uruk culture's Sumerian heartland (Schmandt-Besserat 1992: 39). It is quite possible, therefore, that tokens reached Egypt along the same trade routes that carried cylinder seals and pottery vessels. Predynastic graves and settlement sites in Upper Egypt have occasionally yielded small, cone-shaped objects of fired clay, some examples showing traces of red pigment (Payne 1993: cat. nos. 1948–50; Thomas 2004: 1048, 1049, 1051 fig. 3). Usually identified as gaming-pieces (Payne 1993: 235; Thomas 2004: 1048), they might, in fact, be tokens, and represent another aspect of the Late Uruk administrative system that found a receptive audience among the proto-states of Predynastic Upper Egypt.

Besides accounting practices to establish and proclaim ownership of economic resources, the local elites of Predynastic Egypt were adept at using the medium of art to establish and reinforce the social hierarchy (Wilkinson 1999: 31–4). Here, too, Mesopotamian models were welcomed if they could assist the development of a symbolic vocabulary of power. The remarkable painted tomb T100 at Hierakonpolis (Quibell and Green 1902: pls LXXV–LXXIX; Case and Payne 1962; Payne 1973; Kemp 1973), constructed for a local ruler of the Naqada IIC period, featured a complex frieze of motifs associated with royal power, including the 'master of the beasts' – a man holding apart and restraining two lions – borrowed from contemporary Mesopotamian iconography. Such motifs could have been copied from seals or seal-impressions that entered Egypt attached to imported commodities, although the examples found to date show non-figurative, largely geometric patterns.

As the process of state formation in Egypt gathered pace in the Naqada IID and Naqada III periods (*c.*3300–3000 BC), so too did the level of contact between the Nile Valley and the Uruk culture. The indigenous elites of Upper Egypt adopted a wide range of Mesopotamian iconography (H. Smith 1992) and practices; this reflects the intensity of the ideological effort being mounted to support the major political developments taking place at sites such as Naqada and Hierakonpolis towards the end of the fourth millennium BC. In all cases, the Mesopotamian symbols adopted into Egyptian iconography – and used on objects ranging from ivory knife-handles to ceremonial siltstone palettes – expressed aspects of the complex relationship between the king and the people, and the king and the divine sphere, that were central to the Egyptian ideology of rule, but difficult to express in art. The most prominent examples were the rosette/palmette motif signifying 'divine ruler'; the intertwined serpopards (long-necked quadrupeds), representing the essential duality at the heart of the Egyptian world-view; and the aforementioned 'master of the beasts'. This last was a good example of the Egyptians adopting a Mesopotamian idea but adapting it to their own context: while the two animals (sometimes lions, sometimes snakes) held apart by the ruler might, in a Mesopotamian context, have represented the Rivers Tigris and Euphrates, in the Egyptian symbolic vocabulary they perhaps stood for the opposing forces of nature that it was the king's duty to maintain in balance (Wilkinson 2000b: 28).

Most controversially, it is possible that Egypt also borrowed from Mesopotamia the idea – though not the system – of writing. The earliest hieroglyphic writing known from Egypt comprises small bone labels, originally attached to boxes or jars of commodities, each inscribed with a few signs (Wilkinson 2003a). A large corpus of such labels has been discovered at Abydos, in the tomb of a local ruler of the Naqada III period (*c.*3150 BC); the same burial, tomb U-j, has also yielded pottery vessels inscribed in ink (Dreyer 1998). In both cases, labels and ink inscriptions, the hieroglyphs seem to record the quantity and provenance of commodities (cf. Anselin 2004). They thus seem to support an essentially administrative origin for Egyptian writing (Postgate *et al.* 1995: 465–6). Despite the arguments of some scholars to the contrary (Dreyer 1998), it still seems likely that the invention of writing in Mesopotamia preceded the earliest Egyptian hieroglyphs by 50 to 100 years. Writing offered an ideal solution to the problem of maintaining economic control over an increasingly extensive territory, and may therefore have been adopted by the Egyptian elites of the late fourth millennium BC together with other elements of the Uruk symbolic/administrative 'package'.

A more monumental expression of authority adopted from Mesopotamia was the style of architecture featuring a façade comprising alternating recesses and buttresses (Balcz 1930; Frankfort 1941; Kemp 1975; Wilkinson 1999: 224–6; but see Kaiser 1985 for a different theory concerning the style's origins). In Uruk towns and cities it was used for temples, the most important buildings in Sumerian society. In Egypt, the rulers used it, instead, for the royal palace (hence the term 'palace-façade' applied to it by Egyptologists) and the royal funerary enclosure, which were the most important buildings in Egyptian society. In other words, expressions of power were borrowed, but not the underlying political models. During the process of state formation and the 1st Dynasty, palace-façade architecture became intimately associated with the concepts of royalty and elite status, and remained a key element of Egyptian funerary symbolism as late as the Middle Kingdom (*c.*1820 BC).

The transmission of architectural forms from Mesopotamia to Egypt seems to indicate a form of contact more direct than mere trade: it suggests the movement of individuals from one cultural region to another. The presence of Mesopotamians in Predynastic Egypt is hard to prove, but the discovery of the head from an apparently Sumerian statue in the temple at Abydos (Rice 1990: fig. 36; Wilkinson 2002c) might be significant. Likewise, the clearly Mesopotamian decoration on one side of the carved ivory knife-handle from Gebel el-Arak in Upper Egypt must have been produced by an Uruk craftsman working in Egypt or an Egyptian craftsman well-versed in the Uruk style.

Recent archaeological discoveries at Tell el-Fara'in (ancient Buto) in the north-western Nile Delta may also point to the presence of a Mesopotamian element in the population of late Predynastic Egypt. Strata ranging in date from Naqada IIC–D1 (*c.*3500–3300 BC) to the early third millennium BC yielded small clay pegs (von der Way 1997: pl. 57), identified by their excavator as 'Mosaikstifte' ('mosaic pegs'), in other words decorative architectural elements from a building of Mesopotamian inspiration. Examples of mosaic pegs have been found at a number of Uruk-Period sites, including Uruk itself (Brandes 1968) and the Uruk 'colony sites' of Habuba Kabira (Strommenger 1980: 43, fig. 24) and Hassek Höyük (Behm-Blancke 1989) on the Upper Euphrates. Despite the wide variation in date of the pegs from Buto, most of them can nevertheless be associated with periods of known contact between Egypt and Mesopotamia. They would seem to offer further possible evidence for the transmission of Mesopotamian architectural styles to Egypt (Wilkinson, forthcoming).

The key significance of Buto, however, is that it proves the existence of a northern route for the contacts that took place between Egypt and Mesopotamia in the fourth millennium BC (Moorey 1990). Sherds of imported 'spiral reserved slip' pottery found at Buto (Köhler 1998: pl. 68, photographic pl. 11) in strata dating to Naqada IID2/IIIA1 (*c.*3250 BC) can be associated with phase F of the contemporary Amuq culture in northern Syria, and coincide with the floruit of the Uruk 'colonies' at nearby Habuba Kabira and Jebel Aruda. A Late Uruk cylinder seal found at Ras Shamra (ancient Ugarit) on the Syrian coast completes the evidence for a trade network linking the Uruk heartland with the Nile Delta. Moreover, the appearance around the end of the fourth millennium BC of a ceramic assemblage linking Ras Shamra, Byblos and the Palestinian coastline implies an increasing level of maritime communication in the eastern Mediterranean and provides another context within which contacts between Egypt and Mesopotamia could have taken place.

Some scholars (e.g. Rice 1990; H. Smith 1992) have argued in favour of a southern route around the Arabian peninsula, up the Red Sea and along the Wadi Hammamat to Upper Egypt, but there is little or no archaeological evidence to support this theory, now that the petroglyphs of high-prowed boats from Egypt's Eastern Desert, previously identified as Mesopotamian, can be placed firmly within an indigenous Egyptian iconographic tradition (Wilkinson 2003b). Moreover, a northern route would have been far shorter, and would have followed pre-existing trade networks, with the Uruk 'colony sites' in northern Mesopotamia and southern Anatolia providing staging posts between the Uruk heartland and Egypt. Mesopotamian artefacts and cultural influences arriving in Egypt from the north may have percolated southwards to Upper Egypt via delta ports such as Buto, but also via the Sinai peninsula and Red Sea coast: the relative frequency of Mesopotamian imports in Middle Egypt suggests that an ancient route via the Wadi Asyuti to the Red Sea was, perhaps, brought back into use in the late Predynastic Period, and that the Badari region served as Upper Egypt's 'gateway to the Near Eastern world' (Hartung 2001: 339).

Following the unification of Egypt *c.*3000 BC, the country's rulers consciously turned their backs on foreign modes of expression – except where these had already become thoroughly Egyptianized in their form or context, such as cylinder seals and palace-façade architecture – and set about promulgating an explicitly xenophobic, nationalist state ideology as part of a wider psychological effort to cement the cohesion of the new nation and ensure its loyalty to the king (Wilkinson 2002b). Mesopotamian symbols of authority, such as the 'master of the beasts', were abandoned in favour of equally venerable, indigenous motifs (Wilkinson 2000b: 29). The deliberate rejection of Mesopotamian artistic borrowings in Egypt, for internal political reasons, coincided with major geo-political changes in Mesopotamia itself, reflected in the abandonment of the Uruk colony sites on the Upper Euphrates, the retreat of the Uruk culture back to its Sumerian heartland, and a likely disruption in the trade routes through northern Iran (Feldman 2001: 387). This combination of processes not only cut off Egyptian access to lapis lazuli for three centuries or more, it also effectively severed Egyptian links with Mesopotamia. Contacts between the two cultures seem to have been almost non-existent throughout the third millennium BC, with the possible exception of an indirect link via the site of Ebla in inland Syria which the Akkadian kings of northern Mesopotamia, Sargon (*c.*2334–2279 BC) and Naram-Sin (*c.*2254–2218 BC), claimed to have controlled, and where an inscribed lid of Pepi I (*c.*2354–2310 BC) indicates some degree of contact with Egypt.

IMPERIAL RIVALRY AND INTERNATIONAL DIPLOMACY

In the middle of the second millennium BC, Egypt and Mesopotamia came into sustained contact for a second time. The new context was one of imperial rivalry, as Egypt and the states of northern and southern Mesopotamia, now mature civilizations with expansionist ambitions, sought to extend their areas of political and economic influence in the Near East. Indeed, it was an age of international relations on an unprecedented scale, involving a number of major powers vying for supremacy over the numerous city-states in the Levant (Kuhrt 1995). In the alluvial plains of southern Mesopotamia, a period of political instability had been brought to an end in the early nineteenth century BC by the rise of a strong dynasty based in the city of Babylon. The Babylonian kingdom would dominate the region for the next 1,300 years. Further north, two states emerged by the end of the eighteenth century BC, one in the east centred at Assur on the banks of the Tigris, the other in the west with its heartland in the Upper Euphrates and Upper Khabur valleys. For more than three centuries, these two kingdoms, Assyria and Mitanni, fought not only with each other but also with the Hittite state (Cline 2001) which, from its capital at Boghazköy (ancient Hattusas) on the Anatolian plateau, controlled the western approaches to the northern Levant.

By *c.* 1500 BC, a Hittite attack on Babylon had ushered in the rise of the Kassite dynasty in the south, but had overstretched the aggressors; on his victorious return, the Hittite king Khantilish I was ousted from Syria by the Mitanni who subsequently consolidated their control of the region (Astour 2001: 422). In Egypt, the defeat and expulsion of the Western Asiatic Hyksos rulers by the armies of Kamose and Ahmose at the beginning of the New Kingdom had the effect of drawing the pharaohs into the wider geo-politics of the Near East. Determined both to prevent any repeat of the humiliating foreign occupation and to expand Egyptian economic influence, the warrior kings of the early 18th Dynasty, Thutmose I and Thutmose III, embarked on an epic series of military campaigns to re-establish control over Palestine and extend the borders of Egypt into the Syrian lands to the north. In so doing, Egypt and Mitanni came to blows.

The army of Thutmose I swept through Syria-Palestine and even crossed the Euphrates, enabling the king to erect a boundary stela on the river's eastern bank, an act repeated by Thutmose III half a century later. This gesture was clearly intended to demonstrate that the Egyptian sphere of influence stretched all the way from the Nile to the Euphrates, but it did not signal Egyptian interest in Mesopotamia itself. The reasons may have been both ideological and economic. The land beyond the Euphrates already belonged to another great power, and it was culturally and geographically too remote from Egypt to be a natural part of the pharaoh's territory. Moreover, Egyptian interests in the Near East were primarily economic, and Mesopotamia did not offer access to any desirable resources that could not be obtained more directly from Syria-Palestine. The kingdom of Mitanni was thus never under direct threat from Egypt, but its wider economic and political ambitions certainly were.

The Battle of Megiddo, won by Thutmose III in *c.* 1457 BC against a confederacy of Levantine city-states, backed by Mitanni, marked Egypt's triumphant return to the power-politics of the Near East, after a lull of 25 years. Megiddo occupied a strategically important location in the Jezreel Valley, controlling the main route from Egypt to the northern Levant (Weinstein 2001). By capturing the city and ensuring the loyalty of the local rulers, Thutmose III established Egypt as a major force in the region. This new reality was recognized by the Assyrian ruler (perhaps Ashurnadinakhe) who, a year later, sent tribute to Egypt to maintain good relations. Unfortunately for Assyria, the real threat came not from Egypt but from its nearer neighbour, the kingdom of Mitanni. After Megiddo, Thutmose III launched annual military campaigns for the next 12 years, many of them directed against the city of Kadesh in the Orontes valley. Mitanni, meanwhile, perhaps realizing that territorial expansion to the south was futile in the face of Egyptian aggression, turned its attention eastwards. In *c.* 1463

BC, Saushshatar of Mitanni marched his army into northern Syria, sacked the city of Assur, snuffing out Assyrian independence for the next 100 years (Astour 2001: 423).

With Mitanni dominant in northern Syria and the plains of northern Mesopotamia, and Egypt all-powerful in the southern Levant, the two states had reached a stalemate and sued for peace. Amenhotep II of Egypt negotiated a treaty with Parattarna II of Mitanni, and the new diplomatic alliance was sealed by the marriage of a Mitannian princess (the daughter of Parattarna II's successor, Artatama I) to Amenhotep II's son and heir, Thutmose IV. The pattern was repeated in the following two generations, Gilukhepa of Mitanni (daughter of Shuttarna II) marrying Amenhotep III of Egypt, and Tadukhepa of Mitanni (daughter of Tushratta) marrying first Amenhotep III and then his son Amenhotep IV/Akhenaten. Under Amenhotep III and his successor, Egypt's policy of securing diplomatic alliances through marriage extended also to the Babylonian kingdom (Kozloff *et al.* 1992: 38, 58; Fletcher 2000: 147). To add to his cosmopolitan harem, Amenhotep III took as wives two Babylonian princesses, the daughters of kings Kurigalzu and Kadashman-Enlil I; in the next generation, Akhenaten married the daughter of king Burnaburiash II.

Such intimate relations between the great Near Eastern powers of the mid-second millennium BC – Egypt, Assyria, Babylonia, Mitanni and the Hittites – are documented in unrivalled detail in the Amarna Letters (Moran 1992; Cohen and Westbrook 2000), the archive of diplomatic correspondence from Akhenaten's capital city at Amarna (ancient Akhetaten). The letters span a period of some four decades, from the latter years of Amenhotep III to the reign of his grandson Tutankhamun. They are written in Akkadian, the diplomatic language of the age, and mostly deal with declarations of friendship, discussions of diplomatic gifts, proposals of marriage and lists of the dowries exchanged at the time of diplomatic marriages. They shed light on the mutually suspicious relations between rulers that lay beneath the diplomatic niceties. For example, Kadashman-Enlil I of Babylonia wrote to Amenhotep III: 'My sister whom my father gave you was (already) there with you, and no one has seen her (so as to know) if now she is alive or if she is dead.' The Egyptian king replied that his Babylonian bride was alive and well, and protested against the implied distrust expressed by his Babylonian 'brother'. In a spirit of bridge-building, Amenhotep III sent lavish furnishings for a new palace built by Kadashman-Enlil. The next Babylonian king, Burnaburiash, attempted to start off on a better footing with Egypt, writing to Amenhotep III: 'Just as previously you and my father were friendly to one another, you and I shall now be friendly to one another. Between us, anything else whatsoever is not even to be mentioned.' In a similar vein, Burnaburiash wrote to Akhenaten after the death of Amenhotep III: 'We have inherited good relations of long standing from (earlier) kings.'

Elsewhere in the correspondence, Burnaburiash expressed his frustration at Assyrian truculence and aspirations. An Assyrian renaissance threatened the dominance of Mitanni, and the Amarna Letters show that the Mitannian kings felt increasingly beleaguered. Tushratta wrote to Amenhotep III asking for a new alliance ('May my brother seek friendship with me') and for economic support in the form of gold: 'In my brother's country, gold is as plentiful as dirt . . . May my brother send me in very large quantities gold that has not been worked.' He sent large quantities of lapis lazuli and a statue of the goddess Shushka of Nineveh to Egypt, by way of encouragement, but the pharaoh refused to reciprocate by sending an Egyptian princess to Mitanni as a diplomatic bride. Here we see the limits of Egypt's international policy: while it was acceptable for the Egyptian king to marry foreign princesses (Mitannian and Babylonian), it was clearly felt inappropriate for a daughter of the pharaoh to leave her own country for foreign parts. As so often in the history of Egypt's foreign relations, the practicalities of *realpolitik* and the xenophobic state ideology (which held Egypt to be superior to all other nations) were at odds; in this case, ideology triumphed. Frustrated by the failure to cement a strong alliance with Egypt, Tushratta was all too aware of the growing threat posed by the Hittites under their new, charismatic king, Shuppiluliumash. The Babylonian king Burnaburiash had recognized the threat, too, and had hedged his bets by sending another of his daughters to the Hittite capital as a diplomatic bride (Goelet 2001).

Tushratta's fears proved to be well-founded. Around 1340 BC, Shuppiluliumash sacked the capital of the Mitanni at Washshukanni, and Tushratta was killed in the aftermath of the invasion. Despite the attempts of his successor Artatama II, Mitanni ceased to be a major power and within less than a century its extirpation was complete (Astour 2001). Freed from Mitannian rule, Assyria regained its independence. The Amarna Letters include a single dispatch from Assyria, sent by king Ashuruballit I to Akhenaten late in the latter's reign, and recalling earlier friendly relations between the two states, possibly in the time of Thutmose III: 'When Ashurnadinakhe, my ancestor, wrote to Egypt, 20 talents of gold were sent to him.' Egypt and Assyria once again embarked on closer ties, trading with each other – Egyptian calcite vessels have been found at Assur – and sharing cultural practices in the process, as attested by the simultaneous development in both civilizations of historical (especially battle) narratives, notably the artistic image of the king in his chariot slaying enemies or wild animals (Feldman 2001: 388). As in the late fourth millennium BC, the political and ideological exigencies of the age found expression in a powerful symbolic vocabulary; only, this time, the cultural exchange was perhaps more even-handed between Egypt and Mesopotamia.

By the reign of Tutankhamun, the Hittites had consolidated their position as the great power in the northern Levant. They effectively maintained a buffer zone between Egypt and Mesopotamia during the 19th Dynasty, especially under the terms of the peace treaty concluded between Ramesses II and the Hittite king Muwatallis II in the aftermath of the inconclusive Battle of Kadesh (*c.*1274 BC). Like his 18th Dynasty predecessors, Ramesses II had Babylonian women in his harem, but relations between Egypt and Mesopotamia now entered a lengthy period of only sporadic contact.

CONFRONTATION, CONQUEST AND ECLIPSE

The Hittite empire collapsed around 1200 BC, under pressure from the Kashka state of north-eastern Anatolia and/or the mass population movement known as the Sea Peoples (Cline 2001). This disparate but fearsome coalition swept across the eastern Mediterranean, ravaging towns and cities along the coast and on the island of Cyprus (Steel 2003). Egypt successfully repelled an attack in the reign of Ramesses III, but was weakened in the process. By the time the New Kingdom state came to an end at the death of Ramesses XI (*c.*1069 BC), the political landscape of the Near East had changed fundamentally. The buffer zone that had separated Egypt and Mesopotamia for over two centuries had dissolved, and both civilizations were able once again to embark on expansionist policies that would bring them into direct confrontation.

The evidence for the final period of intensive Egyptian–Mesopotamian relations comes from three major sources, Egyptian inscriptions, the Assyrian royal annals and the Babylonian chronicles. Assyria seems to have taken the first steps to move into the vacuum created by the widespread destruction of city-states along the Levantine littoral (Feldman 2001: 388–9). Ashurnasirpal (*c.*883–859 BC) and Shalmaneser II (*c.*858–824 BC) embarked on military campaigns to extend the borders of the Assyrian kingdom; Sargon II (*c.*721–705 BC) built on these territorial gains and claimed to be the first Assyrian ruler to reach the borders of the Egyptian empire in Palestine. His successor Sennacherib (705–681 BC) set about consolidating Assyria's western territories, a programme that initially received Egyptian backing. A clay bulla found in the palace of Sennacherib at Nineveh, bearing the Assyrian royal seal and that of Shabaqo, the 25th Dynasty king of Egypt, testifies to an Egyptian–Assyrian diplomatic alliance. Friendly relations between the two powers seem to be confirmed by the discovery at Nineveh of three large statues of Taharqo, Shabaqo's successor.

However, such cooperation was short-lived. Seeing an opportunity to extend his own authority, Taharqo reneged on the alliance with Assyria and began to incite discontent among the city-states of Syria-Palestine. In retaliation, Ashurakheddina (historical Esarhaddon) (*c.*680–669 BC) invaded Egypt twice, in 674 BC and again in 671 BC, reaching as far south as Memphis (Spalinger 1974b). At Nahr el-Kelb in Lebanon and at another site in northern Syria, he erected two inscriptions to record his victory over Taharqo. The former was deliberately sited next to an earlier victory inscription of Ramesses II to drum home the point that Egypt was no longer the dominant power in the region. Ashurakheddina's death in 669 BC, en route to Egypt for a third time, gave Taharqo a temporary reprieve. He was able to restore Kushite rule in the delta and with it some of Egypt's wounded pride. However, the Assyrians had scented Egyptian weakness (Spalinger 1974a). The new Assyrian king Ashurbanipal (*c.*669–627) returned to Egypt in 667/666 BC, and appointed a satrap – Nekau, an Egyptian official from the delta city of Sa el-Hagar (ancient Sais) – to govern the newly conquered territory, in accordance with normal Assyrian practice. In 664 BC, Taharqo was succeeded by Tanutamani who moved north from Nubia to claim his inheritance. Welcomed by the Egyptian population at Thebes, he pressed on to the capital, Memphis, where he defeated and killed Nekau. This was the trigger for the Assyrians to launch a full-scale invasion of Egypt. Tanutamani retreated back to his Nubian homeland, leaving Egypt at the mercy of the invading forces. In 663 BC, the Assyrian army sacked the holy site of Thebes, looting the temple treasuries and destroying many of the city's monuments (Aston 2003). This dealt a profound blow to the Egyptian psyche that was only partially healed by the actions of local nobles such as Montuemhat who diligently set about restoring and rebuilding the most important Theban religious buildings (Lichtheim 1980a: 29–33).

Once Tanutamani had fled to Nubia, the Assyrians withdrew their forces from Egypt and confirmed Nekau's son, Psamtik, as vassal ruler. It was not altogether a wise choice. Psamtik promptly declared himself king and set about unifying Egypt under his authority. Nor was Assyria in any position to punish this act of insubordination. It faced threats much closer to home, in the form of its old enemy Babylonia, now in an alliance with the Medes of northern Iran. Sinsharishkun of Assyria (628–612 BC) gave up any lingering hopes of conquering Egypt and, instead, formed a diplomatic alliance with Psamtik. It was not enough to prevent the

Babylonians and Medes from sacking the Assyrian capital, Nineveh, in 612 BC, defeating Sinsharishkun and fatally weakening the Assyrian state. Three years later, Psamtik's successor Nekau II (610–595 BC) sent troops to assist the Assyrian king Ashuruballit II against a second attack by the Babylonians, but the enemy's overwhelming strength proved too much. After more than a millennium of existence the Assyrian empire finally disappeared, absorbed into the Babylonian kingdom of Nabopolassar (626–605 BC) and his successor Nabukudurriusur II (historical Nebuchadnezzar, 605–562 BC). Egypt was left without a major ally in the Near East, and turned increasingly to Greek mercenaries to support its military adventures.

The final chapter in Egyptian–Mesopotamian relations began in 570 BC (Josephson 2001). A disastrous campaign by Egypt against the Libyan coastal state of Cyrene led the Egyptian army to mutiny and depose their king Apries. He fled into exile and, in a desperate bid to regain the throne from the usurper Ahmose II (historical Amasis), sought refuge and assistance at the court of Nabukudurriusur II of Babylon, Egypt's sworn enemy. In 567 BC, with Babylonian assistance (no doubt in return for the promise of overlordship), Apries attempted a counter-coup against Amasis. The invasion failed, and Apries was defeated and killed. The Babylonians soon had troubles of their own to contend with: in 550 BC a charismatic king of Persia, Kurash II (historical Cyrus the Great, 559–529 BC), succeeded in uniting the Medes and the Persians, and set about creating his own empire. In 539 BC, Babylonia finally succumbed to Kurash's armies, the last Babylonian king, Belsharusur (historical Belshazzar, 545–539 BC), failing to see the writing on the wall. Mesopotamian independence, in the north and the south, had been brought to an end by the Iranian conquerors. Egypt would be next, invaded and subjugated by Kurash II's son Kambujia II (historical Cambyses) in 525 BC.

The unstoppable rise of the Persian Empire brought to an end the 3,000-year history of contacts between Egypt and Mesopotamia as great, independent civilizations; but links between two such dominant cultures did not stop altogether. Under the Persians' nemesis, Alexander the Great, Egypt and Mesopotamia found themselves united, albeit briefly, in a single kingdom. Proclaimed king in Memphis, Alexander died in Babylon but was finally laid to rest in Egypt. Under Alexander's Ptolemaic successors, Egypt engaged in active trade with Mesopotamia. Under the Ptolemies' Roman successors, cultural influences moved back and forth between the two regions, as most famously attested by the zodiac ceiling in the Augustan temple of Hathor at Dendera: a Babylonian concept expressed in a quintessentially Egyptian context.

CONCLUSION

Egypt's relations with Mesopotamia over a 4,000-year period were thus characteristic of Egypt's foreign relations more widely. Pharaonic civilization was suprisingly open to foreign influences, even if in outward form it was conservative and intensely nationalistic. Foreign policy, especially during periods of territorial expansion, was largely driven by economic objectives, even if it was cloaked in an ideological mantle. When dealing with foreign powers, pragmatism was as important as conviction, even though the two often seemed to pull in opposite directions. When the two cultures were as strong and influential as Egypt and Mesopotamia, it is scarcely surprising that the contacts between them, at their three key periods of interaction, should have set the agenda for events across the wider Near East.

CHAPTER THIRTY-ONE

EGYPT AND THE MEDITERRANEAN WORLD

———•✦•———

Louise Steel

Ancient Egypt is frequently characterized as isolated and insular, separated by its natural borders from the surrounding civilizations of the ancient world. There is, however, considerable archaeological evidence for external contacts with the cultures of the Mediterranean, specifically the Aegean world and Cyprus, throughout the Bronze Age. The earliest horizon of contact dates to the Old Kingdom and is exclusively with the island of Crete, prior to the emergence of the Minoan palaces. Contacts increase during the Middle Kingdom, Hyksos Period and earlier New Kingdom, but still are focused on Crete in the Aegean, but also beginning to incorporate Cyprus. The final phase, comprising the Amarna Period and 19th Dynasty, is contemporary with the large-scale commodity trade typical of the Late Bronze Age (LBA) eastern Mediterranean and encompasses Cyprus and the Mycenaean world (Warren 1995).

OLD KINGDOM EGYPT AND THE AEGEAN

The earliest evidence for Egyptian interaction with the cultures of the Aegean dates to the Old Kingdom. This is specific to Crete; despite flourishing maritime networks throughout the northern Aegean during this period, there is no evidence for exchange between the latter region and Egypt. The nature and extent of early Egypto-Cretan contacts is unclear, but can be measured in terms of a very small number of artefacts from Early Minoan (EM) levels. It is extremely unlikely that these represent direct trade/exchange; instead, sporadic, down-the-line trade is more probable, possibly via trading middlemen from Syria-Palestine (Phillips 1990: 329–32; 1996: 465–6).

Old Kingdom Egypt was at a very different level of socio-political development from Pre-Palatial Crete. Old Kingdom Egypt can be characterized as a state society, ruled by a powerful political and economic elite presided over by the king. There was a flourishing literate bureaucracy, and centralized control over the procurement of raw materials and their redistribution, and over craft specialization. Crete, on the other hand, is characterized by relatively small, egalitarian village communities. While there might be some evidence for specialization of craft production (specifically ceramics, possibly textiles, probably metal artefacts), this was not centrally controlled. Some individuals might have had the ability to accumulate quantities of luxury, crafted objects, but there is little evidence for the development of an elite class controlling production. There is an horizon of Egyptian imports in EM IIA Knossos, possibly demonstrating that the site was already developing a privileged trading position with Egypt, perhaps overseen by an emergent elite. A second horizon of contacts, represented by significant quantities of Egyptian imports and Egyptianizing objects, is evident in the Middle Minoan (MM) IA period, immediately preceding the appearance of the Minoan palaces.

Two main facets of this early trade can be identified: the movement of raw materials and the exchange of finished luxury goods. Alongside this, there is clear evidence for the transmission of technologies and esoteric knowledge, which might reflect closer interaction between the two societies. Based on the survival of archaeological material, Crete appears to be the main recipient of traded materials, whereas it is extremely difficult to document any Minoan goods in Egypt at this stage. The raw materials include a worked hippopotamus canine found in EM IIA levels at Knossos (Phillips 1996: 459). Minoan craftsmen used imported hippopotamus ivory to make a number of artefacts, predominantly seals and pendants found in tombs in the plain of the Mesara and on the island of Mochlos (Phillips 1996: 460). More unusual is the ivory Cycladic-style figurine found in a burial at Archanes (Sakellarakis and Sakellarakis 1991: fig. 99; Warren 1995: pl. 11/1). Ostrich eggshells are found in apparent religious contexts in EM III levels at Palaikastro in eastern Crete and MM IA Knossos (Phillips 1996: 463). Other materials that were probably imported from Egypt include semi-precious stones – amethyst, carnelian, rock crystal and sardonyx – and gold (Phillips 1990: 325; Warren 1995). The latter needs to be substantiated by isotope analysis; however, Warren (1995: 1) argues that Egypt is more probable than a northern Aegean source.

Egyptian stone vases have been identified in EM settlement levels at Knossos and in a *tholos* tomb at Ayia Triadha (Warren 1995: 1; Phillips 1996: 461). The earliest example is an Early Dynastic obsidian beaker rim found in EM IIA levels at Knossos. Egyptian bowls, ranging in date from Predynastic to the Old Kingdom, also turn up in later Palatial contexts at Knossos and Zakros (Warren 1995: 8). Possibly these survived as heirlooms in Crete, representing luxuries that were not removed from circulation but, instead, had been carefully curated. While it cannot be demonstrated that the export of these objects was not contemporary with their manufacture, it should be noted that they are also carefully curated in Egyptian contexts and turn up in much later contexts. Minoan imitations of Egyptian cylinder vases are found in EM II burials from Mochlos and the Mesara (Phillips 1996: 461).

Imported Egyptian barrel-shaped carnelian beads and cylindrical beads of soft stones are found in the cave burial at Ayios Charalambos in the plain of Lasithi (Betancourt 2005: 451, pl. CIIh–i). Disc-shaped and globular faience beads are found in EM burials from Mochlos and the tombs of the Mesara in southern Crete (Warren 1995: 2; Phillips 1996: 463; Panagiotaki 2000). While the form of the beads and the faience technology are both Egyptian, it appears that these objects are of local Cretan manufacture. Therefore, alongside more concrete aspects of exchange there is some evidence for the transmission of ideas from Egypt to Crete. The locally produced EM ivory seals likewise adopt Egyptian forms such as the squatting ape, the pyramid and fly, and use Egyptian designs on the base (crocodiles, sphinxes and griffins) (Warren 1995). Crouching apes are a typical motif in Egyptian Old Kingdom art, used for amulets and figurines of the god Thoth. This is another example of an Egyptian motif adopted by the Minoans in the EM II–III Period – the earliest example is a seal impression from a burial at Mochlos (Phillips 1996: 460, fig. 2) – and subsequently for seals and pendants, as for example in the cave burial at Ayios Charalambos (Betancourt 2005: 451, pl. CIIj). Whether the amuletic function of these figurines and their ideological content were similarly transmitted is a moot point. A comparable transmission of ideas is evident with the Minoan adoption of the Egyptian scarab. Imported First Intermediate Period scarabs are found with MM IA burials in the Mesara and Archanes (Phillips 1996: 462). The scarab seal was quickly adopted and adapted by Minoan craftsmen; while the form is imitated, the designs on the base are purely Minoan. Nonetheless, the local production of scarabs in Crete was a short-lived phenomenon (see Pini 2000).

The readiness of the Minoans to assimilate Egyptian ideas and technologies is similarly illustrated by the discovery of a clay sistrum in an MM IA burial at Archanes (Sakellarakis and Sakellarakis 1991: fig. 99). This is clearly a Minoan imitation of an Egyptian musical instrument and implies that certain elements of Minoan society had privileged access to esoteric knowledge, specifically the use of a musical instrument. Five clay sistra of Minoan manufacture (made in the light-on-dark style pottery typical of MM II) have been identified in a burial cave at Ayios Charalambos, Lasithi (Betancourt 2005: 450, pl. CIIc), which might demonstrate fairly widespread adoption of this Egyptian musical instrument in Proto-Palatial Crete. The continued use of this instrument into the Palatial period on Crete is illustrated by the Harvester Vase from Ayia Triadha.

MIDDLE KINGDOM TO EARLY NEW KINGDOM EGYPT AND THE MINOAN PALACES

Contacts between Egypt and the Aegean gather pace with the emergence of the palaces in Crete *c.* 1900 BC. Moreover, the nature of relations is transformed into something more in keeping with the gift exchange, diplomatic envoys and tribute systems prevalent in the contemporary Near East. Egypt continues to be a source of raw materials, high-status objects and trinkets. Alongside this there is increasing evidence that the Egyptians were importing luxury finished goods from Minoan Crete. The close nature of the ties between the two cultures is particularly illustrated by the Minoan assimilation of Egyptian ideas and technologies. As the Minoans became progressively more aware of Egyptian culture, they adopted and adapted symbolic material, namely in the form of religious iconography.

The primary class of Minoan material found in Middle Kingdom Egypt is a type of polychrome pottery known as Kamares ware. This is a high-status craft product in its Cretan context, technologically of high quality and very decorative. Its production is centred on the first palace at Phaistos and it was primarily used within the palaces for high-status feasting (Day and Wilson 1998) or in exclusive, religious sites, such as the Kamares cave. Only small quantities of Kamares ware are found outside Crete, in MB I levels in the major Levantine cities of Ugarit, Byblos, Qatna (Betancourt 1998: 5) and Tell el-ʿAjjul. In Egypt it is found in tombs and dumps in mid-12th and 13th Dynasty contexts at Kahun, Lisht, Abydos and Tell el-Dabʿa (ancient Avaris) (Phillips 1990: 328; Warren 1995: 3). Given its localized dissemination in

Egypt and the Levant and its palatial production and consumption back in Minoan Crete, it seems probable that the trade or exchange of the Kamares ware was centrally controlled by the palaces. It was a luxury commodity that was not widely disseminated in Egypt and consequently had little impact on Egyptian culture.

Tell el-Dab'a appears to have been established as a trading site, managing the movement of goods over the North Sinai land route (the Ways of Horus) between the Nile Delta and southern Levant, and also with the Aegean. Based on the material culture of the site, the excavator has argued that the population was largely Canaanite, even the officials who supervised the foreign trade for the 13th Dynasty rulers (Bietak 1995: 19). The Kamares pottery from the site was found in the gardens of the 13th Dynasty palace, although this context was disturbed. Further evidence for the import of finished Minoan artefacts at the site comes from the 13th Dynasty palace tombs. A gold pendant depicting antithetic dogs and a central human figure (Bietak 1995: 19–20, pl. 14/1) stands out from the typical range of Egyptian personal ornamentation. Rather, the technique and style are more consistent with Minoan jewellery, finding close parallels in both the bee pendant from Mallia and the pendant from the Aegina treasure (Higgins 1979). This object might, therefore, represent an item of gift exchange between a Minoan ruler and an Egyptian official.

Occasional finished Egyptian objects are found in Crete. Trinkets include a baboon amulet from a tomb at Ayia Triadha and an amethyst scarab deposited in a religious context at Psychro cave (Phillips 1990: 322, 323). More unusual is the diorite statuette of a Middle Kingdom official, User, found at Knossos, although unfortunately this was not in a fixed context. Such statuettes have a wide distribution beyond Egypt and are typical elements of Middle Kingdom diplomatic exchange (Edel 1990). More emphatic evidence for Minoan integration into diplomatic gift exchange is the alabaster lid inscribed with the cartouche of the Hyksos ruler Khyan, found at Knossos in an MM IIIA context in the Northwest Lustral Basin of the palace at Knossos (Warren 1987: 206–7; Mellink 1995). The lid belonged to a cylindrical jar used as a container for ointment or perfumed oil. Such objects were typical items of gift exchange between rulers in the second millennium BC, paralleled, for example, by an obsidian unguent container sent by Amenemhat III to the prince of Byblos (Mellink 1995: 85). The Khyan lid is one of only a small number of objects from Crete that are inscribed with an Egyptian ruler's *prenomen* and illustrates particularly close ties between Egypt and Crete during the short Hyksos period. In contrast to earlier Egyptian rulers, the Hyksos kings appear to have had special interests in developing maritime trade in the eastern Mediterranean from their base at Tell el-Dab'a. The ointment container from Knossos is one of a number of gift items that Khyan would have sent out to other rulers as tokens of personal interest and to develop friendly trading relations; another extant example is a fragment from an obsidian vase found in debris near Temple 1 at the Hittite capital, Hattusas (Mellink 1995: 86; Warren 1995: 3).

One of the more intriguing aspects of contacts between Egypt and Crete is the perceived Egyptian influence on the developing Minoan iconographic repertoire. There is clear evidence for the adoption and adaptation of various symbols, mythical beasts and possibly also ideologies, which appears to indicate particularly close contacts between people from both cultures. The Egyptian deity Taweret, a hippopotamus goddess associated with popular female cult (childbirth and protection from snakes), is clearly assimilated into Minoan religious ideology at the beginning of the Old

Palace period, contemporary with the 12th and 13th Dynasties of the Middle Kingdom (Weingarten 2000). A clay appliqué plaque in the form of a sphinx was found in Quartier Mu of the town at Mallia, in MM II levels (Warren 1995: 3, pl. 11/2). This is possibly the earliest example of the Egyptian beast known in Crete, and it already displays a mixture of Minoan and Egyptian iconographic traits: the concept of a human-headed feline in reclining pose, the Osiris beard and the tail are all Egyptian, while the face and the flowing wavy locks of hair are purely Minoan. Also from Mallia, Quartiers Mu and Theta, are other appliqué plaques used to decorate cups and jugs, depicting cats sitting in profile in front of trees (Phillips 1995: fig. 1). It has been suggested that the origin of this motif was Egyptian, specifically the fowling scenes that decorate Middle Kingdom tombs such as those at Beni Hasan (Immerwahr 1985; Militello 2000). This would imply that Aegean craftsmen had the possibility of viewing the decoration of Egyptian funerary monuments, though other modes of transfer should perhaps be considered. Phillips (1995), however, suggests that the motif of the cat and the tree was locally inspired in Crete.

A cache of treasure comprising unworked lapis lazuli, silver ingots, later third millennium and early second millennium cylinder seals, and 153 silver bowls and cups was found in the stone foundations of the temple of Montu at Tod in Upper Egypt, stored in four copper chests. The date of the treasure and its origin have been disputed; two of the chests were inscribed with the name of Amenemhat II (12th Dynasty) and traditional interpretations of the treasure assumed it was accumulated and deposited during his reign. However, re-analysis of the stratigraphy suggests that the deposit is later, dating to the reconstruction of the temple during the reign of Thutmose III (Kemp and Merrillees 1980: 290–6; Laffineur 1988: 18). Although it is clear that the final deposition of the cache dates to the reign of Thutmose III, this need not date its initial collection. Possibly some or all of the cache was originally collected during the reign of Amenemhat II; however this presupposes careful curation of these objects over several generations. Warren and Hankey (1989: 131–4, pls 5–11) have argued that many of the vessels found in the Tod treasure have close parallels in the MM IB–II ceramic repertoire. Laffineur (1988) likewise argues for an Aegean origin of the vases, although he attributes them to the early Mycenaean culture of mainland Greece, dating to the sixteenth century BC.

The importance of the trade in perishable goods is difficult to assess, but evidence is accumulating for trade in Minoan woven woollen textiles (Shaw 1970; Barber 1991). In Middle Kingdom Egypt, textiles were restricted to finely woven linens, which were largely undyed and it is likely that coloured woven textiles would have had a tremendous impact on the Egyptians. The contrast between the portrayal of Egyptians in white linen and the Asiatics wearing brightly coloured garments, presumably of wool which absorbs dyes more readily, is apparent in the caravan of Asiatics depicted on the wall of the tomb of Khnumhotep at Beni Hasan (Smith 1998: 201). There is plentiful evidence from the Aegean for production of elaborately woven textiles in bright colours, not only in the form of loom weights from Minoan sites, but also the colourful garb worn by Minoans depicted in their wall paintings (Barber 1991: colour pl. 2; M. Shaw 2000). While no examples of such textiles have survived in Egypt in the archaeological record, the trade in such a commodity was probably the main mode of transfer for the wide range of Minoan decorative motifs adorning the ceilings of Egyptian tombs, such as the Middle Kingdom tomb of

Hapdjefa at Asyut (Shaw 1970; Barber 1991: 338–51, fig. 15.23). This phenomenon is similarly attested in the early New Kingdom (Barber 1991: table 15.1, colour pl. 3). Of particular interest is the tomb painting of the Egyptian official Menkheper-raseneb, dating to the reign of Thutmose III, which shows Minoan envoys bringing tribute to the pharaoh including bolts of textiles (Barber 1991: 335, fig. 15.19). It is plausible, therefore, that decorative textiles were used as wall and ceiling hangings in Egyptian homes (Barber 1998: 15), but rather than placing these in tombs, copies of their designs were painted instead.

EARLY NEW KINGDOM EGYPT

The New Palace Period on Crete (MM IIIB–LM IB) is the time of greatest contact between Egypt and Minoan Crete. In Egyptian terms this coincides with the early New Kingdom: the reunification of Egypt following the expulsion of the Hyksos rulers by the Theban princes who founded the 18th Dynasty, down to the reign of Thutmose III. The early rulers of the 18th Dynasty practised expansionist policies, primarily along the coast of Syria-Palestine but also in Nubia and beyond to the south (to Punt), in search of new sources of luxuries, such as ostrich eggs and exotic animals. This policy was not simply commercial but was aggressive, explicitly expanding Egypt's territories beyond its natural borders, especially in the Levant. The height of this expansionist activity, and also of Egyptian trade, dates to the reign of Thutmose III, possibly as early as his co-regency with Hatshepsut.

Egypt was a possible source of a wide range of raw materials used by Minoan craftsmen, including carnelian, alabaster, rock crystal and amethyst (Warren 1995: 5–6). In the hands of the Minoan craft specialists these became highly prized luxury objects (seal stones, jewellery and vases) both within and beyond Crete; the rock crystal duck vase from Grave Omikron in Grave Circle B at Mycenae, an object acquired by the emergent Mycenaean elite, for example, appears to be a Minoan product imitating Egyptian ivory cosmetic boxes (Mylonas 1973: 203–5, pls 183–5). Other Egyptian imports include ivory, both hippopotamus and elephant, which the Minoans fashioned into small figurines, and ostrich eggs which were transformed into libation vases (*rhyta*) (Warren 1995: 6). Ivory tusks have been found at the palace at Zakros on the coast of Crete, which appears to have had a privileged position in the trade with Egypt (Platon 1974: fig. 25). There is significant pictorial evidence supporting a trade in exotic animals from Egypt, based on their lifelike depiction in Minoan and Theran wall-paintings. The monkeys in Theran and Knossian wall paintings can be identified as *Cercopithecus aethiops aethiops* from Ethiopia or the sub-Saharan *Cercopithecus aethiops tantalus* (Cameron 1968: 3, 5). The walls of building Beta at Thera are adorned with antelopes identified as the East African *Oryx beisa* (Marinatos 1972: 42–3).

Occasional finished objects are also imported from Egypt, primarily Egyptian stone vases. These had a tremendous impact on the Minoan lapidary industry of the New Palace period and a number of much older Egyptian shapes were copied locally in a variety of diorites and gabbros. Other Egyptian stone vessels, some as early as the Early Dynastic or Old Kingdom, were re-worked by Cretan craftsmen into Minoan forms during the New Palace Period (Warren 1995: 8). Whether these should be interpreted as ancient heirlooms in a Minoan or Egyptian context, as traded commodities or as high-status, quality gifts designed to cement relationships between the Minoan elite and the New Kingdom pharaohs is not clear. However, the rare alabaster amphora bearing the cartouche of Thutmose III found in an LM IIIA:1 tomb at Katsamba (Warren 1995: 8, pl. 13/3–4) is surely evidence of official gift exchange, especially in conjunction with the evidence for Cretan emissaries to the court of Hatshepsut and Thutmose III to be discussed below. The context of this vase is crucial for understanding the chronological interrelations between the Aegean and Egypt during the Late Bronze Age. While it has usually been accepted that this vase had been in circulation over several generations in Crete before finally entering the archaeological record, Manning has argued recently that the later reign of Thutmose III, in fact, is contemporary with LM IIIA:1 (S. Manning 1999: 217–18).

Sherds of Egyptian amphorae and other vessels are found at the port of Kommos, on the south coast of Crete, in some quantity. These range in date from LM IB to LM IIIB, but most finds occur in LM IIIA deposits (Phillips 2005: 457). Stylistically this pottery can be assigned to the mid-18th Dynasty, from the end of the reign of Thutmose III into the Amarna Period. It reflects a shift in the emphasis of trade away from sporadic ceremonial exchange towards the commodity trade more characteristic of the fourteenth and thirteenth centuries BC. Moreover, the presence of this pottery at Kommos illustrates continued Cretan involvement in eastern Mediterranean trade into the period usually believed to be dominated by the Mycenaeans of mainland Greece.

The wall paintings of Tell el-Dabʿa

Our understanding of the cultural interaction between Egypt and Crete in the early 18th Dynasty has been dramatically rewritten following excavations at ʿEzbet Helmi. Here, at the western edge of Avaris/Tell el-Dabʿa, a fortified citadel covering an area of 50,000 square metres has been uncovered, dating to the late Hyksos Period and the early 18th Dynasty (Bietak 1997a: 115, fig. 4.28). Several large official buildings have been discovered in this area, including two palaces, F (platform H/I) and G (H/II and H/III) (Bietak 2000: 190–2, fig. 3). Thousands of fragments of wall paintings were found in this area. The main group was found in sumps to the north-east of the ramp of palace F and in the garden. A second group was found to the north of palace G, some of which were still partially *in situ*. Originally both groups were dated to the Hyksos Period (Bietak 1995), but more recent analyses of the stratigraphy demonstrate that these fragments date to the 18th Dynasty occupation of the site (Bietak 1997a: 117; 2000: 192–4). The significance of these fragments is that they appear to belong to the Minoan rather than the Egyptian artistic repertoire and thus have completely challenged the prevailing discourse on relations between Egypt and the Aegean during the second millennium BC.

The technique of the wall paintings also belongs to the Minoan rather than Egyptian craft. The mud-brick walls of the palace were coated with two or three layers of lime plaster, rather than the gypsum plaster more typical of Egyptian wall painting. Ironically, the use of this technique onto a mud-brick background resulted in the lime plaster falling from the palace walls soon after its application, possibly demonstrating a lack of experience of the technique (Bietak 2000: 194). Once the plaster was applied, the surface was smoothed with a stone to a highly polished finish and string impressions for borders were made while the plaster was still wet. Moreover, the first application of paint, the background colour, was made onto the wet surface. The figured decoration was added subsequently when the plaster was dry. This mix of the fresco and secco technique is typical of Minoan art but is unknown in Near East and Egypt (Bietak 1995: 23; 2000: 196). The colour palette is common to both Egypt and the Minoan world; however, certain choices made by the artists indicate them to be working within the Minoan artistic tradition. Most significant is the use of red as a background colour, a colour convention that is typical of the earliest wall paintings from Knossos (Morgan 1995: 33; Bietak 1995: pl. 4/2; 1997a: fig. 4.32) but is unparalleled in Egyptian art. Similarly, the use of blue paint to indicate grey is typically Minoan and only incorporated into Egyptian art in the Amarna Period (Bietak 2000: 196–7). The relief plaster technique used for bull representations and large-scale human figures is another Knossian technique. Likewise, the use of two scales of painting – small friezes and life-size – is paralleled in the Aegean world, on Crete and in the Cycladic islands to the north (Morgan 1995: 31).

The iconography is the most startling aspect of the wall paintings, as it is thoroughly Minoan in concept. There are numerous bull-leaping scenes which have been reconstructed as a miniature frieze. This is a common Minoan motif in a variety of media, chief among them the toreador scenes from Knossos. The costume of the acrobats is also typically Minoan: Minoan loin cloth and boots, and the long flowing wavy locks (Bietak 1995: 23, pls 2, 3/1). These individuals are clearly depicted as Minoans; the only problematic feature is the yellow skin colour, although Bietak suggests this might reflect some Egyptian influence as it was the typical colour convention for females in Egypt (Bietak 2000: 197). Other aspects of the bull-leaping scenes evidently belong to the Minoan artistic canon: the maze background (Bietak 1995: 24, fig. 3, pl. 1/2), the bull-leaper against the background of a maze, and the bull's face depicted frontally rather than in profile (Bietak 1995: 23, pl. 1/1; Morgan 1995: 43). There are also landscape scenes; hunting scenes with antelope, hunting dogs, and in one case a running man; and felines in a flying gallop, a typically Aegean feature (Bietak 1995: 24, pl. 4/1, 2; 1997a: fig. 4.32; 2000: colour pl. A).

There are also several fragments that show large-scale human figures, some slightly less than life-size, others over life-size. These include a bearded male, a motif common in Minoan glyptic (Bietak 1995: 24, pl. 3/2) and a couple of large males found in palace F, one carrying an object over his shoulder, which have particularly close parallels in the wall paintings from Thera (Aslanidou 2005: 464–7, pls CIIIa–c). A fragment of a large-scale female was found in the area of palace G, associated with Egyptian imitations of Minoan *rhyta*; the flounced skirt and double anklets are paralleled by the women adorning the walls of Xeste 3 at Thera (Bietak 1997a: 117; 2000: 199, colour pl. B/a). What is particularly fascinating is that these fragments from Egypt appear to be depicting Minoans (and Aegean islanders?) not only according to foreign (Minoan) artistic conventions but, more specifically, to be representing Minoans as they viewed themselves.

The absence of Egyptian royal symbolism and hieroglyphic inscriptions within an 18th Dynasty palatial context is puzzling. There are, however, examples of emblems that tie into the Minoan palatial (royal?) context, namely the half-rosette frieze and the griffin (Bietak 1995: pl. 4/3; 1997a: fig. 4(35); 2000: 198). Two large-scale griffins are depicted against aquatic plants and there are also fragments of a small-scale griffin (Bietak 2000: colour pl. B/b). All the griffins are purely Aegean in concept, in particular the design of the wing with black spirals with red dots in the centre, between blue lines filled in with red triangles (Bietak 2000: 200). The closest parallel for the detail is the griffin from Xeste 3, Thera; however, the emblematic use of griffins is more characteristic of the Knossian palatial context.

The significance of these evidently Minoan wall paintings is still the subject of considerable discussion. Although they are not unique in the Near East – as analogous paintings have been discovered at Kabri, Qatna and Carchemish in the Levant – the Tell el-Dab'a paintings stand out for their total incorporation of Minoan ritual aspects and ideologies as demonstrated by their iconography. This iconography in its indigenous context served as a form of symbolic communication, and appears to be closely integrated with Minoan religious ideology and elite ceremony. Possibly the Egyptian and Near Eastern wall paintings demonstrate the movement of craft special-ists (Aslanidou 2005: 468; Morgan 1995: 44), or even the development of a common school of wall painting in the Aegean and eastern Mediterranean at the beginning of the Late Bronze Age (Niemeier 1991, 1995). However, this fails to explain the very selective adoption of purely Minoan/Aegean iconography at Tell el-Dab'a, especially with its royal and religious connotations in its home context.

Alternatively, the dissemination of this style in the eastern Mediterranean might illustrate the movement of people who could read this style. One possibility is that the wall paintings indicate a dynastic marriage (Bietak 1995: 26; 1997a: 124), pre-sumably between the earlier rulers of the 18th Dynasty and the court of Knossos. This is supported by the choice of certain motifs, namely the emblematic griffins and the half rosettes. The close association of griffins and females in an Aegean con-text is particularly interesting, possibly relating to Minoan queenship (Marinatos 1995) or a high-status priestess. In this respect, two objects found in the tomb of Ahhotep, the mother of the Egyptian king Ahmose, are of especial import: the Ahmose axe and a dagger (Bietak 1997a: 124; Warren 1995: 5). Both objects have inlaid niello decoration. The axe is adorned with a griffin with the characteristic Aegean wings, and the dagger has a lion in flying gallop chasing a bull in a rocky landscape. Certainly, the wall paintings illustrate a special relationship between the early 18th Dynasty rulers and Minoan Crete, above all Knossos.

Minoans in Egyptian historical sources

There is, surprisingly, very little textual evidence for Minoan activity in the eastern Mediterranean, although the Mari archives of the fifteenth–seventeenth centuries BC mention a 'man from Caphtor'/Captara (Crete?) as one of the recipients in reference to lists of tin sent to Ugarit (Betancourt 1998: 9). These textual sources tell us that Captara (Crete) exported oil, grain, a fermented beverage, textiles and metal weapons to Ugarit and Mari (Knapp 1991: 37–8, 42). A number of Egyptian texts and representations also make direct reference to the Minoans. Various Egyptian texts refer to a place Keftiu which is commonly identified with Minoan Crete (although all too frequently Aegean scholars confuse the name Keftiu with the name of the people) (Sakellarakis and Sakellarakis 1984: 198; Warren 1995: 7). The earliest possible text mentioning 'Horus Kefti' dates to the 12th Dynasty and the reign of Senusret II. However, the vast majority of references date to the 18th Dynasty, in particular the reign of Thutmose III. These include references to the 'ships of Keftiu' in years 3 and 34 of Thutmose III. There is also a series of inscriptions dating to the reign of Amenhotep III, the most intriguing of which is the formula against 'the Asiatic disease' in the language of Keftiu recorded in the London Medical Papyrus. Other New Kingdom references to Keftiu have similar medical connotations; Papyrus Ebers lists medicinal herbs including the Keftiu bean, while the early 19th Dynasty Leiden 'Admonitions' Papyrus mentions Keftiu in a section dealing with mummification.

Scenes depicting foreigners bearing tribute to the Egyptian king are a common iconographic device in the New Kingdom 'Tombs of the Nobles' at Thebes. A number of tombs belonging to high officials of the Egyptian court and dating to the reigns of Hatshepsut, Thutmose III, Amenhotep II and possibly Amenhotep III, spanning a period of around 100 years, depict processions of people who have been identified as Aegean, specifically Minoan (Panagiotopoulos 2001: 265, table 1). The earliest of these representations, in the tombs of Senenmut, Antef and Puyemra, have no inscriptions, whereas the later three tombs, of Useramun, Rekhmira and Menkheperraseneb, state that the people depicted are from 'the Isles in the Middle of the Great Green [Sea]' or more specifically from 'Keftiu' (Panagiotopoulos 2001: 263). In the tombs of Senenmut, Antef and Useramun the individuals are clearly represented as Minoans. They are dressed in Minoan costume, comprising loin cloth, boots and codpiece, with long curly hair and clean shaven, and are slim with narrower waists than the Egyptians (Sakellarakis and Sakellarakis 1984: 200; Strøm 1984: 192; Rehak 1998: 40). The objects being brought as tribute are clearly of Aegean origin – animal *rhyta*, conical *rhyta*, Vapheio style cups – but there are also objects more typical of Near Eastern gift exchange, such as elephant tusks and copper 'oxhide' ingots, which presumably illustrate the circular movement of goods throughout the eastern Mediterranean in diplomatic exchanges (Rehak 1998: 47).

Much has been made of the costume of the people from Keftiu in the tomb of Rekhmira, the vizier under Thutmose III and Amenhotep II. Originally they were painted wearing the Minoan loin cloth and codpiece, but, after the completion of the tomb paintings, this was changed to a kilt, analogous to the costume worn by the individuals in the Procession Fresco, Knossos. The traditional interpretation of this deliberate transformation was that it reflected political changes in the Aegean, with the rising pre-eminence of the Mycenaeans, who were able to oust the Minoans from their privileged trading position with Egypt and the Levant (Immerwahr 1990: 172; Rehak 1996: 36; 1998: 41). More detailed analysis of male costume in Minoan art, however, illustrates that both the loin cloth with codpiece and the kilt are indigenous Minoan costume dating back to the Old Palace Period; the former was worn by particularly active individuals, whereas the elaborate kilts were the preferred costume for males in processions (Rehak 1996: 42–6; 1998: 42–4). By contrast, the kilt does not appear to be a typical item of male dress on the Greek mainland (Rehak 1996: 48–50). The Aegean peoples depicted in the tomb of Menkheperraseneb are less clearly Minoan, perhaps because Aegean peoples were no longer being received in the Egyptian court and their inclusion in procession scenes is little more than a memory; moreover, a Syrian from the same tomb is depicted wearing Minoan shoes and a kilt, suggesting a certain degree of confusion between Syrians and Minoans on the part of the Egyptian artists (Rehak 1998: 47).

It is generally accepted that these tomb paintings refer to real historical events, recording diplomatic envoys from Crete to the Egyptian court in the 18th Dynasty (see discussion in Panagiotopoulos 2001). Vercoutter (1956: 188–9, 194) suggested that these scenes were specifically related to important events in the careers of the Egyptian courtiers and that the reception of foreign tribute was among the more prestigious duties of the vizier. The small number of tombs from a restricted time period which have Aegean procession scenes is certainly worthy of comment; presumably Cretan envoys were unusual, in contrast to the more frequent Asiatic envoys depicted on the tombs of Egyptian nobles. It is notable that the scenes largely date to the reigns of Hatshepsut and Thutmose III, a period of expansion characterized by Egyptian interest in exotic lands, including Punt and Keftiu (Rehak 1998: 48). Although the Aegean procession scenes are displayed alongside scenes of tribute from the Egyptian territories in Syria-Palestine and Nubia, there is no indication that the Minoans were subject to the Egyptians. Instead, the inscription in the tomb of Rekhmira states explicitly that the people from Keftiu had brought tribute because they had 'heard' about the achievements and victories of the pharaoh (Thutmose III) and wanted to present him their gifts and be loyal to him (Panagiotopoulos 2001: 271; Strøm 1984: 193). The importance of gift exchange throughout the eastern Mediterranean is documented not only in the tomb paintings of the Egyptian nobles but also in textual sources, chief among them the Amarna Letters (Zaccagnini 1987; Peltenburg 1991: 167–70). The representations of the Aegean peoples in the eight tombs from Thebes clearly demonstrate that the Minoans participated in this ceremonial gift-giving at least for a short period during the 18th Dynasty.

NEW KINGDOM EGYPT AND MYCENAEAN GREECE

The site of Malkata in western Thebes has yielded intriguing evidence for the close contacts between Egypt and the Aegean in the early fourteenth century BC. A number of painted plaster fragments were recovered from the mud-brick debris of the dismantled palace built to celebrate Amenhotep III's *sed* festival (Kemp 2000b). Technically and iconographically the painted plaster belongs to the Egyptian palatial tradition – the standard Egyptian *tempera* technique executed on gypsum plaster (Nicolakaki-Kentrou 2000: 47). However, a number of fragments display clear Aegeanizing elements. Some of these are reminiscent of the depiction of the emissaries from Keftiu that adorn the walls of the Tombs of the Nobles at Thebes (Wachsmann 1987), such as the way in which the men are depicted without beards and with long flowing wavy locks of hair, and the geometric patterns of their kilts (Nicolakaki-Kentrou 2000: 48). While these scenes can be fitted into the canon of Egyptian art, other motifs appear to be of Aegean origin and included in among Egyptian designs. These include a background of rosettes interspersed with bucrania, Aegean-style rocky landscapes, and marbling. One source of inspiration for these motifs is the monumental wall-painting of the Aegean palaces (both Minoan and Mycenaean); the influence of Aegean textiles should likewise be considered (Barber 1991: 348–50, fig. 15.24).

Although it is not obvious how Egyptian craftsmen would have become aware of such scenes, it is possible that they were among diplomatic envoys and trading missions sent out by Amenhotep III, which appear to have reached the Aegean world. A number of artefacts bearing the cartouche of Amenhotep III and his Queen Tiye are found in the Aegean at six major sites, Mycenae being pre-eminent (Cline 1995: 94). Together with the so-called 'Aegean list' (naming important Aegean centres) inscribed on the statue-base of Amenhotep III at his mortuary temple at Kom el-Hetan, these have been used to reconstruct an Egyptian embassy to the Aegean during the reign of Amenhotep III (Cline 1987, 1995; Hankey 1993: 110; Schofield and Parkinson 1993: 158). This tour also appears to have incorporated the island of Crete, based on the presence of two faience scarabs with the *prenomen* of Amenhotep III from Kydonia and Tomb 4 at Sellopoulo, Knossos (Cline 1994: 147, nos. 125, 128) and a stamp seal bearing the name of his wife Tiye from Ayia Triadha (Cline 1994: 147, no. 142; La Rosa 2000: fig. 1). The date of the posited diplomatic mission is of interest as it coincides with a shift in focus of Egyptian and Near Eastern interests in the Aegean from Crete to mainland Greece in Late Minoan/Late Helladic (LH) IIIA, contemporary with the final destruction of the palace at Knossos. The inscribed Egyptian objects therefore represent formal diplomatic contacts between Amenhotep III and the Mycenaeans when the latter took over the eastern Mediterranean trade routes from the Minoans, presumably with the specific aim of expanding trading relations between the two regions (Cline 1995: 94–5). This might be foreshadowed by an earlier Egyptian embassy in the reign of Amenhotep II, as the Mycenaeans were beginning to become active in the eastern Mediterranean, as attested by two blue faience monkeys inscribed with his *prenomen*, found at Tiryns and Mycenae (Cline 1991).

Trading relations between Egypt and the Aegean, primarily with mainland Greece, during the Late Bronze Age are of a different nature and at a very different scale compared to the relations between the two regions during the earlier second millennium BC. For the most part, they appear to be characterized by large-scale commodity trade incorporating the Aegean, Cyprus, the Levant and Egypt. Other than the possible diplomatic envoys in the reigns of Amenhotep II and III discussed above, there is only scant evidence for diplomatic exchange between the Aegean and Egypt during the later New Kingdom.

The earliest Mycenaean imports into Egypt are unguent containers (squat alabastra) dating to the fifteenth century BC (LH IIA) (Hankey 1993: 112). These are few in number and the bulk of the trade with Mycenaean Greece dates to the fourteenth and thirteenth centuries BC (LH IIIA and B). Egypt appears to be very much at the end of the main eastern Mediterranean maritime trade routes, and the range of Mycenaean vessels identified here is greatly reduced in comparison with the varied exports attested in contemporary Cyprus and the Levant. Some 30 forms are known in Egypt (Hankey 1993: 112), largely closed vessels identified as containers of perfumed oils and unguents. In particular, the Egyptians imported piriform jars, stirrup jars and flasks. Drinking vessels are found, but are rare. Mycenaean imports have been identified at some 23 sites in Upper and Lower Egypt and seven sites in Nubia (Hankey 1993: 113–14). For the most part, Mycenaean pottery occurs in royal or official contexts, namely palatial, official or military establishments, such as the forts along the Ways of Horus. It is also found in rubbish dumps associated with royal establishments, and in domestic contexts, both rich and poor. These include the villages of workmen engaged in royal constructions, chief among them Amarna and

Deir el-Medina. The provision of burials with Mycenaean ceramics is also attested, ranging from tombs of royal officials to more modest burials (see Hankey 1993: 111). The most significant of the funerary deposits is the New Kingdom necropolis at Saqqara used by royal officials (Hankey and Aston 1995).

The high regard that Mycenaean vessels and their contents were accorded in Egypt is evident. In some instances, pottery dating to the Amarna Period (LH IIIA:2 and early LH IIIB) was carefully curated until the Ramesside Period when it was deposited in high-status burials in the Saqqara necropolis (Hankey and Aston 1995: 78). Likewise of significance is the depiction of nine Mycenaean stirrup jars on the wall of the tomb of Ramesses III, together with other treasured commodities such as leopard skins, elephant tusks, metal vases and copper ingots (Hankey 1995: 123, fig. 9). While seven of the jars are painted a dark pink colour, indicating that the originals were probably ceramic, two of the jars are painted green or blue, suggesting the originals were of faience. Certainly, Egyptian craftsmen did choose to imitate these exotic imports in faience and, more unusually, in calcite (Hankey 1995: 123, pls 23–4), which it has been suggested reflects the appeal of these vases to the Egyptian market. Presumably one reason for this appeal was the exotic nature of the contents themselves. It is only during the Amarna Period that the olive was introduced into Egypt, possibly as a result of Egyptian embassies to the Aegean during the reign of Amenhotep III. The garland of olive leaves found in Tutankhamun's outer coffin illustrates the prestige of the newly imported tree. Prior to this, the only sources of oil in Egypt were the castor-oil plant, sesame seeds and the moringa tree. It can, therefore, be concluded that the olive oil being imported from the Aegean was extremely highly prized (Hankey 1995: 117).

The site in Egypt with the greatest quantity of Mycenaean imports is Amarna, the residence of the 'heretic pharaoh' Akhenaten (Hankey 1981; Schofield and Parkinson 1993: 157). The importance of these deposits has usually been to provide a fixed dating point for the Aegean Bronze Age; the vast majority of the imports date stylistically to LH IIIA:2, which is therefore tied in to a very short period in Egyptian history, the Amarna Period. Certainly, the presence of these exotic imports, concurrent with the introduction of the olive, also possibly from the Aegean, is suggestive of particularly close ties between the Amarna pharaohs and the rulers of the Mycenaean palaces in the Argolid. Hankey explicitly links the Amarna deposits of Mycenaean pottery with the find of at least six Egyptian votive faience plaques at Mycenae bearing the *prenomen* of Amenhotep III, the predecessor of Akhenaten (Hankey 1981: 45–6; Cline 1995: 94). She argues that these plaques were diplomatic gifts from the Egyptian to the Mycenaean court, which, in return, sent the Mycenaean pottery (containers of perfumed oils) and possibly also olive trees (Hankey 1995: 117). Curiously, given these apparently close diplomatic and trading links, the Mycenaeans do not appear to be included among the correspondents in the Amarna archives. The only possible mention of Aegean peoples (Mycenaeans?) in Egyptian contexts from the Amarna Period are from Tombs of the Nobles. The tomb of Huya at Amarna is decorated with a scene of foreigners bringing tribute to the pharaoh. The accompanying inscription mentions 'the isles in the midst of the sea', usually interpreted as a reference to the Aegean islands (Schofield and Parkinson 1993: 158). There are also badly preserved depictions of Aegean peoples in the tomb of Horemheb (last ruler of the 18th Dynasty) at Saqqara, which belong to the canon of representations of the people from Keftiu contemporary with the reigns of Hatshepsut and Thutmose III and so need not represent Mycenaeans (Schofield and Parkinson 1993: 159). There is, moreover, only tenuous textual evidence from the Aegean for mention of Egyptians; two joining tablet fragments from Pylos give a man's name, *a-ku-pi-ti-jo* (Egyptian?) (Ventris and Chadwick 1956: 136).

A fascinating addition to the discourse on the close cultural contacts between Mycenaean Greece and Amarna Period Egypt is furnished by a fragmentary painted papyrus from Amarna (Schofield and Parkinson 1993). The papyrus fragments were found in House R 43.2, a chapel dedicated to the pharaoh located at the eastern limits of the official area of the city, probably dating to the latter part of the Amarna Period. It was decorated with battle scenes; one unusually shows Libyan archers attacking an Egyptian (Schofield and Parkinson 1993: fig. 1), and the other shows a group of running warriors wearing Egyptian white linen kilts and helmets. The helmets were outlined in red and painted yellow (Schofield and Parkinson 1993: frontispiece, fig. 2). Some of the warriors also wore tunics of mottled oxhide. Although the helmets are similar to depictions of *gurpisu* helmets worn by Asiatic warriors, an alternative hypothesis is that they might, in fact, represent Mycenaean boars' tusk helmets – a type known from the Greek mainland and Crete from the sixteenth and fifteenth centuries BC and occurring in high-status burials. It is also worth noting that a segment from one such helmet has been identified at Qantir, contemporary with the reign of Ramesses II (Schofield and Parkinson 1993: 166). The oxhide tunics, likewise, have Aegean parallels, on Mycenaean pictorial amphorae (Schofield and Parkinson 1993: 166–9, fig. 5). It is plausible that these specific items of armour were used by the Egyptian artist as ethnic signifiers, to denote Mycenaean warriors in the employ of the Egyptian pharaoh against the Libyans.

The Ulu Burun shipwreck

Nautical archaeology has furnished further insights into the movement of goods throughout the eastern Mediterranean during the Late Bronze Age. Two shipwrecks have been identified off the south coast of Turkey, at Cape Gelidonya (Bass 1967) and Ulu Burun (Bass 1986; Pulak 1997), the latter dating to the late fourteenth century BC, contemporary with the end of the 18th Dynasty in Egypt. The finds from the Ulu Burun shipwreck illustrate the large-scale movement of raw metals, primarily copper (some ten tons) and also one ton of tin (Pulak 1997: 235). The copper was predominantly transported in the form of 'oxhide' ingots, the type shown in Egyptian scenes depicting Syrian tribute-bearers (Bass 1967: 62–7). Metals were not the only cargo on the ship and many of the items recovered are resonant with descriptions of diplomatic exchange recounted in the Amarna Letters (Moran 1992) and can be compared to the Egyptian tomb paintings of tribute being delivered to various New Kingdom pharaohs (Pulak 1997: 251). These commodities include logs of blackwood (*Dalbergia melanoxylon*) from sub-Saharan Africa, originally identified as ebony (Bass *et al.* 1989: 9, fig. 17), cedar logs, an elephant tusk and 13 hippopotamus teeth, three ostrich eggs and some 175 glass ingots, coloured cobalt blue, turquoise and lavender (Pulak 1997: 242). A collection of Egyptian and Canaanite gold and silver jewellery may well be a jeweller's hoard of scrap metal. The most significant piece among this is a unique gold scarab inscribed with the name of Nefertiti, the wife of Akhenaten (Pulak 1997: 244, 250). This scarab clearly shows signs of wear, implying it was in circulation for some time before it was incorporated in the gold hoard, presumably after the end of the Amarna Period. Other specifically Egyptian objects from the shipwreck include scarabs, largely of the Second Intermediate Period, and two duck-shaped ivory cosmetic boxes (Pulak 1997: 244, fig. 13).

EGYPTIAN CONTACTS WITH CYPRUS

Throughout much of its prehistory the island of Cyprus was largely isolated from maritime trading activities of the eastern Mediterranean, and it is not until the second millennium BC that there is any evidence for sustained Egyptian contacts with the island. Earlier material, namely two calcite vases found in Early Cypriot (EC) tombs at Vasilia and Vounous and occasional trinkets of faience from EC tombs at Lapithos and Karmi (Stewart 1962: 203–4, 259–60, 264; Knapp 1990: 152, table 3), illustrate little more than indirect contact between Egypt and Cyprus, possibly via middlemen from the Levant. During the earlier second millennium BC commercial trading contacts were established between Egypt and Cyprus. This can be charted through the movement of certain pottery styles in the Middle Bronze Age, predominantly the circulation of small juglets between Cyprus, Syria-Palestine and Egypt, especially Tell el-Dabʿa (Merrillees 1968; Maguire 1995; Bietak and Hein 2001). Frequently found in tomb assemblages, these small, narrow-necked juglets were presumably containers of a prized luxury commodity such as a perfumed oil. Egyptian-manufactured Tell el-Yahudiyeh ware – a grey pottery with punctured decoration used primarily to make piriform jars – was exported to Cyprus. Here, its distribution, largely concentrated in the eastern Mesaoria, appears to shadow the copper route from the Troodos mountains down to Enkomi on the east coast.

Cypriot Late Bronze Age pottery, in particular Base Ring ware, was exported to Egypt in some quantities from the beginning of the Late Bronze Age, contemporary with the Egyptian New Kingdom (Merrillees 1968). These vessels are largely found in funerary contexts. There has been substantial debate about whether Base Ring juglets were manufactured specifically as containers for opium. This theory is based on their shape and decoration, which Merrillees (1962; 1968: 154–6) has argued explicitly resembled the seed pod of the opium poppy. This supposition has been supported by chemical analyses of the residues found in Base Ring juglets, although the evidence still remains tenuous (Bisset *et al.* 1996: 203–4; Koschel 1996: 159–66). Egyptian imitations of Base Ring juglets in alabaster (Merrillees 1968: 148, 152), faience (Merrillees 1968: 149, 153), glass (Merrillees 1968: 152, 153, 163, 166) and pottery (Merrillees 1968: 152, 162) are attested. Particularly large quantities of Cypriot Middle and Late Bronze Age pottery have been found at Tell el-Dabʿa, including White Slip ware, which previously was considered to be a minor export to Egypt (Bietak and Hein 2001). The apparent abrupt cessation in the trade of Cypriot pottery to Egypt subsequent to the Amarna Period is noted by Merrillees, who relates it to political conditions in the northern Levant, especially increasing Hittite activity in the area and, as a result, the end of economic and diplomatic intercourse between Egypt and Ugarit (Merrillees 1968: 199, 202).

While Cypriot pottery has been found in some quantities in Egypt, rather less was traded in the opposite direction. Even so, small quantities of Egyptian amphorae have recently been identified in Cyprus. One of the first pieces to be identified was an amphora handle stamped with the cartouche of Seti I, found on the surface at Hala Sultan Tekke (Eriksson 1995: 200). Two near-complete amphorae were found in the courtyard of Building C at Hala Sultan Tekke, dating to Late Cypriot (LC) IIIA (twelfth century BC) (Eriksson 1995: 200–1, fig. 2). The necks of the amphorae were broken, probably to open them to gain access to their contents of wine or beer; similar practices have also been attested at Malkata, in Egypt. In addition to the two near-complete amphorae, large quantities of Egyptian marl and silt sherds have also been found at Hala Sultan Tekke. Other sites such as Maa, Pyla, Maroni and Arediou have likewise yielded sherds of Egyptian amphorae in LC IIC–IIIA contexts, suggesting continued Egyptian interests on the island after the Amarna Period. This diverges from the trade in Cypriot pottery to Egypt, which appears to cease after the Amarna Period (Merrillees 1968: 190, 202).

Numerous Egyptian imports and Egyptianizing objects have been identified at Hala Sultan Tekke, attesting to the particularly close links between Cyprus and Egypt during the Amarna Period and later New Kingdom. These include a faience sceptre head inscribed with the cartouche of Horemheb (Åström 1979; 1989: 206–7) and two scarabs inscribed with the cartouche of Ramesses II (Eriksson 1995: 200). The former is very possibly an item of gift exchange. Among a gold hoard from the site there was a signet ring inscribed in Egyptian hieroglyphs with the personal name Nebuwy (Åström 1989: 204). There are also objects of faience, alabaster and glass (Åström 1989: 204), typical grave goods in high-status tombs at other LC IIC sites throughout the island. More unusual is the confirmation that some of the fish bones from the site belong to the Nile perch (*Lates niloticus*), presumably exported to the island as dried fish in baskets (Åström 1989: 204). Other possible items of gift exchange dating to the Late Bronze Age turn up in Early Iron Age tomb groups of the eleventh century BC. These include a Ramesside scarab from Salamis (Barguet 1971: 14–17, fig. 3), a faience bowl, possibly dating to the twelfth century BC, from Kouklia (Karageorghis 1983: pl. XC, fig. CXVI; Peltenburg 1983), and an Amenhotep III commemorative lion's hunt scarab, also from Kouklia (Clerc 1983: 389–92, fig. 7; Karageorghis 1983: pl. CXC). The commemorative scarabs of Amenhotep III were widely distributed throughout the eastern Mediterranean, as far north as Ugarit, and also in Nubia, as a form of gift exchange. Presumably, the Cypriot scarabs reached the island during the Late Bronze Age and were carefully curated over several generations as prized treasures before finally being buried (Clerc 1983: 392).

Egyptian and Near Eastern texts of the second millennium BC further illuminate the nature and extent of contacts with the island of Cyprus. The island has commonly been identified as the ancient kingdom of Alashiya, based on numerous references to Alashiya's copper resources, resonant with increasing exploitation of Cypriot copper resources at this time. The earliest references to Alashiya from Egyptian sources are the Annals of Thutmose III, recorded in the temple of Amun at Karnak. These state that the chief of Alashiya paid tribute to Thutmose of lapis lazuli, wood, horses and copper, the latter comprising the bulk of the tribute. While the Egyptian texts give no precise information as to the location of Alashiya, this can be extrapolated from various Near Eastern documents. Akkadian sources from Mari, Babylon and Alalakh of the eighteenth and seventeenth centuries BC indicate that Alashiya was a town with a mountainous hinterland, the source of its copper. This is corroborated by the

Hittite archives of the fifteenth century BC, which also claim Alashiya to be a vassal state, paying tribute to the Hittite ruler. By the fourteenth century BC, however, it appears that Alashiya played an important role in diplomatic and trade networks of the eastern Mediterranean as an independent state, as is illustrated by the Amarna Letters (Cohen and Westbrook 2000: 7–8).

These archives give a unique insight into the political and economic relations between the rulers of Alashiya and Egypt. Most significantly, the king of Alashiya writes to the king of Egypt as his equal, addressing him as 'brother'. Only the LBA 'super-powers' – the pharaoh, the Hittite king, the king of Mitanni and the king of Babylon – addressed each other as 'my brother', whereas the rulers of the Egyptian vassal city-states in Palestine addressed these powerful rulers as 'father'. The correspondence illustrates a wide-ranging network of diplomatic ties centred on Egypt, and fuelled by the exchange of raw materials and luxuries (Zaccagnini 2000). A recurrent theme is the shipment of Egyptian gold; indeed, Egypt was the main source of this metal in the eastern Mediterranean in the second millennium BC. The ruler of Alashiya sent the pharaoh gifts of copper, ivory, horses and timber, and the sheer quantities involved might indicate that the king of Alashiya exerted some control over the production of copper. This might be substantiated by atomic absorption analysis of copper ingots from the Cape Gelidonya wreck, which suggests a Cypriot source for the copper (Pulak 1997: 237). On the other hand, analysis of 17 bronze objects from Amarna was unable to demonstrate the use of Cypriot copper at the site; while none of the lead isotope compositions was compatible with Cypriot copper, there was some evidence for the use of Egyptian copper sources from Timna in the Sinai (Stos-Gale *et al.* 1995).

The location of Alashiya remains elusive, although it is possible to surmise that it lay within a copper-rich area, and its integration within the diplomatic networks described in the Amarna archives almost certainly places it within the eastern Mediterranean. Even so, given its privileged position in these networks it is extremely improbable that Alashiya was located on the Levantine coast. While many archaeologists equated Alashiya with Late Bronze Age Cyprus, or part thereof, there has been significant resistance to this identification (Merrillees 1987). Recent petrographic analyses of the Alashiya tablets from the Amarna archives, however, have provided clear evidence that their clay source was in southern Cyprus, in the area between two important Late Bronze Age centres: the LC IIC town of Kalavasos-*Ayios Dhimitrios* and the LC IIC–IIIA town of Alassa-Paliotaverna (Goren *et al.* 2003).

Alashiya is one of the places sacked by the 'Sea Peoples' during year 8 of Ramesses III, in *c.* 1189 BC, as listed on his mortuary temple at Medinet Habu (Dothan 1982: 3). This text has been used to date the LC IIC/IIIA destruction horizon within the wider eastern Mediterranean picture of socio-economic collapse at the end of the Bronze Age. Although there is no reference to the economic and political situation in Alashiya, the eleventh-century Egyptian tale of Wenamun (Nibbi 1985; Åström 1989: 202–3) suggests that Alashiya survived the turmoil of the twelfth century BC.

CHAPTER THIRTY-TWO

EGYPT AND THE MODERN WORLD

————•◆•————

Andrew Bednarski

The early nineteenth century is viewed as the age of ancient Egypt's rediscovery by Europeans. This period witnessed the unearthing of ancient mysteries as well as a growing European obsession with a land whose history extended back into obscurity. The driving impetus behind this nineteenth-century fascination is usually credited to an event that took place in 1798, an event that forced Europe to focus its attention on Egypt in an unprecedented military and political manner. It was in this year that Napoleon led his French army across the Mediterranean in an effort to colonize the land of the Nile. In so doing, Egypt was opened up to Europeans as never before. Yet European interest in Egypt significantly predates Napoleon's failed military adventure. Similarly, the impact that the invasion, and its Egyptological by-products, had on the study of the country, across the continent, is far from understood. The goal of this chapter is, therefore, to question the primacy given to certain events in the study of ancient Egypt in the early nineteenth century, as found in many historical accounts of the discipline. It will begin with a brief survey of texts and events recognized as significant to the study of ancient Egypt, from the classical period up to the 1800s. After discussing aspects of early nineteenth-century, British Egyptology, it will then resume this survey, covering phenomena up to the twentieth century. The chapter will then conclude with a discussion of current aspects of, and problems within, the study of ancient Egypt.

BEFORE THE NINETEENTH CENTURY

Egyptology is normally regarded as the product of European enquiry. People living in the geographic region now called Europe have been interested in aspects of pharaonic Egypt for over 2,000 years. Yet why were people such as the ancient Greeks interested in the land and history of Egypt? The answer, regrettably, sounds pedestrian: Egyptian civilization is old. In fact, Egypt was old by the time Greek philosophers and authors first made contact with it. It is this perceived antiquity that appears to have captivated certain writers and sparked interest in the country. It is possible to trace this interest back to such distant historical figures as the seventh-century BC Greek philosopher Thales of Miletus, who appears to have been influenced by Egyptian concepts. More concrete evidence of interest in the land and people of Egypt, however, has been handed down to us through historical accounts, social commentaries and geographies by classical authors, including Hecataeus of Melitus in the sixth century BC, Herodotus in the fifth century, Hecataeus of Abdera in the fourth century, Manetho in the third century, and Diodorus Siculus and Strabo in the first century.

Throughout the Middle Ages and Renaissance, European interest in ancient Egypt continued. People travelled from the continent to Egypt and documented their experiences. Travel accounts from this period are plentiful, and some of them, whether falsified or valid, proved incredibly popular. By the sixteenth and seventeenth centuries, Europeans began to engage with ancient Egypt in new ways. Many travellers appear to have journeyed to Egypt expressly to collect antiquities. It was also during this period that attempts to translate the dead language of the ancient Egyptians were made, as evidenced by Athanasius Kircher's work. The seventeenth century saw the first attempts in Egypt at what we might now recognize as scientific exploration, as epitomized by John Greaves' 1646 study of pyramids. In the eighteenth century an important mission of exploration was undertaken by the Jesuit Claude Sicard, who correctly identified several sites and monuments on the basis of Classical texts. Two other important voyages were undertaken by Frederik Ludvig Norden and Richard Pococke, both of whom provided strong visual records of Egypt's monuments, along with plans and maps, to European audiences. It was also during the eighteenth century that new, European ideologies, reappraising Egypt's place in global politics, were developed. These constructs, as found in the writings of Benoît de Maillet, praised Egypt's pharaonic glory and blamed its 'ruinous' state on its doomed, modern, despotic system of government. Such constructs later lent weight to the ideological imperatives driving Napoleon's invasion.

THE EARLY NINETEENTH CENTURY

The above, cursory survey highlights a long history of intellectual engagement with ancient Egypt, as well as popular and academic knowledge on aspects as diverse as Egypt's antiquities, natural environment, culture and people. Yet despite this intellectual tradition, it is to the nineteenth century that authors turn when discussing the period of utmost importance in the development of Egyptology. At first glance, such a concentration does not seem unwarranted. The French invasion of 1798 and the subsequent British military victory are intertwined with the history of nineteenth-century Egyptology. After all, it was due to French military efforts in Egypt that the Rosetta Stone was discovered and removed. This famous artefact was not alone in its voyage to Europe, however, as numerous antiquities made their way from Egypt immediately after the French invasion. It was also from this invasion that important literary works on Egypt stemmed. A rousing, popular account of the country, and French activities in it under Napoleon, appeared in the form of Dominique Vivant Denon's *Travels*. A more encyclopaedic account of French scholarly efforts in Egypt was the grand *Description de l'Égypte*. Following on the heels of the French invasion came concentrated European exploratory work in Egypt, led by such famous figures as Henry Salt and Bernardino Drovetti. Under such men archaeological sites were explored, large numbers of antiquities amassed, and the core of most of the important museum collections in Europe assembled. With regard to British Egyptology, the early nineteenth century also witnessed the grand exploits of the famous Giovanni Battista Belzoni and the academic ascension of John Gardner Wilkinson. Along with wondrous archaeological discoveries, the groundwork for reconstructing the ancient Egyptian language was set during this period. Significant efforts at translation were, for example, undertaken by numerous men: George Zoëga, Thomas Young, Johan David Åkerblad, Antoine Isaac Silvestre de Sacy, and, of course, Jean-François Champollion. In 1822 efforts at translation witnessed a breakthrough, with Champollion's publication of his famous *Lettre à M. Dacier*. While he expanded this work the following year, it was not until his grammar and dictionary were published that the full extent of his ideas was realized. Despite the validity of much of his work, many of his ideas were disputed into the mid- and late 1800s. Yet the early nineteenth-century exploration of Egypt resulted in more than the acquisition of museum objects, the publication of exploits and attempts to translate hieroglyphics. Interest in the country also resulted in a wave of Egyptomania that swept the world. Architectural design, for example, was deeply affected. The adoption of ancient motifs in architecture was part of the Egyptian Revival, the final phase of Romantic Neoclassicism, and has been recognized as an international movement over the past 200 years (Curl 1994: xvii). Yet, Egyptian influences were not found solely in monumental works and are evident also in a wide range of areas. For example, both furniture, during the French-Empire period, and porcelain capitalized greatly on ancient forms and motifs in the 1800s.

It is with all of these events and developments in mind that authors discuss how early nineteenth-century Europeans engaged with the exploration of ancient Egypt on a scale, and occasionally in manners, not witnessed before. Yet what did these events and developments mean to European audiences? While much has been written on the above phenomena, explorations of what contemporary audiences made of them are rare and usually cursory. If, however, we consider current public interest in ancient Egypt to be significant, and if we attribute this interest to a nineteenth-century 'rediscovery' of the country, then surely the interest of nineteenth-century audiences in Egypt is important. To measure interest in Egypt today we might use data gathered from visitors to specific museum galleries or from tourist surveys. Without such data from the nineteenth century, however, similar investigations for the period require a different approach. To begin with, we must first ask ourselves how best to measure the popularity and acceptance of a phenomenon across a population over many years. How, for example, do we evaluate the reception of a nineteenth-century book that discusses ancient Egypt? When exploring the impact of early Egyptological books on European audiences, it is possible to interpret the number of copies of a work that were printed and sold as evidence of popularity and possible social acceptance. Denon's *Travels*, for example, was translated into German, Dutch, Italian and English, with the English version undergoing three separate editions. In fact, for approximately one and a half centuries the work was continually in print (Ghali 1986: 181–3). This certainly suggests that Denon's work was tremendously popular with European audiences. The most basic, and obvious, reason for its purchase is that, at some point, people wanted to own it. Yet such an answer brings us no closer to evaluating the work's actual reception. In other words, while distribution information tells us that Denon's book sold well, it falls short of telling us what these sales figures meant to those who bought it. What did people actually think of the work once they read it? Did they like it? Did they despise it? Did they regret buying it? Did they sell it on?

The wide distribution of *Travels* raises another issue: is there always a correlation between the fame of a work and its positive reception? A good example of this issue is the perceived impact of the Napoleonic *Description de l'Égypte* in Great Britain in the early nineteenth century. The corpus was born from the disastrous Napoleonic invasion of Egypt, and was the result of 30 years of subsequent effort by French scholars. On production, it incorporated the sum of French knowledge of Egypt and basked in the fame attached to Napoleon's invasion. When mentioned in the context of the history of Egyptology, the work is often assumed to have played a seminal role in the development of the discipline in Great Britain in the early nineteenth century. Such an assumption does not seem unreasonable, given the central role that the corpus appears to have played in the development of French Egyptology, and given its almost global distribution. Yet a closer look at the evidence suggests that the work did not play a great role in the development of Egyptology in Great Britain in the early 1800s (Bednarski 2005). In fact, the reception of the *Description* in Britain appears to have been a much more complex story, with the corpus possibly overlooked in the early part of the century, only to increase in importance as the century progressed. As a result, the case of the *Description* suggests that even a famous, widely distributed work was not necessarily guaranteed a reading audience that wished to engage with it.

Similar questions can be asked about the reception of *events* associated with the history of Egyptology. Possibly the most famous Egyptological event in Great Britain in the early nineteenth century was Belzoni's Egyptian exhibition, held in London in 1821. After years of excavating and amassing antiquities in Egypt, Belzoni returned to his adopted home once archaeological opportunities were no longer viable. After publishing an account of his exploits, he decided to recreate, in Piccadilly, the famous tomb of Seti I from his archaeological data. The event appears to have been financially successful enough for it to be taken to Paris the following year. In short, Belzoni's exhibition appears to have attracted enough people for it to have been a commercial success. Yet, once again, we must ask ourselves what people made of this phenomenon. Can we interpret the attendance of a large number of people at an event as evidence of the acceptance of ideas put forth at that event? Is attendance at an event indicative of more than fleeting interest? Did this exhibition change people's perceptions of ancient Egypt? What impact did this event have on early Egyptological investigations?

In fact, we should take one step back from these examples and questions and address a much larger issue: the general reception of ancient Egypt in the early 1800s. While the term 'rediscovery' has very grandiose connotations, it is important to establish precisely who was interested in the subject of ancient Egypt other than those researching it. Who bought Denon's widely disseminated *Travels* and who visited Belzoni's exhibition? How else did this interest manifest itself? What did the majority of people think about Egypt, and how did they engage with it? Such questions open up vast areas of research and their answers cannot be fully discussed in a single chapter. A more appropriate approach would be to examine the reception of a work or phenomenon country by country before expanding an investigation to draw cross-cultural and trans-national conclusions.[1]

How then does one measure the public response to the study of ancient Egypt in Great Britain between 1800 and 1830? One method of gauging reaction is through examination of British periodicals from the time. After all, it was in literature such as this that new discoveries were announced, and books, such as Denon's *Travels*, and events, such as Belzoni's exhibition, were discussed. The content covered by periodicals was determined by a dynamic relationship between the editors and the reading public to whom they catered. Much like today's readers, nineteenth-century British readers did not simply read what editors wanted them to read. Instead, while the content of periodicals helped to shape the interests of their readers, readers' interests also dictated the content. As a result, periodicals offer a rich, and unique, source of information about their readers' interest in, and response to, a variety of subjects.

While periodicals had been recognized as important by British publishers for quite some time, the early nineteenth century witnessed an explosion of such publications. The number of periodical titles tripled in the first three decades of the 1800s and different kinds of periodicals were increasingly developed. While the number of periodicals grew unevenly throughout the century, the largest proportionate increases seem to have occurred in the earlier decades of the 1800s. Of particular note were increases in the late 1810s, early 1820s and early 1830s. Calculations of the growth of periodicals have been made using the number of titles listed in the *Waterloo Directory of English Newspapers and Periodicals*, series 1, which comprises approximately 20 per cent of the total number of titles. While it should be noted that the titles listed in the *Waterloo* are biased towards subject matter, it has been estimated that there were 475 British journal titles in existence in 1801, with that number growing to approximately 1,000 by 1831 (Dawson *et al.* 2004: 7–9).

Yet British periodical literature is a unique source of information for reasons other than its size and growth in the early nineteenth century. By looking at the articles devoted to the subject of ancient Egypt over many years, this literature allows us to explore both the immediate reception of the subject as well as its long-term reception. Unfortunately, the sheer number, complexity and organization of periodicals available to historians have hampered their use as sources of historical information (Dawson *et al.* 2004: 6). Despite these problems, it is still possible to select historically significant periodicals that cover a broad spectrum of British readers and editors. As a result, a survey of periodical literature can give a rapid sketch of the reception of events and ideas within different segments of British society in the early 1800s.

References to, and passages from, early nineteenth-century periodicals have been used before in histories of Egyptology. This information, however, is generally used by citing often well-known passages concerned with research into Egypt. Authors have used such extracts as evidence to support various historical assertions, but typically without placing the passages in question within a literary or historical context.[2] By examining a range of periodicals over many years, however, it is possible to investigate references to Egypt in a broad, non-Egyptological context. Such an approach helps move away from cursory examinations of isolated journal references specifically concerned with research into Egypt, and construct a more comprehensive historical context.

As an example of what we might learn from an approach of this sort, I have quantified the popularity of Egypt as a subject in 13 British periodicals between 1800 and 1830. These journals are recognized by historians of periodical literature to be the most significant publications of their kind during the early 1800s (Bednarski 2005) and targeted a variety of British readerships. Some were wealthy, well educated and widely read, as was the case with the top five journals listed in Figure 32.1. This group of periodicals shared a similarly high literary status during their publication runs and were closer to books in their size and format. The second category of periodicals, represented by the next six journals, includes works that did not carry the same literary or social weight as the first group. Nonetheless, they played a significant role in the lives of nineteenth-century British readers. In general, the readers of these journals had modest funds that could be spent on reading material, and modest educations, but were interested in a variety of topics. Still other audiences had very specific, scholarly interests, as was the case with the final two publications listed in Figure 32.1. When examined collectively, these journals represent the perspectives of a wide spectrum of British readers and editors. In an exploration of these periodicals, one can read through the indices and tables of contents for each volume, focusing on words

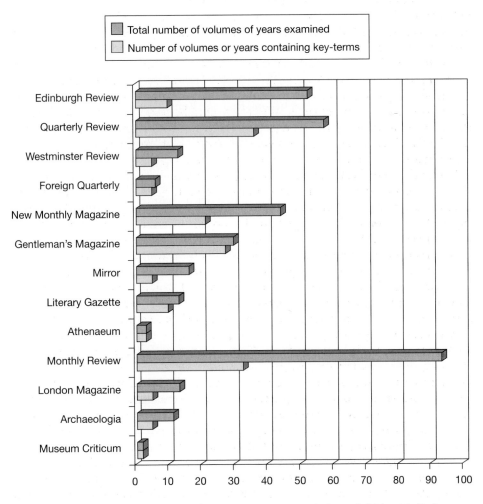

Figure 32.1 The popularity of Ancient Egypt as a topic in 13 British periodicals between 1800 and 1830.

that are central to the study of Egypt during the early nineteenth century. These indices are far from cursory, and include all substantive references within the journal in question. The key terms upon which I focused include Belzoni, Champollion, Demotic, Denon, *Description de l'Égypte*, Egypt, Enchorial, hieroglyphs, Jomard, Rosetta and Young and Figure 32.1 lists the number of volumes, or in the case of the *Literary Gazette* the number of years, examined for each journal. Similarly, the table lists the number of volumes, or with the *Literary Gazette* the number of years, of a periodical that contains key terms between 1800 and 1830.

By quantifying the data in this way, several factors become evident. To begin with, the fact that Egypt is mentioned in all 13 periodicals, each with different goals, political biases and formats, suggests that it was generally a popular theme. How popular that theme was to different journals and readers, however, could vary greatly. To gain a deeper understanding of the variations, it is helpful to compare interest in Egypt with interest in other topics for the period in question. More specifically, a comparison between mention of Egypt and mention of aspects of ancient Greek and Roman civilization might help to contextualize the periodical references.

How then did early nineteenth-century British interest in Egypt compare with interest in classical topics? To address this question I have taken two of the journals listed in Figure 32.1 and searched for terms relevant to the study of ancient Greece and Rome: Aeneid, ancient authors, Athenian, Athens, classic/Classical, Greece, Grecian, Greek, Iliad, Latin, Parthenon, Roman, Rome, Sparta and Spartan. What this search reveals is that these Classical terms can be found in 30 out of the 52 volumes examined of the prestigious *Edinburgh Review*. In other words, the terms relating to aspects of ancient Greece and Rome occur in 58 per cent of the studied volumes. Similarly, a search for the same terms in the *Edinburgh*'s literary rival, the *Quarterly Review*, reveals their occurrence in 32 of the 43 volumes examined (i.e. 74 per cent). These figures, as visually compared with those relating to references to Egypt, are shown in Figure 32.2.

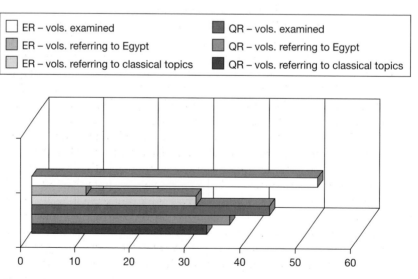

Figure 32.2 The relative popularity of Ancient Egyptian and Classical topics in the *Quarterly Review* and *Edinburgh Review*.

With this comparative data, it might be fair to say that readers and editors of both the *Quarterly* and *Edinburgh* were similarly interested in the subject of ancient Greece and Rome. At the same time, however, interest in Egypt appears to vary considerably between the two journals. It appears that readers and editors of the *Quarterly* were more interested in the subjects of Egypt than those of the *Edinburgh*. Similarly, it might be fair to infer that the readers and editors of the *Edinburgh* were more interested, although not overwhelmingly so, in classical than in Egyptian topics. Yet these differences provoke further questions. If large differences in interest in classical and Egyptian topics are reflected in other journals of the period, then, perhaps the 'rediscovery' of Egypt needs to be understood as a relatively minor occurrence within the context of much more prominent investigations into other past societies. In other words, despite the amount of literature available on early nineteenth-century exploration, the rediscovery of Egypt may have been a scholastic 'storm in a teacup' in nineteenth-century Great Britain.

Such may, in fact, have been the case with efforts to decipher hieroglyphs. While much has been made of the history of British and French efforts to translate the language, it would appear that only a small handful of periodical references in Great Britain discuss this work. As a result, it seems that British attempts at translation went largely undiscussed within British society. If the differences between references to Egypt and aspects of classical civilization are small in other periodicals, then it might be fair to draw an initial conclusion that interest in the relatively new studies into Egypt was on a par with British society's interest in much more established studies of classical civilization. A conclusion of this sort opens up an exciting avenue of enquiry: exactly how important was research into Egypt, versus research into other ancient cultures, in nineteenth-century Britain? In fact, a working hypothesis based on either conclusion will help us to understand better where the study of Egypt resided in the minds of British scholars and the British public during a period regarded as the first few decades of the modern discipline's development, and a period in which new questions of mankind's history were being developed.

As we can see, periodical literature offers much more than anecdotal material for the exploration of nineteenth-century Egyptology. Yet the methods suggested above are not free of problems. To begin with, periodical literature from this period is far from fully understood, and the issues surrounding its production and interpretation are complex. Aside from this fact, anyone interested in using periodical literature must acknowledge that further in-depth research is required to support any assertions drawn from quick statistical analyses. In other words, it is important to read each reference and question the context in which it is found. Only then can we move from a superficial sketch of references to an understanding of what the articles or reviews are saying about the subjects we are analysing. Finally, it should be noted that plentiful, periodical literature is but one source of information on the British public's interaction with Egypt in the 1800s. Other sources, for example, include artistic movements and, of course, non-periodical literature. If combined, these sources will likely complement each other, since artistic and literary ventures were advertised and discussed within contemporaneous periodicals. The early nineteenth century remains a period in which exciting, startling discoveries were made in the field of Egyptology, some of which continue to have an impact on the study of the civilization. It would be a shame not to investigate further the wider historical context in which these discoveries were made, particularly when such rich sources for historical research are available.

AFTER THE EARLY NINETEENTH CENTURY

Important discoveries and developments continued in Egypt throughout the nineteenth and early twentieth centuries. The archaeological traditions evident in the Napoleonic *Description* were continued with the production of Karl Richard Lepsius' *Denkmäler*. The manner in which archaeological investigations were carried out in Egypt was greatly affected by the work of François Auguste Ferdinand Mariette, who founded the Egyptian Antiquities Service (now the SCA) and the first national museum in the Near East. Spectacular finds in the late nineteenth century included the discovery in 1870 of a cache of royal mummies in the Valley of the Kings. An important development, particularly for British Egyptology, was the founding of the Egypt Exploration Fund (now Society) in 1882. The Society was instrumental in amassing antiquities for British and American museums, and continues its long tradition of field-work to this day. It was also during this period that William Matthew Flinders Petrie, a field director for the Fund, established new standards for conducting Egyptian archaeology and trained a generation of excavators. The late nineteenth and early twentieth centuries also saw the growing importance of archaeological data predating the dynastic age. More famous phenomena from this period include Gaston Camille Charles Maspero's publication of the Pyramid Texts and Ludwig Borchardt's discovery of the Berlin Bust of Nefertiti.

Perhaps the most famous archaeological discovery in Egypt was Howard Carter's excavation of the tomb of Tutankhamun in 1922, an event that once again saw Egyptomania sweep the world. Fascination with the boy-pharaoh was, and in some cases continues to be, the result of several historical factors. At the time of its discovery it was the least disturbed king's tomb in Egypt. Prior to its discovery, Tutankhamun was a little-known historical figure. The young king's ascension to the throne and eventual death marks the end of the anomalous Amarna Period. The historical data about his life facilitate speculation rife with political intrigue. Carter's work occurred at a time when new technologies could disseminate both the story and images of the discovery in manners never before imagined; newspapers, movie footage and innumerable consumer objects capitalized on the discovery, catering to the wealthy and the less well-off, which, in turn, both created and fuelled a public fascination with ancient Egypt (Frayling 1992).

Parallel to this famous discovery, the twentieth century demonstrated the usefulness of archaeological investigation, not only for the discovery of inscriptions and the collection of antiquities, but also as a means of developing a holistic comprehension of ancient Egyptian civilization. The long-term, and ongoing, exploration of sites such as Amarna, the capital city of the pharaoh Akhenaten, underscores this fact. The city remains one of the most important sites for the study of settlement archaeology in the Near East. The textual material collected from the ancient village of Deir el-Medina is another case in point. The evidence garnered from both these sites has greatly increased our understanding of ancient Egyptian social organization.

Egyptology has traditionally been concerned with the study and recording of texts. Developments and discoveries were not restricted to archaeology during the late nineteenth century, and our understanding of the ancient Egyptian language greatly advanced through the contributions of numerous scholars during this period. While archaeology in Egypt came into its own in the twentieth century, philological studies also continued to experience great advances. Our comprehension of Middle Egyptian, the classical form of the language, was codified into a grammar by Alan Gardiner. This work remains the foundation for learning the language. At the same time, the broad publication of texts, as undertaken by Kurt Sethe, facilitated the study of the language. Understanding of other forms of ancient Egyptian, including Coptic, developed significantly, and dictionaries such as Erman and Grapow's *Wörterbuch*, now considered a standard tool for studying the language, were created. Epigraphy, the recording of texts, also continues to be of central importance to Egyptology, with the University of Chicago's survey probably the most famous, and long-standing, example.

THE FUTURE

In keeping with the long academic and popular tradition outlined above, interest in ancient Egypt appears to be thriving. Many aspects of ancient Egyptian civilization have become canonical images in Western society. There are few people living in Europe or North America, for example, who would fail to associate the golden burial mask of Tutankhamun with ancient Egypt. Images from, or inspired by, ancient Egypt surround us, their presence and purpose often unquestioned by the people who see them every day. Such images include pyramids on US currency, Egyptian motifs in department stores such as Harrods, or pyramid-shaped buildings in Las Vegas. Documentaries on ancient Egyptian civilization abound, as do weighty, academic, and lighter, popular books. Tourism also remains a vital industry in Egypt, with the majority of people visiting the country intent on seeing its ancient wonders. In short, an intellectual and consumer appetite for ancient Egypt remains strong.

Such interest can manifest itself in ways other than the adoption of Egyptian motifs, speculation on the country's history or tourist visits to Egypt. At times, modern commentators have reinterpreted historical characters from ancient Egypt, or aspects of ancient Egyptian civilization. Different representations of King Akhenaten are a case in point, with the so-called heretic pharaoh adopted as a symbol by marginalized segments of Western society. Akhenaten has, for example, been viewed as holding knowledge from the lost civilization of Atlantis; as a positive role model for disability rights activists; as the first gay man; and, by Afrocentric Egyptology, as an ancestor from a history denied by racist European scholarship (Montserrat 2000). This ongoing engagement with Egyptian civilization across a broad spectrum of groups within Western society demonstrates the influence that the ancient culture continues to exert. It also begs the question why people engage with the study of Egypt beyond a superficial level of curiosity.

In fact, there are more ways than ever before for people to engage with the subject of ancient Egypt and satisfy their appetites. Museums with Egyptian artefacts and monuments from Egypt can be found all over the world. These objects and structures can serve as cultural ambassadors, piquing interest, or as instructional tools, providing a way of following up prior learning. Another increasingly interesting way of interacting with ancient Egypt is through the internet which is revolutionizing the means of historical enquiry and consumption. Continually developing websites, such as the Giza Plateau Mapping Project, provide vast amounts of historical data to anyone with an internet connection, anywhere in the world. Alternative interpretations to standard Egyptological assertions are also readily accessible. Similarly, the internet presents a simple means of purchasing an increasingly wide range of products associated with ancient Egypt, real or imagined.

As the above survey shows, the ways in which Egyptologists engage with ancient Egypt are also continually developing. Along with the refinement of intellectual and methodological tools in the nineteenth and twentieth centuries, new technologies have changed the way in which Egyptologists explore the past. We have greatly improved, for example, our ability to determine the date, structural and chemical composition of ancient materials. New technology, along with a greater concern for the destructive nature of archaeology, has facilitated non-invasive forms of exploration, such as satellite remote sensing and the use of magnetometry. Also, new technology has enabled us to find, gain access to, conserve, protect and even relocate endangered monuments.

Like the tools available to the researcher, however, the challenges faced by Egyptologists are not static. The ecology of Egypt is changing through a combination of natural and man-made factors. The damming of the Nile has stopped the historical distribution of sediments down-river, contributing to increased erosion in the delta. Intensive irrigation and desert reclamation projects have raised the level of groundwater at archaeological sites which, in turn, has put them at risk. Nor should the destructive effects of tourism on the monuments of Egypt be ignored. The sheer number of visitors to the Valley of the Kings, for example, has resulted in humidity levels within many of the tombs rising to dangerous levels. Large numbers of daily visitors to Egypt's funerary monuments have brought inevitable wear-and-tear. The face of the Sphinx, long protected by inert sand, has weathered considerably over the past 200 years, as a result of pollution from Cairo and exposure to the natural elements.

Unexpected pressures also arise from archaeological research. In our bid to record and salvage as much information as possible, there is the danger of continually prioritizing digging over disseminating findings. It is the digging, after all, that usually satisfies funding bodies and secures money for future work. Ironically, such an approach can be more detrimental to the archaeological record than not digging. Excavation partially destroys and transforms data as it records it. With the evidence no longer in the ground, and with a focus on further field-seasons, material runs the risk of sitting unstudied, unpublished and possibly forgotten, in storerooms. In the coming decades Egyptologists and the Egyptian government will have to work together, developing new initiatives and new tools, if they are to face many of these challenges properly. Yet all of these factors, the long history of interest in ancient Egypt, the story of our past successes and failures, the reworking of ancient ideas, the new means of investigation and approaches to research and the problems that we face today, leave the discipline in a dynamic state. The twenty-first century promises to be an exciting time for Egyptology.

NOTES

1 This notion of country-specific reception-studies has a long tradition and is exemplified by works such as Thomas Glick's study of Darwinism (Glick 1974) and Roy Porter and Mikuláš

Teich's examination of the Enlightenment (Porter and Teich 1981). Glick's text contains chapters by individual authors devoted to specific countries, such as England, Germany, France, the United States, Russia, the Netherlands, Spain and Mexico. Similarly, Porter and Teich examine the Enlightenment in national dimensions. The broad lens of their study focuses on the Enlightenment in England, Scotland, France, the Netherlands, Switzerland, Russia and other countries.

2 See Wortham 1971: 30 (his critique of Richard Dalton's drawings of Egyptian monuments is based partly on a review in the *Gentleman's Magazine*; Wortham implies Dalton's drawings had little impact, but he offers no information on the *Gentleman's Magazine* or what such a review would have meant to the reception of Dalton's work); Parkinson 1999: 21–3 (he uses both the *Gentleman's Magazine* and *Archaeologia* as sources of information regarding the Rosetta Stone's acquisition by Britain, but says nothing about the significance of these periodicals to British society); and Adkins and Adkins 2000: 122 (their reference to Thomas Young's translations in *Archaeologia* lacks an explanation of what publishing in this journal meant to authors and readers), 129 (their reference to Young's publications in the *Museum Criticum* lacks similar historical information and does not explain why the authors view it as an obscure publication or what such obscurity would have meant to Young's articles), 142 (a passing reference to a favourable review of Champollion's work in the *Monthly Review* with no further explanation to what this might have meant), and 199 (the reference to the *Quarterly Review*'s article on Champollion's *Lettre à M. Dacier* does not explain what a publication in this very important journal would have meant to both scholars and the wider public).

BIBLIOGRAPHY

———•◆•———

Abd el-Maksoud, M. (1998) *Tell Heboua (1981–1991): Enquête archéologique sur la Deuxième Période Intermédiaire et le Nouvel Empire à l'extrémité orientale du Delta*, Paris: Éditions Recherche sur les Civilisations

Abd el-Raziq, M., Castel, G., Tallet, P. and Ghica, V. (2002) *Les inscriptions d'Ayn Soukhna*, Cairo: Institut Français d'Archéologie Orientale

Adams, B. (1995) *Ancient Nekhen. Garstang in the City of Hierakonpolis*, New Malden: Egyptian Studies Association

Adams, M.D. (1998) 'The Abydos settlement site project: investigation of a major provincial town in the Old Kingdom and the First Intermediate Period', in C.J. Eyre (ed.) *Proceedings of the 7th International Congress of Egyptologists, Cambridge 3–9 Sept. 1995*, 19–30, Leuven: Peeters

Adams, W.Y. (1977) *Nubia: Corridor to Africa*, Princeton, NJ: Princeton University Press

—— (1984) 'The first colonial empire. Egypt in Nubia 3200–1200 B.C.', *Comparative Studies in Sociology and History*, 26: 36–71

—— (1985) 'Doubts about the lost pharaohs', *Journal of Near Eastern Studies*, 44: 185–92

Adkins, L. and Adkins, R. (2000) *The Keys of Egypt: The Race to Read the Hieroglyphs*, London: Harper Collins

Ahmed, S.E.M. (2004) 'The Merowe Dam Archaeological Salvage Project', in D.A. Welsby and J.R. Anderson (eds) *Sudan: Ancient Treasures: An Exhibition of Recent Discoveries from the Sudan National Museum*, 308–14, London: British Museum Press

Albright, W.F. (1954) 'Northwest-Semitic names in a list of Egyptian slaves from the Eighteenth Century B.C.', *Journal of the American Oriental Society*, 74: 222–33

Aldenderfer, M.S. and Stanish, C. (1993) 'Domestic architecture, household archaeology, and the past in the South-Central Andes', in M.S. Aldenderfer (ed.) *Domestic Architecture, Ethnicity, and Complementarity in the South-Central Andes*, 1–12, Iowa City: University of Iowa Press

Aldred, C. (1969) 'The "New Year" gifts to the Pharaoh', *Journal of Egyptian Archaeology*, 55: 73–81

Alexanian, N. and Seidlmayer, S.J. (2002) 'Die Residenznekropole von Dahschur: erster Grabungsbericht', *Mitteilungen des Deutschen Archäologischen Instituts Abteilung Kairo*, 58: 1–28

Allam, S. (1973a) *Hieratische Ostraka und Papyri aus der Ramessidenzeit*, Tübingen: Selbstverlag

—— (1973b) *Das Verfahrensrecht in der altägyptischen Arbeitersiedlung von Deir-el-Medineh*, Tübingen: Selbstverlag

—— (1978) 'Un droit pénal existait-il *stricto sensu* en Égypte pharaonique?', *Journal of Egyptian Archaeology*, 64: 65–8

—— (1985) *Some Pages from Everyday Life in Ancient Egypt*, Cairo: Foreign Cultural Information Department, Egyptian Ministry of Culture

—— (1986) 'Réflexions sur le "code légal" d'Hermopolis dans l'Égypte ancienne', *Chronique d'Égypte*, 61: 50–75

—— (1991) 'Egyptian Law Courts in Pharaonic and Hellenistic times', *Journal of Egyptian Archaeology*, 77: 109–27

—— (1992) 'Legal aspects in the contendings of Horus and Seth', in A. Lloyd (ed.) *Studies in Pharaonic Religion and Society in Honour of J. Gwyn Griffiths*, 137–45, London: Egypt Exploration Society

—— (1994) 'Papyrus Berlin 8523 – Registration of Land-holdings', in B. Bryan and D. Lorton (eds) *Essays in Egyptology in Honor of H. Goedicke*, 1–7, San Antonio: Van Siclen Books

—— (2001) 'Slavery', in D.B. Redford (ed.) *The Oxford Encyclopedia of Ancient Egypt*, vol. 3, 293–6, New York: Oxford University Press

—— (2003) 'Recht im pharaonischen Ägypten', in U. Manthe (ed.) *Die Rechtskulturen der Antike – vom Alten Orient bis zum Römischen Reich*, 15–54, Munich: Beck

—— (2004) 'Justice seigneuriale', in *Droit et Cultures – Revue Semestrielle d'Anthropologie et d'Histoire*, 47: 35–45

—— (2005) 'Eine Prozess-Strafe (O. Berlin 14214)', in Z. Hawass, S. Bedier and K. Daoud (eds) *Studies in Honor of Ali Radwan*, 65–8, Cairo: American University in Cairo Press

—— (2006) 'Archives foncières en Égypte ancienne', in C. Dugas de la Boissonny (ed.) *Terre, forêt et droit – Actes des Journées Internationales d'Histoire du Droit, Nancy 12–15 juin 2002*, 1–18, Nancy: Presses Universitaires de Nancy

—— (forthcoming a) 'Foundations in pharaonic Egypt – The oldest-known private endowments in history', in H. Halm, C. Leitz and W. Röllig (eds) *Die Welt des Orients*, Göttingen: Vandenhoeck & Ruprecht

—— (forthcoming b) 'Some remarks on the *Eisagogeus*', *Journal of Egyptian History*

Allen, J.P. (1988) *Genesis in Egypt: The Philosophy of Ancient Egyptian Creation Accounts*, New Haven, CT: Yale Egyptological Seminar

—— (1994) 'Reading a pyramid', in C. Berger, G. Clerc and N. Grimal (eds) *Hommages à Jean Leclant*, 5–28, Cairo: Institut Français d'Archéologie Orientale

—— (2002a) *The Heqanakht Papyri*, New York: Metropolitan Museum of Art

—— (2002b) 'The Speos Artemidos inscription of Hatshepsut', *Bulletin of the Egyptological Seminar*, 16: 1–17

—— (forthcoming) 'The Second Intermediate Period in the Turin Canon', in *The Second Intermediate Period (13th-17th Dynasties): Current Research, Future Prospects*, Leuven: Peeters

—— (in preparation) *The Advent of Ancient Egyptian Literature*

Allen, T.G. (1974) *The Book of the Dead, or Going Forth by Day*, Chicago, IL: University of Chicago

Alliot, M. (1949) *Le culte d'Horus à Edfou au temps des Ptolémées,* vol. 1, Cairo: Institut Français d'Archéologie Orientale

—— (1954) *Le culte d'Horus à Edfou au temps des Ptolémées*, vol. 2, Cairo: Institut Français d'Archéologie Orientale

Altenmüller, B. (1975) 'Amunsbarke', in W. Helck and E. Otto (eds) *Lexikon der Ägyptologie*, vol. 1, 248–51, Wiesbaden: Harrassowitz

Altenmüller, H. (1998) 'Daily life in eternity – the mastabas and rock-cut tombs of officials', in R. Schulz and M. Seidel (eds) *Egypt: The World of the Pharaohs*, 78–93, Cologne: Könemann

—— and Moussa, A.M. (1975) 'Die Inschrift Amenemhet II. aus dem Ptah-Tempel von Memphis, ein Vorbericht', *Studien zur Altägyptischen Kultur*, 18: 1–48

—— et al. (1970) *Handbuch der Orientalistik*, ed. B. Spuler, Section 1: *Der Nahe und der Mittlere Osten*, Vol. I: *Ägyptologie*, Part 2: *Literatur*, 2nd edn, Leiden and Cologne: Brill

Anderson, J.R. (2004) 'The medieval kingdoms of Nubia', in D. Welsby and J.R. Anderson (eds) *Sudan: Ancient Treasures*, 202–8, London: British Museum Press

Andreu, G. (1987) 'Les titres de policiers formés sur la racine *schena*', *Cahiers de Recherches de l'Institut de Papyrologie et d'Égyptologie de Lille*, 9: 17–23

—— (ed.) (2002) *Les artistes de pharaon: Deir el-Médineh et la Vallée des Rois*, Paris and Turnhout: Brepols

——, Rutschowscaya, M.-H. and Ziegler, C. (1997) *Ancient Egypt at the Louvre*, Paris: Hachette

Andrews, C. (1994) *Amulets of Ancient Egypt*, London: British Museum Press

Anselin, A. (2004) 'Problèmes de lecture et d'écriture – les noms des polities nagadéennes', in S. Hendrickx, R.F. Friedman, K.M. Ciałowicz and M. Chłodnicki (eds) *Egypt at its Origins. Studies in Memory of Barbara Adams*, 547–73, Leuven: Peeters

Anthes, R. (1928), *Die Felsinschriften von Hatnub*, Leipzig: Hinrichs

—— (1930) 'Eine Polizeistreife des Mittleren Reiches in die westliche Oase', *Zeitschrift für Ägyptische Sprache und Altertumskunde*, 65: 108–14

Arkell, A.J. (1961) *A History of the Sudan from the Earliest Times to 1821*, 2nd rev. edn, London: University of London, The Athlone Press

Armelagos, G., van Gerven, D., Martin, D. and Huss-Ashmore, R. (1984) 'Effects of nutritional change on the skeletal biology of northeast African (Sudanese Nubian) populations', in J.D. Clark and S.A. Brandt (eds) *From Hunters to Farmers*, 132–46, Berkeley: University of California Press

Arnold, D. (1962) *Wandrelief und Raumfunktion in ägyptischen Tempeln des Neuen Reiches*, Berlin: Hessling

—— (1991) *Building in Egypt. Pharaonic Stone Masonry*, New York and Oxford: Oxford University Press

—— (1997) 'Royal cult complexes of the Old and Middle Kingdoms', in B. Shafer (ed.) *Temples of Ancient Egypt*, 31–85, London and New York: I.B. Tauris

—— (1999) *Temples of the Last Pharaohs*, New York and Oxford: Oxford University Press

—— (2003) *The Encyclopaedia of Ancient Egyptian Architecture*, trans. S. Gardiner and H. Strudwick, London and New York: I.B. Tauris

—— and Bourriau, J.D. (eds) (1993) *An Introduction to Ancient Egyptian Pottery*, Mainz: von Zabern

Arnold, Do. (1988) 'The Pottery', in D. Arnold, *The Pyramid of Senwosret I, South Cemeteries of Lisht 1*, New York: Metropolitan Museum of Art

Arnold, F. (1990) *The Control Notes and Team Marks, The South Cemeteries of Lisht*, New York: Metropolitan Museum of Art

Aslanidou, K. (2005) 'The Minoan wall paintings from Tell el-Dabʿa/Ezbet Helmi: the life size male figures', in R. Laffineur and E. Greco (eds) *Emporia: Aegeans in the Central and Eastern Mediterranean*, 463–9, Liège and Austin: Université de Liège and University of Texas Press

Assmann, J. (1970) *Der König als Sonnenpriester. Ein kosmographischer Begleittext zur kultischen Sonnenhymnik in den thebanischen Tempeln und Gräbern*, Mainz: von Zabern

—— (1972) 'Palast oder Tempel? Überlegungen zur Architektur und Topographie von Amarna', *Journal of Near Eastern Studies*, 31/3: 143–55

—— (1974) 'Der literarische Text im Alten Ägypten: Versuch einer Begriffsbestimmung', *Orientalistische Literaturzeitung*, 69: 117–26

—— (1989) 'State and religion in the New Kingdom', in W. K. Simpson (ed.) *Religion and Philosophy in Ancient Egypt*, 55–88, New Haven, CT: Yale Egyptological Seminar

—— (1990, 2nd edn 1995a) *Maat. Gerechtigkeit und Unsterblichkeit im alten Ägypten*, Munich: Beck

—— (1992a) *Politische Theologie zwischen Ägypten und Israel*, Munich: Carl-Friedrich-von-Siemens-Stiftung

—— (1992b) *Das kulturelle Gedächtnis. Schrift, Erinnerung und politische Identität in frühen Hochkulturen*, Munich: Beck

—— (1995) *Egyptian Solar Religion in the New Kingdom. Re, Amun and the Crisis of Polytheism*, trans. A. Alcock, London and New York: Kegan Paul

—— (1996) 'Kulturelle und Literarische Texte', in A. Loprieno (ed.) *Ancient Egyptian Literature: History and Forms*, 59–82, Leiden, New York and Cologne: Brill

—— (1997) *Moses the Egyptian. The Memory of Egypt in Western Monotheism*, Cambridge, MA: Harvard University Press

—— (1999a) 'Cultural and literary texts', in G. Moers (ed.) *Definitely: Egyptian Literature. Proceedings of the Symposium 'Ancient Egyptian Literature: History and Forms', Los Angeles, March 24–26, 1995*, 1–15, Göttingen: Seminar für Ägyptologie und Koptologie

—— (1999b) *Ägyptische Hymnen und Gebete*, 2nd edn, Freiburg/Göttingen: Universitätsverlag/ Vandenhoeck & Ruprecht

—— (2001) *The Search for God in Ancient Egypt*, trans. D. Lorton, Ithaca, NY: Cornell University Press

—— (2004) 'Die Zeugung des Sohnes. Ikonizität, Narrativität und Ritualität im ägyptischen Mythos', in J. Assmann, *Ägyptische Geheimnisse*, 59–98, Munich: Wilhelm Fink Verlag

Aston, B.G., Harrell, J.A. and Shaw, I. (2000) 'Stone', in P.T. Nicholson and I. Shaw (eds) *Ancient Egyptian Materials and Technology*, 5–77, Cambridge: Cambridge University Press

Aston, D.A. (2003) 'The Theban west bank from the Twenty-fifth Dynasty to the Ptolemaic Period', in N. Strudwick and J.H. Taylor (eds) *The Theban Necropolis: Past, Present and Future*, 138–66, London: British Museum Press

Astour, M.C. (2001) 'Mitanni', in D. Redford (ed.) *The Oxford Encyclopedia of Ancient Egypt*, vol. 2, 422–4, New York: Oxford University Press

Åström, P. (1979) 'A faience sceptre with a cartouche of Horemhab', in V. Karageorghis (ed.) *Studies Presented in Memory of Porphyrios Dikaios*, 46–8, Nicosia: Lions Club of Nicosia

—— (1989) 'Trade in the Late Cypriot Bronze Age', in E. Peltenburg (ed.) *Early Society in Cyprus*, 202–8, Edinburgh: Edinburgh University Press

Aufrère, S. (1991) *L'univers minéral dans la pensée égyptienne*, 2 vols, Cairo: Institut Français d'Archéologie Orientale

—— (2001a) 'Thèbes victorieuse (*W3st-nḫt*). Allégorie de la guerre et de la science. Histoire d'un concept', *Méditerranées*, 28: 13–40

—— (2001b) 'The Egyptian temple, substitute for the mineral universe', in W.V. Davies (ed.) *Colour and Painting in Ancient Egypt*, 158–63, London: British Museum Press

Ayrout, H.H. (2005) *The Egyptian Peasant*, Cairo: American University in Cairo Press

Badawy, A. (1948) *Le dessin architectural chez les anciens égyptiens*, Cairo: Imprimerie Nationale

—— (1966) *A History of Egyptian Architecture. Volume II. The First Intermediate Period, the Middle Kingdom, and the Second Intermediate Period*, Berkeley and Los Angeles, CA: University of California Press

—— (1968) *A History of Egyptian Architecture. Volume III. The Empire, From the Eighteenth Dynasty to the End of the Twentieth Dynasty*, Berkeley and Los Angeles, CA: University of California Press

—— (1978) *The Tomb of Nyhetep-Ptah at Giza and the Tomb of Ankhmahor at Saqqara*, Berkeley, CA: University of California Press

Bader, B. (2001) *Tell el-Dab'a XIII. Typologie und Chronologie der Mergel C-Ton Keramik*, Vienna: Verlag der Österreichischen Akademie der Wissenschaften

Baer, K. (1960) *Rank and Title in the Old Kingdom*, Chicago, IL: University of Chicago Press

—— (1963) 'An Eleventh Dynasty farmer's letters to his family', *Journal of the American Oriental Society*, 83: 1–19

Bagnall, R.S. (ed.) (1997) *The Kellis Agricultural Account Book*, Oxford: Oxbow Books

Baines, J. (1985) 'Colour terminology and colour classification: Ancient Egyptian colour terminology and polychromy', *American Anthropologist*, 87: 282–97

—— (1991) 'Society, morality and religious practice', in B.E. Shafer (ed.) *Religion in Ancient Egypt: Gods, Myths and Personal Practice*, 123–200, Ithaca, NY: Cornell University Press

—— (1994) 'On the status and purposes of Ancient Egyptian art', *Cambridge Archaeological Journal*, 4: 67–94

—— (1995a) 'Kingship, definition of culture, and legitimation', in D. O'Connor and D.P. Silverman (eds) *Ancient Egyptian Kingship*, 3–47, Leiden, New York and Cologne: Brill

—— (1995b) 'Origins of Egyptian kingship', in D. O'Connor and D.P. Silverman (eds) *Ancient Egyptian Kingship*, 95–155, Leiden, New York and Cologne: Brill

—— (1996) 'Classicism and Modernism in the Literature of the New Kingdom', in A. Loprieno (ed.) *Ancient Egyptian Literature: History and Forms*, 157–74, Leiden, New York and Cologne: Brill

—— (2000) 'Stone and other materials in Ancient Egypt: usages and values', in C. Karlshausen and T. de Putter (eds) *Pierres égyptiennes – chefs-d'œuvre pour l'éternité*, 29–40, Mons: Faculté Polytechnique de Mons

—— (2001a) 'Colour use and the distribution of relief and painting in the temple of Sety I at Abydos', in W.V. Davies (ed.) *Colour and Painting in Ancient Egypt*, 145–7, London: British Museum Press

—— (2001b) 'Egyptian letters of the New Kingdom as evidence for religious practice', *Journal of Ancient Near Eastern Religions*, 1: 1–31

—— and Malek, J. (1980) *Atlas of Ancient Egypt*, Oxford: Phaedon

——, Henderson, J. and Jaeschke, R.L. (1989) 'Techniques of decoration in the Hall of Barques in the temple of Sethos I at Abydos', *Journal of Egyptian Archaeology*, 75: 13–30

Bakry, H. (1968) 'A family from Sais', *Mitteilungen des Deutschen Archäologischen Instituts Abteilung Kairo*, 23: 69–74 and pl. XIX

Balcz, H. (1930) 'Die altägyptische Wandgliederung', *Mitteilungen des Deutschen Instituts für Ägyptische Altertumskunde in Kairo*, 1: 38–92

Baldwin Smith, E. (1938) *Egyptian Architecture as Cultural Expression*, New York and London: Appleton-Century

Baligh, R.O.K. (1997) *Thutmosis I*, unpublished thesis, Yale University

Banks, M. (1996) *Ethnicity. Anthropological Constructions*, London: Routledge

Barber, E.J.W. (1991) *Prehistoric Textiles*, Princeton, NJ: Princeton University Press

—— (1998) 'Aegean ornaments and designs in Egypt', in E.H. Cline and D. Harris-Cline (eds) *The Aegean and the Orient in the Second Millennium*, 13–17, Liège and Austin, TX: Université de Liège and University of Texas at Austin (*Aegaeum* 18)

Bard, K.A. and Carneiro, R.L. (1989) 'Patterns of predynastic settlement location, social evolution, and the circumscription theory', *Cahiers de Recherches de l'Institut de Papyrologie et d'Égyptologie de Lille*, 11: 15–23

Barguet, P. (1953) *La stèle de la famine, à Séhel*, Cairo: Institut Français d'Archéologie Orientale

—— (1971) 'Note sur la date du scarabée égyptien de la tombe T. 1.', in M. Yon, *Salamine de Chypre* II. *La Tombe T. 1 du XIe S. av. J.-C.*, 14–16, Paris: Editions de Boccard

Barker, G., Gilbertson, D., Jones, B. and Mattingly, D. (1996) *Farming the Desert: the UNESCO Libyan Valleys Archaeological Surveys, 1: Synthesis*, Paris, Tripoli, and London: UNESCO Publishing, the Department of Antiquities, Libya, and the Society for Libyan Studies

Barns, J.W.B. (1956) *Five Ramesseum Papyri*, Oxford: Oxford University Press

Barta, W. (1970) *Das Selbstzeugnis eines altägyptischen Künstlers (Stele Louvre C 14)*, Berlin: Hessling

—— (1990) 'Der Palasthorustitel und seine Vorläufer in der Frühzeit', *Göttinger Miszellen*, 117/118: 55–9

Barth, F. (ed.) (1969) *Ethnic Groups and Boundaries*, Boston, MA: Little, Brown and Co

Barulina, H. (1930) 'Lentils of the U.S.S.R. and other countries', *Bulletin of Applied Botany Genetics and Plant Breeding* (Leningrad), supp. 40: 1–319

Basch, M.A. and Gorbea, M.A. (1968) *Estudios de arte rupestre Nubio I yacimentos situados en la orilla oriental del Nilo, entre Nag Kolorodna y Kars Ibrim (Nubia Egipcia)*, Madrid: Ministerio de Asuntos Exteriores/Ministerio de Educacion Nacional

Bass, G.F. (1967) 'Cape Gelidonya: a Bronze Age shipwreck', *Transactions of the American Philosophical Society*, 57, Part 8, Philadelphia: American Philosophical Society

—— (1986) 'A Bronze Age shipwreck at Ulu Burun (Kaş): 1984 campaign', *American Journal of Archaeology*, 90: 269–96

——, Pulak, C., Collon, D. and Weinstein, J. (1989) 'The Bronze Age shipwreck at Ulu Burun: 1986 campaign', *American Journal of Archaeology*, 93: 1–29

Baud, M. (1997) 'Balat/ʿAyn-Asīl, oasis de Dakhla: la ville de la Deuxième Période Intermédiaire', *Bulletin de l'Institut Français d'Archéologie Orientale*, 97: 35–42

——, Colin, F. and Tallet, P. (1999) 'Les gouverneurs de l'oasis de Dakhla au Moyen Empire', *Bulletin de l'Institut Français d'Archéologie Orientale*, 99: 1–19

Beal, R.H. (1992) *The Organization of the Hittite Military*, Heidelberg: Carl Winter

Beaumont, P. (1993) 'Climate and hydrology', in G.M. Craig (ed.) *The Agriculture of Egypt*, 16–38, Oxford: Oxford University Press

Bednarski, A. (2005) *Holding Egypt: Tracing the Reception of the* Description de l'Égypte *in Nineteenth-Century Great Britain*, London: Golden House Publications

Behm-Blancke, M.R. (1989) 'Mosaikstifte am oberen Euphrat – Wandschmuck aus der Uruk-Zeit', *Istanbuler Mitteilungen*, 39: 73–83

Behrens, P. (1984/5) 'Wanderungsbewegungen und Sprache der frühen saharanischen Viehzüchter', *Sprache und Geschichte in Afrika*, 6: 135–216

—— (1986) 'Language and migrations of the early Saharan cattle herders: the formation of the Berber branch', in A. Leahy (ed.) *Libya Antiqua*, 29–50, Paris: UNESCO

Bell, B. (1970) 'The oldest records of Nile floods', *Geographical Journal*, 136: 569–73

—— (1971) 'The dark ages in ancient history, I: the first dark age in Egypt', *American Journal of Archaeology*, 75: 1–26

—— (1975) 'Climate and the history of Egypt: the Middle Kingdom', *American Journal of Archaeology*, 79: 223–69

Bell, L. (1985) 'Luxor temple and the cult of the royal *ka*', *Journal of Near Eastern Studies*, 44: 251–94

—— (1997) 'The New Kingdom "Divine Temple" ', in B. Schafer (ed.) *Temples of Ancient Egypt*, 127–84, Ithaca, NY: Cornell University Press

——, Johnson, J.H. and Whitcomb, D. (1984) 'The Eastern Desert of Upper Egypt: routes and inscriptions', *Journal of Near Eastern Studies*, 43: 27–46

Bender, B. (1999) *The Archaeology and Anthropology of Landscape*, London: Routledge

Bennett, C. (1995) 'King Senakhtenre', *Göttinger Miszellen*, 145: 37–44

Berlev, O. (1967) 'The Egyptian Navy in the Middle Kingdom', *Palestinskij Sbornik*, 17 (80): 6–20

—— (1981) 'The Eleventh Dynasty in the dynastic history of Egypt', in D.W. Young (ed.) *Studies Presented to Hans Jakob Polotsky*, 361–77, East Gloucester: Pirtle and Polson

Betancourt, P.P. (1998) 'Middle Minoan objects in the Near East', in E.H. Cline and D. Harris-Cline (eds) *The Aegean and the Orient in the Second Millennium*, 5–11, Liège and Austin, TX: Université de Liège and University of Texas Press

—— (2005) 'Egyptian connections at Hagios Charalambos', in R. Laffineur and E. Greco (eds) *Emporia: Aegeans in the Central and Eastern Mediterranean*, 449–53, Liège and Austin, TX: Université de Liège and University of Texas Press

Bianchi, R.S. (1998) 'Symbols and meanings', in F.D. Friedman (ed.) *Gifts of the Nile: Ancient Egyptian Faience*, 22–31, London and New York: Thames and Hudson

—— (2001) 'Scarabs', in D.B. Redford (ed.) *The Oxford Encyclopedia of Ancient Egypt*, vol. 3, 179–81, New York: Oxford University Press

Bierbrier, M.L. (1975) *The Late New Kingdom in Egypt (c.1300–664 BC)*, Warminster: Aris and Phillips

Bietak, M. (1975) *Tell el-Dabʿa II: Der Fundort im rahmen einer archäologisch-geographischen Untersuchung über das ägyptische OstDelta*, Vienna: Österreichische Akademie der Wissenschaften

—— (1985) 'Ein altägyptische Weingarten. Tell el-Dabʿa (Auaris) 1985', *Anzeiger der Österreichischen Akademie der Wissenschaften, Philosophisch-historische Klasse*, 122: 267–78

—— (1988) 'Zur Marine des Alten Reiches', in J. Baines, T.G.H. James and A. Leahy (eds) *Pyramid Studies and Other Essays Presented to I.E.S. Edwards*, 35–40, London: Egypt Exploration Society

—— (1990) 'Zur Herkunft des Seth von Avaris', *Ägypten und Levante*, 1: 9–16

—— (1991a) 'Zur Landnahme Palästinas durch die Seevölker und zum Ende der ägyptischen Provinz Kanaʿan', in *Mitteilungen des Deutschen Archäologischen Instituts Abteilung Kairo*, 47: 35–50

—— (1991b) 'Der Friedhof in einem Palastgarten aus der Zeit des späten Mittleren Reiches und andere Forschungsergebnisse aus dem östlichen Nildelta (Tell el-Dabʿa 1984–1987), *Ägypten und Levante*, 2: 47–109

—— (1992) 'An Iron Age Four Room House in Ramesside Egypt', *Eretz Israel*, 23: 10–12

—— (1993) 'The Sea Peoples and the end of the Egyptian administration in Canaan', in A. Biran and J. Aviram (eds) *Biblical Archaeology Today, 1990: Proceedings of the Second International Congress of Biblical Archaeology, Jerusalem, June-July 1990*, 292–306, Jerusalem: Israel Exploration Society/Israel Academy of Sciences and Humanities

—— (1995) 'Connections between Egypt and the Minoan world. New results from Tell el-Dabʿa/Avaris', in W.V. Davies and L. Schofield (eds) *Egypt, the Aegean and the Levant. Interconnections in the Second Millennium BC*, 19–28, London: British Museum Press

—— (1996a) 'Zum Raumprogramm ägyptischer Wohnhäuser des Mittleren und des Neuen Reiches', in M. Bietak (ed.) *Haus und Palast im alten Ägypten*, 24–43, Vienna: Österreichischen Akademie der Wissenschaften

—— (1996b) *Avaris, The Capital of the Hyksos – Recent Excavations at Tell el-Dabʿa. The First Raymond and Beverly Sackler Foundation Distinguished Lecture in Egyptology*, London: British Museum Publications

—— (1997a) 'The center of Hyksos rule: Avaris (Tell el Dabʿa)' (listed in the volume contents under the title 'Avaris, capital of the Hyksos kingdom: new results of excavations'), in E. Oren (ed.) *The Hyksos: New Historical and Archaeological Perspectives*, 87–139, Philadelphia, PA: University Museum, University of Pennsylvania

—— (1997b) 'Dabʿa, Tell ed-', in E.M. Meyers (ed.) *The Oxford Encyclopedia of Archaeology in the Near East*, vol. 2, 99–100, New York: Oxford University Press

—— (2000) 'Rich beyond the dreams of Avaris: Tell el-Dabʿa and the Aegean world – a guide for the perplexed: a response to Eric H. Cline', *Annual of the British School at Athens*, 95: 185–205

—— (2001) 'Dabʿa, Tell ed-', in D. Redford (ed.) *The Oxford Encyclopedia of Ancient Egypt*, vol. 1, 351–4, New York: Oxford University Press

—— (2003a) 'Two Near Eastern temples with bent axis in the eastern Nile Delta', *Ägypten und Levante*, 13: 13–38

—— (2003b) 'Temple or "Bêt Marzeah"?', in W.G. Dever and S. Gitin (eds) *Symbiosis, Symbolism and the Power of the Past: Canaan, Ancient Israel and their Neighbors, From the Late Bronze Age through Roman Palestine. The W.F. Albright Institute of Archaeological Research and the American Schools of Oriental Research Centennial Symposium, Israel Museum, Jerusalem, May 29–31, 2000*, 155–68, Winona Lake, IN: Eisenbrauns

—— (2005) 'The Thutmoside stronghold of Perunefer', *Egyptian Archaeology*, 26: 13–17

—— (forthcoming) 'Where did the Hyksos come from and where did they go?', in *The Second Intermediate Period (13th–17th Dynasties): Current Research, Future Prospects*, Leuven: Peeters

—— and Forstner-Müller, I. (2003) 'Ausgrabungen im Palastbezirk von Avaris: Vorbericht Tell El Dabʿa/Ezbet Helmi 2003', *Ägypten und Levante*, 13: 29–50

—— and —— (2005) 'Ausgrabung eines Palastbezirkes der Tuthmosidenzeit bei ʿEzbet Helmi/Tell el-Dabʿa: Vorbericht für Herbst 2004 und Frühjahr 2005', *Ägypten und Levante*, 15: 65–100

—— and Hein, I. (2001) 'The context of White Slip wares in the stratigraphy of Tell el-Dabʿa and some conclusions on Aegean chronology', in V. Karageorghis, *The White Slip Ware of Late Bronze Age Cyprus*, 171–94, Vienna: Verlag der Österreichischen Akademie der Wissenschaften

—— and Marinatos, N. (2003) 'The Minoan paintings of Avaris', in B. Manley (ed.) *The Seventy Great Mysteries of Ancient Egypt*, 166–9, London and New York: Thames and Hudson

—— and Strouhal, E. (1974) 'Zu den Todesumständen des Pharaos Seqenenreʿ (17. Dynastie)', *Annalen des Naturhistorischen Museums in Wien*, 78: 29–52

Bisset, N.G., Bruhn, J.G. and Zeuk, M.H. (1996) 'The presence of opium in a 3,500 year old Cypriote Base Ring juglet', *Ägypten und Levante*, 6: 203–4

Björkman, G. (1971) *Kings at Karnak: A Study of the Treatment of the Monuments of Royal Predecessors in the Early New Kingdom*, Uppsala: University of Uppsala

Blackman, A. (1914) *The Rock Tombs of Meir*, vol. 1, London: Egypt Exploration Society

—— (1915) *The Rock Tombs of Meir*, vol. 2, London: Egypt Exploration Society

—— (1918) 'The House of the Morning', *Journal of Egyptian Archaeology*, 5: 148–65; reprinted in A. Lloyd (ed.) (1998) *Gods Priests and Men: Studies in the Religion of Pharaonic Egypt*, 197–214, London and New York: Kegan Paul International

—— (1919) 'The sequence of the episodes in the Egyptian daily temple liturgy', *Journal of the Manchester Egyptian and Oriental Institute Society*, 8: 27–53; reprinted in A. Lloyd (ed.) (1998) *Gods, Priests and Men: Studies in the Religion of Pharaonic Egypt*, 215–37, London and New York: Kegan Paul International

—— (1931) 'The Stela of Thethi, Brit. Mus. No. 614', *Journal of Egyptian Archaeology*, 17: 55–61

—— (1988) *The Story of King Kheops and the Magicians, Transcribed from Papyrus Westcar (Berlin Papyrus 3033)*, ed. W.V. Davies, Reading: W.V. Books

Bleiberg, E. (1981) 'Commodity exchange in the Annals of Thutmose III', *Journal of the Society for the Study of Egyptian Antiquities*, 11: 107–10

—— (1984) 'The king's privy purse during the New Kingdom: an examination of *inw*', *Journal of the American Research Center in Egypt*, 21: 155–67

—— (1988) 'The redistributive economy in New Kingdom Egypt: an examination of *B3kw(t)*', *Journal of the American Research Center in Egypt*, 25: 157–68

—— (1995) 'The economy of ancient Egypt', in J. Sasson (ed.) *Civilizations of the Ancient Near East*, vol. 3, 1373–85, New York: Charles Scribner's Sons

—— (1996) *The Official Gift in Ancient Egypt*, Norman, OK: University of Oklahoma Press

—— and Freed, R. (1991) *Fragments of a Shattered Visage: Proceedings of the International Symposium on Ramses the Great*, Memphis, TN: University of Memphis

Bloxam, E. (2002) 'Transportation of quarried hard stone from Lower Nubia to Giza during the Old Kingdom', in A. McDonald and C. Riggs (eds) *Current Research in Egyptology 2000*, 19–28, Oxford: Archaeopress

Boeser, P.A.A. (1909) *Beschreibung der aegyptischen Sammlung der Niederlandischen Reichsmuseum der Altertümer in Leiden*, II part 1, *Stelan*, The Hague: Nijhoff

—— (1911–13) *Die Denkmäler des Neuen Reiches*, 3 vols, The Hague: Nijhoff

Boessneck, J. and von den Driesch, A. (1992a) 'Weitere Tierknochen vom Tell Ibrahim Awad im Östlichen Nildelta', in E.C.M. van den Brink (ed.) *The Nile Delta in Transition: 4th.–3rd. Millennium B.C.*, 97–109, Tel Aviv: L. Pinkhas

—— (1992b) *Tell el-Dab'a VII: Tiere und Historische Umwelt im Nordost Delta im 2. Jahrtausend v. Chr. anhand von Knochenfunden der Ausgrabungen 1975–1986*, Vienna: Verlag der Österreichischen Akademie der Wissenschaften

Bogoslovsky, E.S. (1980) 'Hundred Egyptian draughtsmen', *Zeitschrift für Ägyptische Sprache und Altertumskunde*, 107: 89–116

Bomann, A.H. (1991) *The Private Chapel in Ancient Egypt*, London and New York: Kegan Paul International

Bonneau, D. (1971) *Le fisc et le Nil: incidences des irregularités de la crue du Nil sur la fiscalité foncière dans l'Égypte grecque et romaine*, Paris: Institut de Droit Romain de l'Université de Paris

Bonnet, C. (1990) *Kerma, royaume de Nubie*, Geneva: Mission Archéologique de l'Université de Genève

—— (1991) 'Upper Nubia from 3000 to 1000 BC', in W.V. Davies (ed.) *Egypt and Africa: Nubia from Prehistory to Islam*, 112–17, London: British Museum Press

—— (2000) *Edifices et rites funéraires à Kerma*, Paris: Editions Errance

—— and Valbelle, D. (2005) *Des pharaons venus d'Afrique. La cachette de Kerma*, Paris: Citadeles et Mazenod

Borchardt, L. (1906) *Nilmesser und Nilstandmarken*, Berlin: Koenigliche Akademie der Wissenschaften

—— (1913) *Das Grabdenkmal des Königs Sahure, Band II: Die Wandbilder*, Leipzig: Hinrichs

—— and Ricke, H. (1980) *Die Wohnhäuser in Tell el-Amarna*, Berlin: Gebr. Mann Verlag

Borghouts, J.F. (1994) 'Magical practices among the villagers', in L.H. Lesko (ed.) *Pharaoh's Workers: the Villagers of Deir el Medina*, 119–30, Ithaca, NY: Cornell University Press

Borsch, S.J. (2000) 'Nile floods and the irrigation system in fifteenth-century Egypt', *Mamluk Studies Review*, 4: 131–45

Bourriau, J.D. (1999) 'Some archaeological notes on the Kamose texts', in A. Leahy and J. Tait (eds) *Studies on Ancient Egypt in Honour of H.S. Smith*, 43–8, London: Egypt Exploration Society

——, Nicholson, P.T. and Rose, P.J. (2000) 'Pottery', in P.T. Nicholson and I. Shaw (eds) *Ancient Egyptian Materials and Technology*, 121–47, Cambridge: Cambridge University Press

Bowen, G.E. and Hope, C.A. (eds) (2003) *The Oasis Papers 3. Proceedings of the Third International Conference of the Dakhleh Oasis Project*, Oxford: Oxbow Books

Bowman, A.K. and Rogan, E. (1999) 'Agriculture in Egypt from Pharaonic to modern times', in A.K. Rogan and E. Rogan (eds) *Agriculture in Egypt: From Pharaonic to Modern Times*, 1–32, Oxford: Oxford University Press

Bradbury, L. (1988) 'Reflections on traveling to "God's Land" and Punt in the Middle Kingdom', *Journal of the American Research Center in Egypt*, 25: 127–56

Brandes, M.A. (1968) *Untersuchungen zur Komposition der Stiftmosaike an der Pfeilerhalle der Schicht IVa in Uruk-Warka*, Berlin: Gebr. Mann Verlag

Brandl, B. (1992) 'Evidence for Egyptian colonization of the southern coastal plain and lowlands of Canaan during the Early Bronze Age I Period', in E.C.M. van den Brink (ed.) *The Nile Delta in Transition: 4th-3rd Millennium BC*, 441–76, Tel Aviv: van den Brink

Braun, T.F.R.G. (1982) 'The Greeks in Egypt', in J. Boardman and N.G.L. Hammond (eds) *The Cambridge Ancient History*, 2nd edn, vol. 3, pt 3, 32–56, Cambridge: Cambridge University Press

Breasted, J.H. (1906a) *Ancient Records of Egypt*, vol. 1, Chicago, IL: University of Chicago Press

—— (1906b) *Ancient Records of Egypt*, vol. 2, Chicago, IL: University of Chicago Press

Bresciani, E. (1996) 'Cambyse, Darius I et le droit des temples égyptiens', *Méditerranées*, 6/7: 103–11

Brewer, D.J. and Teeter, E. (1999) *Egypt and the Egyptians*, Cambridge: Cambridge University Press

——, Redford, D. and Redford, S. (1994) *Domestic Plants and Animals: The Egyptian Origins*, Warminster: Aris and Phillips

Brissaud, P. and Zivie-Coche, C. (eds) (1998) *Tanis. Travaux récents sur le Tell Sân el-Hagar, MFFT 1987–1997*, Paris: Éditions Noësis

Broze, M. (1996) *Mythe et roman en Égypte ancienne. Les aventures d'Horus et Seth dans le Papyrus Chester Beatty I*, Leuven: University of Leuven

Brunner, H. (1937) *Die Texte aus den Gräbern der Herakleopolitanzeit von Siut*, Glückstadt: Augustin

—— (1944) *Die Lehre des Cheti, Sohnes des Duauf*, Glückstadt, Hamburg and New York: Augustin

—— (1963) 'Der freie Wille Gottes in der ägyptischen Weisheit', in *Les sagesses du Proche Orient ancien*, 103–17, Strasbourg; reprinted in W. Röllig (ed.) *Das hörende Herz: kleine Schriften zur Religions- und Geistesgeschichte Ägyptens*, 85–102, Freiburg/Göttingen: Universitätsverlag/ Vandenhoeck & Ruprecht

—— (1964) *Die Geburt des Gottkönigs: Studien zur Überlieferung eines altägyptischen Mythos*, Wiesbaden: Harrassowitz

—— (1986) *Grundzüge einer Geschichte der altägyptischen Literatur*, 4th edn, Darmstadt: Wissenschaftliche Buchgesellschaft

—— (1988) *Altägyptische Weisheit: Lehren für das Leben*, Zurich: Artemis

Brunner-Traut, E. (1997) *Altägyptische Märchen: Mythen und ändere volkstümliche Erzählungen*, 11th edn, Munich: Diederichs Verlag

Bruyère, B. (1939) *Rapport sur les Fouilles de Deir el Médineh (1934–1935)*, Cairo: Institut Français d'Archéologie Orientale

Bryan, B. (1992) *The Reign of Thutmosis IV*, Baltimore, MD: Johns Hopkins University Press

—— (2000) 'The 18th Dynasty before the Amarna Period (c.1550–1352 BC)', in I. Shaw (ed.) *The Oxford History of Ancient Egypt*, 218–71, Oxford: Oxford University Press

—— (2001) 'Painting techniques and artisan organization in the tomb of Suemniwet, Theban Tomb 92', in W.V. Davies (ed.) *Colour and Painting in Ancient Egypt*, London: British Museum Press

—— (2006) 'Administration in the Reign of Thutmose III', in E.H. Cline and D. O'Connor (eds) *Thutmose III: A New Biography*, 69–122, Ann Arbor, MI: University of Michigan Press

Bryce, T. (2003) *Letters of the Great Kings of the Ancient Near East. The Royal Correspondence of the Late Bronze Age*, New York: Routledge

Budge, E.A.W. (1898) *The Book of the Dead. The Chapters of Coming Forth by Day*, London: Kegan Paul

—— (1910) *The Chapters of Coming Forth by Day, or the Theban Recension of the Book of the Dead: the Egyptian Hieroglyphic Text Edited from Numerous Papyri*, 3 vols, London: Kegan Paul

Bunimovitz, S. and Faust, A. (2001) 'Chronological separation, geographical segregation or ethnic demarcation? Ethnography and the Iron Age low chronology', *Bulletin of the American Schools of Oriental Research*, 322: 1–10

Burkard, G. (1997) 'An inscription in the Dakhla region', *Sahara*, 9: 152–3

—— and Thissen, H.J. (2003) *Einführung in die altägyptische Literaturgeschichte, I: Altes und Mittleres Reich*, Münster: Lit Verlag

Burmeister, S. (2000) 'Archaeology and migration', *Current Anthropology*, 41: 539–67

Butzer, K. (1975) 'Delta', in W. Helck and E. Otto (eds) *Lexikon der Ägyptologie*, vol. 1, 1043–52, Wiesbaden: Harrassowitz

—— (1976) *Early Hydraulic Civilization in Egypt. A Study in Cultural Ecology*, Chicago, IL: University of Chicago Press

—— (2002) 'Geoarchaeological implications of recent research', in E.C.M. van den Brink and T.E. Levy (eds) *Egypt and the Levant. Interrelations from the 4th through the Early 3rd Millennium B.C.E.*, 83–97, London and New York: Leicester University Press

Cabrol, A. (2000) *Amenhotep III le magnifique*, Paris: Edition du Rocher

Cameron, M.A.S. (1968) 'Unpublished paintings from the "House of the Frescoes" at Knossos', *Annual of the British School at Athens*, 63: 1–31

Caminos, R.A. (1954) *Late Egyptian Miscellanies*, Oxford: Oxford University Press

—— (1956) *Literary Fragments in the Hieratic Script*, Oxford: Oxford University Press

—— (1958) *The Chronicle of Prince Osorkon*, Rome: Pontificium Institutum Biblicum

—— (1964) 'The Nitocris Adoption Stela', *Journal of Egyptian Archaeology*, 50: 71–101

—— (1997) 'Peasants', in S. Donadoni (ed.) *The Egyptians*, 1–30, Chicago, IL and London: University of Chicago Press

Campagno, M. (2004) 'In the beginning was the war: conflict and the emergence of the Egyptian State', in S. Hendrickx, R.F. Friedman, K.M. Ciałowicz and M. Chłodnicki (eds) *Egypt at its Origins. Studies in Memory of Barbara Adams*, 689–704, Leuven: Peeters

Case, H. and Payne, J.C. (1962) 'Tomb 100: the decorated tomb at Hierakonpolis', *Journal of Egyptian Archaeology*, 48: 5–18

Castel, G. (1988) 'Les mines de galène pharaoniques du Gebel el Zeit', *Bulletin de la Société Française d'Égyptologie*, 112: 37–53

—— and Soukiassian, J.-C. (1985) 'Depot de stelas dans le sanctuaire du Nouvel Empire au Gebel Zeit', *Bulletin de l'Institut Français d'Archéologie Orientale*, 85: 285–93

—— and —— (1989) *Gebel El-Zeit I: les mines de galena (Égypte, IIe millenaire av. J.-C.)*, Cairo: Institut Français d'Archéologie Orientale

—— and Tallet, P. (2001) 'Les inscriptions d'El-Harra, oasis de Bahareya', *Bulletin de l'Institut Français d'Archéologie Orientale*, 101: 99–136

Cat. Paris (1998) *Liban, l'autre rive*, Paris: L'Institut du Monde Arabe

Cavillier, G. (2001) *Il farone guerrio: I faraoni del Nuovo Regno alla conquista dell'Asia tra mito, strategia belica e realtà archeologica*, Turin: Tirrenia stampatori

—— (2003) *Thutmosi III: Immagine e strategia di un condottiero*, Turin: Tirrenia stampatori

Černý, J. (1929) 'Papyrus Salt 124', *Journal of Egyptian Archaeology*, 15: 243–58

—— (1956) *Graffiti hiéroglyphiques et hiératiques de la nécropole thébaine (Nos. 1060 to 1405)*, Cairo: Centre d'Étude et de Documentation sur l'Ancienne Égypte

—— (1973) *A Community of Workmen at Thebes in the Ramesside Period*, Cairo: Institut Français d'Archéologie Orientale

—— (1975) 'Egypt: from the death of Ramesses III to the end of the Twenty-first Dynasty', in I.E.S. Edwards, C.J. Gadd, N.G.L. Hammond and E. Sollberger (eds) *The Cambridge Ancient History*, 3rd edn, vol. 2, pt 2, 606–57, Cambridge: Cambridge University Press

—— and Gardiner, A.H. (1957) *Hieratic Ostraca*, vol. 1, Oxford: Griffith Institute

Chapman, J. (1994) 'Destruction of a common heritage. The archaeology of war in Croatia, Bosnia and Hercegovina', *Antiquity*, 68: 120–6

Chartier-Raymond, M., Gratien, B., Traunecker, C. and Vinçon, J.-M. (1994) 'Les sites miniers pharaoniques du Sud-Sinaï, Quelques notes et observations de terrain', *Cahiers de Recherches de l'Institut de Papyrologie et d'Égyptologie de Lille*, 16: 31–77

Chauveau, M. (1991) 'P. Carlsberg 301 – Le manuel juridique de Tebtynis', in P.J. Frandsen (ed.) *The Carlsberg Papyri I – Demotic Texts from the Collection*, 103–27, Copenhagen: Museum Tusculanum Press

Chippindale, C. and Taçon, P. (eds) (2000) *The Archaeology of Rock-Art*, Cambridge: Cambridge University Press

Churcher, C.S. and Mills, A.J. (eds) (1999) *Reports from the Survey of the Dakhleh Oasis 1977–1987*, Oxford: Oxbow Books

Ciałowicz, K. (2001) *La naissance d'un royaume: l'Egypte dès la période prédynastique à la fin de la Ière dynastie*, Krakow: Ksiegarnia Akademicka

Clark, J.E. and Parry, W.J. (1990) 'Craft specialization and cultural complexity', *Research in Economic Anthropology*, 12: 289–346

Clarke, S. and Engelbach, R. (1930) *Ancient Egyptian Masonry. The Building Craft*, London: Oxford University Press

Clerc, G. (1983) 'Appendix I: Aegyptiaca de Palaepaphos-*Skales*', in V. Karageorghis, *Palaepaphos-Skales: An Iron Age Cemetery in Cyprus*, 375–95, Konstanz: Universitätsverlag Konstanz

Clère, J.J. and Vandier, J. (1948) *Textes de la première période intermédiaire et de la XIème Dynastie*, Brussels: Fondation Égyptologique Reine Élisabeth

Cline, E. (1987) 'Amenhotep III and the Aegean: a reassessment of Egypto-Aegean relations in the 14th century BC', *Orientalia*, 56: 1–36

—— (1991) 'Monkey business in the Bronze Age Aegean. The Amenhotep II faience figurines at Mycenae and Tiryns', *Annual of the British School at Athens*, 86: 29–42

—— (1994) *Sailing the Wine Dark Sea. International Trade and the Late Bronze Age Aegean*, Oxford: Tempus Reparatum

—— (1995) 'Egyptian and Near Eastern imports at Late Bronze Age Mycenae', in W.V. Davies and L. Schofield (eds) *Egypt, the Aegean and the Levant*, 91–115, London: British Museum Press

—— (2001) 'Hittites, in D. Redford (ed.) *The Oxford Encyclopedia of Ancient Egypt*, vol. 2, 111–14, New York: Oxford University Press

—— and O'Connor, D. (2005) *Thutmose III: A New Biography*, Ann Arbor, MI: University of Michigan

Cohen, R. and Westbrook, W. (eds) (2000) *Amarna Diplomacy. The Beginnings of International Relations*, Baltimore, MD: Johns Hopkins University Press

Colin, F. (1998) 'Les Paneia d'El-Buwayb et du Ouadi Minayh sur la piste de Bérénice à Coptos: inscriptions égyptiennes', *Bulletin de l'Institut Français d'Archéologie Orientale*, 98: 89–125

—— (2005) 'Kamose et les Hyksos dans l'oasis de Djesdjes', *Bulletin de l'Institut Français d'Archéologie Orientale*, 105: 35–47

Colinart, S. (2001) 'Analysis of inorganic yellow colour in ancient Egyptian painting', in W.V. Davies (ed.) *Colour and Painting in Ancient Egypt*, 1–4, London: British Museum Press

Collier, M. and Quirke, S. (2002) *The UCL Lahun Papyri: Letters*, Oxford: Archaeopress

—— (2004) *The UCL Lahun Papyri: Religious, Literary, Legal, Mathematical, and Medical*, Oxford: Archaeopress

Collin, D., Laisney, D. and Marchand, S. (2000) 'Qaret el-Toub: un fort romain et une nécropole pharaonique. Prospection archéologique dans l'oasis de Bahariya 1999', *Bulletin de l'Institut Français d'Archéologie Orientale*, 100: 145–92

Collin, F. (2005) 'Kamose et les Hyksos dans l'Oasis de Djesdjes', *Bulletin de l'Institut Français d'Archéologie Orientale*, 105: 35–48

Collombert, P. and Coulon, L. (2000) 'Les dieux contre la mer, le debut du "papyrus d'Astarte" (pBN 202)', *Bulletin de l'Institut Français d'Archéologie Orientale*, 100: 193–242

Comaroff, J. and Comaroff, J. (1992) *Ethnography and the Historical Imagination*, Boulder, CO: Westview Press

Cooney, J.D. (1960) 'Glass sculpture in ancient Egypt', *Journal of Glass Studies*, 2: 11–43

Cooney, K.M. (2000) 'The edifice of Taharka by the Sacred Lake: ritual function and the rule of the king', *Journal of the American Research Center in Egypt*, 37: 15–47

—— (2006) 'An informal workshop: textual evidence for private funerary art production in the Ramesside Period', in A. Dorn and T. Hofmann (eds) *Living and Writing in Deir el Medine: Socio-Historical Embodiment of Deir el Medine Texts*, 43–56, Basel: Schwabe

Coulson, W.D.E. (1996) *Ancient Naukratis, Volume II, Part I: The Survey at Naukratis*, Oxford: Oxbow Books

—— and Wilkie, N.C. (1986) 'Ptolemaic and Roman kilns in the Western Nile Delta', *Bulletin of the American Schools of Oriental Research in Jerusalem and Baghdad*, 263: 61–75

Couyat, J. and Montet, P. (1912–13) *Les inscriptions hiéroglyphiques et hiératiques du Ouadi Hammamat*, Cairo: Institut Français d'Archéologie Orientale

Crawford, D.J. (1971) *Kerkeosiris: An Egyptian Village in the Ptolemaic Period*, Cambridge: Cambridge University Press

Curl, J.S. (1994) *Egyptomania: The Egyptian Revival: A Recurring Theme in the History of Taste*, Manchester: Manchester University Press

Czerny, E. (1999) *Tell el-Dab'a IX: Eine Plansiedlung des frühen Mittleren Reiches*, Vienna: Österreichische Akademie der Wissenschaften

—— (2001) 'Ein früher Beleg für *hwt-w'rt* auf einem Siegelabdruck aus Tell el-Dab'a', *Ägypten und Levante*, 11: 13–25

Darby, W., Ghalioungui, P. and Grivetti, L. (1977) *Food: The Gift of Osiris*, London: Academic Press

Daressy, G. (1902) *Fouilles de la Vallée des Rois*, Cairo: Institut Français d'Archéologie Orientale

—— (1928–9) 'Les branches du Nil sous la XVIIIe dynastie', *Bulletin de la Société d'Égyptologie de Genève*, 16: 225–54 and 293–329

—— (1929–31) 'Les branches du Nil sous la XVIIIe dynastie', *Bulletin de la Société d'Égyptologie de Genève*, 17: 81–115 and 189–223

Darnell, D. (2002) 'Gravel of the desert and broken pots in the road: ceramic evidence from the routes between the Nile and Kharga Oasis', in R. Friedman (ed.) *Egypt and Nubia: Gifts of the Desert*, 156–77, London: British Museum Press

—— (forthcoming) *Securing His Majesty's Borders: Middle Kingdom Features on the Routes of the Theban Western Desert*

—— and Darnell, J.C. (forthcoming) *The Rayayna Culture: A New Facet of the Egyptian Predynastic Period*

Darnell, J.C. (1990) 'Articular Km.t/Kmy and partitive KHME', *Enchoria*, 17: 69–81

—— (1995) 'Hathor returns to Medamud', *Studien zur Altägyptischen Kultur*, 22: 47–94

—— (1997) 'The message of King Wahankh Antef II to Khety, ruler of Heracleopolis', *Zeitschrift für Ägyptische Sprache und Altertumskunde*, 124: 101–8

—— (2002a) 'Opening the narrow doors of the desert: discoveries of the Theban Desert Road Survey', in R. Friedman (ed.) *Egypt and Nubia: Gifts of the Desert*, 132–55, London: British Museum Press

—— (2002b) 'The narrow doors of the desert', in B. David and M. Wilson (eds) *Inscribed Landscapes*, 104–21, Honolulu, HI: University of Hawaii Press

—— (2003a) 'The rock inscriptions of Tjehemau at Abisko', *Zeitschrift für Ägyptische Sprache und Altertumskunde*, 130: 31–48

—— (2003b) 'Review of "Katalog der Felsbilder" (R. Váhala and P. Červíček)', *Bibliotheca Orientalis*, 60: 109–15

—— (2003c) 'Die frühalphabetischen Inschriften im Wadi el Hôl', in W. Seipel (ed.) *Der Turmbau zu Babel, Ursprung und Vielfalt von Sprache und Schrift* 3A: *Schrift*, 165–71, Vienna: Kunsthistorisches Museum

—— (2004a) 'The route of Eleventh Dynasty expansion into Nubia: an interpretation based on the rock inscriptions of Tjehemau at Abisko', *Zeitschrift für Ägyptische Sprache und Altertumskunde*, 131: 23–37

—— (2004b) 'Review of "Die Felsinschriften des Wadi Hilal" (H. Vandekerckhove and R. Müller-Wollermann)', *Journal of Near Eastern Studies*, 63: 152–5

—— (2004c) 'A stela of the reign of Tutankhamun from the region of Kurkur Oasis', *Studien zur Altägyptische Kultur* 31: 73–91

—— (forthcoming a) *Theban Desert Road Survey II: Dominion Behind Thebes – the Rock Inscriptions of the Wadi Nag el-Birka*, Part 1

—— (forthcoming b) 'New inscriptions of Predynastic through Early Dynastic date from the Wadi of the Horus Qa-a'

—— (forthcoming c) *The Birth of Victorious Thebes*

—— (forthcoming d) *The Rock Shrine of Pahu, Priest of Amun of Herheramun and other Rock Inscriptions West of Naqada*

—— and Darnell, D. (1997a) 'New inscriptions of the late First Intermediate Period from the Theban Western Desert and the beginnings of the northern expansion of the Eleventh Dynasty', *Journal of Near Eastern Studies*, 56: 241–58

—— and —— (1997b) 'Theban Desert Road Survey', *Oriental Institute Annual Report*, 1996–7: 66–76

—— and —— (2002) *The Theban Desert Road Survey I: The Rock Inscriptions of Gebel Tjauti in the Theban Western Desert, Part 1, and the Rock Inscriptions of the Wadi el Hôl, Part 1*, Chicago, IL: Oriental Institute, University of Chicago

—— and —— (forthcoming) *Oases Lost and Found: Abu Ziyar, Tundaba, and the Integration of the Southern Oases into the Pharaonic State*

—— and Manassa, C. (forthcoming) *Inscribed Material from the Gebel el-Asr Quarries*

——, Dobbs-Allsopp, C., Lundberg, M.J., Zuckerman, B. and McCarter, P.K. (2005) *Two Early Alphabetic Inscriptions from the Wadi el-Hôl: New Evidence for the Origin of the Alphabet from the Western Desert of Egypt*, Boston, MA: American Schools of Oriental Research

Daugé, Y.A. (1981) *Le barbare. Recherches sur la conception romaine de la barbarie et de la civilisation*, Brussels: Révue d'Études Latines

David, A.R. (1973) *Religious Ritual at Abydos, c.1300 BC*, Warminster: Aris and Phillips

—— (ed.) (1979) *The Manchester Museum Mummy Project*, Manchester: Manchester Museum

—— (1981) *A Guide to Religious Ritual at Abydos*, Warminster: Aris and Phillips

David, B. and Wilson, M. (eds) (2002) *Inscribed Landscapes, Marking and Making Place*, Honolulu, HI: University of Hawaii Press

David, R. and Tapp, E. (eds) (1991) *The Mummy's Tale*, London: O'Mara

Davies, B.G. (1999) *Who's Who at Deir el Medina: A Prospographic Study of the Royal Workmen's Necropolis*, Leiden: Nederlands Instituut voor het Nabije Oosten

Davies, N. de G. (1903) *The Rock Tombs of El-Amarna. Part I. The Tomb of Meryra*, London, Egypt Exploration Fund

—— (1905) *The Rock Tombs at el Amarna. Part II. The Tombs of Panehesy and Meryra II*, London: Egypt Exploration Fund

—— (1906) *The Rock Tombs of El Amarna. Part IV. Tombs of Penthu, Mahu, and Others*, London: Egypt Exploration Fund

—— (1908) *The Rock Tombs of El Amarna. Part VI. Tombs of Parennefer, Tutu and Ay*, London: Egypt Exploration Fund

—— (1922) *The Tomb of Puyemrê at Thebes, vol. 1, The Hall of Memories*, New York: Metropolitan Museum of Art

—— (1927) *Two Ramesside Tombs at Thebes*, New York: Metropolitan Museum of Art

—— (1953) *Temple of Hibis, III*, New York: Metropolitan Museum of Art

—— and Faulkner, R.O. (1947) 'A Syrian trading venture to Egypt', *Journal of Egyptian Archaeology*, 33: 40–6

—— and Gardiner, A.H. (1926) *The Tomb of Huy, Viceroy of Nubia in the Reign of Tut'ankhamun (no. 40)*, London: Egypt Exploration Society

Davies, W.V. (1987) *Catalogue of Egyptian Antiquities in the British Museum VII. Tools and Weapons I. Axes*, London: British Museum Publications

—— (1998) 'New fieldwork at Kurgus: the pharaonic inscriptions', *Sudan and Nubia*, 2: 26–30

—— (2001a) 'The dynastic tombs at Hierakonpolis: the lower group and the artist Sedjemnetjeru', in W.V. Davies (ed.) *Colour and Painting in Ancient Egypt*, 113–25, London: British Museum Press

—— (2001b) 'Kurgus 2000: the Egyptian inscriptions', *Sudan and Nubia*, 5: 46–58

—— (2003a) 'Sobeknakht of Elkab and the coming of Kush', *Egyptian Archaeology*, 23: 3–6

—— (2003b) 'Kush in Egypt: a new historical inscription', *Sudan and Nubia*, 7: 52–4

—— (2003c) 'Kurgus 2002: the inscriptions and rock drawings', *Sudan and Nubia*, 7: 55–6

—— (2004) 'The rock inscriptions at Kurgus in the Sudan', in A. Gasse and V. Rondot (eds) *Séhel entre Égypte et Nubie. Inscriptions rupestres et graffiti de l'époque pharaonique*, 149–60, Montpellier: Université Paul Valéry

Dawson, G., Noakes, R. and Topham, J.R. (2004) 'Introduction', in G. Cantor, G. Dawson, G. Gooday, R. Noakes, S. Shuttleworth and J.R. Topham (eds) *Science in the Nineteenth-Century Periodical: Reading the Magazine of Nature*, 1–34, Cambridge: Cambridge University Press

Day, P.M. and Wilson, D. (1998) 'Consuming power: Kamares ware in Protopalatial Knossos', *Antiquity*, 72: 350–8

Deagan, K. (1983) *Spanish St. Augustine. The Archaeology of a Colonial Creole Community*, New York: Academic Press

—— (1998) 'Transculturation and Spanish American ethnogenesis. The archaeological legacy of the Quincentenniary', in J. Cusick (ed.) *Studies in Culture Contact, Interaction, Culture Change, and Archaeology*, 23–43, Carbondale, IL: Southern Illinois University Press

Decker, W. (1965) 'Der Wagen im alten Ägypten', in W. Treue (ed.) *Achse, Rad und Wagen. Fünftausend Jahre Kultur- und Technikgeschichte*, 35–59, Munich: F. Bruckmann

Degas, J. (1994) 'Navigation sur le Nil au Nouvel Empire', in B. Menu (ed.) *Les problèmes institutionnels de l'eau en Égypte ancienne et dans l'antiquité méditerranéenne*, 141–52, Cairo: Institut Français d'Archéologie Orientale

Delmas, A.B. and Casanova, M. (1990) 'The lapis lazuli sources in the ancient East', in M. Taddei (ed.) *South Asian Archaeology 1987*, I (*Proceedings of the Ninth International Conference of the Association of South Asian Archaeologists in Western Europe*), 493–505, Rome: Istituto italiano per il medio ed estremo oriente

Demarée, R.J. (1983) *The 3ḫ Iḳr n Rʿ-stelae: On Ancestor Worship in Ancient Egypt*, Leiden: Brill

De Morgan, J., Bouriant, U. and Legrain, G. (1894) *Les Carrières de Ptolémaïs*, Paris: Leroux

DePauw, M. (2003) 'Notes on transgressing gender boundaries in ancient Egypt', *Zeitschrift für Ägyptische Sprache und Altertumskunde*, 130: 49–59

de Putter, T. (1992) 'Le "problème de Semna" (Nubie) revisité: nouveaux arguments en faveur d'un "event" climatique au moyen empire', in *Atti sesto congresso internazionale di egittologia*, vol. 1, 125–7, Turin: International Association of Egyptologists

—— (1993) 'Les inscriptions de Semna et Koumma (Nubie): niveaux des crues exceptionnelles ou d'un lac de retenue artificiel du moyen empire?', *Studien zur Altägyptischen Kultur*, 20: 255–88

Derchain, P. (1965) *Le papyrus Salt 825 (B.M. 10051). Rituel pour la conservation de la vie en Égypte*, Brussels: Palais des Académies

—— (1971) *Elkab 1. Les monuments religieux à l'entrée de l'Ouady Hellal*, Brussels: Fondation Égyptologique Reine Élisabeth

—— (1975a) 'Le lotus, la mandragore et le perséa', *Chronique d'Égypte*, 50: 65–86

—— (1975b) 'La perruque et le cristal', *Studien zur Altägyptischen Kultur*, 2: 55–74

—— (1975/76) 'Perpetuum mobile', *Orientalia Lovaniensia Periodica*, 6/7 (*Miscellanea in honorem Joseph Vergote*): 153–61

—— (1976) 'Symbols and metaphors in literature and representations of private life', *Royal Anthropological Institute News*, 15: 7–10

—— (1996) 'Auteur et société', in A. Loprieno (ed.) *Ancient Egyptian Literature: History and Forms*, 83–94, Leiden, New York and Cologne: Brill

Der Manuelian, P. (1987) *Studies in the Reign of Amenophis II*, Hildesheim: Gerstenberg

Deshler, W. (1965) 'Native cattle keeping in East Africa', in A. Leeds and A. Vayda (eds) *Man, Culture and Animals*, 153–68, Washington, DC: American Association for the Advancement of Science

Desroches-Noblecourt, C. (1976) *Ramsès le Grand: Catalogue de l'exposition au Grand Palais*, Paris: Galeries Nationales du Grand Palais

—— (1996) *Ramsès II: La veritable histoire*, Paris: Pygmalion

Díaz-Andreu, M. (1996) 'Constructing identities through culture. The past in the forging of Europe', in P. Graves-Brown, S. Jones and C. Gamble (eds) *Cultural Identity and Archaeology*, 48–61, London: Routledge

Dixon, D. (1969) 'A note on cereals in ancient Egypt', in P. Ucko and G. Dimbleby (eds) *The Domestication and Exploitation of Plants and Animals*, 131–42, London: Duckworth

Dodson, A. and Hilton, D. (2004) *The Complete Royal Families of Ancient Egypt*, London and New York: Thames and Hudson

—— and Ikram, S. (2008) *The Tomb in Ancient Egypt*, London and New York: Thames and Hudson

Donker van Heel, K. (1998) 'Use of land in the Kushite and Saite Periods', in B. Haring and R. De Maaijer (eds) *Landless and Hungry*, 90–102, Leiden: Research School CNWS

Dorman, P. (2005) 'The early reign of Thutmose II: an unorthodox mantle of coregency', in E.H. Cline and D. O'Connor (eds) *Thutmose III: A New Biography*, 39–68, Ann Arbor, MI: University of Michigan

Dothan, T. (1982) *The Philistines and Their Material Culture*, Jerusalem: Israel Exploration Society

—— (1989) 'The arrival of the Sea Peoples: cultural diversity in Early Iron Age Canaan', in S. Gitin and W.G. Dever (eds) *Recent Excavations in Israel: Studies in Iron Age Archaeology*, 1–14, Winona Lake, IN: Eisenbrauns

—— and Dothan, M. (1992) *People of the Sea: The Search for the Philistines*, New York: Macmillan

Drenkhahn, R. (1976) *Die Handwerker und ihre Tätigkeiten im alten Ägypten*, Wiesbaden: Harrassowitz

—— (1995) 'Artisans and artists in ancient Egypt', in J.M. Sasson (ed.) *Civilizations of the Ancient Near East*, vol. 1, 331–43, New York: Charles Scribner's Sons

Dreyer, G. (1998) *Umm el-Qaab I. Das prädynastichen Königsgrab U-j und seine frühen Schriftzeugnisse*, Mainz: von Zabern

—— and Ziegler, C. (2002) 'The Predynastic Period', in C. Ziegler (ed.) *The Pharaohs*, 19–27, New York: Rizzoli

Driel-Murray, C. van (2000) 'Leather', in P.T. Nicholson and I. Shaw (eds) *Ancient Egyptian Materials and Technology*, 299–319, Cambridge: Cambridge University Press

Drioton, É. (1939) 'Une statue prophylactique de Ramses III', *Annales du Service des Antiquités de l'Égypte*, 39: 58–89

Dunand, M. (1937) *Fouilles de Byblos, 1926–1932, Atlas*, Paris: Geuthner

—— (1939) *Fouilles de Byblos, 1926–1932, Texte*, Paris: Geuthner

Dunham, D. (1955) *Royal Cemeteries of Kush IV: Nuri*, Boston, MA: Museum of Fine Arts

—— (ed.) (1967) *Second Cataract Forts* II: *Uronarti, Shalfak, Mirgissa*, Boston, MA: Museum of Fine Arts

Durrant, A. (1976) 'Flax and linseed', in N. Simmonds (ed.) *Evolution of Crop Plants*, 190–3, London: Longman

Dziobek, E. (1992) *Das Grab des Ineni Theban Nr. 81*, Mainz: von Zabern

Earle, T.K. (1981) 'Comment on P. Rice's "Evolution of specialized pottery production: a trial model" ', *Current Anthropology*, 22.3: 230–1

Eaton-Krauss, M. (2001) 'Artists and artisans', in D.B. Redford (ed.) *The Oxford Encyclopedia of Ancient Egypt*, vol. 1, 136–40, New York: Oxford University Press

Edel, E. (1962) 'Zur Lesung und Bedeutung einiger Stellen in der biographischen Inschrift S3-rnpwt's I.', *Zeitschrift für Ägyptische Sprache und Altertumskunde*, 87: 96–107

—— (1983) 'Zwei Steinschalen mit ägyptischen Inschriften aus dem Palast von Kâmid el-Lôz', in R. Hachmann (ed.) *Frühe Phönikier im Libanon*, 38–9, Mainz: von Zabern

—— (1990) 'Die hieroglyphische Inschrift auf der Dioritstatuette des User aus Knossos', in S. Israelit-Groll (ed.) *Studies in Egyptology Presented to Miriam Lichtheim, I*, 122–33, Jerusalem: The Hebrew University

—— (1994) *Der Vertrag zwischen Ramses II. von Ägypten und Hattušili III. von Hatti*, Berlin: Gebr. Mann Verlag

Edelstein, E.J. and Edelstein, L. (1945) *Asclepius: A Collection and Interpretation of the Testimonies*, 2 vols, Baltimore, MD: Johns Hopkins University Press

Eder, C. (1995) *Die ägyptischen Motive der Glyptik des östlichen Mittelmeerraumes zu Anfang des 2. Jts. v. Chr.*, Leuven: University of Leuven

Edgerton, W.F. (1947) 'The Nauri Decree of Seti I: a translation and analysis of the legal portion', *Journal of Near Eastern Studies*, 6: 219–30

Edwards, D.N. (2004) *The Nubian Past*, London and New York: Routledge

Edwards, I.E.S. (1971) 'Bill of sale for a set of ushabtis', *Journal of Egyptian Archaeology*, 57: 120–4

—— (1982) 'Egypt: from the Twenty-second to the Twenty-fourth Dynasty', in J. Boardman, I.E.S. Edwards, N.G.L. Hammond and E. Sollberger (eds) *The Cambridge Ancient History*, 2nd edn, vol. 3, pt 1, 534–81, Cambridge: Cambridge University Press

Egberts, A. (1991) 'The chronology of the Report of Wenamun', *Journal of Egyptian Archaeology*, 77: 57–67

—— (2001) 'Wenamun', in D. Redford (ed.) *The Oxford Encyclopedia of Ancient Egypt*, vol. 3, 495–6, New York: Oxford University Press

Eggebrecht, A. (1980) 'Die frühe Hochkulturen: das alte Ägypten', in A. Eggebrecht, J. Fleming, G. Meyer, A. von Müller, A. Oppolzer, A. Paulinyi and H. Schneider (eds) *Geschichte der Arbeit: Vom alten Ägypten bis zur Gegenwart*, Cologne: Kiepenheuer and Witsch

Ehret, C. (1993) 'Nilo-Saharans and the Saharo-Sudanese Neolithic', in T. Shaw and D.W. Phillipson (eds) *The Archaeology of Africa: Food, Metals and Towns*, 104–21, London: Routledge

Eichler, E. (1992) 'Polanyi-Keynes-Warburton: zur Rekonstruktion des altägyptischen Wirtschafts-systems', *Göttinger Miszellen*, 131: 25–31

—— (1993) *Untersuchungen zum Expeditionswesen des ägyptischen Alten Reiches*, Wiesbaden: Harrassowitz

Eide, T., Hägg, T., Pierce, R.H. and Török, L. (eds) (1994–2000) *Fontes Historiae Nubiorum: Textual Sources for the History of the Middle Nile Region Between the Eighth Century* BC *and the Sixth Century* AD, 4 vols, Bergen: University of Bergen

Eigner, D. (1984) *Die monumentalen Grabauten der Spätzeit in der thebanischen Nekropole*, Vienna: Verlag der Österreichischen Akademie der Wissenschaften

—— (2000) 'Tell Ibrahim Awad: divine residence from Dynasty 0 until Dynasty 11', *Ägypten und Levante*, 10: 17–36

Eisa, K.A. (2004) 'Archaeology south of Khartoum: the future prospects of the White Nile', in T. Kendall (ed.) *Nubian Studies 1998: Proceedings of the Ninth Conference of the International Society of Nubian Studies, August 21–26, 1998, Boston, Massachusetts*, 247–9, Boston, MA: Northeastern University

Eiwanger, J. (1984) *Merimde-Benisalâme I: Die Funde der Urschicht*, Mainz: von Zabern

el-Aguizy, O. (1998) *A Palaeographical Study of Demotic Papyri*, Cairo: Institut Français d'Archéologie Orientale

Elayi, J. and Sapin, J. (1991) *Nouveaux regards sur la Transeuphratène*, Turnhout: Brepols

el-Hegazy, S. (2002) 'New Delta site yields burials', *KMT: A Modern Journal of Ancient Egypt*, 13.1: 30–5

el-Khadagry, M. (2002) 'The Edfu offering niche of Qar in the Cairo Museum', *Studien zur Altägyptischen Kultur*, 30: 203–28

el-Kilany, M. (1939) *Flax in Egypt*, Cairo: Egyptian Ministry of Agriculture Technical and Scientific Service (Bulletin 204)

el-Saady, H. (1992) 'The wars of Sety I at Karnak: a new chronological structure', *Studien zur Altägyptischen Kultur*, 19: 285–94

Embabi, N.S. (2004) *The Geomorphology of Egypt. Landforms and Evolution. Volume I: The Nile Valley and Western Desert*, Cairo: Egyptian Geographical Society

Emery, W. (1954) *Great Tombs of the First Dynasty, II*, London: Egypt Exploration Society

Endruweit, A. (1994) *Städtischer Wohnbau in Ägypten: Klimagerechte Lehmarchitektur in Amarna*, Berlin: Gebr. Mann Verlag

Engel, H. (1979) 'Die Siegesstele des Merenptah. Kritischer Überblick über die verschiedenen Versionen historischer Auswertung des Schlußabschnittes', *Biblica*, 60: 373–94

Engelbach, R. (1933) 'The quarries of the Western Nubian Desert: a preliminary report', *Annales du Service des Antiquités de l'Égypte*, 33: 65–74

—— (1934) 'A foundation scene of the Second Dynasty', *Journal of Egyptian Archaeology*, 20: 183–4

Engels, D. (1978) *Alexander the Great and the Logistics of the Macedonian Army*, Berkeley, CA: University of California Press

Engreen, F.E. (1943) 'The nilometer in the Serapeum at Alexandria', *Medievalia et Humanistica*, 1: 3–13

Epigraphic Survey (1932) *Medinet Habu, Volume II: Later Historical Records of Ramses III*, Chicago, IL: University of Chicago Press

—— (1936) *Reliefs and Inscriptions at Karnak, Volume I. Ramses III's Temple Within the Great Enclosure of Amon, Part 1*, Chicago, IL: University of Chicago Press

—— (1941) *Medinet Habu, Volume III: The Temple Proper, Part 1: The Portico, the Treasury, and Chapels Adjoining the First Hypostyle Hall, with Marginal Material from the Forecourts*, Chicago, IL: University of Chicago Press

—— (1986) *The Battle Reliefs of King Sety I*, Chicago, IL: University of Chicago Press

Erichsen, W. (1933) *Papyrus Harris I. Hieroglyphische Transkription*, Brussels: Fondation Égyptologique Reine Élisabeth

Eriksen, T.H. (1992) *Us and Them in Modern Societies: Ethnicity and Nationalism in Mauritius, Trinidad and Beyond*, London: Scandinavian University Press

Eriksson, K.O. (1995) 'Egyptian amphorae from Late Cypriot contexts in Cyprus', in S. Bourke and J.-P. Descoeudres (eds) *Trade, Contact, and the Movement of Peoples in the Eastern Mediterranean.*

Studies in Honour of J. Basil Hennessy, 199–205, Sydney: Mediterranean Archaeology Supplement 3

Erman, A. and Grapow, H. (eds) (1926–50) *Wörterbuch der ägyptischen Sprache im Auftrage der deutschen Akademien*, 7 vols, Leipzig/Berlin: Hinrichs/Akademie-Verlag

Ertman, E.L. (1972) 'The "Gold of Honor" in royal representation', *Newsletter of the American Research Center in Egypt*, 83: 26–7

Evelyn White, H.G. (1932) (ed. W. Hauser) *The Monasteries of The Wâdi ʿN Natroun, Part II: The History of the Monasteries of Nitria and Scetis*, New York: Metropolitan Museum of Art

Exell, K.M. (2006) 'A social and historical interpretation of Ramesside Period votive stelae', unpublished thesis, Durham University

Eyre, C.J. (1984) 'Crime and adultery in ancient Egypt', *Journal of Egyptian Archaeology*, 70: 92–105

—— (1987a) 'Work and the organisation of work in the Old Kingdom', in M.A. Powell (ed.) *Labour in the Ancient Near East*, 5–47, New Haven, CT: American Oriental Society

—— (1987b) 'Work and the organisation of work in the New Kingdom', in M.A. Powell (ed.) *Labour in the Ancient Near East*, 167–221, New Haven, CT: American Oriental Society

—— (1994) 'Feudal tenure and absentee landlords', in S. Allam (ed.) *Grund und Boden in Altägypten (Rechtliche und Sozio-ökonomische Verhältnisse)*, 107–34, Tübingen: Selbstverlag

—— (1998) 'The market women of pharaonic Egypt', in N. Grimal and B. Menu (eds) *Le commerce en Égypte ancienne*, 173–91, Cairo: Institut Français d'Archéologie Orientale

—— (1999) 'The village economy in pharaonic Egypt', in A.K. Bowman and E. Rogan (eds) *Agriculture in Egypt: From Pharaonic to Modern Times*, 33–60, Oxford: Oxford University Press

—— (2005) 'Judgement to the satisfaction of all', in B. Menu (ed.) *La fonction de juger: Égypte ancienne et Mésopotamie*, 91–107, Paris: L'Harmattan

Fakhry, A. (1940) 'Wâdi-el-Natrûn', *Annales du Service des Antiquités de l'Égypte*, 40: 837–48

—— (1973) *Siwa Oasis*, Cairo: American University in Cairo Press

—— (2003) *Bahariyah and Farafra*, 2nd edn, Cairo: American University in Cairo Press

Faltings, D.A. (1998) 'Ergebnisse der neuen Ausgrabungen in Buto. Chronologie und Fernbeziehungen der Buto-Maadi-Kultur neu überdacht', in H. Guksch and D. Polz, *Stationen. Beiträge zur Kulturgeschichte Ägyptens*, 35–45, Mainz: von Zabern

—— (2002) 'The chronological frame and social structure of Buto in the Fourth Millennium BCE', in E.C.M. van den Brink and T.E. Levy (eds) *Egypt and the Levant. Interrelations from the 4th through the Early 3rd Millennium B.C.E.*, 165–72, London and New York: Leicester University Press

Farag, N. and Iskander, Z. (1971) *The Discovery of Neferwptah*, Cairo: Organization for Government Printing Offices

Farina, G. (1938) *Il papiro dei Re: restaurato*, Rome: Dott. G. Bardi

Farout, D. (1994) 'La carrière du *wḥmw* Ameny et l'organisation des expéditions au ouadi Hammamat au Moyen Empire', *Bulletin de l'Institut Français d'Archéologie Orientale*, 94: 143–72

Faulkner, R.O. (1942) 'The Battle of Megiddo', *Journal of Egyptian Archaeology*, 28: 2–15

—— (1947) 'The Wars of Sethos I', *Journal of Egyptian Archaeology*, 33: 34–9

—— (1952) *The Wilbour Papyrus, Vol. 4 Index*, Oxford: Oxford University Press

—— (1958) 'The Battle of Kadesh', *Mitteilungen des Deutschen Archäologischen Instituts Abteilung Kairo*, 16: 93–111

—— (1969) *The Ancient Egyptian Pyramid Texts*, Oxford: Oxford University Press

—— (1973–8) *The Ancient Egyptian Coffin Texts*, 3 vols, Warminster: Aris and Phillips

—— *et al.* (1994–8) *The Egyptian Book of the Dead*, Cairo: American University in Cairo Press

Fecht, G. (1963) 'Die Wiedergewinnung der altägyptischen Verskunst', *Mitteilungen des Deutschen Archäologischen Instituts Abteilung Kairo*, 19: 54–96

—— (1964–5) 'Die Form der altägyptischen Literatur: Metrische und stilistische Analyse', *Zeitschrift für ägyptische Sprache and Altertumskunde*, 91: 11–63; 92: 10–32

Feldman, M.H. (2001) 'Mesopotamia', in D. Redford (ed.) *The Oxford Encyclopedia of Ancient Egypt*, vol. 2, 384–90, New York: Oxford University Press

Fenwick, H. (2004) 'Ancient Roads and GPS survey: modelling the Amarna Plain', *Antiquity*, 78: 880–5

Fèvre, F. (1992) *Le dernier pharaon. Ramsès III ou le crépuscule d'une civilisation*, Paris: Presses de la France

Finnestad, R.B. (1985) *Image of the World and Symbol of the Creator. On the Cosmological and Iconological Values of the Temple of Edfu*, Wiesbaden: Harrassowitz

—— (1997) 'Temples of the Ptolemaic and Roman Periods: Ancient traditions in new contexts', in B.E. Shafer (ed.) *Temples of Ancient Egypt*, 185–237, London and New York: I.B. Tauris

Firth, C.M. and Quibell, J.E. (1935) *The Step Pyramid*, 2 vols, Cairo: Institut Français d'Archéologie Orientale

Fischer, H.G. (1957) 'A god and a general of the oasis on a stela of the Late Middle Kingdom', *Journal of Near Eastern Studies*, 16: 223–35

—— (1959) 'A scribe of the army in a Saqqara mastaba of the early Fifth Dynasty', *Journal of Near Eastern Studies*, 18: 233–74

—— (1961) 'The Nubian mercenaries of Gebelein during the First Intermediate Period', *Kush*, 9: 44–80

—— (1964) *Inscriptions from the Coptite Nome, Dynasties VI-XI*, Rome: Pontifical Biblical Institute

—— (1973) 'Redundant determinatives in the Old Kingdom', *Metropolitan Museum Journal*, 8: 7–25

—— (1977) *The Orientation of Hieroglyphs I, Reversals*, New York: Metropolitan Museum of Art

—— (1989) *Egyptian Women of the Old Kingdom and of the Heracleopolitan Period*, New York: Metropolitan Museum of Art

—— (1991) 'Sur les routes de l'Ancien Empire', *Cahiers de Recherches de l'Institut de Papyrologie et d'Égyptologie de Lille*, 13: 59–64

Fletcher, J. (2000) *Egypt's Sun King: Amenhotep III*, London: Duncan Baird

Forstner-Müller, I. (2001) 'Vorbericht der Grabung im Areal A/II von Tell el-Dab'a', *Ägypten und Levante*, 11: 197–222

—— (2002) 'Tombs and burial customs at Tell el-Dab'a in Area A/II at the end of the MBIIA Period (Stratum F)', in M. Bietak and H. Hunger (eds) *The Middle Bronze Age in the Levant. Proceedings of an International Middle Bronze Age Conference on MBIIA Ceramic Material in Vienna, 24–26 January 2001*, vol. 3, 163–84, Vienna: Österreichische Akademie der Wissenschaften

Foster, J.L. (1975) 'Thought couplets in Khety's "Hymn to the Inundation"', *Journal of Near Eastern Studies*, 34: 1–29

—— (1977) *Thought Couplets and Clause Sequences in a Literary Text: The Maxims of Ptah-Hotep*, Toronto: Society for the Study of Egyptian Antiquities

—— (1993) *Thought Couplets in* The Tale of Sinuhe, Frankfurt am Main, Berlin and Bern: Peter Lang

Foucault, M. (1976–84) *Histoire de la sexualité*, 3 vols, Paris: Gallimard

Fougerousse, F.F. (1946) 'Un atelier de fours à céramique à Tanis', *Kêmi*, 8: 1–28

Franke, D. (1985) 'An important family from Abydos of the Seventeenth Dynasty', *Journal of Egyptian Archaeology*, 71: 175–6

—— (1990) 'Erste und zweite Zwischenzeit: ein Vergleich', *Zeitschrift für Ägyptische Sprache und Altertumskunde*, 117: 119–29

Frankfort, H. (1941) 'The origin of monumental architecture in Egypt', *American Journal of Semitic Languages and Literatures*, 58: 329–58

—— (1948) *Kingship and the Gods*, Chicago, IL: University of Chicago Press

Frayling, C. (1992) *The Face of Tutankhamun*, London: Faber and Faber

Freed, R.E. (1987) *Ramesses the Great: His Life and Works*, Memphis, TN: University of Memphis

——— (1996) 'Stela workshops of Early Dynasty 12', in P. Manuelian (ed.) *Studies in Honor of William Kelly Simpson*, vol. 1, 297–336, Boston, MA: Museum of Fine Arts

French, P. (1992) 'A preliminary study of pottery in Lower Egypt in the Late Dynastic and Ptolemaic Periods', *Cahiers de la Céramique Égyptienne*, 3: 83–93

Friedman, F.D. (1985) 'On the meaning of some anthropoid busts from Deir el-Medina', *Journal of Egyptian Archaeology*, 71: 82–97

——— (1994) 'Aspects of domestic life and religion', in L.H. Lesko (ed.) *Pharaoh's Workers: The Villagers of Deir el Medina*, 95–118, Ithaca, NY: Cornell University Press

——— (1995) 'The underground relief panels of King Djoser at the Step Pyramid complex', *Journal of the American Research Center in Egypt*, 32: 1–42

——— (ed.) (1998) *Gifts of the Nile: Ancient Egyptian Faience*, London and New York: Thames and Hudson

Friedman, R. (1992) 'The Early Dynastic and transitional pottery of Mendes: the 1990 season', in E.C.M. van den Brink (ed.) *The Nile Delta in Transition: 4th.–3rd. Millennium B.C.*, 199–205, Tel Aviv: L. Pinkhas

——— (1996) 'The ceremonial centre at Hierakonpolis Locality HK29A', in A.J. Spencer (ed.) *Aspects of Early Egypt*, 16–35, London: British Museum Press

——— (1999) 'Pots, pebbles and petroglyphs Part II: 1996 excavations at Hierakonpolis Locality HK64', in A. Leahy and J. Tait (eds) *Studies on Ancient Egypt in Honour of H.S. Smith*, 101–8, London: Egypt Exploration Society

——— and Hobbs, J. (2002) 'A "Tasian" tomb in Egypt's Eastern Desert', in R. Friedman (ed.) *Egypt and Nubia: Gifts of the Desert*, 178–91, London: British Museum Press

———, Maish, A., Fahmy, A.G., Darnell, J.C. and Johnson, E.D. (1999) 'Preliminary report on field work at Hierakonpolis: 1996–1998', *Journal of the American Research Center in Egypt*, 36: 1–35

Frood, E. (2003) 'The potters: organization, delivery, and product of work', in J.J. Janssen, E. Frood and M. Goecke-Bauer (eds) *Woodcutters, Potters and Doorkeepers: Service Personnel of the Deir el-Medina Workmen*, 29–62, Leiden: Nederlands Instituut voor het Nabije Oosten

Früz, V. (1980) 'Die kulturhistorische Bedeutung der frühzeitlichen Siedlung auf der Ḥirbet el-Mšāš und das Problem der Landnahme', *Zeitschrift des Deutschen Palästinavereins*, 96: 121–35

Fuller, D.Q. and Smith, L. (2004) 'The prehistory of the Bayuda: new evidence from the Wadi Muqaddam', in T. Kendall (ed.) *Nubian Studies 1998: Proceedings of the Ninth Conference of the International Society of Nubian Studies, August 21–26, 1998, Boston, Massachusetts*, 256–81, Boston, MA: Northeastern University

Gaballa, G.A. (1976) *Narrative in Egyptian Art*, Mainz: von Zabern

——— (1977) *The Memphite Tomb-Chapel of Mose*, Warminster: Aris and Phillips

——— and Kitchen, K.A. (1969) 'The festival of Sokar', *Orientalia*, 38: 1–76

Gabolde, L. (2004) 'La stele de Thoutmosis II à Assouan', in A. Gasse and V. Rondot (eds) *Séhel entre Égypte et Nubie. Inscriptions rupestres et graffiti de l'époque pharaonique*, 129–48, Montpellier: Université Paul Valéry

Gabolde, M. (1995) 'L'inondation sous les pieds d'Amon', *Bulletin de l'Institut Français d'Archéologie Orientale*, 95: 235–58

——— (1998) *D'Akhenaton à Toutânkamon*, Lyon: Institut d'Archéologie et d'Histoire de l'Antiquité

——— and Galliano, G. (eds) (2000) *Coptos: L'Égypte antique aux portes du desert*, Lyon: Musée de Beaux-arts

Gabra, G. (1976) 'Preliminary report on the stela of Ḥtpi from Elkab from the time of Wahankh Inyotef II', *Mitteilungen des Deutschen Archäologischen Instituts Abteilung Kairo*, 32: 45–56

Gale, R., Gasson, P., Hepper, N. and Killen, G. (2000) 'Wood', in P.T. Nicholson and I. Shaw (eds) *Ancient Egyptian Materials and Technology*, 334–71, Cambridge: Cambridge University Press

Galil, J., Stein, M. and Horowitz, A. (1976) 'On the origin of the sycamore fig (*Fiscus sycomorus*) in the Middle East', *Gardens Bulletin*, 29: 191–205

Galvin, M. (1981) *Priestesses of Hathor in the Old Kingdom and the First Intermediate Period*, Ann Arbor, MI: University of Michigan

—— (1984) 'The hereditary status of the titles of the cult of Hathor', *Journal of Egyptian Archaeology*, 70: 42–9

Garbrecht, B. (1983) *Sadd el-Kafara, Die älteste Talsperre der Welt*, Braunschweig: Leichtweiss-Institut für Wasserbau

Gardiner, A.H. (1905) *The Inscription of Mes: A Contribution to the Study of Egyptian Judicial Procedure*, Leipzig: Hinrichs

—— (1909) *The Admonitions of an Egyptian Sage from a Hieratic Papyrus in Leiden (Pap. Leiden 344 Recto)*, Leipzig: Hinrichs

—— (1912) 'The Stele of Bilgai', *Zeitschrift für Ägyptische Sprache und Altertumskunde*, 50: 49–57 and pl. 4

—— (1916) 'The defeat of the Hyksos by Kamose: The Carnarvon Tablet, No. I', *Journal of Egyptian Archaeology*, 3: 95–110

—— (1932) *Late Egyptian Stories*, Brussels: Éditions de la Fondation Égyptologique Reine Élisabeth

—— (1933) 'The Dakhleh Stela', *Journal of Egyptian Archaeology*, 19: 19–30 and pls v–vii

—— (1935a) 'Piankhi's instructions to his army', *Journal of Egyptian Archaeology*, 21: 219–23

—— (1935b) *The Attitude of the Ancient Egyptians to Death and the Dead*, Cambridge: Cambridge University Press

—— (1935c) 'A lawsuit arising from the purchase of two slaves', *Journal of Egyptian Archaeology*, 21: 140–6

—— (1935d) *Hieratic Papyri in the British Museum, Third Series: Chester Beatty Gift*, 2 vols, London: British Museum

—— (1937) *Late-Egyptian Miscellanies*, Brussels: Fondation Égyptologique Reine Élisabeth

—— (1938a) 'The Mansion of Life and the Master of the King's Largess', *Journal of Egyptian Archaeology*, 24: 85–9

—— (1938b) 'The House of Life', *Journal of Egyptian Archaeology*, 24: 157–79

—— (1941) 'Ramesside texts relating to the taxation and transport of corn', *Journal of Egyptian Archaeology*, 27: 22–37

—— (1941–8) *The Wilbour Papyrus*, 3 vols, Oxford: Oxford University Press

—— (1947) *Ancient Egyptian Onomastica I*, London: Oxford University Press

—— (1948) *Ramesside Administrative Documents*, Oxford: Oxford University Press

—— (1951) 'A protest against unjustified tax-demands', *Revue d'Égyptologie*, 6: 115–24

—— (1952) 'Some reflections on the Nauri Decree', *Journal of Egyptian Archaeology*, 38: 24–33

—— (1957) *Egyptian Grammar*, 3rd rev. edn, London: Oxford University Press

—— (1959) *The Royal Canon of Turin*, Oxford: Oxford University Press

—— (1960) *The Kadesh Inscriptions of Ramesses II*, Oxford: Oxford University Press

—— (1961) *Egypt of the Pharaohs*, Oxford: Oxford University Press

—— (1962a) *Tutankhamun's Painted Box: Reproduced from the Original in the Cairo Museum by Nina M. Davies*, Oxford: Griffith Institute

—— (1962b) 'Once again the Proto-Sinaitic Inscriptions', *Journal of Egyptian Archaeology*, 48: 45–8

—— and Sethe, K. (1928) *Egyptian Letters to the Dead*, London: Egypt Exploration Society

——, Peet, T.E. and Černý, J. (1952, 1955) *The Inscriptions of Sinai*, 2 vols, London: Egypt Exploration Society

Gasse, A. (1988) *Données nouvelles administratives et sacerdotales sur l'organisation du Domain d'Amon, XXe-XXIe dynasties, à la lumière des Papyrus Prachov, P. Reinhardt et Grundbuch (avec édition princeps des Papyrus Louvre AF 6345 et 6346–7)*, 2 vols, Cairo: Institut Français d'Archéologie Orientale

Gatto, M.C. (2001–02) 'Two Predynastic pottery caches at Bir Sahara (Egyptian Western Desert)', *Sahara*, 13: 51–60

Germer, R. (2001) 'Flowers', in D.B. Redford (ed.) *The Oxford Encyclopedia of Ancient Egypt*, vol. 1, 541–4, New York: Oxford University Press

Gestermann, L. (1987) *Kontinuität und Wandel in Politik und Verwaltung des frühen Mittleren Reiches in Ägypten*, Wiesbaden: Harrassowitz

Geus, F. (2004a) 'Sai', in D. Welsby and J.R. Anderson (eds) *Sudan: Ancient Treasures*, 114–21, London: British Museum Press

—— (2004b) 'Pre-Kerma storage pits on Sai Island', in T. Kendall (ed.) *Nubian Studies 1998: Proceedings of the Ninth Conference of the International Society of Nubian Studies, August 21–26, 1998, Boston, Massachusetts*, 46–51, Boston, MA: Northeastern University

Ghali, I.A. (1986) *Vivant Denon ou la conquête du bonheur*, Cairo: Institut Français d'Archéologie Orientale

Ghalioungui, P. (1983) *The Physicians of Pharaonic Egypt*, Cairo/Mainz: Al-Ahram Center for Scientific Translations for the National Library of Medicine/von Zabern

Giddy, L. (1980) 'Some exports from the oases of the Libyan Desert into the Nile Valley – Tomb 131 at Thebes', in J. Vercoutter (ed.) *Institut Français d'Archéologie Orientale du Caire. Livre du centenaire 1880–1980*, 119–25, Cairo: Institut Français d'Archéologie Orientale

—— (1987) *Egyptian Oases*, Warminster: Aris and Phillips

Giedion, S. (1964) *The Eternal Present: The Beginnings of Architecture*, London: Oxford University Press

Giveon, R. (1971) *Les bédouins Shosou des documents égyptiens*, Leiden: Brill

—— (1984) 'Soped in Sinai', in *Studien zu Sprache and Religion Ägyptens. Zu Ehren von Wolfhart Westendorf*, 777–85, Göttingen: Hubert & Co

Glanville, S.R.K (1932) 'Records of a royal dockyard of the time of Tuthmosis III: Papyrus British Museum 10056', *Zeitschrift für Ägyptische Sprache und Altertumskunde*, 68: 7–41

Glazer, N. and Moynihan, D.P. (eds) (1963) *Ethnicity. Theory and Experience*, Cambridge, MA: Harvard University Press

Glick, T.F. (1974) *The Comparative Reception of Darwinism*, London: University of Texas Press

Gnirs, A.M. (1996) *Militär und Gesellschaft. Ein Beitrag zur Sozialgeschichte des Neuen Reiches*, Heidelberg: Heidelberger Orientverlag

Goebs, K. (2001) 'Crowns', in D.B. Redford (ed.) *The Oxford Encyclopedia of Ancient Egypt*, vol. 1, 321–6, New York: Oxford University Press

—— (in press) *Crowns in Egyptian Funerary Literature: Royalty, Rebirth and Destruction*, Oxford: Griffith Institute

Goedicke, H. (1956) 'Considerations of the Battle of Kadesh', *Journal of Egyptian Archaeology*, 52: 71–80

—— (1967) *Königliche Dokumente aus dem alten Reich*, Wiesbaden: Harrassowitz

—— (1985) *Perspectives of the Battle of Kadesh*, Baltimore, MD: Johns Hopkins University Press

—— (1986) *The Quarrel of Apophis and Seqenenrê*, San Antonio, TX: Van Siclen Books

—— (2000) *The Battle of Megiddo*, Baltimore, MD: Halgo

Goelet, O. (2001) 'Shuppululiumas', in D. Redford (ed.) *The Oxford Encyclopedia of Ancient Egypt*, vol. 3, 286, New York: Oxford University Press

Goldwasser, O. (1982) 'The Lachish hieratic bowl once again', *Tel Aviv*, 9: 137–8

—— (1984) 'Hieratic inscriptions from Tel Seraʿ in southern Canaan', *Tel Aviv*, 11: 77–93

—— (2006a) 'King Apophis of Avaris and the emergence of monotheism', in E. Czerny, I. Hein, H. Hunger, D. Melman and A. Schwab (eds) *Timelines: Studies in Honour of Manfred Bietak*, vol. 2, 129–34, Leuven, Paris and Dudley: Peeters

—— (2006b) 'Canaanites reading hieroglyphs. Horus is Hathor? The invention of the alphabet in Sinai', *Ägypten und Levante*, 16: 121–60

Golenischeff, V.S. (1913) *Les Papyrus Hieratiques Nr. 1115, 1116 A + B de l'Ermitage à St. Petersburg*, Leipzig: Hinrichs

Goody, J. (1982) *Cooking, Cuisine and Class. A Study in Comparative Sociology*, Cambridge: Cambridge University Press

Gordon, A. (2001) 'Foreigners', in D.B. Redford (ed.) *The Oxford Encyclopedia of Ancient Egypt*, vol. 1, 544–8, New York: Oxford University Press

Goren, Y., Bunimovitz, S., Finkelstein, I. and Na'aman, N. (2003) 'The location of Alashiya: new evidence from petrographic investigation of Alashiyan tablets', *American Journal of Archaeology*, 107: 233–55

Goyon, G. (1957) *Nouvelles inscriptions rupestres du Wadi Hammamat*, Paris: Adrien-Maisonneuve

—— (1974) 'Les inscriptions des carriers et des mines', in *Textes et langages de l'Égypte pharaonique*, 193–205, Cairo: Institut Français d'Archéologie Orientale

Goyon, J.-C. (1974) *Confirmation du pouvoir royal au nouvel an* [*Brooklyn Museum Papyrus 47.218.50*], Brooklyn, NY: Brooklyn Museum

Graefe, E. (1981) *Untersucungen zur Verwaltung und Geschichte der Institution der Gottesgemahlin des Amun I.*, Wiesbaden: Harrassowitz

Graham, A. (2005) 'Plying the Nile, not all plain sailing', in K. Piquette and Love (eds) *Current Research in Egyptology 2003*, 41–56, Oxford: Oxbow Books

—— and Bunbury, J. (2005) 'The ancient landscapes and waterscapes of Karnak', *Egyptian Archaeology*, 27: 17–19

Graindorge-Héreil, C. (1994) *Le Dieu Sokar à Thèbes au Nouvel Empire*, 2 vols, Wiesbaden: Harrassowitz

Grajetzki, W. (2003) *Burial Customs in Ancient Egypt: Life in Death for Rich and Poor*, London: Duckworth

Grandet, P. (1993) *Ramsès III. Histoire d'un règne*, Paris: Pygmalion G. Watalet

—— (1994–9) *Le Papyrus Harris I, BM 9999*, 3 vols, Cairo: Institut Français d'Archéologie Orientale

Grapow, H. (1949) *Studien zu den Annalen Thutmosis III*, Berlin: Akademie Verlag

Gratien, B. (2001) 'Scellements et contrescellements au Moyen Empire en Nubie. L'apport de Mirgissa', *Cahiers de Recherches de l'Institut de Papyrologie et d'Égyptologie de Lille*, 22: 47–69

Graves-Brown, P. (1996) 'All things bright and beautiful? Species, ethnicity and cultural dynamics', in P. Graves-Brown, S. Jones and C. Gamble (eds) *Cultural Identity and Archaeology*, 81–95, London: Routledge

Grenfell, B.P., Hunt, A.S. and Smyly, G. (1902) *The Tebtunis Papyri Part I*, London: Egypt Exploration Society

Griffith, F.L. (1889) *The Inscriptions of Siût and Dêr Rîfeh*, London: Egypt Exploration Fund

—— (1898) *The Petrie Papyri. Hieratic Papyri from Kahun and Gurob (principally of the Middle Kingdom)*, 2 vols, London: Quaritch

—— (1909) *Catalogue of the Demotic Papyri in the John Rylands Library, Manchester*, 3 vols, Manchester: The John Rylands Library

—— (1927) 'The Abydos decree of Seti I at Nauri', *Journal of Egyptian Archaeology*, 13: 193–206 and pls 37–43

Griffiths, J.G. (1960) *The Conflict of Horus and Seth*, Liverpool: University of Liverpool Press

Grimal, N. (1981) *La Stèle Triomphale de Pi(ankh)y au Musée du Caire JE 48862 et 47086–47089*, Cairo: Institut Français d'Archéologie Orientale

—— (1992) *A History of Ancient Egypt*, trans. I. Shaw, Oxford: Blackwell

Groll, S.I. (1983) 'The Egyptian administrative system in Syria and Palestine in the 18th Dynasty', in Manfred Görg (ed.) *Fontes atque pontes, Eine Festgabe für Helmut Brunner*, 234–42, Wiesbaden: Harrassowitz

Grzymski, K. (2005) 'Meroe, the capital of Kush: old problems and new discoveries', *Sudan and Nubia*, 9: 47–58

Gumbrecht, H.U. (1996) 'Does Egyptology need a "Theory of Literature"?', in A. Loprieno (ed.) *Ancient Egyptian Literature: History and Forms*, 3–18, Leiden, New York and Cologne: Brill

Gundlach, R. (1984) 'Scheintür', in W. Helck and W. Westendorf (eds) *Lexikon der Ägyptologie*, vol. 5, 563–75, Wiesbaden: Harrassowitz

—— (1994) *Die Zwangsumsiedlung auswärtiger Bevölkerung als Mittel ägyptischer Politik bis zum Ende des Mittleren Reiches*, Stuttgart: Steiner

—— (2001) 'Temples', in D.B. Redford (ed.) *The Oxford Encyclopedia of Ancient Egypt*, vol. 3, 363–79, New York: Oxford University Press

Gunn, B. (1927) 'The stela of Apries at Mîtrahîna', *Annales du Service des Antiquités de l'Égypte*, 27: 211–37

—— (1943) 'Notes on the Naucratis Stela', *Journal of Egyptian Archaeology*, 29: 55–9

Gutgesell, M. (1989) *Arbeiter und Pharaonen: Wirtschafts und Sozialgeschichte im alten Ägypten*, Hildesheim: Gerstenberg

Habachi, I. (1943) 'Sais and its monuments', *Annales du Service des Antiquitiés de l'Égypte*, 42: 369–407

—— (1954) 'Khata'na-Qantir: importance', *Annales du Service des Antiquités de l'Egypte*, 52, 514–59

—— (1962) 'King Nebhepetre Menthuhotp: his monuments, place in history, deification and unusual representations in the form of gods', *Mitteilungen des Deutschen Archäologischen Instituts Abteilung Kairo*, 19: 16–52

—— (1972a) *The Second Stela of Kamose and His Struggle against the Hyksos Ruler and his Capital*, Glückstadt: Augustin

—— (1972b) 'The destruction of temples in Egypt', in S.A. Hanna (ed.) *Medieval and Middle Eastern Studies in Honor of Aziz Suryal Atiya*, 191–8, Leiden: Brill

—— (1972c) 'Nia, the wab-priest and doorkeeper of Amun-of-the-Hearing-Ear', *Bulletin de l'Institut Français d'Archéologie Orientale*, 71: 67–85

—— (1980) 'The military posts of Ramesses II on the coastal road and the Western Part of the Delta', *Bulletin de l'Institut Français d'Archéologie Orientale*, 80: 13–30

—— (2001) *Tell el-Dab'a I. Tell el-Dab'a and Qantir: The Site and its Connection with Avaris and Piramesse*, Vienna: Österreichische Akademie der Wissenschaften

Haeny, G. (1997) 'New Kingdom "mortuary temples" and "Mansions of Millions of Years" ', in B. Schafer (ed.) *Temples of Ancient Egypt*, 86–126, Ithaca, NY: Cornell University Press

Häggman, S. (2002) *Directing Deir el-Medina. The External Administration of the Necropolis*, Uppsala: Department of Archaeology and Ancient History, Uppsala University

Hall, E.S. (1986) *The Pharaoh Smites His Enemies. A Comparative Study*, Munich and Berlin: Deutscher Kunstverlag

Hall, J.M. (1997) *Ethnic Identity in Greek Antiquity*, Cambridge: Cambridge University Press

Hamilton, G.J. (2006) *The Origins of the West Semitic Alphabet in Egyptian Scripts*, Washington, DC: Catholic Biblical Association of America

Handler, R. (1988) *Nationalism and the Politics of Culture in Quebec*, Wisconsin: University of Wisconsin Press

Hankey, V. (1981) 'The Aegean interest in El Amarna', *Journal of Mediterranean Anthropology and Archaeology*, 1: 38–49

—— (1993) 'Pottery as evidence for trade: Egypt', in C. Zerner (ed.) *Wace and Blegen: Pottery as Evidence for Trade in the Aegean Bronze Age 1939–1989*, 109–16, Amsterdam: J.C. Gieben

—— (1995) 'Stirrup jars at el-Amarna', in W.V. Davies and L. Schofield (eds) *Egypt, the Aegean and the Levant: Interconnections in the Second Millennium B.C.*, 116–24, London: British Museum Press

—— and Aston, D. (1995) 'Mycenaean pottery at Saqqara: finds from excavations by the Egypt Exploration Society of London and the Rijksmuseum van Oudeheden, Leiden', in J.B. Carter and S. Morris (eds) *The Ages of Homer: A Tribute to Emily Townsend Vermeule*, 67–91, Austin, TX: University of Texas Press

Hannig, R. (2003) *Ägyptisches Wörterbuch I, Altes Reich und Erste Zwischenzeit*, Mainz: von Zabern

Hari, R. (1964) *Horemheb et la reine Moutnedjemet ou la fin d'une Dynastie*, Genève: Imprimerie la Sirène

Haring, B. (1993) 'Libyans in the Theban Region, 20th Dynasty', in *Atti del VI Congresso Internazionale di Egittologia*, 159–65, Turin: International Association of Egyptologists

—— (1997) *Divine Households: Administrative and Economic Aspects of the New Kingdom Royal Memorial Temples in Western Thebes*, Leiden: Nederlands Instituut voor het Nabije Oosten

—— (2001) 'Temple administration', in D.B. Redford (ed.) *The Oxford Encyclopedia of Ancient Egypt*, vol. 3, 20–3, New York: Oxford University Press

—— (2004) 'Texts, taxes and temples', *Chronique d'Égypte*, 79: 22–30

Harrell, J.A. (2002) 'Pharaonic stone quarries in the Egyptian deserts', in R. Friedman (ed.) *Egypt and Nubia: Gifts of the Desert*, 232–43, London: British Museum Press

—— and Brown, T.M. (1995) 'An Old Kingdom basalt quarry at Widan el-Faras and the quarry road to Lake Moeris', *Journal of the American Research Center in Egypt*, 32: 71–91

Harpur, Y. (1987) *Decoration in Egyptian Tombs of the Old Kingdom: Studies in Orientation and Scene Content*, London: Kegan Paul International

Hart, G. (1990) *Egyptian Myths*, London: British Museum Press

Hartung, U. (2001) *Umm el-Qaab II. Importkeramik aus dem Friedhof U in Abydos (Umm el-Qaab) und die Beziehungen Ägyptens zu Vorderasien im 4. Jahrtausend v. Chr.*, Mainz: von Zabern

—— (2002) 'Imported jars from Cemetery U at Abydos and the relations between Egypt and Canaan in predynastic times', in E.C.M. van den Brink and T.E. Levy (eds) *Egypt and the Levant: Interrelations From the 4th Through the Early 3rd Millennium B.C.E.*, 306–22, London: Leicester University Press

——, Ballet, P., Béguin, F., Bourriau, J., French, P., Herbich, T., Kapp, P., Lecuyot, G. and Schmitt, A. (2003) 'Tell el-Fara'in-Buto. 8. Vorbericht', *Mitteilungen des Deutschen Archäologischen Instituts Abteilung Kairo*, 59: 199–267

Hartwig, M. (2001) 'Painting', in D.B. Redford (ed.) *The Oxford Encyclopedia of Ancient Egypt*, vol. 3, 1–13, New York: Oxford University Press

—— (2004) *Tomb Painting and Identity in Ancient Thebes, 1419–1372 BCE*, Turnhout: Brepols

Harvey, S.P. (1998) 'The cults of King Ahmose at Abydos', unpublished thesis, University of Pennsylvania

—— (2004) 'New evidence at Abydos for Ahmose's funerary cult', *Egyptian Archaeology*, 24: 3–6

Haslauer, E. (2001) 'Harem', in D.B. Redford (ed.) *The Oxford Encyclopedia of Ancient Egypt*, vol. 2, 76–80, New York: Oxford University Press

Hassan, F. (1981) 'Historical Nile floods and their implications for climatic change', *Science*, 212: 1142–5

—— (1988) 'The predynastic of Egypt', *Journal of World Prehistory*, 2: 135–85

—— (1997) 'The dynamics of a riverine civilization: a geoarchaeological perspective on the Nile Valley, Egypt', *World Archaeology*, 29.1: 51–74

—— (ed.) (2002) *Droughts, Food and Culture: Ecological Change and Food Security in Africa's Later Prehistory*, New York: Kluwer Academic/Plenum Publishers

—— (2005) 'A river runs through Egypt: Nile floods and civilization', *Geotimes*, 50.4: 22–5

Hastings, J. (ed.) (1908) *Encyclopaedia of Religion and Ethics*, vol. 10, Edinburgh: T. & T. Clark

Hawass, Z. (2005) *Tutankhamun and the Golden Age of the Pharaohs*, Washington, DC: National Geographic Society

—— (2006) *Mountains of the Pharaohs*, New York: Doubleday

Hayes, W.C. (1946) 'Royal decrees from the temple of Min at Coptus', *Journal of Egyptian Archaeology*, 32: 3–23

—— (1955) *A Papyrus of the Late Middle Kingdom in the Brooklyn Museum {Papyrus Brooklyn 35.1446}*, Brooklyn, NY: Brooklyn Museum

Heiden, D. (2003) 'New aspects of the treatment of the cult statue in the daily temple ritual', in Z. Hawass (ed.) *Egyptology at the Dawn of the Twenty-First Century, vol. 2: Religion*, 308–15, New York and Cairo: American University in Cairo Press

Heinz, S. (2001) *Die Feldzugdarstellungen des Neuen Reiches. Eine Bildanalyse*, Vienna: Österreichische Akademie der Wissenschaften

Helck, W. (1939) *Der Einfluß der Militärführer in der 18. ägyptischen Dynastie*, Leipzig: Hinrichs

—— (1955a) 'Das Dekret des Königs Haremheb', *Zeitschrift für Ägyptische Sprache und Altertumskunde*, 80: 109–36

—— (1955b) *Urkunden der 18. Dynastie, 1227–1539*, Berlin: Akademie Verlag

—— (1958) *Urkunden der 18. Dynastie, 1776–2179*, Berlin: Akademie Verlag

—— (1960) 'Die ägyptische Verwaltung in den syrischen Besitzungen', *Mitteilungen der Deutschen Orient Gesellschaft*, 92: 1–13

—— (1968) 'Ritualszenen in Karnak', *Mitteilungen des Deutschen Archäologischen Instituts Abteilung Kairo*, 23: 117–37

—— (1970) *Die Lehre des Dw3-Ḥtjj*, 2 vols, Wiesbaden: Harrassowitz

—— (1971) *Die Beziehungen Ägyptens zu Vorderasien im 3. und 2. Jahrtausend v. Chr.*, 2nd edn, Wiesbaden: Harrassowitz

—— (1972a) 'Aufgaben und Steuern', in W. Helck and E. Otto (eds) *Lexikon der Ägyptologie*, vol. 1, 3–12, Wiesbaden: Harrassowitz

—— (1972b) *Der Text des 'Nilhymnus'*, Wiesbaden: Harrassowitz

—— (1974) *Die altägyptischen Gaue*, Wiesbaden: Reichert

—— (1975) *Wirtschaftsgeschichte des alten Ägypten im 3. und 2. Jahrtausend vor Chr.*, Leiden: Brill

—— (1976) 'Die Systematik der Ausschmückung der hypostylen Halle von Karnak', *Mitteilungen des Deutschen Archäologischen Instituts Abteilung Kairo*, 32: 57–65

—— (1977) *Die Lehre für König Merikare*, Wiesbaden: Harrassowitz

—— (1980a) 'Jenseitsgericht', in W. Helck and W. Westendorf (eds) *Lexikon der Ägyptologie*, vol. 3, 249–52, Wiesbaden: Harrassowitz

—— (1980b) 'Maat', in W. Helck and W. Westendorf (eds) *Lexikon der Ägyptologie*, vol. 3, 1110–19, Wiesbaden: Harrassowitz

—— (1981) 'Probleme der Königsfolge in der Übergangszeit von 18. zu 19. Dynastie', *Mitteilungen des Deutschen Archäologischen Instituts Abteilung Kairo*, 37: 207–15

—— (1984) *Die Lehre des Djedefhor und die Lehre eines Vaters an seinen Sohn*, Wiesbaden: Harrassowitz

—— (1988) 'Der "Geheimnisvolle" Mehy', *Studien zur Altägyptische Kultur*, 15: 143–8

—— (1992) *Die Prophezeiung des Nfr.tj*, 2nd edn, Wiesbaden: Harrassowitz

Hendrickx, S. and Friedman, R. (2003) 'Gebel Tjauti rock inscription 1 and the relationship between Abydos and Hierakonopolis during the Early Naqada III Period', *Göttinger Miszellen*, 196: 95–110

Herodotus (1998) *The Histories*, trans. R. Waterfield, Oxford: Oxford University Press

Heywood, A. (2001) 'The use of huntite as a white pigment in ancient Egypt', in W.V. Davies (ed.) *Colour and Painting in Ancient Egypt*, 5–9, London: British Museum Press

Hides, S. (1996) 'The genealogy of material culture and cultural identity', in P. Graves-Brown, S. Jones and C. Gamble (eds) *Cultural Identity and Archaeology*, 25–47, London: Routledge

Higginbotham, C.R. (2000) *Egyptianization and Elite Emulation in Ramesside Palestine*, Leiden: Brill

Higgins, R.A. (1979) *The Aegina Treasure*, London: British Museum Press

Hikade, T. (2001) *Das Expeditionswesen im ägyptischen Neuen Reich: ein Beitrag zu Rohstoffversorgung und Aussenhandel*, Heidelberg: Heidelberger Orientvelag

Hintze, F. (1959/60) 'Eine neue Inschrift vom 19. Jahre König Taharqas', *Mitteilungen des Instituts für Orientforschung*, 7: 330–3

Hobson, C. (1990) *The World of the Pharaohs*, London and New York: Thames and Hudson

Hoch, J.E. (1994) *Semitic Words in Egyptian Texts of the New Kingdom and Third Intermediate Period*, Princeton, NJ: Princeton University Press

Hodder, I. (1979) 'Economic and social stress and material culture', *American Antiquity*, 44: 446–54

—— (1982) *The Present Past. An Introduction to Anthropology for Archaeologists*, London: Batsford

Hoelzmann, P. (2002) 'Lacustrine sediments as key indicators of climate change during the Late Quaternary in Western Nubia (Eastern Sahara)', in T. Lenssen-Erz *et al.* (eds) *Tides of the Desert – Gezeiten der Wüste*, 375–88, Cologne: Heinrich-Barth-Institute

Hogg, M.A. and Vaughan, G.M. (eds) (2002) *Social Psychology*, 3rd edn, London: Prentice Hall

Holladay, J.S. (1997) 'Maskhuta, Tell el-', in E. Meyers (ed.) *The Oxford Encyclopedia of Archaeology in the Near East*, vol. 3, 432–7, New York: Oxford University Press

—— (2001a) 'Yahudiyya, Tell el-', in D.B. Redford (ed.) *The Oxford Encyclopedia of Ancient Egypt*, vol. 2, 527–9, New York: Oxford University Press

—— (2001b) 'Pithom', in D.B. Redford (ed.) *The Oxford Encyclopedia of Ancient Egypt*, vol. 3, 50–3, New York: Oxford University Press

Holmes, D.L. (1999) 'el-Badari district Predynastic sites', in K.A. Bard (ed.) *The Encyclopedia of the Archaeology of Ancient Egypt*, 161–4, London and New York: Routledge

Hölscher, U. (1939) *The Excavation of Medinet Habu vol.II: The Temples of the Eighteenth Dynasty*, Chicago, IL: Oriental Institute, University of Chicago

—— (1941) *The Excavation of Medinet Habu vol. III: The Mortuary Temple of Ramses III, Part 1*, Chicago, IL: University of Chicago Press

Hölscher, W. (1937) *Libyer und Ägypter. Beiträge zur Ethnologie und Geschichte libyscher Völkerschaften nach den altägyptischen Quellen*, Glückstadt, Hamburg and New York: Augustin

Honegger, M. (2004) 'El-Barga', in D. Welsby and J.R. Anderson (eds) *Sudan: Ancient Treasures*, 31–4, London: British Museum Press

Hope, C.A. (1998) 'Early pottery from the Dakhleh Oasis', *Bulletin of the Australian Centre for Egyptology*, 9: 53–60

—— (2002a) 'Early and mid-Holocene ceramics from the Dakhleh Oasis: traditions and influences', in R. Friedman (ed.) *Egypt and Nubia: Gifts of the Desert*, 39–61, London: British Museum Press

—— (2002b) 'Oases amphorae of the New Kingdom', in R. Friedman (ed.) *Egypt and Nubia: Gifts of the Desert*, 95–131, London: British Museum Press

Hornung, E. (1966) *Geschichte als Fest. Zwei Vorträge zum Geschichtsbild der frühen Menschheit*, Darmstadt: Wissenschaftliche Buchgesellschaft

—— (1971) *Das Grab des Haremhab im Tal der Könige*, Bern: Francke Verlag

—— (1982a) 'Pharao Ludens', *Eranos Jahrbuch*, 51: 479–515

—— (1982b, 2nd edn 1996) *Conceptions of God in Ancient Egypt, The One and the Many*, trans. J. Baines, Ithaca, NY: Cornell University Press

—— (1990a, 2nd edn 1999) *The Ancient Egyptian Books of the Afterlife*, trans. D. Lorton, Ithaca, NY and London: Cornell University Press

—— (1990b) *The Valley of the Kings: Horizon of Eternity*, trans. D. Warburton, New York: Timken

—— (1992) *Idea into Image: Essays on Ancient Egyptian Thought*, trans. E. Bredeck, New York: Timken

—— and Staehelin, E. (1974) *Studien zum Sed-Fest*, Basel and Geneva: Ägyptologisches Seminar der Universität Basel/Centre d'études orientales de l'université de Genève

Houlihan, P.F. (1986) *The Birds of Ancient Egypt*, Warminster: Aris and Phillips

Hume, W.F. (1925) *Geology of Egypt*, Cairo: Government Press

Hurst, H.E. (1952) *The Nile*, London: Constable

——, Black, R.P. and Simaika, Y.M. (1963) *Long-term Storage: An Experimental Study*, London: Constable

Huyge, D. (1984) 'Horus Qa-a in the Elkab area, Upper Egypt', *Orientalia Lovaniensia Periodica*, 15: 5–9

—— (2002) 'Cosmology, ideology, and personal religious practice in Ancient Egyptian rock art', in R. Friedman (ed.) *Egypt and Nubia: Gifts of the Desert*, 192–206, London: British Museum Press

Ikram, S. (2003) *Death and Burial in Ancient Egypt*, London: Routledge

—— and Dodson, A. (1998) *The Mummy in Ancient Egypt*, London and New York: Thames and Hudson

Immerwahr, S.A. (1985) 'A possible influence of Egyptian art in the creation of Minoan wall painting', in P. Darque and J.-C. Poursat (eds) *L'iconographie Minoenne*, 41–50, Paris: Editions de Boccard

—— (1990) *Aegean Paintings in the Bronze Age*, University Park and London: Pennsylvania State University Press

Isajew, W. (1974) 'Definitions of ethnicity', *Ethnicity*, 1: 111–24

Iversen, E. (1984) 'The inscription of Herwerre at Serabit-al-Kadem', in *Studien zu Sprache und Religion Ägyptens zu Ehren Wolfhart Westendorf*, vol. 1, 507–19, Göttingen: F. Junge

Jacquet, J. (1983) *Karnak-Nord V. Le trésor de Thoutmosis Ier: étude architecturale*, vol. 1, Cairo: Institut Français d'Archéologie Orientale

Jäger, S. (2004) *Altägyptische Berufstypologien*, Göttingen: Seminar für Ägyptologie und Koptologie

James, T.G.H. (1962) *The Hekanakhte Papers, and Other Early Middle Kingdom Documents*, New York: Metropolitan Museum of Art

—— (1985) *Pharaoh's People: Scenes from Life in Imperial Egypt*, Oxford: Oxford University Press

—— (1991) 'Egypt: the Twenty-fifth and Twenty-sixth Dynasties', in J. Boardman, I.E.S. Edwards, N.G.L. Hammond, E. Sollberger and C.B.F. Walker (eds) *The Cambridge Ancient History*, 2nd edn, vol. 3, pt 2, 677–747, Cambridge: Cambridge University Press

—— (2002) *Ramesses II*, New York: Friedman/Fairfax

—— and Apted, M.R. (1953) *The Mastaba of Khentika called Ikhekhi*, London: Egypt Exploration Society

Janssen, J.J. (1963) 'Eine Beuteliste von Amenophis II und das Problem der Sklaverei im Alten Ägypten', *Jaarbericht van het vooraziatisch-egyptisch Genootschap, Ex Oriente Lux*, 17: 141–7

—— (1975a) 'Prolegomena to the Study of Egypt's Economic History during the New Kingdom', *Studien zur Altägyptische Kultur*, 3: 127–85

—— (1975b) *Commodity Prices from the Ramessid Period*, Leiden: Brill

—— (1979) 'The role of the temple in the Egyptian economy during the New Kingdom', in E. Lipiński (ed.) *State and Temple Economy in the Ancient Near East*, vol. 2, 505–15, Leuven: Department of Orientalistik

—— (1980) *De markt op de oever*, Leiden: Brill

—— (1986) 'Agrarian administration in Egypt during the Twentieth Dynasty', *Bibliotheca Orientalis*, 43: 351–66

—— (1991) *Late Ramesside Letters and Communications*, London: British Museum Press

—— (2004) *Grain Transport in the Ramesside Period: Papyrus Baldwin (BM EA 10061) and Papyrus Amiens. Hieratic Papyri in the British Museum VIII*, London: British Museum Press

Janssen, J.M.A (1946) *De traditioneele egyptische autobiographie voor het nieuwe rijk*, Leiden: Brill

Janssen-Winkeln, K. (1992) 'Das Ende des Neuen Reiches', *Zeitschrift für Ägyptische Sprache und Altertumskunde*, 119: 22–37

—— (1995) 'Die Plünderung der Königsgräber des Neuen Reiches', *Zeitschrift für Ägyptische Sprache und Altertumskunde*, 122: 62–78

—— (1999) 'Die Wahl des Königs durch Orakel in der 20. Dynastie', *Bulletin de la Société d'Égyptologie de Genève*, 23: 51–61

—— (2001) 'Der thebanische "Gottesstaat" ', *Orientalia*, 70: 153–82

Jaritz, H. (1981) 'Zum Heiligtum am Gebel Tingar', *Mitteilungen des Deutschen Archäologischen Instituts Abteilung Kairo*, 37: 241–6

——, Doll, M., Dominicus, B. and Rutishauser, W. (2001) 'Die Totentempel des Merenptah in Qurna: 5. Grabungsbericht', *Mitteilungen des Deutchen Archäologischen Instituts Abteilung Kairo*, 17: 141–70

Jaroš-Deckert, B. (1984) *Das Grab des Jnj-jtj.f. Die Wandmalereien der XI. Dynastie*, Mainz: von Zabern

Jasnow, R. (1992) *A Late Period Hieratic Wisdom Text (P. Brooklyn 47.218.135)*, Chicago, IL: Oriental Institute, University of Chicago

—— (1999) 'Remarks on continuity in Egyptian literary tradition', in E. Teeter and J.A. Larson (eds) *Gold of Praise: Studies on Ancient Egypt in Honor of Edward F. Wente*, 193–210, Chicago, IL: Oriental Institute, University of Chicago

Jeffreys, D.G. (2001) 'High and dry? Survey of the Memphite escarpment', *Egyptian Archaeology*, 19: 15–16

—— and Tavares, A. (1994) 'The historic landscape of Early Dynastic Memphis', *Mitteilungen des Deutschen Archäologischen Instituts Abteilung* Kairo, 50: 143–73

Jéquier, G. (1911) *Le Papyrus Prisse et ses variantes: papyrus de la Bibliothèque Nationale (Nos. 183 à 194), Papyrus 10371 et 10435 du British Museum, tablette Carnarvon au Musée du Caire, publiées en facsimilé*, Paris: Geuthner

Jesse, F. and Kuper, R. (2004) 'Gala Abu Ahmed: eine Festung am Wadi Howar', *Der Antike Sudan: Mitteilungen der Sudanarchäologischen Gesellschaft*, 15: 137–42

Johnson, J.H. (1986) 'The role of the Egyptian priesthood in Ptolemaic Egypt', in L.H. Lesko (ed.) *Egyptological Studies in Honour of Richard A. Parker*, 70–84, Hanover and London: Brown University Press

—— (2003) 'Sex and marriage in ancient Egypt', in N. Grimal, A. Kamal and C. May-Sheikholeslami (eds) *Hommages à Fayza Haikal*, 149–59, Cairo: Institut Français d'Archéologie Orientale

Jones, S. (1996) 'Discourses of identity in the interpretation of the past', in P. Graves-Brown, S. Jones and C. Gamble (eds) *Cultural Identity and Archaeology*, 62–80, London: Routledge

—— (1997) *The Archaeology of Ethnicity. Constructing Identities in the Past and Present*, London: Routledge

Josephson, J.A. (2001) 'Amasis', in D. Redford (ed.) *The Oxford Encyclopedia of Ancient Egypt*, vol. 1, 66–7, New York: Oxford University Press

Junge, F. (2003) *Die Lehre Ptahhoteps und die Tugenden der ägyptischen Welt*, Freiburg/Göttingen: Universitätsverlag/Vandenhoeck & Ruprecht

Junker, H. (1939) 'Phrnfr', *Zeitschrift für Ägyptische Sprache und Altertumskunde*, 75: 63–84

Kaiser, W. (1985) 'Zu Entwicklung und Vorformen der frühzeitlichen Gräber mit reich gegliederter Oberbaufassade', in *Mélanges Mokhtar* II, 25–38, Cairo: Institut Français d'Archéologie Orientale

——, Arnold, F., Bommas, M., Hikade, T., Hoffmann, F., Jaritz, H., Kopp, P., Niederberger, W., Paetznick, J.-P., von Pilgrim, B., von Pilgrim, C., Raue, D., Rzeuska, T., Schaten, S., Seiler, A., Stalder, L. and Ziermann, M. (1999) 'Stadt und Tempel von Elephantine, 25./26./27. Grabungsbericht', *Mitteilungen des Deutschen Archäologischen Instituts Abteilung Kairo*, 55: 63–236

Kampp-Seyfried, F. (1998) 'Overcoming death – the private tombs of Thebes', in R. Schulz and M. Seidel (eds) *Egypt: The World of the Pharaohs*, 248–63, Cologne: Könemann

Kamrin, J. (1999) *The Cosmos of Khnumhotp II at Beni Hasan*, London: Kegan Paul International

Kanawati, N. (1977) *The Egyptian Administration in the Old Kingdom*, Warminster: Aris and Phillips

—— (1980) *Governmental Reforms in Old Kingdom Egypt*, Warminster: Aris and Phillips

Kaper, O.E. (1987) 'How the god Amun-nakht came to Dakhleh Oasis', *Journal of the Society for the Study of Egyptian Antiquities*, 17: 151–6

—— (1997) 'The statue of Penbast: on the cult of Seth in the Dakhleh Oasis', in J. van Dijk (ed.) *Essays on Ancient Egypt in Honour of Herman te Velde*, 231–41, Groningen: Styx Publications

—— and Willems, H. (2002) 'Policing the desert: Old Kingdom activity around the Dakhleh Oasis', R. Friedman (ed.) *Egypt and Nubia: Gifts of the Desert*, 79–94, London: British Museum Press

Kaplony, P. (1963) *Die Inschriften der ägyptischen Frühzeit*, 3 vols, Wiesbaden: Harrassowitz

—— (1968) *Steingefässe mit Inschriften der Frühzeit und des Alten Reiches*, Bruxelles: Editions de la Fondation Égyptologique Reine Élisabeth

—— (1973) *Beschriftete Kleinfunde in der Sammlung Georges Michaelidis*, Istanbul: Nederlands Historisch-Archaeologisch Instituut voor het Nabije Oosten

—— (1977) 'Die Definition der schönen Literatur im alten Ägypten', in J. Assmann, E. Feucht and R. Grieshammer (eds) *Fragen an die altägyptischen Literatur: Studien zum Gedenken an Eberhard Otto*, 289–314, Wiesbaden: Harrassowitz

Karageorghis, V. (1983) *Palaepaphos-Skales: An Iron Age Cemetery in Cyprus*, Konstanz: Universitätsverlag Konstanz

Katary, S.L.D. (1989) *Land Tenure in the Ramesside Period*, London: Kegan Paul International

—— (1999) 'Land-tenure in the New Kingdom: the role of women smallholders and the military', in A.K. Bowman and E. Rogan (eds) *Agriculture in Egypt: From Pharaonic to Modern Times*, 61–82, Oxford: Oxford University Press

—— (2000) 'O. Strasbourg H 106: Ramesside split holdings and a possible link to Deir el-Medina', in R.J. Demarée and A. Egberts (eds) *Deir el-Medina in the Third Millennium AD: A Tribute to Jac. J. Janssen*, 171–208, Leiden: Nederlands Instituut voor het Nabije Oosten

—— (2001) 'Labour on smallholdings in the New Kingdom: O. BM 5627 in light of P. Wilbour', *Journal of the Society for the Study of Egyptian Antiquities*, 28: 111–23

—— (2006) 'The *wsf* plots in the Wilbour Papyrus and related documents: a speculative interpretation', in J.C. Moreno Garcia (ed.) *L'agriculture institutionelle en Égypte ancienne. État de la question et perspectives interdisciplinaires*, 137–55, Villeneuve d'Ascq: Institut de Papyrologie et d'Égyptologie de Lille

Keding, B. (2004) 'The Yellow Nile – settlement shifts in the Wadi Howar region (Sudanese Eastern Sahara) and adjacent areas from between the sixth to the first millennium BC', in T. Kendall (ed.) *Nubian Studies 1998: Proceedings of the Ninth Conference of the International Society of Nubian Studies, August 21–26, 1998, Boston, Massachusetts*, 95–108, Boston, MA: Northeastern University

Kees, H. (1961) *Ancient Egypt: A Cultural Topography*, London: Faber and Faber

—— (1964) *Die Hohenpriester des Amun von Karnak von Herihor bis zum Ende der Athiopenzeit*, Leiden: Brill

Keita, S.O.Y. and Kittles, R.A. (1997) 'The persistence of racial thinking and the myth of racial divergence', *American Anthropologist*, 99: 534–44

Keith-Bennett, J. (1981) 'Anthropoid Busts: II, not from Deir el Medineh alone', *Bulletin of the Egyptological Seminar of New York*, 3: 43–71

Keller, C. (1981) 'The draughtsmen of Deir el-Medina: a preliminary report', *Newsletter of the American Research Center in Egypt*, 115: 7–14

—— (1991) 'Royal painters: Deir el-Medina in Dynasty XIX', in E. Bleiberg and R. Freed (eds) *Fragments of a Shattered Visage: The Proceedings of the International Symposium on Ramesses the Great*, 50–67, Memphis, TN: University of Memphis

—— (2001) 'A family affair: the decoration of TT 359', in W.V. Davies (ed.) *Colour and Painting in Ancient Egypt*, 73–93, London: British Museum Press

Kemp, B.J. (1973) 'Photographs of the decorated tomb at Hierakonpolis', *Journal of Egyptian Archaeology*, 59: 36–43

—— (1975) 'Architektur der Frühzeit', in C. Vandersleyen (ed.) *Das alte Ägypten*, 99–112, Berlin: Propyläen Verlag

—— (1978) 'Imperialism in New Kingdom Egypt (*c.*1575–1087 B.C.)', in P.D.A. Garnsey and C.R. Whittaker (eds) *Imperialism in the Ancient World*, 7–57 and 283–97, Cambridge: Cambridge University Press

—— (1983) 'Old Kingdom, Middle Kingdom and First Intermediate Period *c.*2686–1552 BC', in B.G. Trigger, B.J. Kemp, D. O'Connor and A.B. Lloyd, *Ancient Egypt: A Social History*, 71–182, Cambridge: Cambridge University Press

—— (1989a) 'Appendix: workshops and production at el-Amarna', in B.J. Kemp (ed.) *Amarna Reports 5*, 56–63, London: Egypt Exploration Society

—— (1989b, 2nd edn 2005) *Ancient Egypt: Anatomy of a Civilization*, London and New York: Routledge

—— (1997) 'Why empires rise. Review Feature, Askut in Nubia', *Cambridge Archaeological Journal*, 7: 125–31

—— (2000a) 'Soil (including mud-brick architecture)', in P.T. Nicholson and I. Shaw (eds) *Ancient Egyptian Materials and Technology*, 78–103, Cambridge: Cambridge University Press

—— (2000b) 'The discovery of the painted plaster fragments at Malkata', in A. Karetsou (ed.) *Κρήτη – Αιγύπτος: Πολιτισμικοί Δεσμοί μριών Χιλιετιών*, 45–6, Athens: Kapon Editions

—— and Merrillees, R.S. (1980) *Minoan Pottery in Second Millennium Egypt*, Mainz: von Zabern

—— and Vogelsang-Eastwood, G. (2001) *The Ancient Textile Industry at Amarna*, London: Egypt Exploration Society

—— and Weatherhead, F. (2000) 'Palace decoration at Tell el-Amarna', in S. Sherratt (ed.) *The Wall Paintings of Thera*, vol. 1, 491–523, Athens: Thera Foundation

Kempinski, A. (1974) 'Tell el-ʿAjjûl – Beth Aglayim or Sharuhen?', *Israel Exploration Journal*, 23.3–4: 145–52

Kendall, T. (1989) 'Ethnoarchaeology in Meroitic studies', *Meroitica*, 10: 697–715

—— (1997) *Kerma and the Kingdom of Kush, 2500–1500 BC: The Archaeological Discovery of an Ancient Nubian Empire*, Washington, DC: Smithsonian Institution

—— (1999) 'The origin of the Napatan state: el-Kurru and the evidence for the royal ancestors', in S. Wenig (ed.) *Meroitica 15: Studien zum antiken Sudan*, 3–117, Wiesbaden: Harrassowitz

—— (2002) 'Napatan temples: a case study from Gebel Barkal' (unpublished paper presented at the Tenth International Conference for Nubian Studies, Rome, 9–14 September 2002). Online. Available at: http://rmcisadu.let.uniroma1.it/nubianconference/kendall.doc (accessed 5 June 2007)

—— (2006–7) 'Evidence for a Napatan Occupation of the Wadi Muqaddam: Excavations at Al-Meragh in the Bayuda Desert (1999–2000)', in B. Gratien (ed.) *Hommages Offerts à Francis Geus*, 197–204, Lille: Institut de Papyrologie et d'Égyptologie de Lille

—— (2007) 'Hatshepsut in Kush?', *The Society for the Study of Egyptian Antiquities Newsletter*, Winter 2007: 1–5

—— (in press) 'Why did Taharqa build his tomb at Nuri?', in W. Godlewski (ed.) *Nubian Studies 2006: Proceedings of the 11th International Conference of Nubian Studies, Warsaw University, 27 August–2 September, 2006*, Warsaw: Warsaw University

Kitchen, K.A. (1973, 2nd edn 1986, 3rd rev. edn 1995) *The Third Intermediate Period in Egypt (1100–650 BC)*, Warminster: Aris and Phillips

—— (1975–89) *Ramesside Inscriptions*, 7 vols, Oxford: Blackwell

—— (1977) 'Historical observations on Ramesside Nubia', in E. Endesfelder, K.-H. Priese, W.-F. Reineke and S. Wenig (eds) *Ägypten und Kusch*, 213–26, Berlin: Akademie-Verlag

—— (1985) *Pharaoh Triumphant: The Life and Times of Ramses II*, Warminster: Aris and Phillips

—— (1990) 'The arrival of the Libyans in late New Kingdom Egypt', in A. Leahy (ed.) *Libya and Egypt c.1300–750 BC*, 15–27, London: Centre of Near and Middle Eastern Studies

—— (1993a) 'The Land of Punt', in T. Shaw and D.W. Phillipson (eds) *The Archaeology of Africa*, 587–608, London: Routledge

—— (1993b) *Ramesside Inscriptions, Translated & Annotated: Notes and Comments I: Ramesses, Sethos I and Contemporaries*, Oxford: Blackwell

—— (1996) *Ramesside Inscriptions, Translated & Annotated: Translations II*, Oxford: Blackwell

—— (1999a) *Ramesside Inscriptions. Translated and Annotated. Notes and Comments II: Ramesses II, Royal Inscriptions*, Oxford: Blackwell

—— (1999b) 'The wealth of Amun of Thebes under Ramesses II', in E. Teeter and J. Larson (eds) *Gold of Praise: Studies on Ancient Egypt in Honor of Edward F. Wente*, 235–8, Chicago, IL: Oriental Institute, University of Chicago

—— (2003) *Ramesside Inscriptions. Translated and Annotated. Notes and Comments IV: Merenptah and the Late Nineteenth Dynasty*, Oxford: Blackwell

—— (2004) 'The elusive land of Punt revisited', in P. Lunde and A. Porter (eds) *Trade and Travel in the Red Sea Region*, 25–31, Oxford: Archaeopress

Klemm, R. and Klemm, D.D. (1993) *Steine und Steinbrüche im Alten Ägypten*, Berlin: Springer-Verlag

Klemm, R., Klemm, D.D. and Murr, A. (2002) 'Ancient gold mining in the Eastern Desert of Egypt and the Nubian Desert of Sudan', in R. Friedman (ed.) *Egypt and Nubia: Gifts of the Desert*, 215–31, London: British Museum Press

Kloth, N. (2002) *Die (auto-)biographischen Inschriften des ägyptischen Alten Reiches: Untersuchungen zu Phraseologie und Entwicklung*, Hamburg: Buske Verlag

Klotz, D. (2006) *Adoration of the Ram: Five Hymns to Amun-Re from Hibis Temple*, New Haven, CT: Yale Egyptological Seminar

Klug, A. (2002) *Königliche Stelen in der Zeit von Ahmose bis Amenophis III*, Turnhout: Brepols

Klug, S. (1988) 'Zur Stellung der neolithischen Bevölkerung von Merimde-Benisalame', in S. Schoske (ed.) *Akten des Vierten Internationalen Ägyptologen Kongresses München 1985*, vol. 1, 273–82, Hamburg: Buske

Knapp, A.B. (1990) 'Production, location and integration in Bronze Age Cyprus', *Current Anthropology*, 31: 147–75

—— (1991) 'Spice, drugs, grain and grog: organic goods in Bronze Age Eastern Mediterranean trade', in N. Gale (ed.) *Bronze Age Trade in the Mediterranean*, 21–68, Jonsered: P. Åströms Förlag

Knauf, E.A. (1994) *Die Umwelt des Alten Testamentes*, Stuttgart: Katholisches Bibelwerk

Koch, R. (1990) *Die Erzählung des Sinuhe*, Bruxelles: Éditions de la Fondation Égyptologique Reine Élisabeth

Köhler, E.C. (1992) 'The Pre- and Early Dynastic pottery of Tell el-Fara'in (Buto)', in E.C.M. van den Brink (ed.) *The Nile Delta in Transition: 4th.–3rd. Millennium B.C.*, 11–22, Tel Aviv: L. Pinkhas

—— (1998) *Tell el-Fara'in. Buto III. Die Keramik von der späten Naqadenkultur bis zum Alten Reich (Schichten III-VI, Grabungen der Jahre 1987–1989)*, Mainz: von Zabern

Kohn, H. (1944) *The Idea of Nationalism. A Study of its Origins and Backgrounds*, New York: Macmillan

Kopytoff, I. (1999) 'The internal African frontier: cultural conservatism and ethnic innovation', in M. Rösler and T. Wendl (eds) *Frontiers and Borderlands: Anthropological Perspectives*, 31–44, New York: Peter Lang

Kormysheva, E. (2004) 'On the origin and evolution of the Amun cult in Nubia', in T. Kendall (ed.) *Nubian Studies 1998: Proceedings of the Ninth Conference of the International Society of Nubian Studies, August 21–26, 1998, Boston, Massachusetts*, 109–33, Boston, MA: Northeastern University

Koschel, K. (1996) 'Opium alkaloids in a Cypriote Base-Ring I vessel (bilbil) of the Middle Bronze Age from Egypt', *Ägypten und Levante*, 6: 159–66

Kozloff, A.P., Bryan, B.M. and Berman, L.M. (1992) *Egypt's Dazzling Sun: Amenhotep III and his World*, Cleveland, OH: Cleveland Museum of Art/Indian University Press

Kruchten, J.-M. (1981) *Le Décret d'Horemheb: traduction, commentaire épigraphique, philologique et institutionnel*, Brussels: Éditions de l'Université de Bruxelles

Kubiak, W. (1998) 'The Nile in the urban region of Cairo', *Africana Bulletin*, 46: 23–40

Kuhlmann, K.P. (1992) 'Bauernweisheiten', in I. Gamer-Wallert and W. Helck (eds) *Gegengabe, Festschrift für Emma Brunner-Traut*, 191–209, Tübingen: Attempto Verlag

—— (2002) 'The "Oasis Bypath" or the issue of desert trade in pharaonic times', in T. Lenssen-Erz *et al.* (eds) *Tides of the Desert – Gezeiten der Wüste*, 125–70, Cologne: Heinrich-Barth-Institute

—— (2005) 'Der "Wasserberg des Djedefre" (Chufu 01/1). Ein Lagerplatz mit Expeditionsinschriften der 4. Dynastie im Raum der Oase Dachla', *Mitteilungen des Deutschen Archäologischen Instituts Abteilung Kairo*, 61: 243–89

Kuhrt, A. (1995) *The Ancient Near East c.3000–330 BC*, London and New York: Routledge

Kuper, R. (2002) 'Routes and roots in Egypt's Western Desert: the early Holocene resettlement of the Eastern Sahara', in R. Friedman (ed.) *Egypt and Nubia: Gifts of the Desert*, 1–20, London: British Museum Press

—— and Förster, F. (2003) 'Khufu's "mefat" expeditions into the Libyan Desert', *Egyptian Archaeology*, 23: 25–8

Kurth, D. (1996) 'Der Erfolg des Harurre in Serabit el-Chadim (Inscr. Sinai, Nr. 90)', *Göttinger Miszellen*, 154: 57–63

—— (2003) *Der Oasenmann*, Mainz: von Zabern

Kurzban, R., Tooby, J. and Cosmides, L. (2001) 'Can race be erased? Coalitional computation and social categorization', *Proceedings of the National Academy of Sciences*, 98.26: 15387–92

Kuschke, A. (1979) 'Das Terrain der Schlacht bei Qadeš und die Anmarschwege Ramses' II.', *Zeitschrift des Deutschen Palästina-Vereins*, 95: 7–35

LaBianca, O.S. and Younker, R.W. (1995) 'The kingdoms of Ammon, Moab, and Edom: the archaeology of society in Late Bronze/Iron Age Transjordan, ca 1400–500 BCE', in T.E. Levy (ed.) *The Archaeology of Society in the Holy Land*, 399–415, London: Leicester University Press

Lacau, P. and Chevrier, H. (1977) *Une chapelle d'Hatshepsout à Karnak*, 2 vols, Cairo: Institut Français d'Archéologie Orientale

Lacovara, P. (1997) *The New Kingdom Royal City*, London and New York: Kegan Paul International

Laffineur, R. (1988) 'Reflexions sur le trésor de Tôd', *Aegaeum*, 2, 17–29

Langdon, S. and Gardiner, A.H. (1920) 'The treaty of alliance between Hattusili, King of Hittites, and the Pharaoh Ramesses II of Egypt', *Journal of Egyptian Archaeology*, 6: 179–205

Lange, H.O. (1925) *Das Weisheitsbuch des Amenemope aus dem Papyrus 10,474 des British Museum*, Copenhagen: Bianco Lunos

—— and Schäfer, H. (1902) *Grab- und Denksteine des Mittleren Reichs No. 20001–20780. Vol. I: No. 20001–20399*, Berlin: Reichsdruckerei

La Rosa, V. (2000) 'To whom did the Queen Tiyi scarab found at Hagia Triada belong?', in A. Karetsou (ed.) Κρήτη – Αιγύπτος: Πολιτισμικοί Δεσμοί μριών Χιλιετιών, 86–93, Athens: Kapon Editions

Lauer, J.-P. (1936) *La pyramide à degrés. L'architecture*, 2 vols, Cairo: Institut Français d'Archéologie Orientale

——, Tächolm, V., Laurent, V. and Aberg, E. (1951) 'Les plantes découvertes dans les souterrains de l'enceinte du Roi Zoser à Saqqara (III Dynastie)', *Bulletin de l'Institut d'Égypte*, 32: 121–57

Lawrence, A.W. (1965) 'Ancient Egyptian fortifications', *Journal of Egyptian Archaeology*, 51: 69–94

Leahy, M.A. (1978) *Excavations at Malkata and the Birket Habu 1971–1974. The Inscriptions*, Warminster: Aris and Phillips

—— (1979) 'Nespamedu, "King" of Thinis?', *Göttinger Miszellen*, 35, 31–9

—— (1989) 'A protective measure at Abydos in the Thirteenth Dynasty', *Journal of Egyptian Archaeology*, 75: 41–60

—— (1990) 'Abydos in the Libyan Period', in A. Leahy (ed.) *Libya and Egypt c.1300–750 BC*, 15–27, London: Centre of Near and Middle Eastern Studies

—— (1999) 'More fragments of the Book of the Dead of Padinemty', *Journal of Egyptian Archaeology*, 85: 230–2

Leclant, J. (1960) 'The suckling of the pharaoh as a part of the coronation rites in Ancient Egypt/Le rôle de l'allaitement dans le cérémonial pharaonique du Couronnement', in *Proceedings of the IXth International Congress of the History of Religions. Tokyo and Kyoto, 27.8.–9.9.1958*, 135–45, Tokyo: Maruzen

—— (1961) *Montouemhat quatrième prophète d'Amon prince de la ville*, Cairo: Institut Français d'Archéologie Orientale

Lee, L. and Quirke, S. (2000) 'Painting materials', in P.T. Nicholson and I. Shaw (eds) *Ancient Egyptian Materials and Technology*, 104–20, Cambridge: Cambridge University Press

Lefèbvre, G. (1929) *Inscriptions concernant les grands prêtres d'Amon Romê-Roÿ et Amenhotep*, Paris: P. Guenthner

Legget, W. (1945) *The Story of Linen*, Brooklyn, NY: Chemical Publishing Company

Lehner, M. (1997) *The Complete Pyramids*, London and New York: Thames and Hudson

—— (2002) 'The Pyramid Age settlement of the Southern Mount at Giza', *Journal of the American Research Center in Egypt*, 39: 27–74

Leitz, C. (1989) *Studien zur ägyptischen Astronomie*, Wiesbaden: Harrassowitz

—— (ed) (2002) *Lexikon der ägyptischen Götter und Götterbezeichnungen*, Leuven: Peeters

Lenoble, P. (2004) 'The pre-Christian empire and kingdoms', in D. Welsby and J.R. Anderson (eds) *Sudan: Ancient Treasures*, 186–92, London: British Museum Press

Lesko, B.S. (1989) *Women's Earliest Records from Ancient Egypt and Western Asia*, Atlanta, GA: Scholars Press

Lesko, L.H. (1991) 'Ancient Egyptian cosmogonies and cosmology', in B. Shafer (ed.) *Religion in Ancient Egypt: Gods, Myths and Personal Practice*, 88–122, Ithaca, NY: Cornell University Press

Lichtheim, M. (1945) 'The Songs of the Harpers', *Journal of Near Eastern Studies*, 4: 178–212

—— (1971–72) 'Have the principles of ancient Egyptian metrics been discovered?', *Journal of the American Research Center in Egypt*, 9: 103–10

—— (1975) *Ancient Egyptian Literature. Volume 1: The Old and Middle Kingdoms*, Berkeley, LA and London: University of California Press

—— (1976) *Ancient Egyptian Literature. Volume II: The New Kingdom*. Berkeley, LA and London: University of California Press

—— (1980a) *Ancient Egyptian Literature. Volume III: The Late Period*, Berkeley, LA and London: University of California Press

—— (1980b) 'The praise of cities in the literature of the Egyptian New Kingdom', in S.M. Burstein and L.A. Okin (eds) *Panhellenica: Essays in Ancient History and Historiography in Honor of Truedell S. Brown*, 15–23, Lawrence, KS: Coronado Press

—— (1983) *Late Egyptian Wisdom Literature in the International Context: A Study of Demotic Instructions*, Freiburg/Göttingen: Universitätsverlag/Vandenhoeck & Ruprecht

—— (1988) *Ancient Egyptian Autobiographies Chiefly of the Middle Kingdom: A Study and an Anthology*, Freiburg/Göttingen: Universitätsverlag/Vandenhoeck & Ruprecht

—— (1992) *Maat in Egyptian Autobiographies and Related Studies*, Freiburg/Göttingen: Universitätsverlag/Vandenhoeck & Ruprecht

Liddel Hart, B.H. (1991) *Strategy*, 2nd edn, New York: Meridian

Lightfoot, K.G. and Martinez, A. (1995) 'Frontiers and boundaries in archaeological perspective', *Annual Review of Anthropology*, 24: 471–92

Lippert, S.L. (2003) 'Die sogenannte Zivilprozess-Ordnung – weitere Fragmente', *The Journal of Juristic Papyrology*, 33: 91–135

—— (2004a) *Ein demotisches juristisches Lehrbuch – Untersuchungen zu Papyrus Berlin P 23757 rto*, Wiesbaden: Harrassowitz

—— (2004b) 'Fragmente demotischer juristischer Bücher (pBerlin 23890 a-b, d-g rto und pCarlsberg 628)', in F. Hoffmann and H.J. Thissen (eds) *Res severa verum gaudium: Festschrift für K.-T. Zauzich*, 389–405, Leuven: Peeters

Littauer, M. and Crouwel, J.H. (1979) *Wheeled Vehicles and Ridden Animals in the Ancient Near East*, Leiden and Cologne: Brill

Liverani, M. (1990) *Prestige and Interest. International Relations in the Near East ca. 1600–1100 B.C.*, Padua: Sargon

—— (1994) *Guerra e diplomazia nell'antiquo oriente: 1600–1100 BC*, Rome and Bari: Laterza

Lloyd, A.B. (1975) *Herodotus, Book II: Introduction*, Leiden: Brill

—— (1983) 'The Late Period, 664–323 BC', in B.G. Trigger, B.J. Kemp, D. O'Connor and A.B. Lloyd, *Ancient Egypt: A Social History*, 279–348, Cambridge: Cambridge University Press

Logan, T. (2000) 'The *Jmyt-pr* document: form, function, and significance', *Journal of the American Research Center in Egypt*, 37: 49–73

Lohwasser, A. (1991) *Die Formel Öffnen des Gesichts*, Vienna: Afro-Pub

Loprieno, A. (1988) *Topos und Mimesis. Zum Ausländer in der ägyptischen Literatur*, Wiesbaden: Harrassowitz

—— (1995) *Ancient Egyptian: A Linguistic Introduction*, Cambridge: Cambridge University Press

—— (1996a) 'Defining Egyptian literature: ancient texts and modern theories', in A. Loprieno (ed.) *Ancient Egyptian Literature: History and Forms*, 39–58, Leiden, New York and Cologne: Brill

—— (1996b) 'Linguistic variety and Egyptian literature', in A. Loprieno (ed.) *Ancient Egyptian Literature: History and Forms*, 515–30, Leiden, New York and Cologne: Brill

—— (1997) 'Slaves', in S. Donadoni (ed.) *The Egyptians*, 185–219, Chicago, IL: University of Chicago Press

—— (2001) *La pensée et l'écriture. Pour une analyse semiotique de la culture égyptienne*, Paris: Cybèle

Lorton, D. (1999) 'The theology of cult statues in ancient Egypt', in M.B. Dick (ed.) *Born in Heaven, Made on Earth: The Making of the Cult Image in the Ancient Near East*, 123–210, Winona Lake, IN: Eisenbrauns

Lucas, A. (1962) *Ancient Egyptian Materials and Industries*, 4th edn, revised and enlarged by J.R. Harris, London: E. Arnold

Luft, U. (1978) *Beiträge zur Historisierung der Götterwelt und der Mythenschreibung*, Budapest: Université Loránd Eötvös de Budapest

—— (1992) 'Asiatics in Illahun: a preliminary report', in *Atti Sesto Congresso Internationale di Egittologia*, 291–7, Turin: Il Comitato Organizzativo

Lunn, J. (2005) 'Male identity and martial codes of honor: a comparison of the war memoirs of Robert Graves, Ernst Jünger, and Kande Kamara', *Journal of Military History*, 69: 713–36

Lutz, H. (1922) *Viticulture and Brewing*, Leipzig: Hinrichs

Macadam, M.F.L. (1949, 1955) *The Temples of Kawa*, 4 vols, Oxford: Oxford University Press

Maguire, L. (1995) 'Tell el-Dab'a: the Cypriot connection', in W.V. Davies and L. Schofield (eds) *Egypt, the Aegean and the Levant: Interconnections in the Second Millennium B.C.*, 54–65, London: British Museum Press

Maksoud, M.A. el- (1998) *Tell Heboua (1981–1991)*, Paris: Ministère des Affaires Étrangères

Malek, J. (1986) *In the Shadow of the Pyramids: Egypt during the Old Kingdom*, Norman, OK: University of Oklahoma Press

Manassa, C. (2003) *The Great Karnak Inscription of Merenptah: Grand Strategy in the 13th Century BC*, New Haven, CT: Yale Egyptological Seminar

Manniche, L. (1987) *Sexual Life in Ancient Egypt*, London: Kegan Paul International

—— (1989) *An Ancient Egyptian Herbal*, London: British Museum Publications

Manning, J.G. (1999) 'The land-tenure regime in Ptolemaic Upper Egypt', in A.K. Bowman and E. Rogan (eds) *Agriculture in Egypt: From Pharaonic to Modern Times*, 83–105, Oxford: Oxford University Press

—— (2003) *Land and Power in Ptolemaic Egypt: The Structure of Land Tenure*, Cambridge: Cambridge University Press

Manning, S.W. (1999) *A Test of Time. The Volcano of Thera and the Chronology and History of the Aegean and Eastern Mediterranean in the Mid Second Millennium BC*, Oxford: Oxbow Books

Marchand, S. and Tallet, P. (1999) 'Ayn Asil et l'oasis de Dakhla au Nouvel Empire', *Bulletin de l'Institut Français d'Archéologie Orientale*, 99: 307–52

Marinatos, N. (1995) 'Divine kingship/queenship in Minoan Crete', in P. Rehak (ed.) *The Role of the Ruler in the Prehistoric Aegean*, 37–48, Liège and Austin, TX: Université de Liège and University of Texas Press

Marinatos, S. (1972) *Treasures of Thera*, Athens: Commercial Bank of Greece

Mark, S. (1998) *From Egypt to Mesopotamia. A Study of Predynastic Trade Routes*, College Station/London: Texas A&M University Press/Chatham Publishing

Martin, G.T. (1989) *The Memphite Tomb Horemheb, Commander-in-Chief of Tut'ankhamūn*, London: Egypt Exploration Society

—— (1998) 'The toponym Retjenu on a scarab from Tell el-Dab'a', *Ägypten und Levante*, 8: 109–12

Mass, J.L., Wypyski, M.T. and Stone, R.E. (2002) 'Malkata and Lisht glassmaking technologies: towards a specific link between second millennium BC metallurgists and glassmakers', *Archaeometry*, 44: 67–82

Mathieson, I., Bettles, E., Clarke, J., Duhig, C., Ikram, S., Maguire, L., Quie, S. and Tavares, A. (1997) 'The National Museums of Scotland Saqqara Survey Project 1993–1995', *Journal of Egyptian Archaeology*, 83, 17–53

Mathieu, B. (1996) *La poésie amoureuse de l'Égypte ancienne: recherches sur un genre littéraire au Nouvel Empire*, Cairo: Institut Français d'Archéologie Orientale

Matthäus, H. (1995) 'Representations of Keftiu in Egyptian tombs and the absolute chronology of the Aegean Late Bronze Age', *Bulletin of the Institute of Classical Studies*, 40: 177–94

Mayer, W. and Mayer-Opificius, R. (1994) 'Die Schlacht bei Qadeš: Der Versuch einer neuen Rekonstruktion', *Ugarit Forschungen*, 26: 321–68

Mayfield, J. (1996) *Local Government in Egypt*, Cairo: American University in Cairo Press

McCarthy, B. (2001) 'Technical analysis of reds and yellows in the tomb of Suemniwet, Theban Tomb 92', in W.V. Davies (ed.) *Colour and Painting in Ancient Egypt*, 17–21, London: British Museum Press

McDowell, A.G. (1990) *Jurisdiction in the Workmen's Community of Deir El-Medina*, Leiden: Brill
—— (1999) *Village Life in Ancient Egypt: Laundry Lists and Love Songs*, Oxford and New York: Oxford University Press

McHugh, W., McCauley, J.F., Haynes, C.V., Breed, C.S. and Schaber, G.G. (1988) 'Paleorivers and geoarchaeology in the southern Egyptian Sahara', *Geoarchaeology*, 3: 1–40

McKee, L. (1999) 'Food supply and plantation social order, an archaeological perspective', in T.A. Singleton (ed.) *'I, Too, Am America': Archaeological Studies of African-American Life*, 218–39, Charlottesville, VA: University Press of Virginia

Meeks, D. (1991) 'Oiseaux des carrières et des cavernes', in U. Verhoeven and E. Graefe (eds) *Religion und Philosophie im Alten Ägypten*, 233–41, Leuven: Peeters
—— (2003) 'Locating Punt', in D. O'Connor and S. Quirke (eds) *Mysterious Lands*, 53–80, London: UCL Press
—— (2006) *Mythes et légendes du Delta d'après le papyrus Brooklyn 47.218.84*, Cairo: Institut Français d'Archéologie Orientale
—— and Favard Meeks, C. (1996) *Daily Life of the Egyptian Gods*, Ithaca, NY and London: Cornell University Press

Meinardus, O. (1989) *Monks and Monasteries of the Egyptian Deserts*, Cairo: American University in Cairo Press

Mellink, M.L. (1995) 'New perspective and initiatives in the Hyksos period', *Ägypten und Levante*, 5: 85–9

Menu, B. (1970) *Le régime juridique des terres et du personnel attaché à la terre dans le papyrus Wilbour*, Lille: Institut de la Faculté des Lettres et Sciences Humaines de l'Université de Lille
—— (1982) *Recherches sur l'histoire juridique, économique et sociale de l'ancienne Égypte*, Versailles: B. Menu
—— (1999) *Ramses the Great, Warrior and Builder*, London and New York: Thames and Hudson
—— (2005) 'Les six pharaons législateurs d'après Diodore de Sicile', *Revue Historique du Droit Français et Étranger*, 83: 635–45

Merrillees, R.S. (1962) 'Opium trade in the Bronze Age Levant', *Antiquity*, 36: 287–92
—— (1968) *The Cypriote Bronze Age Pottery Found in Egypt*, Lund: SIMA
—— (1987) *Alashiya Revisited*, Paris: J. Gabalda

Merz, P., Castel, G. and Goyon, J.-C. (1980) 'Installations rupestres du Moyen et Nouvel Empire au Gebel Zeit (pres de Râs Dib) sur la Mer Rouge', *Mitteilungen des Deutschen Archäologischen Instituts Abteilung Kairo*, 36: 299–318

Meskell, L. (1994) 'Dying young. The experience of death at Deir el-Medineh', *Archaeological Review from Cambridge*, 13.2: 35–45
—— (1998a) 'An archaeology of social relations in an Egyptian village', *Journal of Archaeological Method and Theory*, 5.3: 209–43
—— (1998b) 'Intimate archaeologies: the case of Kha and Merit', *World Archaeology*, 29.3: 363–79
—— (1999) *Archaeologies of Social Life: Age, Sex, Class et cetera in Ancient Egypt*, Oxford: Blackwell

—— (2002) *Private Life in New Kingdom Egypt*, Princeton, NJ: Princeton University Press

—— (2004) *Object Worlds in Ancient Egypt: Material Biographies Past and Present*, Oxford: Berg

Metcalf, P. and Huntington, R. (1991) *Celebrations of Death. The Anthropology of Mortuary Ritual*, Cambridge: Cambridge University Press

Meyer, M. (1983) 'Archaeological survey of the Wadi Sheikh Ali', *Göttinger Miszellen*, 64: 77–82

Midant-Reynes, B. (2003) *Aux origines de l'Égypte. Du Néolithique à l'émergence de l'état*, Paris: Fayard

Middleton, A. and Humphrey, S. (2001) 'Pigments on some Middle Kingdom coffins', in W.V. Davies (ed.) *Colour and Painting in Ancient Egypt*, 10–16, London: British Museum Press

Militello, P. (2000) 'Nilotic models and local re-elaboration: the Hagia Triada example', in A. Karetsou (ed.) *Κρήτη – Αιγύπτος: Πολιτισμικοί Δεσμοί μριών Χιλιετιών*, 78–85, Athens: Kapon Editions

Miller, R.L. (1991) 'Counting calories in Egyptian ration texts', *Journal of the Economic and Social History of the Orient*, 34: 257–69

Millet, N.B. (1990) 'The Narmer macehead and related objects', *Journal of the American Research Center in Egypt*, 27: 53–9

Minault-Gout, A. (1985) 'Une inscription rupestre de l'Oasis de Dakhla situé au débouché du *Darb el-Tawil*', in F. Geus and F. Thill (eds) *Mélanges offerts à Jean Vercoutter*, 267–72, Paris: Éditions recherche sur les civilisations

Moeller, N. (2005a) 'An Old Kingdom town at Zawiet Sultan (Zawiet Meitin) in Middle Egypt: a preliminary report', in A. Cooke and F. Simpson (eds) *Current Research in Egyptology II*, 29–38, Oxford: Archaeopress

—— (2005b) 'Les nouvelles découvertes à Tell Edfou', *Bulletin de la Société Française d'Égyptologie*, 164: 29–46

Moers, G. (2001) 'Der Papyrus Lansing: Das Lob des Schreiberberufes in einer ägyptischen "Schülerhandschrift" aus dem ausgehenden Neuen Reich', in M. Dietrich, K. Hecker and J. Hoftijzer (eds) *Texten aus der Umwelt des Alten Testaments. Ergänzungslieferung*, 109–42, Gütersloh: Gütersloher Verlagshaus

Mohammad, A. (1959) 'The administration of Syro-Palestine during the New Kingdom', *Annales du Service des Antiquités de l'Égypte*, 56: 105–37

Möller, G. (1909) *Hieratische Paläographie II*, Leipzig: Hinrichs

Montet, P. (1928) *Byblos et l'Égypte*, Paris: Geuthner

—— (1933) 'La stèle de l'an 400 retrouvée', *Kêmi*, 4: 191–215

—— (1942) *Tanis: Douze années de fouilles dans une capitale oubliée du delta égyptien*, Paris: Payot

Montserrat, D. (1996) *Sex and Society in Graeco-Roman Egypt*, London: Kegan Paul International

—— (2000) *Akhenaten: History, Fantasy and Ancient Egypt*, London and New York: Routledge

Moorey, P.R.S. (1990) 'From Gulf to Delta in the fourth millennium BCE: the Syrian connection', *Eretz Israel*, 21: 62–9

Moran, W.L. (1992) *The Amarna Letters*, Baltimore, MD: Johns Hopkins University Press

Moreno Garcia, J.C. (2000) 'Acquisition de serfs durant la première période intermédiare', *Revue d'Égyptologie*, 51: 123–39

Morenz, L.D. (2005) 'Ein Text zwischen Ritual(ität) und Wissen. Die Inzenierung des Ankhtifi des Hefat as Super-Helden', in B. Dücker and H. Roeder (eds) *Text und Ritual. Kulturwissenschaftliche Essays und Analysen von Sesostris bis Dada*, 123–47, Heidelberg: Synchron

Moret, A. (1902) *Le rituel du culte divin journalier en Égypte*, Paris: Annales du Musée Guimet

Morgan, L. (1995) 'Minoan painting and Egypt. The case of Tell el-Dab'a', in W.V. Davies and L. Schofield (eds) *Egypt, the Aegean and the Levant. Interconnections in the Second Millennium BC*, 29–53, London: British Museum Press

Morkot, R. (2000) *The Black Pharaohs*, London: Rubicon

Morris, E.F. (2005) *The Architecture of Imperialism. Military Bases and the Evolution of Foreign Policy in Egypt's New Kingdom*, Leiden and Boston, MA: Brill

Morris, I. (1987) *Burial and Ancient Society. The Rise of the Greek City-state*, Cambridge: Cambridge University Press

Morrow, M. and Morrow, M. (eds) (2002) *Desert RATS: Rock Art Topographical Survey in Egypt's Eastern Desert*, London: Bloomsbury Summer School

Moussa, A.M. and Altenmüller, H. (1977) *Das Grab des Nianchchnum und Chnumhotep*, Mainz: von Zabern

Muhs, B.P. (2005) *Tax Receipts, Tax Payers and Taxes*, Chicago, IL: University of Chicago Oriental Institute Publications

Müller, W.M. (1899) *Die Liebespoesie der alten Ägypter*, Leipzig: Hinrichs

Müller, V. (1996) *Opfergruben der Mittleren Bronzezeit in Tell el-Dabʿa*, 2 vols, unpublished thesis, University of Göttingen

—— (1998) 'Offering deposits at Tell el-Dabʿa', in C.J. Eyre (ed.) *Proceedings of the Seventh International Congress of Egyptologists, Cambridge, 3–9 September 1995*, 793–803, Leuven: Peeters

—— (2001) 'Bestand und Deutung der Opferdepots bei Tempeln in Wohnbereichen und Gräbern der zweiten Zwischenzeit in Tell el-Dabʿa', in H. Willems (ed.) *Social Aspects of Funerary Culture in the Egyptian Old and Middle Kingdoms: Proceedings of the International Symposium Held at Leiden University 6–7 June, 1996*, 175–204, Leuven: University of Leuven

—— (forthcoming) *Tell el-Dabʿa. Opferdeponierungen in der Hyksoshauptstadt Auaris (Tell el-Dabʿa) vom späten Mittleren Reich bis zum frühen Neuen Reich*, 2 vols, Vienna: Österreichische Akademie der Wissenschaften

Müller-Wollermann, R. (1985) 'Waren Austauch im Ägypten des alten Reiches', *Journal of the Economic and Social History of the Orient*, 28: 121–68

Murnane, W. (1977) *Ancient Egyptian Coregencies*, Chicago, IL: University of Chicago Press

—— (1979) 'The bark of Amun on the Third Pylon at Karnak', *Journal of the American Research Center in Egypt*, 16: 11–27

—— (1980) *United with Eternity: A Concise Guide to the Monuments of Medinet Habu*, Chicago, IL/Cairo: Oriental Institute, University of Chicago/American University in Cairo Press

—— (1985) *The Road to Kadesh – A Historical Interpretation of the Battle Reliefs of Sety I at Karnak*, Chicago, IL: University of Chicago Press

—— (1995a) *Texts from the Amarna Period in Egypt*, Atlanta, GA: Scholars Press

—— (1995b) 'The kingship of the Nineteenth Dynasty: a study in the resilience of an institution', in D. O'Connor and D.P. Silverman (eds) *Ancient Egyptian Kingship*, 185–217, Leiden, New York and Cologne: Brill

—— (1997) '"Overseer of the Northern Foreign Countries": reflections on the administration of Egypt's empire in Western Asia', in J. van Dijk (ed.) *Essays on Ancient Egypt in Honour of Herman Te Velde*, 251–8, Groningen: Styx

Murray, G.W. (1939) 'The Road to Chephren's Quarries', *Royal Geographical Society Journal*, 94: 104–11

Mylonas, G. (1973) *Ο Ο ταφικος κνκλος Β των Μνκηνων*, Athens: Βιβλιοθηκη της Αθηναις Αρχαιολογικης Εταιρειας

Myśliwiec, K. (2000) *The Twilight of Ancient Egypt: First Millennium B.C.E.*, Ithaca, NY and London: Cornell University Press

Na'aman, N. (1975) 'The political disposition and historical development of Eretz Israel according to the Amarna Letters', unpublished thesis, Tel Aviv University

—— (1981) 'The economic aspect of the Egyptian occupation of Canaan', *Israel Exploration Journal*, 31: 172–85

—— (1994) 'The Hurrians and the end of the Middle Bronze Age in Palestine', *Levant*, 26: 175–87

NASA (2006) *Earth Observatory*. Online. Available at: *http://earthobservatory.nasa.gov/Study/Lights2/lights_soil5.html* (accessed 18 January 2006)

National Geographic (1978) *Ancient Egypt: Discovering its Splendor*, Washington, DC: National Geographic Society

Naunton, C.H. (2004) 'Tebe durante la XXV dinastia', in F. Tiradritti and S. Einaudi (eds) *L'Enigma di Harwa: Alla scoperta di un capolavoro del rinascimento egizio*, 83–104, Milan: Anthelios Edizioni

Naville, É. (1886) *Das aegyptische Todtenbuch der XVIII. bis XX. Dynastie*, 3 vols, Berlin: Asher & Co

—— (1892) *The Festival-hall of Osorkon II: In the Great Temple of Bubastis (1887–1889)*, London: Kegan Paul, Trench, Trübner

—— (1893) *The Mound of the Jew and the City of Onias*, London: Egypt Exploration Fund

Nelson, H. (1913) *The Battle of Megiddo*, Chicago, IL: University of Chicago Press

—— (1930) *Medinet Habu I: The Earlier Historical Records of Ramses III*, Chicago, IL: University of Chicago Press

—— (1949) 'The rite of "Bringing the Foot" as portrayed in temple reliefs', *Journal of Egyptian Archaeology*, 35: 82–6

—— and Hölscher, U. (1934) *Work in Western Thebes 1931–33*, Chicago, IL: University of Chicago Press

Nelson, K., Gatto, M.C., Jesse, F. and Zedeño, M.N. (2002) *Holocene Settlement of the Egyptian Sahara, Vol. 2: The Pottery of Nabta Playa*, New York: Kluwer Academic

Nenna, M.-D., Picon, M. and Vichy, M. (2000) 'Ateliers primaires et secondaires en Égypte à l'epoque gréco-romaine', in M.-D. Nenna (ed.) *La route du verre*, 97–112, Lyon: Maison de l'Orient

——, ——, Thirion-Merle, V. and Vichy, M. (2005) 'Ateliers primaries du Wadi Natrun: nouvelles découvertes', *Annales du 16e Congrès de l'Association Internationale pour l'Historie du Verre. London 2003*, 59–63, Amsterdam: AIHV

Newberry, P.E. (1893) *Beni Hasan I*, London: Egypt Exploration Fund

Newman, R. and Halpine, S.M. (2001) 'The binding media of ancient Egyptian painting', in W.V. Davies (ed.) *Colour and Painting in Ancient Egypt*, 22–32, London: British Museum Press

Nibbi, A. (1985) *Wenamun and Alashiya Reconsidered*, Oxford: Bocardo Press

Nicholson, P.T. (1998) 'Materials and technology', in F.D. Friedman (ed.) *Gifts of the Nile: Ancient Egyptian Faience*, 50–64, London and New York: Thames and Hudson

—— and Henderson, J. (2000) 'Glass', in P.T. Nicholson and I. Shaw (eds) *Ancient Egyptian Materials and Technology*, 195–224, Cambridge: Cambridge University Press

—— and Peltenburg, E. (2000) 'Egyptian faience', in P.T. Nicholson and I. Shaw (eds) *Ancient Egyptian Materials and Technology*, 177–94, Cambridge: Cambridge University Press

Nicolakaki-Kentrou, M. (2000) 'Amenhotep III and the Aegean: new evidence on intimacy. The painted plaster fragments from site K at Malkata', in A. Karetsou (ed.) Κρήτη – Αιγύπτος: Πολιτισμικοί Δεσμοί μριών Χιλιετιών, 47–51, Athens: Kapon Editions

Niemeier, W.D. (1991) 'Minoan artisans travelling overseas: the Alalakh frescoes and the painted plaster floor at Tel Kabri (Western Galilee)', *Aegaeum*, 7: 188–201

—— (1995) 'Tel Kabri: Aegean fresco paintings in a Canaanite palace', in S. Gitin (ed.) *Recent Excavations in Israel: A View to the West. Reports on Kabri, Nami, Miqne-Ekron, Dor and Ashkelon*, 1–15, Dubuque: Kendall/Hunt

Nims, C. (1954) 'Popular religion in ancient Egyptian temples', in D. Sinor (ed.) *Proceedings of the 23rd International Congress of Orientalists*, 79–80, London: Royal Asiatic Society

—— (1965) *Thebes of the Pharaohs*, London: Elek Books

Nixon, R. (1951) 'The date palm – tree of life', *Economic Botany*, 5: 2174–301

Nordström, H.-Å. (2004) 'The Nubian A-Group: perceiving a social landscape', in T. Kendall (ed.) *Nubian Studies 1998: Proceedings of the Ninth Conference of the International Society of Nubian Studies, August 21–26, 1998, Boston, Massachusetts*, 134–44, Boston, MA: Northeastern University

Noth, M. (1943) 'Die Annalen Thutmosis III. als Geschichtsquelle', *Zeitschrift des Deutschen Palästinavereins*, 66: 156–74

Nunn, J.F. (1996) *Ancient Egyptian Medicine*, London: British Museum Press

Obsomer, C. (1995) *Sesostris Ier, Étude chronologique et historique du règne*, Brussels: Connaissance de l'Égypte ancienne

O'Connor, D. (1972) 'A regional population in Egypt to circa 600 B.C.', in B. Spooner (ed.) *Population Growth: Anthropological Implications*, 78–100, Cambridge, MA and London: MIT Press

—— (1986) 'The locations of Yam and Kush and their historical implications', *Journal of the American Research Center in Egypt*, 23: 27–50

—— (1987) 'The location of Irem', *Journal of Egyptian Archaeology*, 73: 99–136

—— (1990) 'The nature of Tjemhu Society in the Later New Kingdom', in A. Leahy (ed.) *Libya and Egypt, c.1300–750 BC*, 29–114, London: SOAS and Society for Libyan Studies

—— (1991) 'Mirror of the cosmos: the palace of Merenptah', in E. Bleiberg and R. Freed (eds) *Fragments of a Shattered Visage: The Proceedings of the International Symposium on Ramesses the Great*, 167–98, Memphis, TN: University of Memphis

—— (1993) *Ancient Nubia. Egypt's Rival in Africa*, Philadelphia, PA: University Museum of Archaeology and Anthropology

—— (1996) 'Sexuality, statuary and the afterlife: scenes in the tomb-chapel of Pepyankh (Heny the Black) – an interpretive essay', in P. der Manuelian (ed.) *Studies in Honor of William Kelly Simpson*, vol. 2, 622–33, Boston, MA: Museum of Fine Arts

—— (2003) 'Egypt's view of others', in J. Tait (ed.) *'Never Had the Like Occurred': Egypt's View of Its Past*, 155–85, London: UCL Press

—— and Cline, E.H. (eds) (2001) *Amenhotep III. Perspectives on his Reign*, Ann Arbor, MI: University of Michigan

—— and Reid, A. (2003) *Ancient Egypt in Africa*, London: UCL Press

Ockinga, B.G. and al-Masri, Y. (1988) *Two Ramesside Tombs at El Mashayikh, Part 1*, Sydney: Australian Centre for Egyptology

Ogden, J. (2000) 'Metals', in P.T. Nicholson and I. Shaw (eds) *Ancient Egyptian Materials and Technology*, 148–76, Cambridge: Cambridge University Press

Omlin, J.A. (1973) *Der Papyrus 55001 und seine satirisch-erotische Zeichnungen und Inschriften*, Turin: Museo Egizio

Onstine, S. (2005) *The Role of the Chantress in Ancient Egypt*, Oxford: Archaeopress

Oren, E. (1985) 'Governors' residences in Canaan under the New Kingdom: a case study of Egyptian administration', *Journal of the Society for the Study of Egyptian Antiquities*, 14: 37–56

—— (ed.) (1997) *The Hyksos. New Historical and Archaeological Perspectives*, Philadelphia, PA: University Museum of Archaeology and Anthropology

—— (ed.) (2000) *The Sea Peoples and their World. A Reassessment*, Philadelphia, PA: University Museum of Archaeology and Anthropology

Ortiz, F. (1940) *Contrapunteo Cubano del Tobacco y el Azúcar*, Havana: Montero

Osing, J. (1986) 'Notizen zu den Oasen Charga und Dachla', *Göttinger Miszellen*, 92: 79–85

—— (1999) 'Zum Kultbildritual in Abydos', in E. Teeter and J. Larson (eds) *Gold of Praise: Studies on Ancient Egypt in Honor of Edward F. Wente*, 317–34, Chicago, IL: Oriental Institute, University of Chicago

Otto, E. (1954) *Die biographischen Inschriften der ägyptischen Spätzeit: Ihre geistesgeschichtliche und literarische Bedeutung*, Leiden: Brill

—— (1966) 'Sinuhe und der Schiffbrüchige als lehrhafte Stücke', *Zeitschrift für ägyptische Sprache und Altertumskunde*, 93: 100–11

Pachur, H.-J. (1991) 'Tethering stones as palaeoenvironmental indicators', *Sahara*, 1: 13–32

Panagiotaki, M. (2000) 'Crete and Egypt: contacts and relationships seen through vitreous materials', in A. Karetsou (ed.) *Κρήτη – Αιγύπτος: Πολιτισμικοί Δεσμοί μριών Χιλιετιών*, 154–61, Athens: Kapon Editions

Panagiotopoulos, D. (2001) 'Keftiu in context: Theban tomb-paintings as a historical source', *Oxford Journal of Archaeology*, 20: 263–83

Pantalacci, L. (1998) 'La documentation épistolaire du palais des gouverneurs à Balat-ʿAyn Aṣīl', *Bulletin de l'Institut Français d'Archéologie Orientale*, 98: 303–15

Pardey, E. (2001) 'Provincial administration', in D.B. Redford (ed.) *The Oxford Encyclopedia of Ancient Egypt*, vol. 3, 16–20, New York: Oxford University Press

Parkinson, R.B. (1991a) 'Teachings, discourses and tales from the Middle Kingdom', in S. Quirke (ed.) *Middle Kingdom Studies*, 91–122, New Malden: SIA Publishing

—— (1991b) *The Tale of the Eloquent Peasant*, Oxford: Griffith Institute

—— (1995) ' "Homosexual" desire and Middle Kingdom literature', *Journal of Egyptian Archaeology*, 81: 57–76

—— (1996) 'Individual and society in Middle Kingdom literature', in A. Loprieno (ed.) *Ancient Egyptian Literature: History and Forms*, 137–55, Leiden, New York and Cologne: Brill

—— (1997) *The Tale of Sinuhe and Other Ancient Egyptian Poems 1940–1640 BC*, Oxford: Oxford Unversity Press

—— (1999) *Cracking Codes: The Rosetta Stone and Decipherment*, London: British Museum Press

—— (2002) *Poetry and Culture in Middle Kingdom Egypt: A Dark Side to Perfection*, London and New York: Continuum

—— (2003) 'The missing beginning of "The Dialogue of a Man and His Ba": P. Amherst III and the history of the "Berlin Library" ', *Zeitschrift für ägyptische Sprache und Altertumskunde*, 130: 120–33 and pls 30–1

Partridge, R.B. (2002) *Fighting Pharaohs. Weapons and Warfare in Ancient Egypt*, Manchester: Peartree

Payne, J.C. (1973) 'Tomb 100. The decorated tomb at Hierakonpolis confirmed', *Journal of Egyptian Archaeology*, 59: 31–5

—— (1993) *Catalogue of the Predynastic Egyptian Collection in the Ashmolean Museum*, Oxford: Clarendon Press

Peden, A.J. (2001) *The Graffiti of Pharaonic Egypt*, Leiden: Brill

Peet, T.E. (1923) *The Rhind Mathematical Papyrus BM 10.057 and 10.058*, Liverpool and London: Hodder & Stoughton

—— (1924) 'A historical document of Ramesside age', *Journal of Egyptian Archaeology*, 10: 116–27

—— and Woolley, C.L. (1923) *The City of Akhenaten, Part I: Excavations of 1921 and 1922 at el-ʿAmarna*, London: Egypt Exploration Society

Peltenburg, E.J. (1983) 'Appendix VII. The faience bowl from Palaepaphos-*Skales* T. 58.5. P. 423', in V. Karageorghis, *Palaepaphos-Skales: An Iron Age Cemetery in Cyprus*, Konstanz: Universitätsverlag Konstanz

—— (1991) 'Greeting gifts and luxury faience: a context for orientalising trends in Late Mycenaean Greece', in N. Gale (ed.) *Bronze Age Trade in the Mediterranean*, 162–76, Jonsered: P. Åströms Förlag

Pendlebury, J.D.S. (1951) *The City of Akhenaten, Part III: The Central City and the Official Quarters, vol. 2: Plates*, London: Egypt Exploration Society

Perry, W. and Paynter, R. (1999) 'Artifacts, ethnicity, and archaeology of African Americans', in T.A. Singleton (ed.) *'I, Too, Am American': Archaeological Studies of African-American Life*, 299–310, Charlottesville, VA: University Press of Virginia

Pestman, P.W. (1983) 'L'origine et l'extension d'un manuel de droit égyptien – Quelques réflexions à propos du soi-disant Code de Hermoupolis', *Journal of the Economic and Social History of the Orient*, 26: 14–21

Petrie, W.M.F. (1891) *Illahun, Kahun and Gurob, 1889–90*, London: Kegan Paul

—— (1909) *Qurneh*, London: School of Archaeology in Egypt/Quaritch

—— and Gardiner, A.H. (1886) *Naukratis. Part I, 1884–5*, London: Egypt Exploration Fund

Pflüger, K. (1946) 'The edict of King Haremhab', *Journal of Near Eastern Studies*, 5: 260–76 and pls I–VI

Philip, G. (2006) *Tell el-Dabʿa XV. Metalwork of the late Middle Kingdom and the Second Intermediate Period*, Vienna: Österreichische Akademie der Wissenschaften

Phillips, J. (1990) 'Egypt in the Aegean during the Middle Kingdom', in S. Schoske (ed.) *Akten des Vierten Internationalen Ägyptologen Kongresses München 1985*, 319–33, Hamburg: Helmut Buske Verlag

—— (1995) 'False analogies: the Minoan origin of some so-called "Egyptianizing" features', in S. Metropolitou and Th. V. Tzedake (eds) *Πεπράγμενα του Ζ'Διεθνούς Κρητολόγικος Συνέδριου. Τόμος Α2. Τμήμα Αρχαιολόγικο*, 757–65, Rethymnon: University of Crete

—— (1996) 'Aegypto-Aegean relations up to the second millennium B.C.', in B. Midant-Reynes, L. Krzyżaniak, K. Kroeper and M. Kobusiewicz (eds) *Interregional Contacts in Later Prehistory of Northeastern Africa*, 459–70, Poznań: Polish Academy of Sciences

—— (2005) 'The last pharaohs on Crete. Old contexts and old readings reconsidered', in R. Laffineur and E. Greco (eds) *Emporia: Aegeans in the Central and Eastern Mediterranean*, 455–61, Liège and Austin, TX: Université de Liège and University of Texas Press

Piacentini, P. (1987) 'Egiziani e Asiatici su un relievo della VI dinastia a Deshasheh', in *Studi di Egittologia e di Antichità Puniche* 1, 7–37 and pls I–III, Pisa: Giardini Editori

—— (1990) *L'autobiografia di Uni, Principe e Governatore dell'Alto Egitto*, Pisa: Giardini Editori

Pinch, G. (1982) 'Offerings to Hathor', *Folklore*, 93: 138–50

—— (1983) 'Childbirth and female figurines at Deir el-Medina and el-Amarna', *Orientalia*, 52: 405–14

—— (1993) *Votive Offerings to Hathor*, Oxford: Griffith Institute

—— (1994) *Magic in Ancient Egypt*, London: British Museum Press

—— (2001) 'Red things: the symbolism of colour in magic', in W.V. Davies (ed.) *Colour and Painting in Ancient Egypt*, 182–5, London: British Museum Press

—— (2004) *Egyptian Myth: A Very Short Introduction*, Oxford: Oxford University Press

Pini, I. (2000) 'Eleven Cretan scarabs', in A. Karetsou (ed.) *Κρήτη – Αιγύπτος: Πολιτισμικοί Δεσμοί μριών Χιλιετιών*, 107–13, Athens: Kapon Editions

Pintore, F. (1973) 'La prassi della marcia armata nella Siria egiziana dell'età di el-Amarna', *Oriens Antiquus*, 12: 200–318

Platon, N. (1974) *Ζακος. Το νεον μινωικον ανακτορον*, Athens: Βιβλιοθηκη της Αθηναις Αρχαιολογικης Εταιρειας

Polanyi, K. (1977) *The Livelihood of Man*, New York: Academic Press

Popper, W. (1951) *The Cairo Nilometer: Studies in Ibn Taghri Birdi's Chronicles of Egypt*, Berkeley, CA: University of California Press

Porada, E. (1984) 'The cylinder seal from Tell el-Dab'a', *American Journal of Archaeology*, 88: 485–8

Porphyrius *On Abstinence*, book IV

Porter, B. and Moss, R. (1927–99) *Topographical Bibliography of Ancient Egyptian Hieroglyphic Texts, Reliefs and Paintings*, 8 vols (vol. 8 ed. J. Malek), Oxford: Clarendon Press

Porter, R. and Teich, M. (1981) *The Enlightenment in National Context*, Cambridge: Cambridge University Press

Posener, G. (1940) *Princes et pays d'Asie et de Nubie: Textes hiératiques sur des figurines d'envoûtement du moyen empire*, Brussels: Fondation Égyptologique Reine Élisabeth

—— (1951) 'Les richesses inconnues de la littérature égyptienne', *Revue d'Égyptologie*, 6: 27–48

—— (1952) 'Compléments aux "Richesses inconnues" ', *Revue d'Égyptologie*, 9: 118–20

—— (1957) 'Les asiatiques en Égypte sous les XIIe et XIIIe dynasties', *Syria*, 34: 145–63

—— (1971) 'Syria and Palestine c.2160–1780 B.C.', in I.E.S. Edwards, C.J. Gadd and N.G.L. Hammond (eds) *The Cambridge Ancient History*, 3rd edn, vol. 1 pt 2, 532–58, Cambridge: Cambridge University Press

—— (1976) *L'enseignement loyaliste: sagesse égyptienne du Moyen Empire*, Geneva: Droz

—— (1977) 'La complainte de l'échanson Bay', in J. Assmann, E. Feucht and R. Grieshammer (eds) *Fragen and die altägyptischen Literatur*, 385–97, Wiesbaden: Harrassowitz

Posener-Kriéger, P. (1976) *Les archives du temple funéraire de Néferirkarê-Kakaï (Les papyrus d'Abousir)*, 2 vols, Cairo: Institut Français d'Archéologie Orientale

Postgate, J.N. and Campbell, S. (eds) (2002) *Artefacts of Complexity: Tracking the Uruk in the Near East*, Warminster: Aris and Phillips

Postgate, N., Wang, T. and Wilkinson, T. (1995) 'The evidence for early writing: utilitarian or ceremonial?', *Antiquity*, 69: 459–80

Preisigke, F. and Spiegelberg, W. (1915) *Ägyptische und griechische Inschriften und Graffiti aus den Steinbrüchen der Gebel Silsile (Oberägypten)*, Strasbourg: Trübner

Prisse d'Avennes, E. (1991) *Atlas de l'art égyptien*, Cairo: Zeitouna

Pritchard, J.B. (ed.) (1969) *Ancient Near Eastern Texts Relating to the Old Testament*, 3rd edn, Princeton, NJ: Princeton University Press

Pulak, C. (1997) 'The Uluburun shipwreck', in S. Swiny, R.L. Hohlfelder and H.W. Swiny (eds) *Res Maritimae. Cyprus and the Eastern Mediterranean from Prehistory to Late Antiquity*, 233–62, Atlanta, GA: Scholars Press

Pusch, E.B. (1989) 'Ausländisches Kulturgut in Qantir-Piramesse', in S. Schoske (ed.) *Akten des 4. Internationalen Ägyptologen Kongresses München 1985*, 249–56, Hamburg: Buske

—— (1990) 'Metallverarbeitende Werkstättender frühen Ramessidenzeit in Qantir-Piramesse/Nord – ein Zwischenbericht', *Ägypten und Levante*, 1: 75–113

—— (1995) 'High temperature industries in the Late Bronze Age capital Piramesse (Qantir), II: a quasi-industrial bronze factory, installations, tools and artifacts', in F.A. Esmael (ed.) *Proceedings of the First International Conference on Ancient Egyptian Mining and Metallurgy and Conservation of Metallic Artifacts*, 121–32, Cairo: Egyptian Antiquities Organization Press

—— (1999a) 'Glasproduktion in Qantir', *Ägypten und Levante*, 9: 111–20

—— (1999b) 'Towards a map of Piramesse', *Egyptian Archaeology*, 14: 13–15

—— (ed.) (1999) *Ägypten und Levante*, 9

——, Becker, H. and Fassbinder, J. (1999) 'Palast – Tempel – Auswärtiges Amt? Oder: Sind Nilschlammauern magnetisch zu erfassen?', *Ägypten und Levante*, 9: 135–53

Quack, J.F. (1992) *Studien zur Lehre für Merikare*, Wiesbaden: Harrassowitz

—— (2004) 'Der pränatale Geschlechtsverkehr von Isis und Osiris sowie eine Notiz zum Alter des Osiris', *Studien zur Altägyptische Kultur*, 32: 327–32

—— (2005) *Einführung in die altägyptische Literaturgeschichte*, III. *Die demotische und gräko-ägyptische Literatur*, Münster: Lit Verlag

Quibell, J.E. and Green, F.W. (1902) *Hierakonpolis II*, London: Quaritch

Quirke, S. (1989) 'Frontier or border: the north-west Delta in Middle Kingdom texts', in A. Nibbi (ed.) *The Archaeology, Geography and History of the Egyptian Delta in Pharaonic Times*, 261–75, Oxford: Discussions in Egyptology

—— (1990a) *The Administration of Egypt in the Late Middle Kingdom: The Hieratic Documents*, New Malden: SIA Publishing

—— (1990b) *Who Were the Pharaohs? A History of their Names with a List of Cartouches*, London: British Museum Press

—— (1992) *Ancient Egyptian Religion*, London: British Museum Press

—— (2001a) 'State administration', in D.B. Redford (ed.) *The Oxford Encyclopedia of Ancient Egypt*, vol. 1, 12–16, New York: Oxford University Press

—— (2001b) 'Judgment of the dead', in D.B. Redford (ed.) *The Oxford Encyclopedia of Ancient Egypt*, vol. 2, 211–14, New York: Oxford University Press

—— (2004a) 'Identifying the officials of the Fifteenth Dynasty', in M. Bietak and E. Czerny (eds) *Scarabs of the Second Millennium BC from Egypt, Nubia, Crete and the Levant: Chronological and Historical Implications*, 171–93, Vienna: Akademie der Wissenschaften

—— (2004b) *Titles and Bureaux of Egypt 1850–1700 BC*, London: Golden House Publications

—— (2004c) *Egyptian Literature 1800 BC: Questions and Readings*, London: Golden House Publications

—— and Andrews, C. (1988) *The Rosetta Stone: Facsimile Drawing*, London: British Museum Press

Raedler, C. (2003) 'Zur Repräsentation und Verwirklichung pharaonischer Macht in Nubien: Der Vizekönig Setau', in R. Gundlach and U. Rössler-Köhler (eds) *Das Königtum der Ramessidenzeit*, 129–73, Wiesbaden: Harrassowitz

Raue, D. (2005) 'Eléphantine: cinq campagnes de fouilles dans la ville du IIIe millénaire avant J.-C.', *Bulletin de la Société Française d'Égyptologie*, 163: 8–26

Raven, M. (1982) 'Corn mummies', *Oudheidkundige Mededelingen uit het Rijksmuseum van Oudheden te Leiden*, 63: 7–38

Rawlinson, G. (1964) *The Histories of Herodotus*, London: Dent

Redford, D.B. (1965) 'The co-regency of Tuthmosis III and Amenophis II', *Journal of Egyptian Archaeology*, 51: 107–22

—— (1970) 'The Hyksos invasion in history and tradition', *Orientalia*, 39: 1–51

—— (1972) 'Studies in relations between Palestine and Egypt during the first millennium B.C., 1: the taxation system of Solomon', in J.W. Wevers and D.B. Redford (eds) *Studies on the Ancient Palestinian World*, 141–56, Toronto: University of Toronto Press

—— (1979) 'A gate-inscription from Karnak and Egyptian involvement in Western Asia during the early 18th Dynasty', *Journal of the American Oriental Society*, 99: 270–87

—— (1986) *Pharaonic King-Lists, Annals and Day-books: A Contribution to the Study of the Egyptian Sense of History*, Mississauga: Benben Publications

—— (1992) *Egypt, Canaan and Israel in Ancient Times*, Princeton, NJ: Princeton University Press

—— (1993) *Egypt, Canaan, and Israel in Ancient Times*, Cairo: American University in Cairo Press

—— (1995) 'The concept of kingship during the Eighteenth Dynasty', in D. O'Connor and D.P. Silverman (eds) *Ancient Egyptian Kingship*, 157–84, Leiden, New York and Cologne: Brill

—— (ed.) (2001) *The Oxford Encyclopedia of Ancient Egypt*, 3 vols, New York: Oxford University Press

—— (2003) *The Wars in Syria and Palestine of Thutmose III*, Leiden and Boston, MA: Brill

—— (2004a) *Excavations at Mendes. Volume I. The Royal Necropolis*, Leiden: Brill

—— (2004b) *From Slave to Pharaoh. The Black Experience of Ancient Egypt*, Baltimore, MD and London: Johns Hopkins University Press

Reeves, N. (1990) *The Complete Tutankhamun*, London and New York: Thames and Hudson

—— and Wilkinson, R.H. (1996) *The Complete Valley of the Kings*, London and New York: Thames and Hudson

Rehak, P. (1996) 'Aegean breechcloths, kilts and the Keftiu paintings', *American Journal of Archaeology*, 100: 35–51

—— (1998) 'Aegean natives in the Theban tomb paintings: the Keftiu revisited', in E.H. Cline and D. Harris-Cline (eds) *The Aegean and the Orient in the Second Millennium*, 39–50, Liège and Austin, TX: Université de Liège and University of Texas Press

Rehren, T. and Pusch, E.B. (2005) 'Late Bronze Age glass production at Qantir-Piramesses, Egypt', *Science*, 308: 1756–8

——, —— and Herold, A. (1998) 'Glass coloring works within a copper-centered industrial complex in Late Bronze Age Egypt', in W.P. McCray (ed.) *The Prehistory and History of Glassmaking Technology*, 227–50, Westerville, OH: American Ceramic Society

Reisner, G.A., Dunham, D. and Janssen, J.M.A. (1960) *Semna Kumma*, Boston, MA: Museum of Fine Arts

—— and Reisner, M.B. (1933) 'Inscribed monuments from Gebel Barkal, part 2: the granite stela of Thutmose III', *Zeitschrift für Ägyptische Sprache und Altertumskunde*, 69: 24–36

Renfrew, C. (1996) 'Prehistory and the identity of Europe, or, Don't let's be beastly to the Hungarians', in P. Graves-Brown, S. Jones and C. Gamble (eds) *Cultural Identity and Archaeology*, 125–37, London: Routledge

Reymond, E.A.E. (1969) *The Mythical Origin of the Egyptian Temple*, Manchester: Manchester University Press

Rice, M. (1990) *Egypt's Making*, London: Routledge

Ricke, H. (1950) *Bemerkungen zur ägyptischen Baukunst des Alten Reichs. Bemerkungen zum agyptischen Pyramidenkult*, Cairo: Institut für Ägyptische Bauforschung und Altertumskunde in Kairo

Riefstahl, E. (1968) *Ancient Egyptian Glass and Glazes in the Brooklyn Museum*, Brooklyn, NY: Brooklyn Museum

Riemer, H. (2004) 'News about the Clayton Rings: long distance desert travellers during Egypt's Predynastic', in S. Hendrickx, R.F. Friedman, K.M. Ciałowicz and M. Chłodnicki (eds) *Egypt at its Origins. Studies in Memory of Barbara Adams*, 971–89, Leuven: Peeters

——, Förster, F., Hendrickx, S., Nussbaum, S., Eichhorn, B., Pollath, N., Schonfeld, P. and Wagner, G. (2005) 'Zwei pharaonische Wüstenstationen südwestlich von Dachla', *Mitteilungen des Deutschen Archäologischen Instituts Abteilung Kairo*, 61: 291–350

Riggs, C. (2005) *The Beautiful Burial in Roman Egypt: Art, Identity and Funerary Religion*, Oxford: Oxford University Press

Rilly, C. (2007) *Le méroïtique et sa famille linguistique*, Leuven: Peeters

Ritner, R.K. (1993) *The Mechanics of Ancient Egyptian Magical Practice*, Chicago, IL: Oriental Institute, University of Chicago

Rizkana, I. (1996) 'The Prehistoric House', in M. Bietak (ed.) *Haus und Palast im alten Ägypten*, 175–83, Vienna: Österreichische Akademie der Wissenschaften

Rizzo, J. (2004) 'Une mesure d'hygiène relative à quelques statues-cubes déposées dans le temple d'Amon à Karnak', *Bulletin de l'Institut Français d'Archéologie Orientale*, 104: 511–21

Robins, G. (1983) 'The god's wife of Amun in the 18th dynasty in Egypt', in A. Cameron and A. Kuhrt (eds) *Images of Women in Antiquity*, 65–78, London: Croom Helm

—— (1986) *Egyptian Painting and Relief*, Princes Risborough: Shire Publications

—— (1990) 'Problems in interpreting Egyptian art', *Discussions in Egyptology*, 17: 45–58

—— (1993) *Women in Ancient Egypt*, London: British Museum Press

—— (1994a) *Proportion and Style in Ancient Egyptian Art*, Austin, TX: University of Texas Press

—— (1994b) 'Some principles of compositional dominance and gender hierarchy in Egyptian art', *Journal of the American Research Center in Egypt*, 31: 33–40

—— (1996) 'Dress, undress, and the representation of fertility and potency in New Kingdom Egyptian art', in N. Kampen (ed.) *Sexuality in Ancient Art*, Cambridge and New York: Cambridge University Press

—— (1997) *The Art of Ancient Egypt*, London: British Museum Press

—— (1999) 'Hair and the construction of identity in ancient Egypt, *c.*1480–1350 B.C.', *Journal of the American Research Center in Egypt*, 36: 55–69

—— (2001a) *Egyptian Statues*, Princes Risborough: Shire Publications

—— (2001b) 'Color symbolism', in D.B. Redford (ed.) *The Oxford Encyclopedia of Ancient Egypt*, vol. 1, 291–4, New York: Oxford University Press

—— (2005) 'Cult statues in ancient Egypt', in N.H. Walls (ed.) *Cult Image and Divine Representation in the Ancient Near East*, 1–12, Boston, MA: American Schools of Oriental Research

Roeder, G. (1914) *Naos. Catalogue Général des Antiquités Égyptiennes du Musée du Caire Nr. 70001–70050*, Leipzig: Breitkopf and Härtel

Roehrig, C.H. (ed.) (2005) *Hatshepsut: From Queen to Pharaoh*, New York: Metropolitan Museum of Art

Romano, J. (1990) *Daily Life of the Ancient Egyptians*, Pittsburgh, PA Carnegie Museum of Natural History

—— (1995) 'Jewelry and personal arts in ancient Egypt', in J.M. Sasson (ed.) *Civilizations of the Ancient Near East*, vol. 1, New York: Charles Scribner's Sons

Römer, M. (1989) 'Einige Anmerkungen zur Diskussion über die Ökonomie im alten Ägypten', *Göttinger Miszellen*, 108: 7–20

Rossi, C. (2004) *Architecture and Mathematics in Ancient Egypt*, Cambridge: Cambridge University Press

Rössler-Köhler, U. (1991) *Individuelle Haltungen zum Königtum der Spätzeit. Private Quellen und ihre Königswertung im Spannungsfeld zwischen Erwartung und Erfahrung*, Wiesbaden: Harrassowitz

Roth, A.M. (1991) *Egyptian Phyles in the Old Kingdom: The Evolution of a System of Social Organization*, Chicago, IL: University of Chicago Press

—— (1992) 'The *psỉ-kf* and the "Opening of the Mouth": a ritual of birth and rebirth', *Journal of Egyptian Archaeology*, 78: 57–80

—— (1993) 'Social change in the Fourth Dynasty: the spatial organization of pyramids, tombs, and cemeteries', *Journal of the American Research Center in Egypt*, 30: 33–55

—— (1994) 'The practical economics of tomb-building in the Old Kingdom: a visit to the necropolis in a carrying chair', in D.S. Silverman (ed.) *For His Ka: Essays Offered in Memory of Klaus Baer*, Chicago, IL: Oriental Institute, University of Chicago

—— (2005) 'Hatshepsut's mortuary temple at Deir el-Bahri: architecture as political statement', in C. Roehrig (ed.) *Hatshepsut: From Queen to Pharaoh*, 147–51, New York: Metropolitan Museum of Art

Rothenberg, B. (1972) *Timna: Valley of the Biblical Copper Mines*, London: Thames and Hudson

—— (1988) *The Egyptian Mining Temple at Timna*, London: Institute for Archaeo-Metallurgical Studies

Rothman, M.S. (ed.) (2001) *Uruk Mesopotamia and its Neighbours: Cross-cultural Interactions in the Era of State Formation*, Santa Fe, NM: School of American Research Press

Rowe, A. (1938) 'Provisional notes on the Old Kingdom inscriptions from the diorite quarries', *Annales du Service des Antiquités de l'Égypte*, 38: 391–6

—— (1940) *Four Canaanite Temples of Beth Shan*, Philadelphia, PA: University of Pennsylvania Press

Royce, A.P. (1982) *Ethnic Identity. Strategies of Diversity*, Bloomington, IN: Indiana University Press

Russell, T. (2001) *The Napoleonic Survey of Egypt* (Description de l'Égypte). *The Monuments and Customs of Egypt: Selected Engravings and Texts*, Aldershot: Ashgate

Russmann, E.R. (1980) 'The anatomy of an artistic convention: representation of the near foot in two dimensions through the New Kingdom', *Bulletin of the Egyptological Seminar*, 2: 57–81

—— (2001) *Eternal Egypt: Masterworks of Ancient Art from the British Museum*, Berkeley, CA: University of California Press

Ryan, D.P. (1988) 'The archaeological analysis of inscribed Egyptian funerary cones', *Varia Ægyptiaca*, 4: 165–70

Ryholt, K.S.B. (1997) *The Political Situation in Egypt During the Second Intermediate Period, c.1800–1550 B.C.*, Copenhagen: Museum Tusculanum Press

—— (2000) 'The late Old Kingdom in the Turin King List and the identity of Nitokris', *Zeitschrift für Ägyptische Sprache und Altertumskunde*, 127: 87–100

—— (2005) *The Carlsberg Papyri 6: The Petese Stories II (P. Petese II)*, Copenhagen: Carsten Niebuhr Institute

Rzeuska, T. (2006) *Society and Ceramics: Funerary Pottery and Burial Customs in the Late Old Kingdom at Saqqara*, Warsaw: Nerton

Said, R. (1962) *The Geology of Egypt*, Amsterdam: Elsevier

—— (1975) 'The geological evolution of the River Nile', in F. Wendorf and A.E. Marks (eds) *Problems in Prehistory. North Africa and the Levant*, 7–44, Dallas, TX: Southern Methodist University

—— (ed.) (1990) *The Geology of Egypt*, Rotterdam: Egyptian General Petroleum Corporation

—— (1993) *The River Nile: Geology, Hydrology and Utilization*, Oxford: Pergamon Press

—— and Yousri, F. (1968) 'Origin and pleistocene history of River Nile near Cairo, Egypt', *Bulletin de l'Institut d'Égypte*, 45: 1–30

Sakellarakis, E. and Sakellarakis, Y. (1984) 'The Keftiu and the Minoan thalassocracy', in R. Hägg and N. Marinatos (eds) *The Minoan Thalassocracy: Myth and Reality*, 197–203, Stockholm: Swedish School at Athens

Sakellarakis, J.A. and Sakellarakis, E. (1991) *Archanes*, Athens: Ekdotike Athenon

Saleh, M. and Sourouzian, H. (1986) *The Egyptian Museum Cairo: Official Catalogue*, Mainz: von Zabern

Sandars, N.K. (1985) *The Sea Peoples. Warriors of the Ancient Mediterranean*, London: Thames and Hudson

Sandford, K.S. (1934) *Paleolithic Man and the Nile Valley in Upper and Middle Egypt*, Chicago, IL: University of Chicago Press

—— and Arkell, W.J. (1929) *Paleolithic Man and the Nile-Faiyum Divide: A Study of the Region during Pliocene and Pleistocene Times*, Chicago, IL: University of Chicago Press

Sandison, A.T. (1962) 'Degenerative vascular disease in the Egyptian mummy', *Medical History*, 6: 77–81

Santley, R., Yarborough, C. and Hall, B. (1987) 'Enclaves, ethnicity, and the archaeological record at Matacapan', in R. Auger, M.F. Glass, S. MacEachern and P.H. MacCartney (eds) *Ethnicity and Culture*, 85–100, Calgary: Archaeological Association of the University of Calgary

Sarich, V. and Miele, F. (2004) *Race: The Reality of Human Differences*, Boulder, CO: Westview Press

Sass, B. (1988) *The Genesis of the Alphabet and its Development in the Second Millennium B.C.*, Wiesbaden: Harrassowitz

Satzinger, H. (1977) 'Hieratisch', in W. Helck and W. Westendorf (eds) *Lexikon der Ägyptologie*, vol. 2, 1187–9, Wiesbaden: Harrassowitz

Sauneron, S. (1960, 2nd edn 1980) *The Priests of Ancient Egypt*, New York: Grove Press

—— (1989) *Un Traité Égyptien d'Ophiologie*, Cairo: Institut Français d'Archéologie Orientale

Säve-Söderbergh, T. (1946) *The Navy of the Eighteenth Egyptian Dynasty*, Uppsala and Leipzig: Harrassowitz

—— (1953) *On Egyptian Representations of Hippopotamus Hunting as a Religious Motive*, Uppsala: Gleerup

—— and Troy, L. (1991) *New Kingdom Pharaonic Sites*, Uppsala: Almqvist and Wiksell

Scandone-Matthiae, G. (1990) 'Egyptianizing ivory inlays from Palace P of Ebla', *Annales Archéologiques Arabes Syriennes*, 40: 146–60

Schade-Busch, M. (1992) *Zur Königsideologie Amenophis' III. Analyse der Phraseologie historischer Texte der Voramarnazeit*, Hildesheim: Gerstenberg

Schaedel, H.D. (1936) *Die Listen des grossen Papyrus Harris: ihre wirtschaftliche und politische Ausdeutung*, Glückstadt: Augustin

Schäfer, H. (1904) *Die Mysterien des Osiris in Abydos unter König Sesostris III. nach dem Denkstein des Oberschatzmeisters I-cher-nofret im Berliner Museum*, Leipzig: Hinrichs

—— (1905) 'Ein Zug nach der grossen Oase unter Sesostris I', *Zeitschrift für Ägyptische Sprache und Altertumskunde*, 42: 124–8

—— (1919, 4th edn 1963, rev. edn 1986) *Principles of Egyptian Art*, ed. E. Brunner-Traut, trans. and ed. J. Baines, Oxford: Griffith Institute

Scharff, A. (1922) 'Ein Rechnungsbuch des königlichen Hofes aus der 13. Dynastie', *Zeitschrift für Ägyptische Sprache und Altertumskunde*, 57: 51–68, 1**–24**

—— (1929) *Die Altertümer der Vor- und Frühzeit Ägyptens 1*, Berlin: Karl Curtius

Scheidel, W. (1995) 'Incest revisited: three notes on the demography of sibling marriage in Roman Egypt', *Bulletin of the American Society of Papyrologists*, 32: 143–55

Schenke, H.-M. (1960) 'Die Orakel im alten Ägypten', unpublished thesis, Humboldt University, Berlin

Schenkel, W. (1962) *Frühmittelägyptische Studien*, Bonn: Selbstverlag des Orientalischen Seminars der Universität Bonn

—— (1965) *Memphis-Herakleopolis-Theben. Die epigraphischen Zeugnisse der 7.-11. Dynastie Ägyptens*, Wiesbaden: Harrassowitz

Schiestl, R. (2002) 'Some links between a late Middle Kingdom cemetery at Tell el-Dab'a and Syria-Palestine: the necropolis of F/I, Strata d/2 and d/1 (=H and G/4)', in M. Bietak and H. Hunger (eds) *The Middle Bronze Age in the Levant. Proceedings of an International Middle Bronze Age Conference on MBIIA Ceramic Material in Vienna, 24–26 January 2001*, vol. 3, 329–52, Vienna: Österreichische Akademie der Wissenschaften

—— (2003) *Die Palastnekropole von Tell el-Dab'a, Die Gräber des Areals F/I der Straten d/2 und d/1*, unpublished thesis, University of Vienna

—— (2006) 'The statue of an Asiatic man from Tell el-Dab'a, Egypt', *Ägypten und Levante*, 16: 135–45

Schiff Giorgini, M., Robichon, C. and Leclant, J. (1965) *Soleb*, Florence: Sansoni

Schild, R. and Wendorf, F. (2002) 'Palaeo-ecologic and palaeo-climatic background to socioeconomic changes in the south western desert of Egypt', in R. Friedman (ed.) *Egypt and Nubia: Gifts of the Desert*, 21–7, London: British Museum Press

Schipper, B.U. (2005) *Die Erzählung des Wenamun: Ein Literaturwerk im Spannungsfeld von Politik, Geschichte und Religion*, Freiburg/Göttingen: Universitätsverlag/Vandenhoeck & Ruprecht

Schlichting, R. (1984) 'Stadtgott', in W. Helck and W. Westendorf (eds) *Lexikon der Ägyptologie*, vol. 5, 1250–1, Wiesbaden: Harrassowitz

Schmandt-Besserat, D. (1992) *Before Writing, I: From Counting to Cuneiform*, Austin, TX: University of Texas Press

Schmitt, L. (2005) 'Le temple du Gebel Abou Hassa', *Bulletin de l'Institut Français d'Archéologie Orientale*, 105: 357–404

Schmitz, B. (1976) *Untersuchungen zum Titel s3-nswt, 'Königssohn'*, Bonn: Rudolf Halbert

Schmitz, F.J. (1978) *Amenophis I.*, Hildesheim: Gerstenberg

Schneider, T. (1998) *Ausländer in Ägypten während des Mittleren Reiches und der Hyksoszeit. Teil I. Die ausländischen Könige*, Wiesbaden: Harrassowitz

—— (2003) *Ausländer in Ägypten während des Mittleren Reiches und der Hyksoszeit. Teil 2: Die ausländische Bevölkerung*, Wiesbaden: Harrassowitz

Schofield, L. and Parkinson, R.B. (1993) 'Of helmets and heretics: a possible Egyptian representation of Mycenaean warriors on a papyrus from el-Amarna', *Annual of the British School at Athens*, 88: 157–70

Schott, S. (1958) *Kanais. Der Tempel Sethos I. im Wadi Mia*, Göttingen: Vandenhoeck & Ruprecht

Schulman, A. (1962) 'The N'rn at the Battle of Kadesh', *Journal of the American Research Center in Egypt*, 1: 47–53

—— (1964) 'Siege warfare in pharaonic Egypt', *Natural History*, 73.3: 13–21

—— (1986) 'The royal butler Ramesses-samiaon', *Chronique d'Égypte*, 61: 187–202

—— (1987) 'The great historical inscription of Merenptah at Karnak: a partial reappraisal', *Journal of the American Research Center in Egypt*, 24: 21–34

—— (1988) *Ceremonial Execution and Public Rewards. Some Historical Scenes on New Kingdom Private Stelae*, Göttingen: Vandenhoeck & Ruprecht

Schulz, R. (2002) 'Der Sturm auf die Festung. Gedanken zu einigen Aspekten des Kampfbildes im Alten Ägypten vor dem Neuen Reich', in M. Bietak and M. Schwarz (eds) *Krieg und Sieg. Narrative Wanddarstellungen von Altägypten bis ins Mittelalter*, 19–41, Vienna: Verlag der Österreichischen Akademie der Wissenschaften

Scott, J.W. (1986) 'Gender: a useful category of historical analysis', *American Historical Review*, 91: 1053–75

Seeber, C. (1976) *Untersuchungen zur Darstellung des Totengerichts im alten Ägypten*, Munich and Berlin: Deutscher Kunstverlag

Seidel, M. (1998) 'The hidden tombs of Memphis', in R. Schulz and M. Seidel (eds) *Egypt: The World of the Pharaohs*, 264–9, Cologne: Könemann

Seidlmayer, S. (1996) 'Town and state in the early Old Kingdom. A view from Elephantine', in J. Spencer (ed.) *Aspects of Early Egypt*, 108–39, London: British Museum Press

—— (2000) 'The First Intermediate Period', in I. Shaw (ed.) *The Oxford History of Ancient Egypt*, 118–47, Oxford: Oxford University Press

Serpico, M. and White, R. (2001) 'The use and identification of varnish on New Kingdom funerary equipment', in W.V. Davies (ed.) *Colour and Painting in Ancient Egypt*, 33–42, London: British Museum Press

Serrano, A.J. (2002) *Royal Festivals in the Late Predynastic Period and the First Dynasty*, Oxford: Archaeopress

Sestini, G. (1989) 'Nile Delta: a review of depositional environments and geological history', in M.K.G. Whateley and K.T. Pickering (eds) *Delta: Sites and Traps for Fossil Fuels*, 99–127, Oxford: Blackwell

Sethe, K. (1903) *Urkunden des Alten Reichs, I*, Leipzig: Hinrichs

—— (1905) *Urkunden der 18. Dynastie, I: 1–624*, Leipzig: Hinrichs

—— (1926) 'Ächtung feindlicher Fürsten, Völker und Dinge auf altägyptischen Tongefäßscherben des Mittleren Reiches', *Sitzungsberichte der Preußischen Akademie der Wissenschaften 1926, Phil.-hist. Klasse*, 5, Berlin: Preußischen Akademie der Wissenschaften

—— (1928) *Ägyptische Lesestücke zum Gebrauch im akademischen Unterricht*, 2nd edn, Leipzig: Hinrichs

—— (1935) *Historisch-biographische Urkunden des Mittleren Reiches, I*, Leipzig: Hinrichs

Seyfried, K.-J. (1981) *Beiträge zu den Expeditionen des Mittleren Reiches in die Ost-Wüste*, Hildesheim: Gerstenberg

Shafer, B. (1997) 'Temples, priests and rituals: an overview', in B. Shafer (ed.) *Temples of Ancient Egypt*, 1–30, London and New York: I.B. Tauris

Shalomi-Hen, R. (2006) *The Writing of Gods: The Evolution of Divine Classifiers in the Old Kingdom*, Wiesbaden: Harrassowitz

Shaw, I. (1994) 'Pharaonic quarrying and mining: settlement and procurement in Egypt's marginal regions', *Antiquity*, 68: 108–19

—— (1998) 'Exploiting the desert frontier: the logistics and politics of ancient Egyptian mining expeditions', in A.B. Knapp, V.C. Pigott and E.W. Herbert (eds) *Social Approaches to an Industrial Past*, 242–58, London: Routledge

—— (1999) 'The 1997 survey of the ancient quarrying site of Gebel el-Asr ("The Chephren diorite quarries") in the Toshka region', *Annales du Service des Antiquités de l'Égypte*, 74: 63–7

—— (2000a) 'Egypt and the outside world', in I. Shaw (ed.) *The Oxford History of Ancient Egypt*, 314–29, Oxford: Oxford University Press

—— (ed.) (2000b) *The Oxford History of Ancient Egypt*, Oxford: Oxford University Press

—— (2001) 'Egyptians, Hyksos and military technology: causes, effects or catalysts?', in A.J. Shortland (ed.) *The Social Context of Technological Change. Egypt and the Near East, 1650–1550 BC*, 59–71, Oxford: Oxbow Books

—— (2002) 'Life on the edge: gemstones, politics and stress in the deserts of Egypt and Nubia', in R. Friedman (ed.) *Egypt and Nubia: Gifts of the Desert*, 244–51, London: British Museum Press

—— (2004) 'Identity and occupation: how did individuals define themselves and their work in the Egyptian New Kingdom?', in J.D. Bourriau and J. Phillips (eds) *Invention and Innovation: The Social Context of Technological Change, 2: Egypt, the Aegean and the Near East, 1650–1150 BC*, 12–24, Oxford: Oxbow Books

—— (2006) '"Master of the Roads": quarrying and communications networks in Egypt and Nubia', in B. Mathieu, D. Meeks and M. Wissa (eds) *L'apport de l'Égypte à l'histoire des techniques*, 253–66, Cairo: Institute Français d'Archéologie Orientale

—— and Bloxam, E. (1999) 'Survey and excavations at the ancient pharaonic gneiss quarrying site of Gebel el-Asr, Lower Nubia', *Sudan and Nubia*, 3: 13–20

Shaw, M.C. (1970) 'Ceiling patterns from the tomb of Hepzefa', *American Journal of Archaeology*, 74: 25–30

—— (2000) 'Anatomy and execution of complex Minoan textile patterns in the procession fresco from Knossos', in A. Karetsou (ed.) *Κρήτη – Αιγύπτοζ: Πολιτισμικοί Δεσμοί μριών Χιλιετιών*, 52–63, Athens: Kapon Editions

Shedid, A.G. (1994) *Die Felsgräber von Beni Hassan in Mittelägypten*, Mainz: von Zabern

—— (1998) 'A house for eternity – the tombs of governors and officials', in R. Schulz and M. Seidel (eds) *Egypt: The World of the Pharaohs*, 118–31, Cologne: Könemann

Shortland, A.J. (2000) *Vitreous Materials at Amarna: The Production of Glass and Faience in 18th Dynasty Egypt*, Oxford: Archaeopress

Sikking, L. and Cappers, R.J.T. (2002) 'Eten in de woestijn: voedsel voor mens en dier op doortocht in de Westelijke woestijn van Egypte', *Paleo-Aktueel*, 13: 100–6

Silverman, D.P. (1991) 'Divinity and deities in ancient Egypt', in B.E. Shafer (ed.) *Religion in Ancient Egypt. Gods, Myths, and Personal Practice*, 7–87, London: Routledge

—— (1995) 'The nature of Egyptian kingship', in D. O'Connor and D.P. Silverman (eds) *Ancient Egyptian Kingship*, 49–91, Leiden, New York and Cologne: Brill

Simpson, W.K. (1963a) *Papyrus Reisner*, vol. 1, Boston, MA: Museum of Fine Arts

—— (1963b) *Heka-Nefer and the Dynastic Material from Toshka and Arminna*, New Haven, CT: Peabody Museum

—— (ed.) (2003) *The Literature of Ancient Egypt*, 3rd edn, New Haven, CT and London: Yale University Press

Smith, H.S. (1966) 'Preliminary report on the rock inscriptions in the Egypt Exploration Society's concession at Buhen', *Kush*, 14: 330–4

—— (1972) 'The rock inscriptions of Buhen', *Journal of Egyptian Archaeology*, 58: 43–82

—— (1992) 'The making of Egypt: a review of the influence of Susa and Sumer on Upper Egypt and Lower Nubia in the 4th millennium BC', in R. Friedman and B. Adams (eds) *The Followers of Horus. Studies Dedicated to Michael Allen Hoffman*, 235–46, Oxford: Oxbow Books

—— and Smith, A. (1976) 'A reconsideration of the Kamose texts', *Zeitschrift für Ägyptische Sprache und Altertumskunde*, 103: 48–76

Smith, M. (2000) 'Egyptian invective (review of Thissen 1992)', *Journal of Egyptian Archaeology*, 86: 173–87

Smith, S.T. (1992) 'Intact Theban tombs and the New Kingdom burial assemblage', *Mitteilungen des Deutschen Archäologischen Instituts Abteilung Kairo*, 48: 193–231

—— (1995) *Askut in Nubia. The Economics and Ideology of Egyptian Imperialism in the Second Millennium BC*, London: Kegan Paul

—— (1997a) 'State and Empire in the Middle and New Kingdoms', in J. Lustig (ed.) *Anthropology and Egyptology. A Developing Dialogue*, 66–89, Sheffield: Sheffield Academic Press

—— (1997b) 'Ancient Egyptian imperialism: ideological vision or economic exploitation?', *Cambridge Archaeological Journal*, 7: 301–7

—— (2003) *Wretched Kush: Ethnic Identities and Boundaries in Egypt's Nubian Empire*, London and New York: Routledge

—— (in press) 'A new Napatan cemetery at Tombos', *Cahiers de Recherches de l'Institut de Papyrologie et d'Égyptologie de Lille*

Smith, W.S. (1998) *The Art and Architecture of Ancient Egypt*, 3rd edn, New Haven, CT and London: Yale University Press

Smither, P.C. (1941) 'A tax-assessor's journal of the Middle Kingdom', *Journal of Egyptian Archaeology*, 27: 74–6

—— (1945) 'The Semnah dispatches', *Journal of Egyptian Archaeology*, 31: 3–10

Snape, S.R. (1994) 'Statues and soldiers at Abydos during the Second Intermediate Period', in C. Eyre, A. Leahy and L.M. Leahy (eds) *The Unbroken Reed*, 304–14, London: Egypt Exploration Society

—— (2003) 'The emergence of Libya on the horizon of Egypt', in D. O'Connor and S. Quirke (eds) *Mysterious Lands*, 93–106, London: UCL Press

Snowden, F.M. (1983) *Before Color Prejudice: The Ancient View of Blacks*, Cambridge, MA: Harvard University Press

Soukiassian, G., Wuttmann, M. and Pantalacci, L. (2002) *Le palais des gouverneurs de l'époque de Pépy II, Balat VI*, Cairo: Institut Français d'Archéologie Orientale

——, —— and Schad, D. (1990) 'La ville d'Ayn Asil à Dakhla', *Bulletin de l'Institut Français d'Archéologie Orientale*, 90: 347–58

Spalinger, A.J. (1974a) 'Assurbanipal and Egypt: a source study', *Journal of the American Oriental Society*, 94: 316–28

—— (1974b) 'Esarhaddon and Egypt: an analysis of the first invasion of Egypt', *Orientalia*, 43: 295–326

—— (1979) 'The northern wars of Seti I: an integrative study', *Journal of the American Research Center in Egypt*, 16: 29–47

—— (1985) 'Notes on the reliefs of the Battle of Kadesh', in H. Goedicke, *Perspectives of the Battle of Kadesh*, 1–42, Baltimore, MD: Halgo, Inc.

—— (1986) 'Foods in P. Boulaq 18', *Studien zur Altägyptischen Kultur*, 13: 207–47

—— (2005) *War in Ancient Egypt. The New Kingdom*, Malden, Oxford and Carlton: Blackwell

—— (in press) *Images of Power. The Iconic and Mimetic Nature of New Kingdom War Narratives*

Spanel, D. (1988) *Through Ancient Eyes: Egyptian Portraiture*, Birmingham, AL: Birmingham Museum of Art

Sparks, R.T. (2004) 'Canaan in Egypt: archaeological evidence for a social phenomenon', in J. Bourriau and J. Phillips (eds) *Invention and Innovation. The Social Context of Technological Change 2: Egypt, the Aegean and the Near East, 1650–1150 BC*, 25–54, Oxford: Oxbow Books

Spence, K. (1999) 'Red, white and black: colour in building stone in ancient Egypt', in J. Gage, A. Jones, R. Bradley, K. Spence, E. Barber and P. Taçon, 'What meaning had colour in early societies', *Cambridge Archaeological Journal*, 9.1: 114–17

—— (2004a) 'Royal walling projects in the Second Millennium BC: beyond an interpretation of defence', *Cambridge Archaeological Journal*, 14.2: 265–71

—— (2004b) 'The three-dimensional form of the Amarna House', *Journal of Egyptian Archaeology*, 90: 123–52

Spencer, A.J. (1993) *Early Egypt: The Rise of Civilisation in the Nile Valley*, London: British Museum Press

—— (1999) 'Casemate foundations once again', in A. Leahy and J. Tait (eds) *Studies on Ancient Egypt in Honour of H. Smith*, 295–300, London: Egypt Exploration Society

—— (2001) 'An elite cemetery at Tell el-Balamun', *Egyptian Archaeology*, 18: 18–20

—— (2002) 'The exploration of Tell Belim, 1999–2002', *Journal of Egyptian Archaeology*, 88: 37–51

—— (2006) *Delta Survey*. Online. Available at: www.ees.ac.uk (accessed 10 June 2006)

Spencer, P. (1997) *Amara West I. The Architectural Report*, London: Egypt Exploration Society

Spicer, E. (1962) *Cycles of Conquest*, Tucson, AZ: University of Arizona Press

Spiegelberg, W. (1921) *Ägyptische und andere Graffiti aus der thebanischen Nekropolis*, 2 vols, Heidelberg: C. Winters Universitätsbuchhandlung

Stadelmann, R. (1967) *Syrisch-palästinensische Gottheiten in Ägypten*, Leiden: Brill

—— (1968) 'Die Abwehr der Seevölker unter Ramses III', *Saeculum*, 19.2/3: 156–71

—— (1997) 'The development of the pyramid temple in the Fourth Dynasty', in S. Quirke (ed.) *The Temple in Ancient Egypt: New Discoveries and Recent Research*, 1–16, London: British Museum Press

Stadler, M.A. (2004) 'Rechtskodex von Hermopolis', in B. Janowski and G. Wilhelm (eds) *Texte aus der Umwelt des Alten Testaments – Neue Folge I – Texte zum Rechts- und Wirtschaftsleben*, 185–207, Gütersloh: Gütersloher Verlagshaus

Stager, L.A. (1995) 'The impact of the Sea Peoples in Canaan (1185–1050 BCE)', in T.E. Levy (ed.) *The Archaeology of the Society in the Holy Land*, 332–48, London: Leicester University Press

—— (2002) 'The MBIIA ceramic sequence at Tel Ashkelon and its implications for the "Port Power" model of trade', in M. Bietak and H. Hunger (eds) *The Middle Bronze Age in the Levant. Proceedings of an International Conference on MB IIA Ceramic Materials in Vienna, 24–26 January 2001*, 353–63, Vienna: Österreichische Akademie der Wissenschaften

Stanish, C. (1989) 'Household archaeology. Testing models of zonal complementarity in the South Central Andes', *American Anthropologist*, 91: 7–24

Stanley, D.J. (2005) 'Submergence and burial of ancient coastal sites on the subsiding Nile delta margin, Egypt', *Méditerranée. Revue géographique des pays méditerranéens*, 104: 65–73

——, McRae, J.E. and Waldron, J.C. (1996) 'Nile Delta drill core and sample data bases for 1985–1994: Mediterranean Basin (MEDIBA) program', *Smithsonian Contributions to Marine Science*, 37: 10

Steel, L. (2003) 'The "Sea Peoples": raiders or refugees', in B. Manley (ed.) *The Seventy Great Mysteries of Ancient Egypt*, 176–80, London and New York: Thames and Hudson

Stein, G.J. (1999) *Rethinking World Systems. Diasporas, Colonies, and Interaction in Uruk Mesopotamia*, Tucson, AZ: University of Arizona Press

Steindorff, G. (1935) *Aniba*, Glückstadt: Augustin

Stewart, H.M. (1995) *Egyptian Shabtis*, Princes Risborough: Shire Publications

Stewart, J.R. (1962) 'The Early Cypriote Bronze Age', in P. Dikaios and J.R. Stewart, *Swedish Cyprus Expedition* IV 1A. *The Stone Age and Early Bronze Age*, 205–391, Lund: Swedish Cyprus Expedition

Storey, W. (1976) 'Fig', in N. Simmonds (ed.) *Evolution of Crop Plants*, London: Longman

Stos-Gale, Z., Gale, N. and Houghton, J. (1995) 'The origin of Egyptian copper. Lead isotope analysis of metals from el-Amarna', in W.V. Davies and L. Schofield (eds) *Egypt, the Aegean and the Levant: Interconnections in the Second Millennium B.C.*, 127–35, London: British Museum Press

Strøm, I. (1984) 'Aspects of Minoan foreign relations, LM I–LM II', in R. Hägg and N. Marinatos (eds) *The Minoan Thalassocracy: Myth and Reality*, 191–5, Stockholm: Swedish School at Athens

Strommenger, E. (1980) *Habuba Kabira. Eine Stadt vor 5000 Jahren*, Mainz: von Zabern

Strouhal, E. (1992) *Life in Ancient Egypt*, Norman, OK: University of Oklahoma Press

Strudwick, N. (1985) *The Administration of Egypt in the Old Kingdom*, London: Kegan Paul International

Sweeney, D. (1998) 'Women and language in the Ramesside Period', in C.J. Eyre (ed.) *Proceedings of the Seventh International Congress of Egyptologists, Cambridge*, 1109–17, Leuven: Peeters

Szpakowska, K. (2003) *Behind Closed Eyes: Dreams and Nightmares in Ancient Egypt*, Swansea: Classical Press of Wales

Täckholm, V. and Drar, M. (1950) *Flora of Egypt*, vol. 2, Cairo: Bulletin of the Faculty of Science 28

Tait, W.J. (1991) 'P.Carlsberg 236 – Another fragment of a Demotic legal manual', in P.J. Frandsen (ed.) *The Carlsberg Papyri I – Demotic Texts from the Collection*, 93–101, Copenhagen: Museum Tusculanum Press

Tallet, P. (2003) 'Notes sur la zone minière du Sud-Sinaï au Nouvel Empire', *Bulletin de l'Institut Français d'Archéologie Orientale*, 103: 459–86

Taraqji, A.F. (1999) 'Nouvelles découvertes sur les relations avec l'Égypte à Tel Sakka et à Keswé, dans la région de Damas', *Bulletin de la Société Française d'Égyptologie*, 144: 27–43

Tassie, G. and van Wetering, J. (2003) 'Early cemeteries of the East Delta: Kafr Hassan Dawood, Minshat Abu Omar and Tell Ibrahim Awad', in Z. Hawass and L. Pinch Brock (eds) *Egyptology at the Dawn of the 21st Century, Volume 1: Archaeology*, 499–507, Cairo: American University in Cairo Press

Taylor, J. (2000) 'The Third Intermediate Period (1069–664 BC)', in I. Shaw (ed.) *The Oxford History of Ancient Egypt*, 330–68, Oxford: Oxford University Press

Teeter, E. (1997) *The Presentation of Maat: Ritual and Legitimacy in Ancient Egypt*, Chicago, IL: Oriental Institute, University of Chicago

—— (2001) 'Maat', in D.B. Redford (ed.) *The Oxford Encyclopedia of Ancient Egypt*, vol. 2, 319–21, New York: Oxford University Press

Teissier, B. (1996) *Egyptian Iconography on Syro-Palestinian Cylinder Seals of the Middle Bronze Age (ca. 1920–1550 B.C.)*, Freiburg/Göttingen: Universitätsverlag/Vandenhoeck & Ruprecht

Te Velde, H. (1967) *Seth, God of Confusion: A Study of His Role in Egyptian Mythology and Religion*, Leiden: Brill

Théodoridès, A. (1971) 'The concept of law in ancient Egypt', in J.R. Harris (ed.) *The Legacy of Egypt*, 2nd edn, 291–322, Oxford: Clarendon Press

Thissen, H.J. (1992) *Der verkommene Harfenspieler: eine altägyptische Invektive (P. Wien kilometres 3877)*, Sommerhausen: Gisela Zauzich

Thomas, A.P. (2004) 'Some comments on the Predynastic cemetery at el Mahasna', in S. Hendrickx, R.F. Friedman, K.M. Ciałowicz and M. Chłodnicki (eds) *Egypt at its Origins. Studies in Memory of Barbara Adams*, 1041–54, Leuven: Peeters

Thomas, S. (2000) 'Tell Abqaʿin: a fortified settlement in the western Delta. Preliminary report of the 1997 Season', *Mitteilungen des Deutschen Archäologischen Instituts Abteilung Kairo*, 56: 371–6

—— (2002) 'The wells of Tell Abqaʿin', *Ancient Egypt*, May/June 2002: 22–7

Thompson, D.J. (1984) 'Hellenistic science: its application in peace and war, 9c: agriculture', in F.W. Walbank, A.E. Astin, M.W. Frederiksen and R.M. Ogilvie (eds) *The Cambridge Ancient History*, 2nd edn, vol. 7, pt 1, 363–70, Cambridge: Cambridge University Press

—— (1999a) 'Irrigation and drainage in the early Ptolemaic Fayyum', in A.K. Bowman and E. Rogan (eds) *Agriculture in Egypt: From Pharaonic to Modern Times*, 107–22, Oxford: Oxford University Press

—— (1999b) 'New and old in the Ptolemaic Fayyum', in A.K. Bowman and E. Rogan (eds) *Agriculture in Egypt: From Pharaonic to Modern Times*, 123–38, Oxford: Oxford University Press

Tietze, C. (1985) 'Amarna: Analyse der Wohnhäuser und soziale Struktur der Stadtbewohner', *Zeitschrift für Ägyptische Sprache und Altertumskunde*, 112: 48–84

Toivari-Viitala, J. (2001) *Women at Deir el-Medina*, Leiden: Nederlands Instituut voor het Nabije Oosten

Török, L. (1997) *The Kingdom of Kush: Handbook of the Napatan-Meroitic Civilization*, Leiden: Brill

—— (2002) *The Image of the Ordered World in Ancient Nubian Art: The Construction of the Kushite Mind (800BC–300AD)*, Leiden, Boston and Cologne: Brill

Traunecker, C. (2002) 'The ritualist pharaoh: the religious cult', in C. Ziegler (ed.) *The Pharaohs*, 145–57, New York: Rizzoli

—— and Golvin, J.-C. (1984) *Karnak: Résurrection d'un site*, Fribourg: Office du Livre

Trigger, B.G. (1976) *Nubia under the Pharaohs*, London: Thames and Hudson

—— (1983) 'The rise of Egyptian civilization', in B.G. Trigger, B.J. Kemp, D. O'Connor and A.B. Lloyd, *Ancient Egypt: A Social History*, 1–70, Cambridge: Cambridge University Press

——, Kemp, B.J., O'Connor, D. and Lloyd, A.B. (1983) *Ancient Egypt: A Social History*, Cambridge: Cambridge University Press

Turner, E.G. (1984) 'Ptolemaic Egypt', in F.W. Walbank, A.E. Astin, M.W. Frederiksen and R.M. Ogilvie (eds) *The Cambridge Ancient History*, 2nd edn, vol. 7, pt 1, 118–74, Cambridge: Cambridge University Press

Uphill, E. (1988) *Egyptian Towns and Cities*, Princes Risborough: Shire Publications

Ussishkin, D. (2004) *The Renewed Archaeological Excavations at Lachish (1973–1994)*, vol. 1, Tel Aviv: Yass Publications in Archaeology

Váhala, R. and Červiček, P. (1999) *Katalog der Felsbilder aus der tschechoslowakischen Konzession in Nubien*, Prague: Universitas Carolina Pragensis

Valbelle, D. (1985) *Les ouvriers de la tombe: Deir el-Médineh à l'époque ramesside*, Cairo: Institut Français d'Archéologie Orientale

—— and Bonnet, C. (1996) *Le sanctuaire d'Hathor, maîtresse de la turquoise. Sérabit el-Khadim au Moyen Empire*, Lille: Picard

van den Boorn, G.P.F. (1988) *The Duties of the Vizier: Civil Administration in the Early New Kingdom*, London: Kegan Paul International

van den Brink, E.C.M. (1978) *Tombs and Burial Customs at Tell el-Dabʿa*, Vienna: Institute of Egyptology, University of Vienna

—— (1987) 'A geo-archaeological survey in the north-eastern Delta, Egypt: the first two seasons, a preliminary report', *Mitteilungen des Deutschen Archäologischen Instituts Abteilung Kairo*, 43: 7–24

Vandekerckhove, H. and Müller-Wollermann, R. (2001) *Die Felsinschriften des Wadi Hilâl*, Turnhout: Brepols

Vandersleyen, C. (1998) 'Les guerres de Mérenptah et de Ramsès III contre les peuples de l'ouest, et leurs rapport avec le Delta', in C.J. Eyre (ed.) *Proceedings of the Seventh International Congress of Egyptologists, Cambridge, 3–9 September 1995*, 1197–203, Leuven: Peeters

Vandier, J. (1950) *Mo'alla: La tombe d'Ankhtifi et la tombe de Sébekhotep*, Cairo: Institut Français d'Archéologie Orientale

van Dijk, J. (1993) 'The ritual of breaking the red pots', in 'The New Kingdom Necropolis of Memphis: Historical and Iconographical Studies', 173–88, unpublished thesis, Groningen University

van Seters, J. (1966) *The Hyksos: A New Investigation*, New Haven, CT: Yale University Press

Varille, A. (1954) 'La stèle du mystique Béky (No 156 du Musée de Turin)', *Bulletin de l'Institut Français d'Archéologie Orientale*, 54: 129–35

Vasey, D. (1992) *An Ecological History of Agriculture*, Ames, IA: Iowa State University Press

Ventris, M. and Chadwick, J. (1956) *Documents in Mycenaean Greek*, Cambridge: Cambridge University Press

Ventura, R. (1974) 'An Egyptian rock stela in Timna', *Tel Aviv*, 1: 60–3

Vercoutter, J. (1956) *L'Égypte et le Monde Egéen Préhéllenique. Étude Critique des Sources Égyptiennes, du début de la XVIIIe à la fin de la XIXe Dynastie*, Cairo: Institut Français d'Archéologie Orientale

—— (1994) 'Les barrages pharaoniques: leur raison d'être', in B. Menu (ed.) *Les problèmes institutionels de l'eau en Égypte ancienne et dans l'antiquité méditerranéenne*, 315–26, Cairo: Institut Français d'Archéologie Orientale

Verhoogt, A.M.F.W. (1998) 'Land tenure in late Ptolemaic Egypt: the case of Kerkeosiris', in B. Haring and R. de Maaijer (eds) *Landless and Hungry*, 103–11, Leiden: Research School CNWS

Vermeersch, P.M. (ed.) (2000) *Palaeolithic Living Sites in Upper and Middle Egypt*, Leuven: Leuven University Press

Verner, M. (1992) 'Discovery of a potter's workshop in the pyramid complex of Khentkaus at Abusir', *Cahier de la Céramique Égyptienne*, 3: 55–60

—— (1994) *Forgotten Pharaohs, Lost Pyramids: Abu Sir*, Prague: Academia Skodaexport

—— (2001) *The Pyramids: Their Archaeology and History*, London: Atlantic Books

Vernus, P. (1982) 'La stèle du roi Sekhemsankhtaouyrê Neferhotep Iykhernofert et la domination Hyksôs (Stèle Cairo JE 59635)', *Annales du Service des Antiquités de l'Égypte*, 68: 129–35

—— (1986) 'Études de philologie et de linguistique (V)', *Revue d'Égyptologie*, 37: 139–47

—— (1989a) 'La stèle du pharaon *Mntw-tpi* à Karnak: un nouveau témoinage sur la situation politique et militaire au début de la D.P.I.', *Revue d'Égyptologie*, 40: 145–61

—— (1989b) 'L'eau sainte de Xois', in A. Nibbi (ed.) *The Archaeology, Geography and History of the Egyptian Delta in Pharaonic Times*, 323–35, Oxford: Discussions in Egyptology

—— (2001) *Sagesses de l'Égypte pharaonique*, Paris: Imprimerie nationale

Visweswaran, K. (1998) 'Race and the culture of anthropology', *American Anthropologist*, 100: 70–83

Vittmann, G. (2000) 'Von Kastraten, Hundskopfmenschen und Kannibalen', *Zeitschrift für Ägyptische Sprache und Altertumskunde*, 127: 167–80

Vleeming, S.P. (1991) *The Gooseherds of Hou (Pap. Hou)*, Leuven: Peeters

—— (1993) *Papyrus Reinhardt: An Egyptian Land List from the Tenth Century B.C.*, Berlin: Akademie Verlag

von Beckerath, J. (1964) *Untersuchungen zur politischen Geschichte der Zweiten Zwischenzeit in Ägypten*, Glückstadt: Augustin

—— (1968) 'Die Stele der Verbannten im Museum des Louvre', *Revue d'Égyptologie*, 20: 7–36

—— (1997) *Chronologie des pharaonischen Ägypten*, Mainz: von Zabern von der Way, T. (1984) *Die Textüberlieferung Ramses' II. zur Qadeš Schlacht. Analyse und Struktur*, Hildesheim: Gerstenberg

—— (1992) *Göttergericht und 'Heiliger' Krieg im Alten Ägypten. Die Inschriften des Merenptah zum Libyerkrieg des Jahres 5*, Heidelberg: Heidelberger Orientverlag

—— (1997) *Tell el-Faraʾîn. Buto I. Ergebnisse zum frühen Kontext. Kampagnen der Jahre 1983–1989*, Mainz: von Zabern (*Archäologische Veröffentlichungen* 83)

von Känel, F. (1984) *Les Prêtres-ouâb de Sekhmet et les Conjurateurs de Serket*, Paris: Presses universitaires de France

von Pilgrim, C. (1996a) 'Elephantine im Mittleren Reich: Bemerkungen zur Wohnarchitektur in einer gewachsenen Stadt', in M. Bietak (ed.) *Haus und Palast im Alten Ägypten*, 253–64, Vienna: Akademie der Wissenschaften

—— (1996b) *Elephantine XVIII. Untersuchungen in der Stadt des Mittleren Reiches und der Zweiten Zwischenzeit*, Mainz: von Zabern

—— (2001) 'The practice of sealing in the administration of the First Intermediate Period and the Middle Kingdom', *Cahiers de Recherches de l'Institut de Papyrologie et d'Égyptologie de Lille*, 22: 161–72

——, Bruhn, K.-C. and Kelany, A. (2004) 'The town of Syene. Preliminary report of the 1st and 2nd Season at Aswan', *Mitteilungen des Deutschen Archäologischen Instituts Abteilung Kairo*, 60: 119–48

Wachsmann, S. (1987) *Aegeans in Theban Tombs*, Leuven: University of Leuven

Warburton, D. (1997) *State and Economy in Ancient Egypt. Fiscal Vocabulary of the New Kingdom*, Freiburg/Göttingen: Universitätsverlag/Vandenhoeck & Ruprecht

—— (2003) *Macroeconomics from the Beginning: The General Theory, Ancient Markets, and the Rate of Interest*, Neuchâtel and Paris: Recherches et Publications

Ward, W.A. (1972) 'The "Shasu" Bedouin. Notes on a recent publication', *Journal of the Economic and Social History of the Orient*, 15: 35–60

—— (1982) *Index of Egyptian Administrative and Religious Titles of the Middle Kingdom*, Beirut: American University of Beirut

Warren, P.M. (1987) 'Absolute dating of the Aegean Bronze Age', *Archaeometry*, 29: 205–11

—— (1995) 'Minoan Crete and Pharaonic Egypt', in W.V. Davies and L. Schofield (eds) *Egypt, the Aegean and the Levant: Interconnections in the Second Millennium B.C.*, 1–18, London: British Museum Press

—— and Hankey, V. (1989) *Aegean Bronze Age Chronology*, Bristol: Bristol Classical Press

Wegner, J.W. (2001) 'The Town of Wah-swt at South Abydos: 1999 Excavations', *Mitteilungen des Deutschen Archäologischen Instituts Abteilung Kairo*, 57: 281–306

Weill, R. (1912) *Les Décrets royaux de l'Ancien Empire égyptien*, Paris: Geuthner

Weingarten, J. (2000) 'The transformation of Egyptian Taweret into the Minoan genius', in A. Karetsou (ed.) *Κρήτη – Αιγύπτος: Πολιτισμικοί Δεσμοί μριών Χιλιετιών*, 114–19, Athens: Kapon Editions

Weinstein, J. (1973) *Foundation Deposits in Ancient Egypt*, Ann Arbor, MI: University Microfilms International

—— (1981) 'The Egyptian empire in Palestine: a reassessment', *Bulletin of the American Schools of Oriental Research*, 241: 1–28

—— (1997) 'Yahudiyeh, Tell el-', in E. Meyers (ed.) *The Oxford Encyclopedia of Archaeology in the Near East*, vol. 5, 368–9, New York: Oxford University Press

—— (2001) 'Megiddo', in D. Redford (ed.) *The Oxford Encyclopedia of Ancient Egypt*, vol. 2, 368–9, New York: Oxford University Press

Welsby, D.A. (1996) *The Kingdom of Kush: The Napatan and Meroïtic Empires*, London: British Museum Press

—— and Anderson, J.R. (eds) (2004) *Sudan: Ancient Treasures: An Exhibition of Recent Discoveries from the Sudan National Museum*, London: British Museum Press

Wendorf, F. (ed.) (1968) *The Prehistory of Nubia*, Dallas, TX: Fort Bergwin Research Center

—— and Schild, R. (2002a) 'Implications of incipient social complexity in the late Neolithic in the Egyptian Sahara', in R. Friedman (ed.) *Egypt and Nubia: Gifts of the Desert*, 13–20, London: British Museum Press

—— and —— (2002b) 'The role of storage in the Neolithic of the Egyptian Sahara', in T. Lenssen-Erz *et al.* (eds) *Tides of the Desert – Gezeiten der Wüste*, 41–9, Cologne: Heinrich-Barth-Institute

——, —— *et al.* (2001) *Holocene Settlement of the Egyptian Sahara, 1: The Archaeology of Nabta Playa*, New York: Kluwer Academic

——, Close, A.E. and Schild, R. (1992/3) 'Megaliths in the Egyptian Sahara', *Sahara*, 5: 7–16

Wengrow, D. (2006) *The Archaeology of Early Egypt: Social Transformations in North-East Africa, 10,000 to 2650 BC*, Cambridge: Cambridge University Press

Wenke, R.J., Buck, P.E., Hamroush, H.A., Kobusiewicz, M., Kroeper, K. and Redding, R.W. (1988) 'Kom el-Hisn: excavation of an Old Kingdom settlement in the Egyptian Delta', *Journal of the American Research Center in Egypt*, 25: 5–34

Wente, E. (1973) 'The quarrel of Apophis and Seknenre', in W.K. Simpson (ed.) *The Literature of Ancient Egypt*, 2nd edn, 77–80, New Haven, CT and London: Yale University Press

—— (1990) *Letters from Ancient Egypt*, Atlanta, GA: Scholars Press

Westendorf, W. (1966a) *Altägyptische Darstellungen des Sonnenlaufes auf der abschüssigen Himmelsbahn*, Berlin: Akademie Verlag

—— (1966b) 'Wesen und Ursprung der Maat', in S. Lauffer (ed.) *Festgabe für Dr. Walter Will*, 204–6, Cologne: Heymann

—— (1979) 'Vom Sonnentier zum Sonnenboot', in M. Görg and E. Pusch (eds) *Festschrift Elmar Edel*, 432–5, Bamberg: Görg

Wiener, M.H. and Allen, J.P. (1998) 'Separate lives: the Ahmose Tempest Stela and the Theran eruption', *Journal of Near Eastern Studies*, 57: 1–29

Wiessner, P. (1983) 'Style and ethnicity in the Kalihari San projectile point', *Journal of Anthropological Archaeology*, 48: 253–76

Wildung D. (1977) *Imhotep und Amenhotep – Gottwerdung im alten Ägypten*, München and Berlin: Deutscher Kunstverlag

—— (ed.) (1997) *Sudan: Ancient Kingdoms of the Nile*, Paris and New York: Flammarion

Wilfong, T.G. (1997) *Women and Gender in Ancient Egypt: From Prehistory to Late Antiquity*, Ann Arbor, MI: Kelsey Museum of Archaeology

—— (1998) 'Reading the disjointed body in Coptic: from physical modification to textual fragmentation', in D. Montserrat (ed.) *Changing Bodies, Changing Meanings: Studies on the Human Body in Antiquity*, 116–36, London: Routledge

—— (2002) '"Friendship and physical desire": the discourse of female homoeroticism in fifth century CE Egypt', in N. Rabinowitz and L. Auanger (eds) *Among Women: From the Homosocial to the Homoerotic in the Ancient World*, 304–29, Austin, TX: University of Texas Press

Wilhelm, G. (1981) *Grundzüge der Geschichte und Kultur der Hurriter*, Darmstadt: Wissenschaftliche Buchgemeinde

Wilke, T. (2000) 'Ancient Egypt: an economist's view', *Göttinger Miszellen*, 178: 81–95

Wilkinson, R.H. (1992) *Reading Egyptian Art*, London and New York: Thames and Hudson

—— (1994) *Symbol and Magic in Egyptian Art*, London and New York: Thames and Hudson

—— (2000) *The Complete Temples of Ancient Egypt*, London and New York: Thames and Hudson

—— (2003) *The Complete Gods and Goddesses of Ancient Egypt*, London and New York: Thames and Hudson

Wilkinson, T. (1995) 'A new king in the Western Desert', *Journal of Egyptian Archaeology*, 81: 205–10

—— (1999) *Early Dynastic Egypt*, London and New York: Routledge

—— (2000a) *Royal Annals of Ancient Egypt: The Palermo Stone and its Associated Fragments*, London and New York: Kegan Paul International

—— (2000b) 'What a king is this: Narmer and the concept of the ruler', *Journal of Egyptian Archaeology*, 86: 23–32

—— (2002a) 'Uruk into Egypt: imports and imitations', in J.N. Postgate and S. Campbell (eds) *Artefacts of Complexity: Tracking the Uruk in the Near East*, 237–48, Warminster: Aris and Phillips

—— (2002b) 'Reality versus ideology: the evidence for "Asiatics" in Predynastic and Early Dynastic Egypt', in E.C.M. van den Brink and T.E. Levy (eds) *Egypt and the Levant: Interrelations From the 4th Through the Early 3rd Millennium BCE*, 514–20, London and New York: Leicester University Press

—— (2002c) 'Review of "Umm el-Qaab II. Importkeramik aus dem Friedhof U in Abydos (Umm el-Qaab) und die Beziehungen Ägyptens zu Vorderasien im 4. Jahrtausend v. Chr." (U. Hartung)', *Journal of Egyptian Archaeology*, 88: 256–9

—— (2003a) 'Did the Egyptians invent writing?', in B. Manley (ed.) *The Seventy Great Mysteries of Ancient Egypt*, 24–7, London and New York: Thames and Hudson

—— (2003b) *Genesis of the Pharaohs*, London and New York: Thames and Hudson

—— (forthcoming) 'Cones, nails and pegs: enigmatic clay objects from Buto and their implications for contacts between Egypt and Western Asia in the fourth millennium BC', in A. Dodson and S. Ikram (eds) *Studies in Honour of Barry Kemp*, Cairo: American University in Cairo Press

Willcocks, W. and Craig, J.I. (1913) *Egyptian Irrigation*, London: Spon

Willems, H. (1983–4) 'The nomarchs of the hare nome and Early Middle Kingdom history', *Jaarbericht van het Vooraziatisch-Egyptisch Genootschap 'Ex Oriente Lux'*, 28: 80–102

—— (1988) *Chests of Life. A Study of the Typology and Conceptual Development of Middle Kingdom Standard Class Coffins*, Leiden: Ex Oriente Lux

Willeitner, J. (2003) *Die ägyptischen Oasen: Städte, Tempel und Gräber in der libyschen Wüste*, Mainz: von Zabern

Williams, B. (1980) 'The lost pharaohs of Nubia', *Archaeology*, 33: 14–21

—— (1986) *The A-Group Royal Cemetery at Qustul: Cemetery L*, Chicago, IL: Oriental Institute, University of Chicago

—— (1987) 'Forebears of Menes in Nubia: myth or reality?', *Journal of Near Eastern Studies*, 46: 15–26

—— and Logan, T. (1987) 'The Metropolitan Museum knife handle and aspects of pharaonic imagery before Narmer', *Journal of Near Eastern Studies*, 46: 245–85

Williams, R.J. (1961) 'The alleged Semitic original of the *Wisdom of Amenemope*', *Journal of Egyptian Archaeology*, 47: 100–6

Wilson, P. (2005) 'Two graves and a well at Sais', *Egyptian Archaeology*, 26: 34–5

—— and Gilbert, G. (2003) 'The prehistoric period at Saïs (Sa el-Hagar)', *Archéo-Nil*, 13: 65–72

Winkler, H.A. (1938–9) *Rock-Drawings of Southern Upper Egypt*, 2 vols, London: Egypt Exploration Society

Winlock, H.E. (1936) *Ed-Dakhleh Oasis: Journal of a Camel Trip Made in 1908*, New York: Metropolitan Museum of Art

—— (1947) *The Rise and Fall of the Middle Kingdom in Thebes*, New York: Macmillan

Wiseman, D.J. (1975) 'Assyria and Babylonia c.1200–1000 B.C.', in I.E.S. Edwards, C.J. Gadd, N.G.L. Hammond and E. Sollberger (eds) *The Cambridge Ancient History*, 3rd edn, vol. 2, pt 2, 443–77, Cambridge: Cambridge University Press

Wood, R.C. (1995) *The Sociology of the Meal*, Edinburgh: Edinburgh University Press

Wortham, J.D. (1971) *British Egyptology 1549–1906*, Devon: David and Charles

Wreszinski, W. (1923) *Atlas zur altägyptischen Kulturgeschichte*, Leipzig: Hinrichs

Yoffee, N. and Kamp, K.A. (1980) 'Ethnicity in ancient Western Asia during the early second millennium B.C.: archaeological assessments and ethnoarchaeological perspectives', *Bulletin of the American Schools of Oriental Research*, 237: 85–104

Žába, Z. (1953) *L'orientation astronomique dans l'ancienne Égypte et la précession de l'axe du monde*, Prague: Académie Tchécoslovaque des Sciences

—— (1974) *The Rock Inscriptions of Lower Nubia*, Prague: Universita Karlova

Žabkar, L. (1968) *A Study of the Ba Concept in Ancient Egyptian Texts*, Chicago, IL: University of Chicago Press

Zaccagnini, C. (1987) 'Aspects of ceremonial exchange in the Near East during the late second millennium BC', in M. Rowlands, M. Larsen and K. Kristiansen (eds) *Centre and Periphery in the Ancient World*, 57–65, Cambridge: Cambridge University Press

—— (2000) 'The interdependence of the Great Powers', in R. Cohen and R. Westbrook (eds) *Amarna Diplomacy: The Beginnings of International Relations*, 141–53, Baltimore, MD and London. Johns Hopkins University Press

Zandee, J. (1992) 'The birth-giving creator god in ancient Egypt', in A.B. Lloyd (ed.) *Studies in Pharaonic Religion and Society in Honour of J. Gwyn Griffiths*, 169–88, London: Egypt Exploration Society

Zauzich, K.-T. (1987) 'Einige unerkannte Ortsnamen', *Enchoria*, 15: 169–79

Zivie, A.-P. (1980) 'Du côté de Babylone: traditions littéraires et légendes populaires au secours de l'archéologie', in J. Vercoutter (ed.) *Institut Français d'Archéologie Orientale du Caire. Livre du centenaire 1880–1980*, 511–17, Cairo: Institut Français d'Archéologie Orientale

—— (1985) 'Cavaliers et cavalerie au Nouvel Empire: à propos d'un vieux problème', in *Mélanges Gamal Eddin Mokhtar*, 2: 379–88, Cairo: Institut Français d'Archéologie Orientale

—— (1990) *Découverte à Saqqarah: le vizir oublié*, Paris: Seuil

Zohary, D. (1972) 'The wild progenitor and place of the origin of the cultivated lentil, *Lens culinaris*', *Economic Botany*, 26: 326–32

—— (1987) *Domestication of Plants in the Old World*, Oxford: Clarendon Press

—— and Hopf, M. (1973) 'Domestication of pulses in the Old World', *Science*, 182: 887–94

—— and Spiegel-Roy, P. (1975) 'Beginnings of fruit growing in the Old World', *Science*, 187: 319–27

INDEX

——— •♦• ———

eBooks – at www.eBookstore.tandf.co.uk

A library at your fingertips!

eBooks are electronic versions of printed books. You can store them on your PC/laptop or browse them online.

They have advantages for anyone needing rapid access to a wide variety of published, copyright information.

eBooks can help your research by enabling you to bookmark chapters, annotate text and use instant searches to find specific words or phrases. Several eBook files would fit on even a small laptop or PDA.

NEW: Save money by eSubscribing: cheap, online access to any eBook for as long as you need it.

Annual subscription packages

We now offer special low-cost bulk subscriptions to packages of eBooks in certain subject areas. These are available to libraries or to individuals.

For more information please contact webmaster.ebooks@tandf.co.uk

We're continually developing the eBook concept, so keep up to date by visiting the website.

www.eBookstore.tandf.co.uk